Praise for

THE UPSWING

"Robert Putnam has long been our indispensable guide to contemporary America. His books on social capital, on religion, and on children are essential reading. *The Upswing* is another masterpiece; it weaves seemingly unrelated stories into a grand master narrative of the last hundred years. A triumph."

—Professor Sir Angus Deaton, FBA HonFRSE,
Nobel Prize winner and coauthor of *Deaths of Despair*

"In the most ambitious and compelling of his several exemplary books, Robert Putnam masterfully recasts the history of our country from the Gilded Age to the present. Marshaling data from across such disparate dimensions as residential choices, congressional voting patterns, film and song titles, and even baby-naming and pronoun usage, Putnam builds a phenomenally data-rich portrait of America. He robustly and convincingly demonstrates a startling congruence of trends in the economic, political, social, and cultural realms as they all moved in benign synchronicity toward greater inclusion, equality, engagement, and comity from the Progressive Era until the 1960s, but thereafter morphed in malign unison into today's toxic world of 'metastasizing self-centeredness,' division, distrust, and dysfunction. Putnam concludes with a communitarian catechism about what *we* must now do to get back on that upward path toward the kind of country that all Americans must surely prefer to the one they now inhabit. *The Upswing* is a singularly illuminating book and a clarion call to action."

—David M. Kennedy, Donald J. McLachlan
Professor of History Emeritus, Stanford University

"Americans who feel we are now living in the worst of times will see their spirits lifted and their hopes raised after reading *The Upswing*. Based on a careful analysis of data trends, Robert D. Putnam's compelling narratives reveal why we should take inspiration and instruction from how America's first Gilded Age, a period of despair much like today, turned into the Progressive Era, which moved America in a positive direction for over half a century. *The Upswing* is a must-read for those who wonder how we can once again reclaim our nation's promise."

—William Julius Wilson, Lewis P. and Linda L. Geyser
University Professor Emeritus, Harvard University

"No one understands the United States better than Bob Putnam, and no one else could have written this essential book. *The Upswing* brings together his vast knowledge, love of data, storytelling ability, and passion. It's an astonishing work that reminds Americans we are a great people, shows us what we can accomplish when we come together, and makes clear that we need to do so again. Now."

—Andrew McAfee, MIT scientist, author of
More from Less, and coauthor of *The Second Machine Age*

"*The Upswing* is a revelation—tailor-made for this polarized age and destined to be a central reference point for urgent debates and determined activism. Here, one of America's most renowned public intellectuals gives us a new understanding of our history and a profoundly insightful roadmap for a future we can only create together. Squarely facing race and gender inequity, Putnam and Garrett shed new light on the moral awakening and collective action that a diverse group of Americans sparked more than a century ago—and show how we can build on their example, but also learn from their blind spots, today."

—Xavier de Souza Briggs, Distinguished Visiting Professor,
New York University, and former Vice President, the Ford Foundation

THE
UPSWING

ALSO BY ROBERT D. PUTNAM

Our Kids: The American Dream in Crisis

American Grace: How Religion Divides and Unites Us
(with David E. Campbell and Shaylyn Romney Garrett)

Better Together: Restoring the American Community
(with Lewis M. Feldstein)

*Democracies in Flux: The Evolution of Social Capital
in Contemporary Society* (editor)

Bowling Alone: The Collapse and Revival of American Community

Disaffected Democracies: What's Troubling the Trilateral Countries?
(edited with Susan J. Pharr)

Making Democracy Work: Civic Traditions in Modern Italy
(with Robert Leonardi and Raffaella Y. Nanetti)

Double-Edged Democracy: International Bargaining and Domestic Politics
(edited with Peter B. Evans and Harold K. Jacobson)

Hanging Together: Conflict and Cooperation in the Seven-Power Summits
(with Nicholas Bayne)

Bureaucrats and Politicians in Western Democracies
(with Joel D. Aberbach and Bert A. Rockman)

The Comparative Study of Political Elites

The Beliefs of Politicians: Ideology, Conflict, and Democracy in Britain and Italy

THE UPSWING

How We Came Together a Century Ago and How We Can Do It Again

ROBERT D. PUTNAM

With Shaylyn Romney Garrett

Swift

SWIFT PRESS

First published in the United States of America by Simon & Schuster, Inc. 2020

First published in Great Britain by Swift Press 2020

1 3 5 7 9 8 6 4 2

Copyright © Robert D. Putnam, 2020

Interior design by Ruth Lee-Mui

The moral right of the author has been asserted

Offset by Tetragon, London
Printed in England by CPI Group (UK) Ltd, Croydon, CRO 4YY

A CIP catalogue record for this book is available from the British Library

ISBN: 978-1-80075-002-9

To Rosemary, love of my life
—*Robert D. Putnam*

To Sophia Eve and Aeon Elijah, my brightest hopes for the future
—*Shaylyn Romney Garrett*

CONTENTS

1. What's Past Is Prologue   1

2. Economics: The Rise and Fall of Equality   21

3. Politics: From Tribalism to Comity and Back Again   69

4. Society: Between Isolation and Solidarity   109

5. Culture: Individualism vs. Community   163

6. Race and the American "We"   200

7. Gender and the American "We"   245

8. The Arc of the Twentieth Century   283

9. Drift and Mastery   315

Acknowledgments   343

Notes   351

Index   447

THE
UPSWING

1

WHAT'S PAST IS PROLOGUE

". . . what's past is prologue, what to come, in yours and my discharge."
—William Shakespeare, *The Tempest*

In the early 1830s a French aristocrat named Alexis de Tocqueville traveled to America at the behest of his government, with a mission to better understand the American prison system. At the time the United States was a fledgling democracy, barely half a century old, and many nations looked to it as a bold experiment. It was an open question as to whether securing liberty and equality by means of a constitution and a participatory government would, or could, succeed.

Tocqueville traveled widely in the newly formed nation, taking detailed notes filled with observations and insights that only an outsider's perspective could yield. He reflected on almost every aspect of American public life, speaking to countless citizens, observing daily interactions, and examining the various communities and institutions that made up the new nation. Above all, he noted a fierce commitment to personal liberty among the descendants of rugged pioneers who had fought so hard for it. But he also observed the coming together of people for mutual purposes, in both the public and private spheres, and found that a multiplicity of associations formed a kind of check on unbridled individualism. Keenly aware of the dangers of individualism (a term he coined), Tocqueville was inspired by what he saw in America: Its citizens were profoundly protective of their independence, but through associating widely and deeply, they were able to overcome selfish desires, engage in collective problem solving, and work together to build a vibrant and—by comparison to Europe at that time—surprisingly egalitarian society by pursuing what he called "self-interest, rightly understood."[1]

Though far from perfect in its execution—indeed, this was an America built upon the genocide of Native Americans, the enslavement of African Americans, and the disenfranchisement of women, and Tocqueville was well aware of the evils of slavery—what Tocqueville saw in our nation's democracy was an attempt to achieve balance between the twin ideals of freedom and equality; between respect for the individual and concern for the community. He saw independent individuals coming together in defense of mutual liberty, in pursuit of shared prosperity, and in support of the public institutions and cultural norms that protected them. Though there were blind spots still to be addressed, and dangers lurking in some of its flaws and features, democracy in America, Tocqueville felt, was alive and well.[2]

Were Alexis de Tocqueville to travel to America once again—further on in our national story—what might he find? Would America fulfill its promise of balancing individual liberty with the common good? Would equality of opportunity be realized, and indeed produce prosperity for all? And would shared cultural values, respect for democratic institutions, and a vibrant associational life be the promised antidotes to tyranny? Let's look at an end-of-century balance sheet.

On the broad question of prosperity, things could hardly be better. Huge advances in communication, transportation, and standards of living have brought to almost all Americans a degree of material well-being unmatched in our history. Increasing educational opportunities have made strides toward leveling the social and economic playing field. A wide variety of goods priced for mass consumption as well as innovative new forms of entertainment—all made available in increasingly convenient ways—have improved the daily lives of nearly everyone. On the whole, Americans enjoy a degree of educational opportunity, abundance, and personal freedom of which previous generations only dreamed, a fact which might prompt an observer to paint a rosy picture of this America: widespread progress and prosperity driven by education, technological innovation, and sustained economic growth.

And yet this prosperity has come at a cost. While industries spawned by technological advance have allowed huge corporations to produce un-paralleled profits, very little of this wealth has trickled down. The poor may be better off in real terms than their predecessors, but the benefits of economic growth have remained highly concentrated at the top. Extremes of wealth and poverty are everywhere on display.

Class segregation in the form of an entrenched elite and a marooned underclass is often a crippling physical, social, and psychological reality for those striving to get ahead. Young people and new immigrants enter the labor force filled with the hope that the American Dream can be theirs through persistence and hard work. But they often become disillusioned to find how great their competitive disadvantage is, and how difficult it is to make the leap to where the other half lives. American idealism increasingly gives way to cynicism about a rigged system.

But the departure from our past is visible not only in rising inequal-ity and resultant pessimism—it is also apparent in the institutions that increasingly define our nation. Corporate conglomerates are replacing local and craft economies in almost every sector, including agriculture. America's rugged individuals struggle against the loss of identity, au-tonomy, and mastery as they are subsumed into the anonymous labor of hyper-consolidated corporate machines and forced to pool meager wages to make ends meet. Corporate monopolies have hoarded profits and gained unrivaled economic influence through a wave of mergers. Because of corporations' outsized power, workers' leverage has eroded, and capitalists cite their responsibility to shareholders and market forces as justification for keeping pay low. Corporations search at home and abroad for ever-more-vulnerable populations to employ at ever-lower wages.

In important ways, life is much improved at the bottom of American society, which makes some commentators optimistic that things will only get better. But these gains have come mostly at the price of long hours in insecure low-wage work. Slavery has been abolished, of course, but the still ruthless reality of structural inequality condemns many people of color to a life of intergenerational poverty, and in some ways the situation of black Americans is actually worsening. And women still struggle to participate equally in a society that manifestly favors male wage earners. The economic well-being of the middle class is eroding, and soaring private debt has become a common buttress to lagging incomes.

The economic power of corporations has in turn become political power. While profits mount, so, too, does corporations' creativity in evading financial and ethical responsibility to the public systems that allow them to flourish. Commercial giants successfully fend off feeble efforts to regulate them by buying off politicians and parties. Politicians collect exorbitant amounts of money from wealthy donors which they use to win elections, creating a dangerous mutuality between wealth and power. Interest groups also relentlessly pressure elected officials both to prop up corporate agendas and, paradoxically, to get out of the way of the free market. Thus, huge swaths of an increasingly interdependent economy go largely unregulated, and the system as a whole occasionally careens out of control. But the stratospherically wealthy remain insulated, even though their reckless actions often contribute to the crashes.

Inadequate regulation further fuels an irresponsible use of America's vast natural resources. The nation's GDP soars, but wildlife is disappearing at a dismaying rate, fuel sources and raw materials are exploited indiscriminately, and effluence threatens lives. And while large portions of the country have been set aside as public lands, their fate is vehemently debated, as business interests pressure the government to open protected areas for mining, grazing, and fuel extraction—citing the need for natural resources to feed a voracious economy. The rights and cultures of the native peoples who inhabit and hold those lands sacred are pushed aside in favor of business interests. Furthermore, contaminated products—including food—are sold without regard to the health or safety of consumers. The corporate mentality of the age seems to be focused solely on gaining economic advantage no matter the consequences.

Books and newspapers of the day are filled with reports of scandal in both the personal and professional lives of society's leaders, as journalists work to reveal the rotten core of an America run amok. Politicians are regularly exposed for corruption—trading in power and patronage and taking advantage of their positions in increasingly creative ways. Sex scandals are also common among the elite, and even prominent religious leaders are not immune. Crime and moral decay are the ubiquitous subjects of popular entertainment, contrasting indulgence at the top and indigence at the bottom.

As an after-the-fact attempt at carrying out their civic duty, many of America's wealthiest donate large sums of money to various philanthropic causes. This largesse erects buildings, founds institutions, and shores up cultural infrastructure, but usually in exchange for the donor's name being immortalized upon a facade. Industry leaders are often idolized for rising from humble backgrounds by employing the "true grit" of entrepreneurship and become social and cultural icons despite morally questionable actions. The message to ordinary Americans is that anyone can go from rags to riches *if* they are willing to do whatever it takes.

Indeed, many of the corporate titans who dominate the American imagination live by an ideology of individualism that barely masks selfishness and an air of superiority. A philosophy of supreme self-reliance is common, and the pursuit of unfettered self-interest is considered a laudable ethic to live by. The idea that one must do what is best for oneself at every turn—and that only those willing to live by this code deserve to prevail in the economy—has been translated into a subtle but powerful cultural narrative about the unimpeachable fairness of the market and the undeservingness of the poor. Redistributive programs are often criticized as wasteful and an irresponsible use of resources. But lavish displays of luxury, flamboyant parties, global travel, and opulent mansions are the social currency of the elite—all propped up by a growing underclass of largely immigrant laborers.

A drift toward self-centeredness in private life is matched in the public square. In politics, an overfocus on the promotion of one's own interests at the expense of others' has created an environment of relentless zero-sum competition and a repeated failure of compromise. Public debates are characterized not by deliberation on differing ideas, but by demonization of those on the opposing side. Party platforms move toward the extremes. And those in power seek to consolidate their influence by disenfranchising voters unsupportive of their views. The result is a nation more and more fragmented along economic, ideological, racial, and ethnic lines, and more and more dominated by leaders who prove shrewdest at the game of divide and conquer. The inevitable result is political gridlock and a hobbled public sector. Decaying infrastructure, inadequate basic services, and outmoded public programs are a national embarrassment. Citizens rightly despair of elected officials ever being able to accomplish anything at all.

This climate has also created a pervasive disillusionment with the nation's political parties. Neither seems capable of addressing America's problems, and many voters are turning to third parties for better options. Libertarian leanings are common while, at the other pole, socialism gains adherents. And a rising tide of populism has captured the enthusiasm of many, especially those in rural areas. America's democratic institutions strain under the burden of polarization.

In addition to this economic and political malaise, social and cultural discontent are also rising. In an America transformed by the rapid forward march of technology, new forms of communication and transportation have disconnected and reconnected people in countless ways, rearranging identities, beliefs, and value systems. Some optimistically tout the breaking of barriers and narrowing of distances between people, while many others experience loneliness, isolation, and atomization as traditional social structures give way.

The increasingly global information age is inundating people with news from every corner of the earth, and this explosion of information threatens to overwhelm the individual trying to make sense of it all. New ideas in science, philosophy, and religion upend traditional touchstones at an astonishing pace. And a culture dominated by commerce and consumption has made advertising a ubiquitous—and often lamentable—part of daily life in America. Even the reliability of the free press, that critical component of any democratic system, has become questionable, as a drive for profit overpowers a responsibility to the truth.

A fevered pace of life is often blamed for widespread stress and anxiety. Demand for stimulants of all kinds is on the rise as Americans hurry to keep up and strive to get ahead. The growing demand for productivity at all costs is claiming the physical health and emotional well-being of many individuals and families. The combined effect of these powerful technological, economic, political, and social forces is a sort of dizzying vertigo—a pervasive sense that the average person has less and less control over the forces shaping his or her individual life. Anxiety is mounting among the young, who face unprecedented challenges, and appear likely to live shorter, less rewarding lives than their parents did. This nation seems no longer recognizable or intelligible to those brought up in an earlier age, turning many older Americans toward nostalgia for a bygone era.

Some Americans have reacted to these many forms of dislocation by turning on their perceived adversaries in an increasingly cutthroat social and economic contest. Racism and gender discrimination persist and are even intensified. Indeed, the progress toward racial equality achieved in an earlier era has in many ways reversed. White supremacist violence is on the rise—often encouraged, rather than prevented, by white authorities. Tensions flare continually and conflict often turns bloody, while trust in law enforcement deteriorates with each successive clash. Massive new waves of immigrants—bringing to America ideas and religious beliefs thought to be strange and threatening—are met with hate and violence. Nativism is common and considered by many to be culturally acceptable and even patriotic. Support for restricting, and even halting, immigration from certain countries and from groups with alien political or religious views is growing. The number of immigrants entering the country illegally soars. Meanwhile, ideologically motivated terrorists ignite a backlash against all immigrants, including crackdowns by law enforcement, nationwide raids sponsored by the attorney general, and threats to civil liberties. In greater numbers than ever before, Americans seem to have stopped believing that we are all in this together.

Almost as often as we are turning on one another, Americans are responding to uncertainty and insecurity by turning to self-destructive behaviors and beliefs. Substance abuse is rampant—taking a tragic toll on family formation and claiming many lives. Materialism, too, holds out an empty promise of relief. Also attractive is a descent into cynicism and spectatorship or the adoption of an apocalyptic worldview: the American experiment has failed, and the best we can hope for is to start from scratch once it all comes apart. Whether the response is lashing out, turning inward, tuning out, or giving up, Americans are becoming increasingly paralyzed by disagreement, disillusionment, and despair. Indeed, many Americans seem to agree these days on only one thing: This is the worst of times.

Worried observers—as Tocqueville certainly would be—use words like "oligarchy," "plutocracy," and even "tyranny" to warn of the subtle reemergence of overlapping economic and political power structures that America's founding was supposed to have banished. Still others lament that the country is on the wrong track morally and culturally. Does democracy in America, they wonder, stand on the verge of ruin?

Though it would appear so in every way, the nation of which we have just written is *not* today's America. The foregoing balance sheet is actually a historically accurate portrait of this country in another era, at the opening of the *twentieth* century, just fifty years after Tocqueville wrote his stirring depiction of a thriving democracy.

The United States in the 1870s, 1880s, and 1890s was startlingly similar to today.[3] Inequality, political polarization, social dislocation, and cultural narcissism prevailed—all accompanied, as they are now, by unprecedented technological advances, prosperity, and material well-being. The parallels are indeed so striking that the foregoing description could have been written virtually word-for-word about our nation today. Looking back to a time Mark Twain disparagingly called the Gilded Age turns out to feel eerily like looking in the mirror.

Of course, other commentators have already spotted this troubling similarity. They have rightly warned that without a change in course, Americans today will have been guilty of allowing an ugly chapter in our history to repeat itself. But this comparison—remarkably apt as it is—inevitably begs the question of what actually came to pass the last time our nation found itself in such a troubling state of affairs. Clearly, the doomsday prophecies and despairing anxieties of the late 1800s were never fulfilled—the fear that the American project was headed irretrievably off the rails proved unfounded. So how did we get from the last American Gilded Age to our current predicament? What happened in the intervening century?

This book is an attempt to answer these questions. As such, it is neither a detailed assessment of our current troubles, nor an exhaustive portrait of the turn of the last century. Rather, we seek to provide a more sweeping historical perspective, aided by a vast array of newly compiled statistical evidence. This evidence provides a fresh and striking data-based portrait of the past 125 years of our nation's history, which is summarized in Figure 1.1.

The trends illustrated below represent a compendium of scores of different measures of century-long phenomena in four key areas: economics, politics, society, and culture. (The underlying numbers that comprise these four curves will be explored in the next four chapters.) As we looked closely at each of these facets of American life, we asked the basic question of whether things have been improving or deteriorating since the turn of the twentieth century. In other words, over the past 125 years, since the last Gilded Age, has America been moving toward

- greater or lesser economic equality?
- greater or lesser comity and compromise in politics?
- greater or lesser cohesion in social life?
- greater or lesser altruism in cultural values?

When charting the answers to these questions side by side, we found an unmistakable—even breathtaking—pattern. In each unique case, the trend line looks like an inverted U, starting its long upward climb at roughly the same moment, and then reversing to a downward descent within a remarkably similar time frame.[4]

FIGURE 1.1: **ECONOMIC, POLITICAL, SOCIAL, AND CULTURAL TRENDS, 1895–2015**

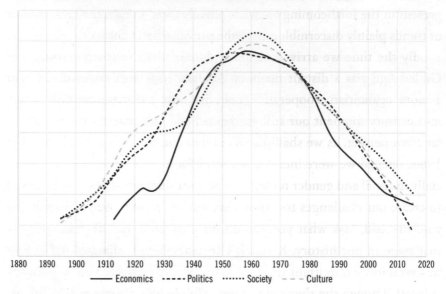

Source: See endnote 1.4. Data LOESS smoothed: .2.

A great variety of measures shows that on the heels of the first American Gilded Age came more than six decades of imperfect but steady upward progress toward *greater* economic equality, *more* cooperation in the public square, a *stronger* social fabric, and a *growing* culture of solidarity. Throughout the first two thirds of the twentieth century we actually narrowed the economic chasm born in the Gilded Age, making progress not only during the Great Depression and World War II, but for decades both before and after. In that same period we gradually overcame extreme political polarization and learned to collaborate across party lines. We also steadily wove an ever-stronger network of community and family ties. And our culture became more focused on our responsibilities to one another and less focused on our narrower self-interest. In short, America experienced a dramatic, multifaceted, and unmistakable upswing.

During these decades Americans became—perhaps more than ever before—focused on what we could accomplish together. And this sense of shared responsibility and collective progress was not simply some victory lap after overcoming the Great Depression and defeating the Axis powers, as many have suggested. As this chart makes clear, and as the data we shall present in the forthcoming chapters prove, it was, in fact, the culmination of trends plainly discernible across the previous half century.

By the time we arrived at the middle of the twentieth century, the Gilded Age was a distant memory. America had been transformed into a more egalitarian, cooperative, cohesive, and altruistic nation. At this mid-century moment our still segregated and still chauvinist society was far from perfect, as we shall discuss in detail in later chapters, but as the 1960s opened we were increasingly attentive to our imperfections, especially in racial and gender terms. Our new president described us as poised to tackle our challenges together. "Ask not what your country can do for you," he said, "ask what you can do for your country." To Americans at that stage in our history, Kennedy's argument that collective well-being was even more important than individual well-being was hardly counter-cultural. Though the rhetoric was powerful, to his contemporaries he was stating the obvious.

Over the first six decades of the twentieth century America had become demonstrably—indeed measurably—a more "we" society.

But then, as the foregoing graph indicates, and as those who lived through that period know too well, in the mid-1960s the decades-long upswing in our shared economic, political, social, and cultural life abruptly reversed direction. America suddenly found itself in the midst of a clear downturn. Between the mid-1960s and today—by scores of hard measures along multiple dimensions—we have been experiencing *declining* economic equality, the *deterioration* of compromise in the public square, a *fraying* social fabric, and a *descent* into cultural narcissism. As the 1960s moved into the 1970s, 1980s, and beyond, we re-created the socioeconomic chasm of the last Gilded Age at an accelerated pace. In that same period we replaced cooperation with political polarization. We allowed our community and family ties to unravel to a marked extent. And our culture became far more focused on individualism and less interested in the common good. Since the 1950s we have made important progress in expanding individual rights (often building on progress made in the preceding decades), but we have sharply *regressed* in terms of shared prosperity and community values.

JFK had foreshadowed the transformation that was to come, because his idealistic rhetoric was, in retrospect, proclaimed from a summit to which we had painstakingly climbed, but were about to tumble right back down. And though that summit was certainly not nearly as high as America could hope to climb toward equality and inclusion, it was closer than we had yet come to enacting the Founders' vision of "one nation . . .with liberty and justice for all." Thus, Kennedy's call to put shared interest above self-interest may have sounded at the time like reveille for an era that was opening—a new frontier of even greater shared victories—but with the perspective of the full century, we can now see that instead he was unwittingly sounding taps for an era that was about to close.

Over the past five decades America has become demonstrably—indeed measurably—a more "I" society.

Generally speaking, each of the trends we uncovered is recognized in the relevant scholarly literature, although they have largely been examined separately. Rarely have scholars recognized the striking concurrence of a multiplicity of factors that followed the same curvilinear course in the twentieth century.[5] Furthermore, examinations of these trends have most often focused exclusively on the second half of the curve—America's downturn—ignoring the equally notable first half—America's upswing. By contrast, our study aims to achieve a broad analysis of many different variables over a much longer period of time in order to expose the deeper structural and cultural tendencies that have roots in the opening decades of the twentieth century and that have culminated in today's multifaceted national crisis.

By using advanced methods of data analysis to combine our four key metrics into a unified statistical story, we have been able to discern a single core phenomenon—one inverted U-curve that provides a scientifically validated summary of the past 125 years in America's story. This meta-trend, represented in Figure 1.2, is a phenomenon we have come to call the "I-we-I" curve: a gradual climb into greater interdependence and cooperation, followed by a steep descent into greater independence and egoism. It has been reflected in our experience of equality, our expression of democ-

racy, our stock of social capital, our cultural identity, and our shared understanding of what this nation is all about.

FIGURE 1.2: **COMMUNITY VS. INDIVIDUALISM IN AMERICA, 1890–2017**

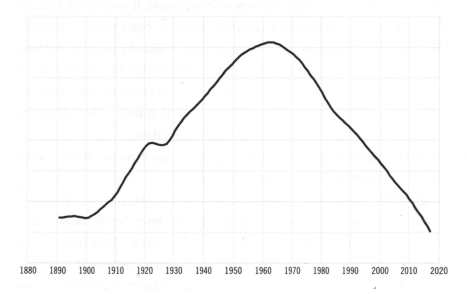

Source: See endnote 1.4. Data LOESS smoothed: .1.

In each of the next four chapters of this book we will consider a single
core trend: economics, politics, society, and culture, and reflect upon how
its unfolding has contributed to our nation's upswing toward a "we" ethos
and subsequent downturn toward an "I" ethos. As we zero in on each inverted U-curve, we will take a deep dive into the myriad underlying statistical measures that comprise the overarching trend but, equally important,
we explore its historical context—the unique confluence of circumstances,
forces, and factors that likely contributed to its formation. As a result, in
the historical narratives throughout this book we will revisit certain characters and events several different times as we view the century's unfolding
through our four basic analytical lenses—economics, politics, society, and
culture.

Two additional analytical perspectives that we will apply to this time period, devoting a separate chapter to each, are race and gender. Indeed, no discussion of "I" and "we" in the twentieth century could be complete without asking the question of how these trends were or were not reflected in the experience of traditionally excluded groups. However, because our analysis necessarily relies upon data sets that span 100+ years of history, we spend far less time in this book discussing the experience of Latinos, Asian Americans, Native Americans, and other peoples of color than we do African Americans. This is certainly not because these groups and their unique stories are unimportant, but because the statistical sources on which this book relies do not consistently single out other peoples of color alongside African Americans until late in the twentieth century, making it nearly impossible to discern long-term trends in a rigorous way. Our discussion of race is therefore focused on African Americans, and our mention of other racial and ethnic minorities is limited.

While aggregate measures of economic inequality, political polarization, social fragmentation, and cultural narcissism all follow a strikingly similar inverted U-curve over the course of our 125-year period, the story is far more complex when it comes to measures of racial and gender equality. Because African Americans, women, and many others had to fight to achieve even basic forms of equality and inclusion during the first two thirds of the twentieth century, it might be fair to assume that any supposed "we" America was moving toward in this period was inherently racist and sexist. Indeed, it is imperative for this study to consider the very real possibility that the "we" taking shape at this time was a fundamentally white, male "we."

The broad-strokes histories of both race and gender in twentieth-century America are often characterized not as an inverted U-curve, but as something resembling a hockey stick. In other words, widespread intolerance, inequality, and oppression are often thought to have been the unchanged norm for blacks and women until the watershed changes of the mid-Sixties Civil Rights and feminist revolutions led to improvements at an unprecedented pace. However, this cartoon history is in important respects misleading. A close reading of the data, which we will present in later chapters, indicates that a surprising number of gains in both racial and gender equality happened well before 1970—and in fact constituted a long period of progress that corresponds to the story told by the variables charted above. It seems that as America's sense of "we" was expanding over the first two thirds of the century, blacks and women actually benefited as racial and gender disparities in education, income, health, and voting gradually narrowed. We will therefore argue that the rights revolutions of the 1960s and 1970s must be seen not as a bolt from the blue, but rather as the culmination of more than four decades of progress. This progress was most often made in persistently segregated spheres, was (in the case of race) driven largely by black Americans themselves rather than by institutional change, and was certainly far from sufficient, but it is nevertheless a vitally important part of the history of equality and inclusion in the twentieth century.

Furthermore, our examination of race in twentieth-century America will show that the decades after 1970—the period Americans often believe brought about the greatest gains in racial equality—actually represented a marked slowdown of progress for black Americans. (The story of gender equality is somewhat different, as we shall explain in detail in Chapter 7.) This period of deceleration is as surprising as it is clear, but *also* corresponds to the story told by the curves charted above. It seems that as America took a more individualistic and narcissistic turn after 1970, we simultaneously took our "foot off the gas" in pushing toward true racial equality. This surprising and even counterintuitive story, which focuses not on absolute levels of racial equality, but the *rate of change over time*, challenges some popularly accepted ideas about the history of race relations in this nation. Thus, when it comes to racial equality the shape of the curves looks different, but the phenomenon underlying the data turns out to be a subtle and unexpected confirmation of the story of America's I-we-I century. We will lay out this case in detail in Chapters 6 and 7, which is why the preceding chapters will address questions of race and gender only lightly.

And yet, despite the real and often underemphasized progress African Americans and women were making early in the century, our analysis also reveals the undeniable ways in which the mid-century "we" was nonetheless highly racialized and gendered, and just how far short of the goal we were, even at a time when America's comity and cohesion were at an unprecedented high. It is thus critical to avoid nostalgia about the 1950s as some sort of "golden age" in America's quest for an egalitarian society—exactly because of the experience of people of color, women, and other embattled groups. Indeed, we will see clear evidence of the fact that America's failure to create a fully inclusive, fully egalitarian "we" over the first two thirds of the century played a critical role in the nation's larger turn toward "I." Why this is and what it could mean for the challenges we face today will be one of the more thought-provoking questions this book will take on. And it may turn out to be a key that unlocks a greater understanding of why today—half a century after the Civil Rights and women's revolutions—we find ourselves in a society still deeply divided along racial and ethnic lines and still struggling to define and achieve gender equality.

Our ongoing failure to achieve racial and gender equality and inclusion is a deeply troubling aspect of our national life—indeed one that violates foundational principles of the American project. However, it is far from the only problem our country now faces. In politics we're fighting in exceptionally angry ways; in economics the gap between rich and poor is tremendous in virtually all aspects of life; in social life we are often lonely, disconnected, and despairing; and our "selfie" culture continually reveals itself to be blindly narcissistic. Today we find ourselves living in an extremely polarized, extremely unequal, extremely fragmented, and extremely self-centered nation, a fact of which we are all painfully aware. For nearly fifty years, across party lines and with only a few short interruptions, most Americans—by a two to one margin or more over the last decade—have said that our country "is on the wrong track."[6] A recent study by the Pew Research Center revealed that Americans are "broadly pessimistic" about the future, with clear majorities predicting that the gap between rich and poor will widen, that the country will become yet more divided politically, and that the US will decrease in importance on the world stage over the next thirty years.[7] The American Psychological Association reports that "the future of our nation" is a bigger source of stress among average Americans than even their own finances or work.[8]

How did we get here? Until we can answer that question, we shall be condemned to plunge further down an ever-darkening path.

The 1960s represented an extraordinarily important hinge point in the history of the twentieth century—a moment of inflection that changed the course of the nation. But, as this book will argue, accurately answering the question of how we got here is only possible when viewing the Sixties as a *second* inflection, not a first. The coming apart set in motion in the mid-1960s, though deeply salient to those who lived through it, was a phenomenon whose effects were largely equal and opposite to what had happened as the century opened. Only when our lens zooms out far enough to consider both of these hinge points together can we begin to get an accurate picture of how we have arrived at our current predicament—and how we might navigate our way out again. Indeed, our hope is that by presenting a new, evidence-based story spanning the past 125 years of our nation's history we might begin to bridge the "OK Boomer"[9] generational divide—and the many other lines of fracture facing our nation—in order to construct a shared vision for the future that we can all work toward *together*.

Rebecca Edwards, a historian of the Gilded Age, observed that "the lessons one draws from a period of history depend to a large degree on one's choice of beginning and ending points."[10] This book will argue that the historical period from which we must take our instruction today doesn't start in the 1960s. Looking back only that far has taken many commentators down the road of nostalgia—leaving them little more to do than lament some paradise lost and argue about whether and how we should re-create it. In other words, looking to the moment when an upswing culminated turns out not to be very instructive. Looking to the moment of its inception proves far more fruitful, especially when the context of that moment bears a striking resemblance to the context in which we find ourselves today. As represented in the subtitle of this book, our thesis is not that we should return nostalgically to some peak of American greatness, but that we should take inspiration and perhaps instruction from a period of despair much like our own, on the heels of which Americans successfully—and measurably—bent history in a more promising direction.

If, as Shakespeare wrote, "what's past is prologue," then what follows surely depends upon us gaining a right understanding of where we've been. The seldom remembered second half of the Shakespearean epigram—"what to come, in yours and my discharge"—reveals not a pessimistic statement of historical determinism, but rather a more realistic and even optimistic argument that the past merely sets the agenda for choice going forward. Coming to see our past more clearly serves to better prepare us to gain mastery over our future.

Let us begin, then, at the beginning.

This book will trace the roots of today's problems to the last time these same problems threatened to engulf our democracy. It contains an evidence-based story about how we have arrived at our current predicament. We will examine how economic inequality, political polarization, social fragmentation, cultural narcissism, racism, and gender discrimination each evolved over the course of the last 125 years—not merely the last fifty. Doing so will unearth some unexpected twists and turns, and will challenge some settled truths among pundits and historians about the twentieth century—the "American Century."

Rather than citing some recent event or offering a narrative of long-run decline, we will argue that the state of America today must be understood by first acknowledging that within living memory, each of the adverse trends we now see was going in the opposite direction. And we will show that, to a surprising degree, century-long trends in economics, politics, society, and culture are remarkably similar, such that it is possible to summarize all of them in a single phenomenon: The story of the American experiment in the twentieth century is one of a long upswing toward increasing solidarity, followed by a steep downturn into increasing individualism. From "I" to "we," and back again to "I."

The Upswing is a history of the United States in the twentieth century, but it is avowedly a simplified history, and it leaves out much that is also important. But in so doing, it accentuates real trends that are highly relevant to our current set of challenges. This book is, therefore, an exercise in macrohistory, and as such it will be controversial among historians. Furthermore, writing contemporary history is always precarious, because our understanding of the past evolves as the future unfolds. Peaks, valleys, and inflection points take on new meaning in the light of each new decade. But we borrow our motto from Alfred North Whitehead: "Seek simplicity and distrust it."[11] Finally, this book is not primarily about causal analysis. It is about narratives. Narratives, as we use the term, are not merely entertaining tales, but events linked together in trends inter-braided by reciprocal causality. The strands of a narrative are inextricable, but still interpretable, and therefore instructive as we look to the future.

As Tocqueville rightly noted, in order for the American experiment to succeed, personal liberty must be fiercely protected, but also carefully balanced with a commitment to the common good. Individuals' freedom to pursue their own interests holds great promise, but relentlessly exercising that freedom at the expense of others has the power to unravel the very foundations of the society that guarantees it. Looking back over the full arc of the twentieth century, we will see these ideas and their consequences borne out in vivid historical and statistical detail. And finally we will turn to the implications of our findings for reformers today. For the arc we describe is not an arc of historical inevitability, but an arc constructed by human agency, just as Shakespeare suggested.

Perhaps the single most important lesson we can hope to gain from this analysis is that in the past America has experienced a storm of unbridled individualism in our culture, our communities, our politics, and our economics, and it produced then, as it has today, a national situation that few Americans found appealing. But we successfully weathered that storm once, and we *can* do it again. If ever there were a historical moment whose lessons we as a nation need to learn, then, it is the moment when the first American Gilded Age turned into the Progressive Era, a moment which set in motion a sea change that helped us reclaim our nation's promise, and whose effects rippled into almost every corner of American life for over half a century.[12] Understanding what set those trends in motion, then, becomes of critical importance. We will therefore close our book by examining the inflection that set the stage for the twentieth century's communitarian climb, attempting to glean lessons from the story of those who, during the last American Gilded Age, refused to let go of the reins of history, and took deliberate action to reverse its course. In their story, more than in the story of those who lived through a supposed golden age, we may find the tools and inspiration we need today to create another American upswing—this time with an unwavering commitment to complete inclusion that will take us toward a yet higher summit, and a fuller and more sustainable realization of the promise of "we."

2

ECONOMICS: THE RISE AND FALL OF EQUALITY

Our story of America's I-we-I century begins with a look at trends in economic prosperity and material well-being over the past 125 years, as well as how evenly distributed economic gains and losses have been during that time.

So how are we Americans doing? Let's begin with creature comforts. Here sunny-side optimists like Steven Pinker[1] seem to have a strong case, and we must begin by acknowledging the long-run aggregate improvements. As measured by the luxuries—and even the length—of our lives, American prosperity has advanced steadily and powerfully for a century and more, based in part on technological advances, in part on an entrepreneurial spirit, and in part on wise public investments, especially in education and infrastructure. But we shall shortly offer abundant evidence that long-term gains conceal sharp inequalities in the distribution of income, wealth, and well-being among Americans.

PROSPERITY, HEALTH, AND EDUCATION: AN OVERFLOWING CORNUCOPIA

Since 1900, Americans have become, on average, healthier, wealthier, and if not wiser, then at least more educated, although as we shall see, the education story is somewhat more complicated. These decades have seen our lifespan nearly double and have witnessed the transition from outhouses to iPhones, from dusty wagons on dirt roads to the advent of space tourism, from cracker-barrel country stores to drone deliveries.

Objective measures show remarkable, virtually uninterrupted progress over more than a century. The simplest measure of this progress is provided by Figure 2.1, showing year-by-year growth in gross domestic product (GDP) per capita.[2]

FIGURE 2.1: LONG-TERM REAL GROWTH IN US GDP PER CAPITA, 1871–2016

Source: C. I. Jones, "The Facts of Economic Growth." See endnote 2.2.

Economists have shown that (as is clear from Figure 2.1), the slope of this upward curve in economic prosperity has been remarkably constant at 2 percent per year since the beginning of the Industrial Revolution. Indeed, over the century after 1871 the only visible deviation from the steady pulse of the American economy was the Great Depression (when GDP per capita fell nearly 20 percent in four years), followed by the World War II catch-up boom. However, as economist C. I. Jones reports, "To me this decline stands out most for how anomalous it is. Many of the other recessions barely make an impression on the eye: over long periods of time, economic growth swamps economic fluctuations."[3]

Economists have devoted much thought and energy to explaining this continuous growth—which was once considered "a stylized fact,"[4] that is, a fact so widely accepted that almost no one disputes it. More recently, the growth rate seems to have slowed significantly after 1970, falling below the long-term rate of 2 percent a year, perhaps because technological innovation is no longer leading to steady growth in productivity.[5] That discovery should dampen any cheery optimism about the 2 percent "stylized" growth rate continuing into the future. But for most of the period we cover in this book material progress seemed steady and assured.

Many scholarly tomes—and many political campaigns—have debated potential explanations, but for our purposes, the central factor appears to be technological and educational progress, powerfully fostered by both public and private investment. The specific technologies and forms of education that have been most relevant have, of course, varied across this century—from high schools and telephones and automobiles in the first half of the period to universities and microchips and biotech in the second half. But like the little engine that could, the American economy chugged relentlessly upward, decade after decade, powered primarily by technology and education.

This same steady, upward trajectory is mirrored in many measures of creature comfort that have enriched the daily lives of ordinary Americans. A few charts illustrate how our material existence has been gradually transformed for the better since 1900.

Take our dwellings. Figure 2.2 shows that decade after decade the average American home has steadily expanded, nearly doubling in size since the end of the nineteenth century. Meanwhile, inside those ever-larger homes the convenience of flush toilets—enjoyed by fewer than one in seven Americans in 1900—became virtually universal over the next seven decades, as did time- and labor-saving household appliances, such as vacuum cleaners, which spread from 10 percent of American homes to

90 percent in the half century between 1920 and 1970.[6] In short, decade by decade for more than a century American homes have become larger, more comfortable, and easier to maintain. Of course, not all Americans live in equally luxurious homes, and we shall turn our attention to inequality in the next section of this chapter, but on average American standards and expectations for housing have soared upward.

The same is true of transportation. Here a single illustration will suffice, as Figure 2.3 displays the remarkably sustained surge in Americans' love affair with the automobile over more than a century.[7] Indeed, the only periods of brief stagnation were during the Great Depression, World War II (when automobile production was halted for the duration), and the recent Great Recession. In fact, between 1915 and 2015 the number of vehicles per 1,000 inhabitants in the U.S. exploded from 25 to 820—a growth rate of 3.5 percent per year across an entire century!—a stark statistical indicator of dramatically improved ease and comfort of transportation for hundreds of millions of ordinary Americans.

FIGURE 2.2: **AMERICAN HOMES GET LARGER (1891–2010)**

Source: Moura, Smith, and Belzer, "120 Years of U.S. Residential Housing Stock and Floor Space." See endnote 2.6.

FIGURE 2.3: CARS PROLIFERATE, 1900–2015

Source: *Transportation Energy Data Book*, Department of Energy, Table 3.6.

Scores of similar charts could be added to show the steady proliferation of life-improving gadgets—from telephones to refrigerators to clothes washers to electronic entertainment.[8] The bottom line for long-run trends in the material conditions of the average American can be neatly summed up in a slightly edited mid-century advertising slogan from DuPont—"better things for better living—through technology."

Even more elemental evidence of steady material progress in America over the last 125 years comes from statistics on life and death. Figure 2.4 focuses on the dramatic, century-long decline in infant mortality: As the twentieth century opened, out of every 1,000 births, 129 babies died before their first birthday, but as the twenty-first century opened, that tragic toll had been slashed to barely 7. To be sure, as we shall emphasize later in this book, important racial and class disparities persisted, but all parts of American society benefited from this enormous advance.

Figure 2.5 widens our lens to look at the comparable trend for life expectancy across the full life cycle. (The singular deviation from this remarkable record of steadily improving health is explained by the astonishingly lethal influenza pandemic of 1918.) Americans born in 1900 could expect to live on average to age 47. Their children (born, let's say, in 1925) could expect to live to age 59, their grandchildren (born in 1950) to age 68, their great-grandchildren (born in 1975) to age 73, and their great-great grandchildren (born in 2000) to age 77. Within barely one century the lifespan of the average American lengthened by three decades.

FIGURE 2.4: **INFANT MORTALITY, 1890–2013**

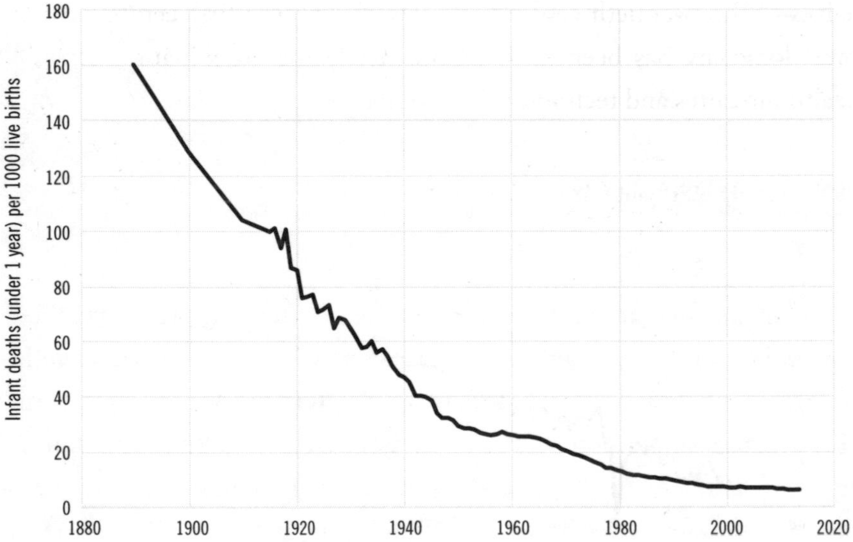

Source: *Historical Statistics of the United States*, Table Ab 920.

This seemingly inexorable improvement in population health actually represents two quite different eras during which different causes of mortality were mastered. The gains in the first half of the twentieth century derived from advances in public health (especially clean water), improved nutrition, and the development of antibiotics.[9] Death rates from infectious diseases fell by 90 percent in the first half of the century, accounting for the lion's share of rising life expectancy. The benefits in this first era were concentrated among children, while very little progress was made against the maladies of older Americans.

By contrast, during the second half of the century, after the defeat of infectious diseases, medical advances in the form of pharmaceuticals (Lipitor, for example), medical technology that allows early diagnosis, and surgical techniques (angioplasty, for example) sharply reduced death rates among the elderly, first from heart disease and then increasingly from cancer. The public anti-smoking campaign was another important contributor though its effects were necessarily lagged, as deaths caused by packs smoked in the middle of the century occurred decades later. In short, across both halves of the twentieth century and into the twenty-first century, Americans' longevity has been steadily enhanced by a combination of public health measures and technological progress.

FIGURE 2.5: LIFE EXPECTANCY, 1900–2017

Source: National Center for Health Statistics.

Both Figure 2.4 and Figure 2.5 hide important social inequalities in health—especially along racial and class lines—and we will focus intently on those disparities in this and succeeding chapters. Nevertheless, it remains true that the average American today enjoys substantially better health and will live longer than her parents and (still more) her grandparents or great-grandparents.

In the last few years, however, that line not only stopped ascending, but began to descend.[10] This unfortunate change can be largely attributed to sharp rises in fatalities due to drugs, alcohol, or suicide—more commonly known as "deaths of despair."[11] In their 2020 book, *Deaths of Despair and the Future of Capitalism*, economists Anne Case and Angus Deaton offer powerful evidence of the growing incidence of deaths of despair and trace the origins of this trend to deep-seated social inequities.[12] Drug overdoses, in particular, have recently spiked, reflecting an opioid epidemic related to social strife, impediments to economic mobility, and lethal misconduct by the pharmaceutical industry.[13] While these deaths of despair afflict the entire nation, they especially affect rural communities, working-class individuals, and young adults.[14] The emergence of deaths of despair in recent years is important not merely because of the human tragedies they reveal, but because they are a warning signal that the broader social trends discussed in this book may bring yet more calamities.

Nonetheless, the overall case for long-term American optimists seems strong. We might term this perspective on the twentieth and early twenty-first centuries "the view from Silicon Valley or MIT." Every decade and indeed almost every year our material and physical lives have steadily improved—primarily because of underlying technological progress.

In fact, this diagnosis is shared by the American people: When the Pew Research Center asked Americans in 2017 to name the biggest improvements to life over the past half century, we overwhelmingly cited technology (42 percent) and medicine and health (14 percent), and when asked to predict the biggest improvements to life over the next half century, technology (22 percent) and medicine and health (20 percent) again topped the list.[15]

A third domain of American life—education—at first glance appears to show exactly the same steady and substantial rate of improvement, although more closely examined, educational trends are subtly different.

As the twentieth century opened, "common schools" providing free public elementary education were already widespread in the US, with the important exception of the African American population in the South.[16] The US had virtually the highest literacy and educational rates in the world. However, secondary and college education were still confined to a small fraction of the population.

Building on that sturdy foundation, during the twentieth century two major educational revolutions in America led first to nearly universal high school education and then to widespread college education. Americans typically complete our formal education as young adults and maintain that level of education throughout the rest of our lives, so population-wide measures of educational attainment change slowly, just as a bathtub full of water changes temperature more slowly than the flow at the faucet. Even after a major advance in educational access, the impact of that advance is obscured by the persistence of generations educated (or not) decades earlier. Thus, to see the immediate effects of educational innovations, we need to focus on the educational attainments of successive *youth* cohorts. This distinction is the familiar accounting distinction between "stock" and "flow" measures, and we focus here on "flow" measures.

The *high school* revolution was fostered by the "high school move-ment" in the early 1900s and was marked by the creation of free public high schools, beginning in small towns of the West and Midwest, then spreading to urban areas across the North, and finally throughout the en-tire country.[17] As Figure 2.6 shows, as late as 1910 fewer than one in every ten young people received a high school degree, but within barely five decades that mark of educational attainment exploded to nearly seven in ten, as public high schools sprouted in communities across the land. (The only exception to this uninterrupted growth came during World War II, when many young men were away at war.) Educational advancement in the half century after 1910 was so rapid that its effects were visible within individual families. Of young people coming of age in the mid-1960s, three quarters were high school graduates, as compared to fewer than half of their parents and barely one tenth of their grandparents.

This remarkably successful institutional innovation led *both* to a mas-sive increase in the productivity of American workers (thus accounting for

the lion's share of overall economic growth in this period) *and* to an increase in upward mobility, because universal high school education leveled
the playing field.[18] Economic growth and social equality moved steadily
upward in tandem, contrary to some presumptions that equality and
growth are incompatible. As the Sixties opened, no end of that educational,
economic, and social progress was in sight.

Then, however, as Figure 2.6 shows, suddenly America took its foot
off the educational gas pedal and began coasting (and even slowing), initiating a surprising pause in high school expansion that would last for more
than four decades.[19] Only as the twenty-first century opened did the incidence of high school graduation begin once again to rise, though the post-
2000 increase was probably later, smaller, and less sustained than the
inflated official figures shown in Figure 2.6 suggest. The latest research
suggests that the high school graduation rate, properly measured, is perhaps 5 percentage points higher than it was a half century ago, compared
to a rise of more than 70 percentage points in the previous half century.[20]

FIGURE 2.6: **HIGH SCHOOL GRADUATION RATE, 1870–2015**

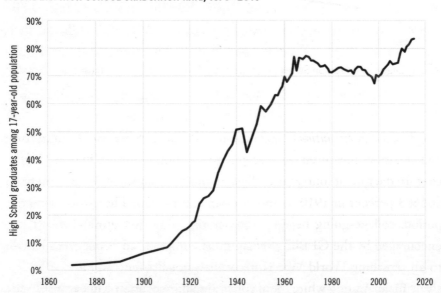

Source: *Historical Statistics of the United States*; National Center for Educational Statistics.

So although educational attainment as measured by high school graduation has risen over more than 125 years, that inexplicable and prolonged
halt after the mid-1960s will merit revisiting later in this book, because it
turns out that many other measures of social progress halted at the very
same time.[21]

FIGURE 2.7: **COLLEGE GRADUATION RATE, 1910–2013**

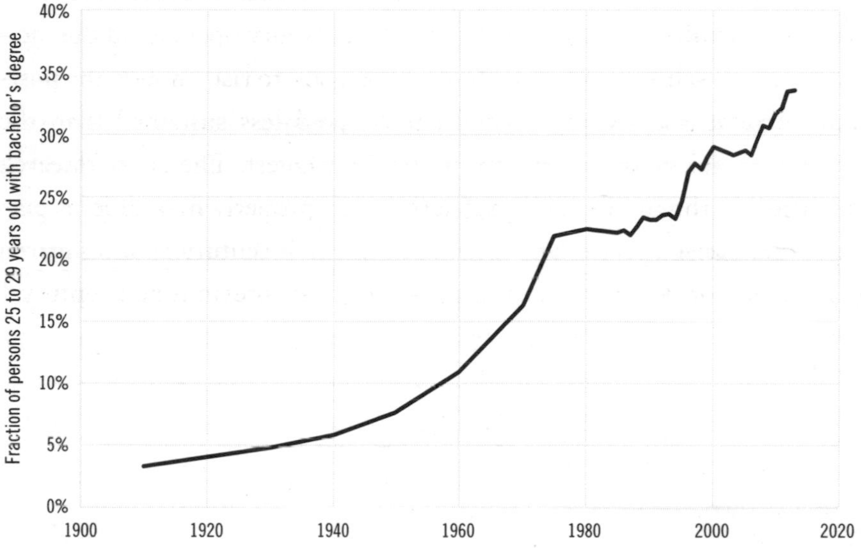

Source: Digest of Education Statistics, National Center for Educational Statistics.

The *college revolution* occurred somewhat later in the twentieth century
and at a more measured pace, as Figure 2.7 shows. For the first half of the
century the rate of four-year college graduation edged slowly upward from
about 3 percent in 1910 to about 8 percent in 1950. Then in the postwar
period, college-going began a steeper rise. The first upward thrust was
encouraged by the GI Bill offering greatly discounted[22] college education
to all returning World War II veterans—mostly white and almost exclusively male. Among white men, college-going accelerated in earnest in the
early 1960s, temporarily widening preexisting gender and racial disparities.

However, within a decade more ambitious college aspirations began to spread among women and nonwhites, as well, and by the early 1980s both the gender and the racial gaps had begun to narrow.[23] In short, in the first three quarters of the twentieth century the fraction of all young Americans with college degrees rose at an accelerating pace from 3 percent to 22 percent. Then, in 1975, roughly a decade after the "foot off the gas" pause in high school graduation rates, a similar pause of almost two decades interrupted the century-long progress in college graduation rates. Not until the end of the twentieth century did measures of educational attainment resume growth.

In sum, like all the measures of progress explored in this section of this chapter, educational gauges show marked advancement over more than a century, but unlike the indicators of material and physical well-being, educational progress has not been entirely uninterrupted, perhaps in part because—unlike material and medical progress—educational progress relies less directly on inexorable technological advance and more on social institutions and behavioral change. We will return to this puzzling "foot off the gas" phenomenon later in the book, but for now it must remain an anomaly. The basic story of this section is simple: On average, by many important measures, life in America has gotten better and better for more than a century.

ECONOMIC EQUALITY

Obviously, nationwide averages conceal more gains for some groups and fewer gains or even losses for others; that is how averages work. But the distribution of gains and losses matters, and the purpose of the rest of this chapter is to survey how that distribution has changed since the end of the nineteenth century.[24] What have been the ebbs and flows of economic equality over the last 125 years?

As we observed in Chapter 1, economic disparities in the first Gilded Age were massive, as millions of poor immigrants, impoverished (though now emancipated) blacks, and the native-born white working class confronted the moneyed robber barons of the economic elite. Statistics on the evolution of inequality in the last half of the nineteenth century are sketchy, but the net rise in nationwide economic inequality over this period appears to have been modest, offset in part by the substantial boost in black economic circumstances within the South implied by Emancipation. However, at the very top, the slice of the growing pie seized by the very richest Americans swelled. Roughly speaking, the top 1 percent's share of national income nearly doubled from less than 10 percent in 1870 to approaching 20 percent in 1913.[25] Inequalities in income, wealth, and status were vast and seemed destined to grow in perpetuity.

What followed instead was a surprisingly durable turn toward a halcyon period of roughly six decades during which economic inequalities were substantially reduced—what economic historians call the "Great Leveling" or "Great Convergence."[26] Dating this period is not an exact science, but the most recent and widely accepted account of US economic history, by Peter H. Lindert and Jeffrey G. Williamson, dates it from roughly 1913 to roughly 1970.[27] Precise magnitudes and timing vary according to what part of the income distribution we focus on—the very top, the broad middle, or the poor at the very bottom—and depending on whether we look at "market" income or instead take account of government taxes and transfers. But virtually all evidence confirms the same broad pattern. As Lindert and Williamson explain,

> What happened during the Great Leveling was much broader than just a decline in the top income shares. Inequality diminished even within the middle and lower ranks. And the Great Leveling was not just a manifestation of government's redistribution from rich to poor with taxes and transfers. Incomes became more equal both before and after those taxes and transfers.[28]

INCOME

Figure 2.8 illustrates this trend, focusing for simplicity's sake on the share of national income held by the top 1 percent of Americans.[29] (For purposes of consistency, all the charts in this book are oriented so that "up" means "more equality," "more community," and so forth. Accordingly, in this case the vertical axis is oriented such that "up" reflects a smaller proportion of income held by the top 1 percent of families.) The ascent of the two lines in Figure 2.8 (one representing market incomes and the other representing incomes after taxes and transfers, such as Medicaid) from 1913 to the mid-1970s is gradual and somewhat uneven, but that upswing reflects the steady increase in economic equality over that period. No matter how we measure it, the gap between rich and poor gradually narrowed over those sixty years.

The lower line represents the less equal distribution of income before taxes and transfers, and the upper line represents the more equal distribution after taxes and transfers, so the space between the two lines represents the net effect of government redistribution. Before taking account of taxes and transfers, the richest 1 percent of Americans in 1913 claimed 19 percent of the national income, but by 1976 their share had been nearly halved to 10.5 percent. After taxes and transfers, share of national income

FIGURE 2.8: INCOME EQUALITY IN THE UNITED STATES, 1913–2014

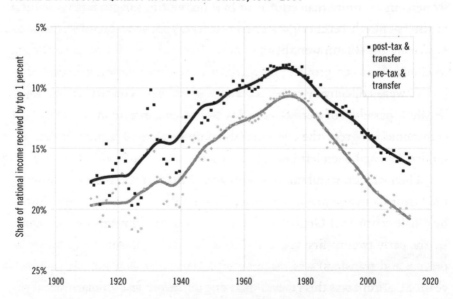

Source: Piketty, Saez, and Zucman, *QJEcon* May 2018. Data LOESS smoothed: .2.

received by the top 1 percent had been cut even more, from 18 percent to 8 percent. (By 2014, these figures had doubled all the way back to 20 percent before tax and transfers and 16 percent after tax and transfers.) We shall shortly discuss in more detail how the evolution of taxes and transfers over the last 125 years has affected inequality. Nevertheless, after all the qualifications, virtually every technical specification shows the same basic curve: six decades of convergence and ever greater equality. The point is not that overnight America became absolutely equal, but that in the first decade or two of the twentieth century our national trajectory changed—instead of becoming less and less equal, we were becoming more and more equal.

As we saw earlier in this chapter, these same six decades also witnessed substantial growth in the aggregate American economy; virtually everyone, rich and poor alike, benefited from this growth. However, during the Great Convergence low- and middle-income groups gained a *growing* share of the *expanding* pie. Lindert and Williamson estimate that over this period "the real income per family of the top 1 percent rose by 21.5 percent in the United States, while . . . average real family income for the bottom 99 percent . . . more than tripled."[30] In other words, for the first two thirds of the twentieth century greater national prosperity and greater equality in sharing the wealth went hand in hand. In those decades we did not have to choose between growth and equality, as some economic theories have it—we were collectively richer *and* more equal. Mid-century America was hardly a paradise of perfect equality, but after more than sixty years of continuous progress, the chasm between opulence and penury of the first Gilded Age had been left behind.

Then suddenly and unexpectedly in the mid-1970s, Figure 2.8 shows, the Great Convergence was reversed in a dramatic U-turn, to be followed by a half century of Great Divergence, that is, plunging income equality. By the early twenty-first century income inequality in America (especially pre-tax and transfers) was reaching an intensity unseen for one hundred years. So abrupt was this reversal that one of the earliest scholarly accounts of it was subtitled "A Tale of Two Half-Centuries."[31] In the most recent half century, in vivid contrast to the previous half century, what growth there was came at the expense of equality, and the rich captured the lion's share of the growth dividend.

WEALTH

Understanding this inverted U-curve in the distribution of *income* in America is one purpose of this book, but first, let's glance at the equivalent trend in the distribution of *wealth*.[32] Wealth—not how much we earn in a year, but how much we accumulate over the years from savings and inheritance—has always been much more unequally distributed than income, because roughly half of all families have essentially zero net worth,[33] in effect living paycheck to paycheck. But the degree of wealth inequality, like the degree of income inequality, has varied a lot over the decades, and perhaps not surprisingly, trends in the two are closely correlated. Figure 2.9 displays how the distribution of wealth in America has evolved over the last century.[34]

FIGURE 2.9: **DISTRIBUTION OF WEALTH IN THE UNITED STATES, 1913–2014**

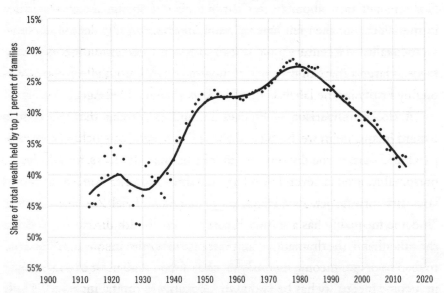

Source: Piketty, Saez, and Zucman, *QJEcon* May 2018. Data LOESS smoothed: .2.

No facet of the first Gilded Age had been more glaring than the extremes of wealth. Even in 1913 the wealthiest 1 percent owned 45 percent of the country's total wealth, and during the Roaring Twenties their share rose for a couple of years to 48 percent, as Figure 2.9 shows. In the following six decades, however, their share was more than halved to 22 percent, in large part by financial regulation and progressive taxation on income and estates, though in part because of redistributive spending. In other words, mirroring the great convergence in income was a great convergence in wealth.

However, in recent decades the top 1 percent's share of our national wealth surged back to nearly 40 percent by 2014 and has continued to increase.[35] The top 1 percent in recent years have garnered roughly 20 percent of household *income*, but nearly 40 percent of household *wealth*. The share of *wealth* held by that top 1 percent nearly doubled from less than 25 percent of total national wealth in the early 1980s to more than 40 percent in 2016. In fact, the top *0.1* percent of American families now hold about 20 percent of household wealth, almost as much as at the peak of the first Gilded Age.[36] Conversely, the share of national wealth held by the poorest 95 percent of the population nearly doubled during the Great Convergence from about 28 percent in the late 1920s to about 54 percent in the 1980s, but then fell sharply away, approaching the depths of colossal inequality of a century ago. In short, the top 1 percent now have nearly twice as large a share of the nation's wealth as the bottom 90 percent, thoroughly justifying the labeling of our age as a new Gilded Age.[37]

A closer comparison of Figures 2.8 and 2.9 reveals that the U-turn toward inequality in wealth lagged about five to ten years behind the comparable U-turn in the distribution of income (mid-1980s vs. mid-1970s)—presumably, it takes several years of multimillion-dollar bonuses to afford your first private jet. As Emmanuel Saez and Gabriel Zucman observe, "Income inequality has a snowballing effect on wealth distribution."[38] On the other hand, the dramatic recent increase in wealth inequality has begun to feed back into income inequality: Since about 2000 most of the increase in income inequality has been due to inequality in capital income.[39] These two forms of economic inequality are thus mutually reinforcing.

Emmanuel Saez, a leading scholar in this field, concludes:

U.S. income and wealth concentrations both fell dramatically during the first part of the 20th century, and remained low and stable during three decades after World War II, but there has been a sharp increase in inequality since the 1970s. The United States now combines extremely high labor income inequality with very high wealth inequality.[40]

THE GREAT CONVERGENCE

The second half of Figures 2.8 and 2.9 is much discussed in contemporary political and economic commentary, focusing on the Great Divergence between rich and poor. Pundits and politicians properly bemoan the widening gap between rich and poor, and their narratives typically begin with the troubled times of the 1970s. However, the more interesting and ultimately more encouraging tale we seek to tell begins a half century earlier with the *first* half of the inverted U-curve—the Great Convergence of the first two thirds of the twentieth century.

As we shall shortly review, the institutional, social, and cultural seeds of the Great Convergence were sown in the Progressive Era from roughly 1890 to 1910. Those seeds did not germinate overnight, however. Examined closely, the distribution of income and wealth oscillated widely between 1910 and 1930, as shown in Figures 2.8 and 2.9. National solidarity during Woodrow Wilson's war to make the world "safe for democracy" had transitory egalitarian effects. With the return of "normalcy" under conservative Warren Harding and the stock bubble of the Roaring Twenties, however, the top-end concentration of wealth and income of the Gilded Age quickly returned. In that same period, however, Claudia Goldin and Lawrence Katz discovered a substantial increase in equality within the working and middle classes.[41] Beneath the choppy weather at the top, the deeper tide of economic inequality had begun to turn.

With the Crash of 1929 the bacchanal among the 1 percent abruptly ended, even before Franklin Roosevelt took power in 1933 with his New Deal programs. Those programs, based in large part on innovations from the Progressive Era, unleashed the full force of the Great Convergence, as we shall shortly see. World War II required massive tax increases and further encouraged the sense that "we are all in this together," and measures of economic equality jumped even higher, just as during World War I. That both world wars were associated with a rapid increase in equality seems to confirm the view of the nineteenth-century sociologist Émile Durkheim that shared wartime adversity fosters strong norms of solidarity and thus equality, as well as the more recent theory that war is "The Great Leveler."[42]

In this postwar era, however, unlike after World War I, those egalitarian norms long outlasted wartime solidarity and controls, for war's end in 1945 did not trigger a reversion to severe inequality as it had in the 1920s. On the contrary, as Figures 2.8 and 2.9 clearly show, for decades after World War II the gap between rich and poor continued to narrow. Poor and middle-income Americans' share of the bounty of postwar prosperity grew, further reducing income inequality, in sharp contrast to the Roaring Twenties. "From 1945 to 1975," sociologist Douglas Massey has written, "under structural arrangements implemented during the New Deal, poverty rates steadily fell, median incomes consistently rose, and inequality progressively dropped, as a rising economic tide lifted all boats."[43] In fact, during this period the dinghies actually rose faster than the yachts. Economists Thomas Piketty, Emmanuel Saez, and Gabriel Zucman report that over these postwar decades the post-tax and transfer income of the poorest 20 percent grew three times faster than the income of the richest 1 percent—179 percent vs. 58 percent.[44]

Why economic egalitarianism long outlasted World War II, unlike World War I, will prove to be an interesting puzzle, because it suggests that the distribution of income was driven by something more basic than wartime exigencies. Something had changed between the first postwar era and the second, and the search for that something will carry us through the succeeding chapters of this book. Be that as it may, by the early 1970s the sacrifices (and wage and price controls) of World War II were hardly visible in the rearview mirror, yet the egalitarian norm that "we're all in this together" apparently persisted.

THE GREAT DIVERGENCE

But then, as we have seen, came the sharp U-turn away from economic equality. Economic historians Lindert and Williamson describe the breadth of the sea change: "Like the earlier leveling, the rise in inequality widened gaps all up and down the income ranks, and not just a rise in the share going to the top 1 percent."[45]

In the early 1970s workers' real wages began a long period of stagnation that would last for nearly half a century, even though the economy as a whole continued to grow. Initially, the middle class and the upper class together pulled away from the working class and the poor. Then in the 1980s, the top began pulling away from the middle, in effect transferring 8 percent of total national income from the bottom 50 percent to the top 1 percent. Finally, by the 1990s the very top (the top 0.1 percent) increasingly pulled away from everyone else, including the rest of the top 1 percent.[46] To be sure, the gap between the top 10 percent (essentially high-income professionals) and everyone else has continued to widen over these years, but the most rapidly growing—and indeed, breathtaking—gaps have been concentrated at the very top.[47] Over the four decades between 1974 and 2014, inflation-adjusted annual market income fell $320 for households at the 10th percentile (the bottom tenth), rose $388 for those at the 20th percentile (the bottom fifth), rose $5,232 for those at the national median, rose $75,053 for households in the top 5 percent, rose $929,108 for those in the top 1 percent, and rose $4,846,718 for those in the top 0.1 percent. There are no misprints in that sentence![48]

In stark contrast to the decades of the Great Convergence, when average Americans garnered a growing share of a growing pie, during the decades of the Great Divergence, the growth of the pie has been monopolized by a smaller and smaller group at the top. The resulting change is huge. If today's income were distributed in the same way that 1970 income was distributed, it is estimated, the bottom 99 percent would get roughly $1 trillion more annually, and the top 1 percent would get roughly $1 trillion less.[49]

This growing economic inequity is linked with growing inequality in other spheres of society, including our children's prospects for upward mobility and even our physical health.

Evidence from the first half of the twentieth century is too sparse to be certain about trends in socioeconomic mobility, but the best evidence is that upward mobility—the likelihood that a child born into a poor home would do better than his or her parents—rose during the first half of the twentieth century, in part because of the high school revolution. Economist David Card and his colleagues term this era "the Golden Age of Upward Mobility."[50] As we saw earlier in this chapter, during the first two thirds of the century a higher and higher fraction of American youth graduated from high school and college. Thus, more and more children born and educated in this period surpassed their parents in education and likely earned more, as well.

However, as we also saw in the previous section, that overall educational progress stalled in the early 1970s, and with it, upward mobility. We know from the pathbreaking work of Raj Chetty and his colleagues that beginning with young adults who reached their adult earning levels in the late 1960s, upward mobility in terms of income has been steadily declining. "Children's prospects of earning more than their parents have fallen from 90 percent to 50 percent over the past half century."[51] They attribute most of this decline in mobility precisely to the increasingly unequal distribution of economic growth. Scattered, but consistent, evidence also suggests that economic mobility rose from the birth cohort of the mid-1910s (who reached their adult earning levels in the mid-1940s) to the birth cohort of the late 1930s (who reached their adult earning levels in the mid-1960s), as shown in Figure 2.10. That in turn suggests that intergenerational economic mobility may have followed the same path as income inequality over the decades—rising during the Great Convergence up until about 1970 and then sharply falling for the next half century.[52]

As we saw earlier in this chapter, the health of the "average" American improved steadily throughout most of the twentieth century. However, that "average" conceals different trajectories for different parts of the population. Although evidence on trends in health by social class during the first part of the twentieth century is scattered, it appears that between roughly

FIGURE 2.10: **THE RISE AND FALL OF INTERGENERATIONAL ECONOMIC MOBILITY, 1947–2010**

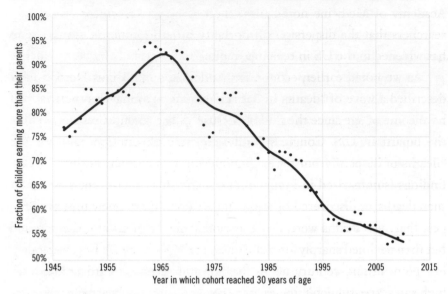

Source: Berman, "The Long Run Evolution of Absolute Intergenerational Mobility," Data LOESS smoothed: .25.

1880 and roughly 1960 health disparities by race and class narrowed, as the health of minorities and the working class improved even more rapidly than was true among the white middle and upper classes. Improvements in public health measures, which had powerful effects on morbidity and mortality, were concentrated in areas with many have-nots.[53] For example, Peter Lindert and Jeffrey Williamson describe a "spectacular" convergence in infant mortality across income classes in these years.[54]

However, while the health of the population as a whole has generally continued to improve in recent decades, class (and perhaps racial) gaps in some health indices have begun to widen in the last four decades. It appears that earlier health gains among the have-nots have slowed and, in some cases, even reversed. A review of more than a dozen recent studies published in the British medical journal *The Lancet* concluded that over the last three to four decades, "socioeconomic gaps in survival have . . . increased. Life expectancy has risen among middle-income and high-income Americans whereas it has stagnated among poor Americans and even declined in some demographic groups."[55] A group of experts convened by the National Academy of Medicine noted that "there is broad agreement among researchers that the dispersion of mortality by socioeconomic status (SES) has widened in the US in recent decades."[56]

As we noted earlier, economists Anne Case and Angus Deaton have described a wave of "deaths of despair" among working-class whites who have come of age since the middle 1970s.[57] More recently, researchers for the bipartisan U.S. Congress Joint Economic Committee have tracked "deaths of despair" from the beginning of the twentieth century.[58] Their findings (summarized in Figure 2.11) clearly show the recent upsurge in such deaths, as discovered by Case and Deaton, but the new findings suggest that such deaths were also common at the beginning of the century, but then declined sharply after the onset of the Progressive Era, reaching a low point in mid-century before beginning to climb toward today's very high rates. We still don't understand the etiology of the "deaths of despair" syndrome, but the work of Case and Deaton strongly suggests that economic distress and inequality are implicated. In other words, there is ample

FIGURE 2.11: **THE RISE AND FALL OF DEATHS OF DESPAIR, 1900–2017**

Source: "Long-Term Trends in Deaths of Despair." Joint Econ Committee. Data LOESS smoothed: .15.

reason to fear that the Great Divergence has now spread into noneco-
nomic domains like social mobility and health, just as the preceding Great
Convergence had egalitarian consequences beyond its immediate economic effects.

Inequality can be measured in terms not merely of individuals, but
also of regions. So it is reasonable to ask how regional inequality—the difference in economic well-being between affluent places and impoverished
places—has changed across the last 125 years. It is widely accepted that
regional inequalities declined steadily for the first seven or eight decades of
the twentieth century, following exactly the same path as individual equality during the Great Convergence. The single most important driver of
this regional convergence was the South's long, steady catching up with
the rest of the country, partly because of a natural convergence among different parts of a single economic unit and partly because of explicit federal
policies to help the South.[59]

It is also broadly agreed that that regional convergence halted in the late
1970s, just about the same time that the Great Convergence in individual
incomes was ending, though researchers differ on whether regional convergence at that point actually reversed, leading to growing regional inequality. Much of that disagreement turns on measurement differences that are
too arcane to describe here, but those who think that regional divergence is
growing typically point to the emergence of the "knowledge economy" and
its concentration in a few high-tech meccas, especially on the two coasts.
During the Trump years these regional disparities have become a central
issue in the national public debate, as our politics become increasingly polarized regarding what to do about regions that have been "left behind." So
the debate about regional inequality is far from academic, and only future
research will show whether the parallel between individual inequality and
regional inequality is complete or not, and if so, what can be done about it.[60]

HOW DID WE GET HERE?[61]

What caused the Great Convergence, and then what caused the Great Divergence? In recent years we have heard much debate about the latter, but

relatively little about the former. It turns out that these are not two separate issues, because to a considerable extent the same factors are responsible for both the upswing in equality until the 1970s and the downturn after that.

International factors are no doubt a significant part of the backstory, because the same basic U-shape across the twentieth century is found in most advanced countries.[62] Globalization is a plausible suspect, because international flows of people and goods and money tended to diminish in the first half of the twentieth century and then to intensify in the second half.[63] Other Western countries have experienced the same international pressures, however, while seeing a much less dramatic increase in inequality, suggesting that U.S. domestic institutions and policies have played a major role. Careful studies have found the overall impact of immigration on U.S. income inequality to be minor, and to have no impact at all on high-end inequality, which is precisely where the shifts in income distribution have been the most marked.[64]

The impact of international trade on inequality is a hotly contested issue. For many years economic studies tended to downplay the effects of trade on wage inequality, assuming that workers who lost jobs in one industry would soon find them in another, but in the first decade or two of the twenty-first century that consensus began to shift, and scholars now put somewhat greater weight on the impact of trade on wage structures. The effects of trade on inequality have been studied much more heavily during the Great Divergence than during the Great Convergence. That said, it is probably a fair summary of the existing literature that the impact of trade on both halves of the equality U-curve has been significant, though modest.[65] Moreover, even if it's true that imports have helped the American economy as a whole, while hurting industrial workers, we still need to explain why the overall gains have not been redistributed to compensate the losers. That is fundamentally a political question, not an economic one, and as such, it is one that we need to postpone until our discussion of politics in the next chapter.

In short, the long, inverted U-curve of economic equality and inequality that has so deeply affected Americans may in part be the product of global trends, but it was driven substantially by domestic factors, as well, and those factors are our focus here. To a remarkable degree domestic institutional and social reforms that had their origins in the first decade of the twentieth century turn out to explain both the rise and then the fall of economic equality, because those reforms themselves waxed and waned in precisely the same century-long rhythm as equality and inequality. The U-curve that describes the ups and downs of economic equality is paralleled by—and very likely caused at least in part by—the ups and downs of a set of institutional changes that were first sketched and implemented during the Progressive Era.

In other words, Progressive Era social innovations and institutional reforms put the US on a new path toward greater economic equality, laying the foundations for the Great Convergence that lasted until the 1970s. Progressive Era reformers, both dreamers and doers, created innovations such as the public high school, labor unions, the federal tax structure, antitrust legislation, financial regulation, and more.[66] Those creations did not immediately close the income gap, given the turbulence of the Twenties, but they were the necessary foundations for further developments (especially during the New Deal, but not only then) that underpinned the Great Convergence.

Conversely, by the 1970s those earlier social innovations and institutional reforms had all begun to fade and even to be reversed. The growth of education "paused" around 1965, as we saw earlier in this chapter; unions had begun their long decline by 1958; in the mid-1960s tax cuts began to make the tax structure more regressive; after 1970, deregulation, especially of financial institutions, overturned the reforms begun in the Progressive Era; and most subtle, but also perhaps most important, the collective norm that "we are all in this together" was replaced by a libertarian (sometimes misleadingly called "neoliberal") norm that we're not. These changes underlay the pivot toward inequality in the mid-1970s that we saw in Figure 2.8.

Since one popular interpretation of these shifts in policy and of the consequent shifts in income and wealth distribution fingers the Reagan Revolution after 1981 as the chief culprit, it is significant that in virtually every case the key turning points occurred a decade or more *before* the presidency of Ronald Reagan. In short, the presidential election of 1980 and the subsequent unfolding of Reaganism was a lagging indicator of this sea change in the American political economy. The reversal of the social and policy innovations from the first decades of the twentieth century was probably the proximate cause of the Great Divergence in the twenty-first century, just as their original invention had been the proximate cause of the Great Convergence.[67] Let us briefly review the evidence.

Educational Innovation and Technological Change

Most experts agree that a primary cause of the Great Convergence was the interplay between technological advance and the educational innovations (especially the public high school) that emerged from the Progressive Era around 1910. Other things being equal, more widespread education means more equality, as the increased supply of high-skilled workers puts downward pressure on higher incomes, while the decreased supply of low-skilled workers puts upward pressure on lower incomes. That dynamic is offset by technological progress, which increases the demand for (and hence the incomes of) high-skilled workers and lowers the incomes of low-skilled workers. Hence, the title of the groundbreaking book that aims to explain the ups and downs of income equality over our period is *The Race Between Education and Technology*.[68]

The massive growth of public secondary education beginning in the early twentieth century and of college education after World War II—see Figures 2.6 and 2.7—had two important consequences: It raised the rate of national economic growth, and it increased the rate of upward mobility, by giving a fairer start to kids from the wrong side of the tracks. A third, related consequence is that these reforms raised Americans' skill levels and thus boosted the relative income of the middle and working class. In the first two thirds of the century, while the demand for skill edged upward, that change was eclipsed by the rapid increase in the supply of high school and college graduates.[69] Because the American labor force became by far the best educated in the world, the balance between education and technology tipped in favor of equality.

In the final third of the twentieth century, however, the race between technology and education was reversed. The twin pauses in high school and college growth in the 1970s, clearly visible in Figures 2.6 and 2.7, halted the long, steady increase in the supply of skilled workers. At the same time, what economists call "skill-biased technological change" (or SBTC) began to increase the relative demand for ever more highly skilled workers. High school education was fine for the assembly lines that dominated economic growth from the 1920s to the 1970s, but it was inadequate for the high-tech labs that replaced those assembly lines in the last decades of the twentieth century.

Most economists agree that technological change has been an important contributor to the recent growth of inequality. Nevertheless, if the educational push that had begun in the Progressive Era had been renewed and accelerated after the 1970s, the magic combination of growth and equality might well have continued. But instead we Americans collectively took our feet off the educational accelerator in the 1970s and began to coast. Almost immediately, the long, gradual upward trend in equality was reversed, as we saw in Figure 2.8.

In broad outline, this is probably now the single most widely accepted explanation for the Great Convergence and Great Divergence.[70] However, it works much less well in explaining the waning and waxing gap between the top 1 percent and the rest of the American labor force, especially the explosive widening of that gap in recent years. Moreover, while this explanation is sometimes described as "market-based," because it emphasizes changes in the labor market, in fact its roots lie much deeper in politics and even morality.

The rapid growth of public high schools and universities from 1910 to 1975 did not happen by accident. It required major public investment, and it emerged from a nationwide grassroots reform movement, as Claudia Goldin has emphasized.[71] Why did Americans so enthusiastically support public educational investments from 1910 to 1970? And why did that popular support then wane? That is the sense in which "we" took our foot off the accelerator. Why we did so is an important conundrum to which we shall return.

Unions[72]

In the Gilded Age union organizing provided a potential counterweight to the captains of industry, representing the norm of mutualism and solidarity against the norm of individualism. Unions spread rapidly but unevenly in the late nineteenth and early twentieth centuries. However, they faced firm opposition from owners and managers and from the courts in the name of the individual freedom of workers and owners.[73]

The Knights of Labor, based on the premise that workers of all types should be enrolled in "one big union," had boomed from 28,100 members in 1880 to 729,000 six years later, but then fell back to 100,000 in 1890 and collapsed in 1894 in the face of internal conflicts between the skilled and unskilled, as well as between blacks and whites. Its leading role was soon taken over by the American Federation of Labor, along with a series of unions organized along craft and industrial lines—mine workers (founded in 1890), electrical workers (1891), longshoremen (1892), garment workers (1900), teamsters (1903), and so on. In barely seven years (1897–1904) nationwide union membership almost quadrupled from 3.5 percent of the nonagricultural workforce to 12.3 percent. This time union efforts proved more durable, and union membership would not fall below the new high-water mark for the rest of the century.[74]

Strikes became the workers' weapon of choice in the struggle with management, and in the decades after 1870 America acquired "the bloodiest and most violent labor history of any industrial nation in the world."[75] On neither side was this tussle a polite effort to seek compromise through collective bargaining. Both sides used violence—from the notorious street battles of the Homestead steel strike in 1892, to the equally violent Pullman strike in Chicago in 1894, to the anthracite coal strike in Pennsylvania in 1902. In 1894 Democratic president Grover Cleveland and his attorney general, Richard Olney, crafted a strategy to use court injunctions to break the Pullman strike, but by 1902 the Progressive Republican president Teddy Roosevelt appointed the Anthracite Coal Commission that ended the miners' strike, giving de facto recognition to the union. Against the backdrop of fears among the "haves" of anarchy and revolution by the "have-nots," mutualism and compromise had begun to win out over individualism and conflict, though it would be several decades before a new model of labor relations would emerge.

Union membership oscillated up and down in these early years, depending on the state of the economy and the political climate, but the secular trend was ascendant. In the background was a growing rejection (and not just among workers themselves) of pure laissez-faire capitalism in favor of "industrial democracy" that linked workers' rights to their role as equal citizens in a democratic community.[76] Renewed antiunion efforts by conservatives during the 1920s reduced union membership by a third from a peak of 5 million just after World War I to 3.5 million in 1929. This "pause" or even reversal of Progressive Era innovations during the 1920s will become a recurring feature of our historical narrative in this book, but even before the advent of the New Deal, the growth of unions resumed in 1930, just as the job-crushing Great Depression was getting under way (see Figure 2.12).

Recurrent bouts of joblessness in the late nineteenth century had long undermined unionization, so most observers were surprised when union membership began to grow in the 1930s. To be sure, new legislation would eventually make it easier for unions to organize. The National Labor Relations Act (NLRA) of 1935 is most famous, but even prior to Franklin Roosevelt's election, the landmark Norris-LaGuardia Act of 1932 had removed certain legal and judicial barriers against union organizing. This earlier bill was cosponsored by two Progressive Republicans and signed into law by a third—Herbert Hoover.

Legislation was not the sole explanation for renewed union growth, however, for the resumption of growth after the slump of the 1920s predated this legislation. Much of union growth in the 1930s was bottom-up: Most workers in this period were organized by unionization strikes, not by NLRA elections.[77] Legislation was important, but workers themselves were coming to feel solidarity toward one another, even occasionally across ethnic and racial lines.[78]

In short, the argument sometimes heard that the New Deal itself accounts for the growth of unions in the 1930s is an oversimplification,

although the New Deal and World War II are clearly part of the story behind the remarkable growth between 1935 and 1945. In 1929 only about
10 percent of workers were members of unions, but by 1945 that figure had
risen to about 35 percent. Probably an even larger fraction of Americans
were members of a union family, and during this period unions enjoyed
wide public approval. Gallup polls showed union supporters steadily outnumbered critics by more than three to one throughout the three decades
from 1936 to 1966.[79] It was a period in which most Americans had come to
appreciate the virtues of solidarity.

FIGURE 2.12: **UNION MEMBERSHIP, 1890–2015**

Source: Freeman, "Spurts in Union Growth"; Hirsch and Macpherson, "Unionstats." Data
LOESS smoothed: .2. See endnote 2.80.

By the 1960s, however, membership rates in unions (and their social
and cultural salience, to which we shall return in Chapter 4) had begun a
long, seemingly inexorable slump, so that by the 2010s unions were left
with substantial membership only in the public sector (especially among
teachers), despite innovative efforts to organize low-paid workers in the
service sector. Much ink has been spilled exploring the causes of this long

decline, and this is not the place for an extended review of that debate.[80] Among the most important factors are:

- Structural changes in the American economy that have shifted employment from blue-collar production workers to white-collar workers, many in the service and knowledge industries. However, even within specific sectors and industries union membership is way down, so the bleaching of blue collars to white explains barely one quarter of the total membership decline.[81]

- Reinvigorated employer and conservative opposition, symbolized by the Taft-Hartley Act of 1947 (passed over Harry Truman's veto) that limited unions' room for action, and by the breaking of a national air traffic controllers strike by the new Reagan administration in 1981.[82] (A burst of state legislation in the 1960s allowed substantial growth in public sector unions, but this trend halted in the opening decades of the twenty-first century.) The rise of the Sun Belt was fostered by union weakness in the socially conservative South and in turn weakened unions nationally.

- Union blunders, including irksome public sector strikes and revelations of union corruption, especially in the Teamsters Union, which damaged the public legitimacy of unions.[83]

- The devitalization of unions as a site for social connection, in part because of growing individualism on part of younger workers, who preferred watching television in isolating suburbs to bowling with the guys in the union hall, a factor to which we shall return in Chapter 4.[84] Social connections like these waned in importance across the country after the 1960s, reducing the role of unions to mere collective bargaining agents.

The ups and downs of union membership had important economic consequences, but the underlying causes of these fluctuations were as much political, sociological, and cultural as merely economic.

What does a comparison of the trends in income equality in Figure 2.8 with the trends in union membership in Figure 2.12 tell us? First, in the two decades between 1899 and 1920 the union membership rate had roughly tripled. Hence, unionization was a leading indicator of the Great Convergence, anticipating the turn toward income equality by a decade or two. Similarly, the steady six-decade slide of unions after 1958, about a decade or two before the turning point of income distribution, was a leading indicator of the Great Divergence. Otherwise, the inverted U-curve of union membership in Figure 2.12 is a perfect mirror of the inverted U-curves of income and wealth equality in Figures 2.8 and 2.9.[85] That correlation certainly does not in itself prove that one caused the others, because both union membership and economic inequality could have been responding to some other factor yet to be discovered. The parallel is striking, and it is only the first of many such parallels that we shall discover in this book.

Our focus in this chapter is on equality in the distribution of income and wealth. The historical record of unions is mixed on racial and gender equality,[86] a topic to which we return in Chapters 6 and 7. In terms of economic or class equality, however, many recent studies have confirmed that the growth of unions boosted income equality from the 1930s to the 1960s, and that the post-1960s decline in unions has contributed to the Great Divergence. During the Great Convergence unions increased the incomes of what would otherwise have been low-income households, thus compressing the income distribution.[87] Conversely, the decline of unions has fostered income inequality during the Great Divergence.[88]

Only a fraction of these effects comes from the direct impact of collective bargaining on the incomes of union members.[89] Studies have found that unionization had an equalizing impact even on the nonunionized labor force,[90] on broader norms of equity,[91] and on CEO pay during the Great Convergence.[92] During the Great Convergence unions also provided powerful support for political forces that were working for greater income equality. For all these reasons, several independent studies suggest that roughly one quarter of the post-1970s decline in income equality could be explained by the fall in unionization.[93] Unions are another important example, like the high school movement, of a "we" social innovation from the early 1900s whose development over the ensuing six decades contributed to the Great Convergence and whose decline after mid-century contributed to the ensuing Great Divergence.

Public Economic Policy

In addition to social innovations like unions, Progressives also confronted the massive inequality gap with innovations in public policy.[94] These policy reforms of the Progressive Era did not eliminate the gap between rich and poor, certainly not overnight. Political reverses in the 1920s stalled the trend toward greater equality for a decade. But then came the New Deal, and the trend resumed with even greater force, reinforced by World War II, and continuing for a quarter century afterward. Prominent among these policy innovations were (1) progressive taxation of personal and corporate income and estates, (2) regulation of large financial institutions, and (3) minimum wage rules.

This is not the place for an extended treatment of these policies. Our purpose here is only to show that—not by accident—activities in each of those policy areas followed precisely the same inverted U as income equality itself. In other words, to understand both the Great Convergence and the Great Divergence, we must understand why the policy choices made by Americans and our leaders favored equality from the early 1900s until the 1970s and then in a remarkably short period reversed course and undermined equality. This story turns out to be as much about politics as about economics, and not merely party politics.

Taxing and Spending[95]

As the gap between the superrich and everyone else grew during the first Gilded Age, support for progressive tax reform spread across the political spectrum and across the country. Progressive tax innovations began at the state level. "In the 1890s fifteen states instituted taxes on large inheritances; more than 40 states had inheritance taxes in place in the 1910s."[96] The first federal income tax (apart from a temporary tax to support the

Civil War), as well as the first inheritance tax, were approved with bipartisan support in 1894. A conservative Supreme Court struck down the taxes
as unconstitutional a year later, but Progressive pressures to redress the
mammoth economic disparities in the country nevertheless continued to
mount. Republican president William Howard Taft proposed a constitutional amendment in 1909, and by 1913 this proposal had a sufficiently
broad bipartisan consensus (encompassing two thirds of both houses of
Congress and three fourths of the states) to amend the Constitution and
institute the first permanent federal income tax. Both the level and the
progressivity of this tax were initially low, but the principle that rich folks
should pay more than poor folks had been established. World War I, the
New Deal, and World War II pushed both the level and the progressivity
of the federal income tax ever upward to a high plateau from the 1940s to
the mid-1960s.

The solid line in Figure 2.13 traces a by now familiar inverted U-curve
in the progressivity of the federal income tax in its first one hundred years,
with a turning point in the mid-1960s. After that high point, federal income tax progressivity plummeted under presidents of both parties, from
John F. Kennedy to Donald J. Trump, nearing the lows of the 1910s and
1920s by century's end. (To be sure, Figure 2.13 also shows that occasional
recent presidents, both Republican and Democratic, have sought to halt
the plummet and restore some progressiveness to the tax code; this list
includes George H. W. Bush, Bill Clinton, and Barack Obama.)

Because the federal income tax represents only a small fraction of all
taxes collected in the US, the gray line in Figure 2.13 shows the ups and
downs of a measure of the progressivity of *all* taxes (including state and
local taxes, federal payroll taxes for Social Security, corporate and estate
taxes). This measure is calculated independently from the measure of federal income taxes, using independent sources of data, and yet the two are
very closely correlated.[97] Changes in the progressivity of all taxes are only
in part driven by federal income tax rates. In fact, payroll taxes are regressive, and increases in those taxes (disguised as Social Security insurance
premiums) have been responsible for much of the total trend toward more

regressive taxation since the 1950s.[98] Since Figure 2.13 encompasses many different forms of taxation by different levels of government run by different parties across the country, the changes over time cannot simply reflect partisan propensities to "soak the rich," but must reveal more pervasive changes in patterns of political power and economic egalitarianism. In short, trends in the progressiveness of U.S. taxation—increasing during the first half of the twentieth century and decreasing during the second half—have amplified both the upswing in equality before 1970 and the downswing after 1970.

FIGURE 2.13: **PROGRESSIVITY OF FEDERAL INCOME TAX AND OF ALL TAXES, 1913–2015**

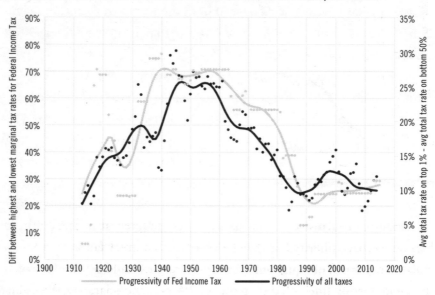

Source: Federal income tax: Tax Policy Center. Data LOESS smoothed: .2. Total tax: Piketty, Saez, and Zucman, *QJEcon* May 2018. Data LOESS smoothed: 0.15.

Two other tax innovations of the Progressive Era reformers were also important contributors to both the Great Convergence and the Great Divergence. The federal corporate income tax was instituted in 1909 and is generally estimated to be borne by shareholders and thus basically progressive. As shown in Figure 2.14, the top corporate tax rate has risen and fallen in the familiar U-shape curve, rising steadily from 1 percent in 1909 to its peak of 53 percent in 1968–1969, then falling from 1970 to 2018, when President Trump's tax cut sharply lowered it to 21 percent, the lowest rate in eighty years.[99]

FIGURE 2.14: FEDERAL CORPORATE TOP TAX RATE, 1909–2018

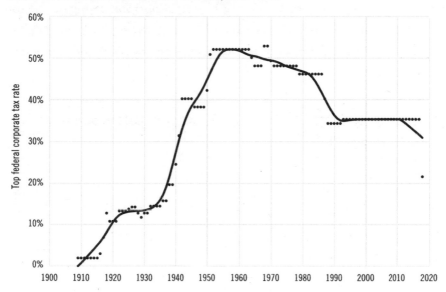

Source: Tax Foundation; World Tax Database; IRS. Data LOESS smoothed: 0.15.

A third Progressive Era tax reform was directed at inequality in inherited wealth. Inherited advantage embodied in great family fortunes so violated the norm of equal opportunity—that all should begin life's race at the same starting line—that even the wealthiest beneficiaries of the Gilded Age like John D. Rockefeller and Andrew Carnegie favored the taxation of large estates.[100] Both the top estate tax rate and the size of estates covered by the tax show a clear inverted U-curve, rising from 1916 to 1941 (especially 1931–41), then drifting slowly upward until 1976, when all estates over $300,000 were subject to the tax and the top rate was 77 percent.[101] Interestingly, this increase in the stringency of the estate tax is not simply attributable to FDR, the New Deal, and wartime budgetary needs. In fact, the sharpest rise ever in the estate tax (1930–32) was passed under the aegis of Herbert Hoover![102]

But during the four decades after 1976, following the now familiar inverted U-curve, the top rate of the estate tax fell, and the threshold at which it applies rose, as shown in Figure 2.15. In 2016 the Trump tax cuts exempted estates up to $5.5 million, and the top rate dropped to 40 percent, dropping the impact of the estate tax virtually back to the levels of the Gilded Age.

FIGURE 2.15: **TOP ESTATE TAX RATE AND SIZE OF EXEMPTION, 1916–2017**

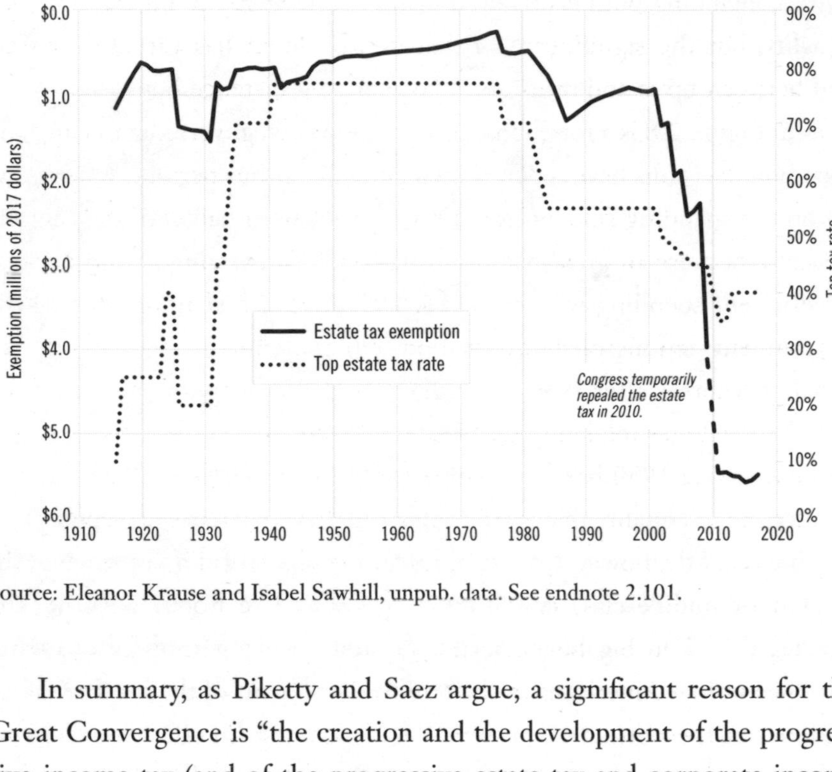

Source: Eleanor Krause and Isabel Sawhill, unpub. data. See endnote 2.101.

In summary, as Piketty and Saez argue, a significant reason for the Great Convergence is "the creation and the development of the progressive income tax (and of the progressive estate tax and corporate income tax)."[103] Moreover, Emmanuel Saez and his colleagues have pointed out the interesting fact that there is a strong correlation between tax progressivity and *pre*-tax income equality. In other words, it is not simply that high taxes lop off top incomes, but that the determination of the pre-tax income distribution and the determination of tax progressivity are somehow intertwined, perhaps because both are responding in part to the same external factor or perhaps for some other reason.[104] Be that as it may, our brief review of long-run changes in the progressivity of American taxes suggests that underneath the surface of party platforms and tax lobbyists and tax-writing committees and revenue officials in thousands of jurisdictions across the country a broad century-long ebb and flow of egalitarianism was at work.

Government fiscal policy encompasses spending as well as taxing. As we noted earlier in this chapter, the net effect of government fiscal activities, including both taxes and transfers, is modestly to improve income equality, but the significance of that improvement has varied over time and between taxes and transfers. The changing distance between the two lines in Figure 2.8 is a rough measure of how much government taxing and spending decisions have reduced inequality in various periods. Progressivity on the spending side increased throughout both halves of the century, basically because of growth in the total size of government and because government spending was on net redistributive. Thus, up to about 1980 government actions on both taxation and spending tended to enhance equality, whereas after 1980 tax changes tended to increase inequality, but spending changes tended to decrease inequality, so that in total, taxes and spending since 1980 have modestly reduced income inequality, buffering the decline in equality that would otherwise have been even steeper.

Importantly, however, most of this expanded spending represents the growth of middle-class entitlement programs like Social Security and Medicare.[105] The big beneficiaries of these growing transfer programs have been older Americans in the middle 40 percent of the income distribution, not the bottom 50 percent. That spending (in effect, transferring money from younger people to older people) has made the *age* distribution of income more egalitarian, mostly ending the scourge of elderly poverty that in the 1960s outraged social reformers like Michael Harrington, author of *The Other America*. However, that new spending has *not* had such a marked effect on the *class* distribution of income, which also concerned Harrington.[106] The only battle of the War on Poverty that was won was the War on Elder Poverty. These transfers have not much narrowed the gap between the top 1 percent and the bottom 50 percent. "The bottom half of the adult population has thus been shut off from economic growth for over 40 years, and the modest increase in their post-tax income has been absorbed by increased health spending," conclude economists Piketty, Saez, and Zucman.[107]

One way to see this skewing of the American welfare state over the last half century is to compare the average monthly "welfare" benefit per family with the average monthly Social Security benefit for a retired worker and spouse, as shown in Figure 2.16. From the mid-1930s to about 1970 (our now familiar turning point) those two forms of assistance—to the "poor" and to the "elderly"—kept pace, reaching roughly $900 in 1970 in 2003 dollars. But over the ensuing 30 years the average real Social Security benefit kept rising, reaching $1,483 in 2001, whereas the average real welfare payment fell steadily, reaching $392 in 2001.[108] Indexing Social Security payments, but not welfare payments, for inflation drove a wedge between these two groups.[109]

FIGURE 2.16: **SOCIAL SPENDING ON THE ELDERLY AND ON THE POOR, 1936–2001**

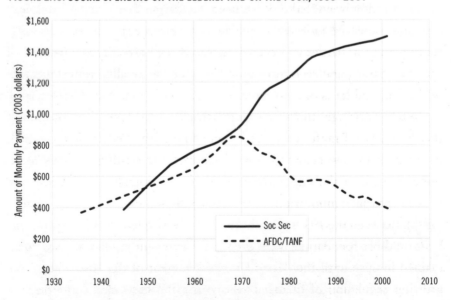

Source: Robert Sahr, *PS* 2004. See endnote 2.108. Data LOESS smoothed: 0.15.

In sum, during the Great Convergence, both taxation and spending moved in a progressive direction, so government redistribution was a major contributor to growing equality. With the advent of the Great Divergence, by contrast, taxes became more regressive, though spending continued to be more progressive, softening the post-1980 trend toward inequality, at least for the aging middle class. The net effect of government fiscal activity is less marked in explaining the Great Divergence, while market and other nonmarket forces were more important. It is important to remember, however, that government nonfiscal actions (or inactions) can also have a powerful indirect effect on income inequality; one important example is regulatory policy, to which we now turn.

Financial Regulation

The anticompetitive behavior of the big trusts and monopolies, and especially misbehavior by large financial institutions, was one of the main themes of Gilded Age protest. Financial panics in 1873 and 1893 (due to reckless and often fraudulent and corrupt financial speculation, especially in banks and railways) led to long, deep depressions, with rising rural poverty and industrial joblessness, which in turn led to the rise of populist movements and parties and eventually the Progressive Era reforms. All of that has strong parallels in American life today, especially in the aftermath of the financial crisis of 2008 and the Great Recession.[110]

Not surprisingly, financial regulation was a major policy innovation of the Progressive Era (for example, the creation of the Federal Reserve with its supervisory powers and the succession of "trust-busting" initiatives). In the aftermath of the Great Depression, these controls were greatly enhanced with such innovations as the Securities and Exchange Commission (SEC). Between the 1930s and the 1950s successive federal administrations built on those foundations with even more stringent regulation, which remained intense until the deregulation movement of the late 1970s. This growing regulation of financial services during the Great Convergence led to substantial reductions in the incomes of financiers. Since those who work at Wall Street firms and big banks are very prominent in the top strata of the income distribution, the reduction in their incomes was an important force for equalization.[111]

As Figure 2.17 shows, deregulation of financial markets began in the 1970s, under the influence of free market economists, producing yet another familiar inverted U-curve. Almost inevitably, economists Thomas Philippon and Ariell Reshef have shown, financial deregulation led to a rise in the incomes associated with the financial services industry.[112] Indeed, they estimate that this factor alone accounts for 15–25 percent of the total increase in income inequality during the Great Divergence.

Anticompetitive and unregulated market concentration is, of course, much discussed today in realms beyond finance, just as it was 125 years ago. Then as now, the issue was clearest in the most technologically advanced sectors—railroads, telephones, iron and steel then; the internet and pharmaceutical giants today—though in both eras anticompetitive practices were common in many industries. We have not found comparable data for market concentration or market regulation across the 125 years in nonfinancial sectors that would allow us to construct a chart equivalent to Figure 2.17, but the principle seems as likely to apply at the beginning of the twenty-first century as it did at the end of the nineteenth century.[113] In Chapter 5 we shall explore the intellectual roots of the deregulation movement of the 1970s in the New Right of the 1960s.

Minimum Wage

A final example of public policy that mirrors and helps explain the rise and fall of economic equality during the twentieth century is minimum wage policy. Various states had experimented with minimum wage laws during the first decades of the century,[114] but it was not until late in the New Deal that the federal government followed in the same path. Thereafter the inflation-adjusted national minimum wage traced essentially the now familiar inverted U-curve, reaching its peak in 1968, almost precisely the same time as the other curves we've explored in this chapter (see Figure 2.18).

FIGURE 2.17: **REGULATION AND DEREGULATION OF FINANCIAL MARKETS, 1909–2006**

Source: Thomas Philippon and Ariell Reshef, *QJEcon* Nov 2012. See endnote 2.112.

In recent years the rise and fall of the minimum wage has attracted much attention as an important contributor to the Great Convergence and Great Divergence, and many states and localities have recently raised their minimum wage levels in an effort to reverse income inequality.[115] Economists are sharply divided on whether the direct effect of minimum wage laws on wage levels is offset, in whole or in part, by their indirect negative effects on low-wage employment opportunities. The raft of new state and local initiatives may soon help settle that argument, but in the meantime, a reasonable view is that there has probably been some effect on inequality at the lower end of the income distribution, though not at the top end, where the most massive inequalities have been concentrated in recent years.[116]

Perhaps the most striking implication of the minimum wage history is how closely it follows the same inverted U, with its origins at the state level in the Progressive Era, coming to the national level in the 1930s, peaking in the late 1960s, and then declining exactly at the same time as all the other factors causally linked to income inequality. Across a very wide range of public policy, then, we can see a broad pendular swing—for a half century and more in the direction of greater equality and then for at least a half century back in the direction of greater inequality. And since these policies themselves have affected the final distribution of income in the country, it is hardly surprising that the policy pendulum seems almost perfectly correlated with the outcome pendulum. But the underlying causality may not be so simple as that correlation implies.

FIGURE 2.18: US REAL MINIMUM WAGE, 1938–2020

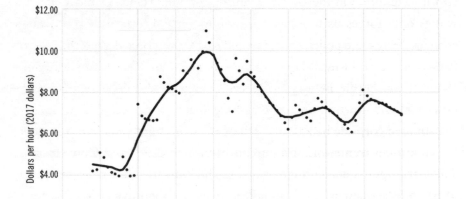

Sources: Department of Labor; Federal Reserve. Data LOESS smoothed: 0.15.

SOCIAL NORMS

Many economists who have closely examined growing income inequality over the last half century have emphasized the same factors that we have just outlined. "In the United States," argue Thomas Piketty, Emmanuel Saez, and Gabriel Zucman, "the stagnation of bottom 50% incomes and the upsurge in the top 1% coincided with reduced progressive taxation, widespread deregulation (particularly in the financial sector), weakened unions, and an erosion of the federal minimum wage."[117]

On the other hand, policy is not (as economists say) "exogenous," that is, it is not an external factor, like sunspots, whose causes in turn we can afford to ignore. On the contrary, noting the importance of those policy swings only forces us to explain the timing and direction of the policy changes. Why were policies that favored equality in force during the Great Convergence, and why did they all then change in the decade or so around 1965? It can hardly be a coincidence that all these independent factors moved up and down in one century-long synchronized leap, like a single well-trained corps de ballet.

In a wider framework, the origins of the trends in economic equality likely lay largely outside the purely economic sphere. Politics seem likely to be an important part of the backstory, as we shall discuss in the next chapter.[118] On the other hand, as we noticed when discussing Reaganism, the causal role of politics itself may be complicated. The pivot from egalitarian to inegalitarian policies and outcomes predated Reagan's landslide arrival in the White House, so in that sense politics seems to have been a lagging indicator of economic change, not a leading indicator, though we shall revisit that intriguing question several times throughout this book.

Changing social norms are likely to be an important part of the story on both the up and the down sides of the curve. Economics as a profession is usually reluctant to cite such "soft" factors, in part because they are so difficult to measure. Nevertheless, many of the best economists studying the Great Convergence and the Great Divergence, including Paul Krugman, Thomas Piketty and Emmanuel Saez, Anthony Atkinson, and Peter Diamond, agree that it is impossible to explain the dramatic swing in economic equality without taking norms about fairness and decency into account.[119]

The fierce and growing hostility to "plutocracy" at the opening of the twentieth century reflected moral outrage about inequality that had been absent during the Gilded Age with its emphasis on social Darwinism and the rights of ownership. This normative change was temporarily disrupted by the Red Scare of the 1920s, but the utter devastation of the Great Depression gave renewed force to the ideals of social solidarity instead of naked individualism, even among Republicans like Herbert Hoover.[120] The widely shared sacrifices of World War II strongly reinforced egalitarian norms among the Greatest Generation, who would then dominate American society and politics for a quarter century after the war. Executive compensation during that period was undoubtedly held in check by norms of fairness and decorum and what we might call the "outrage" factor.[121]

In Chapter 5 we shall explore more directly how dramatically the culture of America shifted toward individualism during the 1960s. But a single comparison illustrates how this shift affected executive compensation. In the early 1960s George Romney was a titan of business, the chairman and CEO of American Motors, and he was compensated handsomely. In 1960, his top-paid year, he made just over $661,000 (roughly $5.5 million today). Nevertheless, he also frequently turned down bonuses and pay raises that he viewed as excessive. In 1960, for example, he refused a $100,000 bonus, and in a five-year period he turned down a total of $268,000 (roughly 20 percent of his total earnings during the period). He feared the effects that overcompensation could have on executives: Overly generous pay could lead to "the temptations to success [that] could distract people from more important matters."[122] Moreover, he paid over a third of his income in taxes.

Fifty years later, his son Mitt pulled in $21.7 million in 2010, roughly four times his father's peak income. Of this, he paid an effective tax rate of 13.9 percent, roughly one third the rate his father had paid. We know of no evidence Mitt has ever voluntarily returned any of his compensation, though he and his wife gave away $3 million in charitable donations in 2010, including $1.5 million to the Mormon Church. During the presidential campaign of 2012 he said, "There are 47% of the people . . . who are dependent upon government, who believe that they are victims. . . . These are people who pay no income tax. . . . And so my job is not to worry about those people. I'll never convince them that they should take personal responsibility and care for their lives." When his father ran for president in 1968, just as the six-decade trend in social norms from "I" to "we" was peaking, he never said anything like that.[123]

This is doubtless an extreme case. Most executives in the 1960s were not so generous as George, and few today make as much as Mitt. Nevertheless, their respective outlooks on economic equality provide a perfect window into how norms around compensation and economic fairness have shifted over the past half century. Indeed, these shifts in norms provide a potentially compelling explanation for shifts in inequality throughout the twentieth century, as well as for the shifts in public policies, such as educational investments or tax progressivity, that show the same mid-Sixties turning point. We shall turn back to the question of changing social norms in Chapter 5.

Meanwhile, we can summarize what we have learned about trends in economic equality in a surprisingly simple chart, because the trends we have examined here match one another so closely. Figure 2.19 combines all the relevant charts in this chapter into a single curve, which illustrates the inverted U-shape we saw over and over again in the various measures here examined.[124] This curve charts the foundational efforts to improve economic equality during the Progressive Era, the temporary reversals during the Roaring Twenties, and the sharply renewed thrust toward greater equality from the 1930s, culminating in the Great Convergence in about 1960. Then we see the accelerating reversal toward ever-greater inequality during the Great Divergence that has persisted into the twenty-first century. The broader implications of this economic pattern—one facet of what we are terming the I-we-I curve—and what might have caused it will be clarified in our subsequent chapters.

FIGURE 2.19: **ECONOMIC EQUALITY, 1913–2015**

Source: See endnote 1.4. Data LOESS smoothed: .1.

3

POLITICS: FROM TRIBALISM TO COMITY AND BACK AGAIN

The Founding Fathers famously failed to anticipate the rise of political parties in their new republic, but they thoroughly understood that, as James Madison put it in Federalist 10: "The latent causes of faction are . . . sown in the nature of man." Disagreement is a constant, permanent feature of politics, especially democratic politics. But how disagreement is framed and resolved is not a constant across American history. Historians have chronicled how the intensity of our political battles has ebbed and flowed—from the "Era of Good Feelings" (1815–1825), for example, to the fratricidal violence of the Civil War forty years later.

In this chapter we ask how political conflicts have been framed and reframed over the last century and a quarter. Our task is initially descriptive—what have been the ups and downs of political polarization in America since the late nineteenth century? It will turn out that by many measures polarization has traced an inverted U-curve over this period, a curve uncannily like the curve for economic equality that we found in the previous chapter. Toward the end of this chapter we'll step beyond simple description to ask about the implications of extreme polarization for American democracy.

What exactly polarization means and how we measure it has roiled political science in recent decades, but one chart has been widely accepted as the beginning point for the debate. Almost all political scientists accept the basic curvilinear version of twentieth-century party history portrayed in Figure 3.1, though the second half of the curve has been much more explored than the first half of the curve. The chart shows that in the late nineteenth century cross-party collaboration was low and declining (in other words, partisan conflict was high and rising).[1] (As explained in Chapter 2, to avoid confusion, throughout this book we orient all charts so that "up" means more equal, less polarized, more connected, and more communitarian.) The Gilded Age was a period of intense political polarization. With the opening of the new century and the rise of the Progressive movement came a turning point, however, and collaboration across party lines became steadily more common, slowing only briefly in the Roaring Twenties before reaching a new higher plateau of cooperativeness in the New Deal and World War II. That cooperative trend leveled off in the 1950s, but not until the 1970s did partisanship begin to become more intense and bipartisan collaboration rarer.[2] The last five decades of steadily accelerating

FIGURE 3.1: **CROSS-PARTY COLLABORATION IN CONGRESS, 1895–2017**

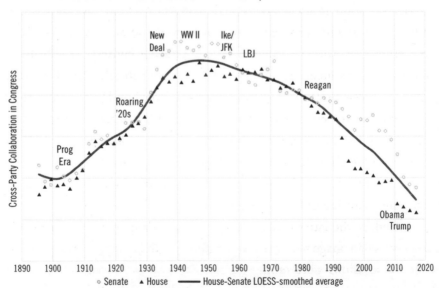

Source: Congressional Roll-Call Votes Database 2019. Data LOESS smoothed: .2.

partisanship have produced the deeply polarized world in which we live today. This chapter begins with a historical account of the political ups and downs that underlie Figure 3.1. In the latter half of the chapter we turn to quantitative evidence of the various dimensions, causes, and consequences of polarization and depolarization, asking "so what?"

THE UPS AND DOWNS OF PARTY POLITICS SINCE THE FIRST GILDED AGE

In recent decades polarization has largely occurred along the familiar left-right, liberal-conservative ideological dimension, but polarization has not always been about ideological distance.[3] Party conflict in the late nineteenth century was crystallized along somewhat different lines from our own times, but in both periods—then and now—politics were polarized, as Figure 3.1 illustrates. Both periods involved intense sectarian bitterness, and in both, polarization rested on strong internal party cohesion and zero-sum inter-party conflict that resisted compromise and demonized opponents, with no common ground and each side's victory defined as the other side's loss.

Political divisions in the late nineteenth century were rooted in the Civil War—the Republican "bloody shirt" waved in the North against the Democratic "solid South"—and in regional economic differences—the agricultural South and West vs. the industrial Midwest and Northeast—but those differences were seldom "ideological" in our contemporary understanding. For example, the sole Democratic president elected in the half century between 1860 and 1912, the so-called Bourbon Democrat Grover Cleveland, mostly sided with conservative business interests, though he also stood alone in vetoing racist anti-immigration legislation in 1897. Polarization in the Gilded Age was not primarily about the size of the state vs. the free market, though that issue would become the dominant cleavage in party politics during the next century.

Instead, in the late nineteenth century, party alignments were largely tribal—vast patronage networks competing for spoils. Reinforcing regional economic divisions were ethnic divisions and a cultural and urban-rural cleavage not entirely unlike the cultural and urban-rural cleavage today. Prohibition (and undergirding that, religious conservatism) was a major dividing line in American politics from the 1890s until the 1930s, when it was effectively removed from the national agenda by repeal.[4] Though lacking today's ideological overlay, conflict between the parties was intense, as illustrated by a contemporary political cartoon by Thomas Nast (Figure 3.2). As today, cross-party coalitions were relatively rare.[5]

FIGURE 3.2: THOMAS NAST ON SECTARIAN BITTERNESS IN 1870

Source: *Harper's Weekly* 13, Feb. 26, 1870. Courtesy of Harvard University Library.

As the Gilded Age climaxed in the 1890s, polarization intensified. The Panic of 1893 (ushering in one of the worst economic downturns in US history) triggered widespread, violent conflict between labor and capital. The realigning election of 1896, pitting the Democrats' William Jennings Bryan against Republican William McKinley, was one of the most bitterly contested, vitriolic, and closely fought of the post–Civil War period. As illustrated in Bryan's famous "Cross of Gold" peroration, the parties acrimoniously disputed tariffs and monetary policy. His arms outstretched in the image of the crucified Christ, Bryan thundered

> Having behind us the producing masses of this nation and the world, supported by the commercial interests, the laboring interests, and the toilers everywhere, we will answer their demand for a gold standard by saying to them: "You shall not press down upon the brow of labor this crown of thorns; you shall not crucify mankind upon a cross of gold."[6]

The party conflict underlying the election of 1896 remained as much sectoral and regional as class-based or ideological, as most Republicans represented industrial constituencies, especially in the North and East, and most Democrats represented agricultural areas, especially in the South and West. In the 1896 House elections, for example, 86 percent of the victorious Republicans came from industrial districts, whereas 60 percent of the victorious Democrats came from agricultural districts.[7]

The tide of strikes, violence, and eventually anarchist terrorism that had begun to spread across the industrializing North in the 1870s would not recede until the 1920s.[8] At the same time, with the end of Reconstruction in 1877, white repression of blacks in the South became more violent, culminating in the imposition of Jim Crow segregation across the region, ratified by the Supreme Court in 1896 in *Plessy v. Ferguson*. A wave of black lynchings surged in the 1880s, reaching the appalling rate of an atrocity every other day in 1892, and despite Northern handwringing, would persist for decades.[9] No matter how horrific the plight of blacks, however, race would not become prominent on the national party agendas until later in the twentieth century.[10] In Chapter 6 we shall return to the history of racial repression in this era, as well as to the complicated saga of racial progress and regression in the subsequent century. For now, the crucial point is that at the turn of the twentieth century, American politics, both North and South, was violently riven as it had not been for nearly half a century.

The very intensity of these partisan divisions prevented major new problems from being recognized and resolved. In the eyes of increasing numbers of voters, the two traditional political parties and their leaders were not helping the country to address newly pressing issues. Third parties like the Populists, the Free Silver Party, and the Socialists arose, and gradually reform coalitions began to cut across party lines. The Progressive movement (and eventually Teddy Roosevelt's Progressive or "Bull Moose" Party) embodied this discontent. By 1912 such third parties would receive 35 percent of the national popular vote for president, the high-water mark for third parties in American history and a symptom of public discontent with the polarized party system.[11]

The new issues jostling for a place on the national agenda included insurance for the elderly, the jobless, and the disabled; progressive income and estate taxation; environmental regulation; labor reform; the overweening power of big business monopolies; women's suffrage; campaign finance reform; and universal health insurance. (The parallels to our contemporary political agenda are striking.) Initially, support for such reforms had been concentrated among progressive Democrats, but as the new century opened, Progressivism also found strong champions among liberal Republicans, like Teddy Roosevelt, and the Republican Party began to split into the "stand-patters" and the emerging "Progressive" wing. This cross-party Progressive movement had first surfaced at the state and local level in the 1880s and 1890s, but gained power at the national level with TR's unexpected ascent to the presidency after McKinley's assassination in 1901. As we shall see in the next chapter and again in the concluding chapter, activists and social movements in civil society from radical unionists to settlement house organizers to reformist local politicians to church leaders played a crucial role in this process.

As political scientist Hans Noel has observed, "Progressives disrupted existing party coalitions. . . . A progressive element crosscut the parties and eventually reshaped them."[12] Indeed, by 1912 all three major candidates—TR, William Howard Taft, and Woodrow Wilson—claimed the Progressive mantle. Their policies were not identical, nor were all members of their parties progressive, but all three supported antimonopoly initiatives and a progressive federal income tax. Even though TR's Bull Moose Party lost in the three-way presidential race, that party's platform of 1912 helped set the progressive policy agenda for Wilson's presidency, the New Deal, and beyond.[13]

One mark of the incipient blurring of party lines in the Progressive Era (visible in Figure 3.1) is that the major reforms of that period were enacted during both Republican and Democratic administrations with support (and opposition) from both sides of the aisle. On ten major reforms passed between 1906 and 1919, including the Interstate Commerce Commission, the Pure Food and Drug Act, the federal income tax, the direct election of senators, the tariff cuts of 1913, the Federal Reserve, the Clayton Antitrust Act, child labor regulation, Prohibition, and women's suffrage, the administration in power received, on average, the support of 78 percent of the House and Senate members of its own party, as well as 40 percent of the votes of the opposing party.[14] Party-line votes were beginning to be replaced by bipartisan coalitions.

After World War I, the rise of the cross-party Progressive movement continued to moderate partisan polarization, especially in Congress, though at a less dramatic pace than during the prewar high tide of Progressivism. Congressional reform reduced the power of centralized leadership structures, and more legislating began to happen in committees, where a cross-party coalition (renewed and formalized in a bipartisan Progressive Coalition) could more freely operate independently of the two parties.[15] Even trade policy—a key axis of partisan division in the nineteenth century—became less polarized along party lines in the 1920s, with cross-party coalitions on tariff issues. And even in presidential politics, in 1920 both parties weighed the possibility of nominating the progressive Republican Herbert Hoover as their candidate, with Franklin D. Roosevelt writing privately, "Hoover is certainly a wonder. I wish I could make him President of the United States."[16]

The Progressive movement did not eliminate polarization, to be sure, but in reflecting reformist, egalitarian, and even communitarian sentiments among leaders of both major parties, it laid the groundwork for decades of declining polarization. This Progressive trend not only influenced congressional voting, as shown in Figure 3.1, but also brought into politics a new generation of reformers in both parties who would dominate presidential politics for decades to come. Though not all remained lifelong Progressives, eight of the ten Republican presidential nominees and six of the eight Democratic nominees in the first half of the twentieth century had launched their careers as members of the broad Progressive movement at the turn of the century.[17] In politics, just as in the economic policies that we reviewed in the previous chapter, the Progressive Era cast a long shadow over the first half of the twentieth century.

In the 1920s, however, the immediate impact of Progressivism began to fade, and convergence between the Republicans and Democrats seemed to slow. After TR, many Republicans began to distance themselves from the Progressive idea of using government to address social issues. After the rapid expansion of government during World War I, Republican Warren Harding was elected under the banner of "return to normalcy." His successor, Calvin Coolidge, had come into politics as a Progressive twenty years earlier, but as president in 1925, while cutting taxes and spending, he averred that "the chief business of the American people is business."[18]

The election of 1928 reflected the deepest conflicts in American society at the end of the nineteenth century—over immigration, religion, Prohibition, small town vs. cosmopolitan city. It pitted the Catholic, urban New Yorker Al Smith against Herbert Hoover, a former mining engineer who had earned a reputation as a Progressive humanitarian and had derived from his Quaker upbringing a genuine commitment to community and to service. His biographer Kenneth Whyte calls Hoover a liberal Republican, "progressivism incarnate," especially the more technocratic version of Progressivism.[19] As president, facing the unprecedented collapse of the global economy in 1929, Hoover was a prisoner of orthodox conservative economic theories of the time that were skeptical of government action, but in other respects he was and saw himself as an heir of the Progressive Era.[20]

The trauma of the Great Depression, Franklin D. Roosevelt's sweeping victory in 1932, and the subsequent New Deal turned many Republican Progressives into reactionaries. After his landslide loss in 1932 Hoover became an increasingly cranky critic of Roosevelt and the New Deal. Throughout the 1930s affluent, conservative businessmen, led by the reactionary American Liberty League, launched vicious attacks on FDR as a "traitor to his class," to which Roosevelt responded insouciantly, "I welcome their hatred," labeling them "economic royalists."[21]

On the other hand, as the New Deal proceeded, cross-party alliances and alignments became more common, not less, reducing party polarization. The New Deal increasingly divided progressive Democrats from conservative Southern Democrats and liberal Republicans from conservative Republicans.[22] Behind the scenes a strong cadre of liberal Republicans, centered in the still powerful Northeast, sought to revive their party by coming to terms with FDR's social welfare policies, while attacking his economic "statism." Alf Landon, the ill-fated centrist Republican nominee in 1936, ran on a middle-of-the-road platform that endorsed key elements of the New Deal.[23]

After an even bigger rout in 1936 than in 1932, even more Republican leaders recognized the need to accept much of the New Deal. In 1938 the rapidly rising New York governor Thomas E. Dewey (who would become the Republican presidential nominee in 1944 and 1948) called himself a "New Deal Republican," and on the eve of the 1940 election Senator Arthur Vandenberg, a deeply conservative isolationist, wrote a widely noticed article "The New Deal Must Be Salvaged."[24]

Meanwhile, during FDR's second term conservative Southern Democrats became increasingly disaffected from the New Deal, partly (but only in part) because of the issue of race. Some scholars attribute the depolarization of the late 1930s to the defection of Southern Democrats from the New Deal coalition on racial issues.[25] That fact—and thus racism—was clearly an important part of the story, but it cannot account for the surprising support of the New Deal from Republicans. On average, the nine major New Deal reforms—the Reconstruction Finance Corporation, the Agricultural Adjustment Act, the Tennessee Valley Authority (TVA), the National Industrial Recovery Act, the National Housing Act, the Works Progress Administration, Social Security, the National Labor Relations Act, and the Fair Labor Standards Act—were supported by 81 percent of congressional Democrats, but also by nearly half (47 percent) of congressional Republicans.[26]

In short, both parties were internally divided—on race, foreign policy, and socioeconomic policy—while the stances of their presidential standard-bearers were unexpectedly convergent. The historical realities of party politics during the Great Depression are at odds with a common view of this as a period torn by titanic battles along party lines. In the 1890s hard times had produced intense party polarization, but in the 1930s even harder times coincided with an almost unprecedented degree of cross-party collaboration. While obviously incomplete, this degree of bipartisan collaboration contrasts sharply with party politics today.

In 1940 the divided Republicans nominated the now forgotten Wendell Willkie as their presidential candidate. Willkie, a successful businessman who had been a progressive Democratic activist until he switched his allegiance only months before his nomination, had gained national recognition for opposing early New Deal industrial policy, especially the TVA, but was (like FDR) an internationalist and (even more than FDR) an advocate of racial and gender equality. As in 1936, the 1940 GOP platform and its nominee endorsed the core New Deal achievements, including regulation of financial institutions, collective bargaining, unemployment allowances, and even Social Security, though both still railed against New Deal "statism" and the "arrogance" of FDR.

Moreover, the 1940 Republican platform endorsed the Equal Rights Amendment and decried discrimination against blacks—in other words, on both racial and gender equality, Republicans in 1940 were actually to the left of the Democrats.[27] Only gradually between the 1930s and the 1970s would African Americans themselves move from their historic commitment to the party of Lincoln to a new and equally firm commitment to the party that sponsored the New Deal and then the Civil Rights Acts of 1964.[28]

The 1940 campaign itself was, like most campaigns, harshly competitive, but immediately afterward Willkie urged cooperation with the Roosevelt administration wherever possible and FDR reciprocated. In the end Willkie failed to vanquish the Republican old guard, but the political imperative of coming to terms with the New Deal persisted even after he had vanished from the scene. In short, during the Depression years of the 1930s, long before Pearl Harbor launched the United States into World War II, the convergence between the Republican and Democratic parties that had begun in the Progressive Era and slowed in the 1920s resumed and even accelerated, exactly as Figure 3.1 illustrates.

Not surprisingly, partisan differences reached their twentieth-century nadir during World War II. In 1944 Governor Dewey of New York finally reached the head of the line for the Republican nomination. As presidential historian Paul Boller wrote, "Dewey waged a campaign which was a model of consensus liberalism. Endorsing most of the New Deal's social legislation, and supporting Roosevelt's foreign policy—including participation in post-war international organizations—Dewey centered his criticisms almost entirely on the management of the New Deal and of the wartime economy."[29] On the other hand, as Figure 3.1 shows, bipartisanship was not much greater between 1941 and 1945 than it had been in 1939 nor than it would be in the decades after the war. In other words, just like the trend toward economic equality that we examined in the previous chapter, collaboration across party lines was no mere temporary wartime parenthesis, but the intensification of a depolarization that had been clearly visible for nearly half a century and would remain so for another quarter century after the war's end.

For more than two decades after World War II American politics remained much less tribalized and polarized, as compared to the intense and even violent conflicts at the outset of the twentieth century or the party vitriol that would characterize the early part of the twenty-first century. An informal content analysis of all inaugural addresses from 1901 to 2017 shows that those in the 1949–1965 period (Truman, Eisenhower, Kennedy, and Johnson) were distinctive in their emphasis on shared values, fairness, and unity, rather than self-reliance, individualism, and identity.

In 1953, for example, the Republican thirty-fourth president recited his own prayer after taking the oath of office: "Especially we pray that our concern shall be for all the people regardless of station, race or calling. May cooperation . . . be the mutual aim of those who . . . hold to differing political faiths." And in 1965 the Democratic thirty-sixth president spoke more eloquently of racial and economic justice than any other president of the twentieth century, saying that "Justice requires us to remember: when any citizen denies his fellow, saying: 'His color is not mine or his beliefs are strange and different,' in that moment he betrays America." It is not easy to imagine the forty-fifth president using such rhetoric.[30]

A gradual rise in an emphasis on racial equality in both parties was one aspect of this surge in "we" values. Eisenhower, for example, actively implemented Truman's 1948 executive order that integrated the US military. Civil rights became temporarily a bipartisan issue, as progressive Northern Democrats joined with liberal Northern Republicans, though their actions remained an inadequate response to racial inequality. But this bipartisanship on race would not last.

However, the egalitarian and communitarian surge in the postwar

period was distinctive entirely apart from racial issues. As we saw in the preceding chapter, economic outcomes continued to become more equal in this
era. Dwight Eisenhower, elected in 1952 as the first Republican president in
a generation, had actually considered running as a Democrat before accept-
ing the Republican nomination. He campaigned in 1952 as an ideologically
conservative Republican, but he governed as a moderate and was the least
partisan president of modern times. His domestic policies in fact did not
differ much from those offered by Adlai Stevenson, his Democratic oppo-
nent in 1952 and 1956. Eisenhower described his stance as "modern Republicanism." He wrote his brother Edgar on November 8, 1954, "Should any
political party attempt to abolish social security, unemployment insurance,
and eliminate labor laws and farm programs, you would not hear of that
party again in our political history." When confronted by the Republican
old guard during his first term, he even mused privately about founding a
new party called "The Middle Way," seeking common ground between the
Republicans and Democrats. He was an entirely appropriate president for
the mid-century peak of party depolarization.[31]

Some historians in retrospect term this period a "conservative consensus," and by comparison to the mid-1960s, it was indeed conservative.
In fact, however, Eisenhower extended core elements of the New Deal,
including Social Security, minimum wage regulations, and labor laws. In
1954 he expanded Social Security coverage to 10 million farm and service
workers who had been excluded from the original New Deal program in
part because they were disproportionately black and female. One of his
first acts as president was to create the new Department of Health, Education, and Welfare, and during his tenure, social welfare spending as a
percent of GNP rose from 7.6 percent in 1952 to 11.5 percent in 1961.[32]

While acknowledging the burden of high tax rates, a legacy of wartime, Ike emphasized that Americans also wanted an expansion of Social
Security, unemployment insurance, more public housing, better health
care, more schools, and massive investment in infrastructure. (The Interstate Highway system was his proudest domestic achievement.) These
things cost money, and that money would have to come from taxes, he
explained, in sharp contrast to Republican tax- and budget-cutting after

World War I. All this from a Republican president, collaborating with the moderate Democratic congressional leaders, Sam Rayburn and Lyndon Baines Johnson, to produce policies that a later generation of Republican leaders would castigate as "tax and spend liberalism."[33]

Still, we must not exaggerate the mood of an "era of good feelings" in the early 1950s, a period of intense anticommunism during which the Red Scare and Korean War occasioned frequent accusations of treachery. In 1954 Senator Joseph McCarthy called the period running from FDR to Ike "twenty years of treason." In 1960 Senator Barry Goldwater, the leader of the right wing of the Republican Party, looking back at the 1950s, complained that Ike "ran a dime store New Deal."[34] Nevertheless, at mid-century, mainstream political values included collegiality, compromise, and bipartisanship. Defending the moderate partisanship of this era, two-time Republican presidential nominee Thomas Dewey argued that "the resemblance of the parties is the very heart of the strength of the American political system."[35]

In the 1960 election both Kennedy and Richard Nixon ran centrist campaigns with relatively few domestic policy differences. Kennedy was in practice a conservative Democrat, despite his occasional liberal rhetoric. Quoting Jefferson, JFK warned liberals that "Great innovations should not be forced on slender majorities."[36] His emphasis on moving by bipartisan consensus, reinforced by the Senate filibuster, encouraged policy stagnation—most vividly in the field of race and civil rights, but not only there. As Americans would learn in the twenty-first century, however, policy stagnation could also be produced by polarization itself.

By the early 1960s, however, the right wing of the GOP, sidelined for nearly thirty years, had openly revolted. Barry Goldwater's call for "a choice, not an echo" reflected this mood, as he articulated the reborn libertarianism of the New Right. In 1964, crushing the liberal wing of the Republican Party, Goldwater argued that "extremism in the defense of liberty is no vice," and "moderation in the pursuit of justice no virtue." But that polarizing choice was premature for the electorate as a whole, and Goldwater was trounced by Johnson, who had correctly predicted his cross-partisan appeal would translate to an electoral blowout: "You ask a voter who classifies himself as a liberal what he thinks I am and he says a liberal. You ask a voter who calls himself a conservative what he thinks I am and he says I'm a conservative."[37] That was partisan politics at low tide.

Buoyed by his landslide victory in 1964, LBJ moved to the left on issues of race and inequality, beginning to open an ideological divide that would widen steadily for the next half century. Nevertheless, across LBJ's far-reaching Great Society initiatives (the War on Poverty, Civil Rights, Voting Rights, Medicare/Medicaid, federal aid to education, and immigration reform—the very issues at the core of intense party polarization in our own period, a half century later), all major bills were supported by majorities or substantial minorities within *both* parties. On average, these bills were supported by 74 percent of congressional Democrats and 63 percent of congressional Republicans, a fact forgotten by later Republicans who would rail against the leftist extremism of the Great Society programs.[38] Behind the scenes LBJ cooperated with Senator Everett Dirksen, the titular head of congressional Republicans, just as he himself had done with Ike a decade earlier. In 1968 Richard Nixon ran on a Republican platform that accepted all the major Great Society reforms, just as Ike had accepted the core of the New Deal in the 1950s. This campaign would prove the high tide of liberal Republicanism and another low-water mark for party polarization in the twentieth century.

As president, Nixon proved to be an ambiguous and transitional figure. In domestic policy, he was (with the important exception of race and civil rights) a moderate. Though highly partisan, opportunistic, paranoid, and vengeful in pursuing power, he was ideologically flexible and accepted liberal policies. Apart from TR, as historian James Patterson pointed out, "Nixon was easily the most liberal Republican President in the twentieth century."[39] He kept Great Society programs more or less intact; raised social spending; sponsored the Environmental Protection Agency, the Clean Air Act, the Occupational Safety and Health Act, and the National Endowment for Arts and for the Humanities; signed Title IX, which ended sex discrimination in education; opined that "I am now a Keynesian in economics";[40] and even proposed a national health insurance system and a guaranteed annual income, though without following through on either proposal.

On the overriding issue of race, however, Nixon led Republicans sharply to the right, partly in response to the third-party candidacy of the race-baiting ex-governor of Alabama, George Wallace. That Nixon intended to do so was initially not so clear. For example, his first secretary of housing and urban development (HUD) was George Romney, president of the American Motors Company and father of future Republican presidential nominee Mitt Romney, who exemplified the last gasp of progressive Republicanism.[41] Romney's Republicanism didn't see the world as a zero-sum contest between capital and labor, white and black, friend and enemy, us and them. As secretary of HUD, he was implacable that minorities deserved access to quality housing in affluent white suburbs. But in the new Republican Party he had become a political liability, a fossil from earlier in the century, and he was forced from his position by Nixon in 1972.

The 1960s and early 1970s were a period of flux in party politics on both sides of the aisle. The Democrats' move to the left on civil rights, gender rights, and social rights coupled with the Republicans' incitement and exploitation of the white backlash to the civil rights victories produced ever greater social, cultural, and political polarization. Southern Democrats left the party over civil rights legislation, just as liberal Republicans were marginalized by their party's shift to the right on those same issues. On both sides the centrist party establishment was weakened, and racial conflict was the primary cause.

In 1964 the Republicans had nominated the most conservative candidate in many decades, and in 1972, as the New Left took over the grass roots, the Democrats nominated George McGovern, probably the most left-wing candidate ever nominated by a major party.[42] In the short term, these "choice, not echo" candidates were drubbed, but both foreshadowed a period of increasingly stark choices.

By the late 1960s bipartisanship was going out of fashion. In 1968 George Wallace complained "there's not a dime's worth of difference" between the major parties, and in 1972 the country's leading liberal pundit, David Broder, lamented the lack of party polarization: "What this country needs is some unvarnished political partisanship."[43] He may have been channeling a 1950 report from the American Political Science Association, "Toward a More Responsible Two-Party System,"[44] which had called for greater party distinctiveness in place of Tweedledum-Tweedledee parties. Wallace, Broder, and the political scientists were about to get what they wanted.

Partisan tribalism began to reemerge—slowly at first, but then with gathering speed and force. The polarization that began in the late 1960s was initially driven primarily by race, as the two parties became more distinct and more internally homogeneous. Johnson and Nixon (ironically, each a moderate within his own party) were the twin progenitors of that turn toward polarization, Johnson by signing the Civil Rights bills in 1964-65 that (as he himself reportedly had foretold[45]) cost the Democrats their conservative, Southern wing, and Nixon by following an essentially racist "Southern strategy" in 1968 to bring those same conservative Southerners into the Republican fold.[46]

In the aftermath of Watergate, Vietnam, and the myriad other conflicts of the late 1960s and early 1970s (to be discussed in Chapter 8), Presidents Gerald Ford and Jimmy Carter temporarily tacked back toward the middle, trying to press the pause button on growing polarization. By 1975, however, Ronald Reagan was raising an impassioned banner of "no pale pastels, but bold colors," and after 1980 the Reagan Revolution pulled the Republican Party further and further to the right, a movement that would last well into the twenty-first century.[47] The polarization that had begun with civil rights spread quickly across many other issues, as the parties took opposing stances on issues that had not previously been partisan, thus extending and reinforcing the basic polarization. These increasingly polarizing issues include:

- "Big government": As we have seen, during the postwar period Republicans like Eisenhower had defended high taxes as the necessary price to pay for expanded public services. But with the advent of the New Conservatism in the 1960s under the aegis of Barry Goldwater and the economist Milton Friedman, Republicans moved sharply to the right.[48] "Big government" and "tax and spend" liberal policies, they now argued, caused deficits, inflation, and unemployment, while government regulation interfered with the efficiency of the free market.[49] "Government is not the solution to our problem," Ronald Reagan argued in his 1981 inaugural address; "government is the problem."[50] By the 1990s

Democrats under Bill Clinton began to follow the Republicans to the right on issues like welfare, crime, and deregulation, but never fast enough to keep pace with the Republicans; and this widening ideological gap soon became the dominant dimension of polarization. Democrats on the left, like Jesse Jackson, objected in 1995 to establishment Democrats' move toward the center: "what we've got now in the United States is one party, two names. We've got Republicans and Republicans Lite," in effect echoing Goldwater's complaints of three decades earlier.[51]

- Abortion and religion: In the late 1960s Democrats had been *more* likely to be churchgoers than were Republicans.[52] At the time of the 1973 *Roe v. Wade* decision, the abortion issue did not divide Americans by party or religion. The first reaction of Southern Baptists was actually to support the *Roe* decision. But by 1976 (and especially during the 1990s) partisanship, religiosity, and attitudes toward abortion began to swing into the nearly perfectly polarized alignment that became central to early-twenty-first-century party division. Unexpectedly, this realignment occurred mostly by Americans adjusting their religious convictions and their views on abortion to fit their increasingly polarized party affiliation, rather than the reverse.[53] Partisanship was on its way to becoming the master cleavage in American society and party identity the primary force field.

- The environment: The Nixon administration had initially responded favorably to the renascent environmental movement, with the creation of the Environmental Protection Agency and the passage of the Clean Air Act of 1970. With the advent of Reaganism, however, the Republicans became steadily more skeptical about environmentalism, a trend capped by their leaders' uncompromising denial of climate science in the twenty-first century.

- Education: Roughly 40 percent of Republicans in the House and Senate had voted alongside roughly 80 percent of Democrats in favor of the landmark Elementary and Secondary Education Act of 1965, part of LBJ's War on Poverty. But as the issue of school desegregation heated up and free market orthodoxy permeated the Republican Party in the 1980s, the two parties began to divide on the issue of public vs.

private or charter schools, a division that would remain into the next century. Eventually, even a technical debate about reading pedagogy between "phonics" and "whole language" approaches became the subject of the party-inflected "Reading Wars."[54]

So the renewed party polarization of the last half century began with race—the one constant and central conflict in American history—but polarization soon came to be about much more than race.[55] By the years of Obama and Trump, bipartisanship in Congress had become virtually nonexistent; on six major votes of this period, the administration received support from 95 percent of their own party, but only 3 percent of the opposition.[56] Statistically speaking, party polarization was rapidly approaching mathematical perfection.

Racial conflict had initially shifted both parties away from the moderate center in a kind of symmetrical polarization, but the dynamics of the polarization since 1975 have been far more asymmetrical, as the evolution of party attitudes on particular issues just outlined illustrates. On issue after issue, Democrats remained mostly on the center-left, whereas the Republican center of gravity moved further and further to the right, as shown in Figure 3.3. In other words, bipartisanship has disappeared from American politics over the last half century largely because the Republican Party has become steadily more extreme. At least part of the explanation for this rightward shift is the investment by wealthy, highly conservative business elites in a sustained effort to shift American politics rightward, an effort signaled, symbolically at least, in a memo by Lewis F. Powell, Jr. in 1971, articulating a coordinated, long-term political strategy.[57] This was one way in which the accelerating top-end inequality described in the previous chapter encouraged the rapid increase in polarization that we review in this one, though as we will later argue, the causal arrows here do not point in only one direction.

Political scientist Nolan McCarty has summarized virtually all nonpartisan assessments, "During the period of increased polarization, the main driver has been the increasing conservatism of the Republican party."[58] Whether this asymmetry will persist in the years ahead depends on whether the Democratic Party and especially congressional Democrats move left, but as Figure 3.3 suggests, if history is any guide, it would likely take decades for any such shift to play itself out. The result of these moves and countermoves: In contemporary America, party polarization and tribalization has reached an intensity unseen since the Civil War with no end in sight.

FIGURE 3.3: **ASYMMETRIC POLARIZATION IN THE US HOUSE OF REPRESENTATIVES, 1879–2019**

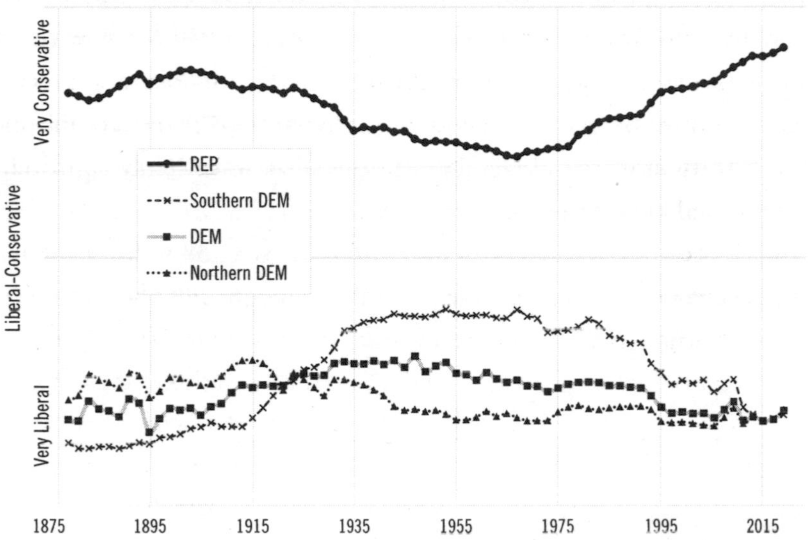

Source: Jeffrey B. Lewis et al., Congressional Roll-Call Votes Database (2019).

DIMENSIONS, CAUSES, AND CONSEQUENCES OF POLARIZATION

Thus far we've explored the historical narrative of polarization and de-polarization decade by decade and even year by year. In this section we zoom out to a wide-angle view of the full trend across the last 125 years and explore possible causes and consequences of that longer curvilinear pattern. In Figure 3.1 we saw how that pattern played out in congressional voting trends, but any single measure like that might be misleading. Our confidence in that larger pattern can be strengthened if we can confirm it with other measures.

Figure 3.4 offers one such measure, based on national newspaper accounts of party conflict among elected officials in arenas not limited to congressional roll call votes.[59] This indicator varies from year to year, depending on the issues that happen to be on the national agenda at any given time. Nevertheless, the basic trend is unmistakable, and it confirms the inverted U that appears in congressional voting. Party conflict was high (and thus cross-party comity was low) in the closing years of the Gilded Age in the 1890s. With the onset of the Progressive Era party conflict began to diminish and continued to do so for the next four decades. Just as in congressional voting, cross-party collaboration as reflected in the national press reached a peak during World War II, and just as in congressional voting, that period of relative party harmony endured virtually undiminished until the 1960s. Finally, this chart displays the practically uninterrupted half century of rapid polarization after 1970, culminating in the unprecedented partisan conflict of the early decades of the twenty-first century. In short, this independent measure confirms the familiar inverted U pattern shown in Figure 3.1 in all essentials.

FIGURE 3.4: **CROSS-PARTY COMITY VS. CONFLICT AS REPORTED IN THE NATIONAL PRESS, 1890–2013**

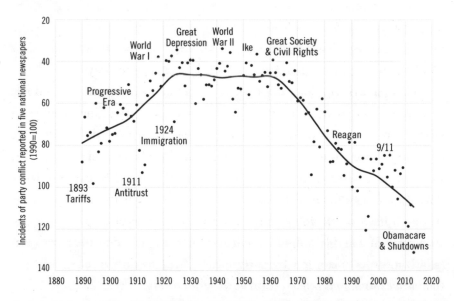

Source: Azzimonti, "Partisan Conflict and Private Investment." Data LOESS smoothed: .25.

POLARIZATION AT THE MASS LEVEL

The measures of polarization at the level of political institutions and leaders that we've explored thus far are available for the entire period from the 1890s to the 2010s, showing both the depolarization until mid-century and the resurgence of polarization after 1970.[60] As we now turn to measures of polarization among ordinary citizens, our evidence is mostly limited to the period after 1970, when systematic opinion polling became common. With a few important exceptions, we are unable to assess trends in polarization among ordinary Americans during the half century when the parties were becoming less polarized. In effect, for the most part we are unable to see the first act of the play, because the curtain was only raised for the second act, though in a few cases we can catch glimpses of the end of the first act.

One of the few measures of partisanship among ordinary voters available for the entire period, is "split ticket" voting, that is, when voters choose one party for president and a different party for Congress. In a depolarized period, split ticket voting is common, since the differences between the parties seem modest, whereas in a polarized period such mixed loyalties among voters are rare. During the highly polarized Trump era, for example, national attention has been closely focused on a few such cases (Republicans elected in Hillary Clinton districts or Democrats in Trump districts), precisely because they are so rare, but forty years ago nearly half of all members of Congress were cross-pressured in that way.

This pattern of change might, in principle, reflect either top-down or bottom-up dynamics, that is, changes in voters' party-line loyalties or changes in party nominating behavior (vetting their candidates to get rid of RINOs ["Republicans in Name Only"] or DINOs). In either case, the trend in split ticket voting echoes our familiar inverted U-curve of party polarization, as shown in Figure 3.5.[61] Polarization at the level of voters seems to have neatly followed polarization at the level of political elites with a lag of roughly a decade. This lag suggests, but doesn't prove, that polarization has been led by party leaders, with voters gradually sorting themselves to match polarization at the elite level.

On one direct measure of cross-party attitudes among ordinary

FIGURE 3.5: THE RISE AND FALL OF TICKET-SPLITTING, 1900–2016

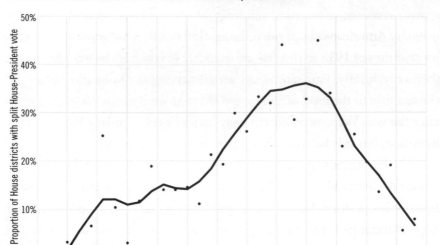

Source: Fiorina, *Unstable Majorities*, Fig. 7.4. Data LOESS smoothed: .25.

citizens we are lucky to have evidence from well before the 1970s' turning point in party polarization. According to very early Gallup polling data from the late 1930s on the now standard question about presidential support, partisan differences in evaluations of the incumbent president traced the familiar U-shaped curve of depolarization and then repolarization.[62] (See Figure 3.6, which shows the discrepancy between approval of the president by voters from his own party and his approval rating among his partisan opponents.) For more than a decade from September 1937 to June 1948 Democratic and Republican voters steadily *converged* in their judgments about the president. Recall that this is the period in which Wendell Willkie and Thomas Dewey led the Republicans toward accommodation with the New Deal. To be sure, these eleven years of depolarization also encompassed World War II, consistent with the idea that wars (or at least, popular wars) cause national convergence.

However, exactly as in the cases of the economic convergence that we examined in the previous chapter and the political depolarization at the elite level that we examined earlier in this chapter, this mass depolarization persisted into the 1970s, thirty years after war's end, so it cannot have been a mere remnant of wartime solidarity. Party polarization in the views of ordinary Americans about the president did not touch the prewar levels of polarization of 1938 until 1984, nearly forty years after the war ended, and then only briefly. Partisanship in presidential evaluations did not return consistently to the level of prewar polarization until about 2005, sixty years after the war. Wartime solidarity may be part of the explanation for depolarization, but it is far from the main story.

The latest years in Figure 3.6 show that this measure is now approaching its statistical limit in which *all* voters from the president's own party approve his performance, while *no* voters from the opposite party approve his performance.[63] Between 2013 and 2019, approval from the president's own party averaged about 88 percent compared to about 8 percent from the opposition party, a discrepancy of roughly 80 percentage points! By contrast, in January 1947 41 percent of Republicans approved of Harry Truman, compared to only 61 percent of Democrats; and in February 1964 64 percent of Republicans, compared to 84 percent of Democrats,

FIGURE 3.6: **PARTISANSHIP IN PRESIDENTIAL APPROVAL, 1938–2019 (GALLUP POLLS)**

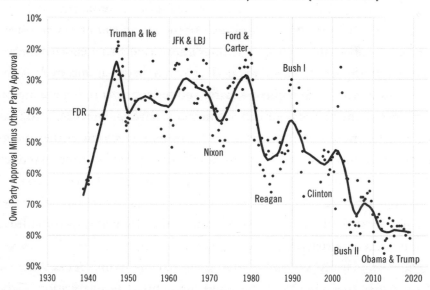

Source: Gallup Polls. See endnote 3.62. Data LOESS smoothed: .1.

approved of LBJ. We have become so accustomed to thinking of extreme polarization as normal that we have nearly forgotten that as late as the opening years of the Reagan Revolution the partisan discrepancy was typically about 30 percentage points, corresponding roughly to approval by two thirds of the president's own party supporters and one third of opposition voters.

These first two measures of mass depolarization (split ticket voting and presidential approval) didn't really begin to reverse until the 1980s, a full decade after repolarization had begun at the congressional level. On the other hand, as we shall now see, voting along party lines at the electoral level (which had been generally *declining* in the 1950s and 1960s) began to rise in the 1970s, and the trend in what is termed "affective polarization" (that is, how we *feel* about the other party) seems to have turned at the end of the 1980s. In short, as a rough rule of thumb, many measures of political polarization at both the mass and elite levels began to increase in the 1970s and to accelerate in the 1980s, but polarization at the mass level tended to lag polarization at the elite level by a decade or so.

After 1952, when the earliest systematic surveys of voters' attitudes and behavior began, we can begin to measure the direct impact of party identification on voters' behavior, as well as the degree to which voters inherited their parents' partisan loyalties. These indicators of party polarization and tribalism among ordinary Americans turn out to trace the familiar U-curve, falling from 1952 to the mid-1970s and rising thereafter.[64] From the 1950s to the 1970s, voting behavior seemed *less and less* determined by party loyalty and family traditions. At the same time, identification with either political party became more muted, with fewer extreme partisans and more independents. Analysts at the time called this trend "dealignment," and this rough equivalent of depolarization looked set to continue into the indefinite future.

But in the 1970s—once again, that familiar turning point—those trends suddenly reversed, as more and more of the electorate began to describe themselves as "strong" Democrats or "strong" Republicans, and that identity became a more and more powerful predictor of actual voting. The correlation between a voter's long-term party identification and his or her actual vote had declined between 1952 and 1976, but it then unexpectedly began to rise sharply.[65] In the ensuing half century the alignment between voters' party affiliation and their ideological positions on specific issues, as well as their actual vote, became steadily stronger, as partisan lines in the electorate became ever more strictly and coherently drawn.

Many readers may assume that elite polarization (parties moving away from the center) will have caused a rise in independents who are unhappy with the choice between these two parties, though we know from other evidence that many voters are playing "follow the leader" in their policy views. More people are likely today than thirty years ago to say that they are "independents," rejecting both parties, but the evidence suggests that that category is quite heterogeneous, including many self-camouflaged partisans, and that it coexists with a trend toward stronger partisan commitment among partisans. Some self-described "independent" voters actually behave more like partisans in that they are nowadays less likely to switch from election to election. One possible interpretation is that a growing fraction of partisan, follow-the-leader voters are highly polarized and tribal, turning off many other voters, who may be choosing the "independent" title as a way of symbolically separating themselves from tribalization.[66]

Writing in 2008, political scientists Joseph Bafumi and Robert Y. Shapiro observed that

> this partisanship has voters more strongly anchored than ever before by left/right ideological thinking. What followed from the mid-1970s to [now] have been decades of an increasing connection between individuals' expressed partisanship and their self-reported ideology and a stronger connection between both partisanship and expressed liberal-conservative ideology and the opinions of Americans on policy-related issues. This kind of partisan and ideological sorting and polarizing process increasingly reflected, and in turn further fueled, an even more pronounced partisan and ideological conflict among political leaders in both parties.[67]

This stricter partisan alignment, Bafumi and Shapiro concluded, was associated with the aftermath of the political turmoil of the 1960s, including the Southern party realignment over race and the emergence of newer issues such as abortion, women's rights, religion, environmentalism, and so on, exactly as we have described in our earlier narrative of national party politics.[68]

Our discussion of mass political polarization has focused on party polarization and political tribalism, not on patterns of agreement or disagreement on specific foreign and domestic issues, like global warming or health insurance or deregulation, for three related reasons. First, we have no good measures of the voters' views on specific issues before the onset of survey research in the 1960s. Second, one of the most robust findings of the ensuing half century of research is that most ordinary voters are ill-informed about the details of public issues, so much so that they entirely lack views on many issues of the day.[69] Most people have more urgent everyday things to worry about than policy debates. Finally, recent political science research has found that voters tend to adjust their policy positions to fit their "tribal" party loyalties, rather than the other way around.[70] Sports fans typically feel a strong affinity for their team, even though they could not offer a reasoned explanation for their attachment. Similarly, political scientists Christopher Achen and Larry Bartels argue that "group and partisan loyalties, not policy preferences or ideologies, are fundamental in democratic politics,"[71] and Michael Barber and Jeremy C. Pope find that "group loyalty is the stronger motivator of opinion than are any ideological principles."[72] Partisan identification is more a tribal affiliation than an ideological commitment, and that is a crucial part of the story of party polarization.

In accord with this growing emphasis on partisan tribalism, voters' evaluations of presidential candidates' personal traits became ever more defined by partisan loyalties. After 1980, partisans of each party increasingly ascribed only positive traits to their candidate and only negative traits to the opposing candidates. Data indicate "partisans increasingly perceive the other party's candidate as *personally* flawed."[73] This pattern reflects the affective polarization that is, as we shall shortly see, a key feature of contemporary political life.

The correspondence between one generation's political identity and the next generation's actual political behavior is another subtle marker of political tribalism, since it represents the power of family traditions to mold contemporary political behavior. The correlation between a voter's party identification (and vote) and his or her parents' party identification steadily *declined* between 1958 and the late 1960s[74] (meaning less tribalism), but then rose sharply between the late 1960s and 2015 (indicating more tribalism).[75] In the absence of survey data, we will likely never know how tight that intergenerational correlation was in the first half of the twentieth century, but at a minimum we do know that as the curtain of our ignorance about the behavior of individual voters began to lift with the advent of the first few electoral surveys in the 1950s, tribalism was declining and would continue to decline for the next twenty years. Then in the early 1970s that measure of tribalism began to strengthen, and by now it is stronger than ever recorded.

Even in local affairs far from the pinnacles of national politics, mass polarization became increasingly common after the early 1970s, not because of who showed up, but because of who didn't. Participation in public meetings, local civic organizations, political parties, and political rallies by self-described middle-of-the-roaders fell by more than half between 1973 and 1994. Participation by self-described "moderate" liberals or conservatives declined by only about one third. Among people who described themselves as "very" liberal or "very" conservative, declines in participation were even more muted. Ironically, at the same time that more and more Americans described their political views as "middle of the road" or "moderate," the extremes on the ideological spectrum accounted for a bigger and bigger share of those who actually attend meetings, write letters, serve on civic committees, and even go to church. Because moderate voices have fallen silent, more extreme views have gradually become more dominant in grassroots American civic life. Even though many Americans remain self-described moderates, local civic life has become steadily more polarized.[76]

In the widely discussed book *The Big Sort*, published in 2008, political observers Bill Bishop and Robert Cushing argued that Americans are increasingly sorting themselves into politically homogenous and geographically segregated enclaves, with growing cultural and lifestyle differences

between the two party-tribes as both cause and consequence of this sorting on the basis of partisan identity. Social scientists have been skeptical
that the available evidence supports these claims, although recent evidence
seems more consistent with the *Big Sort* hypothesis. [77] Still, the most prudent judgment regarding a *geographic* Big Sort over the last half century
must remain for now the prudent Scottish verdict: Not proven.

However, there has clearly been a *sociological* Big Sort. As a result of the
growing coherence and consistency of Americans' political views and party
and social affiliations, partisan prejudice and even hostility have begun to
pervade the private lives of ordinary Americans.[78] Cross-cutting ties and
"inconsistent" identities (e.g., a liberal Republican or a conservative Democrat, an evangelical Democrat or an African American Republican) once
softened partisan prejudice, but those are rarer now.[79] The Pew Research
Center found that in 2016, 75 percent of Americans reported no political
disagreements within their own circle of friends, up from about 65 percent
as recently as 2000.[80] Political tribalism is on the rise. A less pejorative
term for "tribalism" might be "team spirit," but however we label it, it has
become the conceptual twin of party polarization in Congress and other
political institutions that we explored earlier in this chapter.

Thus, as Americans have increasingly sorted themselves more consistently between the two political parties, and as social identities have
aligned more completely with partisan loyalties, interparty prejudice and
even anger have been heightened. Interpersonal partisan hostility has increased.[81] American voters increasingly see supporters of the other party as
extreme ideologically and flawed personally. Both Democrats and Republicans increasingly dislike, even loathe, their opponents. Out-party stereo-
typing in assessing the "intelligence" of Americans rose from 6 percent in
1960 to 48 percent in 2008; out-party bias in perceptions of "selfishness"
rose from 21 percent to 47 percent. In slightly more than two decades
(1994–2016) the rate of "extremely unfavorable" views of our party opponents rose steadily from less than 20 percent to about 56 percent.[82]

This pattern also shows up in 0–100 "feeling thermometer" scores, as
measured in the National Election Study.[83] Although feelings about one's
own party have always been warmer than attitudes toward the opposition,

in-group feelings have *not* changed much over the years, remaining steady at about 70°. However, between 1978 and 2016 average warmth toward the opposing party fell steadily from just below neutral (48°) to quite cool (30°), as shown in Figure 3.7.[84] (Earlier data measuring attitudes toward "Democrats" or "Republicans" rather than toward the parties as such suggest that partisan hostility had actually been declining throughout the 1960s until the precipitous increase in partisan hostility began in the mid-1970s.[85])

Partisan hostility as measured in these feeling thermometers is now even more intense than racial or religious hostility, both of which have declined over the years. In other words, partisan cleavages have widened just as racial and religious cleavages have gradually (and surprisingly) narrowed.[86] Indeed, as political scientists Shanto Iyengar and his colleagues have recently argued, "the most significant fault line in the second decade of the twenty-first century [in America] is not race, religion, or economic status but political party affiliation."[87] In short, partisanship at the level of ordinary Americans is increasingly framed as "us" against "them," not merely in public life, but even in private life.[88]

FIGURE 3.7: **INTERPARTY FEELINGS STEADILY COOL, 1978–2016**

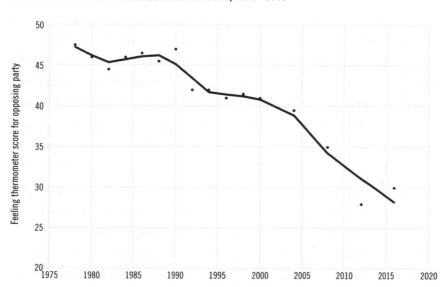

Source: American National Election Studies. Data LOESS smoothed: .33.

This increasing affective polarization has influenced even attitudes to intermarriage. Between 1960 and 2010 opposition to one's offspring marrying an out-partisan rose from 4 percent to 33 percent among Democrats and from 5 percent to 49 percent among Republicans.[89] This partisan prejudice shows up both in online dating and in actual marriages, as people are increasingly choosing their partners on the basis of political affiliation, even more than on the basis of education or religious orientation.[90] Over the last half century marriage across racial and religious lines has become much more common than either used to be,[91] whereas marriage across party lines has become much less common.[92] This increasing agreement between husband and wife about politics in turn strengthens the inheritance of party identity by the next generation, since we know that children are more likely to inherit party identity when both parents agree politically. In this very intimate way, over the last half century partisanship has gradually replaced religion as the main basis of "tribal" affiliation in America.[93]

If partisan identity has become stronger than other social identities, like regional or occupational or class or religious or even racial identity over the last half century, as we have just seen, then a reasonable question (given the substantial evidence we have already compiled on the century-long U-curve of polarization and depolarization) is whether the reverse process was happening 1900–1965, and if so, why? Identity can be divisive, to be sure, but identity itself is malleable, not ineluctably fixed, and can, in fact, be a source of unity. As we shall argue in Chapter 5, a widening sense of "we" seems to have characterized American identities in the 1900–1965 period. So perhaps partisan identity and affective polarization waned over the half century from the polarized, tribal Gilded Age to the depolarized America in mid-century, though without direct evidence of the strength of partisan identity in that earlier period (because of the curtain that obscures that first act) that hypothesis must remain unproven. The bottom line: We can't be sure about the trend in polarized feelings among ordinary Americans over the last 125 years, but we can be sure about the basic U-curve in party polarization.

EXPLANATIONS?[94]

Which causes what—elite or mass polarization—has been a source of lively, chicken-egg debate among political scientists over the last several decades.[95] The ups and downs of tribalization have been reflected in the views of both ordinary citizens and elected officials, but that correlation doesn't tell us what caused what—were citizens inducing more/less moderation among leaders, or were leaders presenting more/less polarized choices to voters?

There is broad consensus that members of Congress are increasingly ideologically divided by party, but the evidence of mass polarization on specific issues is more contentious. What is clear is that voters are increasingly sorting themselves out in terms of ideological consistency—there are fewer liberal Republicans and conservative Democrats, and the issue positions of Republican partisans and Democratic partisans have increasingly diverged. Partisan consistency in voting has increased, as we have seen.

However, even when the evidence for mass polarization is clear, it is possible that voters have merely responded to more polarized alternatives put forward by the party elites. Polarization appears to have begun at the elite level in the 1970s, but spread to the electorate as a whole in the 1980s, as voters, responding to the increasingly disparate options offered by leaders and encouraged by activists, sorted themselves into opposing camps.[96] The patterns of elite and mass polarization do not conclusively prove whether the causal impetus for change came from the party leaders or the voters. Probably it was a bit of both, with feedback in both directions, as voters' partisan hostility and leaders' refusal to compromise are two sides of a vicious feedback loop. When public trust in partisan opponents is low, politicians have little incentive to compromise, and when politicians don't compromise, they signal to their supporters that staunch opposition is appropriate.

The balance of opinion among experts currently is that in this elite-mass interaction the primary impetus is top-down. Elites send polarizing messages to the electorate in an effort to win support with partisan appeals. And often voters change their views on issues as a result of these messages from their own party leaders. As leaders "signal" increasingly divergent views on specific issues, that divergence can quickly spread to their followers.[97] One recent example: A long-term bipartisan consensus on U.S.-Russian relations was rapidly converted to mass polarization after 2016, as President Trump, in effect, signaled to his base that sympathy for Russia was now the appropriate policy view. Another example mentioned earlier is the case of views about abortion, which seems to have become more polarized among ordinary voters in response to signals from political leaders.[98] This top-down causality is consistent with the fact that mass polarization has tended to lag elite polarization by a decade or two.

Some scholars put special emphasis on pundits and political activists as the mainspring of party polarization, inducing more extremism among both elected officials and ordinary citizens.[99] The ideological gap between Republican and Democratic activists grew substantially after the 1960s, and as we have seen, the folks who still show up in local civic life are increasingly coming from the ideological poles. Activists and social movements appear to have played a strong role in encouraging extremism and in extending the dimensions of conflict to include identity-based issue groupings over time. These choices are communicated by the media and articulated by political leaders seeking electoral advantage. Combined, these factors may well have encouraged the electorate to sort itself into partisan camps.

A comparison of the inverted U-shaped charts in this chapter and the preceding one shows that economic inequality and political polarization have moved in lockstep over the last 125 years. But as generations of students of social science have learned to recite, correlation doesn't prove causation. Nolan McCarty, Keith T. Poole, and Howard Rosenthal, the pioneers in this field of scholarship, initially argued that inequality caused polarization,[100] but it is now widely agreed that the timing doesn't fit. Our own analyses show that inequality is, if anything, the lagging variable (meaning that rising inequality has shown up later than rising polarization), which makes it unlikely to be the primary driver in this relationship. More recently, political scientists Bryan J. Dettrey and James E. Campbell have argued that "income inequality does not appear to have been a significant cause of growing polarization," while economists John V. Duca and Jason L. Saving conclude that causation between inequality and polarization runs in both directions.[101] The fact that inequality and polarization are highly correlated over time also is consistent with the possibility that both are the consequences of some unidentified third factor, a possibility that we shall explore in subsequent chapters.

Scholars and pundits have offered a wide variety of other possible causes of the polarization of the last half century, but much less attention has been given to the long trend toward depolarization in the first half of the twentieth century, and many of the proffered explanations fit poorly with the actual history of party politics in that period. In fact, even for the later period of increasing polarization after 1970, evidence in support of many putative causal factors is weak. This is true of the role of individual politicians, or of electoral or legislative institutions, like gerrymandering or campaign finance.[102] Change in the mass media (from "yellow journalism" in 1900 to Uncle Walter Cronkite in mid-century to Fox News and Twitter feeds today) is a plausible suspect in this mystery, but research has found no clear answer to which is cause and which effect.[103] We shall return to the task of understanding the full 125-year cycle of falling and rising polarization later in this book.

CONSEQUENCES OF POLARIZATION?

Democracy requires fair, vigorous competition between political parties who seek voter support in the political marketplace. Indeed, one influential theory of democracy argues that party competition is the very definition of democracy.[104] The most important limitation on American democracy during the first half of the twentieth century was precisely that racial equality was excluded for the most part from the agenda of party competition, and conversely, the single most important gain for American democracy between the 1920s and the 1960s was the emergence of racial equality as a central issue in party competition. So party difference is, in itself, healthy for democracy.

On the other hand, the intense and pervasive political polarization of the last half century has manifestly impaired American democracy. Any contemporary observer of US politics is aware of the debilitating impact of this polarization on public life. Tennessee Republican Senator Howard Baker, "The Great Conciliator" who served in the Senate from 1967 to 1984, famously lauded the political value of recognizing that "the other fellow might be right." In that less-polarized era, politicians' stock-in-trade was the ability to see both sides of an issue and thus to look for win-win solutions, but as that skill or inclination has waned, disputes have become increasingly difficult to resolve.[105]

At the level of ordinary citizens, as political philosopher Danielle Allen has pointed out, in a democracy when our side is defeated, we need to understand that to accept losing in the short run is essential to preserve the long-run goal of democracy. "Any life in a democracy involves losses as well as wins, so a part of having a sturdy ethos of democratic citizenship is to know how to process that loss and stay in the game."[106] Polarization undermines that ethos.

Nolan McCarty has laid out clearly why polarization in America has increased gridlock in national policymaking.[107] Our Madisonian separation of powers, checks and balances, and federalism, coupled with the ever-present possibility of a senatorial filibuster, multiplies the number of veto points, making it much easier to say "no" than "yes." Getting to "yes" is even harder without give-and-take between the parties. This constitutional effect is magnified during periods of close competition between the parties, when control of executive and legislative branches is more likely to be narrowly divided between the two parties. Probably not coincidentally, extreme polarization has coincided at the two ends of our U-curve with such "insecure majorities," exacerbating gridlock.[108] It is no accident that most substantial legislative reform programs of the last 125 years—the Progressive Era reforms, the New Deal, the Great Society, and even the Reagan Revolution—had substantial support from both sides of the aisle.[109]

One consequence of both the incivility and the gridlock that come from polarization is that American government has become less effective—less able to manage our national fortunes, including addressing persistent economic and ethnic inequality. A striking trend of our time is the decline of public confidence in our political institutions themselves, though political scientists disagree about whether that is a cause or an effect of polarization. In mid-century both Republican and Democratic citizens tended to trust (or occasionally distrust) the government, regardless of which party was in power, but in the mid-1960s overall trust in the government began to decline, especially among the supporters of the out-party (whichever that happened to be). As this cycle continued, overall confidence in government ratcheted down, while the gap between the in-party and the out-party grew. Party polarization has led to a growing polarization in trust in government.

We lack opinion polls from the nineteenth century, but political scientists Marc J. Hetherington and Thomas J. Rudolph speculate that public trust in government was lower in the Gilded Age, when (as we have seen earlier in this chapter) polarization was higher.[110] Trust in government, we might thus conjecture, rose until the 1960s, reflecting the manifold social and economic successes of the long mid-century period of party convergence. A bit of early survey data (shown in Figure 3.8) suggests that trust in government was rising from 1958 to 1964. Thereafter, however, trust in government plummeted from 77 percent of Americans in 1964 to 29 percent in 1978, undermined by the Vietnam war, the Watergate scandal, and the racial and economic troubles of the late 1960s and early 1970s. Trust in government modestly and temporarily rebounded during both the Reagan and the Clinton periods of prosperity, but then plunged even further after 2000 and has remained impervious to the economic booms of the twenty-first century. This standard index of trust in government now oscillates between 15 and 20, compared to its peak of about 75 percent sixty years ago. Figure 3.8 summarizes this astonishing collapse of confidence among ordinary Americans that government can be made to work, a trend that matches the now familiar pattern of party polarization during this period.

Falling trust in the federal government is part of a larger pattern of rising political cynicism on the part of ordinary Americans. Public cynicism and political alienation have followed the same discouraging pattern,

FIGURE 3.8: DECLINING TRUST IN GOVERNMENT, 1958–2019

Source: Pew Research Center, "Public Trust," April 2019. Data LOESS smoothed: .12.

with the same two temporary respites during the Reagan and Clinton booms, so that over the last six decades the sense of political efficacy of the average citizen has plummeted from about 70 percent to about 30 percent. As party polarization has increased, public disdain for both political parties has grown considerably, just as it did in the Gilded Age a century ago, leading then to the rise in support for third parties. A few examples will illustrate the breathtaking change over the last sixty to seventy years.

- In 1964, asked to choose whether the government was run on behalf of (1) "a few big interests" or (2) "the benefit of all," Americans optimistically chose the latter by a whopping margin of more than two to one (64 percent to 29 percent). By 2018 after a half century of growing economic inequality and political tumult, that sanguine assessment had been completely submerged by successive waves of mounting cynicism, interrupted only temporarily by the economic booms of the 1980s and 1990s. By now, as Figure 3.9 shows, those saying "the benefit of all" are outnumbered by those saying "a few big interests" by more than three to one (21 percent to 76 percent). At the same time, the fraction of Americans agreeing that "the people running the country don't really care what happens to you" has risen massively in the last half century from 26 percent in 1966 to 82 percent in 2016.

FIGURE 3.9: **POLITICAL ALIENATION, 1964–2018**

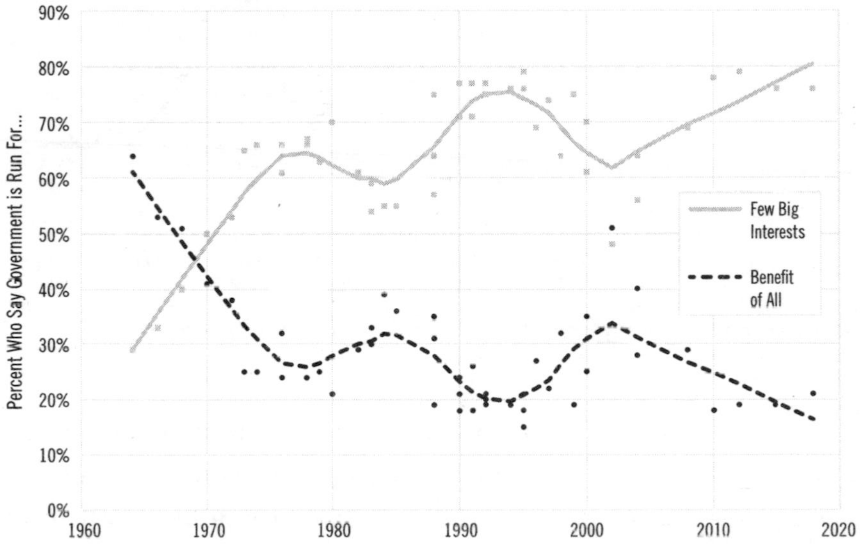

Source: Pew Research Center, "Amer. Democracy," April 2018. Data LOESS smoothed: .3.

- Finally, Figure 3.10 compiles evidence from several independent long-term survey archives to provide a consistent picture of trends in political cynicism and its opposite, political efficacy, over the last two thirds of the century.[111] In the 1950s, it appears, political efficacy was rising, but across the six decades between 1960 and today efficacy rose (and cynicism fell) only momentarily between the dot-com boom of the late 1990s and the powerful, but fleeting rally-round-the-flag moment of 9/11. In short, decades of polarization have taken a visible toll on Americans' faith in democratic politics, just as they did in the first Gilded Age a century ago.

FIGURE 3.10: **POLITICAL EFFICACY VS. POLITICAL CYNICISM, 1952–2016**

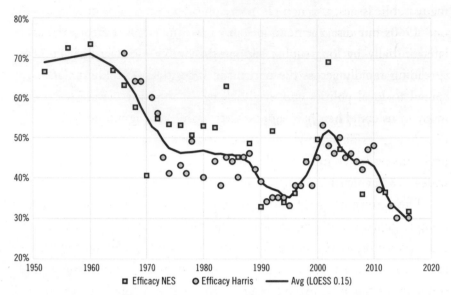

Source: American National Election Studies; Harris Poll. Data LOESS smoothed: .15.

The most important reason to worry about polarization is that in the long run extreme polarization can produce democratic breakdown. Drawing on their best-seller *How Democracies Die*, political scientists Steven Levitsky and Daniel Ziblatt have expressed this concern most cogently:

> When societies divide into partisan camps with profoundly different worldviews, and when those differences are viewed as existential and irreconcilable, political rivalry can devolve into partisan hatred. Parties come to view each other not as legitimate rivals, but as dangerous enemies. Losing ceases to be an accepted part of the political process and instead becomes a catastrophe.[112]

So what have we learned about polarization in this chapter? We have discovered that as the twentieth century opened, American politics was riven by deep, even violent political rivalries, but that over the ensuing six decades Americans gradually learned to cooperate across party lines to solve shared problems. Of course, we continued to disagree vigorously on many public issues, as is natural in any pluralist democracy, but then in the mid-1960s our disagreements began to become more rancorous, stimulated initially by long-suppressed conflicts over racial justice, but then spreading rapidly across the entire spectrum of issues. The polarization spread to local politics and eventually even into our private lives, until many of us could hardly imagine living in the same community. Polarization led to gridlock, preventing government from responding even to problems on which most people actually agreed. The inevitable result was widespread cynicism and alienation from basic democratic institutions.

The pattern was so clear and widespread that it can be summarized in a single chart, combining trends in bipartisan collaboration in Congress, cross-party comity as reported in the national press, ticket-splitting by voters,[113] and cross-party concordance in presidential approval. Figure 3.11 summarizes this broad trend in political amity over the last 125 years.[114] It can be readily compared with the comparable charts at the end of

FIGURE 3.11: POLITICAL COMITY, 1895-2015

Source: See endnote 1.4. Data LOESS smoothed: .20.

Chapters 2, 4, and 5, showing the equivalent long-term trends in economics, society, and culture.

Before drawing up a balance sheet about the broader implications of these trends, it will be important to explore the social and cultural dimensions of change in American society since the end of the nineteenth century, to which we turn in the next two chapters.

4

SOCIETY: BETWEEN ISOLATION AND SOLIDARITY

As we recalled in Chapter 1, Alexis de Tocqueville has been the patron saint of American communitarians since his voyage to our land in the 1830s. But individualism, he also argued, was an inevitable consequence of equality in America. Thus recognizing the competing claims of community and the individual, Tocqueville described how Americans sought a synthesis of the two in a chapter he entitled "How the Americans combat individualism by the principle of self-interest rightly understood."[1]

In this chapter we explore how Americans have navigated between the poles of individualism and community in the last 125 years. We begin, as Tocqueville did, with civic associations and other manifestations of community engagement. We devote special attention to two forms of association prominent for much of this period: religious institutions and labor unions. We then turn to the most nearly universal form of social solidarity and connectedness, exploring changing patterns of family formation over this same century and a half. Finally, we turn briefly to the evidence on the psychological manifestation of social solidarity and connectedness—social trust.

As we range across this broad social terrain of bowling leagues, prayer groups, and family, we shall discover a broadly similar pattern: In each of these forms of social solidarity seemingly so distant from economics and politics, we shall discover a remarkable resemblance. Social solidarity (membership in civic associations, churches, unions, and even family formation) was at a relatively low point during the first Gilded Age, began to rise during the Progressive Era toward a high point in the 1960s, and then declined steadily into the second Gilded Age, a path remarkably parallel to the inverted U-curve that we have observed in the two preceding chapters. For each of these dimensions of social solidarity we offer a historical narrative of the change, supplemented by relevant quantitative evidence.[2]

CIVIC ASSOCIATIONS

At the end of the Civil War, America remained, as it had been at the time of Tocqueville's visit, predominantly a land of small farms, small towns, and small businesses. By the end of the nineteenth century, three decades later, America was rapidly becoming a nation of cities, teeming with immigrants born in villages in Europe or America, but now toiling in factories operated by massive industrial combines. Millions of Americans left family and friends behind on the farm when they moved to Chicago or Milwaukee or Pittsburgh, and millions more left community institutions behind in a Polish shtetl or an Italian village when they moved to the Lower East Side or the North End.

These migrants were living now, not merely in a new community, but in a setting so unfamiliar and disjointed that many doubted that it deserved to be called "community" at all. Indeed, at the opening of the twentieth century all Americans, not just migrants, had just lived through profoundly disorienting social change. "We are unsettled to the very roots of our being," wrote Walter Lippmann in 1914. "There isn't a human relation, whether of parent and child, husband and wife, worker and employer, that doesn't move in a strange situation. . . . We have changed our environment more quickly than we know how to change ourselves."[3]

But even as these problems were erupting, Americans were beginning to address them. Within a few decades around the turn of the century, a quickening sense of crisis, coupled with inspired grassroots and national leadership, produced an extraordinary burst of social inventiveness and political reform. In fact, as we shall shortly see, most of the major community institutions in American life at the close of the twentieth century were invented or renewed in that most fecund period of civic innovation.

Optimists, then as now, enthused that new technologies of communication would allow human sympathy wider scope. In William Allen White's 1910 utopian vision the new technological advances harbored the possibility of "making the nation a neighborhood. . . . The electric wire, the iron pipe, the street railroad, the daily newspaper, the telephone . . . have made us all one body. . . . There are no outlanders. It is possible for all men to understand one another. . . . Indeed it is but the dawn of a spiritual awakening."[4]

On the other hand, more cautious Progressives like John Dewey and Mary Parker Follett were concerned with how to sustain face-to-face ties. Although they recognized and honored the larger new society, they also cherished older, smaller personal networks.

> The Great Society created by steam and electricity may be a society [wrote Dewey], but it is no community. The invasion of the community by the new and relatively impersonal and mechanical modes of combined human behavior is the outstanding fact of modern life.[5]
>
> Real solidarity [added Follett] will never be accomplished except by beginning somewhere the joining of one small group with another. . . . Only by actual union, not by appeals to the imagination, can the . . . varied neighborhood groups be made the constituents of a sound, normal, unpartisan city life. Then being a member of a neighborhood group will mean at the same time being a member and a responsible member of the state.[6]

Prescient Progressives also worried about the professionalization of social organization. Sociologist Robert Park wrote: "All the forms of communal and cultural activity in which we . . . formerly shared have been taken over by professionals and the great mass of men are no longer actors, but spectators."[7] Social reformers were caught on the horns of a dilemma.

In social service, in public health, in urban design, in education, in neighborhood organization, in cultural philanthropy, even in lobbying, professional staff could often do a more effective, more efficient job on the task
at hand than well-meaning volunteers. However, to disempower ordinary
members of voluntary associations could easily diminish grassroots civic
engagement and foster oligarchy. As we shall soon see, that same problem
would resurface more than half a century later.

One striking feature of the revitalization of civic life in America in the
last decades of the nineteenth century was a veritable boom in association-
building. To be sure, the American penchant for clubs dated to the earliest
years of the republic.[8] Some associations (like the Independent Order of
Odd Fellows) dated from the first third of the nineteenth century, and many
others dated from the Civil War and its aftermath.[9] In the late nineteenth
and early twentieth centuries a new generation of civic entrepreneurs built
a massive new structure of civic associations on these earlier foundations.
In Peoria and St. Louis, Boston and Boise and Bowling Green, Galves-
ton, Denver, and San Francisco citizens organized clubs and churches
and lodges and veterans' groups and ethnic associations and professional
groups.[10] A so-called "club movement" swept across the land, emphasizing
self-help and amateurism. Handbooks appeared on how to establish a boys'
club or a women's club. In 1876 Henry Martyn Robert published *Robert's
Rules of Order* to bring order to the mushrooming anarchy of club and committee meetings.

Between 1870 and 1920 civic inventiveness reached a crescendo unmatched in American history, not merely in terms of numbers of clubs,
but in the range and durability of the newly founded organizations. Social
historian Theda Skocpol and her colleagues have shown that half of *all*
the largest mass membership organizations in American history—the fifty-
eight national voluntary organizations that *ever* enrolled at least 1 percent
of the adult male or female population—were founded in the decades between 1870 and 1920.[11] As Figure 4.1 shows, the number of such large
membership associations grew dramatically in the Gilded Age and Progressive Era, but after 1910 relatively few were added during the rest of the
twentieth century.[12]

FIGURE 4.1: **FOUNDING DATES OF 58 MAJOR NATIONAL MEMBERSHIP ORGANIZATIONS, 1800–1990**

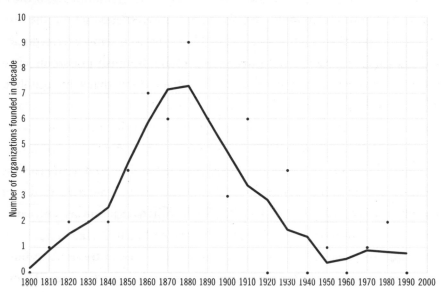

Source: Theda Skocpol, *Diminished Democracy*, 26–29. Data LOESS smoothed: .33.

Both local and national studies tell essentially the same story: The organizational seeds planted from the Gilded Age into the Progressive Era proved exceptionally hardy, and throughout the next six decades they flowered into an intensely Tocquevillian America.[13] Indeed, most broad-gauged, chapter-based civic institutions of American life at the end of the twentieth century were founded in several decades of exceptional social creativity around the beginning of that century. From the Red Cross to the NAACP, from the Knights of Columbus to Hadassah, from Boy Scouts to the Rotary Club, from the PTA to the Sierra Club, from the Gideon Society to the Audubon Society, from the American Bar Association to the Farm Bureau Federation, from Big Brothers to the League of Women Voters, from the Teamsters Union to the Campfire Girls, it was hard to name a major civic institution in American life at the close of the twentieth century that was *not* invented in these few decades at the opening of the twentieth century.[14]

America a century ago was much more gendered and racialized than it is today, and most of the organizations founded in that period were seg-regated by sex and race. The most prominent examples of organizational proliferation were fraternal groups, like the Moose and the Eagles. By 1910, historian David Beito calculates, "a conservative estimate would be that one third of all adult males over age nineteen were members." In part, fraternalism represented a reaction against the individualism and anomie of this era of rapid social change, asylum from a disordered and uncertain world. Mutual aid, resting on the principle of reciprocity—today's donor becomes tomorrow's recipient—was a core feature of the groups. Beito observes, "By joining a lodge, an initiate adopted, at least implicitly, a set of values. Societies dedicated themselves to the advancement of mutualism, self-reliance, business training, thrift, leadership skills, self-government, self-control, and good moral character." In the early twentieth century fra-ternal organizations were joined by new service clubs (Rotary, Kiwanis, Lions, the Jaycees, and the like) and by professional associations. These newer groups offered business contacts, a more modern face, and more outward civic zeal.[15]

Though many of the new organizations that emerged at the end of the nineteenth century were closed to women and minorities, this flurry of organizational innovation was not confined to white males, for growth was substantial among women and ethnic minorities, and in fact, even more rapid among blacks than whites. Virtually all these organizations, re-gardless of race and gender, tended to encompass both middle-class and working-class members, as Skocpol emphasizes, and served the same func-tions of mutual aid and moral uplift.[16] Segregation by race and gender may now be repugnant to our values. However, as an ascendant form of social capital, civic organization, though largely segregated at the turn of the cen-tury, was definitely not limited to middle-class white males.

Women's groups, founded in response to the rapid increase in wom-en's education in the post–Civil War era, gradually shifted their focus dur-ing this period from reading and conversation to grassroots mobilization on behalf of social and political reform on issues like temperance, child labor, women's employment, urban poverty, kindergartens, and especially, women's suffrage, culminating at the end of the Progressive Era in the

Eighteenth and Nineteenth Constitutional Amendments.[17] By the turn of the century, one newly elected president, Sarah Platt Decker, exclaimed to her group, "we prefer Doing to Dante, Being to Browning. . . . We've soaked in literary effort long enough."[18] In 1890 this network of women's organizations was linked together to form the General Federation of Women's Clubs.

A more or less spontaneous grassroots crusade of 1873–1874 resulted in the formation of the mammoth Woman's Christian Temperance Union (WCTU). "Do Everything" was the motto of Frances Willard, leader of the WCTU, and with her at the helm, it soon became a vehicle for broader moral and social reform.[19] The National Congress of Mothers, formed in part from the kindergarten movement in 1897, went on to organize local school groups of parents and teachers. In 1924 the Congress of Mothers was formally renamed the National Congress of Parents and Teachers (later the PTA).[20] Interestingly, some women's groups even bridged profound class gaps. For example, young immigrant women struggling to create a trade union in the garment industry of the Lower East Side of Manhattan received powerful political and financial support from the Women's Trade Union League, actively sustained by Progressive socialites from the Upper East Side like Anne Morgan, daughter of J. P. Morgan, the most powerful capitalist in the world.[21]

As illustrated by the Knights of Columbus, B'nai B'rith, and Prince Hall Freemasonry (an organization for black Masons), various ethnic groups tended to spawn their own fraternal organizations. The benevolent society for mutual aid was the bedrock of many immigrant communities, providing financial security, camaraderie, and even political representation. According to historian Rowland Berthoff, "the immigrants, who had been accustomed to a more tightly knit communal life than almost any American could now recall, were quick to adopt the fraternal form of the American voluntary association in order to bind together their local ethnic communities against the unpredictable looseness of life in America."[22]

The growing importance of associations among blacks followed much the same pattern, including mutual aid, burial, and social associations, and fraternal and women's groups. In his classic study *The Philadelphia Negro* at the turn of the century, W. E. B. Du Bois emphasized the importance of black societies, such as the Odd Fellows and Freemasons, in furnishing "pastime from the monotony of work, a field for ambition and intrigue, a chance for parade, and insurance against misfortune"—virtually the same benefits that attracted millions of whites into such organizations in these years. African American fraternal groups would go on to play a powerful role in the struggle for civil rights during the first two thirds of the twentieth century. The church played a role of unique importance in social capital formation within the African American community. And so did black women's clubs, such as the National Association of Colored Women's Clubs, founded in 1896, a strong advocate for social and racial justice, and still active more than a century later. At the same time, associations arose that linked blacks and whites together in support of social reform—above all, the NAACP and the Urban League.[23]

Progressive Era reformers made youth development a special focus of their organizational energies. In an extraordinary burst of creativity, in less than a decade (1901–1910) most of the nationwide youth organizations that were to dominate the twentieth century were founded—the Boy Scouts and Girl Scouts, Campfire Girls, the 4-H, Boys Clubs and Girls Clubs, Big Brothers and Big Sisters. In a stroke of marketing genius, the new organizations combined enduring social values—"A Scout is trustworthy, helpful, friendly, courteous. . ."—with the pure fun of camping, sports, and play.[24]

As a social movement, Progressivism evades any simple classification as "top-down" or "bottom-up." Many of the new fraternal, civic, and reform organizations represented the recruiting efforts of national headquarters and national leaders, while others sprang up in response to local initiatives. Some, like the 4-H and the Grange, were actually the creation of the federal government. More important still was the lateral diffusion of initiatives from one community to another: Initiatives born in one part of the country were picked up and developed elsewhere, as local activists intent on rebuilding community ties learned from one another. In fact, the wave of association-building of the late nineteenth century actually had begun in the small towns of the heartland, not in the cosmopolitan metropolis.

As social historian Skocpol notes, "this method of organizational expansion was very reminiscent of the techniques used by Methodist and Baptist circuit-riding clergy to disseminate new congregations, like wildfire, across the pre–Civil War United States."[25]

This period of institutional ferment ended around 1920, having laid the foundations on which civic America would rest for the next one hundred years. In the half century after 1920 the organizations founded in the Gilded Age and Progressive Era steadily expanded, both in membership and in geographic coverage. Many of them were, in effect, franchise-form organizations, designed for rapid diffusion, and that is what happened from 1920 to 1960. Franchise-form commercial organizations had begun with Singer Sewing Machines in 1880 and auto dealerships in the 1890s, and this pattern was quickly adopted by the contemporaneous new civic organizations. Invented once, the organizations then replicated themselves endlessly to meet a seemingly inexhaustible demand from Americans for ways to connect.

The first Rotary club, for example, was invented in Chicago in 1905 by Paul Harris, a young lawyer, just arrived in Chicago from a small town, who lacked useful social connections and felt "desperately lonely" in the urban maelstrom. Within four years his Chicago club had two hundred members, and within six years Rotary clubs existed in every major city in America. Imitative competitors like Kiwanis and Lions (and dozens more) spread rapidly across the country. Nationwide membership in service clubs grew exponentially to 300,000 by 1920 and several million by 1930, a quarter century's rate of diffusion that would not be rivaled until Ray Kroc's invention of the McDonald's franchise system nearly half a century later.[26] Service clubs were hardly alone in experiencing rapid growth in these years, for the same was true of many older fraternal organizations, like the Elks, the Moose, and even the Odd Fellows. After setbacks during the Great Depression, service clubs, fraternal groups, and virtually all other civic associations in the country experienced a remarkable boom during the quarter century during and after World War II.

The secret to the rapid diffusion of these organizations was a kind of "sociability in a box"—handbooks that explained the organization of a local chapter, mission statement, code of ethics, officers and committees, membership obligations (such as attendance at weekly meetings), slogans, meeting rituals designed to build solidarity (for example, a period set aside each week for members to recognize recent achievements of other members), and a commitment to social responsibility and community service (such as Kiwanis Pancake Day fundraisers, Rotary Scholarships, or Lions Club blindness prevention). The Boy and Girl Scouts, the Audubon Society, the Red Cross, the National Urban League, and Jack-and-Jill (for black middle-class kids) all illustrated the ubiquity and usefulness of the franchise form for rapid growth and diffusion.

Many of these new forms of "instant" sociability were castigated by critics as middle-class, low-brow, conformist "Babbitry," but that critique overlooks their innovative importance as a new form of community to replace the rural barn raisings, quilting bees, and small-town neighborliness that had been rendered obsolete by the economic advances and demographic turmoil of the late nineteenth century. It is also remarkable how uniform were the commitments of these new organizations—male and female and of all ethnic backgrounds—to the ideals of community service and social solidarity.[27]

The membership rolls of such diverse civic associations reveal a strikingly parallel pattern across the twentieth century. This pattern is summarized in Figure 4.2, which is a composite of the changing membership rates from 1900 to 2016 for thirty-two diverse national, chapter-based organizations, ranging from B'nai B'rith and the Knights of Columbus to the Elks Club and the PTA.[28] In each case we measure membership as a fraction of the pool of members in the population—4-H membership as a fraction of all rural youth, Hadassah membership as a fraction of all Jewish women, and so on. Embodied in the broad outline are a number of crucial facts about associational life in American communities throughout the twentieth century.

For most of the twentieth century growing numbers of Americans were involved in such chapter-based associations. The long upward wave in this figure reflects the fact that virtually every year more women belonged to women's clubs, more rural residents belonged to the Grange,

FIGURE 4.2: **MEMBERSHIP RATE IN NATIONAL CHAPTER-BASED ASSOCIATIONS, 1900–2016**

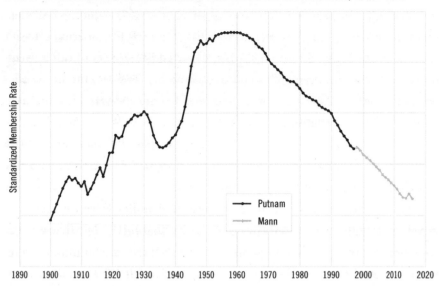

Source: Putnam, *Bowling Alone*, 53–55; Taylor Mann.

more youths belonged to the Scouts, more Jews belonged to Hadassah and B'nai B'rith, and more men belonged to fraternal clubs. As the decades passed, America seemed more and more to fit Tocqueville's description of us as a nation of joiners.

The interruption in the 1930s in this generally rising line of civic involvement is mute evidence of the traumatic impact of the Great Depression on American communities. The membership records of virtually every adult organization in this sample bear the scars of that period. In some cases the effect was a brief pause in ebullient growth, but in others the reversal was extraordinary. Membership in the League of Women Voters, for example, was cut in half between 1930 and 1935, as was membership in the Elks, the Moose, and the Knights of Columbus. This period of history underlines the impact of acute economic distress on civic engagement.

Most of these losses had been recouped, however, by the early 1940s. World War II occasioned a massive outpouring of patriotism and collective solidarity, and at war's end those energies were redirected into community life. The two decades following 1945 constituted one of the most vital periods of community involvement in American history. As a fraction of potential membership, the "market share" for these thirty-two organizations skyrocketed. The breadth of this civic explosion encompassed virtually every organization on the list, from "old-fashioned" ones like the Grange and the Elks (roughly a century old in the 1960s) to the newer service clubs like the Lions and the League of Women Voters (roughly four decades old in the 1960s).

By mid-century, civic engagement as measured by membership and involvement in a wide variety of groups—religious organizations, sports groups, charitable groups, unions and professional groups, neighborhood associations, hobby groups, parent groups, book clubs, youth groups, fraternal organizations, veterans organizations—was very high by any standard. Across lines of race and gender, most Americans belonged to one or more of these groups, and our national rate of civic involvement was at or near the top of the world rankings. Community groups across America seemed to stand on the threshold of a new era of expanded involvement. Except for the civic drought induced by the Great Depression, the seedlings planted by the Progressives had shot up year after year, cultivated by assiduous civic gardeners and watered by increasing affluence and education. Each annual report registered rising membership. Churches and synagogues, as we shall shortly see, were packed, as more Americans worshipped together than only a few decades earlier, perhaps more than ever in American history.

Already by the late 1950s, however, this burst of community involvement began to tail off. By the late 1960s and early 1970s, membership growth began to fall further behind population growth. On average, across all these organizations, membership rates began to plateau in 1957, peaked in the early 1960s, and began a period of sustained decline by 1969. Membership rates had more than doubled between the early 1940s and the early 1960s, but by 2000 the results of that massive postwar boom in joining had been entirely erased. The decline would continue uninterrupted through the first two decades of the twenty-first century, and by 2016 more than a century's worth of civic creativity had vanished.

These averages conceal some important differences among the experiences of the various organizations. For example, the effects of the Great Depression varied from organization to organization, with massive declines in the Masons and Hadassah, while membership in youth organizations like the 4-H, Boy Scouts, and Girl Scouts seems to have been immune to the economic distress affecting adults. The postwar boom appears in virtually every case, but for the Grange and the General Federation of Women's Clubs the good times had ended by the mid-1950s, whereas other organizations, like the appropriately named Optimists, remained on a higher plateau until the 1980s. NAACP membership spiked sharply during World War II, collapsed in the early 1950s, regained its highest levels during the Civil Rights movement in the early 1960s, and then stagnated and slumped again from the 1970s onward.

Behind each of these membership records are scores of individual tales of leadership success and failure, organizational tenacity and strategic blunders, and the vicissitudes of social life and politics, but the common features across these very diverse organizations—rapid growth from 1900 to the 1950s, interrupted only temporarily by the Great Depression, slowing in the 1960s, and then rapidly reversing from the 1970s on—represents a mosaic of evidence on changing civic involvement in American communities. Even after we explore the details of each organization's rise and decline, we are left with the remarkable fact that each of these very different and very long-lived organizations followed this same pattern.

We pause here to consider one possible exception—the rapid rise of nonprofit Washington-based national associations. The sheer number of nonprofit organizations exploded over the last three decades of the twentieth century, more than doubling from 10,299 to 22,901 between 1968 and 1997, according to the *Encyclopedia of Associations*.[29] Could the older chapter-based organizations simply have been replaced by these new nonprofits, so that the decline in membership shown in Figure 4.2 is an illusion?

In fact, relatively few of the new nonprofit associations actually have mass membership. Sociologist David Horton Smith found that nearly half of the groups in the 1988 *Encyclopedia of Associations*, such as the Animal Nutrition Research Council, the National Conference on Uniform Traffic

Accident Statistics, and the National Slag Association, had no individual members at all. Even among associations that actually had members, average membership fell from 111,000 in 1956 to 13,000 in 1998. In other words, while the number of "associations" more than doubled, the average individual membership was roughly one tenth as large—more groups, but most of them much smaller.[30] The organizational eruption between the 1960s and the 1990s represented a proliferation of letterheads, not a boom of grassroots participation.

As Theda Skocpol has argued in *Diminished Democracy: From Membership to Management in American Civic Life* (2003), the proliferating new organizations are professionally managed advocacy organizations, not membership associations. She explains that the social movements of the 1960s and 1970s

> inadvertently helped to trigger a reorganization of national civic life, in which professionally managed associations and institutions proliferated while cross-class membership associations lost ground. In our time, civilly engaged Americans are organizing more but joining less . . . [These new movements] synthesized grassroots protest, activist radicalism, and professionally led efforts to lobby government and educate the public. . . . Between the 1970s and the 1990s older voluntary membership federations rapidly dwindled, while new social movements and professionally managed civic organizations took to the field in huge numbers, redefining the goals and modalities of national civic life. The universe of very large American membership associations today is much less concerned with brotherhood, sisterhood, fellow citizenship, and community service than ever before in the nation's long history.[31]

Though these new groups often depend on financial support from ordinary citizens and may speak faithfully on their behalf, for the vast majority of their members the only act of membership consists in writing a check for dues or perhaps occasionally reading a newsletter. Few ever attend any meetings of such organizations—many never have meetings at all—and most members are unlikely ever knowingly to encounter any other member. Membership in the newer groups means moving a pen, not making a meeting.

Mail-order "membership" turns out to be a poor measure of civic engagement. For example, Greenpeace became the largest environmental organization in America, accounting for more than one third of all members in national environmental groups at its peak in 1990, through an extremely aggressive direct mail program. At that point Greenpeace leaders, concerned about the spectacle of an environmental group printing tons of junk mail, temporarily cut back on direct mail solicitation. Within three years Greenpeace "membership" had hemorrhaged by 85 percent.[32]

Even if we restrict our attention to actual chapter-based organizations with real members, such as those represented in Figure 4.2, however, membership figures for individual organizations are an uncertain guide to trends in Americans' involvement in voluntary associations. First, over a century or more the popularity of specific groups may wax and wane. If newer, more dynamic organizations have escaped our scrutiny, the picture of decline in Figure 4.2 might apply only to "old-fashioned" organizations, not to all community-based organizations. Second, "card-carrying" membership may not accurately reflect actual community engagement.

To address these two issues, we turn from the organizational records that we have relied on thus far, and instead explore survey evidence, which can encompass organizational affiliations of all sorts and can distinguish formal membership from actual involvement. Survey coverage is sparse until the early 1970s, so the price we pay for greater sensitivity to the nature of membership is coverage of a shorter span of time, the same unavoidable dilemma we have encountered in earlier chapters. Nevertheless, it turns out that the available survey evidence reinforces the story we've told so far.

The scant survey evidence available prior to 1970 is consistent with the organizational records showing that formal membership in voluntary associations among ordinary Americans was stable or modestly declining between the mid-1950s and the mid-1970s.[33] After the mid-1970s the survey evidence becomes richer, and our judgments about trends can be more confident. Three major survey archives contain relevant information: The

General Social Survey (GSS), the Roper Social and Political Trends archive, and the DDB Needham Life Style archive.[34]

How has group membership in general changed over the last half century? The GSS asked about formal organizational membership from the early 1970s to the early 1990s, but unfortunately this major national survey has not asked about organizational membership in the last quarter century. The GSS data suggest that formal membership rates slipped only slightly during those two decades, from about 75 percent of Americans to about 70 percent.

This modest conclusion, however, is drastically altered when we examine evidence on more active forms of participation than mere card-carrying membership. Service as an officer or committee member was once very common among active members of American organizations.[35] Sooner or later, in the heyday of civic America the overwhelming majority of active members in most voluntary associations were cajoled into playing some leadership role in the organization. How did the number of Americans who fit this bill change over the later part of the twentieth century?

Between 1973 and 1994 (the last time this question was posed by the Roper researchers) the number of men and women who took *any* leadership role in *any* local organization—from "old-fashioned" fraternal organizations to New Age encounter groups—was cut in half. Across the two decades, whites were more likely than blacks to hold a leadership role, but the trend was similar in both races. The leadership rate among whites fell from 17 percent to 9 percent between 1973 and 1994, while the rate among blacks fell from 12 percent to 7 percent. By this measure, across racial lines, virtually half of America's civic infrastructure was obliterated in barely two decades.[36]

Eighty percent of life, Woody Allen is said to have quipped,[37] is simply showing up. The same might be said of civic engagement, and "showing up" provides a useful standard for evaluating trends in associational life in our communities. In thirty-one annual surveys between 1975 and 2005 by DDB Needham researchers more than 106,000 Americans were asked "how many times in the last year did you attend a club meeting?" Figure 4.3 shows that this form of civic engagement steadily dwindled over those three decades. In 1975–1976, American men and women attended twelve club meetings on average each year—essentially once a month.[38] By 2005 that national average had shrunk by two thirds to four meetings per year. In 1975–1976, 64 percent of all Americans attended at least *one* club meeting in the previous year. By 2005 that figure had fallen to 33 percent. In short, in the mid-1970s nearly two thirds of Americans still attended club meetings, but by the mid-2000s two thirds of Americans never did. (Once again, there is no evidence of significant racial differences in these trends.) By comparison to other countries, we may still seem a nation of joiners, but by comparison to our own past, we are not—at least if "joining" means more than nominal affiliation.

FIGURE 4.3: **CLUB MEETING ATTENDANCE DWINDLES, 1975–2005**

Source: DBB Needham Life Style surveys, updated. Data LOESS smoothed: .33.

Thus, two different survey archives suggest that active involvement in local clubs and organizations fell by half to two thirds in the waning decades of the twentieth century. This estimate is remarkably consistent with evidence of an entirely different sort. Each decade between 1965 and

1995 national samples of Americans were asked to complete "time diaries," recording how they spent every minute of a randomly chosen "diary day." From these sets of diaries we can reconstruct how the average American's use of time gradually evolved over the three decades between 1965 and 1995.[39]

Broadly speaking, our time allocations have not changed dramatically over this period—we have averaged roughly eight hours of sleep a night throughout the decades, for example—but there are some important exceptions. Screen time consumes more time now than it used to, while we spend less time now on housework and childcare. Except for a small slice of upper-middle-class professionals, average work hours in America have declined over the last half century. Nevertheless, the diaries show that the time we devote to community organizations has fallen steadily over this period.[40]

The average American's investment in organizational life (apart from religious groups, which we shall examine separately) fell from 3.7 hours per month in 1965 to 2.9 in 1975 to 2.3 in 1985 and 1995. On an average day in 1965, 7 percent of Americans spent some time in a community organization. By 1995 that figure had fallen to 3 percent of all Americans. Those numbers suggest that nearly half of all Americans in the 1960s invested some time each week in clubs and local associations, as compared to less than one quarter in the 1990s.[41]

In absolute terms the declines in organizational activity and club meeting attendance were roughly parallel at all educational and social levels. However, because the less well educated were less involved in community organizations to begin with, the relative decline was even greater at the bottom of the hierarchy.

The organizational collapses reported here come from entirely different streams of evidence—different sampling techniques, different survey organizations, different questions, different sorts of organizations. That they converge so closely in their estimate that active involvement in local organizations fell by more than half in the last several decades of the twentieth century is as persuasive as the fact that Southwestern tree rings and Arctic ice cores and British Admiralty weather records all confirm global warming.

To summarize: Organizational records suggest that for the first two thirds of the twentieth century Americans' involvement in civic associations of all sorts rose steadily, stalled only temporarily by the Great Depression. In the last third of the century, by contrast, only mailing list membership continued to expand, with the creation of an entirely new species of association whose members never actually meet. We could surely find individual exceptions—specific organizations that successfully sailed against the prevailing winds and tides—but the broad picture is one of declining involvement in community organizations. Over the last half century or so card-carrying membership in civic organizations has edged downward by perhaps one quarter. More important, active involvement in clubs and other voluntary associations has been sliced in half.[42]

Many Americans continue to claim that we are "members" of various organizations, but most Americans no longer spend much time in community organizations—we've stopped doing committee work, stopped serving as officers, and stopped going to meetings. And all this despite rapid increases in education that have given more of us than ever before the skills, the resources, and the interests that once fostered civic engagement. In short, for nearly half a century now Americans have been dropping out of organized community life in droves, exactly the opposite of what was happening a century ago.

RELIGION AND PHILANTHROPY[43]

Religious institutions have long been the single most important source of community connectedness and social solidarity in America. Even in our secular age, roughly half of all group memberships are religious in nature—congregations, Bible study groups, prayer circles, and so forth—and roughly half of all philanthropy and volunteering is carried out in a religious context. For many Americans religion is less a matter of theological commitment than a rich source of community. And involvement in a faith community turns out to be a strong predictor of connection to the wider, secular world.

Active members of religious congregations are more likely than

secular Americans to give generously to charity, and not merely in the offering plate, but also to secular causes. Regular churchgoers are more than
twice as likely to volunteer as demographically matched Americans who
rarely attend church, and to volunteer not merely for church ushering, but
also for secular causes.[44] Religious Americans are two or three times more
likely than matched secular Americans to belong to secular organizations,
like neighborhood associations, Rotary, or the Scouts, and to be active in
local civic life. Rigorous statistical analysis suggests (surprisingly, perhaps,
to secular Americans) that the link between religious involvement and civic
do-gooding is not spurious, but probably causal. In short, trends in religious engagement are key indicators of trends in social connection more
generally.[45]

Traditionally, Americans have been substantially more active in religious institutions than other people, and we have often thought of our
religiosity as a stable national trait. However, like other forms of social
connectivity, religion has seen ups and downs across American history. Sociologists Roger Finke and Rodney Stark showed that Americans in the
colonial era were not nearly so religiously observant as suggested by our
national mythology.[46] At the time of the Revolution fewer than one in five
Americans were members of any religious body, and the figure had risen to
only 34 percent by 1850.[47]

On the other hand, across American history there have been periodic
waves of intense religiosity, called "Great Awakenings." Conventionally,
the First Great Awakening is said to have occurred in the 1750s, followed
by a Second Great Awakening in the 1820s and 1830s, and a Third Great
Awakening beginning around 1860. Each such Awakening was characterized by a sharp increase in religious engagement, especially in evangelical
churches and new religious movements.

By the time of the Gilded Age at the end of the nineteenth century,
however, such religious fervor had subsided. In public, religious rhetoric
was omnipresent, as throughout most of our history. Protestantism was
culturally dominant, but with increasing immigration from Catholic countries, religion was becoming a sectarian, divisive force, even provoking
anti-Catholic violence along the Eastern seaboard. Nativist, ethnocentric,

anti-Semitic, and racist sentiments were common, often entangled with religious intolerance.

On the other hand, in their daily lives most Americans were "unchurched" or "churchless." Like contemporary religious "nones," those who profess no religious identity, these secular Americans were not necessarily unbelievers, but they were unattached to religious institutions by membership, attendance, or contributions.[48] Ray Stannard Baker, a renowned Progressive Era muckraking journalist, wrote in 1910:

> Not only have the working classes become alienated from the churches especially from the Protestant churches but a very large proportion of well to do men and women who belong to the so-called cultured class have lost touch with church work. Some retain a membership, but the church plays no vital or important part in their lives. . . . And what is more this indifferentism is by no means confined to the "wicked city" but prevails throughout the country in small towns and villages as well as in large cities—except possibly in a few localities where "revivals" have recently stirred the people.[49]

The distinguished historian of American religion Sydney Ahlstrom reports that only 43 percent of the total population claimed any church affiliation in 1910, and a *Washington Post* article in 1909 offered a very similar estimate that the unchurched population in America "probably outnumbers our church members in the proportion of about three to two."[50]

During the Gilded Age, Protestant theology tended to ignore the social and moral questions posed by Jesus' "blessed are the poor" Beatitudes, focusing instead on personal piety and salvation. Ahlstrom emphasizes this individualistic focus of Gilded Age religion, arguing that

> Concentrating upon the individual sinner led inexorably to a preoccupation with exceedingly personal sins. The resultant erosion of social ethics was noted even in colonial times, but the full effect of this tendency was not manifest until after the Civil War, when the rise of huge corporate entities began to complicate the moral life of nearly all Americans. . . .

Revivalism tended to become socially trivial or ambiguous to the point of irrelevance. It was precisely these tendencies which made pious Christians like [Walter] Rauschenbusch so harsh in their judgments of evangelicalism.[51]

Not again until the rapid rise a century later of the "prosperity gospel"—the evangelical argument that personal religiosity leads to personal prosperity—would American religion encompass such a materialistic interpretation of religion's significance.[52] To be sure, denominational diversity has long been great in American religious life. Religious institutions are anything but uniform or monolithic in America. So when generalizing about trends in American religion, we will need to be attentive to that diversity.

As the Progressive Era opened, mainline Protestants began to pivot from individualism toward concern with the broader community, best exemplified by the Social Gospel movement, an effort by liberal Protestant leaders to bring pressing social problems such as urban poverty to the attention of their middle-class parishioners and to highlight the importance of social solidarity over individualism.[53] The movement was not numerically dominant among turn-of-the-century Protestants, but it was a leading indicator of cultural change. The Social Gospel represented a reaction against individualism, laissez-faire, and inequality; it was an attempt to make religion relevant to new social and intellectual circumstances.

Walter Rauschenbusch was a Christian theologian and Baptist pastor who was a key figure in the Social Gospel and "Single Tax" social reform movements that flourished in the United States in the early twentieth century. Raised in upstate New York, Rauschenbusch had begun his ministry in Hell's Kitchen in Manhattan, where he confronted joblessness, poverty, malnutrition, and above all the death of innocent children. He turned from his pietistic calling of saving individual souls to what he called the "Social Gospel," applying Christian morals to social reform. Baptism was, he wrote, "not a ritual act of individual salvation but an act of dedication to a religious and social movement."[54] His influence would persist for decades within mainline Protestantism; his book *Christianity and the Social Crisis*

(1907) leaving, Martin Luther King, Jr. said, "an indelible imprint on my thinking."

Rauschenbusch was hardly alone. The phrase "What would Jesus do?" (paradoxically now common among conservative Christians) was popularized in a best-selling 1899 novel by Charles Sheldon, a Congregational minister in Topeka, Kansas, whose theology was shaped by a commitment to Christian Socialism. His book was an evangelical attack on economic inequality, drawing on Jesus' proclamation that it would be easier for a camel to get through a needle's eye than for a rich man to enter the kingdom of God.

> What would Jesus do? . . . It seems to me sometimes as if the people in the big churches had good clothes and nice houses to live in, and money to spend for luxuries, and could go away on summer vacations and all that, while the people outside the churches, thousands of them, I mean, die in tenements, and walk the streets for jobs, and never have a piano or a picture in the house, and grow up in misery and drunkenness and sin.[55]

In this communitarian turning, many churches adopted a model of what religious historian E. Brooks Holifield terms "the social congregation."

> Thousands of congregations transformed themselves into centers that not only were open for worship but also were available for Sunday school, concerts, church socials, women's meetings, youth groups, girls' guilds, boys' brigades, sewing circles, benevolent societies, day schools, temperance societies, athletic clubs, scout troops, and nameless other activities. . . . Henry Ward Beecher advised the seminarians at Yale to "multiply picnics" in their parishes, and many congregations of every variety proceeded beyond picnics to gymnasiums, parish houses, camps, baseball teams, and military drill groups.[56]

The turning of religious thinking outward toward social ills fit the reformist mood of the Progressive Era, but it was certainly not universally accepted among Protestants. Indeed, by the early decades of the twentieth century many "fundamentalist" Protestants began to split away from the "modernist" theology of the mainline Protestant denominations, especially in the South and Midwest. This division would become the hallmark of Protestantism throughout the twentieth century, with mainline churches having the upper hand during the first half of the century and evangelicals (mostly heirs of the fundamentalists, though no longer so austere and inward-focused) increasingly dominant in the second half.

As the culture of industrial America was becoming more secular at the turn of the twentieth century, most religious denominations showed increased sensitivity to social solidarity, some even more so than the Protestants. Catholics tended to be more sympathetic to the plight of the poor, not least because more Catholics belonged to the immigrant laboring classes. With his 1891 encyclical *Rerum Novarum*, Pope Leo XIII "rejected laissez-faire theories of economic liberalism, and laid the central planks of modern Catholic social teaching, based on the rights to a just wage and to form unions, the call for a more equitable distribution of wealth and the duty of the state to ensure social justice in the economy."[57]

As always, the church played a predominant role in the black community. Evelyn Higginbotham, a leading historian of the African American church, observes that "it housed a diversity of programs including schools, circulating libraries, concerts, restaurants, insurance companies, vocational training, athletic clubs—all catering to a population much broader than the membership of individual churches. The church . . . held political rallies, clubwomen's conferences, and school graduations."[58] In short, a socially reformist Christianity was a central inspiration for much of the social activism of the period. On the verge of nominating Theodore Roosevelt for president in 1912, delegates to the Progressive convention broke spontaneously into a chorus of "Onward, Christian Soldiers!"[59]

Not all the social engagement of religion in the Progressive Era was focused on what we would today term "progressive" causes. The most important conservative example was the temperance movement, which reached its highwater mark with passage of the Prohibition amendment to the Constitution in 1919. This movement divided Americans along religious lines, especially "dry" Protestants from "wet" Catholics, and also illustrated how even conservative religion in this era pointed outward to community reform, not merely inward to individual salvation.

How did Americans' involvement in organized religion evolve in the decades after the Progressive Era? Figure 4.4 synthesizes quantitative evidence on church membership from the late nineteenth century, drawing on *Historical Statistics of the United States* from 1890 to 1989, when the Census Bureau itself collected this information, and then from Gallup poll surveys from 1990 to 2018.[60] Church membership, the best available evidence suggests, rose gradually but steadily during the first half of the twentieth century from about 45 percent of the adult population in 1890 to about 60 percent on the eve of World War II.

FIGURE 4.4: **CHURCH MEMBERSHIP, 1890–2018**

Source: *Historical Statistics of the US*, Gallup. See endnote 4.60. Data LOESS smoothed: .15.

The anxieties of World War II heightened American religiosity—no atheists in foxholes, it was said. Exactly like the economic and political trends we examined in the previous two chapters, however, the invigorated religious observance did not fade after the war, but accelerated.[61] Postwar affluence and the onset of the Cold War against "godless communism" encouraged a paradoxical mixture of material optimism and respect for traditional values, including both patriotism and religion. The boom in churchgoing was fueled by men and women who had survived the Great Depression as teenagers and World War II as grunts and girlfriends, and were now ready at last to settle into a normal life, with a steady job, a new house and car, and a growing family. Then, as now, getting married, settling down, and raising children were associated with more regular churchgoing.

Generationally, the postwar upsurge was concentrated among twenty-somethings, among whom weekly church attendance skyrocketed from 31 percent in February 1950 to an all-time record of 51 percent in April 1957, an astonishing change in barely seven years, implying millions of new churchgoers every year.[62] These GIs and their wives (and widows) would form the bedrock of American religious institutions (and of civic institutions, as well) into the next millennium, long after their own children (the Boomers) and grandchildren (the Millennials) had begun to move away from religion.[63]

The tsunami of religious involvement during the 1950s was massive, reaching levels probably unrivaled in American history. This outpouring is clear in the membership figures summarized in Figure 4.4, and it shows up as well in the best available continuous data on attendance at religious services, summarized in Figure 4.5. The methodological details about this latter measure have been much debated, and the sharp peak in 1944 is surely attributable to the unusual stress of wartime, but virtually all experts agree that the period from the late 1940s to the early 1960s was one of exceptional religious observance in America.[64]

This postwar surge had no partisan or denominational cast. Republicans and Democrats, liberals and conservatives, Catholics and Protestants and Jews—all thronged the pews. (Americans of the twenty-first century might be surprised that as late as the mid-1960s religiously observant Americans were more likely to be Democrats than Republicans, even among whites.[65])

Religious vitality was marked not merely by increasing attendance, but by the institutional commitment embodied in church membership we saw in Figure 4.4.[66] Church-building and Bible-publishing set new records to

FIGURE 4.5: **RELIGIOUS ATTENDANCE IN AMERICA, 1939–2018**

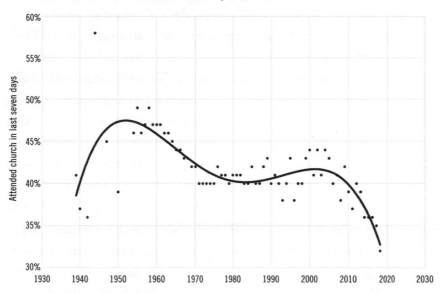

Source: Gallup Polls. See endnote 4.64.

accommodate all those new worshippers.[67] As Andrew Cherlin observed, "People wanted a religious experience that made them feel at home. Inhabiting the sacred space of a church or synagogue gave them a sense of membership in a community."[68]

It was not simply religious fervor that brought people to church in postwar America. For many of the families packing the pews, religious attendance was less an act of piety than an act of civic duty, like joining the PTA or Rotary, whose membership rolls, as we just saw, were also exploding in these same years. Religion represented the unifying theme of national purpose or what sociologist Robert Bellah would later term "civil religion."[69] Sydney Ahlstrom aptly summed up the civic dimension of the 1950s religious boom:

Religion and Americanism were brought together to an unusual degree. This was especially true of the 1950s, when President Dwight D. Eisenhower served for eight years as a prestigious symbol of generalized religiosity and Americans' self-satisfied patriotic moralism. The president even provided a classic justification for the new religious outlook. "Our government," he said in 1954, "makes no sense unless it is founded on a deeply felt religious faith—and I don't care what it is."[70]

Ike's nonsectarian, deist argument was criticized by some as theologically suspect, but whatever the mix of theological rigor and ecumenical togetherness, America was clearly a very religious place in the 1950s. Speaking of what would later be labeled "nones," that is, people without any religious identification, Will Herberg, preeminent chronicler of postwar American religion, observed that "their ranks are dwindling. . . . The pervasiveness of religious identification may safely be put down as a significant feature of the America that has emerged in the last quarter of a century."[71] Most Americans expected the religious boom—like the contemporary boom in other forms of community engagement—to continue. In 1957, 69 percent of Americans told Gallup pollsters that "religion is increasing its influence on American life." Within barely a decade, those expectations would be shattered.

The Sixties represented a perfect storm for American institutions of all sorts—political, social, and religious.[72] Ahlstrom aptly summarized this period in the long sweep of American religious history.

> The decade of the Sixties was a time, in short, when the old foundations of national confidence, patriotic idealism, moral traditionalism, and even of historic Judeo-Christian theism, were awash. . . . It was perfectly clear to any reasonably observant American that the postwar revival of the Eisenhower years had completely sputtered out, and that the nation was experiencing a *crise de conscience* of unprecedented depth.[73]

Maurice Isserman and Michael Kazin, preeminent chroniclers of the Sixties, conclude that "Nothing changed so profoundly in the United States during the 1960s as American religion."[74]

Alongside other major institutions, religious institutions suffered a dramatic loss of both public confidence and self-confidence. Mainline Protestant churches, accustomed to more than a century of social dominance, were especially struck by demoralization. The most widely discussed theo-logical book of the 1960s, liberal Protestant Harvey Cox's *The Secular City* (1965), criticized religious institutions as overly bureaucratic, hierarchical, and beholden to donors, thus inhibiting their own mission in the world. He called on readers to pursue "creative disaffiliation," which meant the abandonment of churches beholden to "institution-centered thinking."

For most mainline Protestants "disaffiliation" meant leaving the tra-ditional denominations. Among Catholics, by contrast, divided over the liberal reforms of Vatican II (a major Catholic reform council held in 1962–1965), formally leaving the church was initially less common than simply ignoring its precepts, including regular attendance at Mass. Attendance at Mass fell so rapidly during the Sixties that Catholics alone accounted for much of the total decline in religious attendance, but the number of self-identified Catholics did not immediately decline. Leaving the Church entirely became much more common with the gradually emerging clerical sex abuse scandals of the 1990s.

The Sixties also witnessed unprecedented religious experimentation outside traditional channels.[75] Some Boomers, interested in what they called the "spiritual," but disdaining conventional religion, were dubbed "seekers," looking for new spiritual homes. Much less highfalutin but more evocative was the emergence of "Sheilaism," named after a woman quoted by Robert Bellah and his colleagues in their best-seller *Habits of the Heart* (1985):

> "I believe in God. I am not a fanatic. I can't remember the last time I went to church. My faith has carried me a long way. It's Sheilaism. Just my own little voice. . . . My own Sheilaism . . . is just try to love yourself and be gentle with yourself."[76]

Amidst this exaltation of personal truth, "religious certainty begins to erode and a certain degree of religious relativism is inevitable."[77] Tradi-tional religious *communities* were gradually being replaced by religious (or at least spiritual) *individuals*. Few of the religious innovations of the 1960s would survive as significant elements on the American religious scene, but the very diversity of the spiritual menu laid before the seekers was symptomatic of disarray in conventional American religion. "Spirituality has become a vastly complex quest in which each person seeks in his or her own way."[78] The religious "we" was giving way to the religious "I."

The most substantial indication of the change wrought by the Sixties' earthquake was the rapid decline in religious observance itself. Weekly church attendance nationwide nosedived from 49 percent in 1958 to 42 percent in 1969, by far the sharpest decline on this measure ever recorded.[79] It is hard to imagine a more clearly defined generational phenomenon: Among those over 50 (the World War II generation and their elders) there was virtually no decline at all, while among those aged 18–29 (the early Boomers), weekly religious attendance was cut nearly in half, from 51 percent in April 1957 to 28 percent in December 1971. As the Boomers aged, they would become somewhat more conventionally observant, but they would always remain much less observant than their parents had been at an equivalent age. Just as the Boomers' parents had been largely responsible for the postwar surge in religiosity, the Boomers themselves were largely responsible for the collapse in religiosity two decades later.

Perhaps the most sensitive seismometer recording this religious temblor was provided by the American people themselves. Recall that as late as 1957 fully 69 percent of Americans had observed that "the influence of religion in America is growing." Barely five years later that number had fallen to 45 percent, and it continued to fall to 33 percent in 1965, 23 percent in 1967, and 18 percent in 1968, finally bottoming out at 14 percent in 1970. Almost overnight, it seemed, America had turned from God's country to a godless country.

The rapid change in religious observance in the Sixties and an equally rapid change in sexual mores in those same years were closely intertwined. As we shall see in Chapter 8, traditional sexual norms, especially with respect to premarital sex, changed almost overnight. And in turn, attitudes toward sexual norms (like premarital sex) strongly predicted which Americans moved away from religion during the 1960s and 1970s. A very similar (though slightly slower) revolution would transform attitudes toward homosexuality and then attitudes toward religion three decades later.[80]

Many Americans experienced the social, sexual, and religious changes of the 1960s as "liberation," but others were deeply unhappy about the direction the country had taken, especially about sexual permissiveness, but also about school prayer and other church-state issues. Their reaction to the Sixties soon produced a backlash strong enough to be visible nationally. For the next two decades, these people—conservative in both religion and politics—swelled the ranks of evangelicals and stanched the hemorrhage of religious engagement of the Sixties, a kind of aftershock to the Sixties' earthquake. Figures 4.4 and 4.5 show that the sharp decline in church membership and attendance that had occurred during the earthquake of the Sixties slowed to a halt in the 1970s and 1980s. The most important result of this temblor was that conservatism (theological, social, moral, and political) and religion became increasingly identified, especially in the public eye, as the Religious Right. To many religious Americans, this collaboration represented an appropriate retort to the excesses of the Sixties.

A growing number of their fellow citizens, however, were not so sure. As the 1990s opened, a backlash against the growing public presence of conservative Christians manifested itself in the increasing numbers of Americans who objected to the political influence of religious leaders and organized religion more generally. Young Americans in particular came to view religion as judgmental, homophobic, hypocritical, and partisan.[81] All these were warning signs that a second aftershock was about to roil the American religious landscape. The rise of the so-called nones after 1990 marked unmistakably the onset of this third temblor.

Who were these nones? Historically, whatever their degree of religiosity, almost all Americans have identified with one religion or another.[82] In response to standard questions in the 1950s about "what is your religious preference?" the overwhelming majority expressed some sort of religious identity, just as Will Herberg had said. Only a very small fraction responded by saying "none."[83] The earthquake of the Sixties had increased the national incidence of such nones from about 5 percent to about 7 percent, but that figure remained virtually unchanged for two decades.

Around 1990, however, the fraction of Americans who said they were "none of the above" suddenly began to rise, and at virtually the same time the fraction of people who said that they "never" attended church also began to rise, as is shown in Figure 4.6.[84] This turning point would prove one of the most decisive in recent American religious history. As Figure 4.4 and Figure 4.5 had shown, the decline of religious engagement that had begun in the 1960s and paused during the 1970s and 1980s accelerated once again as the twenty-first century opened.

FIGURE 4.6: **EMPTYING PEWS AND MULTIPLYING "NONES," 1972–2018**

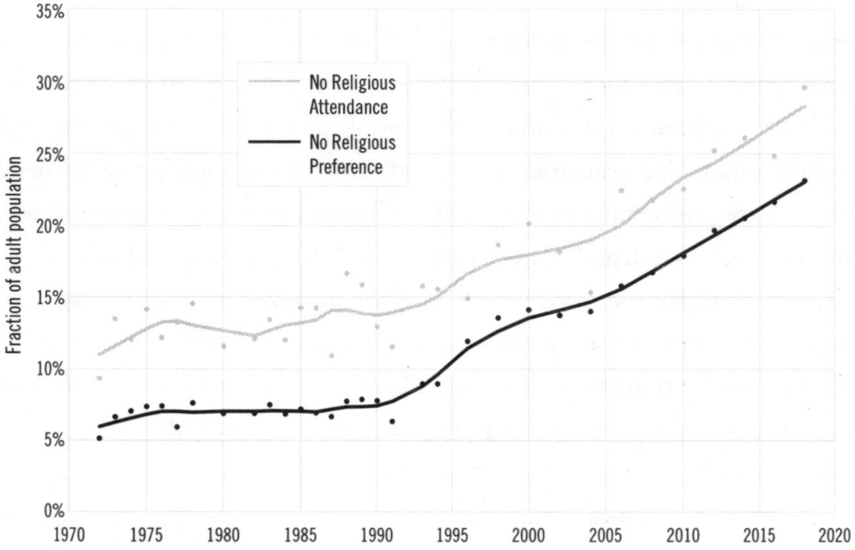

Source: General Social Survey. Data LOESS smoothed: .25.

Americans of all races have moved away from organized religion over the last half century. But the church has long played a more significant role in the life of nonwhites than among whites, whether measured by belief, or belonging, or behavior.[85] So it is worth asking whether the disengagement from church charted in Figure 4.6 applies equally to nonwhites and whites. Until recent decades too few Latinos appeared in nationally representative surveys to allow reliable estimates of their religious engagement. Between 1972 and 2016 the fraction of white Americans who never attended church roughly tripled from about 11 percent to 31 percent, while among black Americans that fraction also tripled from about 6 percent to 20 percent.

The fraction of nones among whites quadrupled from about 6 percent in 1972 to 24 percent in 2016, while among blacks that fraction also quadrupled from about 5 percent in 1972 to 20 percent in 2016. In short, both nonwhites and whites disengaged from organized religion at the same pace over these nearly five decades, though nonwhites remained more observant than whites.[86]

Like the earlier turning points we have discussed, the rise of the nones in the 1990s was heavily driven by generational factors. Americans who reached adulthood after 1990 had markedly more liberal views on homosexuality and related issues than the generations before them, and these same young people increasingly rejected religious intervention in politics and indeed organized religion itself. They constituted the lion's share of the new nones. The dramatic contrast between a young generation increasingly liberal on certain moral and lifestyle issues and an older generation of religious leaders consumed by the political fight against gay marriage was one important source of the third temblor. Michael Hout and Claude S. Fischer, who have a good claim to having first spotted the significance of the rise of the nones, attribute the trend, as we do here, to political backlash and generational succession, both rooted in cultural changes and conflicts in the 1960s.[87]

In the early decades of the twenty-first century cohorts of older Americans, of whom barely 5 percent say they have no religious affiliation, are being replaced by cohorts of millennials of whom roughly 35 to 40 percent say they have no religion. That generational succession has massively and continuously lowered the average level of religious engagement in America, and leads some scholars even to conclude that "secularization," to which America was long thought to be immune, has at last reached our shores.[88] Be that as it may, a commitment to individual autonomy now plays a larger role in Americans' religious affiliations than it has for at least a century.

Stepping back from the details of the canvas of American religious history in the twentieth century, we can see unmistakably the same inverted U-shaped pattern that we have seen repeatedly in earlier chapters. During the first two thirds of the twentieth century Americans gradually became more engaged with organized religion, whether measured by church membership or church attendance. But then at the now familiar turning point in the early 1960s, all those trends reversed course, declining sharply throughout the 1960s and early 1970s, pausing during the 1980s and 1990s, and then plunging ever downward in the twenty-first century.[89]

This same historical U-curve appears in the imperfect records of philanthropy, both religious and secular. Fragmentary evidence suggests that Protestant and Catholic giving (as a fraction of disposable income) was severely constrained during the Great Depression, but that was followed by a sustained rebound between 1945 and the 1960s, just as church membership and church attendance were booming. Then, however, much better data covering all major Christian denominations show a long, steady decline, exactly coinciding with the long decline in church membership and attendance. Per capita religious giving as a fraction of income fell by roughly 60 percent over the half century between 1968 and 2016.[90]

Imperfect but comprehensive records of all nationwide personal giving (both religious and secular) as a fraction of national income show a classic inverted U-curve, rising steadily and nearly doubling from 1929 to 1964 but then turning back downward from 1964 to 1996. For a decade between 1996 and 2005 total national philanthropy unexpectedly shot upward by nearly one third, only to fall back equally sharply in the following decade. This temporary spurt in generosity puzzled experts for some years, but further investigation showed that it was driven entirely by megagifts during the boom years from the mid-1990s to the Great Recession, while the rate of giving in the population as a whole continued to fall. Measures of the "average" gift were pulled way up by a few high outliers. By contrast, giving to United Way, the largest single charity in America and one focused almost entirely on small gifts, fell uninterruptedly in the nearly six decades between 1961 and 2017, with no evidence whatsoever of an increase in the 1996–2005 boom years. In short, philanthropy among most Americans has fallen steadily since the mid-1960s, only partially and temporarily offset by megagifts from the newly mega-rich.[91]

This is exactly what happened in the previous Gilded Age, as Rockefeller, Andrew Carnegie, and some of their peers, immensely rich as a by-product of the massive increase in inequality, doled out megagifts. It may seem hard to be critical of the generosity of Bill Gates, Warren Buffett, and Mark Zuckerberg, but their personal charity shouldn't conceal the metastasizing self-centeredness among middle-class Americans since the peak of our generosity in the 1960s.[92]

WORKER SOLIDARITY

In Chapter 2 on economic inequality we discussed in detail the rise of labor unions as economic institutions in the first half of the twentieth century and their collapse after 1960. But unions were, at the height of their importance, also social institutions, and in that guise, they merit additional attention in this chapter.

The growth of union membership in the first Gilded Age required the development of a shared sense of identity and shared interests to create working-class solidarity. Unionism in the nineteenth century had encountered widespread worker resistance embedded in the traditional ideal of the individual craftsman reluctant to sacrifice his independence and his status as a skilled worker on behalf of workers on the far side of historic occupational and ethnic or racial cleavages. Why should a Polish locomotive engineer put his livelihood at risk to benefit a black or Chinese gandy dancer merely because they both happened to work for the same large corporation? Labor agitation inevitably involves a dilemma of collective action, tempting some workers (strikebreakers or "scabs") to defect from the union side. That temptation was especially great for African Americans and other ethnic minorities excluded from unions by white prejudice.

Thus, successful unionization inherently involves remolding identities. Only intensive efforts by union organizers to build solidarity among all workers could hope to overcome that dilemma. In the words of the classic union song, written by labor activist Ralph Chaplin in 1913,

> *What force on earth is weaker than the feeble strength of one?*
> *But the union makes us strong.*
> *Solidarity forever, solidarity forever, solidarity forever,*
> *For the union makes us strong.*[93]

American workers were not class-conscious in the European sense, but they did come proudly to identify themselves as "working-class."[94] For the unionization drives of the 1930s and 1940s to be successful, union leaders and workers had to overcome racial and ethnic divisions.[95]

Replacing individualism with collective identity was thus an essential part of the rise of unions. Economic historians Thomas C. Cochran and William Miller, writing in the 1940s, emphasized that unions were an important part of their members' social lives, not merely a means to gain material improvements.

> Collective action by labor had roots far more complex than simple questions of wages and hours. . . . Labor unions were but a part of the mass movement into clubs, lodges and fraternal orders. Working for the union and empowering the delegates to do battle with the boss was a reassertion of the individual's power over his environment. Mutual benefit policies gave a feeling of security in the face of industrial accidents and seasonal unemployment, while union socials, dances, picnics and lectures offered stimulating leisure-time activity.[96]

In those years unions became a prominent institution in social and economic life, and even in American culture, as illustrated in Figure 4.7, which shows the frequency of references to unions in all US published books from 1880 to 2008. Unions appeared in novels and detective stories and even poetry, mostly not because of their economic standing, but because of their importance in daily life. Union locals provided medical clinics, resorts, radio stations, sports teams, educational classes, and a myriad of opportunities for informal social connections.[97] At their peak in the 1960s roughly one third of all American adults belonged to a union family, a figure that would fall to 13 percent by 2018.[98]

We earlier charted the quantitative rise and fall of membership in unions in Figure 2.12 and explored the economic, political, and social factors behind that trend, including structural changes in the economy and an active campaign by corporate management and conservative politicians at all levels of government over many decades to reduce the membership

FIGURE 4.7: CULTURAL SALIENCE OF UNIONS, 1880–2008

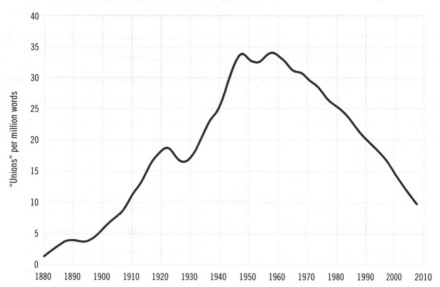

Source: Ngram. See page 169 below and endnote 5.19. Data LOESS smoothed: .15.

and the power of unions. Moreover, as membership numbers were dwindling, the meaning of union membership itself shriveled from social solidarity to the purely representational function of collective bargaining. The solidarity of union halls is now at most a fading memory of aging men.[99] "Solidarity forever" was a norm that had lost all appeal to the individualistic Boomers and their successors. As an older laid-off manufacturing worker in Youngstown expressed this loss, decrying lack of solidarity from other union members: "they have lost the understanding of the brotherhood of the union shop, the camaraderie, the understanding. They're only concerned about 'me, me, me.' . . . That's why I think the strength of the union is fading."[100]

FAMILY FORMATION[101]

We've seen that America's major community institutions from civic associations to churches to unions rose and then fell in one synchronized century-long arc from individualism to community and back to individualism—from

"I" to "we" to "I." Perhaps surprisingly, a similar rhythm can be detected in the most fundamental unit of society—the family.

In the case of those three earlier institutions, we examined both quantitative and qualitative trends—how many people belonged to associations or churches or unions, and what kind of associations or churches or unions. We pose the same two questions now in our examination of trends in family formation: quantitatively, how many men and women got married and formed families over the last 125 years, and what kind of families did they form? Any simplified history of a social institution as complicated as the family in a variegated nation over a turbulent century will miss many important subtleties, but as in the previous sections, we can discern one broad pattern that affected most families in America over this period.

As the twentieth century opened, family formation in America was far from universal and surprisingly late. Relative to patterns earlier or later, many young adults in the Gilded Age lived with their parents well into their twenties and married only later in life—if at all, for many people remained lifelong "bachelors" and "spinsters," unmarried and childless. When marriage did occur, it was unlikely to cross class lines. To be sure, most Americans in that age (as in all ages) eventually married and had children. But as in the case of Gilded Age religion, a surprising number of Americans were "nones," when it came to having a nuclear family of their own.

Gradually, however, throughout the first half of the twentieth century, young men and women began to leave home and marry earlier. They were increasingly unlikely to remain single, and when they married, they were more likely to marry across class lines and to have children at a younger age. By 1960 early marriage and children were part of the lives of virtually all Americans.

In the second half of the century, however, young Americans began to stay longer in their parents' homes, and to postpone and even eschew marriage and children. Singletons became more common, perhaps more common than ever in America history.[102] In short, in the two "I" periods at the beginning of the twentieth and twenty-first centuries, fewer people married and had kids, and those who did, married later and had kids later, whereas in the mid-century "we" period, for virtually all Americans that "we" began with their nuclear family.

The last several decades have seen a profusion of many new types of family—same-sex families, cohabiting families, "fragile" families, and so on, and this profusion itself deserves close attention.[103] It is far from our purpose here to dismiss those newer types of family as illegitimate. But for the most part such nontraditional families were rare throughout the twentieth century, and reliable evidence about them is rarer still, so we devote less attention to them than we would if we were writing entirely about the twenty-first century.

Let's begin with some basic data on the changes in the incidence and timing of marriage between the last Gilded Age and our own. Figure 4.8 depicts the changing age at first marriage for American men and women from 1890 to 2016, oriented so that younger is "up." It shows that in the two Gilded Ages at the beginning and at the end of the twentieth century family formation began relatively late in life for both men and women. In 1890 the average age at first marriage was 22 for women and 26 for men, while in mid-century such family formation began earlier—at roughly 20 for women and roughly 23 for men. The sharp reduction in the average age of marriage in the late 1940s is obviously related to the return of the GIs after World War II, but the gradual trend toward early marriage had begun decades earlier, and it would persist for decades after war's end. However, by 2016 the average age at first marriage had risen to about 27 for women and nearly 30 for men. The Boomers' parents married young, but that was much less true of the Boomers themselves and the subsequent generations, as is clear in Figure 4.9, which compares the marriage rates of successive generations at the same stage in their life cycles. Marriage today comes on average about seven years later in life than in the 1960s, though only about four years later than was true a century ago.

These data, in one respect, understate the larger curvilinear pattern, since by definition "age at first marriage" ignores people who never get married. Figure 4.10 offers a broader perspective on the rise and fall of marriage between 1900 and 2015, showing what fraction of all American adults in their prime marriageable years (30–44) were, in fact, married.[104]

FIGURE 4.8: **MEDIAN AGE AT FIRST MARRIAGE, 1890–2016**

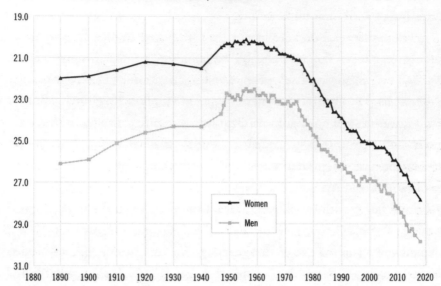

Source: Census Bureau, decennial censuses; since 1947, Current Population Survey.

FIGURE 4.9: **GENERATIONAL DIFFERENCES IN MARRIAGE RATES**

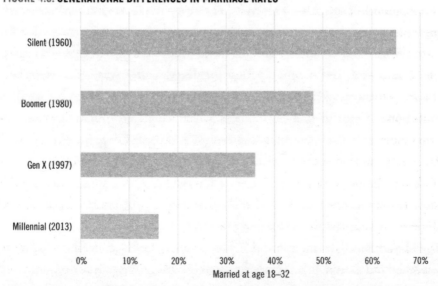

Married at age 18–32

Source: https://www.pewsocialtrends.org/2014/03/07/millennials-in-adulthood/sdt-next-ame
rica-03-07-2014-0-02/.

FIGURE 4.10: **THE RISE AND FALL OF MARRIAGE (1880–2017)**

Source: IPUMS USA: Version 9.0, 2019, https://doi.org/10.18128/D010.V9.0.

In sum, at our now familiar mid-century "togetherness" peak in 1960, 80 percent of Americans in middle age (30–44) were married, and on average they had married at age 21. By contrast, in 1900 only about 65 percent of that same age group were married, and on average they had married at age 24, and by 2018 only 45 percent of those of that age group were married and on average they had married at about 28. Representing hundreds of millions of momentous personal decisions by ordinary Americans, it is remarkable that family formation over this 125-year period followed exactly the same rhythms as civic and religious and union engagement.

Evidence on when young people have moved out from their parents' home confirms this same story. Early in the twentieth century and again late in the twentieth century roughly one in three young adults (aged 25–29) delayed family formation by living with their parents, but that fraction bottomed out at about one in ten (and thus delay in family formation was at a minimum) around 1970. As shown in Figure 4.11, at the peak period of family formation around 1970 virtually all young Americans had set up housekeeping on their own by their late 20s, the vast majority of them married. But before and after that period, family formation was delayed for many young people.

FIGURE 4.11: THE RISE AND FALL OF INDEPENDENT LIVING BY YOUNG ADULTS (25–29), 1900–2016

Source: https://www.pewresearch.org/wp-content/uploads/sites/3/2010/10/752-multi-genera tional-families.pdf (1900–2008) and https://www.pewresearch.org/fact-tank/2018/04/05/a-rec ord-64-million-americans-live-in-multi-generational-households/ (1940–2016).

It was not merely the incidence and timing of marriage that evolved over this period, for the institution of marriage itself was changing in tandem. A leading family sociologist, Andrew Cherlin, has explained that in the late nineteenth century most marriages represented a kind of utilitarian bargain between two individuals who each needed what the other had to offer. In that era, the archetypal bargain involved the man providing material support, while the woman cared for children and the home.

During the Progressive Era, Cherlin explains, a new model of "companionate marriage" arose, based on romantic love, friendship, and partnership rather than convenience and self-interest.[105] To be sure, companionate marriage was still gendered and far from egalitarian, because the male breadwinner model persisted, but the new model of marriage was definitely different from the nineteenth-century marriage of convenience.[106]

The ideal of companionate marriage became steadily dominant among American couples during the first half of the twentieth century, reaching its apotheosis in the 1950s. More Americans married, married young, and had kids faster in the 1950s than in any other decade of the twentieth century. "The only path to respectable adulthood was marriage," Cherlin points out, "and people walked down that path quickly: about half of all women were married by age twenty."[107]

Cherlin notes the close connection between the changing nature of the mid-century family and the other trends explored in this chapter. "The 1950s family and the 1950s church supported one another," he observes,[108] and he might have added the 1950s community groups to the pairing, for it is no accident that PTA membership peaked exactly in this period. In 1954 *McCall's* magazine coined the term "togetherness" to describe this new family, "this new and warmer way of life, not as women alone or men alone, isolated from one another, but as a family sharing a common experience."[109]

That way of framing companionate marriage would eventually undermine the male-headed household, overturning the culture of *Father Knows Best* and *Leave It to Beaver.* Conceptions of the family were about to take a sharp turn in an individualist direction, almost in synchrony with the comparable turn toward a more individualist perspective on religion.[110] "Love and marriage go together like a horse and carriage," sang Dinah Shore and Frank Sinatra in 1955. "All you need is love," retorted the Beatles twelve years later.

In the 1970s and 1980s popular magazines began publishing articles about the importance of privacy, self-development, individual growth, and identity apart from marriage. Cherlin explains:

A new style of marriage was emerging in which both the wife and the husband were expected to develop a separate sense of self. . . . They asked themselves questions such as: *Am I getting the personal satisfaction I want from my marriage?* and *Am I growing as a person?* The result was a transition from the companionate marriage to what we might call the individualized marriage.[111]

This cultural shift was obviously related to the simultaneous women's movement (which we discuss in more detail in Chapter 7), but it was not limited to the gender balance within marriage; marriage itself was becoming more optional and more fragile. The cultural shift toward individualized marriage contributed to a sharp rise in divorce and cohabitation.

Expressive individualism framed marriage as a limited liability contract dissolvable with a "no fault" divorce—"expressive divorce." For at least a century, divorce rates in America had followed a very slow, steady upward curve. Demographers Arland Thorton, William G. Axinn, and Yu Xie report, "In fact, this trajectory has been so persistent that demographers in the 1890s accurately predicted the divorce rate nearly 100 years later in the 1980s. With some fluctuations associated with depressions and wars, the American divorce rate increased slowly but steadily throughout the century from 1860 to 1960."[112] During the 1950s and 1960s (the heyday of the companionate marriage) the divorce rate dipped below the long-term trend, and then rose sharply above the long-term trend in the 1970s and 1980s. The Boomers' parents had shunned divorce, but among the Boomers and their children, divorce was unusually common.[113]

After the sharp shift in norms about premarital sex in the late 1960s that we shall describe in more detail in Chapter 8, America saw an explosive increase in cohabitation.[114] The fraction of all couples who were cohabiting (sometimes called "common-law marriage" earlier in the century) had probably drifted slightly downward from 1880 to 1960, but was almost certainly less than 1 percent. By 2000 it had risen many-fold to roughly 10–15 percent of all couples, and that trend continued in the twenty-first century. By 2013 nearly two thirds of women aged 19–44 had ever cohabited.[115] By 2019, 69 percent of American adults say that cohabitation "is acceptable, even if the couple don't plan to get married," though 53 percent say that "society is better off if couples who want to stay together eventually get married."[116]

Unlike some northern European countries, however, in contemporary

America cohabitation is not "marriage without a license," but typically a short-term relationship. More than half of all cohabitations end within two years.[117] For college graduates cohabitation nowadays frequently ends in ordinary marriage, but for the bottom two thirds of the American class hierarchy, where cohabitation is more common, it typically ends with both partners moving on to new partners, often with children in tow, thus producing complex, fragile families. In other words, for most Americans cohabitation is generally less stable than marriage.[118]

In either case, as Cherlin says, "cohabitation carries with it the ethic that a relationship should be ended if either partner is dissatisfied; that, after all, is part of the reason why people live together rather than marrying. . . . Consequently, the spread of cohabitation involves the spread of an individualistic outlook on intimate relations, an outlook that makes people more likely to dissolve a union—whether marital or not—if they find it personally unfulfilling."[119] In short, "the advance of individual rights, as laudable as it may be, has made marriage less necessary and, when it occurs, less stable."[120]

In the early twenty-first century the trend away from conventional life partnerships and toward purely individual lives accelerated beyond cohabitation, as the fraction of singletons among young adults rose sharply. Among Americans between 18 and 34, the number living without any steady romantic partner rose from 33 percent in 2004 to 51 percent in 2018. In our personal lives, not just our public life, for better or worse, the "I" had begun entirely to supplant the "we."[121]

The cultural, social, and economic changes between the early twentieth century and the early twenty-first century affected not only when and whether people got married and stayed married, and how they conceived the marriage, but also who married whom. Generally speaking, upper- and middle-class Americans have long had somewhat higher marriage rates than their working- and lower-class compatriots, no doubt because economic stringency makes it harder to sustain a marriage. This class gap in marriage rates is itself correlated with the rise and fall of economic inequality, the rhythm of which we examined in Chapter 2. The class gap in marriage rates was highest between 1890 and 1910 and after 1970—the two periods of high and rising inequality. The class gap was lowest between 1920 and 1970, when inequality was relatively low.[122]

Moreover, the likelihood that Americans would marry within or across class boundaries follows this same pattern, according to sociologist Robert Mare. This is hardly surprising, since high rates of intermarriage imply permeable class barriers, while low rates of intermarriage imply rigid class barriers. "Spousal resemblance on educational attainment was very high in the early twentieth century, declined to an all-time low for young couples in the early 1950s, and has increased steadily since then. These trends broadly parallel the compression and expansion of socioeconomic inequality in the United States over the twentieth century."[123] Mare's curves for class intermarriage, in fact, mirror exactly our familiar inverted-U. Another way of describing this same pattern is that during the two Gilded Ages of the late nineteenth and early twenty-first centuries, men and women were less likely to marry and especially unlikely to marry outside their own social class, whereas at the peak of family formation in the 1950s and 1960s they were more likely both to marry and to marry outside their social class.

Thus far we've focused on trends in marriage, but how about trends in parenthood? Measuring and accounting for trends in birth rates is a notoriously complex statistical task, as very long-term trends (the so-called "demographic transition" from high to low birth rates that typically accompanies industrialization) interact with short-term effects (like the reductions in birth rates associated with wars or cyclical economic upheaval).[124] Leaving aside nonmarital births, lower and later rates of marriage directly produce lower birth rates, so the ups and downs of marriage that we've already explored should be expected to have left some mark on American birth rates over the last century, and they have.

Mothers' mean age at first birth, unsurprisingly, follows the same inverted U-curve, at least from the 1930s to the 2010s. The available statistical coverage is incomplete, but in 1950 in the midst of the postwar Baby Boom, the median age of a mother at her first birth was less than 21, while by 2016, after six decades of steady rise, it was nearly 27, and for female college graduates more than 30.[125]

A standard account of birth rates over this period puts the emphasis on the long-term "demographic transition" toward lower birth rates that began in the US at the beginning of the nineteenth century, augmented by more effective birth control in the twentieth century, briefly and only temporarily interrupted by the Baby Boom of the 1950s.[126] However, that theory does not entirely fit the trend in whether couples decided to have children at all or not. "Trends in lifetime levels of childbearing in [the twentieth] century form a single, massive wave that peaked with women who married and began to bear children in the decade following World War II," Cherlin observes.[127]

Figure 4.12 presents evidence on childlessness among successive cohorts of women throughout the twentieth century. Across the century as a whole, roughly 25 percent of women remained childless, but that fraction varied sharply over the decades. The difference between the two lines in Figure 4.12 (childless at 30 and childless at 45) represents women who, for whatever reason, did not have children until late in their childbearing years.[128] Thus, for

FIGURE 4.12: MOTHERHOOD AMONG SUCCESSIVE COHORTS OF WOMEN, 1900–2010

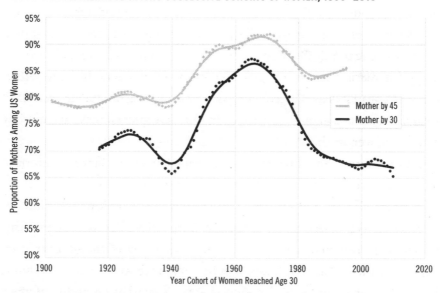

Source: National Center for Health Statistics. See endnote 4.128.

example, Figure 4.12 shows that roughly 67 percent of all women born around 1910 had had at least one child by 1940, while roughly 33 percent remained childless in 1940, because their normal childbearing years coincided with the depths of the Great Depression. With postwar prosperity, however, an additional 12 percent of that cohort had become mothers by 1955, contributing importantly to the Baby Boom, and leaving only about 21 percent of that cohort still childless by the time they reached 45. '

We can see in this chart evidence not merely of the temporary impact of the Depression baby bust and postwar Baby Boom, but also of the now familiar longer wave in family formation. The youngest women to appear in this chart were born in 1980 and reached 30 in 2010. In that Millennial generation the fraction of women who had become mothers by age 30 (about 65 percent) was relatively low and virtually identical to the rate among women in the "birth dearth" 1910 cohort of the Great Depression when they reached 30 in 1940. Figure 4.12 shows that both cohorts were nearly three times more likely to be childless (about 33 percent) compared to the cohort of women who were that age in the mid-1960s (about 12 percent). That intergenerational contrast makes vivid how thoroughly transformed the process of family formation has become over the last century.

We have thus seen that many aspects of Americans' decisions about family formation followed the same inverted U-curve that we have seen in inequality and polarization in the two previous chapters and in the other forms of community connectedness discussed earlier in this chapter. As a nation of families, we moved from individualism to togetherness and then back to individualism.

What accounts for the U-curve in family formation—fewer, later marriages and more childless couples at the beginning and end of the twentieth century; and more marriages, earlier marriages, and more children in the middle? Our discussion thus far may have left the impression that the primary driver of this trend was changing social norms about when and whether family formation is appropriate, but that is not the only story. Another highly plausible explanation is not cultural, but economic. If marriage and having kids depend on a couple being able to afford both, then one might expect that affluent couples in boom times would marry and have children early, while poorer couples in hard times would postpone or even forgo family formation.

During certain periods of the last century that economic explanation seems entirely plausible. For example, marriage and childbearing were much delayed during the Great Depression, and we know from many accounts that economic hardship was directly responsible for that fact. "The boys have no jobs," said one unmarried Chicago woman at the time. "I want a man with a job," said another.[129] On the other hand, recent experience seems in certain respects to contradict that economic account. For example, despite unprecedented prosperity for upper-middle-class couples in recent years, they have delayed marriage and childbearing longer than nearly any other group of Americans over the last 125 years.

A full accounting of the ups and downs of family formation over the last 125 years is beyond the scope of this chapter.[130] That said, it appears that both economic and cultural explanations are necessary, and neither alone is sufficient. The first Gilded Age was a time of great inequality, to be sure, but as we also saw in Chapter 2 it was in the aggregate a time of unprecedented affluence. Yet in that very period, many people remained unmarried and childless, especially well-educated women.[131] That suggests that cultural factors may have played an important role in the period. During the 1930s economic factors were clearly dominant. The postwar pattern of very early family formation was probably influenced both by economic prosperity and by the culture of "togetherness" that Andrew Cherlin described. And over the last half century affluence has been associated with late family formation, while poverty has been associated with early childbearing and unstable or nonexistent marriage—"fragile families."[132]

We do not claim that the I-we-I story is the full explanation for the ups and downs of family formation over the last 125 years. Indeed, factors other than culture and economics, such as changes in birth control and especially changing gender roles that we shall discuss in Chapter 7, are doubtless also relevant. However, we do suggest that the I-we-I curve is an important part of the story.

Decisions about whether and when to get married and have children are deeply personal. It is not our intent either to condemn or to praise late family formation, though some evidence suggests that kids may do better when they are raised in stable families by somewhat older parents.[133] Our purpose is merely to point out the remarkable shifts in the choices that Americans have made over the last 125 years.

SOCIAL TRUST

This chapter has focused on social networks because those networks are the visible sinews of community and undergird a valuable norm of generalized reciprocity. That norm amounts to a version of the Golden Rule: As philosopher Michael Taylor has pointed out,

> each individual act in a system of reciprocity is usually characterized by a combination of what one might call short-term altruism and long-term self-interest: I help you out now in the (possibly vague, uncertain and uncalculating) expectation that you will help me out in the future.[134]

When Tocqueville visited the United States in the early nineteenth century, he was struck by how Americans resisted temptation to take advantage of each other and instead looked out for their neighbors, not because Americans obeyed some impossibly idealistic rule of selflessness, but rather because we pursued "self-interest rightly understood."[135] An effective norm of generalized reciprocity enables that reconciliation of self-interest and good neighborliness. And where such a norm prevails, its effectiveness is manifest in generalized social trust. Political scientists Wendy M. Rahn and John E. Transue observe that "social, or generalized, trust can be viewed as a 'standing decision' to give most people—even those whom one does not know from direct experience—the benefit of the doubt."[136]

Hence, we conclude this survey of trends in social solidarity in America over the last century or so with a review of the evidence of trends in social trust.[137] Since social trust has not been measured by, say, the decennial US Census, we must rely on survey evidence asking Americans simply whether they trust one another, which once again precludes any direct measure of social trust in the early years of the twentieth century.

Fortunately, this topic was measured in some of the earliest scientific surveys, first posed as a very simple question, "Do you agree or disagree that most people can be trusted?" That version was asked repeatedly from the mid-1940s to the mid-1980s. Meanwhile, in 1960 a more balanced version of this question about social trust began to be used by survey researchers: "Generally speaking, would you say that most people can be trusted, or that you can't be too careful in dealing with people?" That "two-handed" version quickly became a global standard for measuring trust, and by now it has been used hundreds of times in the US and thousands of times around the world. Naturally, by offering two options, the two-handed version elicits fewer "can be trusted" responses—roughly a 15 percentage-point difference—but since both versions were used in parallel for several decades, we can, with cautious adjustment, splice the results from the earlier and later versions, as in Figure 4.13, to sketch a tentative picture of the rise and fall of social trust in America over nearly eighty years.

The best evidence suggests that social trust rose from the mid-1940s to the mid-1960s and thereafter fell. Agreement that "most people can be trusted" hit a momentary high of 73 percent during World War II, slipped back slightly to about 65 percent in the immediate postwar years, and then rose further to about 77 percent between 1957 and 1964, before slipping to 71 percent in 1966 and then falling much further to 56 percent by 1983.[138]

Meanwhile, the more balanced version made its inaugural appearance in 1960, recording 58 percent trusting, the highest level of generalized social trust on the "two-handed" question that would be registered in America for at least six decades. By the 2010s, social trust in America had collapsed to 33 percent. In round numbers, in the early 1960s nearly two thirds of Americans trusted other people, but two decades into the twenty-first century two thirds of Americans did not.

Both versions of the question converge on the early 1960s as the high point of generalized social trust over these eight decades. Piecing this evidence together, it appears that social trust was high and rising into the 1960s. By the late 1960s, however, this beneficent trend was reversed, initiating a long-term nearly uninterrupted decline in social trust, a trend repeatedly confirmed by scholars.[139] In sum, middle-aged Americans in the 1960s were living in a more trusting society than the one in which they had grown up, but also in a more trusting society than the one their children would inherit.

FIGURE 4.13: SOCIAL TRUST, 1942–2018

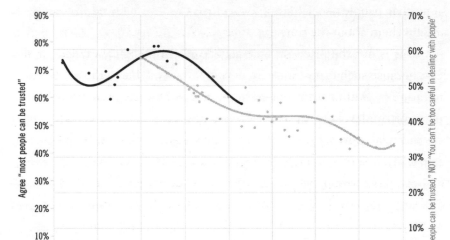

Source: Roper Center for Public Opinion Research.

Researchers also agree that the observable decline in social trust since the 1970s is in part generational. That is, successive birth cohorts of Americans seem to have been "imprinted" with different default levels of social trust. (Of course, everyone's trust is also influenced by many other things besides their generation, including their age, their race and social class, their personal experiences in life, and so forth.[140]) As older, more trusting cohorts have gradually been replaced by newer, less trusting cohorts, the average level of trust in the country has declined.

To the extent that cohorts born in earlier decades—say those born in the 1920s, who came of age in the 1940s, or those born in the 1950s, who came of age in the 1970s—retained a level of trust roughly corresponding to the average trust in the society in which they were raised, we can use the differences among successive cohorts to estimate the level of trust in previous decades. This approach is tricky, both because the analysis of generational differences is notoriously complicated and because the approach requires us to estimate when exactly in one's lifetime one is "imprinted" by the wider world. However, recent decades have seen notable progress in grappling with the former problem, and scholars generally assume that people's social attitudes are decisively influenced by the world around them about the time that they reach maturity.[141]

This is not the place for an extended methodological exposition, not least because such expositions are now readily available in the professional literature.[142] Suffice it for our purposes to say that the best available estimates of the levels of trust across successive generational cohorts, using this indirect approach, are given in Figure 4.14. Strikingly, both the real-time analysis shown in Figure 4.13 and the cohort-based analysis in Figure 4.14 converge to support the idea that social trust in America traced a curvilinear pattern over the last 100 years, starting from relatively low levels of trust prior to the 1930s, rising to higher levels of trust from 1940 up to a peak around 1960, then reversing course, with steadily falling trust from the mid-1960s to the beginning of the twenty-first century.

FIGURE 4.14: GENERATIONAL DIFFERENCES IN SOCIAL TRUST, 1910–2010

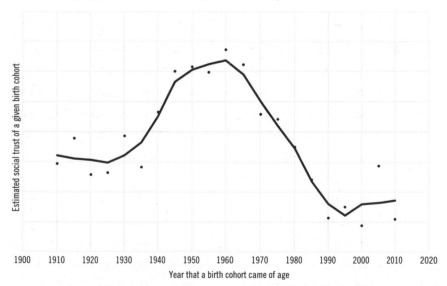

Source: April K. Clark, "Rethinking the Decline in Social Capital," Fig. 4(a) M2.

We don't want to exaggerate the precision of these estimates, given the inevitable limitations of the evidence. Nevertheless, our best estimates of long-run trends in social trust neatly match the other trends in social solidarity reviewed in this chapter: steadily increasing civic and religious engagement and family formation from the Progressive Era until the 1960s apogee, and then steadily declining solidarity for the next half century and more.[143]

What have we learned in this chapter? Figure 4.15 summarizes the broad trend in social solidarity over the last 125 years, combining the trends for civic engagement, religion, unions, family, and social trust.[144] It shows that except for a pause in the 1920s and early 1930s, Americans became steadily more connected socially from the 1890s to the 1960s, but then virtually all our measures show a steady, unrelenting decline in social connectedness over the last half century. This chart can be readily compared with the charts at the end of Chapters 2, 3, and 5, showing the equivalent long-term trends in economics, politics, and culture. In Chapter 8 we shall explore how and why these curves overlap.

FIGURE 4.15: **SOCIAL SOLIDARITY, 1890–2017**

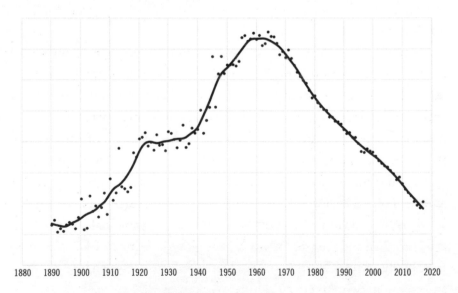

Source: See endnote 1.4. Data LOESS smoothed: .10.

5

CULTURE: INDIVIDUALISM VS. COMMUNITY[1]

The relationship between the individual and the community is one of the timeless dualisms of social thought. As early as 1623 the English poet John Donne penned the original communitarian epigram: "No man is an island, entire of itself . . . any man's death diminishes me, because I am involved in mankind; and therefore never send to know for whom the bell tolls; it tolls for thee."[2]

The contrast between individualism and community is not perfectly unidimensional, with the individual at one pole and the community at the other. The Bill of Rights in the US Constitution captures the subtlety: It enshrines individual rights, but it is also a quintessential part of a constitution that virtually all Americans worship. So does the Bill of Rights mark the US as individualist or communitarian? Or take the US frontier, symbolized in countless westerns by a lone cowboy riding into the sunset, but also symbolized by a wagon train in which settlers sustain and protect one another. Individualist or communitarian? The evolving dialectic between the individual and the community is an important feature of American history. In this chapter we trace the fluctuating balance between individualism and community in American culture over the last 125 years.

Cultural studies require narrative and nuance, and we aim at that here,

but we also draw on unexpected quantitative evidence to gauge the fluctuations. Cultural essentialists sometimes assume that culture is a fixed
national characteristic, like "Chinese culture" or "Western culture," that
determines institutions and behavior, but we have a different view. "Culture," as we use the term, is not uniform across a society nor across time—
quite the contrary—and it is not an uncaused first cause of social change.
As we will show in Chapter 8, culture is one strand in a skein of interacting
social and economic and political influences.

Since the term "culture" is so widely used across many different disciplines, its meaning has been the subject of wide-ranging conceptual and
definitional debates, especially in literary studies and cultural studies, particularly in anthropology. While those debates are important and often fascinating, our purposes here are simpler and more immediate. By culture we
mean *beliefs, values, and norms about fundamental aspects of American society*.
Conventionally, measures of culture in this limited sense rest heavily on
surveys, but as we have seen in earlier chapters, surveys are essentially un-
available for the first half of our period. Census data, so useful in our earlier
chapters, contain very little direct information about cultural change. Instead, we rely heavily here on narratives of intellectual and cultural history,
alongside a new quantitative tool that enables us to explore the corpus of
American literature over the last century or two. We have also discovered
a few behavioral measures of culture that we shall introduce throughout
this chapter, and fortunately they are completely consistent with the more
abundant, but "softer" evidence that is most readily available to us.

Michele Gelfand, a cultural psychologist, has emphasized the power
of culture:

> culture . . . is largely invisible. We rarely recognize how powerful it is! One
> of the most important aspects of culture that we take for granted is our
> social norms. We follow norms constantly. And we rarely recognize how
> much we need norms: social norms are the glue that keeps us together,
> they give us our identity and help us to coordinate and cooperate at such a
> remarkable level. . . . But . . . some groups have much stronger norms than
> others; they're tight. Others have much weaker norms; they're loose.[3]

Gelfand is most interested in differences among groups, whereas we focus on differences across time, but her distinction between "tight" and "loose" norms is closely related to our distinction between communitarian and individualist norms.

Following the literary critic Lionel Trilling, "culture," as we use the term, always entails a contest, a dialectic, a struggle.[4] American history and myth have always contained elements of both individual and community—the cowboy and the wagon train. "There is no period in American history when thinkers have not wrestled with the appropriate balance of power between self-interest and social obligation," observes intellectual historian Jennifer Ratner-Rosenhagen.[5] Examined closely, the relative emphasis on the individual and the community in American culture has varied over long periods of time, a pendulum swinging irregularly from one pole to the other and back again.[6]

But this pendulum doesn't swing by itself. It is pushed one way or the other by social actors, sometimes by leaders, but often by grassroots activists. As it swings, it alters what pundits have recently called the "Overton window," making some policies more promising and acceptable or at least conceivable and others less so. "The Overton window is the range of ideas tolerated in public discourse, also known as the window of discourse. The term is named after Joseph P. Overton, who stated that an idea's political viability depends mainly on whether it falls within this range, rather than on politicians' individual preferences."[7] As our culture becomes more in-dividualist, for example, policies that rest on the assumption that "we're all in this together," like redistributive taxes, become unthinkable, while policies like deregulation become more plausible. And as the pendulum swings back toward the communitarian pole, the plausibility of those poli-cies reverses. For this reason, culture is not simply flotsam and jetsam on the tides of history, of interest only to effete literati or connoisseurs of pop culture, but an active ingredient in the dynamics of political, economic, and social life.

GILDED AGE/PROGRESSIVE ERA STRUGGLES OVER INDIVIDUALISM AND COMMUNITY (1870-1920)

Abraham Lincoln, though presiding over the most violent period in American history, was by background and instinct a communitarian and an egalitarian Whig.[8] His strong personal and moral commitment to equality of opportunity was second only to his commitment to America's constitutional order. He sought to the very end to avoid fracturing the union, and as the war was ending, in his second inaugural address he urged that after the war America should be reunited as one community "with malice toward none, with charity for all." With Lincoln's assassination, however, followed by the end of Reconstruction in 1877 and the full onset of the Industrial Revolution, his egalitarian emphasis on shared values gave way in both parties to the inegalitarian individualism of the Gilded Age.

At the 1893 World's Fair celebrating industrial change, the historian Frederick Jackson Turner reflected on whether American individualism, which had been fostered by the frontier then just closing, would be undermined by the emerging urban, industrial society.[9] Recent research has confirmed that frontier life was indeed associated with a culture of bootstrap self-reliance and hostility to economic redistribution, an imprint still visible a century later.[10] In this way, the frontier had encouraged American individualism generally, just as Turner had speculated, and its closing might portend a turn away from it. As we have said, the frontier was also symbolized by communitarian wagon trains and barn raisings, but both Turner and the recent research suggest that the more enduring legacy of the frontier was individualism.

At just about this time, an unanticipated and unrelated scientific thesis conceived across the Atlantic—Charles Darwin's *On the Origin of Species*—unexpectedly reinforced the individualism of the Gilded Age. Despite Darwin's disavowal of the term, an English acolyte, Herbert Spencer, began to propound "social Darwinism," based on the apparently Darwinian principle of the "survival of the fittest."[11] A noted American sociologist, William Graham Sumner, followed Spencer in applying "survival of the fittest" to human society, arguing that "some people were better at the contest of life than others. . . . The good ones climbed out of the jungle of savagery and passed their talents to their offspring, who climbed still higher. . . . Attempts to overrule evolution—as by alleviating the plight of the poor— were both immoral and imprudent."[12]

That version of social Darwinism, launched around 1870, reached its peak influence between 1890 and 1915 and swept through much of the intellectual and upper middle classes as the Gilded Age waxed and then began to wane. Social Darwinism gave birth to scientific racism,[13] to eugenics, and to a pseudo-biological defense of laissez-faire capitalism. Scientific racism offered a convenient rationale for the contemporary efforts of Southerners and their Northern sympathizers of the so-called "Redemption Era" to impose Jim Crow oppression and ridicule on freed slaves. To wealthy residents of Manhattan's Upper East Side, disturbed by muckraker Jacob Riis's appalling photographs of destitute slum-dwellers of the Lower East Side in *How the Other Half Lives* (1890), social Darwinism gave reassurance that they deserved their wealth. Many came to believe that the ills of the Gilded Age were the inevitable price of progress. Cutting-edge science was blended with ancient bigotry to promote the principle of "every man for himself." In short, the haves deserved what they had, and the devil take the have-nots. The cultural movement toward unmitigated individualism approached its zenith.

Other educated middle-class Americans, however, increasingly rejected that view. As historian James Kloppenberg has observed, "Although historians have discovered too many varieties of progressivism to make possible a simple characterization of a coherent movement, it is clear that a diverse array of new political ideas and reform proposals appeared in the first two decades of [the twentieth] century."[14] Progressives differed among themselves in many ways, but they shared a critique of hyper-individualism. They argued that individualism betrayed American values and had caused the economic and social crises roiling the country.

Progressives sought to use a scientific approach to bring about the moral betterment of society, and were largely reformist and pragmatic, rather than radical, in temperament, but were fiercely committed to democratic practices and more egalitarian socioeconomic outcomes. Many had grown up in racially and religiously homogeneous small towns, and they longed for that sense of community in the newly industrializing cities. They sought to provide a new, more communitarian narrative of modernization that could knit together haves and have-nots, immigrants and native-born Americans,[15] and their views gradually gained ground.

At the same time, reformers across the land were working locally to build networks to help improve social life, support local schools, foster a more engaged "new civics" education, create community centers, and discuss urgent national issues like women's suffrage, capital punishment, and racial equality. It was in just this context that in 1916 L. J. Hanifan, an obscure West Virginia rural educator and active Progressive, introduced the concept "social capital," to denote what he and his colleagues were aiming at. "Go to, now, let us be social," they urged, against the dominant culture of unbridled individualism. John Dewey himself, a leading communitarian Progressive and educational reformer, appears to have been the progenitor of Hanifan's coinage of "social capital," certainly in spirit and probably in fact. The concept behind the term pervaded the Progressive Era, but the term itself virtually disappeared from common usage until its reappearance at the end of the twentieth century, once again in service of a communitarian critique of hyper-individualism.[16]

Changes in religious outlook in the early years of the twentieth century also played an important role in cultural change, influencing even many essentially secular thinkers. As we discussed in the previous chapter, American Protestantism in the second half of the nineteenth century had focused largely on individual salvation, but around the turn of the new century a more socially engaged theology emerged under the label of "Social Gospel." The Social Gospel emphasized that community and equality lay at the heart of the Christian message, and reformist Social Gospelers attacked the philosophy of social Darwinism. "On the Catholic side," wrote Marta Cook and James Halpin, "Pope Leo XIII's 1891 encyclical, *Rerum Novarum*, served as the intellectual and theological basis for a new generation of social activism among American Catholics," including Dorothy Day, cofounder of the Catholic Worker Movement, who would lead Catholic radicalism into the 1950s.[17]

We can, as it happens, reinforce this historical narrative of cultural change with evidence produced by a remarkable tool of the Internet Age. Google has digitized millions of books containing over half a trillion words in English dating back to the sixteenth century. Using the website http:// books.google.com/ngrams, it is possible to display the relative frequency of any word or group of words over long periods of time and thus to estimate trends in the cultural salience of words or concepts. We will frequently draw on Ngram evidence based on all books published in America from roughly 1880 (when our period of interest begins) to 2008 (the last year for which the archive is available).[18] Scholars who have pioneered the use of Ngrams for historical studies of culture term the field "culturomics."[19] They argue that Ngrams provide a new and more rigorous way of exploring and quantifying cultural change, so that claims about culture become more than merely subjective.[20]

This method "is based on the premise that books are a tangible and public representation of culture."[21] To be sure, writers and the written word are not the sole barometer of cultural change, but books have the advantage of systematically registering similarities and differences across time. The Google archive covers an extremely broad range of genres—detective stories, history books, gardening books, children's books, poetry, public affairs commentary, self-help books, scientific and medical textbooks, travel guides, romance novels, cookbooks, and so forth—but it does not allow the user to limit which genres are used, so it is best interpreted as a broad indication of what literate Americans were writing and reading in any given period.[22]

One instructive measure of the waxing and waning of the emphasis on the individual or the community in American culture from the first Gilded Age to today's second Gilded Age turns out to be the changing relative frequency of two phrases that were born in the second half of the nineteenth century—"survival of the fittest" and "social gospel." Figure 5.1 shows that "social gospel" hardly appeared in any books published before 1890, whereas Americans were already writing very often about "survival of the fittest" in that period.[23] By 1920, on the other hand, attention to "social gospel" was rising rapidly, whereas attention to "survival of the fittest" had begun to fade. The cultural passage from the Gilded Age to the Progressive

Era is reflected in this indicator—a measurable change from social Darwinism to the Social Gospel.

**FIGURE 5.1: CULTURAL SALIENCE OF "SURVIVAL OF THE FITTEST" AND "SOCIAL GOSPEL,"
1880–2008**

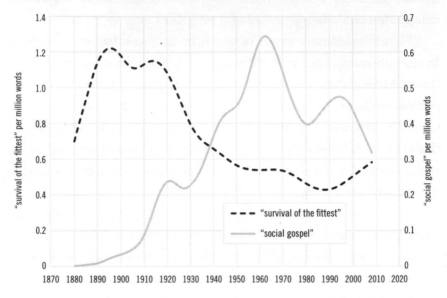

Source: Ngram. Data LOESS smoothed: .10.

Glancing briefly ahead in our narrative, Figure 5.1 also shows that the
cultural salience of "survival of the fittest" faded throughout most of the
twentieth century, only to win a new lease on life in the twenty-first century. By contrast, the salience of the "social gospel" rose steadily until about
1960. From the Sixties on, however, that communitarian concept has faded
from our cultural milieu. In the rest of this chapter, we shall see consistent
and often even sharper evidence of this pattern—a fading of individualist
themes from American cultural debates during the first two thirds of the
twentieth century, paired with a rise of communitarian sentiment in these
same decades (often with a brief pause in the 1920s), followed by a sharp
reversal of those trends from the 1970s into the twenty-first century. This is,
of course, an I-we-I rhythm that is already familiar from previous chapters.

This conflict between individualism and communitarianism was explicitly debated in the last decades of the nineteenth century and the first

decades of the twentieth century. Communitarian sentiment, though not yet dominant nationally, was at the heart of the Progressive mood. Teddy Roosevelt, Jane Addams, and other progressives were explicit in rejecting "individualism," and endorsing (in Addams's words) "a cooperative ideal of mutual assistance," not merely charity or philanthropy, which she and her fellow reformers saw as patronizing forms of aid.[24]

TR was even more emphatic about our communitarian obligations. In his address on the "new nationalism" at the dedication of the John Brown Memorial Park in Osawatomie, Kansas, on September 1, 1910, he spelled out the philosophy that undergirded his Progressivism. Speaking to Civil War veterans, Roosevelt explicitly echoed Lincoln's communitarian themes and his Whiggish concern for community and equality of opportunity, pursued, if necessary, by government redistribution from the haves to the have-nots.

> The essence of any struggle for healthy liberty has always been, and must always be, to take from some one man or class of men the right to enjoy power, or wealth, or position, or immunity, which has not been earned by service to his or their fellows. That is what you fought for in the Civil War, and that is what we strive for now. . . . We grudge no man a fortune which represents his own power and sagacity, when exercised with entire regard to the welfare of his fellows. . . . We grudge no man a fortune in civil life if it is honorably obtained and well used. It is not even enough that it should have been gained without doing damage to the community. We should permit it to be gained only so long as the gaining represents benefit to the community. This, I know, implies a policy of a far more active governmental interference with social and economic conditions in this country than we have yet had.[25]

America was reversing its post–Civil War trajectory of cultural, political, and economic individualism, and communitarian obligations had an improbable new upper class tribune.

Roosevelt, Addams, and their Progressive colleagues had a variety of labels for the alternative vision toward which they were grappling.

"Christian socialism," "neighborliness," and even the more mundane "community" were common terms, but the most widely used were "association" (or "associationism") and "cooperation."[26] We can again turn to Ngram for quantitative confirmation of the changing cultural salience of these concepts. As Figure 5.2 shows, these communitarian ideals rose and persisted for the first two thirds of the twentieth century, but after 1970 they would all steadily recede.[27] Figure 5.2 also includes "socialism," because that concept attracted some activists in the Progressive movement, but not Addams, not TR, and not many others, who were put off by doctrinaire Marxism. Despite the ideological and political resonance of "socialism," "association" and "cooperation" were much more salient throughout the twentieth century. The attentive reader will spot in Figure 5.2 the familiar inverted U pattern that we have noted throughout previous chapters.

TR's Bull Moose Party was beaten by the equally progressive (or nearly so) Woodrow Wilson in 1912. In the fall of 1916, in an effort to attract TR's 1912 four million votes, Wilson led congressional approval of the final

FIGURE 5.2: CULTURAL SALIENCE OF "ASSOCIATION," "COOPERATION," AND "SOCIALISM," 1880–2008

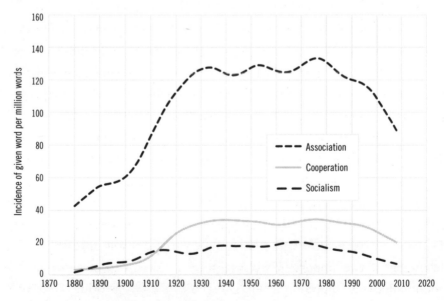

Source: Ngram. Data LOESS smoothed: .15.

tranche of national progressive legislation on child labor, the eight-hour workday, the estate tax, and a more progressive income tax. The Overton window had begun to shift to encompass more progressive policies, the culmination of a quarter century of cultural change and grassroots organizing.

FANFARE FOR THE COMMON MAN: 1920–1950[28]

After World War I the communitarian thrust of American politics and culture seemed to dissipate during the giddy, materialist interlude of the Roaring Twenties, remembered more for "flapper" dance crazes, Prohibition, gangsters, and stock market gyrations than for enduring policy or intellectual innovations. Prosperity, presided over by Wall Street financiers, seemed to reanimate, if only temporarily, the myth that opportunity was open to all but the lazy.

Ironically, Herbert Hoover, who coined the term "rugged individualism" and would preside unhappily over the crash that ended the Roaring Twenties, had Progressive roots and was a firm communitarian. In a widely admired book, *American Individualism*, published in 1923, Hoover argued for a paradoxical blend of individualism and communitarianism.[29] In the words of historian James Kloppenberg, Hoover insisted "in good progressive fashion that laissez-faire was irresponsible, and that individualism without equal opportunity was repressive. The only individualism worth having—American individualism—must combine personal initiative with a deep spiritual commitment to the value of public service and the importance of cooperation."[30] Hoover wanted what he called an "associative state," in which the government would encourage voluntary cooperation among corporations, consumers, workers, farmers, and small businessmen.

As president, as we saw in Chapter 3, Hoover enacted orthodox conservative economic policy, a departure from his previous embrace of Progressive ideas, and that orthodoxy failed him with the onset of the Great Depression. Nevertheless, the Hoover of the 1920s was an excellent illustration of two important facts: (1) that good conservatives could be communitarians—opposing "big government," but favoring collective action to redress injustice—and (2) that the Progressive Era torrent of communitarianism had not dried up, but simply gone underground during the Roaring Twenties.

For American writers of the 1920s known as "The Lost Generation"—including Ernest Hemingway, F. Scott Fitzgerald, Gertrude Stein, and Ezra Pound—the millions of deaths in the trenches of World War I, followed by millions more in the horrific pandemic of 1918, had destroyed all illusions, including the illusion that kindness and altruism were normal human traits. They had lived through profound loss, alienation, and despair, and their heroes were left to celebrate inner strength and the individual. In "hip" circles, too, the Twenties were highly individualistic, favoring free love and flouting convention. Both the war and the pandemic fostered nihilism.

The stock market crash of 1929 dropped the curtain on the Roaring Twenties. The idea that joblessness was due to character flaws was hard to reconcile with the reality of the Depression, as unemployment shot up from about 3 percent in 1929 to about 25 percent in 1933. Individual effort could hardly solve such a massive collective problem. A commission of Episcopal bishops argued that "it is becoming increasingly evident that the conception of society as made up of autonomous, independent individuals is as faulty from the point of view of economic realism as it is from the standpoint of Christian idealism. Our fundamental philosophy of rugged individualism must be modified to meet the needs of a co-operative age."[31] Historian Charles Beard argued that "the cold truth is that the individualist creed of everybody for himself and the devil take the hindmost is principally responsible for the distress in which Western civilization finds itself."[32]

In literature, social conscience and social realism prevailed, culminating in John Steinbeck's *Grapes of Wrath* (1939). In cinema these were the years of Frank Capra's celebration of community spirit in films like *Mr. Smith Goes to Washington* (1939) and *It's a Wonderful Life* (1946). As Capra said, "My films must let every man, woman, and child know that . . . peace and salvation will become a reality only when they all learn to love each other."[33]

In politics, too, the New Deal reanimated the communitarianism of the Progressive Era, not least because many New Dealers had themselves come of age in the Progressive movement. FDR had been a communitarian progressive from his days at Harvard in 1900–1903, likely having picked up this commitment from his role model and fifth cousin, then in the White House. As a young state senator in 1912, fighting for conservation for the Adirondacks, FDR had argued that it was necessary to establish the "liberty of the community," the right of the community to require certain responsibilities of its members.[34] Experience in the Social Gospel movement and the settlement house had been especially influential among New Dealers, many of whom (like Harry Hopkins, one of FDR's closest advisors; Treasury Secretary Henry Morgenthau, Jr.; the pioneering secretary of labor, Frances Perkins; and the president's wife, Eleanor) had acquired their ideals as young people during the Progressive Era.[35]

Politically, as well as culturally, seen from the perspective of the twentieth century as a whole, the New Deal was a continuation of the Progressive Era, interrupted only temporarily by the pause in the 1920s. The Great Depression and revival of concern for the community, not merely the isolated individual, had the effect once again of shifting the Overton window, making massive government intervention more plausible and laissez-faire policies less credible.

It was not merely in New Deal domestic policy that the communitarian spirit pervaded the 1930s. As early as January 1931 Congress had authorized, and President Hoover had appointed, a War Policies Commission to assure that should there be a war in the future, its burden would fall equally on everyone. The commission's executive secretary was a promising young Army officer named Dwight Eisenhower. The commission was a response to growing popular feeling that "merchants of death" had profited from World War I, and reaction to its report across party lines was overwhelmingly favorable. In other words, the idea that "we're all in this together" was widely shared nearly a decade before America's actual involvement in World War II.[36]

The foremost anthem for mid-century America was the monumental "Fanfare for the Common Man" penned in 1942 by composer Aaron Copland, and inspired in part by a speech made earlier that year by Vice President Henry A. Wallace, in which Wallace proclaimed the dawning of the "Century of the Common Man." As Figure 5.3 shows, the term "common man" had appeared first in American literature in the Progressive Era, rose steadily in

FIGURE 5.3: CULTURAL SALIENCE OF "COMMON MAN," 1880–2008

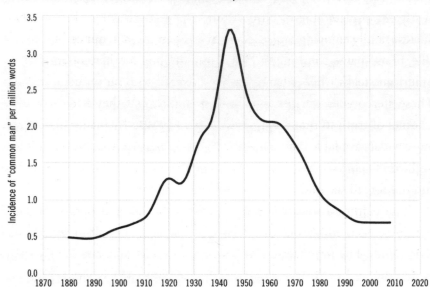

Source: Ngram. Data LOESS smoothed: .10.

the first half of the century (except for the familiar pause in the 1920s), peaked in 1945, and then faded in cultural salience throughout the rest of the century, its waning accelerating after the Sixties. By 1942 "common man" had become a powerful cultural symbol of national solidarity, social equality, and communitarianism that Wallace and Copland appropriated.[37]

A virtually uninterrupted boom and ever-increasing prosperity were the most important features of the quarter century after the war. Poverty declined by almost half from 1945 to 1975. The postwar boom obviously helped, but so, too, did the fact that in that era (as we saw in Chapter 2) the poor and working classes were receiving a fairer share of the growth. Meanwhile, the number of families receiving Social Security checks increased by 4.5 million (nearly five-fold) from 1950 to 1960, and overall benefit expenditure rose from $960 million to $10.7 billion. By the early 1960s, 50 percent of major labor union contracts contained a guaranteed cost-of-living adjustment.[38]

From the New Deal through World War II and into the postwar period, the exaltation of shared values, social solidarity, and the ordinary middle-class American way of life intensified. Contemporary advertising neatly encapsulated these cultural stereotypes—portraying a happy, white, nuclear family enjoying unprecedented leisure time, surrounded by affordable, brand-name consumer goods, with a smiling mother cooking up all-American steaks while a handy father tinkered with an outboard engine. These stereotypes were exaggerated, of course, but they had more than a kernel of truth in them, as unprecedented prosperity made this lifestyle more widely available than it had ever been. In the arts, too, Norman Rockwell's middlebrow paintings in *The Saturday Evening Post* both reflected and reinforced the mid-century moral and cultural consensus.

The culture associated with postwar affluence and optimism could rightly be accused of "blandness," but it was not materialism shorn of all civic values. The term "American Dream" had originally been popularized by James Truslow Adams in 1931, who explained, "It is not a dream of motor cars and high wages merely, but a dream of a social order in which each man and each woman shall be able to attain to the fullest stature of which they are innately capable, and recognized by others for what they are, regardless of the fortuitous circumstances of their birth."[39]

That high-minded understanding of the "American Dream" persisted into the 1960s. As Nobel Laureate economist Robert Shiller has observed, "it meant freedom, mutual respect and equality of opportunity. It had more to do with morality than material success." References to the American Dream became even more common in the 1960s, Shiller points out, including "Martin Luther King Jr.'s 'I Have a Dream' speech in 1963, in which he spoke of a vision that was 'deeply rooted in the American Dream.' [King] said he dreamed of the disappearance of prejudice and a rise in community spirit. . . . But as the term became more commonplace, its connection with notions of equality and community weakened. In the 1970s and '80s, home builders used it extensively in advertisements, perhaps to make conspicuous consumption seem patriotic."[40]

In the decades after the Sixties, Shiller goes on to show, the "American Dream" as used by politicians and ordinary citizens was steadily converted into a symbol of individual material success, such as homeownership, not collective moral success. This conversion is a useful reminder that the same term might come to symbolize quite different ideals, as the underlying culture changes. Bland the Fifties may indeed have been—and as we will discuss at length in the next two chapters, the Fifties were also thoroughly imbued with long-standing racial and gender bias—but a sense of shared citizenship and egalitarian values played a predominant role in American culture of the era.

Reacting against the twin, still vivid ideological extremes of Nazi Germany and communist Russia, American political thinkers at mid-century emphasized a nonideological, nonextreme centrism. Emblematically, in his best-selling book *The Vital Center* (1949), Arthur Schlesinger, Jr. defended liberal democracy and a state-regulated market economy against the totalitarianism of communism and fascism, seeking, as he put it, to "restore the balance between individual and community."[41]

Solidarity, even shared across racial lines, remained a sufficiently dominant ideal that in the early 1960s leaders—even advocates of controversial causes—could appeal to it as a fundamental value. In April 1963, staking his case for liberation on that shared morality, Martin Luther King, Jr. pleaded from the Birmingham jail to his critics in the white Southern clergy: "We are caught in an inescapable network of mutuality, tied in a single garment of destiny."[42] King's Civil Rights movement was rooted in communitarian values and community-building. Two months after King's Birmingham Letter (and five months before he himself would be felled in Dallas), JFK responded in the same key:

> The rights of every man are diminished when the rights of one man are
> threatened. . . . We are confronted primarily with a moral issue. It is as old
> as the scriptures and is as clear as the American Constitution. The heart of
> the question is whether all Americans are to be afforded equal rights and
> equal opportunities, whether we are going to treat our fellow Americans
> as we want to be treated.[43]

King's letter did little to convince his local critics, to be sure, but its deeper resonance with the national culture roused for the first time a wave of national support for the Civil Rights movement. Swinging the sturdy

hammer of the Exodus narrative widely embraced across racial and religious lines—"Set my people free!"—MLK broke the shackles of Jim Crow
segregation on the bedrock of shared values.[44] And Bull Connor's fire hoses
and police dogs had a powerful impact on white Northern opinion precisely because they flouted those same shared values.

   To be sure, civil rights activists were often alleged by white Southerners and their Northern supporters to be subverting those same widely
shared values, and the white South often invoked "community standards"
as a pretext for resisting integration. So the practical meaning of the shared
values was contested, but their existence meant that the struggle took place
on moral and cultural ground that in fact gave crucial legitimacy to advocates of integration.

   In this period, in short, however divergent their policy views, Americans
largely shared a common moral discourse, a reality that would become noticed only when it disappeared over the next half century. Concepts like
unity, agreement, and compromise became increasingly common in national
discourse between the 1920s and the 1960s, as shown in Figure 5.4, though

**FIGURE 5.4: CULTURAL SALIENCE OF "AGREEMENT," "COMPROMISE," AND "UNITY,"
1880–2008**

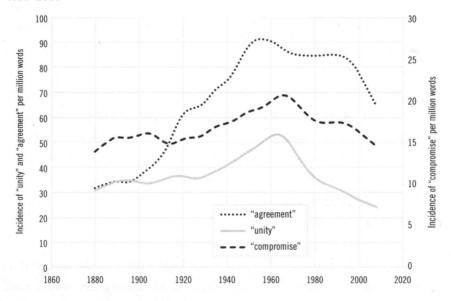

Source: Ngram. Data LOESS smoothed: .15.

all three would fade away just as abruptly in the half century after 1960. Thus, unembellished quantitative evidence reinforces the continued ascendance of communitarian values in American culture of the 1950s and 1960s.

RUMBLES OF DISSENT: THE 1950s

So far in this book we've focused on patterns of social change from the 1910s to the 1960s that seem broadly commendable—more economic equality, more political comity, and more social solidarity. You couldn't have too much of a good thing, it seemed. The cultural story is more complicated, because although the familiar inverted U-curve is empirically unmistakable in the cultural domain, too, many reasonable Americans might reverse the normative polarity here. For example, an increasingly communitarian culture might seem to some a sign of the rise of repressive conformity, while a move toward individualistic culture might seem to symbolize the dawning of liberation. And in fact, one of the virtues of the 1960s' pivot away from communitarianism was greater tolerance and support for diversity and racial and gender equality, as we shall discuss at length in the next two chapters. However, the post-1960s tolerance was mostly of a live-and-let-live sort, not the embracing tolerance and moral solidarity of Martin Luther King's "beloved community," and it definitely did not entail tolerance of political opponents, as we saw in Chapter 3.

The dark side of communitarianism became readily visible in Senator Joseph McCarthy's attacks on "subversives" in the early 1950s. Though the more tolerant Ike despised McCarthy and McCarthyism, even he sought to exclude "deviants" from government service.[45] The Red Scare (and the contemporaneous Lavender Scare aimed at homosexuals) gradually waned, but concern that the balance had shifted too far toward "conformity" and community standards began to spread, especially among intellectuals. Marie Jahoda, a social psychologist who had fled prewar fascism in Europe, observed in 1956 that "Many observers of the current crisis of civil liberties in this country agree with regard to one of its aspects: this is a time of growing conformism . . . of severely restricted tolerance for deviation from the medium and mediocre."[46]

The cultural reflection of this mood appeared in growing commentary on "subversion" and "deviance" in the 1950s and 1960s, since subversion and deviance were defined as deviation from what were said to be widely shared community standards (see Figure 5.5). Strikingly, however, within a decade or two discussion about subversion and deviance would subside almost as quickly as it had grown, with the rise of cultural individualism in the 1970s and beyond. Concern about dissent was, in effect, a leading, but transitory indicator of the cultural turn that was to come.

FIGURE 5.5: CULTURAL SALIENCE OF "SUBVERSION" AND "DEVIANCE," 1880–2008

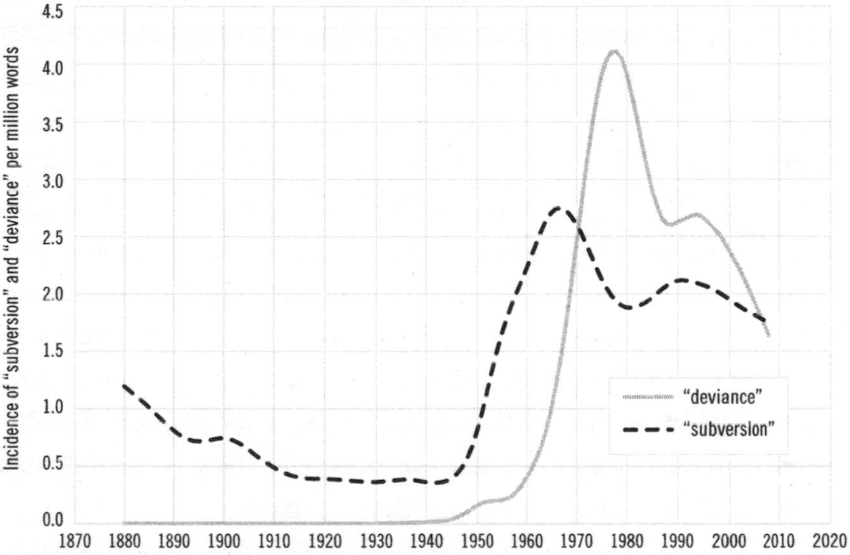

Source: Ngram. Data LOESS smoothed: .10.

On the surface, American society in the 1950s seemed characterized by an unusual consensus, but appearances could be deceiving. Subtle observers could see deeper signs of growing cultural and intellectual dissent, flickering beneath the surface. Cultural rebellion against convention, repression, and consumerism emerged. In the field of literature, the 1950s brought *Catcher in the Rye* by J. D. Salinger, *Lord of the Flies* by William Golding, the beatniks inspired by Jack Kerouac's *On the Road*, and other books that reflected rebellion against the mid-century insistence on conformity. In cinema, this trend was embodied in James Dean, the lead actor in the hit movie of 1955, *Rebel Without a Cause*, who was killed in an auto accident at age twenty-three and who was nominated posthumously for an Academy Award for the film. Dean became an instant cultural icon, representing disillusionment and social estrangement to young people growing up in the 1950s. The decade's best works of fiction were dark reflections of youthful anxiety and hinted at seismic cultural shifts to come.

Increasing numbers of scholars and public intellectuals in the late 1950s and early 1960s were also concerned about the growing "we-ness" of America and decried the trend toward conformity. *The Lonely Crowd*, David Riesman's 1950 runaway best-seller, contrasted (unfavorably) the "other-directed" American of the mid-twentieth century with the "inner-directed" American of the nineteenth century.[47] The "inner-directed" personality emphasized individual drive, initiative, and competition, while the "other-directed" personality took his cues from friends, bosses, and peers, seeking to "get along with others." The other-directed person's forte was not individual drive and innovation, but selling his own affable personality and seeking to fit in. For millions of young Americans, Riesman's polarity was morally loaded: It was bad to be other-directed and good to be inner-directed. In *The Lonely Crowd* Riesman had adopted a stance as neutral observer, not moralist, but in his 1954 *Individualism Reconsidered*, he urged Americans to find "the nerve to be oneself when that self is not approved of by the dominant ethic of a society."[48] His young readers were avidly listening.

William H. Whyte's 1956 social commentary *The Organization Man* and Sloan Wilson's 1957 novel *The Man in the Gray Flannel Suit* were classics in the same genre as *The Lonely Crowd*. *The Organization Man* was critical of "belongingness," "togetherness," "sociability," conformity, classlessness, and the "social ethic," which Whyte defined as a "contemporary body of thought that makes morally legitimate the pressures of the society against the individual." The flaw in the social ethic, in Whyte's eyes, was not its suggestion that the individual had an obligation to society per se. Rather, the problem was that people came to believe that "society's needs and the needs of the individual are one and the same," with the result that anyone who expressed discontent was considered psychologically maladjusted.[49]

FIGURE 5.6: **CONFORMITY**

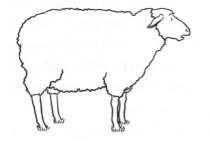

GREGORY

"Sure, I follow the herd—not out of brainless obedience, mind you, but out of a deep and abiding respect for the concept of community."

CartoonCollections.com

Source: Alex Gregory, *The New Yorker*, June 30, 2003. Reprinted with permission.

That these weighty tomes unexpectedly became best-sellers testified to the fact that similar concerns were spreading among millions of American readers. Their grievances embodied an impending turn away from a culture of conformity—and thus community—that spread rapidly in the late 1950s and peaked in the mid-1960s. As American society turned from "we" to "I" in the late 1960s, these complaints of excessive "we"-ness declined and would disappear by the late 1970s. As the problem they had identified began to dissipate in a more individualistic America, the complaints no longer seemed necessary or even novel. Hydrological engineers are said to believe that "the dam leaks before it breaks,"[50] and in effect, this cultural indicator was an early warning sign that the pendulum had swung too far toward the communitarian pole for comfort.

Conformity is the dark twin of community, for communitarianism almost by definition involves social pressure to conform to norms. If the communitarian "we" is defined too narrowly, however, then conformity to social norms punishes dissidents and deviants, whether political or sexual or racial. That was no less true in mid-twentieth-century America than it had been in seventeenth-century Salem, and it was no accident that Arthur Miller underscored that parallel in his 1953 play *The Crucible*.

During the first half of the twentieth century, this potential disadvantage of community had been virtually undiscussed. As the I-we-I pendulum swung

ever upward in the 1950s, however, Americans suddenly became more aware
of this dark side of community. That awakening to the fact that we might have
too much of a good thing was reflected in a sudden increase in the number of
books dealing with "conformity" (see Figure 5.7). With the 1960s' turn from
"we" to "I"—a pivot that we shall discuss in more detail in Chapter 8—that
preoccupation with conformity declined almost as quickly as it had arisen.
Whether that cultural shift was itself a cause of the 1960s' turn, or merely a
reflection, is a difficult question to which we shall return in Chapter 8.

FIGURE 5.7: **CULTURAL SALIENCE OF "CONFORMITY," 1880–2008**

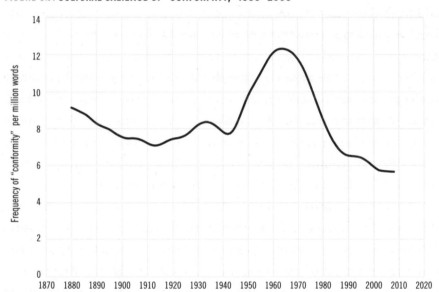

Source: Ngram. Data LOESS smoothed: .10.

Why do we emphasize these rumbles of individualistic dissent in the
1950s? In part, as we have argued, they seem to have been signals of an
impending cultural shift. But equally important for our argument, they
are implicit evidence that, in fact, postwar America was predominantly
"other-directed" and communitarian. Why so many complaints about conformity unless conformity was, in fact, prevalent? However, our discussion
of conformity has rested thus far on literary evidence. We know that people
were writing (and reading) a lot about conformity in the 1950s. But were

Americans actually more conformist, more "other-directed" in the 1950s than now? Fortunately, we have strong, experimental evidence on that very point.

In 1950 social psychologist Solomon Asch conducted a simple experiment on visual perception whose results astounded psychologists and the general public.[51] Subjects were asked to decide which of three comparison lines matched the length of a target line. Crucially, these judgments were made in the presence of other participants. Only one of the participants in the experiment was the naive subject, while the others were confederates of the experimenter and were instructed to give manifestly incorrect answers. Although those answers seemed plainly wrong to most of the naive subjects, as post-experiment interviews revealed, about one third of the time they went along with the majority anyway. In other words, people were willing to ignore the simple evidence before their eyes in order to conform to the group consensus. For many observers, these results threatened their image of America as the land of individualism and autonomy. The experiment became an instant classic, replicated many times in the 1950s and early 1960s. All confirmed that Americans were remarkably willing to suppress their own judgment in the face of social pressure.

Yet as the replications continued into the 1970s and 1980s, the size of the Asch effect diminished and then disappeared. Eventually researchers failed to detect even minimal levels of conformity, suggesting that "Asch's results were a child of the 1950s, the age of 'other-directed' people made famous by David Riesman."[52] Asch subsequently agreed that cultural and social pressures for conformity in mid-century America could have contributed to his finding, and that the later failures to replicate it were not lab failures, but rather evidence of real social change: "Historical circumstances may have altered this supposedly rock-bottom condition."[53]

In other words, the culture of community and conformism that peaked in America from the 1950s to the 1960s was not a figment of the imagination of social critics, but was embodied in the actual behavior of ordinary Americans. The history of "the Asch social pressure effect" is a rare instance in which changing lab results were evidence not of scientific incompetence, but of wider social and cultural change.

In sum, reformers in the 1950s were properly worried about the constraints that conformity placed on individualism and (as we shall see in Chapters 6 and 7) about the persistence of racial and gender inequality. Those combustible concerns, ignited by the sparks of the 1960s, would help to reverse the fundamental trends of the first two thirds of the century, and set us on a different course. That new course would indeed bring more cultural freedom and diversity, though at a cost to the earlier communitarian values, a cost mostly unnoticed as one century unspooled and gave way to the next.

THE RISE OF INDIVIDUALISM IN THE 1960s AND BEYOND

The sharp critiques of the 1950s from J. D. Salinger and James Dean to David Riesman and William Whyte were couched in social-psychological terms. They did not frame their complaints in terms of political ideology—Riesman's book was subtitled "A Study of the Changing American Character" and Dean's "rebel" famously had no "cause." It was constraint in American society and repression in the American psyche that these cultural critics worried about, not constraints on the American marketplace nor repression in American politics. At virtually the same time, however, a pair of seemingly independent developments extended the critique of America of the 1950s into the realm of political ideology. Strikingly, this occurred simultaneously on both the Right and the Left, giving rise to the New Right and the New Left.

On the Right the challenge had originated with Ayn Rand and Friedrich Hayek and eventually included orthodox economists like Milton Friedman. These "libertarians," as they began to be called, appealed to younger conservatives because their ideas seemed fresh and attractive in an era of flatness and tired "big government." Hayek (*Road to Serfdom*, 1944) and Rand (*The Fountainhead*, 1943; *Atlas Shrugged*, 1957) reacted against "collectivism" gone wrong under communism and Nazism. Hayek was the better thinker, but Rand was a better novelist. *Atlas Shrugged* is sometimes said to be the most widely read book of the twentieth century, trailing only the Bible.[54]

Rand had a genius for quotable, controversial aphorisms: "Nobody has ever given a reason why man should be his brother's keeper" and "Altruism is incompatible with freedom, with capitalism and with individual rights."[55] Gordon Gekko's "Greed is good" from the 1987 film *Wall Street* simply echoed Rand. Rand's libertarianism was so accessible that it became virtually biblical to successive generations of conservative political leaders— from Margaret Thatcher and Ronald Reagan to Alan Greenspan and former speaker of the House of Representatives Paul Ryan.

Atlas Shrugged was the source for a right-wing meme that would endure well into the twenty-first century: "makers" and "takers." (Rand called them "producers" and "looters.") According to this meme, society is composed of two classes of people: those who make stuff and those who take stuff. The takers take from the makers, usually using the power of government. The makers, like the eponymous Atlas, bear the entire weight of society. All that is required for freedom and prosperity is for Atlas to "shrug" off the feckless takers. A direct line runs between *Atlas Shrugged* and Mitt Romney's infamous observation more than half a century later in the 2012 election campaign that 47 percent of the country is a "taker class" that pays little or nothing into the federal government but "believe they are entitled to healthcare, to food, to housing, to you name it."[56]

Rand's influence has become especially pronounced in Silicon Valley, where her overarching philosophy that "man exists for his own sake, that the pursuit of his own happiness is his highest moral purpose, that he must not sacrifice himself to others, nor sacrifice others to himself," as she described it in a 1964 *Playboy* interview,[57] has an obvious appeal for self-made entrepreneurs. In 2016 *Vanity Fair* anointed her the most influential figure in the technology industry, surpassing Steve Jobs.[58]

The New Right, inspired by Rand's extreme libertarianism, stressed the virtues of individualism, unfettered capitalism, and inequality over egalitarianism and collectivism. In this light the twenty-first-century revival of the term "survival of the fittest," which we noticed in Figure 5.1, is unsurprising, since it was the slogan of choice for the libertarians of the first Gilded Age.

Gradually, individual "choice" became the touchstone for all conservatives. As Paul Ryan put it, "In every fight we are involved here on Capitol Hill . . . it is a fight that usually comes down to one conflict: individualism versus collectivism."[59] To be sure, free market fundamentalism, undergirded by libertarianism, was not the only route followed by post-1960s conservatives; others explored themes of law and order, racism, and evangelical Christianity. In today's Trump world what counts as conservatism is much in turmoil, but for the half century between 1960 and 2016 conservatism shifted starkly away from the solidarity and compassion of the 1950s Republicans (later dismissed as "Republicans in Name Only") to libertarian individualism.

The impact of this cultural shift went well beyond politics. For example, the dominant philosophy of business management during the "we" era (as epitomized by George Romney) had been that corporate decisions should take into account a wide range of constituencies beyond the owners—employees, customers, suppliers, and even the wider community within which they operated—what would later be called "stakeholders." But the newer libertarian philosophy of the 1970s argued for sharply narrowing the focus of business management to a single group—the shareholders of the company's stock—and closely linking the income of managers themselves to the stock price. "Shareholder value" (that is, the stock price) became the single metric for managerial success; this term first appeared (according to Ngram) in 1976 and then exploded in usage after 1980. The CEO of General Electric from 1981 to 2001, Jack Welch, converted that idea from theory to the dominant business culture and by 1999 was named "Manager of the Century" by *Fortune* magazine.

Meanwhile, in the very same years an equal and opposite evolution was more slowly getting under way at the far-left end of the spectrum, as the Old Left was replaced by the New Left, similarly eager to replace institutionalized solidarity with individual liberation. While the New Right wanted to remove the fetters from capitalist entrepreneurs, the New Left wanted to free people from oppressive community bonds. Francis Fukuyama in *The Great Disruption* (1999) emphasized that both Left and Right have taken freeing people from constraints as their central goal. For the Left, constraints are on lifestyles; for the Right, constraints are on money.[60]

Leftist thinkers and activists in the late 1950s and early 1960s pursued the ideal of participatory democracy by turning against highly organized elites. C. Wright Mills wrote *The Power Elite* (1956) with the goal of mobilizing the resistance of a "New Left." His ideas were echoed by more abstract thinkers, such as Herbert Marcuse, whose *One-Dimensional Man* (1964) argued that the political triumph of "technical rationality" had brought about "a comfortable, smooth, reasonable, democratic unfreedom" in American society, as managerial techniques achieved "freedom from want" at the cost of "the independence of thought, autonomy, and the right to political opposition."[61]

Unlike the New Right that had attacked solidarity in favor of extreme individualism from the beginning, the New Left in its early years was communitarian in both its philosophy and its strategy. The 1962 Port Huron Statement of the Students for a Democratic Society, drafted by Tom Hayden and widely read on campuses throughout the 1960s, laid out the ideals of participatory democracy, racial equality, economic justice, and peace as a guide to the Left. In historical perspective the Port Huron Statement marked an inflection point on the Left, a high point of communitarianism, condemning "egoistic individualism," while praising self-expression as against conformism.[62]

During the second half of the Sixties more individualistic strands in the New Left counterculture became more dominant. The term "New Left" itself exploded into common usage between 1963 and 1968 (according to Ngram). The New Left was more heterogenous and fractious than the New Right, but in general members of the New Left shared disillusionment with the state, and all emphasized deconstruction of repressive institutions and assertion of self-autonomy. Outside the purely political sphere, as we'll discuss in Chapter 8, the libertine hippie slogan "If it feels good, do it" became the watchword for the Left for the Sixties.

The transition away from the Old Left toward a more individualistic New Left was neatly encapsulated in a 1966 mass meeting at Berkeley about an antiwar campus strike. It was a microcosm of the future of the Left: (1) the original Left, heavily influenced by labor unions and the Civil Rights movement, and (2) the growing hippie and New Left subculture. Todd Gitlin's autobiographical account reveals who won out in the merger.

In December 1966, Berkeley antiwar protestors tried to evict a Navy recruiting table from the student union. The police intervened. Afterward, at a mass meeting to discuss a campus strike, someone started singing the old union standby, "Solidarity Forever." Voices stumbled; few knew the words. Then someone started "Yellow Submarine," and the entire room rollicked into it, chorus after chorus. With a bit of effort, the Beatles' song could be taken as the communion of hippies and activists, students and non-students, all who at long last felt they could express their beloved single-hearted community. (It did not cross the collective mind that "Yellow Submarine" might also be taken as a smug anthem of the happy few snug in their little Utopia.)[63]

Most interpretations of the 1960s are framed in terms of the political struggle between the Left and the Right, a struggle in which the initial victories of the Left (the Great Society and the Civil Rights revolution) triggered a conservative backlash, putting in power the Right, which has largely dominated American politics ever since. In Chapter 3 we acknowledged that narrative, but we also argued that the more durable and pervasive change was from communitarianism to individualism, a dimension that is conceptually and empirically distinct from the left-right spectrum. The shift in the Sixties was less from left to right (or the reverse) than from we to I, a shift that was entirely visible on both extremes, as the Old Right gave way to the New Right and the Old Left gave way to the New Left. Both the New Right and the New Left seemed fresh and attractive, whereas the communitarian ideals had come to seem stale and constraining.

For the most part the New Right had much more long-term success than the New Left. The Republican Party in 2018 was much more like the New Right of the 1950s than the Democratic Party was like the New Left of the 1960s. In only one domain did the legacy of the New Left linger and expand into the twenty-first century, and that involves the concept of "identity."

Here, too, the cultural innovation did not begin in politics, but in social psychology. In 1958 the term "identity crisis" was introduced into the American lexicon by the psychologist Erik Erikson to describe a common phase in human development.[64] The new term resonated widely in an America where millions of young people craved independence and sought to craft a personal identity. The term "identity crisis" spread rapidly across

America in the next two decades and then began to fade from view. However, by then the concept of "identity" itself had begun to spread beyond developmental psychology to gender and racial identity in the 1970s and 1980s and to identity politics by the 1990s.[65]

"Identity" itself, unmodified by race, or gender, or politics, rapidly became an important theme in American culture after mid-century, as our trusty Ngram tool reveals with great clarity. The frequency of the word "identity" in American literature increased more than five-fold over the second half of the twentieth century, as Figure 5.8 shows. Identities, of course, can be collective—"we Democrats," "we whites," "we women"—but over much of this period "identity" referred as much to personal identity as to collective identity. Of all references to "identity" charted in Figure 5.8, fewer than 3 percent involved "identity politics," "gender identity," "racial identity," "black identity," "white identity," "class identity," and virtually all other demographic identities combined. In short, the rapidly increasing salience of identity in American culture in the second half of the twentieth century began in young adult psyches far from race and gender and class and politics. Although identity was eventually reflected in those spheres, too, at its core it represented an emphasis on "I."

One final indication of the changing weight that Americans gave in the mid-1960s to the competing claims of the individual and the community involved the balance between rights and responsibility. An emphasis on individual rights, of course, has profound roots in American political culture dating to before our national founding. National commitment to a "Bill of Rights" was demanded by the states as a precondition for ratification of the Constitution. Historically, however, our strong normative commitment to rights has been counterbalanced by strong commitment to our civic responsibilities. "Citizenship offers many benefits and equally important responsibilities," we tell all new citizens. "Below [in this pamphlet] you will find several rights and responsibilities that all citizens should exercise and respect."[66]

We can therefore get some measure of the changing balance between individualism and communitarianism by examining (see Figure 5.9) the changing cultural balance between "rights" and "responsibility" in our national literature.[67] Overall, "rights" is a more common word in American

FIGURE 5.8: CULTURAL SALIENCE OF "IDENTITY," 1880–2008

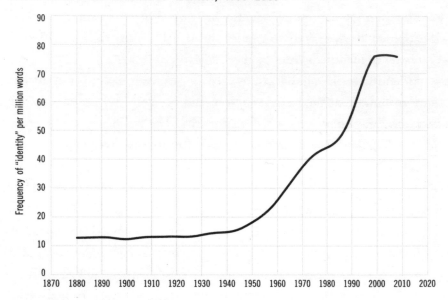

Source: Ngram. Data LOESS smoothed: .10.

English than "responsibility," but that edge has varied enormously over time. From the Gilded Age to about 1960 American writers put ever increasing stress on "responsibility" (as compared to "rights")—not just civic responsibilities, of course, but also family responsibilities, religious responsibilities, and so forth. Over that period, as Figure 5.9 shows, the ratio of "responsibility" to "rights" in American publications rose from one to four in 1900, when "responsibility" was a relatively rare word, to four to five in 1960, when "responsibility" was nearly as commonly used as "rights." By contrast, between 1960 and 2008, "responsibility" became rarer and "rights" more common, so that the ratio of the first word to the second fell back to about one to three.

Beginning in the Sixties, "rights talk" (as philosopher Mary Ann Glendon properly dubbed it[68]) became ever more prominent. Communitarian constitutional scholars have criticized the "rights revolution" on normative grounds, but whether the shift was good or bad is less relevant here than simply the fact and timing of the shift. The emphasis on individual rights— civil rights, women's rights, gay rights, consumer rights, children's rights, and so forth—has expanded steadily over the last half century and shows

FIGURE 5.9: RELATIVE CULTURAL SALIENCE OF "RESPONSIBILITY" AND "RIGHTS," 1880–2008

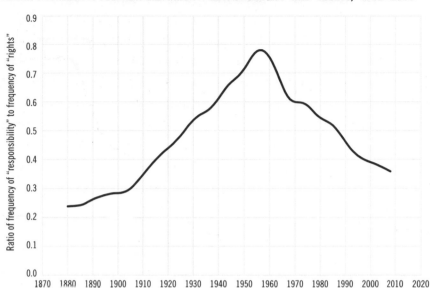

Source: Ngram. Data LOESS smoothed: .10.

no sign of waning. Though initially framed as a progressive value, "rights" soon became a normative framework accepted across the political spectrum—"rights of the unborn," "gun rights," or even "white rights."[69] Figure 5.9 offers particularly crisp evidence of the swing of the pendulum in American culture from individualism to communitarianism from 1900 to the Sixties, and back to individualism from the Sixties to today.

Cultural change in America in the years after the 1960s is vividly portrayed in the sequence of Ngrams that we have offered so far in this chapter. In virtually every case the salience of ideas and themes that emphasize individualism has surged up to replace ideas and themes that emphasize unity, agreement, association, cooperation, compromise, and—lest we forget—conformity. However, some of the most salient evidence of change in the last half century involves generational change, as the generations who came of age during and after the 1960s were more likely to be socialized in favor of individual autonomy. Significantly, studies of how parents have raised their children over this period show that parental values have shifted from obedience to autonomy and self-expression.[70]

Anecdotal evidence strongly suggests that Americans have become lit-
erally more self-centered. Sales of "self-help" books soared in the 1960s
and 1970s.[71] "Selfies" have come to dominate our photographic behavior,
and we now speak of "sharing a selfie," although the meaning of the verb
"to share" has subtly changed. It once referred to other-directed behavior,
or in the words of an older dictionary definition, "to give a portion of something to another." More recently, however, its meaning has become more
"inner-directed" or (according to the Merriam-Webster dictionary online)
to "talk about one's thoughts, feelings, or experiences with others."[72] For
many younger Americans, presenting a "curated self" online has become
de rigueur. As early as 1979 social observers like Christopher Lasch argued
that Americans were becoming increasingly narcissistic.[73]

The most substantial quantitative evidence on this trend has been
gathered by social psychologist Jean Twenge, under the rubric of *The Narcissism Epidemic* (coauthored with W. Keith Campbell, 2009) and *Generation
Me* (2014). In one of her earliest studies, she cited the astonishing fact that
in 1950, 12 percent of students agreed with the statement, "I am a very
important person." By 1990 that figure had risen to 80 percent![74] Twenge's
interest is not in the incidence of a clinically defined personality trait, but
in broader social and cultural change: "the fight for the greater good of
the 1960s" turning into "looking out for number one by the 1980s."[75] Initially, Twenge's pioneering work was criticized on methodological grounds,
but as she steadily improved the scope of her evidence, the scientific community has revised its assessment, which is now generally supportive. Her
latest work definitely suggests a long-term increase in self-centeredness
among American youth. "No single event initiated the narcissism epidemic; instead, Americans' core cultural ideas slowly became more focused
on self-admiration and self-expression. At the same time, Americans' faith
in the power of collective action or the government was lost."[76] She and
others offer abundant evidence for a monotonic increase since the 1960s in
self-focus, which matches our account of cultural change, but virtually no
one has extended this analysis to the full twentieth century, largely because
of the absence of systematic survey data prior to the 1960s.

That very absence of earlier survey data has required us in this chapter to rely almost exclusively on narratives and Ngrams to trace the pendular swing between individualism and community. However, as it happens, one solid, century-long behavioral measure comes from a very simple choice that faces almost all of us at one time or another: What names do we give our newborns?

Concentration of parental baby-naming choices on fewer names implies tighter social constraints on appropriate baby names, whereas a wider dispersion of parents' choices reflects a desire to assert individuality. Individualistic people give their children rare names, reflecting a desire to stand out, as opposed to common names, which reflect instead a desire to fit in. Among advanced countries, those whose inhabitants have more idiosyncratic names rank higher on the Hofstede index of cultural individualism, representing "a preference for a loosely-knit social framework in which individuals are expected to take care of only themselves and their immediate families."[77] We borrow our baby names measure of individualism from social psychologists—including Jean Twenge. This measure has been found to correlate strongly with other proxies for individualism in multiple contexts by economists and sociologists, as well as psychologists.[78]

The advantage of this measure of individualism is that it is based on the actual choices of succeeding generations of all American parents, not on the somewhat mysterious processes that influence American authors' changing word choices. Strikingly, this objective indicator of cultural change turns out to be remarkably synchronized with the changes as reflected in our Ngram word counts.

Data on baby names year by year since 1879 is readily available from the US Social Security Administration.[79] The most sensitive and robust measure of the degree of concentration of parental choices on a limited number of names is the Gini index, a measure of statistical dispersion.[80] As Gabriel Rossman of UCLA writes, "Gini is basically a better version of taking the ratio of a high percentile and a low percentile. If you have exactly two people with exactly equal wealth (or exactly two names with equal numbers of babies) then you'd have a very low Gini."[81] When the index (as oriented in this chart) is high, most children are given conventional names like John and David and Susan and Mary. When the index is low, many more children are given unusual names like Silas and Jaden and Harper and Maude. (The basic trend in baby-naming persists even with controls for immigration and "foreign" names.[82]) Figure 5.10 shows that this unusual measure of conventionality and individualism matches our I-we-I curve almost perfectly over the last 125 years, including even the "pause" in the 1920s. The figure also shows that since the 1920s, boys have been given more conventional names than girls and that this gender distinction has widened over the decades. Nonetheless, the pendular swing from idiosyncratic names to conventional names and back again has followed perfectly the same pattern as more literary measures of culture.

FIGURE 5.10: CONVENTIONALITY (VS. INDIVIDUALISM) IN BABY NAMES, 1890–2017

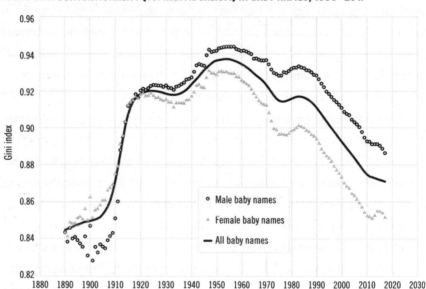

Source: Social Security Administration. "All baby names" data LOESS smoothed: .10.

PRONOUN USAGE

Social psychologist James Pennebaker in his fascinating book *The Secret Life of Pronouns* (2011) explains that our usage of the first-person plural and first-person singular pronouns is remarkably revealing. Use of "we" is more common in strong marriages and close-knit teams, for example.

Similarly, high-status, confident people, focused on the task at hand, not on themselves, use fewer "I" words. Frequent use of "I" is associated with depression and suicide; indeed, researchers have reported that pronouns are actually more reliable in identifying depression than negative emotion words, like "sad." On the other hand, in the aftermath of community trauma (such as 9/11; Princess Diana's death; or a mass campus shooting) use of "I" declines, researchers have found, whereas use of "we" increases. Frequent use of "I" seems to be a signal of individual isolation, whereas "we" is typically a sign of solidarity and collective identification.[83]

Pennebaker cautions that "we" has multiple meanings—he identifies at least five. "We" can mean "my friends and I, *not* you," or the royal "we" (as in "we are not amused"), or "every person on earth" (as in "we face global catastrophe"), or even "you" (as in "how are we feeling today?"). Of course, "we" most conventionally means "you and I." By contrast, there are not multiple usages of "I," so it is a cleaner indicator of psychological and cultural focus.[84] But comparing "I" and "we" over time provides an unexpectedly clear index of individual and community salience.

In recent years scholars have turned to Ngram to explore the frequency of "I" and "we" across time and space, as a tool for measuring individualism. Patricia Greenfield[85] and Jean Twenge and her colleagues[86] have independently found evidence for a long-term shift toward language that evinces greater "individualistic and materialistic values" over the last two centuries. On the other hand, both have focused on "I," ignoring "we," and neither has focused specifically on the full period of our interest in this book. Both looked particularly for one-way trends (like modernization), not ups and downs, and Twenge did not extend her work back before 1960.

In fact, over the period from 1900 to 1965 the word "I" appeared less and less often in American publications, but after 1965 (as both Greenfield and Twenge reported) that trend reversed itself, and in a paroxysm of self-centeredness the word "I" became ever more frequent. The frequency of the word "I" in all American books actually doubled between 1965 and 2008. "We" is less common in general, and its changes over time are less marked, but Figure 5.11 combines both pronouns by showing the ratio of "we" to "I" over the period from 1875 to 2008 in American literature of all sorts.

Taking that full span of time allows us to see the accelerating individualism of the Gilded Age 1875–1900, supplanting the Lincolnian era of communitarianism. Then comes the reinvigorated communitarian reversal of the Progressive Era in the "we" spurt from 1900 to 1916, the familiar pause of the 1920s and the renewed "we"-ness during the Depression and then World War II. We can see the remarkable increase in "we"-ness in the 1950s and early 1960s, a very abrupt turning point in 1967, followed by what Tom Wolfe would call the "Me Decade."[87] Finally, we can see the long plunge toward ever more intense individualism over the last half century. This chart closely matches the narrative that intellectual and cultural historians have given of the twentieth century. The convergence of these entirely independent streams of evidence gives us considerable confidence in our description of the I-we-I curve in this book.[88]

FIGURE 5.11: FROM "I" TO "WE" TO "I" IN AMERICAN BOOKS, 1875–2008

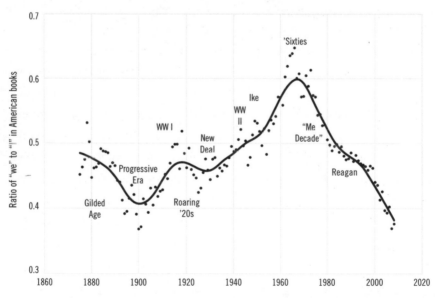

Source: Ngram. Data LOESS smoothed: .20.

As we have done with each of our analytical lenses so far, we can conveniently summarize the main empirical findings of this chapter in a single graph. Figure 5.12 tracks how a composite index of American culture varied along that community-individual continuum between 1880 and 2017. This curve is, in effect, a weighted average of all the principal curves that we have seen in this chapter.[89] It shows the by now familiar pattern. Our further statistical analysis confirms that of all the noisy, chaotic, year-to-year fluctuations of these ten cultural indicators over a century and a quarter, 70 percent can be attributed simply to the common I-we-I pendulum.[90] In other words, the communitarianism indicators fluctuate across the years in impressive lockstep.

But we can't ignore the fact that "we" is, as we noted earlier, a slippery pronoun. That possibility is very vivid in the case of Charts 5.11 and 5.12. Was the American "we" of the 1950s and 1960s a truly national "we," or was it instead a white, affluent, male "we," excluding blacks, many women, and the poor? To this broad and fundamental question, we devote the next two chapters of this book.

FIGURE 5.12: **CULTURE: COMMUNITY VS. INDIVIDUALISM, 1890–2017**

Source: See endnote 1.4. Data LOESS smoothed: .10.

6

RACE AND THE AMERICAN "WE"

Throughout the preceding chapters we have outlined the multiplicity of ways in which America's trajectory toward economic equality, political comity, social cohesion, and cultural communitarianism combined to produce a clear upswing during the first two thirds of the century, which then abruptly reversed course during the last third. To a remarkable extent, the interconnected phenomena we have examined so far can be summarized in a single statistical trend, which we have come to call the I-we-I curve.

However, the argument that America was for more than six decades moving toward a more equal, cohesive, and expansive "we" must also take into consideration the contested nature of the very concept of "we." Just how expansive was it, really? What kind of American community were we building toward during the upswing? Did our nation's "coming together" come at the expense of traditionally excluded groups? How was the upswing reflected—or not—in the experience of people of color[1] and women?

THE COLOR LINE

In 1903, W. E. B. Du Bois, one of America's most influential scholars and activists, wrote, "the problem of the twentieth century is the problem of the color-line."[2] As the nation was poised to begin what would be a sixty-year upward climb toward a more capacious sense of "we," Du Bois called attention to what would be one of the greatest challenges—and most enduring exceptions—to America's communitarian ideal.

In the Reconstruction years immediately following the Civil War and the abolition of slavery many African Americans had made remarkable strides toward equality. Finally, they were able to apply their labor toward ownership of land, satisfy a long-felt desire for literacy and learning, organize community associations, help rewrite Southern states' constitutions, exercise the vote, and achieve elected office—all of which they did in earnest. In fact, during Reconstruction some two thousand black men held government posts ranging from sheriffs and mayors to US senators and congressmen.[3]

But by the end of the nineteenth century the hope that Reconstruction would bring about racial equality was little more than a bitter memory. Under the banner of Southern Redemption, violent oppression of African Americans raged in the South, intensifying whenever blacks stood up to claim their new rights. Some four hundred black people were lynched between 1868 and 1871 alone.[4] The tactic of reclaiming white dominance by violence was augmented in the 1870s, 1880s, and 1890s by more creative measures, such as restrictive Black Codes and the disenfranchisement of African Americans through poll taxes, literacy tests, and election fraud.[5] Even so, Northern Republicans could not rally enough white support to continue Reconstruction in earnest.[6] Southern manipulation of the legal system and a series of backroom political dealings doomed Reconstruction to failure. As America moved through the Gilded Age, Northerners increasingly looked the other way as over eight million African Americans slid into a state-sanctioned and violently enforced form of second-class citizenship.[7] In establishing the doctrine of "separate but equal," the 1896 Supreme Court ruling in the *Plessy v. Ferguson* case dealt a final blow to any hope of genuine equal rights and freedoms for people of color. As the nineteenth century ended, the outlook for African Americans was bleak indeed.

As the new century opened, day-to-day life for black Americans—who were still overwhelmingly concentrated in the South—was defined by what came to be called Jim Crow, a system of laws, customs, and codes that institutionalized discrimination and disadvantage. Stark segregation and social exclusion were the norm. All public amenities and institutions including restrooms, public conveyances, and schools were separate and woefully unequal. Violence and brutality—aided and abetted by law enforcement—were the punishment for even the smallest transgression, real or imagined. And the convict-lease system exploited blacks' labor to enrich railway contractors, mining companies, and plantation owners as well as the states who received generous revenue from renting out their prisoners.[8] Economic prospects were grim, with most black laborers trapped in the abusive systems of sharecropping and tenant farming, which offered no hope of landownership, and no path out of abject poverty.[9]

Thus, in the opening decade of the twentieth century, by almost every measure, the black-white gap in America was enormous. Life expectancy for people of color in 1900 was just 33 years, compared to 47.6 years for whites.[10] Black children were only about half as likely as white children to be enrolled in school,[11] and the schools they attended were dismally underfunded and overcrowded, which, combined with the legacy of slavery, resulted in a black literacy rate of just 55.5 percent, compared to 93.8 percent for whites.[12] Only about one fifth of African American household heads owned their own homes in 1900, less than half the rate of white homeownership.[13] And while the census did not record labor earnings by race until 1940, in their definitive history of inequality in America, Peter Lindert and Jeffrey Williamson have used other data to offer a reconstructed picture, estimating that blacks earned less than half as much as whites at the beginning of the twentieth century.[14]

The absolute standing of both black and white Americans generally improved in the ensuing 125 years, as indicated in Chapter 2, but this fact tells us little about racial equality. Thus, in attempting to understand how racial equality evolved over the course of the twentieth century, in this chapter we will examine *relative* comparisons of black and white well-being, rather than the absolute standing of blacks. When the relative standing of blacks improved, that implies that blacks were making even more progress than whites, thus narrowing the racial gap; and when the relative standing of blacks failed to improve, that implies that the racial gap was not narrowing, even though in absolute terms they (like whites) might have been better off than before.

Jim Crow, which was the defining experience of life for most African Americans during the first two thirds of the twentieth century, constituted a glaring exception to the many ways in which, during that same period, the nation was moving toward a more expansive American "we." Accordingly, when it comes to trends in racial equality over the course of the twentieth century, a commonly held view is that all was discrimination, exclusion, and inequality until the lightning-bolt changes of the mid-1960s. This could be described as a sort of "hockey stick" story, which, charted against our now familiar inverted U-curve, would look by contrast like a flat line indicating virtually no improvement for six decades, followed by a sharp, dramatic upturn after mid-century.

In many ways the "hockey stick" image is accurate. The persistent exclusion of people of color from the white American mainstream after the abolition of slavery is an indelible blot upon this nation's history. However, the story is more complex than it appears. As we looked closely at a variety of measures spanning the twentieth century, two surprises emerged. First, progress toward equality for black Americans didn't begin in 1965. By many measures, blacks were moving toward parity with whites well before the victories of the Civil Rights revolution, despite the limitations imposed by Jim Crow. And second, *after* the Civil Rights movement, that long-standing trend toward racial equality slowed, stopped, and even reversed. Unlike the "hockey stick" image, these trends embody a too-slow but unmistakable decades-long drive toward equality, followed by a period in which Americans took our collective "foot off the gas," so that progress slowed and even in some cases reversed. [15] Let's examine these long-term trends in racial equality in four key areas: health, education, economics, and voting.[16]

Health

Due to a combination of environmental factors, poverty, discrimination, and a lack of healthcare access affecting nearly all African Americans, there were substantial health gaps between black and white populations at the beginning of the twentieth century: Black Americans were expected to live only 69 percent as long as their white counterparts, black death rates were 1.4 times as high as white death rates, black infants died 1.8 times more frequently than white infants, and black mothers died in childbirth 1.8 times more frequently than white mothers. But all of these gaps narrowed steadily, albeit unevenly, for the first half to two thirds of the century. Figure 6.1, charting the relative life expectancy of blacks versus whites over the twentieth century, is one illustration—relatively continuous progress toward equality between the races was made from 1900 through the late 1950s.[17] During this period white life expectancy rose steadily, of course, as we described in Chapter 2, but black life expectancy rose even more rapidly. To be sure, we must not ignore that throughout the entire period

FIGURE 6.1: **LIFE EXPECTANCY, BLACK-WHITE RATIO, 1900–2017**

Source: National Center for Health Statistics, "Death Rates and Life Expectancy at Birth."

black lives have been shorter, but it is significant—indeed, unexpected—that the racial gap was steadily narrowing from 1900 to 1960.

Though black Americans had made important gains during the first two thirds of the century, thereafter, progress virtually halted. By 1995 the life expectancy ratio (whites living 10 percent longer than blacks) was exactly the same as it had been thirty-five years earlier. Despite modest relative progress in the two decades since then (now whites live on average only 5 percent longer than blacks, partly because of a surprising increase in premature deaths among working class whites), this is a clear "foot off the gas" phenomenon.[18]

Other measures of relative health outcomes between racial groups over the course of the twentieth century echo this pattern. Nationally, the black-white ratio of age-adjusted death rates shows a marked improvement during the first half of the century, followed by steady worsening between 1955 and 2000. The gap in infant mortality between blacks and whites narrowed sharply from 1915 to 1945, widened somewhat from 1945 to 1965, then shrank sharply until 1970, after which progress toward racial parity suddenly halted. Today black infants are more than twice as likely to die within their first year of life as white infants, just as they were in the early 1960s.[19]

Overall, nationwide data for the entire twentieth century show, surprisingly, that the black-white health gap significantly narrowed from 1900 to the late 1960s, during America's broader upswing, but thereafter remained stubbornly stuck. And the timing of this stagnation in progress corresponds remarkably closely to the larger turn from "we" to "I," which we have seen again and again throughout this book. Why and how were blacks narrowing inequality gaps with whites in the pre–civil rights period, and why did that progress slow and even stop afterward? Later in this chapter we shall explore this puzzle and others like it.

Education

Just as with health and health care, at the beginning of the twentieth century African Americans faced enormous disparities in both educational outcomes and access, as compared with white Americans. (Recall that more than 90 percent of African Americans in 1900 lived in the South.) The vast majority of black elementary school students and about half of older black schoolchildren had no access to education whatsoever, and what schools did exist were racially segregated and of far inferior quality to their white counterparts. But by the end of the century, the racial gap on most absolute measures of educational inputs and outcomes had narrowed dramatically, and school segregation, especially in the South, had plummeted. However, just as with health outcomes, the particular shape of the trends toward educational equality over the course of the century reveals some surprises.

The first half of the twentieth century brought significant improvements in the relative racial equality of educational access. School attendance rates provide one example. According to education scholar James D. Anderson, in the South the elementary school attendance gap between blacks and whites was virtually eliminated between 1900 and 1940, as shown in Figure 6.2.[20] To be sure, this schooling was racially segregated

FIGURE 6.2: GROWTH IN SOUTHERN ELEMENTARY SCHOOL ATTENDANCE RATES BY AGE AND RACE, 1900 AND 1940

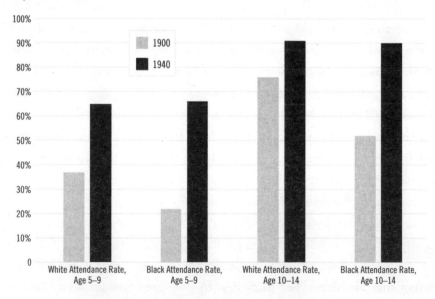

Source: Anderson, *The Education of Blacks in the South*, 151, 182.

and very unequal in quality, as the US Supreme Court would belatedly recognize in *Brown v. Board of Education* in 1954.

Parity in educational access was not similarly achieved in high school attendance, but the racial gap did narrow significantly during that same period—from Southern high school attendance rates of 4 percent for white youth and just 0.39 percent for black youth in 1890 (a ratio of ten to one) to 54 percent for white youth and 18 percent for black youth in 1933 (a ratio of three to one).[21] By 1960 Southern high school attendance rates were at 82 percent for whites, and 69 percent for blacks (a ratio of 1.2 to one).[22] Looking at Southern school attendance rates by race and sex across age groups (from age 5 through age 20) and regardless of school grade, economist Robert A. Margo has found a similar narrowing of the racial attendance gap between 1890 and 1950.[23] And though we did not find comparable data on black-white college attendance ratios, absolute enrollment numbers for black students in the South expanded dramatically over this time period, from 2,168 enrolled in college in 1900 to 29,269 in 1935,[24] to 63,000 in 1952.[25]

Comparable data on school enrollment and attendance by race in Northern states during the first half of the twentieth century is harder to come by. It does appear, however, that absolute black enrollment rose in Northern states as a result of the Great Migration (a phenomenon which we will discuss in detail below), perhaps contributing to a narrowing of attendance gaps nationally. For example, in his case study of black education in Philadelphia—a major destination for black migrants—historian Vincent P. Franklin found that the number of black public schools in that city expanded from nine in 1910 to fifteen in 1937. And between 1910 and 1950, African American enrollment in all public schools in Philadelphia grew by 677 percent.[26]

A slightly different measure of educational equality is educational attainment—not how many schools existed or how many students attended them, but how many individuals obtained degrees. On this measure, reliable national data are more readily available. As with rates of attendance, the fastest and most dramatic progress toward parity between blacks and whites finishing high school was achieved before 1970. In this case, however, progress began somewhat later, as illustrated in Figure 6.3. But after 1970, the relative rate at which blacks were completing college dropped, then flatlined, and never recovered its previous upward trajectory. In fact, today black Americans are completing college at a *lower rate* compared to whites than they were in 1970. The relative rate at which African Americans were finishing high school was less severely stalled, but still markedly slower after the Civil Rights revolution than before—and it still has not achieved equality today.

It is important to keep in mind that as we showed in Chapter 2, overall educational levels (white and black) rose steadily among successive cohorts of young Americans from roughly 1900 to roughly 1965. In this chapter, however, we are focused on racial differences against that backdrop, so we focus on the *relative* standing of blacks compared to whites, such that equality means a ratio of 1.0. Figure 6.3 shows that despite the fact that white educational attainment was rising throughout this period, between

FIGURE 6.3: **RACIAL EQUALITY IN EDUCATIONAL ATTAINMENT, 1920–2018**

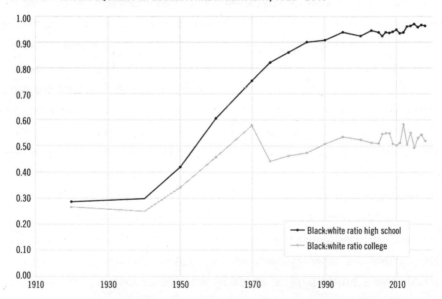

Source: National Center for Education Statistics, Table 104.20; Current Population Reports, Series P-20, various years; Current Population Survey, 1970 through 2018.

1940 and 1970 black educational attainment was rising *even faster*, so the black-white gap was narrowing, as blacks began to catch up with whites. But after 1970 that "catch-up" progress drastically slowed (in the case of high school) and actually ended (in the case of college)—well before racial parity had been achieved.

Of course, *quantity* is not the same as *quality*. Racial disparities in educational quality were stark at the beginning of the century. Indeed, immediately following Reconstruction, measures such as the black-white ratio in per-pupil spending and the black-white ratio in school year length had worsened significantly. However, even those trends began to reverse early in the century—around 1910.[27] According to Lindert and Williamson, by measures of per-pupil spending and teacher-student ratios, educational quality for African Americans slowly improved from 1910 to 1950 within the South.[28] Furthermore, between 1940 and 1954, aggregate Southern spending on black schools increased 288 percent, as compared with only 38 percent for white schools.[29] Teacher salaries in the South similarly converged, with black educators making 85 percent more in 1950 than they had in 1940, closing the black-white teacher earnings ratio by 23 percentage points.[30] Southern black educational facilities remained systematically substandard,[31] but overall, despite Jim Crow, such inequalities were shrinking.

Thus, the quantity and quality of education available to black Americans expanded dramatically in the first half of the century, a surprising fact that corresponds to the larger story of America's turn from "I" to "we." However, the vast majority of schools during the first half of the twentieth century were racially segregated—by law in the South, and often de facto in the North.[32] School segregation has had a particularly detrimental effect on racial equalization not only because of resource disparities, but also because for most of the century white schools generally offered a liberal arts curriculum, whereas black schools usually provided only vocational training, resulting in the tracking of African Americans into inferior jobs, a fact which has lifelong consequences.[33]

Nevertheless, looking at the national trend toward school integration over the course of the twentieth century, change began much earlier than is often believed.[34] School integration seems to have increased from very low levels at the beginning of the twentieth century to higher (but still inadequate) levels until 1960, because of blacks' movement out of the completely segregated South into the somewhat less segregated North. Then, for the next decade, that long, slow increase sharply accelerated, largely because of the effect on the South of the Supreme Court's decision in *Brown v. Board of Education*.

Remarkably, however, even the sharp upward trend toward school integration, which began after *Brown*, leveled off in the early 1970s, after which a modest trend toward *re*-segregation began.[35] Thus, in the same moment that a near century-long trend toward racial convergence on measures of quantity and quality of education halted, the national project of desegregation also stagnated and even began to reverse course. And troubling disparities between majority-white and majority-black schools (in class sizes, per-pupil spending, teacher pay, and curricular tracking) persist today.[36]

Thus, measures of the drive for racial equality in the quality, quantity, and integration of education also show a clear "foot off the gas" pattern, with progress being made in the first two thirds of the century, followed by stagnation beginning in roughly the 1970s—precisely when America began its downward plunge from "we" to "I."

Economic Outcomes

Overall, African American incomes rose relative to white incomes for the first two thirds of the century. Although there is very little literature examining economic outcomes by race in the decades between 1900 and 1940, what data do exist suggest modest progress toward racial parity in income during this period.[37] And most scholars agree that income levels by race converged at the greatest rate between 1940 and 1970.[38] According to economist Thomas N. Maloney, the black-white wage ratio for males jumped from .48 to .61 during the 1940s, an increase of 27 percent, which is remarkable given that it occurred during the Jim Crow period,[39] but which can in large measure be explained by a massive black exodus from the South, which was accelerating during this time.[40]

The most recent scholarship on racial convergence in income equality indicates that the leading cause of the gains black Americans were making during these decades was in fact the Great Convergence, which we discussed in Chapter 2. The very same factors that were creating income equalization across the American economy at this time were also driving equalization between white and black workers, especially as black workers moved to places where they could access better jobs. In fact, far from leaving African Americans out, the Great Convergence disproportionately benefited them (partly because they had so much ground to gain), so that the racial gap in earnings narrowed significantly during America's "we" decades.

Conversely, according to sociologist Robert Manduca, "black-white family income disparities in the United States remain [in 2018] almost exactly the same as what they were in 1968," and "a key and underappreciated driver of the [persistent] racial income gap has been the national trend of rising income inequality."[41] In other words, racial disparities in income narrowed during America's "we" epoch and have stopped narrowing during America's "I" epoch.

Of course, absolute equality was and remains a distant goal. In fact, progress toward income equality between blacks and whites—as we have now seen in many other measures—flatlined or outright regressed after the late 1970s, as Figure 6.4, as well as much other data, suggests.[42] As Robert A. Margo writes, the black-to-white income ratio improved on average 7.7 percentage points per decade between 1940 and 1970. This was by no means a rapid enough convergence, but had this rate of change continued, the income ratio "would have been 0.88 in 2010, instead of its actual value of 0.64."[43] The critical result of widening, rather than further narrowing, of the national income gap during America's "I" decades is that the difference between median black and white earnings today is "as large as it was in 1950."[44]

Furthermore, labor force participation rates among African Americans have continued to decline and incarceration rates among young black men

FIGURE 6.4: BLACK-WHITE INCOME EQUALITY, 1870–2010

Source: Lindert and Williamson, *Unequal Gains* (2016), 190.

have exploded in recent decades, factors which many scholars feel bias the black-white income ratio upward—meaning that the reality of the stagnation since 1970 may be even worse than it appears. After correcting for these factors, many economists have argued that there was essentially *no* relative economic progress for black men between 1970 and 2010—a bleak picture indeed.[45]

One countervailing phenomenon, however, is that gains in professional sector employment for African Americans accelerated in the latter third of the century, thanks to antidiscrimination measures and growing educational mobility, improvements that were concentrated in the South. But the resultant emergence of an upwardly mobile black middle class coincided with the deepening poverty of a downwardly mobile black "underclass," creating significant intra-racial divides between the richest and poorest African Americans. There is great political disagreement about the meaning of this divergence. Nevertheless, even taking into account the growth of the black middle class, black Americans have, on average, experienced flat or downward economic mobility during the last third of the century.[46]

Thus, America's upswing toward greater and greater economic equality was, on average, disproportionately *helpful* for African Americans, and our downturn toward greater and greater economic inequality was, on average, disproportionately *harmful* to them.

Because wealth is highly correlated with income and employment, it may not be surprising that racial equality in homeownership charts a similar trajectory, as shown in Figure 6.5. The first notable increase in relative homeownership rates (shown here as the ratio of black homeownership rates to white homeownership rates) occurred between 1900 and 1910, and is largely attributable to black farmers moving out of tenancy and into farm ownership in the South—a phenomenon that occurred essentially against all odds during the hostile climate of Jim Crow.[47] But this ratio also improved significantly between 1930 and 1970,[48] because as blacks migrated northward (a phenomenon discussed in detail below) they increasingly

FIGURE 6.5: **BLACK-WHITE HOMEOWNERSHIP RATIO, 1900–2017**

Source: 1900–1970, IPUMS; 1973–2017, Current Population Survey. See endnote 6.47.

gained access to affordable homes previously occupied by whites, who, especially after 1940, were migrating to the suburbs in large numbers.[49] Of course, black Americans' access to mortgages and more desirable neighborhoods was limited by redlining and related practices during these decades. But, notably, just as it became illegal for lenders and realtors to discriminate on the basis of race, gains in black homeownership stalled, then declined slowly, finally taking a nosedive in the wake of the 2008 financial crisis. In 2017 black-white inequality in homeownership was as high as it had been in 1950.

Ironically, policies meant to encourage low-income homeownership in the 1970s were in fact exploited by racist practices in the real estate industry to suppress black homeownership, which is one explanation for the stagnation.[50] And, more recently, when subprime lenders went looking for borrowers in the 1990s, they disproportionally targeted black Americans, who refinanced or bought homes under predatory lending conditions. When the bubble burst in 2008, many lost those homes to foreclosure, which is reflected in the recent downturn in homeownership seen in Figure 6.5.[51] In short, the black-white wealth gap remains enormous, since homeownership accounts for much of the wealth of ordinary Americans.[52]

Once again, we see the unexpected pattern of change in black-white ratios of material well-being over the last 125 years: Incomplete, but substantial progress toward racial equality over the half century before 1970, but then a surprising halt to this progress over the subsequent half century.

Voting

At the dawn of the twentieth century, African American political involvement was abysmally low by virtually every measure. In the South, political disenfranchisement was a cornerstone of white supremacy and Jim Crow.[53] Between 1867 and 1908, nearly 620,000 black registered voters were purged from the Southern rolls, leading to a drop in voter registration rates of 84.5 percent.[54] Given that nearly nine in ten black Americans lived in the South as of 1910,[55] this regional pattern of disenfranchisement dominated the national portrait for the first two decades of the century.

But the period from 1920 to 1956 saw a surprising increase in the number of registered black voters in the South as well as a reduction in racialized voting restrictions, which resulted in regional progress toward greater equality of political access between blacks and whites. Scholars attribute these developments to a combination of the NAACP's legal campaigns, the Urban League's black voter registration drives, and the widespread repeal of poll taxes in the face of opposition from poor white Southerners.[56] There was a particular surge in black voter registration in the 1940s, thanks in part to the lowering of the voting age in 1943 and the 1944 Supreme Court ruling in *Smith v. Allwright*, which outlawed white primaries. The number of registered Southern black voters increased more than seven-fold from 1940 to 1956. Although these new voters accounted for only about a quarter of the Southern black population, progress toward equality was on the rise at mid-century.

Race-based disenfranchisement was far less common outside the South, so it is likely that the northward migration of large numbers of blacks after 1915 augmented the trend toward greater political participation already under way in the South. In her case study of political participation in Chicago, for example, political scientist Dianne Pinderhughes has found high levels of voter registration and voter turnout in presidential elections between 1920 and 1940 among black residents, even compared to other native-born and immigrant groups.[57] Turnout in presidential races among registered voters in black wards reached over 70 percent at its peak in 1936.[58] Pinderhughes attributes these high levels of black voter participation to mobilization by African American church networks, to the symbolic importance of political participation for former residents of the Jim Crow South, and to the competitive incentives for politicians amidst the political realignments of the Great Depression.[59] Taken together, the evidence suggests a significant national increase in black voting in the first half of the twentieth century.

Political access and representation of African Americans nationwide at mid-century was still far less than that of whites, with much progress to be made. More rapid improvements would come after 1965. However, progress toward black political participation long before the landmark 1965

Voting Rights Act is often obscured by the magnitude of that historic victory. Yet in a now familiar pattern, after the Voting Rights Act black voter registration in the South virtually flatlined, fluctuating between roughly 55 percent and 65 percent after 1970, as shown in Figure 6.6; in fact, black voter registration in the South in 2018 was slightly lower (65 percent) than in 1970 (66 percent).[60]

FIGURE 6.6: **BLACK SOUTHERN VOTER REGISTRATION RATES, 1940–2018**

Source: Voter Education Project; Current Population Survey. See endnote 6.60.

National voter turnout by race over the course of the century is harder to track, especially before 1948. However, the data indicate that nearly all of the gains toward equality in voter turnout occurred between 1952 and 1964—*before* the Voting Rights Act passed—and that modest gains made between 1964 and 1968 then almost entirely halted for the rest of the century—a shocking fact, entirely consistent with the other "foot off the gas" phenomena we have observed, as well as our now familiar turning point from "we" to "I."

What is striking about these trends in African Americans' progress toward equality in health, education, economic outcomes, and voting is both how similar they look to one another, and how different they look from the "hockey stick" story often assumed in discussions of the history of race in the twentieth century. In actuality, undeniable and often quite significant progress toward equality between black and white Americans was made *before* the 1960s Civil Rights revolution. During the period when much of America was marching toward a stronger sense of "we," black Americans were also moving into that "we" in important ways. [61]

Just what might explain this unexpected pattern, and how much of it was due to efforts by blacks themselves, are important topics to which we will shortly return. But first we need to explore the manifest limitations on black Americans' progress toward racial equality.

THE PERSISTENT REALITY OF EXCLUSION

The picture of progress over the first two thirds of the century we have just seen obscures the ongoing inequality of social and political access between the races. Many of the strides African Americans were making toward parity with whites during that time were taking place in separate and persistently unequal spheres. Equalization is thus an inadequate marker of inclusion, for the "we" America was building toward in that period was still highly racialized.

The unequal status of black Americans was readily apparent in their ongoing lack of political representation, despite their increasing political participation. This is clearly reflected in the number of black members of Congress, which did not rise significantly until after 1965, as Figure 6.7 illustrates—a clear "hockey stick" pattern of change.[62]

Black Americans' exclusion from the mainstream was a concomitant of a widespread culture of white supremacy, as historian Henry Louis Gates, Jr. has documented in vivid detail in his book *Stony the Road: Reconstruction, White Supremacy, and the Rise of Jim Crow* (2019). The most prominent example of this was the rebirth of the KKK in 1915 in response to the film *Birth of a Nation*. Scientific racism, the belief in the biological inferiority of nonwhite people, pervaded the academy and popular culture for decades before and after Reconstruction. Racist depictions of African

FIGURE 6.7: **BLACK AMERICANS IN US CONGRESS, 1883–2019**

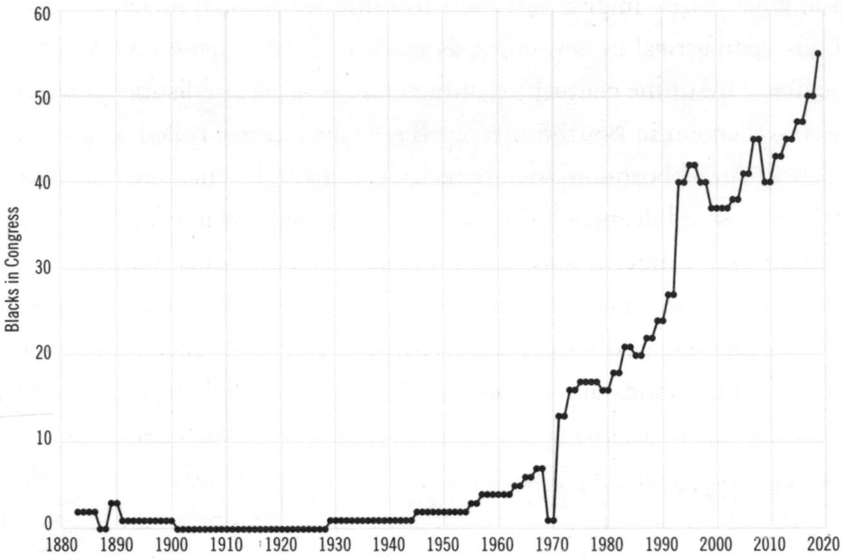

Source: Congressional Research Service. See endnote 6.62.

Americans in entertainment and advertising, narratives of black men as sexual predators, and gruesome postcards celebrating lynchings were common in the South, but also the North, for much of the twentieth century.[63] Only in the 1970s did representation of people of color in the media begin to break with the viciously racist stereotypes of the 1950s and 1960s.[64] And racial intermarriage was feared and decried—as well as outlawed in many states—until the Supreme Court declared such legal restrictions unconstitutional in 1967, unleashing another long-delayed change.

Another important example of racial exclusion is that of job quality and job security. Even as the postwar boom was lifting the employment prospects and pay of all workers, whites were moving into more secure, unionized jobs, while blacks were employed largely in what historian Thomas J. Sugrue has called the "meanest and dirtiest" jobs, thanks to employer discrimination and union local exclusion, among other factors. These jobs were more vulnerable to economic shocks and offered less long-term security, making it more likely that African Americans would suffer in tough economic times, which, as the century wore on, they did.[65]

But by far the most consequential form of racial exclusion has been residential. Black migrants tended to settle in majority-black neighborhoods upon arrival in new cities, as was typical for most ethnic groups in the first third of the century, resulting in the creation of distinct pockets of black settlement in Northern cities. But as the century rolled on and various white neighborhoods lost their distinctive ethnic character, racial segregation instead deepened. African American homeownership was on the rise during this time, as we saw in Figure 6.5. But black families attempting to buy homes in white neighborhoods were met with massive resistance. White residents used a variety of tools to preserve the racial character of their neighborhoods and confine black residents to ghettoized enclaves, including restrictive housing covenants, violence, and such real estate practices as racial steering. When black residents did manage to successfully relocate, block-busting and white flight ensued, causing entire neighborhoods to flip their racial makeup in an incredibly short period of time. This process began the expansion of systematic residential segregation between 1920 and 1940. Indeed, some recent research, using more fine-grained measures of segregation, suggests that in all areas of the country, North and South, urban and rural, segregation doubled nationally from 1880 to 1940.[66]

But residential segregation truly accelerated and consolidated between 1940 and 1970, thanks to overlapping federal policies,[67] discriminatory realtor practices, and organized white resistance to the second wave of the Great Migration—a phenomenon one group of scholars has termed "collective action racism."[68] In the process, financial considerations came to further strengthen white homeowners' opposition to residential integration, even when they otherwise harbored no racial animosity. As one white resident put it, picketing outside the house of the first black family to move onto his block, "He's probably a nice guy, but every time I look at him I see $2,000 drop off the value of my house." By 1970, in the average metropolitan area, an astonishing 80 percent of black Americans would have had to move to a different census tract in order to achieve racially integrated neighborhoods.[69] As a result, at a time when white Americans were increasingly purchasing high-quality homes in suburban rings, black

Americans remained disproportionately confined to older properties in the urban core.[70]

Meanwhile, black males were being subjected to increasingly high rates of incarceration for most of the century, a reality which, like residential segregation, has brought devastating consequences to the African American community. As Figure 6.8 indicates, racial inequality in incarceration rose steadily from 1926 to 2000, especially (but not only) during the War on Drugs.[71] Prison reform in the last two decades has gradually reduced this inequality, though it is still much higher today than it was during the first half of the century. In other words, incarceration is quite unlike the other trends we have examined—racial inequality on this metric rose almost uninterruptedly throughout the twentieth century.

Thus, even as black Americans were moving toward equality of outcomes with their white counterparts in health, education, income, and voting—a surprising fact that is often underemphasized in the story of race in America—they were nonetheless being systematically excluded from equal opportunity, equal access, and the cultural mainstream in many

FIGURE 6.8: **BLACK-WHITE INCARCERATION RATIO, 1926–2017**

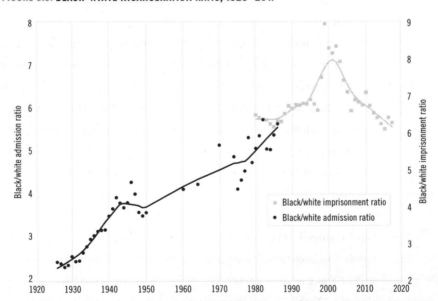

Source: US Department of Justice, Bureau of Justice Statistics. See endnote 6.71. Data LOESS smoothed: .35.

ways. But the surprising *timing* of trends toward equalization brings us to our next question: How did black Americans achieve measurable progress toward equality during a period marked by ongoing—and often severe— segregation and exclusion?

THE GREAT MIGRATION

The first explanation encompasses one of the most dramatic demographic shifts in American history. Beginning around 1915 and continuing until roughly 1970, some six million black Americans—a large fraction of all black Americans—fled the violent oppression of the Jim Crow South to the relative freedom and safety of Northern industrial cities and the West. In 1915, only 10 percent of African Americans lived outside the South, but by 1970, that number had grown to 47 percent.[72] This vast outmigration was often triggered on a local level by white terrorism, but was fueled over time by flooding and crop failures in the South, labor shortages in Northern factories following World War I, significant changes in the South's "King Cotton" economy, and campaigns undertaken by the black press to convince African Americans of the better life that awaited them outside the South. As a result, growth in the African American population in Northern cities was rapid and dramatic. The number of blacks in Cleveland, to take one typical example, was just under 8,500 in 1910. By 1920 it had jumped to almost 35,000, and by 1930 had reached nearly 72,000.[73]

Though the prospects for blacks in Northern cities were in no way equal to those of whites, for those who migrated the difference from the rural South was stark. Consider the experience of Price Davis, an African American who moved from North Carolina to New York City during the Great Migration:

> Everything changed. The whole atmosphere changed. I got there at Washington, D.C., changed buses and a black woman come up and she told me . . . "You can sit wherever you want to sit on the bus." I said, "I can?" She said, "Yeah" . . . I did not move to the front but I did not sit in the back. I moved middle ways. When I got to New York, got a cab and

went to Harlem, I looked around. I saw a black policeman directing traffic. I said, "Oh, my God, this is the Promised Land!"[74]

Of course, in countless ways, the North was no "Promised Land." In many
Northern cities Jim Crow was a culturally sanctioned reality, often enforced with violence. The Chicago race riot of 1919—which lasted six days
and left thirty-eight people dead—is just one example. And recent scholarship has also documented the many ways in which segregation was in fact
also legally codified in the North.[75] And yet, despite persistent racism and
ongoing inequalities, the North was a place where African Americans could
begin to live in relative peace and comfort, access better educational opportunities, own their own businesses, vote, and hold elected office.

The Great Migration was in one sense a double migration, because
blacks were moving not merely from the extremely racist Jim Crow South
to the somewhat less racist North, but also from impoverished and even
primitive rural areas to metropolitan areas with modern amenities. In
other words, as blacks moved from farms to cities in both the South and
the North, they moved not only out of places in which they were treated as
worse than second-class citizens, but also into places that had an infrastructure of public goods. Though still largely segregated, black Americans'
overall access to institutions such as public hospitals and public schools
increased dramatically as they migrated.

And their earning power greatly increased. The labor demands created
first by the war effort and then by the Immigration Act of 1924, which dramatically slowed the inflow of workers from Europe, opened opportunities for black Americans to find employment in Northern industrial cities.
In fact, many Northern factories sent representatives to Southern states
specifically to recruit black laborers. In 1915, a factory wage in the urban
North was typically two to three times what blacks could earn in the rural
South—and the difference was even greater for the few who managed to
enter skilled trades and professions.[76]

Furthermore, as more and more African Americans migrated, they
were also better positioned to benefit from a period of unprecedented national economic growth as well as the dramatic upward wage compression

that took place from 1940 to 1970, phenomena which we touched on above and discussed at length in Chapter 2. The Great Convergence led to disproportionate gains for those who were worst off to start with, especially African Americans.[77] In fact, relative income gains during this period were even more dramatic for black women than black men, the former of whom had actually achieved *greater* median incomes than white women by 1970.[78]

And though largely isolated from the white mainstream, black artists, businesses, schools, theaters, nightclubs, literary societies, churches, and voluntary associations proliferated in migrant destinations, providing a strong sense of identity, community, and support for the millions starting anew in strange cities. In this way, blacks contributed significantly to the overall mushrooming of associational life in America over the first half of the century, which we discussed in Chapter 4.[79]

In short, the narrowing of the black-white inequality gap was one of the *intentions* of the black migrants, and it had the intended effect. However, improvements in the relative well-being of black Americans during the first half of the century came not only because of the more benign environments migrants encountered in the urban North, nor simply as a result of the postwar economic boom. They were also driven by slow but measurable changes in the South. Because of the economic pressure the outmigration exerted on the Southern economy, whites in the South initially resorted to the usual tactics of intimidation and violence to keep vital black labor from fleeing northward, and when this failed, began exploring ways to incentivize blacks to stay by responding to local African American mobilization and making life in the South more livable.[80] To take just one example, there were *no* public four-year black high schools in the entire states of Georgia, Mississippi, South Carolina, Louisiana, or North Carolina in 1916, but by 1926, every major Southern city had established at least one public high school for black students.[81] As Isabel Wilkerson, a master chronicler of the Great Migration, put it, "the former Confederacy was made better in part by the pressures put upon it by those who made the sacrifice to leave it."[82]

The Great Migration has been called the great untold story of racial reorganization in the twentieth century. It is considered "untold" in part because many of the migrants chose not to share stories with their children of their lives under Jim Crow—or their heroic efforts to escape it—preferring instead to make a clean break from the centuries-long trauma that had prompted their move out of the South.[83] But it has also been underemphasized as historians have foregrounded the landmark victories of the 1964 Civil Rights Act, and the subsequent legislation and federal programs that built upon it.[84] And yet, its impact cannot be overstated. Wilkerson describes its significance this way:

> The history of African-Americans is often distilled into two epochs: the 246 years of enslavement ending after the close of the Civil War, and the dramatic era of protest during the civil rights movement. Yet the Civil War-to-civil rights axis tempts us to leap past a century of resistance against subjugation, and to miss the human story of ordinary people, their hopes lifted by Emancipation, dashed at the end of Reconstruction, crushed further by Jim Crow, only to be finally, at long last, revived when they found the courage within themselves to break free.[85]

Indeed, the movement of millions of black Americans, intent upon claiming their place within the American "we," played a critical role in catalyzing a slow but steady trend toward equalization of outcomes between whites and blacks over the first half of the century, as depicted in the foregoing figures. This is largely because, though far from perfect, life was better in almost every way for black Americans outside the South.[86] In the North and West, African Americans were also far more able to engage in mutual aid; organize cooperatives and institutions that brought social, educational, and economic advancement; develop a powerful voice through art, literature, and activism; build political power; and advocate for change[87]—acts of courage and persistence that, perhaps more than anything else, explain the progress outlined above.

In short, the Great Migration, in which millions of black Americans uprooted their lives for a chance to improve their lot, was a powerful force for narrowing racial disparities, even though in the places they resettled the treatment of blacks was still far from equal to whites.

PUBLIC AND PRIVATE INITIATIVES

A second explanation for the surprising strides toward equality made by black Americans during the first half of the century lies in interventions undertaken by the white establishment. Early in the century, philanthropic foundations channeled resources toward institutions serving African Americans by funding black nursing schools, upgrading black hospital facilities, paying the salaries of black doctors hired by public health departments, launching highly effective initiatives for disease eradication, and subsidizing patient care.[88]

And from 1914 to 1932, a school construction program by the Chicago-based Rosenwald Foundation partnered with black communities to support the building of 4,977 schools for rural black youth, expanding elementary education to 883 counties in fifteen Southern states.[89] By the time this program came to a close, as many as 36 percent of Southern black school-aged children might have attended one of these schools. This program alone was very effective at closing the racial gap in years of schooling completed—for cohorts born between 1910 and 1925, roughly 40 percent of the total progress was due to Rosenwald schools. The program has also been shown to have had significant positive effects on literacy and cognitive test scores of rural Southern blacks. [90]

Some historians have argued that such initiatives were undertaken by white elites for selfish reasons, complicating the idea that these efforts were driven by an ethic of inclusion.[91] Nonetheless, their effect was to dramatically improve life expectancy, infant mortality rates, school enrollment rates, and educational attainment for African Americans, thereby narrowing racial disparities in overall well being.

Federal interventions, too, played an important role in driving the steady equalization of outcomes between the races in the first two thirds of the twentieth century. Beginning in the Progressive Era, Northern reformers championed public initiatives that had disproportionately positive effects on the health and well-being of blacks, who were by far the most underserved Americans. Programs to improve water and sewer systems,[92] provide education and treatment for diseases such as tuberculosis,[93] and bring healthcare to rural regions[94] are but a few examples. Furthermore, historians have noted that the turn of the century was a "golden age" for public education generally, with Progressive reformers leading the charge toward expanding funding for schools—a phenomenon which, particularly in the Northern cities to which African Americans were migrating, was at least partially responsible for the increases in attendance rates early in the century.[95]

Historian Edward Beardsley has also shown that World War I was a key turning point in increasing federal intervention in the South, as the military induction process increased awareness of just how large regional health disparities were, and the wartime commitment to federal spending in the name of national defense provided political cover for public health initiatives benefiting Southern blacks. Federal dollars arrived to support the draining of wetlands that harbored malarial mosquitoes, mandatory testing programs for venereal disease, bureaus of child hygiene, and TB sanatoria, all of which disproportionately improved black health outcomes.[96] The New Deal also brought rural health cooperatives that extended care to black agricultural workers, as well as sanitation projects, and Works Progress Administration-funded school inspection and child nutrition programs.[97] Federal investments expanded further as part of mobilization efforts during World War II, including massive subsidies extended to black medical schools and, in 1946, the Hill-Burton program, providing $75 million in grants to states for hospital construction based on need, the greatest of which was concentrated in the rural South.[98]

Some scholars are dubious about the impact of federal programs on the welfare of blacks, because many were systematically denied benefits. The 1935 Social Security Act included matching funds for maternal/infant care and aid for dependent children, for example, but excluded agricultural and domestic workers, categories that accounted for two thirds of all black Americans.[99] And Southern state health officials often made little attempt to reach black recipients even when they did qualify for aid: Edward Beardsley has calculated, for example, that New Deal spending on disabled children in Georgia reached 40 percent of qualified white residents, but only 2 percent of black ones.[100]

THE LONG CIVIL RIGHTS MOVEMENT

All of the factors outlined above—migration into better circumstances, the opening up of industrial jobs, pressure on Southern states to improve conditions, the efforts of private philanthropists and public reformers, the creation of the modern welfare state, and the war efforts and postwar boom—combined to produce slow but steady improvements in the relative well-being of black Americans during the first half of the twentieth century.

And yet, by far the most consequential force for positive change was the organizing and advocacy of blacks themselves. The simultaneous upward climb toward racial parity but persistent exclusion from the mainstream that they experienced during the first two thirds of the century fueled a growing activism among African Americans who resisted oppression and called for true equality and full inclusion. As more and more blacks migrated out of the South, black institutions in the North such as churches, colleges and universities, advocacy groups, and political organizations gained power and influence. A new ability to focus cultural and political narratives, organize community action, partner with white allies, and catalyze activism around racial justice gave birth to the Civil Rights movement—long before the famed lunch counter sit-ins and legal battles of the 1950s or the 1963 March on Washington.

When recounting the history of the Civil Rights movement, it is common to focus on the decade between the 1954 *Brown v. Board* decision and the passage of the Civil Rights Act in 1964 and the Voting Rights Act in 1965. However, recent accounts of racial justice in twentieth-century America have come to emphasize the critical agitation for, and progress toward, racial inclusion during the first half of the century.[101] The term "long Civil Rights movement"[102] has come into use to describe the efforts of two generations of African Americans who not only migrated northward, but fiercely challenged racism throughout the long, dark reign of Jim Crow. Their determined efforts created enough cracks in the exclusionary social, political, and legal structures of this nation to facilitate the dramatic changes of the 1960s—which essentially burst forth as from a dam that could no longer hold.

Though a detailed account of the long Civil Rights movement could fill volumes, it is useful here to highlight a few key actions and victories which took place well before the period we typically associate with watershed change, and which both coincided with and nudged the slow but steady movement toward racial equality discussed above.

The National Association for the Advancement of Colored People (NAACP), one of the most influential organizations in the fight for racial justice, was founded in 1909 under the leadership of W. E. B. Du Bois, who partnered with prominent white Progressives to agitate for change. The new organization advocated boycotts of the 1915 racist film *Birth of a Nation* with mixed success.[103] In 1917, following the brutal St. Louis race riots that left forty-eight dead, the NAACP organized some ten thousand African Americans to march in silence down Fifth Avenue in New York City to protest racial violence.[104] It was the very first mass protest of its kind.[105] In 1919 the NAACP championed the Dyer Anti-Lynching Bill, which was subsequently endorsed by President Warren Harding and passed the House of Representatives by a large majority in 1922, only to be filibustered by Southern Democrats in the Senate.[106] Though legislative victories for racial justice in this era were few, it was a time when civil rights agitators consolidated into a national movement that was gaining influence, exposure, and white allies drawn largely from the ranks of Progressive reformers.

With the stock market crash in 1929 and the subsequent Great Depression, African Americans were the first to lose their jobs and were ultimately hit the hardest. Though still inadequate and (as noted above) unfairly distributed, in absolute terms Roosevelt's New Deal provided more federal economic support to African Americans than at any time since Reconstruction.[107] The New Deal provided jobs for black Americans in the Civilian Conservation Corps, Works Progress Administration, and Public Works Administration, and many of its departmental staffs included advisors for "Negro affairs," none more famous than Mary McLeod Bethune, who ensured that the National Youth Association offered employment and vocational training to blacks.[108] In response to such developments, increasing numbers of African Americans came to see FDR and his New Deal as their best political hope, and helped to ensure Roosevelt's reelection in 1936 by leaving the Republican Party for the Democrats in record numbers.

Indeed, several scholars have argued that the racial realignment of the nation's political parties was more gradual and was more driven by grassroots organizing and shifting ideologies than is often believed. Beginning in the early 1940s, Northern Democrats began to champion civil rights legislation, which some scholars consider to have been a "trial run" for later victories. In historical perspective, this development was the direct political consequence of the Great Migration, as white northern Democrats responded to the growing numbers of black voters among their constituents. Bills proposed in this period tackled both political equality (outlawing the poll tax and federalizing soldier voting) and economic equality (mandating fair employment practices and ending discrimination in education by making school lunch funding conditional on states' compliance with anti-discrimination measures).[109] And as we noted in Chapter 3, support for such initiatives was sometimes even stronger among Republicans than Democrats.

The growth of African American activism and the white establishment's support for equal rights were both accelerated by World War II, which fundamentally changed the tenor of the conversation about black-white equality and racial inclusion in America. As black servicemen came home from fighting for democratic principles, their willingness to submit to undemocratic realities at home frayed, and their motivation grew not only to leave the South in greater numbers, but to join the political effort for change. Accordingly, NAACP membership jumped from 50,000 to 450,000 during World War II,[110] and the 1940s brought yet more agitation both at the grassroots and national levels. One example among many was the action of Navy veteran Otis Pinkert, who earned three promotions in the war but on the train ride home was forced to sit in a segregated car. When he got to his hometown of Tuskegee, Alabama, he expressed his anger by picketing a store that sold primarily to blacks but employed only whites. He succeeded in shutting the store down and getting a black manager installed in exchange for ending the protest.[111] Similar efforts by returned black servicemen to register to vote, cast ballots, or claim even a modicum of respect after their service to the nation and the world were met with threats and violence, primarily in the South.[112] But victories such as Pinkert's were slowly becoming more frequent, and so fueled courage and conviction on the part of black Americans, who continued to knock on the door of the American "we."

The desegregation of the armed forces became another focal point for activists during World War II. In 1941 A. Philip Randolph, founder of the Brotherhood of Sleeping Car Porters, the first predominantly African-American labor union, threatened to bring 100,000 African Americans to march on Washington, following the Roosevelt administration's disappointing decision to continue segregating the military. In order to stave off the demonstration, FDR issued Executive Order 8802, banning racial discrimination in federal agencies and defense industries employed in the war effort.[113]

World War II raised the hopes of both blacks and whites for a turning point in the struggle for racial justice. The scientific racism that had pervaded the academy and provided a basis for discrimination had been discredited in the wake of the Holocaust.[114] Civil rights leaders and the international press highlighted the hypocrisy of fighting for human rights abroad, while tolerating racism at home.[115] Thus foreign policy pressures became a major motivation for postwar and Cold War administrations to act on civil rights. In 1948 Harry Truman had secured election in part by maintaining a strong plank for civil rights in the Democratic Party platform, continuing the process of wooing African Americans to its ranks. He made good on that promise by establishing the President's Committee on Civil Rights, which ultimately produced a 178-page report advocating sweeping reforms. As a result, Truman issued the long-awaited ban on segregation in the military.[116]

In 1944, after studying race relations at the behest of the Carnegie Foundation, Swedish economist Gunnar Myrdal published an unsparing account of white racism entitled *An American Dilemma*. The book's emphatic message was that the time was ripe in America for an inevitable reckoning between the reality of discrimination and the "American Creed" of democratic equality. "Not since Reconstruction has there been more reason to anticipate fundamental changes in American race relations, changes which will involve a development toward American ideals," Myrdal wrote, optimistically.[117] The book was a best-seller and Myrdal's analysis was well received by both African American and white intellectuals. "The near unanimity in support of Myrdal's message," historian James Patterson writes, "reflected the rising expectations among liberals for racial and ethnic progress at the close of the war."[118] This optimism was also fueled by the unprecedented political comity of the postwar era, which we discussed in detail in Chapter 3. The liberal consensus was increasingly responsive to civil rights activists who insisted that the time for more proactive steps to ensure racial equality was at hand.

In addition to an increasing political focus on civil rights, a growing cultural focus on racial tolerance was also taking hold at mid-century. One example was a book cover distributed to students by the Institute for American Democracy, an offshoot of the Anti-Defamation League. It featured a DC Comics image of Superman advising a group of kids against discrimination:

> "And remember, boys and girls, your school—like our country—is made up of Americans of many different races, religions and national origins so . . . if YOU hear of anybody talk against a schoolmate or anyone else because of his religion, race, or national origin—don't wait. Tell him that THAT KIND OF TALK IS UN-AMERICAN!" [119]

In its promotion of Myrdal's ideal of the "American Creed," it is a classic example of the liberal antiracist optimism that characterized mid-century America.

Though exaggerated, that optimism nonetheless met with judicial and legislative successes. Supreme Court decisions in 1950 striking down segregation in state universities opened a pathway for change that led pioneering African American lawyer Thurgood Marshall to look for a case that would raise the issue of segregated elementary and secondary education. In 1954 that case produced the landmark decision in *Brown v. Board of Education*.[120] Of course, the Supreme Court's mandate to desegregate schools with "all deliberate speed" left significant room for foot-dragging, and President Eisenhower wasn't exactly zealous in defending *Brown*. But shortly thereafter, Congress passed the first federal civil rights legislation since Reconstruction—the Civil Rights Act of 1957, which was hailed at the time by *The New York Times* as "incomparably the most significant domestic action of any Congress in this century."[121] The act aimed primarily to ameliorate the fact that, despite significant gains to that point, a meager 20 percent of black Americans were registered to vote. Though it only had a limited impact on black voting,[122] the policy established the United States Commission on Civil Rights, the activities and reports of which contributed to a shift in public opinion, and further opened the way for subsequent legislative victories.

The Reverend Dr. Martin Luther King, Jr., who by the late 1950s had emerged as a powerful civil rights leader, began forcefully and eloquently calling for an end to America's hypocrisy. Though King remains the most venerated leader of the Civil Rights movement, other black leaders, such as Ella Baker and Fannie Lou Hamer, along with the efforts of many African American organizations, including the Student Nonviolent Coordinating Committee (SNCC) and the Southern Christian Leadership Conference (SCLC), brought about unprecedented protests ranging from nonviolent sit-ins at Southern segregated lunch counters starting in 1960; Freedom Rides by integrated teams of students in 1961, which attempted to force the implementation of laws requiring the integration of interstate transit; the 1963 March on Washington, when some 300,000 civil rights advocates assembled to call for immediate federal action; and Freedom Summer of 1964, when young black and white activists joined forces in an effort to register African Americans to vote.

John F. Kennedy became president at the crest of this wave of activism. However, JFK was slow to prioritize civil rights, focusing instead on national security at the height of the Cold War.[123] Nevertheless, he soon began actively identifying the Democratic Party with the Civil Rights movement, moved more blacks into the federal government, and encouraged the Justice Department to take a more active role in prosecuting voting rights cases. Zeroing in on domestic issues and the "dreams" Kennedy was not able to accomplish, his successor, Lyndon Johnson, quickly put civil rights at the center of his agenda. As a Southerner and master coalition-builder, he secured passage of the watershed Civil Rights Act of 1964, the Voting Rights Act of 1965, and the Fair Housing Act of 1968, as well as a raft of Great Society programs aimed at lifting all Americans, especially black Americans, out of poverty. He also secured the appointment of Thurgood Marshall to the Supreme Court in 1967, the Court's first African American justice, another landmark of racial inclusion.

Though victories were painfully slow and met with resistance at every turn, the groundwork for the revolutionary breakthroughs of the 1950s and 1960s had been laid throughout America's ascent from a selfish and fragmented "I" society toward a more altruistic and cohesive "we" society. Of course, it was largely African American activism that pushed for an expansion of America's "we" to include blacks, a fact of which President Johnson was well aware: "The real hero of this struggle is the American Negro," he said in his 1965 speech to Congress. "He has called upon us to make good the promise of America. And who among us can say that we would have made the same progress were it not for his persistent bravery, and his faith in American democracy?"[124] The critical influence of the long Civil Rights movement—and the Great Migration, which fueled it—was to challenge the nation at last to bring about equality and inclusion for all.

CHANGING WHITE ATTITUDES

The Civil Rights revolution was a culmination of a multiplicity of forces lifting African Americans toward equality and inclusion throughout the century. Yet another such force was a marked decline in racist attitudes among whites during the first two thirds of the century.

Scholars of public opinion broadly agree that, concurrent with the Great Migration and the long Civil Rights movement, a substantial decline in explicit or "traditional" white racism started well before mid-century and continued into the 1980s.[125] The earliest public opinion polls beginning in 1942 show that this shift toward support for racial equality was manifested in the realms of schools, transportation, public accommodations, residential choice, black presidential candidates, and interracial marriage, to name a few (see Figure 6.9). Research in the mid-1960s showed that white support for the principle of racial equality was highest among younger, well-educated adults—that is, the *parents* of the boomers. By the 1990s support for the principle of racial equality among white adults had become so nearly universal that pollsters stopped asking these questions, except about racial intermarriage. Responses to that question showed that the long-term trend toward greater support for the principles of racial equality continued into the twenty-first century.

FIGURE 6.9: **WHITE SUPPORT FOR SELECTED PRINCIPLES OF RACIAL EQUALITY, 1942–2011**

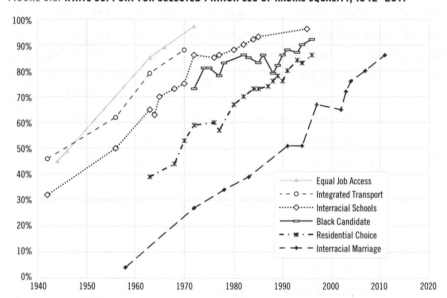

Source: Schuman et al., *Racial Attitudes*; Krysan and Moberg, *Portrait*. See endnote 6.125.

This trend is especially clear in examining cohort data, which tracks generational changes over time. From generations who were raised at the beginning of the twentieth century to generations who were raised at mid-century, there was a steady progression toward less prejudice—with each generation adopting a more liberal and inclusive view of race relations. And since the most prejudiced cohorts of whites had been socialized in the earliest decades of the twentieth century, we can be reasonably sure that the underlying trend was already underway when the curtain lifted on public opinion as measured in contemporary surveys.

Thus, as more prejudiced cohorts died out and less prejudiced cohorts came of age, white adults as a group became far less likely to tell pollsters that their black counterparts were inherently or biologically inferior, and far more likely to say that they supported integrated social spaces and institutions, at least in principle. As with all generational change, this one occurred less by changing minds, and more by changing the generational composition of the adult population.

This massive change in white attitudes on the principles of racial equality was significant in the sweep of history, and it was an important part of the backdrop to both the Civil Rights movement and America's upswing. On the other hand, as the Civil Rights revolution moved forward, issues of implementation of those principles by government policy, such as affirmative action, came to the fore, and on those issues white resistance was both more substantial and more resistant to change, a fact to which we will return below. And even progress in white support for the *principles* of racial equality slackened as the twentieth century ended, partly because the engine of cohort replacement generated less aggregate progress after the pre–World War II generations had passed from the scene.

In other words, the intergenerational shifts in attitudes slowed after the 1960s: The parents of the Boomers were much more liberal on questions of race than their own parents had been, but the Boomers were not so much more liberal than their parents, and the difference between the Boomers and their children was even less than the difference between the Boomers and their parents. The intergenerational motor of change in white racial attitudes was slowing and, with a lag, that slowing showed up in a declining rate of change among whites as a whole.

Thus, most of the fading of traditional white racism throughout the twentieth century occurred prior to the 1970s, lending credence to the idea that racist attitudes were liberalizing even as America's "we" was expanding. Indeed, a 1964 Gallup poll showed that Americans favored the Civil Rights Act by a nearly two-to-one margin (58 percent to 31 percent), and in April 1965, fully 76 percent expressed support for the forthcoming Voting Rights Act.[126] This gradual embrace of principles of integration and inclusion—decades in the making and almost certainly influenced by both the Great Migration and the activities of the long Civil Rights movement—was an important factor in Johnson's ability to secure the breakthrough legislation that ended de jure segregation.

At a critical juncture in his quest to secure the passage of the Voting Rights Act, President Johnson gave a speech to Congress in which he anticipated the difficult road ahead in fully securing racial equality and inclusion in America. "Even if we pass this bill the battle will not be over," he warned. But "we shall overcome," Johnson concluded, emphatically embracing a popular anthem of civil rights demonstrators. In so doing he had, both rhetorically and legislatively, folded the black "we" into the American "we" as never before—leaning into the liberalizing attitudes of white Americans, and adding his hope to Martin Luther King, Jr.'s "dream" that the strength of this widening "we" would hold.[127]

WHITE BACKLASH

Substantial progress toward white support for black equality was made in the first half of the twentieth century, progress visible both in contemporary surveys and in generational analysis. When push came to shove, however, many white Americans were reluctant to live up to those principles. But as La Rochefoucauld has said, "Hypocrisy is the tribute that vice pays to virtue." It would be wrong to dismiss the massive change in white acceptance of the principle of racial equality over the course of the full twentieth century, but it would also be wrong to assume that that conversion was translated directly into practice.

Tragically, just as the Civil Rights movement began to see major success, and especially as the government undertook affirmative actions to bring about integration, the fragile national consensus that had enabled that change began to erode. While equality and inclusion sounded good in principle, white Americans quickly began to voice concerns about the pace of change. Although clear majorities supported the 1964 Civil Rights

Act, a national poll conducted shortly after its passage showed 68 percent of Americans wanting moderation in its enforcement. In fact, many felt that the Johnson administration was moving too fast in *implementing* integration. Remarkably, the proportion of survey respondents expressing this view jumped from 34 percent in March of 1965 to 45 percent in May, as the 1965 Voting Rights Act moved through Congress.[128]

Government enforcement of the new legislation was also increasingly met with organized resistance and violent backlash on the part of disaffected whites. Sociologists Doug McAdam and Karina Kloos call this the "white resistance movement," and argue that it developed first in the South in the early 1960s, then spread to the rest of the country in the mid- to late 1960s, "in opposition to the African American freedom struggle in both its traditional civil rights and increasingly threatening 'black power' incarnations."[129]

This "white resistance" was virulent, and often violent. Nineteen-sixty-five saw "Bloody Sunday," when state troopers attacked, whipped, clubbed, and tear gassed demonstrators attempting to march from Selma to Montgomery, Alabama. Then, in 1968, King, who had led African Americans to unprecedented victories by calling for love, nonviolence, and mutual understanding, was silenced by a bullet. MLK joined Medgar Evers, Jimmie Lee Jackson, and scores of others killed in the 1950s and 1960s in response to their nonviolent agitation for racial justice.[130] The nation experienced an intense outpouring of grief, anger, and yet more violence as riots broke out in more than 130 cities across the country.[131]

The backlash was not confined to the South, nor merely a phenomenon of mob violence—it quickly took on serious implications for political candidates as well. According to McAdams and Kloos, by the mid-1960s "the degree of racial polarization in the country had grown to such an extent that for a candidate to openly court the black vote was to invite significant defections among his or her white constituents," who increasingly saw Great Society programs through a racial lens.[132]

The Kerner Commission, appointed by President Johnson in July 1967 following riots in Detroit and Newark, reported in February 1968 that the riots were indisputably the result of African Americans' justified outrage at rampant racism, police brutality, and inescapable poverty. But Johnson rejected the commission's recommendations of sweeping reforms to end the ghettoization of African Americans and increase federal investments in poverty reduction, suggesting that his fine-tuned political sensitivity had detected a sea change in white attitudes in the seven months after he created the commission.[133]

Indeed, in 1968, just months after Dr. King was killed, Alabama governor George Wallace (who just three years earlier had presided over Bloody Sunday) ran for president and captured 13.5 percent of the popular vote. Nearly 10 million Americans across regional lines had voted to elect an unrepentant segregationist to the highest office in the land,[134] casting a pall over all the victories that had marked the first two thirds of the twentieth century and exposing the fact that, for all that had been achieved, Americans' commitment to extending the full rights and privileges of citizenship to all was still gravely compromised.

Even though Wallace had siphoned off a significant percentage of Republican voters, Richard Nixon's shrewd exploitation of what McAdam and Kloos call "the politics of racial reaction" made possible his 1968 presidential victory. His "much-ballyhooed 'southern strategy,'" they write, "is more accurately seen as a reflection of the emerging dynamic than a bold new direction on his part." They go on to argue that Wallace's surprising success was "nothing short of a revelation to political strategists in both parties," who thenceforth understood that grasping the critical balance of power meant appealing to a growing white backlash. Accordingly, President Nixon began to shift his rhetoric to a racially conservative stance and appointed conservative judges who began to roll back civil rights victories. He thereby successfully won over Wallace's supporters, capturing every Southern state and winning a landslide reelection in 1972. As we noted in Chapter 3, this was the key turning point in the U-curve of party polarization.[135]

As the 1970s wore on, politicians increasingly understood that while Americans could abide the slow, steady, and separate progress of black Americans, when progress demanded a reorganization of power structures, reallocation of resources, reformation of cultural norms, and genuine integration, backlash would ensue. This was nowhere more evident than in controversies over government-mandated integration of schools by bus-ing, which met intense white resistance. But backlash was also manifest as whites fled to the suburbs to avoid the neighborhood integration encour-aged by the 1968 Fair Housing Act.

Indeed, when examining attitudes toward policies meant to establish racial equality (often called "racial policies" for short), scholars have found not only that white respondents remain widely opposed, but also that their support has been generally trending downward since 1970. White support for policies that ban discrimination and legal segregation in the realms of schools, public accommodations, and employment has slipped since the early 1970s.[136] Meanwhile, white support for affirmative action pro-grams that provide compensatory government assistance or preferential treatment to black Americans has remained very low since 1970, whether respondents are asked about direct spending, government aid, school ad-missions, or employment practices.[137]

Similarly, in the post–civil rights era, although white respondents in-dicated increasing levels of support for integration when *small* numbers of black individuals were involved (that is, when there were only a "few" black children in an integrated school or only a single black family next door), they were far less supportive when large proportions of black individuals were involved, suggesting limits to their commitment to racial tolerance.[138]

When asked about the causes of racial inequality, very few white re-spondents at the end of the century were still citing the "low ability" of black Americans. Yet their most common alternative explanation was nei-ther racial discrimination nor low opportunity—responses that had been in decline during the last decades of the century—but "low motivation," a perspective that seems to simply transmute racist attitudes from innate to non-innate grounds.[139] And though measures of traditional white racism generally show century-long generational declines, cohort analysis shows a *slowing* of this process in recent decades.

Thus, despite the very real trend toward liberalizing attitudes about racial inclusion during the first two thirds of the century, this progress was very clearly followed by a significant white backlash against the measures required to make inclusion a reality.

AMERICA TAKES ITS FOOT OFF THE GAS

Nevertheless, in the wake of watershed judicial and legislative victories between 1963 and 1966, African Americans moved more rapidly toward social, legal, and political inclusion than ever before. This was particularly true in the realms of political representation, racial intermarriage, the integration of public spaces and institutions and the media, and the entry of black Americans into professional schools and upper-middle-class occupations.

And, as we discussed above, though blacks had not achieved equality, by the mid-1960s their incomplete advance toward parity with whites in health, educational attainment, income, homeownership, and even voting had already been under way for decades. We might reasonably have expected, therefore, that as exclusionary laws changed, and more and more barriers to full inclusion came down, preexisting trends toward equalization between the races would continue or even accelerate. However, the disheartening reality of the last third of the twentieth century was a marked *deceleration* of progress, and in some cases even a reversal.

During the closing decades of the twentieth century:

- Gains in relative life expectancy for black Americans stagnated, beginning to improve again only at the start of the twenty-first century.[140]
- The closing of the black-white gap in infant mortality rates plateaued, and in recent years the infant mortality rate for black Americans has increased.[141]
- Black/white ratios in high school and college degree attainment showed little or no improvement.
- Progress toward income equality between the races reversed, and in the aggregate the black-white income gap widened significantly.[142]
- Relative rates of black homeownership plateaued and even declined.
- Schools began to resegregate.[143]
- The trend toward generational liberalization of white attitudes slowed.

In measure after measure, the *rate* of positive change was actually *faster* in the decades preceding the Civil Rights revolution than in the decades that followed. And in many cases, progress then stopped or reversed.

In the words of U.W. Clemon, an African American lawyer who won a precedent-setting Alabama school desegregation case over forty years ago—and has recently taken up a remarkably similar legal battle in the very same county—"I never envisioned that I would be fighting in 2017 essentially the same battle that I thought I won in 1971."[144]

One important explanation for why America took its "foot off the gas" instead of continuing to press for equality, integration, and a more inclusive "we" is simply that white Americans vocally—and often violently—opposed the measures required to do so. Meanwhile, many black Americans, too, began to lose faith in the promises of the liberal establishment, and in the project of integration, which seemed excruciatingly slow in coming. In 1978 the *New York Times* reported survey data indicating that even though most black Americans recognized in general the liberalizing attitudes of their white neighbors, 44 percent felt that whites didn't "care one way or another" about helping them get a "better break."[145]

Thus, the cultural shift from "we" to "I" in the mid-1960s was intimately bound up with the white backlash to the Civil Rights revolution, and the shift from Jim Crow racism to a new kind of white racism, sometimes called "laissez-faire racism." In 1997 Lawrence Bobo and his colleagues argued that "Support for segregation, revulsion at interracial marriage, and belief in the inherent inferiority of blacks were the ideological cornerstones of the Jim Crow era. Collective racial resentments are among the centerpieces of the new laissez-faire racism era."[146] And Donald Kinder and Howard Schuman observed in 2004, citing Mary Jackman, "whites come to champion the idea of individualism . . . because it provides them with a principled and apparently neutral justification for opposing policies that favor black Americans."[147]

The broad national shift from "we" to "I" in economics, politics, society, and culture that we have documented in the previous four chapters clearly harmed blacks as much as whites, and perhaps more. An individualistic

America is not more hospitable to racial minorities than a more communitarian America, and indeed sometimes less.

RACE AND THE I-WE-I CURVE

One possible interpretation of America's broader climb from "I" to "we" during the first two thirds of the twentieth century is that, because it coincided with the stark racism and exclusion of Jim Crow, the "we" America was building toward came at the expense of African Americans. Some might argue that it was, quite simply, a white male "we" under construction in this period—one that had no room for anyone else, and whose strength was ultimately derived from its exclusivity.

However, this view fails to take into account the ways in which blacks were moving toward equality with whites during that same period, as well as the slow but significant victories of the long Civil Rights movement, which prevailed upon the white establishment to widen the "we" in important (though ultimately insufficient) ways across many decades. As one writer reflecting upon race relations in America put it, these changes were "at once not enough of a difference and all the difference in the world."[148] By the late 1960s the work of widening was not nearly complete, but America had come closer to an inclusive "we" than ever before in its history.

Indeed, the fact that landmark civil rights legislation, which would permanently alter legal race relations in America, passed at the very peak of the I-we-I curve suggests that an expanding sense of "we"—which we have argued was taking hold in many ways in the run-up to the 1960s—was in fact a prerequisite for the dismantling of "the color line." Without what historian Bruce Schulman calls the "expansive, universalist vision" America had been building toward in the preceding decades,[149] it is hard to imagine that such watershed change—so long and so violently resisted—would have been possible.

Furthermore, the "foot off the gas" phenomenon we have noted—in which progress toward many measures of racial equality was in fact faster before roughly 1970 and then slowed, stalled, and reversed thereafter—largely coincides with the nation's larger shift away from a widening "we"

and back toward a narrowing "I." Long-delayed moves toward racial inclusion had raised hopes for further improvements, but those hopes went unrealized as the nation shifted toward a less egalitarian ideal. Thus, the idea
that a supposed white male "we" had to be dismantled in order to pave the
way for racial progress is unsupported by the data, when viewed from the
perspective of the full century. For as that "we" came apart, racial progress
in many important realms came to a halt.

Of course, the very real white backlash against black liberation is an
important part of the story of how and why America turned from "we"
back to "I." In fact, it is certainly possible that America's larger turn toward "I" was, in important respects, a response to the supreme challenge
of sustaining a more diverse, multiracial "we" against a backdrop of deep,
historically embedded, and as yet unresolved racism. For example, economist Charles Ballard argues that a "protracted backlash against the civil
rights movement" has been crucial in producing the more general anti-
egalitarian surge over the past fifty years.[150] And sociologists Doug Mc-
Adam and Karina Kloos make a similar claim with regard to the effect
of racial resentment on the larger turn away from political liberalism and
big government.[151] Furthermore, historian Bruce Schulman argues that the
embrace of identity politics and culture in the 1970s, which we discussed
in the preceding chapter, fueled the rise of a competitive ethos and the
abandonment of a broader cooperative ethic in the public square. The result, he believes, was a fractured notion of citizenship—based less on broad
commonality and more on claiming rights and privileges associated with a
narrowed sense of group identity.[152]

If rising inequality, declining social capital, paralyzing political polarization, surging cultural narcissism, and a fractured notion of the common
good (the defining elements of America's broader turn toward "I") had
somehow been the necessary price to pay for finally achieving black-white
equality, some might say it was worth it. But the fact is that this equality
has yet to be realized, despite the shift from "we" to "I." And that shift has
harmed African Americans just as much—if not more—than everyone else.
Furthermore, much of the twentieth century's progress toward equality
took place *not* amidst America's fracturing "I" moment, but rather during

its long, earlier move toward an imperfect but nonetheless more expansive "we."

In 1945, forty-two years after W. E. B. Du Bois first described the "color-line" as the defining problem of the twentieth century, African American sociologists St. Clair Drake and Horace R. Cayton published *Black Metropolis*, a groundbreaking study of the contradictions and complexities of life on Chicago's South Side in the throes of the Great Migration. They painted a vivid and often damning portrait of life in a starkly segregated corner of America—but one that was nonetheless filled with people pursuing, and in ways never previously possible, participating in, the American Dream. Though exclusion from mainstream America still defined the black experience at mid-century, great changes were well under way. "The color-line is not static," the authors concluded. "It bends and buckles and sometimes breaks."[153]

And so one lesson of the complex history of race in twentieth-century America is perhaps simply this: "We" can be defined in more inclusive or exclusive terms, and that inclusiveness can gradually change over time. But a selfish, fragmented "I" society is not a favorable environment for achieving racial equality. Furthermore, any attempt to create an American "we" that is not fully inclusive, fully egalitarian, or genuinely accommodating of difference will contain the seeds of its own undoing. Finding new and ever-more inclusive ways to achieve Martin Luther King, Jr.'s unrealized vision of the "beloved community"—a true multiracial and multicultural "we"—is as urgent as ever, and will play a critical role in determining whether America is ultimately able to reverse its downward drift and move forward into another upswing.

7

GENDER AND THE AMERICAN "WE"

In the foregoing chapter we considered the question of how the experience of African Americans did or did not map onto our nation's twentieth-century upswing, asking the critical question of whether the evidence suggests that America's "we" decades came at the expense of people of color. In this chapter we turn that same question to the experience of women. How does looking at the century through the lens of gender confirm, contradict, or complicate the story of America's I-we-I century?

As we saw in our examination of African Americans, writing in the aggregate about any subgroup within our diverse nation is a perilous endeavor, because it inevitably obscures important geographic, economic, cultural, and idiosyncratic differences of experience. This is especially true when the group we are considering is "women," who represent roughly half the population. Furthermore, in defining such a broad group upon which to train our interest, we also must acknowledge the fact that this group contains within it every other marginalized group, introducing the issue of intersectionality, and the possibility that layered forms of discrimination may produce experiences and outcomes not fully captured by data that utilize a single form of categorization.[1] Thus, reminding the reader that this study is an exercise in macrohistory, and thereby inevitably involves the simplification of complex stories, we offer a broad-strokes account of how the remarkably robust phenomenon of our now familiar inverted U-curves was reflected and/or refracted by gender.[2]

AMERICAN WOMEN AT THE DAWN OF THE TWENTIETH CENTURY

Though women have been calling for equality and inclusion since the creation of the American republic,[3] the founding of the American women's movement is widely considered to have taken place at Seneca Falls in 1848. At what became the first national gathering addressing women's rights, almost three hundred people convened at a church in upstate New York to discuss "the condition and rights of women," and passed resolutions calling for equal rights in twelve areas, including ownership of property, education, access to employment, the ability to participate in the public sphere, and—most controversial of all—the right to vote.[4] Thus, Seneca Falls launched what has been called in retrospect the "first wave" of the American women's movement.[5]

According to historian Christine Stansell, by 1900 "many of the demands broached at Seneca Falls had been tentatively won: college education, access to the professions, eased restrictions in property rights, [and] child custody."[6] Of course, the benefits of these changes accrued primarily to the most privileged women and did nothing to address ongoing racial and ethnic discrimination. Furthermore, at this time women were widely expected to fulfill narrowly defined roles as wives and mothers, and marriage and employment were largely considered mutually exclusive. Still, opting out of marriage during the opening decades of the twentieth century became increasingly attractive for middle-class, educated "New Women," who had a desire to put their education to use outside the home and eagerly took advantage of emerging opportunities to do so.

Overall, however, only about 20 percent of women participated in the formal labor force as the century opened.[7] The majority of these working women were single, poorly educated, and from low-income households, and thus seeking wage labor out of necessity.[8] Their experience diverged markedly from their more privileged counterparts, and they often faced extremely adverse working conditions, as exemplified by the devastating fire at the New York City Triangle Shirtwaist Factory in 1911, which took the lives of 146 people, most of them immigrant women and girls. The fight for better pay and conditions for working-class women was thus an important early component of women's activism.

But tragedies such as the Triangle fire also galvanized a new generation of middle-class female reformers, who began to argue that as more and more women entered the industrial economy, issues of labor, poverty, and class should play a crucial role in women's emancipation. And many female activists, inspired by the communitarian ideals of the Progressive movement, began to recast the long and still ongoing fight for women's suffrage as something that could not be separated from the larger goals of creating a wider American "we."[9]

However, this Progressive vision that many female reformers began to champion, as well as the rights-based narratives being put forward by their more feminist sisters, was nonetheless highly racialized. The racism that came to characterize the early-century women's movement was especially striking, given that many early feminists had initially found common cause with enslaved African Americans, and had found their voice as passionate participants in the abolitionist movement that preceded the Civil War. But in 1870 the Fifteenth Amendment, which legally gave the vote to black males, had been ratified, and despite the fact that granting the vote to women had been demanded and vigorously debated alongside the issue of black male suffrage, "sex" was conspicuously absent from the protected categories of the amendment. This fact incensed some white suffragists and had the effect of driving a wedge between the movements for racial justice and gender equality, and even caused a rift among suffragists themselves.[10] Thus, the early-twentieth-century women's movement was diverse and multifaceted, encompassing many different subgroups, whose activism and agendas converged and diverged variously over time.

Yet another example of this reality is the younger, more spirited generation of feminists who began to fill the ranks of the women's suffrage movement at the turn of the twentieth century, and who were not afraid to employ more controversial and confrontational tactics to advance their cause. They helped push the seventy-two-year struggle to success, and the Nineteenth Amendment, which granted the vote to women, was finally ratified in 1920.[11] This watershed victory, along with progressive child labor legislation, protective laws for and increasing unionization of female workers, the opening of new opportunities for education and careers, and slowly changing cultural ideas about sexuality and womanhood, meant that many American women felt a new optimism about the future of their gender. "The twentieth century was expected to bring, if not utopia, then still something grand and shining between men and women," writes Stansell. "Here was a feminism that promised to propel women into a dazzling future with enthusiastic men at their side."[12]

While the goal of full and harmonious gender equality is still an elusive one, over the ensuing century women have nonetheless achieved substantial gains—women's roles in society have been vastly recast and reimagined, rights and opportunities have been greatly expanded, female labor force participation has tripled, many battles for safer and more equitable working conditions have been won, job categories previously closed to women have opened, and women have even surpassed men in educational attainment and voting rates. While these gains were highly uneven across different groups of women, economic historian Claudia Goldin has referred to these and other century-long trends as "a grand gender convergence."[13]

So how, exactly, did this progress unfold? Popular historical narratives about the forward march of gender equality in the twentieth century generally take one of two forms:

- A "first wave" of feminist activism achieved significant gains, by far the greatest of which was the right to vote. But according to this narrative, these gains were followed by a decades-long period of stagnation and even retrenchment in women's activism and thus gender equality, necessitating a "second wave" of mobilization, which began in the 1960s. As this story goes, the "feminist revolution" of the 1960s and 1970s is what finally made possible the widespread progress we see today. A related but slightly different version of this narrative downplays the achievements of early-twentieth-century women's activism, arguing that it made very little difference for most women's lives, and that almost *all* of the appreciable progress toward equality and inclusion for women can be attributed to the 1960s women's movement.

- A second narrative (which we find more persuasive) suggests that the story of women's march toward equality and inclusion is in fact more complex than the oft-repeated first narrative might suggest. While some indicators quite clearly fit a story of long-delayed progress, many other measures indicate that women were in fact making *steady* progress toward equality and inclusion throughout the century—which progress neither stagnated between two waves of activism nor was held at bay until the 1960s. And, despite the fact that gender parity has yet to be achieved on many dimensions, there has been little appreciable slowing down of progress in recent decades, unlike the phenomenon that we saw over and over again in the case of race. On the contrary, once women began to move toward educational, economic, and political equality (whether early in the century or much later), that progress largely continued unabated.[14]

Thus, a closer look at several different empirical measures of gender parity across the full century will not reveal one simple story, but may correct some common misconceptions about the rate and timing of women's remarkable but still incomplete march toward full and equal participation in the American "we."

WOMEN IN EDUCATION

As we discussed in Chapter 2, in the early 1900s the availability of free high school education vastly expanded nationwide, as reflected in the precipitous increase in overall graduation rates depicted in Figure 7.1.[15] Both attendance and graduation rates were higher for girls than boys, particularly in the early decades of the century. In 1900, fully 60 percent of all high school graduates were female, and according to economic historians Susan B. Carter and Mark Prus, when it comes to attendance,

"girls outnumbered boys by over four to three among whites and over
three to two among blacks through the second decade of the twentieth
century."[16]

The fact that many young men were attracted to the burgeoning industrial sector at a young age often meant they dropped out of school,
contributing to the early-century female edge. But another reason that so
many girls attended secondary school in the opening decades of the twentieth century was that the rapidly expanding clerical sector offered clean,
respectable, and less physically demanding jobs to young women who had
a secondary education. In fact, by the 1930s, most clerical jobs required a
high school diploma, creating a clear economic incentive for completion of
secondary school. Thus, structural changes to the economy slowly created
a greater return on education, particularly for white females.[17]

When the Depression forced large numbers of young men out of
work, however, many of them returned to school, and the size of the female lead began to shrink. The gap spiked during World War II, while

FIGURE 7.1: **TOTAL HIGH SCHOOL GRADUATION RATE AND GENDER BALANCE, 1870–2018**

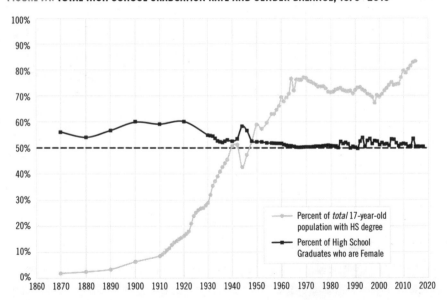

Source: *Historical Statistics of the United States*; National Center for Educational Statistics.

young men went off to war, but then returned to its long-run equilibrium. As Figure 7.1 demonstrates, for the remainder of the century, slightly more than half of all high school graduates were women—a fact which still holds true today. Notably, this stability in the gender ratio among high school graduates had persisted through a century of uneven, but remarkable growth in the rate of high school graduation. Slightly more than half of high school graduates were women in the 1880s and 1890s, when only 5 percent of American youth graduated from high school, and slightly more than half of high school graduates today are women, when nearly 90 percent of young people graduate from high school. Gender equity in high school education has been a constant for a century and a half.

When it comes to college education, however, the story is quite different, as illustrated in Figure 7.2. Men started the twentieth century with a marked advantage over women, whose opportunities to attend college were new and very limited. In 1900, less than 20 percent of college

FIGURE 7.2: GENDER BALANCE AMONG NEW COLLEGE GRADUATES, 1870–2017

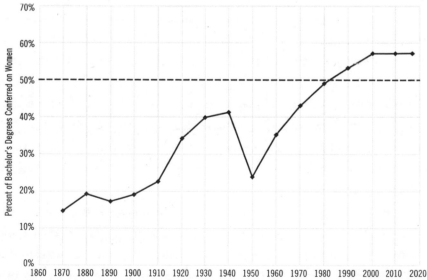

Source: U.S. Census; Current Population Survey; National Center for Education Statistics.

graduates were women, but that fraction climbed throughout the century. As a result, the gender gap in college graduation generally narrowed over the century—with the notable exception of the 1950s, which saw a temporary increase in the gender gap. At this time college-going among men increased rapidly, boosted by the GI Bill, while many women forewent or delayed college in order to start families (the Baby Boom).[18] In addition, some scholars have also posited that the GI Bill had the effect of privileging male enrollment in higher education, and have documented cases in which spots for women were temporarily restricted in order to make room for war veterans.[19] Thus, women as a proportion of undergraduate students declined somewhat in the 1950s, creating a temporary lapse in progress toward gender parity in higher education. But this setback turned out to be temporary and by the 1980s women had caught up to men in college graduation rates, and then began to surpass them. Females are now substantially more likely to obtain a bachelor's degree than males, a fact which holds across all racial and ethnic groups with the exception of Asian Americans.[20] Gender equality was more delayed in postgraduate education, but there too progress became rapid in the second half of the twentieth century, as shown in Figure 7.3.

In sum, starting in the late nineteenth century from a position far behind men in both undergraduate and graduate education, women made substantial progress toward gender equality from about 1900 to about 1930/1940. In mid-century this progress was disrupted by the Second World War and its aftermath, but then progress toward full gender equality resumed and accelerated around 1950 for bachelor's and master's degrees and around 1970 for doctoral degrees, and by 2017 fully 57 percent of bachelor's degrees, 59 percent of master's degrees, and 53 percent of PhDs were awarded to women.[21]

The very same pattern applies to professional degrees in fields like law and medicine—long delay in progress toward equality, followed by rapid progress in the last three decades of the twentieth century. To explain this dramatic uptick after 1970, Claudia Goldin identifies several factors that encouraged women to seek higher education, especially career-oriented

FIGURE 7.3: GENDER BALANCE IN GRADUATE DEGREES, 1870–2017

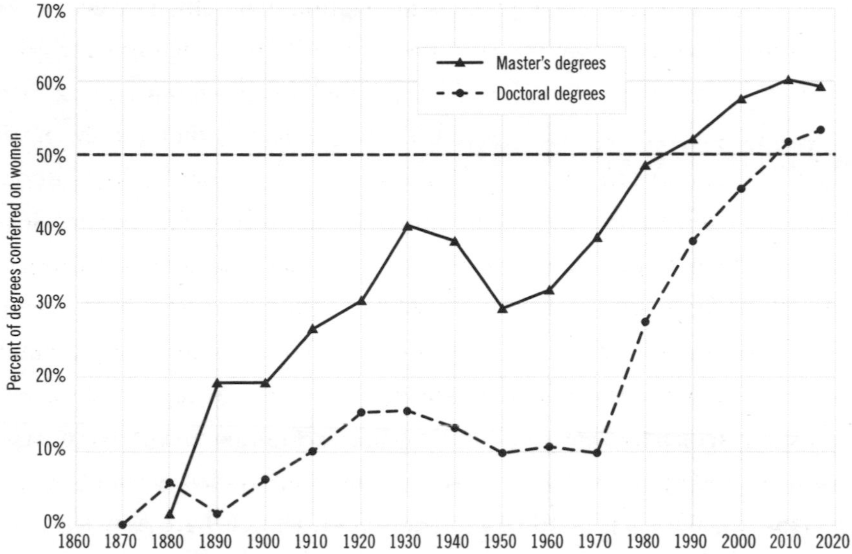

Source: U.S. Census; Current Population Survey; National Center for Education Statistics.

education: the influence of post-Sixties feminism in encouraging an independent mind-set, an increase in divorce rates and women's resultant need to support their families economically, the advent of the birth control pill, which allowed delayed childbearing, and young women seeing older counterparts participating in the workforce in greater numbers and with greater longevity. "As a result," Goldin concludes,

> [young women] increased their investments in formal schooling, majored in career-oriented subjects, and continued on to professional and graduate schools in far greater numbers. They had longer horizons than did previous generations and an altered identity that placed career ahead, or on equal footing, with marriage.[22]

In the case of educational equity over the course of the twentieth century, therefore, we see a clear example of long-delayed progress in regard to advanced degrees. But even more striking were women's essentially steady,

century-long gains in both secondary education and college attainment—
trends which laid important groundwork for late-century changes in economic equality.[23]

THE ECONOMICS OF GENDER EQUALITY

Was women's progress toward educational parity—and even the surpassing
of men in high school, college, and postgraduate attainment—reflected in
economic outcomes?

One of the most common images that springs to mind when we look
back on twentieth-century feminism is Betty Friedan's portrait of unhappy, unfulfilled housewives—who, by her account, were still largely im-
prisoned by both motherhood and domestic servitude when she published
The Feminine Mystique in 1963. However, powerful as this image has been
in shaping twentieth-century gender narratives, in fact, women had been
on a steady march into the workplace beginning as early as 1860, as

FIGURE 7.4: FEMALE LABOR FORCE PARTICIPATION RATE, 1860–2016

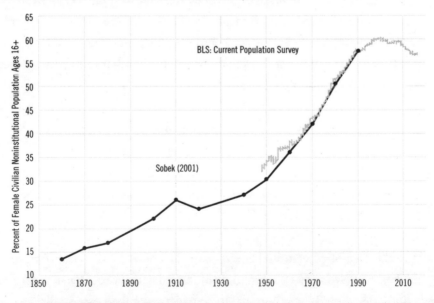

Source: Matthew Sobek, "New Statistics on the U.S. Labor Force, 1850–1990," *Historical
Methods* 34 (2001): 71–87; Current Population Survey. Data for 1860 exclude slaves.

charted in Figure 7.4.[24] We see that women's labor force participation actually grew steadily from 1920 to 1990 (with some acceleration after 1950), progressively closing the gender gap in employment over the span of the entire century. Interestingly, this measure shows no sign of any effect of the 1965–1975 women's movement on overall female labor force participation.[25]

Over the course of the entire century, more and more women worked outside the home, and women became an ever-larger percentage of the wage labor force, ultimately representing roughly 47 percent of all paid workers today.[26] As Figure 7.4 indicates, the entry of women into the workforce began to tail off as the twenty-first century opened, a fact which scholars attribute mostly to the ongoing lack of family-friendly work policies and affordable and/or public childcare options, but also to a recent resurgence of traditional attitudes about male breadwinning and female homemaking, two facts to which we will return. And though much has been written about the cost to women and the economy of this particular

FIGURE 7.5: **LABOR FORCE PARTICIPATION RATES OF MEN AND WOMEN, 1890–2018**

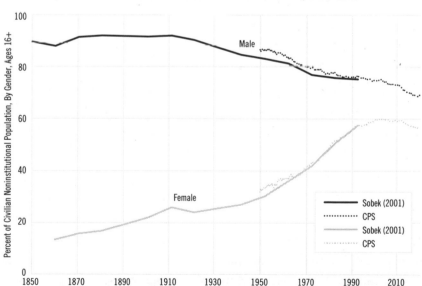

Source: Matthew Sobek, "New Statistics on the U.S. Labor Force, 1850–1990," *Historical Methods* 34 (2001): 71–87; Current Population Survey. Data for 1860 exclude slaves.

slowdown, it did not actually reflect a retrenchment in gender *parity*, because the male labor force participation rate was also in decline at this time.

In fact, when charting male and female participation in paid work side
by side over the full century (Figure 7.5), we see a clear and more or less
steady closing of the gender gap, with almost no interruptions. This trend
toward growing parity holds for all ethnic groups and ages, with the important exception of women over 55. However, exactly when and how women
of different races entered the workforce varies somewhat.[27] The trend also
holds at every level of family income—however, labor force participation
in the twentieth century increased much more *rapidly* in high-income than
low-income households. This is due largely to the opening of white-collar
jobs for educated women in the clerical, sales, and service sectors. Significantly, the trend also holds within all marital statuses, with the largest
increase in employment rates among married women.[28]

The shape of these trends seems to tell the story of a steady march
toward equality in the workforce between men and women, a phenomenon
which started before America's larger climb toward a more capacious "we,"
and continued long afterward. However, data about labor force participation is merely a measure of quantity—how many women had jobs—not
quality—how women were being compensated, treated, and fulfilled in
their work. Indeed, a crucial component of Friedan's call to arms was the
demand for *meaningful* work outside the home.

One thought-provoking question when looking at steadily increasing
female labor force participation is why more and more women have entered the workplace. Is it indeed to seek fulfillment and meaning, or is it
out of growing economic necessity? While we do not have full-century
data, the DDB Needham Life Style Survey, conducted between 1978 and
1999, asked women this very question. Their responses are charted in Figure 7.6. Remarkably, in the aftermath of Friedan's call to arms, the number of women reporting that they worked because they *wanted to* stayed
flat over this period, while the number of women reporting they worked
because they *had to* nearly doubled. This contrast reflects the economic
challenges more and more working-class Americans have encountered
after the 1970s—America's "I" decades—which we documented in detail

in Chapter 2, as well as the significant increase in single-parent families during this same period, which we discussed in Chapter 4.

Generally speaking, discussions of broad trends in women's employment have interpreted increasing labor force participation as a mark of welcome progress toward gender equity. One subtle, but important implication of Figure 7.6, however, is to question whether the steady movement of women into the paid labor force during the 1970s, 1980s, and 1990s (shown in Figures 7.4 and 7.5) is actually a mark of women moving toward increasingly fulfilling lives. If more and more women are able to enjoy the personal and economic fruits of professional employment, that is no doubt a plus for gender equity. If, however, poor women from minority communities are increasingly forced away from their children and into the labor market—as many were by the welfare reforms of the 1990s—it is much less clear that we should count that as a plus for gender equity. It might, on the contrary, be seen as a kind of increased class discrimination analogous to the trends that we examined in Chapter 2 on economic equality.

Furthermore, despite a steady, century-long trend toward gender

FIGURE 7.6: **WORKING OUT OF NECESSITY OR BY CHOICE AMONG AMERICAN WOMEN, 1978–1999**

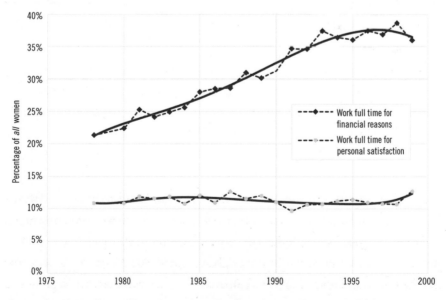

Source: DDB Needham Life Style Survey, in Putnam, *Bowling Alone*, pp. 196–98.

parity in labor force participation, the move toward equal pay has been far less straightforward. Between 1890 and 1955, women did in fact see a steady increase in earnings, leading to a considerable jump in pay equity, as illustrated in Figure 7.7. (The vertical axis is easily interpretable into the "$0.77" dollar that women received in 2012, compared to a "$0.61" dollar in the 1960s.) However, that trend essentially reversed for the three decades thereafter. Only in the 1980s did women begin again to make meaningful progress toward wage equality, but in very recent years this progress has once again stagnated.[29]

FIGURE 7.7: RATIO OF FEMALE TO MALE EARNINGS FOR FULL-TIME, YEAR-ROUND WORKERS, 1890–2012

Source: Goldin, *Understanding the Gender Gap*, 59.

In the case of earnings, the lagged effect of so-called "second wave" feminism and the 1964 passage of Title VII of the Civil Rights Act is much clearer. Title VII officially barred sex discrimination in pay and compensation. The ultimate effects of this change to the law were slow in coming, however, as the chart above indicates—largely because enforcement of the act depended upon women initiating lawsuits alleging discrimination, which often took years to reach a conclusion. Furthermore, by 1969, the Equal Employment Opportunity Commission (EEOC) had received over fifty thousand reports of sex discrimination, and the agency was simply overwhelmed by the task of investigating them all.[30] But by 1980, more than a decade of legislative and judicial victories finally began to result in steep progress toward pay equity for women. In addition to diminishing discrimination, the narrowing of the pay gap in the latter decades of the twentieth century also reflects the higher educational attainment of women, including their increasing choice of educational tracks that lead to more lucrative jobs, as well as their ambitious pursuit of entry into traditionally men's occupations.[31]

However, in 2017 a typical working woman still made only 84 cents for every dollar earned by a typical working man, a gender wage gap of 16 percent.[32] According to the Institute for Women's Policy Research, "if change continues at the same slow pace as it has for the past fifty years, it will take 42 years—or until 2059—for women to finally reach pay parity."[33] And the situation is considerably more dire for women of color, who generally make far less than the 84 cents, and whose pace of progress toward pay equity has been significantly slower. At current rates, "Black women's median annual earnings would reach parity with White men's in 2119, and Hispanic women's in 2224."[34] Furthermore, the fact that women have achieved—and even exceeded—educational parity with men has not yet had a fully equalizing effect on wages. As the Georgetown University Center on Education and the Workforce has reported, "at all levels of educational attainment, women earn, on average, 25 percent less than men," and in general "women have to have a PhD in order to make as much as men with a BA."[35] Thus, despite more rapid improvement during the last third of the twentieth century than ever before, gender wage equality remains an elusive goal.

And despite having entered the workforce in remarkably large numbers, women still shoulder a far greater share of housework and childcare responsibilities than men.[36] Some observers emphasize this imbalance, the limits it places upon women's ability to work long hours, and the frequency with which women must take breaks from work and career to care for children or elders as major reasons for the stubborn continuation of the pay gap.[37] Some pay disparity is also clearly due to discrimination, as women are denied advancement or raises. Women today are about twice as likely to report experiencing such discrimination in the workplace as men, [38] and economists often note a certain percentage of the gender pay gap that is "unexplained" by all other factors.

But by far the biggest reason for the narrowing but still significant gender pay gap has been the persistent reality of occupational segregation. Occupational segregation is tracked using a measure called the Index of Dissimilarity, which calculates how equally distributed between men and women is employment in a given job category. If women make up 47 percent of the total workforce, as they do today, then zero occupational segregation (or a zero on the Index of Dissimilarity) would mean that, on average, in every single job category (from nursing, to engineering, to retail, to financial planning) 47 percent of the employees are women and 53 percent of the employees are men. However, as illustrated in Figure 7.8, in 1900 the Index of Dissimilarity was nearly 70, meaning that 70 percent of females would need to move into male-dominated professions (or vice versa) in order to achieve occupational parity. Thus the rate of occupational segregation by gender in the American workforce was extremely high at the beginning of the twentieth century.

But the long-term trend shows very little change until 1960, with slow improvement thereafter, and marked improvement only after 1970.[39] This trend is another case in which the 1960s feminist revolution seems to have had an important effect, by finally opening up many job categories long closed to women.[40] And yet, still today, nearly 50 percent of all workers would have to reshuffle occupational categories in order to achieve gender parity by profession.[41] This fact has important implications for pay disparities, because in general, male-dominated job categories are compensated more highly than female-dominated job categories. Thus, a major reason why women earn less than men is that they are concentrated in jobs that, in general, pay less.[42]

How did occupational segregation come to be such an enduring feature of the American economy? Burgeoning American industries in the late nineteenth century (such as iron and steel, lumber, mining, and

FIGURE 7.8: OCCUPATIONAL SEGREGATION, 1900–2017

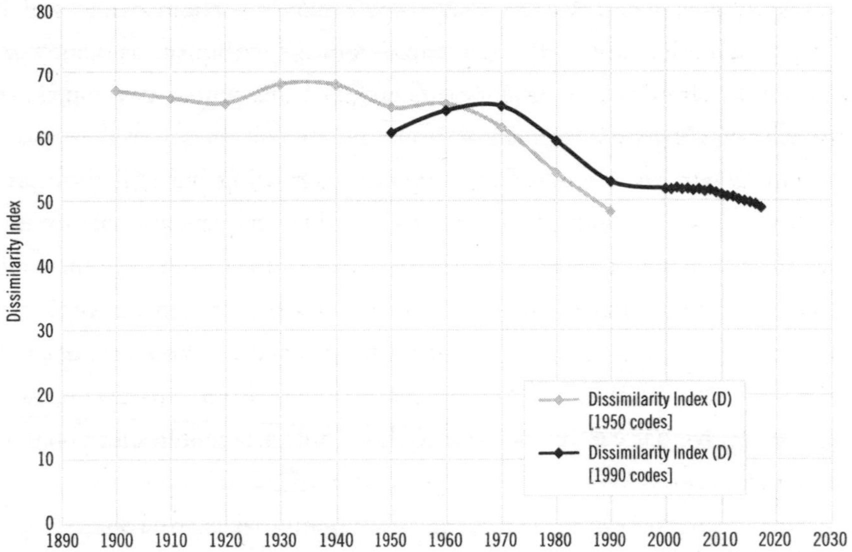

Source: US Census; IPUMS; American Community Survey. See endnote 7.39.

machinery) created very little demand for female labor, leaving women who sought work outside the home to factory jobs producing textiles, apparel, and canned goods—typically in positions with no qualifications for entry, no opportunity for advancement, and payment by the piece.[43] However, at the turn of the twentieth century, corporations began to compound in size, retail stores became considerably larger, and sectors such as communications and public utilities expanded dramatically. These structural changes to the economy created a growing demand for clerical workers—most of which was met by women. Women represented 18.5 percent of all white-collar workers in 1900, but that number had increased nearly two-fold by 1930, to 33.2 percent. Similarly, women occupied 20.2 percent of clerical and sales positions in 1900, doubling to 40.4 percent by 1930.[44] No longer were women—especially educated women—strictly confined to informal employment, such as taking in laundry or boarders, nor limited in their options for formal employment to grueling, low-level industrial jobs.

However, this "spectacular" transformation in women's work, as Claudia Goldin calls it, also ushered in an enduring practice of gendering in the workplace that created discriminatory limitations on women's advancement and pay. Despite the fact that women were increasingly working in the same factories, stores, and companies as men, they were restricted to certain job categories, hired at lower starting rates, and "dead-ended" in positions that offered no upward mobility. Furthermore, even in cases when women could and did advance due to growing levels of skill and experience, their pay increase was far slower than that of men on a similar track, particularly in office jobs and professional and corporate positions.[45] And despite the fact that many more women were remaining employed after marriage during this time, many companies nonetheless maintained "marriage bars," policies which kept married women out of certain positions, or meant that women could lose their jobs or be demoted upon getting married.

During World War II, such forms of occupational segregation and discrimination against women often gave way to the demands of production but, especially in heavy industry, these gains were short-lived. According to historian James Patterson, as the war ended "the biggest losers were the women who had found industrial work during the war: these jobs either disappeared amid the rush of demobilization or were given to veterans who returned to civilian life."[46] Rosie the Riveter was thus able to find better work and better pay during the war, a fact which appealed to women who might otherwise have opted out of work, and raised expectations for equality overall. But once the war was over, returning heavy industry and manufacturing jobs to men required reviving old narratives that such work was "too hard" for women, leaving them to return to segregated industries and more menial positions.

Yet not all wartime occupational gains were wiped out with the arrival of peace. In the 1950s, the debate on female employment shifted from whether or not women, or even married women and mothers, should work at all to the conditions of their employment. And women entered (gendered) professions at a very high rate. Clerical jobs multiplied, and elementary school teachers were in particularly high demand due to the Baby Boom. Blue-collar women in the 1950s moved into some new fields as well—especially as demand in the thriving economy outstripped the supply of male workers. Marriage bars also began to decline in the 1940s and were virtually eliminated by 1950.[47] And part-time work became increasingly available after the war, making it easier for women to combine work and family responsibilities.

Thus, despite demobilization, the robust trend toward female employment continued, albeit in once again starkly sex-segregated jobs characterized by inequitable pay. Nonetheless, female labor leaders at this time mostly advocated for the right of married women to work, for maternity benefits for mothers, and for a restoration of the public childcare provision that the war had brought.[48] They generally did not challenge the sexual division of labor, and focused their wage demands on equal pay for *comparable* work, in order to address the fact that in a gender-segregated economy most women simply did not do work that was precisely equal to men's.[49] The postwar era, then, was not a time when all working women returned home, nor was it a moment of quiescence in women's activism and advocacy for equality—though it is often portrayed that way.

It is true, however, that in the aftermath of the war millions of women did *voluntarily* quit their wartime jobs, and when surveyed, about half cited "family responsibilities" as the reason.[50] But many of these women likely expected to return to work after marriage and childbearing. It may also be true that ongoing occupational segregation and pay inequity, as well as the loss of wartime opportunities, discouraged many women from pursuing careers after the war.[51] Furthermore, in the postwar years the cultural value placed upon motherhood and domesticity increased. However, the long-term trend to that point in the century was toward greater and greater numbers of women working outside the home, most of whom were much more concerned with labor conditions than with Friedan's "problem that has no name." Nevertheless, a keen disillusionment was certainly felt among a postwar generation of women who faced a strong cultural expectation to find fulfilment either at home or in underpaid, sex-segregated, dead-end employment—factors which both fueled the unprecedented birth rates responsible for the Baby Boom generation, and likely contributed to the rise of critiques such as *The Feminine Mystique*.

Moreover, women who tried to combine a career with homemaking still faced an uphill battle at mid-century.[52] As noted above, despite women working more and more over the course of the century, the expectation that housework and childcare were primarily the woman's responsibility remained basically unchanged, creating what many call the "double shift," where women essentially worked two jobs—paid employment outside the home and an unpaid job inside the home.

Alongside the multiple forms of discrimination that have limited women's choice, compensation, and fulfillment in the workplace, sexual harassment is also a long-standing issue. The prospect of unwanted sexual advances in the workplace and the expectation of sexual favors in exchange for career advancement has long been a concern for advocates of women's rights. According to legal scholars Janet Halley, Catharine MacKinnon, and Reva Siegel, "women in the early feminist and labor movements never managed to organize a sustained assault on the set of practices we have come to call 'sexual harassment,' but they did articulate an indictment of the practices that anticipated many of the arguments that women in the modern feminist and labor movements voiced in the 1970s." It was the efforts of these early feminists to bring attention to the issue that finally brought about a legal ban, which was included in Title VII of the 1964 Civil Rights Act. But it was pioneering female lawyers, advocates, and theorists in the 1970s who helped bring to light women's stories and to properly define sexual harassment and fine-tune the concept's application in courts of law.[53]

Indeed, consciousness around the discriminatory realities women faced in the economy began to rise just as the Civil Rights movement entered its most visible and successful phase, and in the 1960s a reinvigorated women's movement was born. Though landmark legislation finally pronounced economic discrimination against women illegal, as noted above, it took a decade or more of legal action and advocacy before real changes in workplace discrimination, gender pay inequity, occupational segregation, and sexual harassment were truly seen and felt. It also took time for women to see returns on newly mandated educational equality, created by Title IX. The effects of these transformations were uneven among different categories of women, but where they took hold, the effect was indeed dramatic.

Where they didn't take hold was mostly among poor women and women of color, many of whom today fill the ranks of service jobs long considered "women's work," thereby feeding into ongoing gender *and* racial wage gaps.[54] Thus, any narrative of economic change that hinges on second wave feminism seems to best fit the experience of upper-class white women. Furthermore, because of an ongoing lack of affordable and/or public childcare and eldercare options, as well as the continued gendering of housework and care work, women entering higher-paid professions largely rely on lower-class women and women of color to provide domestic labor and childcare—meaning that class inequality has to a large extent underpinned the expansion of gender equality in the workplace.[55] Just as Chapter 2 showed the growing importance of class divisions in the economy as a whole over the last half century, there is at least some evidence that the same is true among women. But the solutions to this particular problem will require a wider societal rethinking of how to collectively manage the human care work women have so long shouldered, in order to allow them full freedom of choice without a further widening of class gaps.

Thus, the picture of progress toward economic equality between men and women over the course of the twentieth century is mixed, and the movement toward gender equality occurred at different rates and times, depending on the measure, and the subgroup of women in question. Nevertheless, women moved toward parity with men in a number of ways during the first half of the century, with accelerating progress thereafter. The "grand gender convergence" of the twentieth century is not yet complete, however, leaving significant unfinished business as we look to the future.[56]

WOMEN IN THE PUBLIC SQUARE

Though nineteenth-century women had played an active role in public campaigns advocating for causes such as the abolition of slavery, temperance, consumer protection, and improved conditions for the poor and working classes, they were nonetheless adamantly denied the vote and the chance to hold public office.

Not surprisingly, therefore, in their first electoral outing after the adoption of female suffrage in 1920, women's turnout was 32 percentage points lower than men's turnout, but in years that followed women quickly began to close that gap, as indicated in Figure 7.9. Thus, women had begun cultivating their political voice as voters long before the women's movement of the 1960s. This narrowing of the gender gap in voting continued throughout the century, though at a slightly slower pace after 1965, which is somewhat unexpected, given that this was a critical date in extending the franchise to women of color, who had effectively been denied it under Jim Crow. Overall, however, the gender gap in voting has narrowed more or less steadily since the ratification of the Nineteenth Amendment, and has resulted in a distinct female advantage in today's electorate. Women now play a critical role in the outcome of elections, voting at a rate roughly 4 percent higher than men.[57]

In addition to steadily increasing their influence at the ballot box,

FIGURE 7.9: **GENDER DIFFERENCES IN VOTER TURNOUT, 1920–2016**

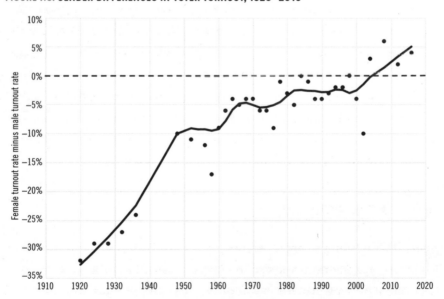

Source: Corder and Wolbrecht; ANES. See endnote 7.57. Data LOESS smoothed: .25.

women have also long engaged in advocacy work to bring about greater gender equality. Despite the very common usage of the "waves" metaphor to describe the shape of women's political activism over the course of the twentieth century, this framework is in fact increasingly contested.[58] Though legislative and judicial victories for women's equality from 1920 to 1965 were scant, it was in no way a period of dormancy during which women retreated into the private sphere. Women worked through voluntary organizations to pursue their various goals and made inroads into the previously male-dominated political parties, acting as canvassers, campaign aides, convention speakers, and even delegates, though in small numbers.[59]

Furthermore, women of color and working-class women—whose stories have often been left out of mainstream historical accounts—were especially active during this period, advocating for better working conditions, better pay, union representation, and racial justice. In fact, it was the trailblazing African American attorney Pauli Murray who insisted that the prohibition of sex discrimination in employment be added to the Civil Rights Act. Political scientist Kristin A. Goss has described this underemphasized phase of women's advocacy as a period of "swells between the waves." "By almost any metric," she writes, "the post-suffrage years were boom years for women's organizations: the number of groups grew, memberships increased, policy coalitions continued to form, and Congress increasingly sought out women's point of view. Even when one women's group faded from view, another took its place."[60]

This proliferation of women's organizations also underscores the fact that the women's movement has never been a monolithic phenomenon with a single agenda. Indeed, for much of the twentieth century, women's groups were split as to whether they wanted legislation specifically protecting women (which had been the predominant goal of Progressive Era reformers and the early activities of the Department of Labor's Women's Bureau, established in 1920) or gender-blind legislation aimed at equal rights. While some women's organizations ardently supported the Equal Rights Amendment (introduced in Congress in 1923), others felt it would undermine existing protective labor laws, and bring about more harm than good for women workers. However, the 1940s represented a clear shift away from protective labor laws, many of which were abandoned in the interest of wartime production, meaning that the fear of losing them was no longer an obstacle to supporting the ERA. The number of women's groups endorsing the ERA increased, and soon both parties' platforms included commitments to equal rights and equal pay for women. The Republican Party was first to endorse the ERA, and by and large was the early leader on issues involving strict gender equality. Prominent female Democrats, on the other hand, were more supportive of laws to protect the health, safety, and economic welfare of women (and workers more generally).[61] The tension between prioritizing special protections for women versus equal rights remained salient even into the 1960s, but the balance shifted markedly toward equal rights thereafter. Only at this time, Goss argues, did the women's movement take on a more narrow conception of women's identity and female issues.[62] Making this shift to a rights-based, identity politics agenda clearly contributed to the achievement of watershed change on questions of equality, but also fundamentally altered the nature of women's influence on policymaking—for better and for worse.

One of the most important developments in the twentieth-century struggle for gender equality in America was President Kennedy's establishment of the Presidential Commission on the Status of Women, which occurred in 1961—some five years before the women's revolution found its organizational footing. The commission, initially headed by Eleanor Roosevelt, put forward a report in 1963 that demonstrated the seriousness of the problem of gender discrimination. Consequently, the Equal Pay Act was passed in 1963, and the Civil Rights Act—with the inclusion of "sex" as a protected category—in 1964. Historian Dorothy Sue Cobble has argued that these early victories "were the culmination of some twenty-five years of political activism" on the part of women.[63] The commission's report was unsparing in its revelations about the still starkly gendered and often inegalitarian state of American life. However, the fact that the status of women was an important national issue *before* the advent of "second wave feminism" strongly suggests that America's widening sense of "we" was already—and increasingly—sensitive to the inclusion of women.

That being said, during this time very few women managed to attain public office. In fact, several states refused to recognize that women's suffrage meant that women could hold office, and disallowed the practice as late as the 1940s.[64] As a result, the number of female elected officials was slow to increase. Figure 7.10 charts the number of women serving in the U.S. Congress, which barely budged until 1970. The chart for state legislatures looks very much the same.[65] The first female governor was not elected until 1974, and women have been equally slow in obtaining judgeships—it was 1981 when Sandra Day O'Connor joined the Supreme Court. Such advances came more readily after President Carter initiated an affirmative action program to help correct gender imbalances in 1974. By 2003 21 percent of federal judges were women, and 29 percent of state supreme court judges were women.[66] The 116th Congress, elected in 2018, is made up of 24 percent women, the highest percentage in U.S. history and a considerable jump from the previous year. And twenty-five of the one hundred U.S. senators are now women.[67]

FIGURE 7.10: **WOMEN IN US CONGRESS, 1917–2019**

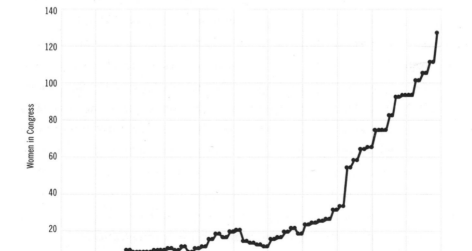

Source: Congressional Research Service.

Thus, while women voted at greater and greater rates throughout the century—eventually surpassing men in voter turnout—their presence in elected leadership roles was significantly postponed, at least in part by discrimination, and still is only (at best) halfway to proportional representation. Nevertheless, both before and after suffrage women have organized and advocated for their concerns, and those concerns have increasingly become priorities for both parties. However, women's issues are not uniform—as a large and diverse constituency, not all women have the same views about how to advance their cause, or which issues should take precedence—a fact which has at times complicated the pursuit of legislative guarantees of gender equality, and even left many women out of the conversation.

CHANGING ATTITUDES TOWARD GENDER EQUALITY

Another part of the oft-repeated story of women's liberation in the twentieth century is the idea that women were continually oppressed by widespread anti-egalitarian ideas for the majority of the century, and that these conservative attitudes about gender roles began to change significantly only after the women's movement of the Sixties. Historians who have put forward this view often base their argument on one or two mid-century public opinion polls which, by their interpretation, show strong opposition to feminism and enduring support for traditional ideas about women. However, such a momentary snapshot cannot possibly capture change over time, nor do standard interpretations of these polls reflect the actual nuance of participants' responses.[68] While it is true that attitudinal changes were particularly rapid from 1970 to 1990, the idea that beliefs about gender equality and women's roles had been basically static until 1970 is simply unsupported by the data. Our analysis actually reveals large gains in attitudes favorable to gender equality in the preceding decades as well.

As we have seen in previous chapters, one of the challenges in determining long-run change in attitudes is that survey data were sparse or nonexistent before polling became regular in the early 1970s. However, it is nonetheless possible to reconstruct something of a "fossil record" of early-century attitudes by breaking down late-century polling data into birth cohorts. This is because scholars have repeatedly shown that an individual's attitudes about social norms are largely determined by socialization that occurs early in life, and tend to hold fairly steady over that individual's life cycle.[69] Thus, if a person born in the opening decades of the century was asked their opinion about gender equality in 1970, it is fair to assume that, by and large, the opinion they express more accurately reflects the social norms of their youth than the social norms of the moment in which they were surveyed. However, such nuances are not reflected when it is simply reported that, in the aggregate, a certain percentage of Americans surveyed in 1970 held a certain view. Beneath that statistic inevitably lie significant generational differences of opinion. It is also true, therefore, that when it is later reported that the percentage of Americans holding a particular attitude has changed, much of that change is due to changing people (as older generations are replaced by younger generations) rather than changing minds. We saw evidence of this "cohort replacement" phenomenon when we examined change over time in attitudes about racial equality in Chapter 6, and a similar trend is visible when we look at change over time in attitudes about gender equality.

To begin with, Figure 7.11 shows how attitudes toward gender roles changed from the 1970s until the early twenty-first century, as measured by the following five survey items.

1. If your party nominated a woman for president, would you vote for her if she were qualified for the job? (Yes)
2. Women should take care of running their homes and leave running the country up to men. (Disagree)
3. Do you approve or disapprove of a married woman earning money in business or industry if she has a husband capable of supporting her? (Approve)
4. Most men are better suited emotionally for politics than are most women. (Disagree)
5. It is much better for everyone involved if the man is the achiever outside the home and the woman takes care of the home and family. (Disagree)

At first glance, this chart would seem to indicate that the women's revolution of the Sixties had the effect of changing many minds about these questions.

FIGURE 7.11: SUPPORT FOR GENDER EQUALITY, 1972-2014

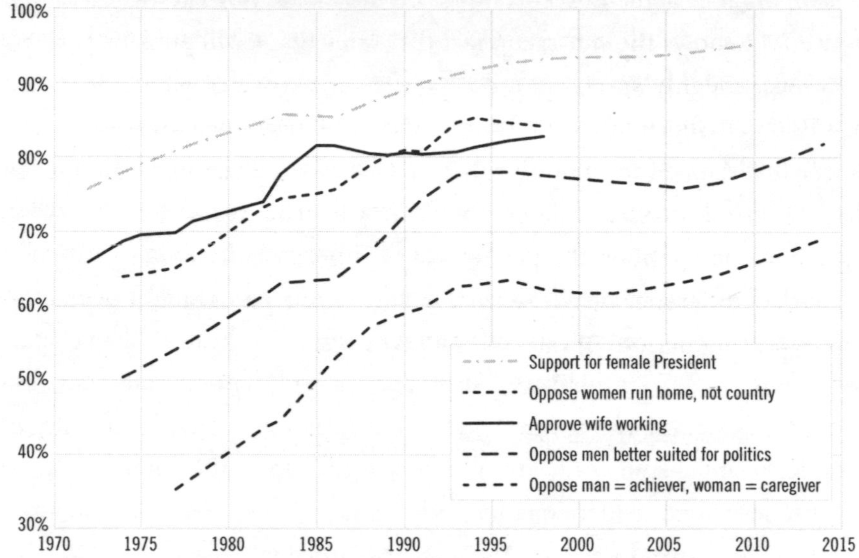

Source: General Social Survey. Data LOESS smoothed: .33.

However, when the same data are broken down by birth cohort (and for simplicity combined into a single index), as in Figure 7.12 below, it becomes clear that, in fact, there were and are significant intergenerational differences of opinion.[70] Men and women born and socialized in the first several decades of the twentieth century (represented in the lowest line of Figure 7.12) were, even when interviewed a half century later, much more traditionalist in their view of gender roles than men and women born and socialized just prior to World War II (in the next two lines up). In turn, that group (broadly speaking, the parents of the Boomers) were more traditionalist than the Boomers (the fourth and fifth lines from the bottom) were. But the difference, in turn, between the Boomers and *their* children was much smaller. In other words, the Boomers, raised in the 1950s and 1960s, were much more egalitarian in their view of gender roles than their parents, raised in the 1920s and 1930s. And in turn that cohort were much more egalitarian than *their* parents, raised around the turn of the twentieth century.

The implication is that in terms of the socializing environments of successive generations, most of the rejection of the more traditional gender division of labor actually occurred before the 1970s, not after. Conversely, Figure 7.12 shows the surprising fact that on average Millennials (born in the 1980s, roughly speaking) are no more supportive of gender equality than Boomers (born in the 1950s, roughly speaking), since their lines have entirely overlapped in the twenty-first century! In effect, just as the rings of a tree trunk display differences in climate in previous decades, thick rings indicating periods of rapid growth, so the successive curves in Figure 7.12 reflect differences in the social climate in previous decades, with wider gaps indicating periods of rapid change.

FIGURE 7.12: **SUPPORT FOR GENDER EQUALITY, BY BIRTH COHORT, 1972–2014**

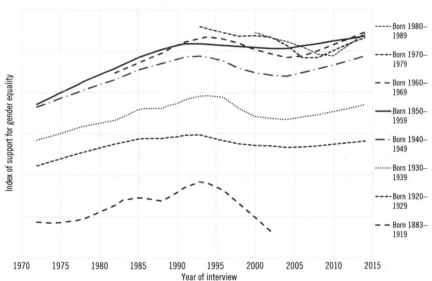

Source: General Social Survey. Data LOESS smoothed: .5.

Though it is often reported otherwise, this form of analysis reveals that much of the change in attitudes about gender equality from the Seventies

onward actually occurred *by subtraction*. That is, people who came of age
in the first quarter of the twentieth century were much less supportive of
gender equality than people who came of age after them (reflecting generational differences in socialization), which implies that feminism was
gradually but steadily gaining acceptance during the first half of the century. People who came of age in the 1960s were much more supportive
of gender equality than their parents, who were themselves more so than
their parents had been at the same age. And as those older generations
passed away between the 1970s and the 1990s, their departure from the
population meant that the Americans who remained were by default—that
is, without any individual changing his or her mind—becoming progressively more liberal in their attitudes toward gender. In other words, the
Grim Reaper did a lot of the work of increasing Americans' overall support
for women's liberation during the closing decades of the century.

Historians have noted changes in gender socialization over the early
decades of the twentieth century and have provided some interesting examples of and explanations for it, including changing ideas about parenting, the advent of clubs like Girl Scouts (a Progressive Era invention),
which encouraged female achievement, the rise of companionate marriage
(discussed in Chapter 4), an increasing preference for small families, and
the political socialization of women (and men) through activism. Another
explanation for women's increasing commitment to gender equality in the
1930s, 1940s, and 1950s is a theory developed by political scientist Roberta
Sigel called "relative deprivation." Essentially, as women became progressively more conscious of their abilities and ambitions, they felt increasingly
shortchanged by social norms and began adjusting their own views as a
result. Sigel makes this argument specifically about women in the 1980s,
but it likely applies to women throughout the century.[71]

Of course, many things besides birth cohort have influenced attitudes toward gender in recent decades, including many individual men
and women changing their outlook through consciousness-raising. Many
people during the last half century actually *were* changing their minds in
a more egalitarian direction. This "period effect" is indicated by the shape
of the parallel curves, which, had there been no mind-changing, would

have been perfectly flat. As second wave feminism marched on, significant numbers of people within each cohort gave progressively more egalitarian responses to the questions. This change is visible in Figure 7.12 in the gentle rise in support for gender equality visible within each birth cohort between the mid-1970s and the mid-1990s. Thus, the second part of the explanation for the total growth in support for gender equality in the 1970s and 1980s is in fact the influence of the women's movement, which does appear to have created a widespread change in cultural norms. However, to highlight this period effect alone means that we lose the surprising but quite clear evidence of even more substantial changes that began decades earlier in the twentieth century.

Finally, the above charts also show that the pace of change toward a liberalization of attitudes dramatically slowed down as the twenty-first century arrived. The differences in outlook on gender roles between the Millennials and the Gen-Xers are modest and inconsistent. In fact, among post-Boomer generations, egalitarian attitudes even seem to have retreated somewhat, a fact which has been confirmed by targeted polling of Gen-Xers and Millennials. This is one gender-based measure we found that shows the "foot off the gas" phenomenon we saw over and over in the case of race.[72]

We can summarize our basic findings about the timing of change in gender attitudes across the last 100 years by displaying how, on average, the attitudes of successive cohorts differed from one another. This is shown in Figure 7.13, which presents the same data as Figure 7.12, but in a slightly simplified fashion. All four phenomena described above are apparent: The steady century-long trend toward liberalization of attitudes about gender, the ever-so-slightly increased pace of that liberalization among Americans who came of age during the 1960s, the gradual slowing of the pace of that liberalization after 1970, as post-Boomer cohorts entered adulthood, and the slight but surprising reversal of this trend in recent years.[73] Figure 7.13 suggests that the bulk of progress in Americans' support for gender equality over the last 100 years occurred among Americans socialized *before* 1970. In effect, the women's movement seems to have lit a match to what was already well-cured kindling.

A recent study of over forty years of survey data tracking high school

FIGURE 7.13: ESTIMATED GENERATIONAL DIFFERENCES IN SUPPORT FOR GENDER EQUALITY

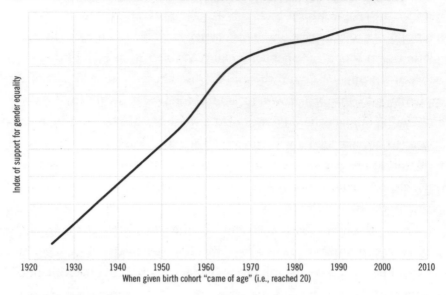

Source: General Social Survey. Data LOESS smoothed: .33.

seniors' responses to various questions relating to gender roles and egalitarian attitudes found that youths' attitudes became increasingly egalitarian with regard to women having equal opportunity to work and lead from roughly 1970 to 1990, and then plateaued. And with regard to gender dynamics in the family, after liberalizing for almost twenty years, young people's beliefs became markedly more traditional after roughly 1995, with increasing percentages feeling that men should be breadwinners and make the decisions in the home.[74] Millennial men are also considerably more likely than Gen-X or Boomer men to say that society has already made sufficient changes in creating gender equality in the workplace.[75]

Though the slowing down of liberalizing attitudes about gender in recent decades (especially among younger Americans) is quite clear, explanations of why this happened are not totally coherent. Some scholars have suggested that it reflects a new cultural framework on the part of younger women, which extends a feminist rhetoric of choice to include stay-at-home mothering as a legitimately "feminist" option. This theory points to the increasing replacement of an "equal opportunity" framework—common in the 1970s and 1980s—with "work-family accommodation" rhetoric, which advocates for measures that support women who combine work and motherhood, and which is more common in today's women's advocacy.[76] Other observers argue that post-Boomer women are simply more individualistic, and therefore less concerned with collective action or movement politics as a way of achieving equality or overcoming discrimination.[77] Still others attribute the change to the practical difficulties parents face in dual-earner households, especially in the absence of public policies supporting work-family balance.[78] Finally, there is also scholarship on an alleged "new sexism" among men since the 1990s.[79]

Despite these wildly diverse explanations, there is a growing consensus that the mid-1990s was a time when resurgent traditionalism regarding male and female roles, especially with regard to caregiving, came to coexist with more feminist beliefs about women's equal capacity to work and equal right to choose to earn a living. But exactly how and why this came to be is still not clear.[80] And the effect of very recent forms of feminism such as the #MeToo movement remains to be seen.

Though the recent generational trend toward resurgent traditionalism is puzzling, what is by far most striking when viewing attitudinal data broken down by cohorts is the distinct evidence that most liberalization in gender attitudes actually occurred *before* the 1970s, a fact which complicates a simplistic story of women's liberation taking off only in the last third of the century. Surprisingly, the vast majority of progress toward mainstream acceptance of egalitarian attitudes toward gender did not begin with—or even much accelerate after—the 1960s women's movement.[81]

FROM EVOLUTION TO REVOLUTION

If women had been on a steady march into the workplace, attending high school and college at ever-greater rates, participating in the public sphere more and more, and seeing chauvinistic attitudes gradually fading—all at significant and fairly steady rates over the course of the century—why then did the 1960s feminist revolution feel so urgent? What motivated women to found new advocacy organizations, organize mass protests, and take to the streets to demand liberation?

The first answer is that—much as we saw in the case of African Americans—though significant and often underrecognized trends toward equalization for women had indeed characterized the first two thirds of the century, in many important and often egregious ways, women were still experiencing limitation and exclusion. As outlined above, very little progress had been made by the 1960s for women seeking entry into professional schools and occupations, and very few women held public office, despite high levels of female voting. Occupational segregation, pay inequity, sexual harassment, and job loss due to pregnancy were persistent realities that ever-greater numbers of working women faced every day. And mainstream media depictions of women were narrowly focused on marriage, home, and family. Furthermore, many restrictions on women's personal freedom and self-determination persisted: in 1960 a woman could not open a line of credit if unmarried, or without her husband's signature, if married. In many states women were de facto (and in some cases de jure) excluded from jury service; and in still others they could not obtain a no-fault divorce or legally access contraception. Abortions were outlawed, and any open discussion of female sexuality was largely considered taboo. Women were not allowed to attend military academies, or participate in many sports. The Equal Rights Amendment—under debate for forty years—had (and has) yet to achieve ratification. Outright gender discrimination in many domains was still legal, acceptable, and widely practiced. Indeed, in many ways, it was the very progress women *had* made before the 1960s that fueled a growing discontent with these inegalitarian realities. Ever-greater numbers of women were reaching adulthood educated, ambitious, and independent-minded, only to find their agency and options artificially curtailed.[82]

A second answer is that, even though attitudes toward women were in fact liberalizing in the first half of the century, in the postwar years, suburbanization, a cult of domesticity promoted by mainstream media and advertising, and a widespread push for cultural conformity had created an image and expectation of womanhood that in many ways contradicted women's otherwise gradual but significant progression toward equality. The 1950s were in many ways a moment of pause and even retrenchment in an otherwise forward march toward cultural liberalization. Betty Friedan's critique was thus accurately responsive not only to cultural expectations, but also to real (though temporary) setbacks in educational and pay equity, the post-war resurgence of occupational segregation, and reversals in the public provision of childcare—all of which immediately preceded its publication.

Another important reason is that, as had happened in the nineteenth century, women saw activism for racial equality and inclusion as both an inspiration and a model for seeking gender equality and inclusion. As the Civil Rights movement gained momentum and won important victories in the 1950s and 1960s, feminists were encouraged and emboldened to press their own case. As the entire nation became more rights-conscious, and a culture of protest swept the country, more space opened up for demanding gender rights in the context of the fight for civil rights.

Soon, the National Organization for Women (NOW) was formed to mobilize women and pressure employers to follow—and the federal government to enforce—antidiscrimination measures, and also to draw attention to a wider array of women's issues including abortion and reproductive health access, violence against women, and lesbian rights. One of the most visible actions NOW organized was the 1970 national Women's Strike for Equality, which celebrated the fiftieth anniversary of the ratification of the Nineteenth Amendment. It drew tens of thousands of women to rallies, marches, and sit-ins across the country with the slogan "Don't iron while the strike is hot!"

Some of the women's movement's most significant legal victories after the formation of NOW included:

- Executive Order 11246, extending full affirmative action rights to women in 1967
- The Equal Employment Opportunity Act of 1972
- Title IX, which was added to the Amendments to the Higher Education Act in 1972 to include gender as a protected class in federally aided education
- The Women's Educational Equity Act (1974), which outlined federal protections against gender discrimination in education
- *Roe v. Wade*, which legalized abortion in 1973
- The Equal Credit Opportunity Act of 1974

- The Pregnancy Discrimination Act of 1978
- A 1975 law requiring military academies to admit women
- The initial outlawing of marital rape and legalization of no-fault divorce

But perhaps the most heralded victory of gender activism during the last third of the twentieth century is the transformation of cultural norms and social attitudes about women. Feminist theory exploded at this time, and prompted truly revolutionary debates about power structures and patriarchy, many of which were captured succinctly in the movement's mantra, "the personal is political." Many women who lived through this turbulent period experienced it as a complete transformation in how "the second sex" was perceived and what paths were open to them.[83] And yet, as the public opinion data presented above clearly show, this change was built upon many decades of slow but steady progress, rather than coming as a bolt from the blue, and also owed much of its punch to the effect of older, more traditionalist generations dying out. Moreover, both legislative victories and changing attitudes toward women were building upon persistent female activism as well as slow and steady transformations in women's economic, educational, and political status—all of which had in fact been under way for many decades of the twentieth century.

Economic historian Claudia Goldin has described the transformation of women's roles in American society as occurring in four phases—the first three, which, in her framework encompassed the late nineteenth century to the late 1970s, were what she calls "evolutionary," and the fourth phase, beginning in the late 1970s and continuing until today, has been what she terms "revolutionary." "The evolutionary phases led, slowly, to the revolutionary phase," she writes, adding that "the revolutionary part of the process—like many revolutions—was preceded by fundamental, long-run, and evolutionary changes that were necessary but not sufficient."[84] Though she is referring here primarily to economic indicators, her description certainly applies more broadly—from women's pursuit of education and political participation, to legal and attitudinal changes touching questions of gender equality. Changes in the first half of the twentieth century were real and quietly transformational and, though inadequate, were a critical part of the story of when and how women succeeded in achieving broader and deeper forms of participation in the American "we."

WOMEN AND THE I-WE-I CURVE

Throughout this book we have argued that in a great many respects the 1925–1965 period was one of building toward an increasingly encompassing American "we"—a time when egalitarian values triumphed, comity and cohesion improved, an ethic of generosity and solidarity prevailed, and a shared commitment to the common good took hold. However, as we noted in the previous chapter on race, it is critical to consider the very real possibility that the "we" taking shape over the first two thirds of the century was essentially inclusive of white males only. Because African Americans, women, and many other groups have struggled mightily over the past hundred years (indeed, far longer) to attain even basic forms of equality and inclusion, it might be fair to assume that any supposed "we" that was built in the twentieth century was inherently racist and chauvinist.

However, just as we saw in the case of race, when we look at long-run empirical trends in gender equality over the course of the century, it becomes difficult to argue that women were entirely left out of the "we" until late in the century, or completely left behind by a persistently male-centric conception of America that had to be torn down in order for progress to begin. Trends in gender equality certainly do not mirror the I-we-I curve—we have cited far too many examples of ways in which women's equality and inclusion were held back until the end of the century. And yet, neither does the story of gender in the twentieth century disconfirm our more general conclusions—we uncovered far too many examples of women, too, making steady, appreciable progress toward equality and inclusion during America's upswing. And the watershed change women experienced alongside African Americans in the 1960s and 1970s was only possible as a culmination of progress decades in the making. Furthermore, the intertwining "I" phenomena of rising economic inequality, rising rates of female-headed households, and concurrent slow progress on wage equality in recent decades have been especially hard on women—realities that to some extent echo the "foot off the gas" phenomenon we saw in the case of African Americans in the same time period.

Overall, America's "we" at mid-century was never expansive enough, nor is it today. But long-run trends in gender equality offer a slightly more optimistic picture than do trends in racial equality. Women have, by and large, had greater and more lasting success at participating in the "we" and gaining from its benefits than have African Americans generally, or African American women, who experience multiple dimensions of disadvantage.[85] Indeed, there is still more work to do for *all* women to be able to make their full contribution to the American project. And in important ways the path forward remains fraught.

In 1965, the Report on the Status of Women created by President Kennedy's commission was turned into a widely read, mass-market book. It included both an introduction and an epilogue written by the famed anthropologist Margaret Mead. She noted that the report and its recommendations left two key issues unresolved. First, the question of who would handle the "very important aspects of home life" once women had achieved equal participation in the workforce. Second, the divide between the advancement of educated women and the poverty and stagnation of the women who worked for them. "There will be those who are working very hard at what they want to do, with the assistance of poor help in the home, in the office, and in the laboratory," Mead rightly predicted.[86]

Mead was remarkably prescient in her observations. Though the commission's report was in some ways the beginning of the end of women's struggle toward equality and inclusion, it also came at a moment in which America was perched on a precipice of history, the downslope of which would increasingly pit the needs and interests of some groups against those of others, and would culminate in a far more divided nation. Unfortunately, there is little evidence that women's progress toward full equality was accelerated by our national shift toward an "I"-centered America. Creating a community that values the contributions of all, limits the opportunities of none, and offers prosperity without prejudice, will define any lasting renewal of American democracy—for people of color, for women, and for other marginalized groups who still struggle for equality and inclusion. Indeed, for all of us.

8

THE ARC OF THE TWENTIETH CENTURY

WIDE-ANGLE HISTORY

In this chapter we aim to see the forest, not merely the trees and leaves. We begin with a summary of the broad changes that have animated the four thematic chapters—economics (Chapter 2), politics (Chapter 3), society (Chapter 4), and culture (Chapter 5). We step back from detailed narratives of specific topics, specific variables, and specific decades to ask how America changed over the last 125 years in terms of the balance between the individual and the community. This wide-angle overview will allow us to spot one obvious pivot point over these decades—the Sixties, broadly defined. So in the second half of this chapter we shall zoom in for a close-up view to understand exactly when, how, and perhaps why the pivot occurred.

Most of the topics explored in this book have been actively studied by others in recent years—including a study by one of us, *Bowling Alone* (2000). Our contribution in this book is different from those previous studies in two respects. First, we explore the last 125 years, not merely the last ten or even the last fifty. Second, we explore four broad dimensions of social change together, not one at a time.

The benefits of this wide-angle, time-lapse approach are familiar in natural science. Early astronomy began studying the universe in a single band of radiation—visible light—at one point in time, viewing the night sky through a telescope. Later astronomers began to study the sky over longer periods of time, and to measure the entire electromagnetic spectrum, creating infrared astronomy, X-ray astronomy, and so on. Recently, multispectral astronomy has emerged, allowing images from separate spectra to be integrated and observed over longer periods of time. For example, our contemporary understanding of supernovae is based on multispectral images collected over time.[1]

Similarly, by measuring social change over an unusually long period and across multiple dimensions (economic, political, social, cultural) simultaneously, we can detect and investigate previously unnoticed patterns. We greatly value and indeed rely on research that is narrower in time and scope, like studies of economic inequality since the Great Recession, or studies of party polarization after the Southern realignment of the 1970s, or studies of family formation among working-class whites in the last several decades, but we seek to frame such studies in a broader context.

In the previous chapters, we have recounted many diverse historical patterns that seem on the surface utterly unconnected—wages, split ticket voting, baby-naming, club membership, philanthropy, marriage rates, congressional voting, unionization, and even pronoun usage. Our challenge in writing this book was well framed by a popular historian of the first half of the twentieth century, Frederick Lewis Allen.

> Sometimes the historian wishes that he were able to write several stories
> at once, presenting them perhaps in parallel columns, and that the human
> brain were so constructed that it could follow all these stories simultane-
> ously without vertigo, thus gaining a livelier sense of the way in which
> numerous streams of events run side by side down the channel of time.[2]

In our case, we have discovered an unexpected and remarkable synchronicity in trends in four very different spheres over the last 125 years, as summarized in Figure 8.1. We have seen each of these four individual graphs at the end of the relevant chapters; here we simply bring them together in a single chart, allowing us to see just how similar the trends in the four spheres are to one another.

FIGURE 8.1: ECONOMIC, POLITICAL, SOCIAL, AND CULTURAL TRENDS, 1895–2015

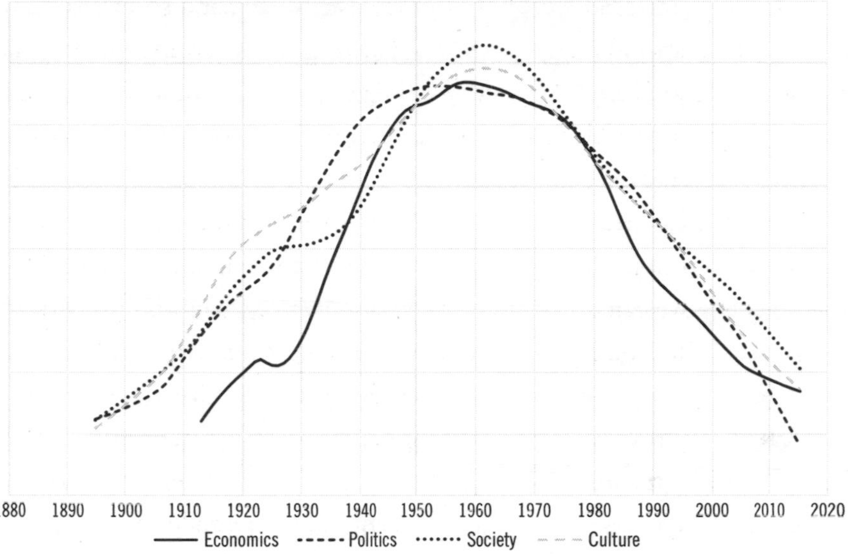

Source: See endnote 1.4. Data LOESS smoothed: .2.

Viewed together, the intertwined curves of Figure 8.1 embody a broad and yet parsimonious narrative of American economics, politics, society, and culture over the last 125 years.[3] The Gilded Age had brought great material advance to America, but it had also brought inequality, polarization, social disarray, and cultural self-centeredness. Then in a decade or two at the turn of the twentieth century the Progressive movement—diverse in its politics, its demographics, and its ideologies and with little philosophic coherence except for a commitment to community—undertook initiatives that over time redirected the course of history.

For roughly half a century these separate "streams of events"—sometimes rushing forward together, sometimes tumbling over one another, and occasionally pausing in a stagnant eddy—shaped an America that was more equal, less contentious, more connected, and more conscious of shared values than the America of the Gilded Age. But then—unexpectedly, though not without forewarning—the diverse streams simultaneously reversed direction, and since the 1960s America has become steadily less equal, more polarized, more fragmented, and more individualistic—a second Gilded Age.

That is the core story recounted thus far in this book. This inverted U-curve is admittedly a simplified macrohistory of these 125 years, potentially controversial because it omits much that is important, above all, the nuanced and complicated curves regarding race and gender that we discussed in the previous two chapters. At the same time this simplification highlights trends that helped produce America's current malaise. In this chapter and the next we step back to ask what it has all meant and may yet mean for our country.

Quantitative analysis confirms that to a remarkable degree the scores of successive charts of change in economics, politics, society, and culture that populate this book reflect a single pattern that we label (in shorthand) the "I-we-I curve." All these diverse variables are very closely intercorrelated over time. Underneath the many different variables there seems to be a single latent variable represented by the basic I-we-I curve.[4]

To be sure, this latent variable is not the only thing influencing any given indicator. The year-by-year scores on individual economic, political, social, and cultural indicators are affected by many other influences. The real value of the minimum wage, for example, was affected when Congress happened to adjust it upward, and party-line voting was influenced by which candidates were on the ticket in a given year. The striking fact, however, is that so many diverse indicators, though influenced by many idiosyncratic forces, show strong evidence of the basic inverted U-curve. This commonality strongly suggests that the I-we-I curve traces a fundamental arc of social change in America over the last 125 years, an arc whose influence seeped into the most varied nooks and crannies of American life.

So one big question is: What caused this pattern?

We have looked carefully for systematic differences among these various measures—were some variables "leading" or "lagging" indicators? If so, that might give us valuable clues about what is going on. However, the very simultaneity of these changes makes it virtually impossible to distinguish what might be causing what, just as it's impossible to tell which bird is leading a flock in flight that simultaneously changes direction.

There are virtually no leading indicators among the dozens of variables that we've measured. The only systematic discrepancy that we've detected (using high-tech econometric analysis) is, unexpectedly, what appears to be a modest tendency for economic inequality, especially wealth inequality, to lag the others. Initially, we suspected that economic inequality was the master driver of these linked trends, but the statistical evidence suggests that economic inequality is, if anything, slightly more likely to be the caboose of social change than the engine.[5]

Nor can we argue that politics is the key to the I-we-I curve. One or two of our empirical indicators of depolarization crested before the other curves, but our best single measure of polarization throughout the twentieth century, congressional voting, does not fit the idea that political polarization preceded the other factors we've discussed.

Bits of evidence seem to suggest that cultural change might have led the way, contrary to the common belief (perhaps derived from Marxism) that culture is merely froth on the waves of socioeconomic change. Contrary to economic determinism, the turn away from social Darwinism began several decades before the trend toward greater economic equality was firmly in place. Conversely, at the time that the cultural rumbles of the 1950s foretold the turn away from community, the increase in inequality still lay decades in the future. These bits of evidence are tantalizing, but this evidence is too weak to support any definitive claim.

In short, at this stage the available evidence offers virtually no indication of an uncaused first cause of the I-we-I syndrome. All the birds in this flock wheeled around at almost precisely the same time, seemingly leaderless. That fact seriously complicates any effort at causal analysis.

Another obstacle to any straightforward causal analysis is the very breadth of indicators encompassed by our story. Any simple "X → Y" claim would run afoul of the wide range and diversity of our Ys. A specific explanation (X in our notation) that might work for Y_1 (say, income inequality) seems unlikely also to explain Y_2 (say, club membership), Y_3 (say, split ticket voting), Y_4 (say, baby names), and so on through the scores of Ys we've examined. We shall return to this issue of causation momentarily, but we already see that it is prima facie unlikely to be a simple case of "X → Y."

This book is about change and turning points in equality, polarization, social solidarity, and individualism, not about static levels. At a turning point what changes is the direction of change, not immediately the level. When you step on the gas, your car does not immediately reach top speed, and when you put on the brakes, the car's momentum slows, but your speed does not instantly go to zero. The same is true in society; because of social inertia, change rarely occurs instantly.

The Progressive Era, for example, witnessed a sea change away from the increasing inequality and polarization and social fragmentation of the Gilded Age toward equality, comity, and community, but the *level* of equality, comity, and community did not change overnight. Equality and community in 1920 were still low by the standards of the 1960s, after the underlying trend had run its course. What did change in the 1900–1920 period was the direction of change, and in the long run, that was fundamental.

Similarly, the 1960s represented an unmistakable turning point away from "we" toward "I," a turning point we shall explore in the second half of this chapter, but in terms of the *level* of equality, polarization, marriage rates, and the like, 1970 was not dramatically different from 1960. What changed dramatically in the 1960s was the direction of our nation's momentum, and as we shall see, that change in the direction of change was perfectly visible to Americans at the time.[6] "Change in direction of change" sounds esoteric, but in fact turning points are probably easier to sense in real time than more gradual, year-to-year changes between the turning points.

The inverted U-curve at the heart of our narrative is not perfectly smooth or symmetrical. In particular, the trend in the first half of the century was not strictly linear, though it was mostly monotonic, that is, increasing or pausing, but rarely reversing and never for long. The biggest shifts toward "we" occurred before roughly 1920 and then again after roughly 1935, separated by a visible pause centered in the 1920s. This pause during, or just after, the Roaring Twenties can be seen in most of our curves— economic equality, polarization, religious engagement, club membership, family formation, public policy, and even baby names. In other words, if we had stopped to analyze America in the early 1930s, the longer-term trends would not have been obvious or predictable.[7]

In most conventional accounts of the history of twentieth-century America, the New Deal and World War II together constituted the central pivot point, dividing the twentieth century into "before" and "after." For many purposes that traditional account captures important features of American history, especially in foreign policy. However, from the perspective offered in this book, twentieth-century American history pivoted in the 1960s, not the 1940s, as we have repeatedly seen in previous chapters.

Given the tensions between community and individualism, it is natural to use the metaphor of a pendulum, swinging back and forth between those two poles. As a pendulum moves steadily in one direction, countervailing forces begin to build up, and the pendulum eventually reverses direction. After the reversal, movement in the opposite direction accelerates, but as the pendulum moves toward the opposite pole, it slows in response to equilibrating forces, until it reaches the other pole and once again reverses. This metaphor leads naturally to a search for equilibrating forces, especially as the pendulum nears one pole or the other. What events rupture people's confidence in current institutions and behavioral patterns? What events tear us apart or knit us together? Which ideas come to seem outdated, and which ideas now seem fresh and more attractive, and why? Something like that happened during the 1960s, and later in this chapter we will explore those very questions.

Not surprisingly, some acute observers of American history have used this pendular metaphor, as we occasionally do. The economist Albert O. Hirschman in *Shifting Involvements* wrote about cycles of "private interest" and "public action," a distinction akin to (though not identical to) our own distinction between individualism and community.[8] The former are periods when people care most about personal gain and do not relate to the larger community or support public actions. The latter are periods of collectivist, pro-government thinking and action. Hirschman pointed out that for such a pendular pattern to exist, something *outside* the private interest/public action framework—some "exogenous variable"—must cause these shifts in involvement. The answer he found was disappointment—namely, that people become disenchanted by one mode of thinking and shift to the other. At some point, the growing imbalance between the vices of one mind-set and the virtues of the other reaches a tipping point, as when adding grains of sand to a balance. The pendular reversal can be seen as backlash to excesses of the previous period. In our case, by the 1960s, communitarian views seemed clichéd and out-of-date, whereas the individualistic views on both left and right seemed innovative. That countervailing pressure can be seen, for example, in the rapid rise of critiques of conformity in the 1950s that we noted in Chapter 5.[9]

On the other hand, the pendulum metaphor has serious weaknesses for our purposes. In social life, unlike the physical world, there is no mechanical equilibrium. A physical pendulum is moved at a perfectly smooth pace by the law of gravity. By contrast, the curves that we have examined in all four spheres display fits and starts, periods of rapid change and interludes of stasis. More important, as we have discussed in virtually all our chapters, human agency and leadership are essential. Change, whether for the better or for the worse, is not historically inevitable. The pendulum metaphor (like some cyclical theories of history) implies that the pivots in the 1900s and the 1960s (and conceivably one in the 2020s) were (or are) preordained, but we do not believe that. Since our American pendulum is moved by human agency, we doubt that the turning point in the 1960s was ineluctable, as the pendulum metaphor implies, simply because America had reached some maximum possible level of "we-ness."[10]

CAUSATION

There's a lot we don't know about causation. Precisely because the curves are so closely intertwined, our conventional tools for causal analysis, such as looking at leads and lags, fail us. Moreover, there are almost certainly different causal backgrounds to each of our empirical indicators, and equally certainly, there must be complicated feedback loops. For example, economic inequality at one stage might encourage polarization, while at a subsequent stage polarization might foster inequality.[11] Such feedback loops preclude any simple causal story. But causal investigation in science often is the last step, not the first step in understanding, especially where true experiments are impossible, such as in astronomy and much of social science. In such cases, describing a phenomenon and speculating about causes is a significant contribution, and we aspire to that in this book. If future researchers find our description and our speculations plausible, they will doubtless make progress on understanding causation.

Social scientists and historians typically differ in their approach to explanation. When we speak to quantitative social scientists about the I-we-I curve, they often say that they would fully believe our story only if we can identify a "cause" of the curve; but when we speak to historians they usually say that if we did identify a "cause" of the curve, they would not believe our story, because "history is always more complicated than that." In short, social scientists tend to prefer causal analysis, while most historians prefer narratives.[12]

Robert Shiller, a Nobel Prize–winning economist, has recently argued that historians may be on to something that social scientists should not ignore. Shiller's book *Narrative Economics* opens with him reminiscing about an enlightening undergraduate history class in which he read an account of the 1920s by, coincidentally, Frederick Lewis Allen, the same historian whose image of "streams of events run[ning] side by side down the channel of time" we cited earlier in this chapter. Shiller writes that what he learned in that class about the causes of the Great Depression was far more useful in understanding that period of economic and financial turmoil than standard econometric accounts.[13]

Be that as it may, this book is primarily about trends and narratives, not certifiable causes. The various trends we have identified are braided together by reciprocal causality, so it is difficult and even misleading to identify causes and effects. In the twentieth century the American experiment followed a long arc of increasing solidarity and then increasing individualism. That arc had implications for equality, for politics, for social capital, and for culture. It led to an increasingly zero-sum, tribal view of society and, eventually, to Trumpism. The trends in economics, politics, society, and culture were entwined in an inextricable, but still interpretable skein.

Some might be tempted to ascribe this syndrome ultimately to cultural dynamics—I to we to I. But what then explains culture? Material conditions? Structural change? Social movements? Politics? Do ideas drive change or respond to it? Max Weber, perhaps the leading social theorist of the last two centuries, saw culture as a historical process that at times leads social change and at other times simply reinforces it. According to Weber, people are very much motivated by material interests. But using a striking metaphor, he argued that culture can act like a switch on railroad tracks: "Not ideas, but material and ideal interests directly govern men's conduct. Yet very frequently the 'world-images' that have been created by 'ideas' have, like switchmen, determined the tracks along which action has been pushed by the dynamic of interest."[14]

For the reasons just laid out, we eschew broad causal interpretations of the I-we-I curve, but it is useful to summarize briefly some of the causes most frequently suggested by other researchers. These factors are implausible as simple causes for the full set of inverted U-curves, but they may well be implicated in a more complex interpretation.

- When pundits ponder nowadays why our politics are so polarized, or our economy so biased, or our families so weakened, or our churches so empty, or our culture so self-centered, two of the most commonly cited culprits are "*young people these days*" and the *internet*. However, amidst the tangle of possible causes that we review in this chapter, one thing is perfectly clear: Neither Millennials nor Twitter and Facebook can possibly be blamed for the I-we-I curve. The longer time frame of our study gives those alleged culprits an ironclad alibi. The declines of the last half century predate the Millennial generation and the internet by decades. But if youth and social networking are not the problem, they may well be part of the solution. We shall turn to that possibility in the next chapter.
- Many accounts of political, economic, social, and cultural decline of the last half century begin with the more cohesive America of the 1950s, and ask why things have gotten worse.[15] Was it the Boomers? Working women? The welfare state? The pill? TV? Such accounts contain insights, but that basic framing of the causal question makes sense only if we begin the story in the postwar era. (For example, the impact of TV

on the decline of social capital now seems less significant, given the longer and broader perspective of this book, than it did at the writing of *Bowling Alone* twenty years ago.) Finding a single "cause" that could explain *both* the ups *and* the downs of what we are calling the I-we-I curve is more challenging.

- *Big, centralized government*, with the proliferation of federal bureaucracies and the expansion of public welfare programs, is sometimes said to have undercut the mediating institutions of civil society, "crowded out" private generosity, and sapped individual initiative. This is a common explanation among conservative commentators, who attribute the reversal from we to I in the 1960s to the welfare state.[16] Empirical evidence for "crowding out" is modest, for across states in the US and across countries in the world, the correlation between big government and social solidarity appears to be, if anything, faintly positive, not negative.[17]

  However, the more fundamental problem with the big government explanation is that by most measures (all spending, or spending on the welfare state in real per capita terms, or spending as a fraction of GDP; number of government employees) the size of government lagged behind the I-we-I curve by several decades. Federal government spending and the number of employees rose steadily in tandem with the I-we-I curve from 1900 to 1970 and kept rising until they leveled off after the 1980s. That is exactly opposite of the pattern that we would expect if big government killed civil society. In fact, the empirical evidence strongly suggests that government size is a *consequence* of the I-we-I curve, not a *cause*. The best evidence is that the size of government responded to changes in Americans' sense that we are all in this together, and that growth of government did not cause increased individualism.[18] Libertarians as a matter of philosophy might prefer increased individualism, but their theory of what caused what cannot be correct.

- What about *war* as the cause? In 1897 the French sociologist Émile Durkheim had found that social solidarity rises during wars, lowering (for example) suicide rates.[19] Barely a decade later the American sociologist William Graham Sumner argued that "the exigencies of war with outsiders are what make peace inside. . . . Loyalty to the group, sacrifice for it, hatred and contempt for outsiders, brotherhood within, warlikeness without—all grow together, common products of the same situation."[20]

Certainly World War II entailed shared sacrifice and national solidarity among Americans. "Together We Can Do It" became a national slogan during the war, alongside massive civilian service programs and propaganda that emphasized bridging differences, such as Hollywood's famed multiethnic foxhole.[21] World War II no doubt contributed to the shape of the I-we-I curve. However, as we have noted in earlier chapters, the increases in economic equality, political comity, civic engagement, family formation, philanthropy, and cultural solidarity began decades before World War II and continued for decades afterward, so war cannot be the primary cause of the inverted U-curve.

- *Economic inequality*: Many commentators, focused on trends in health, political polarization, social integration, and trust simply assume, without good evidence, that the hard facts of economics must have driven the soft facts of politics, society, and culture.[22] We do not doubt—indeed, we insist—that economic inequality is a central strand in the causally braided I-we-I syndrome. However, as we have seen, economic inequality seems to be, if anything, a slightly lagging indicator, so it can hardly be the master cause of the syndrome.

- *Does material abundance or material adversity foster a focus on the self?* Does prosperity or hard times encourage social solidarity? It turns out that both sides in this theoretical pairing have persuasive advocates.

  - Some argue that affluence encourages a focus on "we," whereas hard times produce a focus on "I." In the midst of the postwar boom, a widely read book, *People of Plenty* by historian David Potter (1954), emphasized that material abundance was fundamental to the consumerist consensus in American society.[23] More recently, Tyler Cowen has argued that economic dynamism before 1973 allowed for policies that promoted equality, and conversely, the post-1970s stagnation explains the trend toward inequality and political dysfunction. That stagnation has in turn been explained by the end of a long period (1880–1940) of high innovation and productivity growth.[24]

When people are affluent and satisfied, so the argument goes, they can afford to be more generous toward others. Without low-hanging fruit, however, politics becomes much more contentious. In times of austerity, constraints on both household and government budgets make people look inward to protect their offspring and insure themselves against growing uncertainty. When material constraints lessen, I can be more generous of spirit, whereas if material constraints tighten, I hunker down and worry about my immediate self-interest.

This argument has been recently reinforced by work by Send-hil Mullainathan and Eldar Shafir in experimental microeconomics, framed in terms of the impact of scarcity on people's focus of attention.[25] The general premise is that folks with scarce resources are prone to tunnel vision, diverting their attention toward their immediate needs and away from everything outside of that tunnel. Conversely, material abundance allows altruism.

• On the other hand, other observers argue, the high joblessness and economic insecurity of the Great Depression coincided with an upsurge of "we're all in this together" sentiment both in civil society and in public policy. Analogously, economic historian Eric Hobsbawm argued that postwar affluence and economic security led to the rise of "an absolute a-social individualism," a "society consisting of an otherwise unconnected assemblage of self-centred individuals pursuing only their own gratification." Affluence undermined collective institutions, eroded moral norms, and ushered in an age that worshipped the self over and against society.[26] In a similar vein, political scientist Ronald Inglehart famously argued that it was the "post-materialist" children of the postwar boom (unlike their parents, raised during the Great Depression) who valued individual autonomy and self-actualization.[27] Inglehart's intuition, framed at the peak of postwar affluence, was that as material constraints loosen, people feel freer to focus on self-development and individuality, not merely on satisfying their material needs and getting along with others. On that theory, too, prosperity produces an "I" society.

•   In fact, we have been unable to detect any consistent correlation, positive or negative, between prosperity or hard times and the I-we-I curve. Communitarianism rose through both the Great Depression and the long postwar boom, while individualism was high during the economic distress of the 1890s and the 1970s, as well as during the booms of the 1980s and 1990s and 2010s. More specifically, we find no significant year-by-year correlation of the I-we-I curve and the unemployment rate, one way or the other.

• *Backlash against gender and racial liberation.* As discussed in Chapters 3, 6, and 7, we do find evidence of backlash in explaining the reversal of the I-we-I curve after the rights revolutions of the Sixties. In our judgment it would be going too far to say that race and gender together are the "master cause" of the curve, since both women and African Americans made progress through the long upward curve of "we," in large part through their own efforts, but backlash is certainly a central part of the explanation for the post-1960s reversal. In this case, feedback loops complicate things, but in the end it is impossible to talk about causation and the I-we-I curve—or anything else in American history—without considering race and gender.

• Finally, a common interpretation of the decline of community in the last half century attributes it to *globalization*, including both international trade and immigration. (A version of this interpretation seems to underlie President Trump's policies to "Make America Great Again.")

    •   As a matter of fact, the curves for both international trade as a fraction of the total US economy and foreign-born as a fraction of the total US population track the I-we-I curve reasonably closely.

        - Imports and exports as a fraction of the US GDP declined sharply from 11 percent in 1900 and 15 percent in 1920 to about 5–7 percent from 1930 to 1969, as Depression-era trade wars and World War II caused the collapse of world trade. Then, however, for the half century after 1970 globalization caused international trade as a fraction of the US economy to increase sharply from about 7 percent to about 27 percent.

        - Foreign-born inhabitants as a fraction of the US population fell from a high of about 15 percent in 1910 to a low of about 5 percent in 1965, a decline attributable to the imposition of strict immigration limits by the Immigration Act of 1924. The Immigration and Nationality Act of 1965 reopened America to immigrants and the fraction of immigrants (legal and illegal) rose steadily over the next half century from 5 percent to about 14 percent.[28]

- So judging simply by matching curves, global flows of goods and people are closely correlated with the I-we-I curve. Going behind these crude numbers, however, the hypothesis that either trade or migration "caused" the I-we-I curve is less firmly based on evidence. Most specific studies of international trade offer mixed evidence about the effects of trade on the distribution of income, and that is to speak only about the links of trade to economic inequality. It is even harder to imagine how increasing trade flows could cause people to marry later or attend church less often or give their children unusual names or use the first personal singular more often.

- The argument that immigration encourages self-centeredness seems at first glance more difficult to refute. Indeed, one of us attained some notoriety for suggesting that ethnic diversity causes people to hunker down. But that study added that the linkage works only in the short run.[29] In the long run and with proper policies, we argued, social divisions can eventually give way to "more encompassing identities" that create a "new, more capacious sense of 'we.' "

- Indeed something like that happened in the United States during the four decades between 1924, when immigration was shut off, and 1965, when immigration reform reopened America's door.[30] During the long upswing of the I-we-I curve Americans became increasingly comfortable with ethnic diversity and increasingly open to immigration reform. It is no accident that the bipartisan Immigration and Nationality Act of 1965 was passed by Congress at precisely the peak of the I-we-I curve. At the time of the law's passage, fully 70 percent of Americans across party lines favored it.[31] Far from immigration preventing a rise in social and cultural solidarity, the opposite seems equally likely: The greater the solidarity of a society, the more open it becomes to immigration and diversity.

♦ In the case of economic inequality the role of immigration has been much debated, but the argument that over the long run immigration causes inequality is not strong. As Anne Case and Angus Deaton have recently summarized the empirical evidence, "immigration, although it has attracted a great deal of attention, cannot have been the main cause of the long-term stagnation of working-class wages nor for the removal of a ladder up to the middle class. . . . The National Academy of Sciences, in its 2017 report on immigration, concluded its review of the evidence on wages in the words 'particularly when measured over a period of ten years or more, the impact of immigration on overall native wages may be small or close to zero.'"[32]

We do not claim that the case for some impact of globalization on the I-we-I curve is open-and-shut, but we do claim that the case for it as the primary cause—a case now being made by white nationalist groups—is implausible.

So far in this chapter we've used a wide-angle lens to get as comprehensive a picture as possible of what happened to America between the first Gilded Age at the end of the nineteenth century and the second Gilded Age at the beginning of the twenty-first century. That view has enabled us to spot with unexpected clarity the point at which the balance between the individual and the community shifted. In the second half of this chapter we now zoom rapidly in to focus on the decade—indeed, the specific years—in which that pivot occurred. How did it happen that America came into the Sixties as a "we" nation and came out an "I" nation?

THE SIXTIES AS THE HINGE OF THE TWENTIETH CENTURY

The Sixties is one of the most debated epochs in American history, but if there is one thing that virtually all scholars agree upon, it is that America changed dramatically in a very short period of time. In such diverse realms as popular music, fashion, the arts, race relations, sexual norms, gender roles, drug use, political institutions, religious practice, and consumption habits, rapid and highly visible transformations took place in the 1960s. The changes in America between roughly 1960 and roughly 1975 were so head-spinning as to be palpable to most people living through them.[33]

It is customary to use big historical events, like World War II or the Great Depression, as landmarks for understanding big historical trends. But many such trends move slowly in patterns that are less evident to contemporary observers, and are (like some ancient ruins) visible only to observers at thirty thousand feet. The long uptrend in egalitarian community from 1900 to the 1960s was like that, and only recently has the long downtrend after 1970 become apparent to contemporaries. But the actual turning point of the Sixties was manifest at the time.

Political philosopher Mark Lilla has discerned this same before-and-after contrast, though he frames it in terms of presidential leadership, not wider social trends.

> The Roosevelt Dispensation pictured an America where citizens were involved in a collective enterprise to guard one another against risk, hardship, and the denial of fundamental rights. Its watchwords were solidarity, opportunity, and public duty. The Reagan Dispensation pictured a more individualistic America where families and small communities and businesses would flourish once freed from the shackles of the state. Its watchwords were self-reliance and minimal government.[34]

While we agree with Lilla about the contrast in political culture between the 1930s and the 1980s, the evidence in this book strongly suggests that the turning point can be dated much more precisely to the 1960s.

There are major debates among historians about how to evaluate the Sixties, in large part because of disagreements about the preceding era. Historians who view the Fifties as conformist and oppressive welcome the Sixties' liberation and individualism, whereas those who cherish the achievements of the "mid-century consensus" condemn the chaos of the Sixties. (As we gain greater distance from the Sixties, the debates of historians have obviously become more nuanced and complex than this simple dichotomy.) But the areas of agreement among historians of the Sixties are equally important.[35]

- Almost all historians agree that a major historical turning point took place between roughly 1968 and 1974—a "revolution," a "renaissance," a "fracture," a "shock wave," a point after which "everything changed," creating a "new America."[36] Maurice Isserman and Michael Kazin, for example, argue that the Sixties ushered in a moment of historical rupture on the scale of the American Civil War, dividing the twentieth century into a pre- and post-Sixties world, a change from which "there is no going back, any more than the lost world of the antebellum South could have been restored after 1865."[37]

- Most historians also agree on an important distinction between the first half of the 1960s and the second half—"years of hope" and "days of rage," as Todd Gitlin famously put it.[38] Widely shared prosperity, the Civil Rights movement (culminating in the 1964 Civil Rights Act and the 1965 Voting Rights Act), and progress toward equality, democracy, and tolerance (symbolized by the Great Society of 1964–1965 and the immigration reform of 1965) represented the "years of hope." By contrast, the Vietnam war protests (1966–1970), urban unrest (1965–1969), the rise of the Black Panthers (1966–1968), the "law and order" counterattack (1968–1972), the convulsions of 1968, and the stagflation and rancorous gas lines of the 1970s represented "days of rage." In the first half of the Sixties various left-wing reform movements coalesced into "The Movement," whereas in the second half "The Movement" splintered into fractious sects. Meanwhile, on the right during the second half of the decade, the "silent majority" fueled backlash against the liberal establishment, whether over race, "tax-and-spend," crime, or cultural pluralism. In short, there were two "Sixties," not one, and the second one spilled into the early 1970s.[39]

- The vast majority of scholars describe the post-1960s age as an individualistic one, in the sense that American politics, culture, and intellectual life increasingly prioritized the self over and against society. Historian Eric Hobsbawm, for example, argues that "the cultural revolution of the later twentieth century can thus be best understood as the triumph of the individual over society, or rather, the breaking of the threads which in the past had woven human beings into social textures."[40] The result: a crisis of authority in virtually every social institution, from government to religion, from unions to the family, leading to disillusionment and disengagement. Whether they approved or disapproved of the U-turn, most observers and indeed most Americans at the time recognized it.[41]

In other words, mainstream America entered the Sixties in an increasingly "we" mode—with communes, shared values, and accelerating efforts toward racial and economic equality—and we left the Sixties in an increasingly "I" mode—focused on "rights," culture wars, and what would be almost instantly dubbed the "Me Decade" of the 1970s. Rather like a swimmer making a flip turn, Americans entered the 1960s moving toward community, but midway through the decade abruptly changed direction and left the 1960s behind, moving toward individualism. In this half of this chapter we seek to document and understand that rapid turning point.

Because the Sixties are darkly associated in historical memory with cultural conflict, political polarization, and economic malaise, we need to remember the sense of optimism and what historian James Patterson terms "Grand Expectations" of accelerating affluence that prevailed as the decade opened. The backdrop was the postwar prosperity, which gathered even more speed in the booming economy of the 1960s. This virtually uninterrupted, generally accelerating, and widely shared boom was the most important feature of the quarter century after World War II, raising aspirations and expectations. Real median family income rose by 30 percent during the Sixties, and the poverty rate was cut from 22 percent in 1959 to 11 percent in 1973.[42]

The economy was not the only thing booming in the Sixties: The Baby Boom of the 1950s rolled on, reinforcing national optimism, even as the earliest Boomers were thronging into universities. As we showed in Chapter 2, a rapidly growing fraction of this rapidly growing pool of adolescents was converging on overcrowded campuses, a portentous development that would leave its mark on the second half of the decade. Taken together, these economic and demographic booms contributed to the national mood of great expectations.

Moreover, entering the 1960s, the United States was still under the spell of our unparalleled victory in World War II—the so-called "good war" that conjoined our highest national ideals (defeating fascism and spreading democracy) to our unmatched global power—military, economic, cultural, diplomatic. Most Americans were proud of our country and confident about our national institutions. (Recall the evidence on trust in government that we reviewed in Chapter 3.) We could not see over the horizon, however, and few suspected that we were riding for a fall.

To be sure, the Cold War and the threat of thermonuclear war had preoccupied us and shadowed our self-confidence during the 1950s, but John F. Kennedy's campaign rhetoric in 1960 was rooted in optimism that after the dozy years of Ike, a new generation could, as he said in his acceptance speech at the Democratic convention, "get the country moving again."[43] With the advent of the new administration and its New Frontier almost nothing seemed beyond our power—go to the moon in a decade, bring about enduring global peace, even perhaps shed at last our centuries-old legacy of racism.

In 1958 economist John Kenneth Galbraith (soon to become an advisor to JFK) in *The Affluent Society* had described the post–World War II United States as flourishing in the private sphere but impoverished in the public sector, with inadequate social and physical infrastructure and persistent income disparities. Even though we now see that America in the late 1950s was near an apogee of shared affluence, Galbraith's book gave voice to ambitions for further advance and expressed the unfulfilled aspirations of a "we"-focused America. It was the high tide of egalitarian optimism.[44] In the first half of the Sixties this increasingly encompassing sense of "we," coupled with rising national self-confidence, would produce a succession of social movements, though where exactly those movements would lead no one could yet know.

Between March 1962 and February 1963 no fewer than four groundbreaking, best-selling popular tracts described deep social problems in America that the authors argued should (and could) be addressed. Each book helped trigger a major intellectual and social movement that would reverberate well into the next century.

- Michael Harrington's *The Other America: Poverty in the United States* (published in March 1962) helped to start the Great Society.
- Rachel Carson's *Silent Spring* (published in September 1962) generated a half century of environmentalism.
- James Baldwin's *The Fire Next Time* (published in January 1963) eloquently implored Americans to transcend "the Negro Problem" and foreshadowed the grim racial strains of the next half century.[45]
- Betty Friedan's *The Feminine Mystique* (published in February 1963) inspired a new feminism that would develop over the next half century, though not always in ways that Friedan would applaud.

These authors (two women, two men; one African American, three whites) and their books were products of the rising tide of "we-ness" during the first half of the century. (Three of the four had been born between 1921 and 1928; only Carson, born in 1907, was of a slightly older generation.) Consistent with the pervasive ethos in which they were raised, all argued for collective action to address shared public problems.[46] They were radicals, but not cynics. They were deeply critical of mid-century America, but they assumed that mid-century Americans could be rallied to their causes. They were focused on the ways in which America was falling short of its own ideals, but they did not reject those ideas as bankrupt or give up on shared goals.

These high aspirations also embodied high expectations. America had big problems, but we could fix them. We were poised for further progress. However, if those expectations proved excessive and we encountered turbulence on the voyage, we were (unknowingly) also poised for rancorous disillusionment. This reversal of fortune and mood occurred more rapidly than anyone could have imagined in 1963. Not coincidentally, the four issues highlighted by these books—inequality, the environment, race, and gender—remain *the* central issues in American politics nearly sixty years later, an agenda left unfulfilled after the turn to "I."

The change that lay just over the horizon in 1963 would be so momentous that for people living through it, history seemed to pivot almost overnight. An intriguing quantitative measure of how fateful a decade it turned out to be is how many books historians have written focused specifically on the Sixties. It sometimes seems that more books have been devoted to the 1960s than to all the other decades of the twentieth century combined. In fact, virtually every year between 1964 and 1974 (and even a single month) has been the focus of a major book on that year (or month) as one that "transformed America," or "changed America forever," or "rocked the world," or in which simply "everything changed."

- John Margolis, *The Last Innocent Year: America in 1964*
- James Patterson, *The Eve of Destruction: How 1965 Transformed America*
- Jon Savage, *1966: The Year the Decade Exploded*
- Victor Brooks, *1967: The Year of Fire and Ice*
- Mark Kurlansky, *1968: The Year That Rocked the World*
- Rob Kirkpatrick, *1969: The Year Everything Changed*
- Andreas Killen, *1973 Nervous Breakdown: Watergate, Warhol, and the Birth of Post-Sixties America*
- Jim Robenalt, *January 1973: Watergate, Roe v. Wade, Vietnam and the Month That Changed America Forever*

In all of American history only the Founding and the Civil War seem to have inspired the same intensity of historiographical interest as the Sixties, a telling pair of parallels.

I, ME, MINE

We often think of the earthquake of the Sixties in political terms, but it was perhaps most palpable in culture, especially pop culture. As we noted earlier, the Sixties cultural revolution took the form of a youthful rejection of the suffocating "we" of the 1950s in favor of liberation and individualism. Ronald Inglehart argued that the material affluence of the 1960s had freed the younger generation to turn to "self-actualization." "Man does not live by bread alone, especially if he has plenty of bread" was the adroit way Inglehart summarized his thesis.[47] And it was a short step from self-actualization to narcissism. Charles Reich's best-seller *The Greening of America* proclaimed a revolutionary new "Consciousness III," a rejection of "society, the public interest, and institutions as the primary reality," and an embrace of "the individual self [as] the only true reality."[48]

This shift was perhaps most obvious in the world of pop music, where the pivot from "we" to "I" was so visible and so quick that we can almost date it to the month. The mid-Sixties rock band Buffalo Springfield caught winds of the change when they sang "Something's happening here/What it is ain't exactly clear." One of the most influential artists of that momentous decade was Bob Dylan, whose roots were in acoustic guitar and folk music, as exemplified by his early hits, "Blowin' in the Wind" (1963) and "The Times They Are A'Changin'" (1964). His contemporaries and collaborators included Joan Baez, Woody Guthrie, Pete Seeger, and Peter, Paul and Mary, all of whom became world famous for their social commentary and calls for brotherly love. The early Dylan, like his peers, was a balladeer for social justice.

But in July 1965 at the Newport Folk Festival, Dylan's famous mid-concert turn from acoustic anthems to electric rock aroused strong (and mostly negative) reactions, including among his fellow musicians. Nevertheless, in the succeeding years, Dylan moved deliberately from inspiring community-building and social protest to expressing his individuality. It is thus not surprising that Dylan's popularity persisted long into the "I" period, whereas that of his peers—who did not follow this broader cultural turn—did not.[49]

The Beatles were another pop phenomenon embodying much more than music—they symbolized a generation coming of age.[50] Like Dylan, the Beatles in the early 1960s sang in harmony about togetherness—"I Want to Hold Your Hand" (1963); "All You Need Is Love" (1967); "With a Little Help from My Friends" (1967). But already by 1966 they had become more attuned to isolation and alienation, when they wrote of Eleanor Rigby and Father McKenzie: "All the lonely people / Where do they all come from?"

By 1970 the Beatles had split up and begun to follow distinct paths, morphing from a team making music together into individuals on separate voyages of self-discovery. The last track they finished recording as a band was written by George Harrison, its lyrics serving simultaneously as his personal protest about the group's fractious dynamics and as a remarkably literal depiction of the broader Sixties' turn from "we" to "I."[51]

All I can hear, I me mine / I me mine, I me mine.

Six months later, John Lennon replied in his solo hit, "God":

I don't believe in Beatles / I just believe in me.

The idea of self-love as a virtue, not a vice, became a New Age "thing" in the late 1960s and 1970s. The refrain "learning to love yourself . . . is the greatest love of all" was originally recorded in a song for the 1977 Muhammad Ali biopic *The Greatest*. (In later years the phrase would reappear in smash hits by Whitney Houston and Olivia Newton-John.) The lines typified the cultural turn toward individualism. It is impossible to imagine Nat "King" Cole or Ella Fitzgerald or even Elvis Presley rhapsodizing about self-love.

Ironically, Muhammad Ali himself was not an advocate of self-love— quite the contrary. In 1975, speaking to students at Harvard, he uttered what might be the shortest poem in history: "Me? We!"[52] He could not have known that as he spoke, a sea change in American culture was under way that would, in effect, reverse the word order and punctuation.

CONCATENATED CRISES

The Sixties was not only a cultural turning point, but a time when a concatenation of multi-dimensional and otherwise unrelated public crises brought many long-simmering conflicts to a boil:

- The assassinations of JFK, RFK, and MLK
- The Vietnam War
- Student upheavals
- The Civil Rights revolution

- The urban crisis and urban riots
- Domestic terrorism and nihilistic violence
- The women's movement
- The pill and the sexual revolution
- The counterculture and the drug epidemic
- Unprecedented questioning of traditional religious and family values
- A series of environmental crises
- Watergate and Nixon's resignation
- Stagflation and oil shortages and economic malaise

In a fundamental sense these were all largely independent and unrelated phenomena—whatever "caused" the pill was not what "caused" Vietnam, and whatever "caused" the drug epidemic was not what "caused" the oil shortages. But together, these various crises seem to have had a synergistic effect, producing something like a national nervous breakdown. It was the ultimate perfect storm, and the intensity of the storm itself contributed to the sharp cultural and political pivot.

For some, it all started on November 22, 1963, the day John F. Kennedy was gunned down in Dallas. JFK had embodied the national optimism of the early 1960s, and his assassination was a senseless tragedy that struck deep at the heart of American innocence. But this was only the first of a series of assassinations that would rock America in the 1960s.

Next came Martin Luther King, Jr. on April 4, 1968. King's eerie prediction that he might not live to see the Promised Land for which he had fought so long and hard compounded the sense of loss. Much of the nation had looked to him as a shining beacon of hope and a stalwart proponent of peace amid what had been, and would continue to be, an ugly and violent struggle to bring justice to the black community.[53] The divisions and disillusionment that took over the Civil Rights movement after Dr. King's death struck deep at our collective resolve to fight the good fight.

Two months later on June 8 Robert F. Kennedy was assassinated in the midst of a presidential bid. RFK is an intriguing illustration of the rapid personal transformations of the mid-1960s.[54] His loyal service to Joe McCarthy in the 1950s had represented the intolerant dark side of community, but he was deeply shaken by his brother's assassination in 1963. In his subsequent turn toward racial and economic justice and away from the Vietnam War, he had become a crusading champion of the downtrodden, and an establishment voice echoing Dr. King's call for a more encompassing "we." At the moment of his assassination he was reaching across lines of race, class, generation, and even ideology. "Might have beens" are not evidence, but his example poses an important, if unanswerable question about whether able leadership might have delayed or even averted the pendulum's reversal. Robert Kennedy's death struck deep at America's fraying sense of hope.

As the Sixties wore on, violence increasingly seemed the currency of the day. Vietnam, America's first televised war, seemed endless as it played out in bloody episode after bloody episode. Mass protests went unheeded by a succession of presidents, and frustrations mounted. The demonstrations at the Democrats' 1968 Chicago convention found New Deal veterans inside, and young activists outside protesting—while being attacked by working-class cops. The bitter losses of Vietnam struck deep at our belief in American greatness.

The fact of the Baby Boom meant that throughout the 1960s and 1970s, the ratio of adults to children in society was dramatically lower than in the normal population pyramid, leading toward a *Lord of the Flies* slippery slope.[55] Dominated by young, educated whites seeking greater inclusion for themselves and oppressed minorities, violent protests became an epic struggle for control of traditional power structures, which struck deep at our faith in American institutions.

At the same time, the nation's inner cities were exploding with violence as well. The urban riots that flared from 1965 to 1969—the worst in America in one hundred years—were, on the part of racial minorities, a bitter expression of impatience with the pace of social change and with America's failure to make good on the promises of civil rights legislation. For the whites and law enforcement officers who fought back, the riots were an occasion to unleash latent anger about the effects of desegregation and the loss of dominance. And for everyone else who watched on TV, they were a terrifying display of the worst of human nature on every side. A mad five-year spasm of brutal, murderous nihilism followed, embodied in the headline-grabbing Charles Manson Family murders (1969), the Weather-men bombings (1969–1974), and the violent actions of Patty Hearst and the Symbionese Liberation Army (1974–1975). Such senseless violence struck deep at our confidence in public safety and the rule of law.

Meanwhile, another, more subtle form of revolt was sweeping the nation. The women's movement, while it brought long-delayed forms of equality, caused intense debate about the effects on the nuclear family. Simultaneously, the sexual revolution was challenging behavioral norms through popular culture as well as legal reforms. The FDA approved the birth-control pill for contraceptive use in 1960, and in 1965 the U.S. Su-preme Court declared it unconstitutional for states to outlaw the use of birth control by married couples. In principle and increasingly in practice, birth control separated sex from marriage.

The change in sexual mores came with breathtaking speed. The frac-tion of all Americans who believed that premarital sex was "not wrong" doubled in barely four years from 24 percent in 1969 to 47 percent in 1973. For the most part this was a classic case of generational change, as a well-defined cohort of young people, four fifths of whom accepted sex be-fore marriage, barged into a population of their elders, four fifths of whom rejected that idea—producing a revolution in moral views.[56] In the eyes of many, women's liberation and the sexual revolution struck deeply at the most basic unit of society.

Alongside women's liberation came counterculture. The hippie move-ment reached its apex during 1967's Summer of Love. But the movement's initial focus on "free love," communal living, and spiritual transcendence soon gave way to increasingly hedonistic exploits, hard drugs, and "do your own thing" permissiveness. The once-so-optimistic communes con-structed in the springtime sun of the 1960s collapsed in the winter rains of the 1970s. What followed almost inevitably was a growing disillusion-ment with the failed ideals of the early 1960s—what Todd Gitlin would call *The Twilight of Common Dreams*.[57] The shocking rejection of the status quo struck deep at cultural consensus, and left an entire generation of adults feeling that "nothing less than the soul of America was at stake,"[58] as the groundwork was laid for the "culture wars" of the next half century.

While parents and pundits worried about America's moral decay, environmental decay was increasingly evident across the nation. The previous decades' blithe utilization of chemicals and technologies that had been insufficiently tested for safety was shown in the Sixties to have devastating long-term impacts on human health and the environment. *Silent Spring* struck deep at America's naive hope of (as the DuPont chemical company had bragged during the 1950s) "better living through chemistry."

Among the most unsettling of the chaotic events of this troubled era was Watergate. The dark underbelly of American politics was exposed to a shocked public as tales of burglaries, blackmail, enemies lists, covert surveillance, and "hush money" dominated the headlines month after month. As a calamitous bookend to a heart-wrenching decade, Watergate left America stunned, and struck deep at our faith in honorable leadership.[59]

As the Sixties ended, so, too, it seemed, did America's promise of prosperity. Given rising public discontent, especially over the Vietnam War, both Johnson and Nixon decided neither to raise taxes nor to choose between guns and butter. That fainthearted policy led to a combination of high inflation and high unemployment that had until then seemed virtually impossible economically, so a new term and a new measure had to be invented. The term was "stagflation," and the measure was called the "misery index." Stagflation was compounded by the oil embargoes and resultant gas lines of the 1970s. Economic misery began to accelerate in the late 1960s, by the 1970s rivaling the hardship of the Great Depression and exceeding the distress of the later Great Recession of 2008–2009. These economic crises, extending from the late 1960s to the mid-1970s and thus helping to justify the commonly used moniker "the Long Sixties," struck deep at America's self-confidence, and brought down the curtain on postwar prosperity. The I-we-I curve had already begun to turn, but this economic malaise sealed it.

Each of these multiple and intersecting crises rent the apparent economic, political, social, and cultural unity of the Fifties. The speed and thoroughness with which this transformation ultimately overtook America was astonishing to all who lived through it. In the words of one POW who had left for Vietnam in 1965, and returned to America in 1972, "We came home to quite a different world—it was like Rip Van Winkle waking up after nearly six years in a prison camp. It was just unbelievable that our culture had changed to that point."[60]

Though many critics had been uneasy about the constraints of the mid-century consensus, few could have foreseen that within a few short years harmony in America would be replaced by cacophony. The Long Sixties seemed to confirm that the earlier consensus had led to a dead end. Everything seemed out of control, leading to a widespread sense of ill-defined discord.[61]

"Alienation," "anomie," "estrangement," and "malaise" all soared as Ngram buzzwords during the Long Sixties. The mood was encapsulated in 1979 by a nationally televised address by President Jimmy Carter—summarizing virtually all of the events and trends that we have described in this section—a talk that he titled a "Crisis of Confidence" but that was quickly and appropriately dubbed "the malaise speech." Together, the crises of the second half of the Sixties undermined the national self-confidence of the first half and subtly lowered our collective and egalitarian aspirations.

The 1970s were famously dubbed "The Me Decade" by Tom Wolfe in an evocative 1976 essay.[62] Detailing the explosive popularity of the self-help movement and New Age spirituality, Wolfe identified a national turn inward that followed on the heels of the dizzying vertigo of the preceding years. Americans forswore mass protests over big issues in favor of psycho-therapists and religious gurus who were supposed to focus on what was wrong with them as individuals. In short, the Seventies were a decade in which people stopped aspiring to fix society and started to think only of fixing themselves.

As historian James Patterson summarized this period,

> Many of the would-be Tocquevilles who searched for the essence of the United States in the mid-1970s—and later—were almost as pessimistic as the headline writer who wrote, "THINGS WILL GET WORSE BE-FORE THEY GET WORSE." Americans, they said, had become disoriented, fractious, alienated and divided into ever more self-conscious groups that identified themselves narrowly by region, gender, age, religion, ethnicity, and race.[63]

The Boomers who had entered the Sixties in idealistic togetherness exited the Seventies in grumpy self-centeredness. As philosopher Richard Rorty wrote in *Achieving Our Country* (1998), "It is as if, sometime around 1980, the children of the people who made it through the Great Depression and into the suburbs had decided to pull up the drawbridge behind them."[64] The full effects of that momentous directional shift are now abundantly clear as we view subsequent decades from the perspective of the next century.

LESSONS FROM THE SIXTIES TURNING POINT

We saw earlier that it is fruitless to look for a single cause of the we-to-I pivot that occurred during the long Sixties. The various economic, political, social, and cultural trends that we have described in this book had themselves been bound in a self-reinforcing equilibrium for decades, but that equilibrium itself was completely upended by the turmoil described above. The virtuous cycle among the elements of the movement toward an expanding "we" suddenly reversed and became a vicious cycle. Now, growing polarization produced growing individualism, which in turn produced growing inequality, which produced growing social isolation, which produced in turn more polarization, in what seemed to be an endless downward spiral.

But, as we have emphasized previously, the turning point was about more than circumstances and crises. Human agency exercised in response to those crises played a central role. As historian Bruce Schulman wrote,

> For the entire postwar era, from the 1940s to the 1970s, reformers had . . . pushed towards widening the circle of the "we," downplaying difference and including more in "us." . . . But during the early 1970s, Americans retreated from that expansive, universalist vision. Instead of widening the "we," the nation reconstructed itself as a congeries of many narrower units.[65]

As we have emphasized in earlier chapters, the reformers of the 1960s had good reasons for seeking to expand individual rights. Indeed, so much was achieved and set in motion in the realm of personal rights in the 1960s that it might be hard not to look at that decade as a time when the yoke of repression and conformity was finally broken, individuals were freed to be who they wanted to be, and America was held to account for its failings in guaranteeing liberty and equality under the law. However, as we have also seen in the preceding chapters, the net effect of these progressive and forward-thinking movements was—often ironically—to emphasize individualism and individual rights at the expense of widely shared communitarian values. The movements of the 1960s to "liberate" individuals in many cases had the unintended side effect of elevating selfishness. The reformers and revolutionaries sought inclusion, but in its pursuit they ushered in alienation. Thus, the Sixties deserve our attention today in large part so that we might learn from the efforts of that generation of reformers—so that today's pursuit of shared aspirations for a better future does not culminate in another rancorous "Twilight of Common Dreams."

Reformers in the 1950s had rightly worried about the constraints that conformity placed on individualism as well as the persistence of racial and gender inequality. They questioned who the mid-century "we" really included, and wondered what trade-offs were required for the particular form of "consensus" it represented. Those combustible concerns, ignited by the sparks of the 1960s, were enough to reverse the fundamental trends of the first two thirds of the century, and set our nation on an entirely different course. That new course would indeed bring more individualism, but at a cost to the earlier values—a fact too long ignored.

A thoughtful retrospective on mid-century America makes clear its deficiencies: the shortcomings of a society that undervalued individuality and diversity and gave woefully insufficient attention to racial and gender justice. Nonetheless, the empirical evidence we have gathered in this book also makes clear that we have paid a high price for the Sixties' pivot—the indefensible economic inequality of the second Gilded Age, the political polarization that is enfeebling and endangering our democracy, the social fragmentation and isolation that ignore the basic human need for fellowship, and most fundamentally, the self-centeredness that itself makes it so difficult to achieve the unity of purpose required to change our national course.

What seems "normal" to any of us depends on when we personally entered the story. To many older Americans today who lived through at least part of America's upswing and then witnessed the extraordinary reversals outlined above, the extreme inequality, polarization, social fragmentation, and narcissism of today—represented even in the highest offices of the land—are anything but normal. And thus they are understandably eager *not* to normalize it. Meanwhile, to Gen Xers, Millennials, and younger Americans, deepening inequality, polarization, isolation, and narcissism may seem normal because this is the America into which they were born. The downturn is the only reality they have experienced, and they may not be fully aware of how historically unusual today's "normal" really is. But as we have abundantly documented, within living memory, *all* of these troubling realities were in fact in retreat.

One contribution of this book, we hope, is to help narrow the "OK Boomer" generational divide by introducing a new, evidence-based narrative that encompasses the ups and downs of an entire century, thereby setting a clearer agenda for choice going forward. Indeed, bridging this difference in perspective may turn out to be a critical component of constructing a new shared vision of our nation's future. Just how all Americans might work together to engineer another upswing is the final question this book takes on.

9

DRIFT AND MASTERY

In 1888 American Progressive Edward Bellamy wrote a best-selling novel entitled *Looking Backward, 2000–1887*. In it, the protagonist Julian West falls asleep in 1887 and wakes up in the year 2000 to find the America he had known completely changed. The cutthroat competition of his own Gilded Age had been replaced by cooperation; and the individualistic "winner take all" mind-set by a deep sense of mutual responsibility and mutual aid. West tours this society with a sense of wonder at the hopeful possibility of democratic citizens choosing to organize their institutions around a shared sense of destiny.

We have now, in reality, lived through more than the 113-year period over which Bellamy imagined "looking back." However, were his protagonist to walk the streets of today's America, he would, unfortunately, find himself quite at home—in a reality more similar to his native one than the utopia he had envisioned. Unprecedented prosperity coupled with vast disparities between rich and poor, gridlock in the public square, a fraying social fabric, and widespread atomization and narcissism reign today, just as they did then.[1]

It is, of course, not surprising that our lived reality has not conformed to Bellamy's utopian dream. Imaginative fiction is often thought-provoking, but rarely prophetic. What *is* surprising, however, is that in the half century following the publication of Bellamy's novel, America did indeed slowly climb closer to his idealized society than ever before. We became measurably more equal, more willing to work together and compromise, more able to come up with innovative solutions to vexing problems, more concerned with the common good. And then we sharply reversed our course, undid decades of progress on those fronts, and re-created a world more starkly similar to Bellamy's Gilded Age than has existed at any other period in our history.

The stunning similarities between the last American Gilded Age and today have been noted by numerous commentators. And yet, as this book's introductory narrative laid bare—and as we have now seen through countless hard measures spanning an extensive array of economic, social, political, and cultural phenomena—the parallels are even wider and deeper than many have supposed. Today we find ourselves once again in a moment characterized by profound challenges on nearly every side, and by the palpable risk of plunging even deeper into a national downturn. But we also now have the benefit of not only looking forward to imagine a brighter future, as Bellamy did, but looking backward in search of understanding how one was actually created—on the heels of a moment so very similar to our own.

This book has revealed various sector-specific ways in which America's highly unequal, polarized, socially disconnected, and culturally self-absorbed late-nineteenth-century society experienced measurable and near-simultaneous upswings toward equality, inclusion, comity, connection, and altruism as the twentieth century opened. Indeed, uncovering the striking confluence of these phenomena—constituting one of the most dramatic and multifaceted turning points in the history of this nation—is, we hope, a significant contribution, providing a new lens through which to understand the twentieth century. However, leaving our story there fails to take full advantage of the lessons of history, which is why we devote one final chapter to exploring how America's last upswing came to be, and how we might engineer another one today.

FROM DRIFT TO MASTERY

Several years after Bellamy wrote *Looking Backward*, Walter Lippmann, another American Progressive—barely twenty-five years of age at the time—published a small volume entitled *Drift and Mastery* (1914). Eschewing the "constructing of utopias" to which his predecessors were often prone, Lippmann instead devoted himself to "an attempt to diagnose the current unrest and to arrive at some sense of what democracy implies."[2]

In the utterly new world of the early twentieth century—transformed by urbanization, industrialization, an increasing dependence on wage labor, the mushrooming of corporations and consolidations of every kind, the rewriting of social norms and customs, a rapidly growing and diversifying population, and raging debates about the role of individuals, institutions, and government in managing the challenges these conditions created—what was the democratic citizen to do?

At a time when American democracy suffered from the "drift" of overwhelming despair, Lippmann called for the "mastery" of history by an active, inventive, and disciplined citizenry. Of the prospect of engendering an upswing out of a downward drift, he contended, "it has to be done not by some wise and superior being but by the American people themselves. No one man, no one group can do it all. It is an immense collaboration."[3] Americans, in other words, had to eschew the corrosive, cynical slide toward "I" and rediscover the latent power and promise of "we."

Unlike Bellamy's unfulfilled dreams, Lippmann's prescription hewed remarkably close to what actually happened as America transitioned into the new century. The reformers responsible for turning the Gilded Age into the Progressive Era included immigrants and elites, women and men, blacks and whites, housewives and career politicians, unionists and capitalists, college graduates and factory workers, top-down bureaucrats and bottom-up activists, Republicans and Democrats, and nearly everyone in between. The movement was so diverse as to be barely coherent and was home to contradictory impulses, but together, the Americans who took up the nonpartisan mantle of "Progressives" ultimately put in place a stunningly diverse and sweeping set of reforms and innovations—many of which form the basis of American society as we know it today.

The secret ballot; the direct primary system; the popular election of senators; the initiative, referendum, and recall; women's suffrage; new forms of municipal administration; the federal income tax; the Federal Reserve System; protective labor laws; the minimum wage; antitrust statutes; protected public lands and resources; food and drug regulation; sanitation infrastructure; public utilities; a vast proliferation of civic and voluntary societies; new advocacy organizations such as labor unions, the ACLU, and the NAACP; the widespread provision of free public high schools; and even the spread of public parks, libraries, and playgrounds all owe their origins to the efforts of a diverse array of Progressive reformers.

On average, since the Bill of Rights, constitutional amendments have been approved once every thirteen years. As a mark of how monumental the innovations of the Progressive Era were, the four amendments that traversed the hurdle-ridden path to ratification between 1913 and 1920 represent the biggest burst of amendments since the Bill of Rights, rivaled only by the three post–Civil War amendments on slavery.

In an attempt to understand its historical significance, many observers today look to the culmination of the Progressive Era—the enumeration of Teddy Roosevelt's Square Deal domestic agenda (1910), the creation of the Progressive Party (1912), and the passage of sweeping federal legislation (1913–1920)—and conclude that it was a coordinated political project to expand the size, reach, and power of the federal government.[4] However, this narrative fails to account for the vast, pluralistic upsurge of cultural critique, impassioned agitation, and citizen-led reform that began long before a Progressive occupied the White House.

In the words of historian Richard Hofstadter, the Progressive movement is best characterized as "that broader impulse toward criticism and change that was everywhere so conspicuous after 1900." This interpretation maps quite strikingly onto the timing of the broader social, economic, cultural, and political upswing we have documented in this book, which, when observed in the aggregate, shows a clear change in the country's overall trajectory beginning around 1900. "As all observant contemporaries realized," Hofstadter continues,

> Progressivism in this larger sense was not confined to the Progressive Party but affected in a striking way all the major and minor parties and the whole tone of political life. . . . While Progressivism would have been impossible without the impetus given by certain social grievances . . . it was a rather widespread and remarkably good-natured effort of the greater part of society to achieve some not very clearly specified self-reformation.[5]

Though their initial goals were not always clear or coherent, Progressives had two things in common—a compelling desire to repudiate the downward drift of our nation, and a galvanizing belief in the power of ordinary citizens to do so. In their diverse stories—more so than their specific politics, policies, or programs—we may find a blueprint for how to create a similar turning point today.[6]

FROM PRIVILEGE TO PASSION

Frances Perkins was born in 1880 in Boston, Massachusetts, to a middle-class Yankee family who valued education and took pride in their colonial roots. As an undergraduate at Mount Holyoke College she had been introduced to Progressive politics by a professor who tasked her students with visiting factories and interviewing laborers about their working conditions. After graduation, Perkins began teaching at a Chicago-area girls school and continued to learn about the plight of the working poor as a volunteer at Jane Addams's Hull House.

At Hull House she rubbed shoulders with an impressive array of influential Progressives, and saw firsthand the social problems which, until then, she had mainly encountered only in books. She attended fiery labor speeches and thought-provoking lectures, and found herself questioning the detached, conservative politics of her parents and becoming increasingly drawn to fight for the rights of the downtrodden.

Rather than continuing to pursue a respectable career as a teacher, Perkins took a position in Philadelphia investigating the sexual exploitation of immigrant and African American women by illegitimate employment agencies and rooming houses—carefully keeping the details of her job from her family. She studied economics at Wharton, then moved to New York City to earn a master's degree in political science from Columbia. Once in New York she threw herself into the women's suffrage movement, attending protests and passing out literature on street corners. She also continued her advocacy for workers' rights as head of the New York Consumer's League.

In 1911, Perkins was attending a tea with a group of society women at an apartment just off Washington Square when she heard an uproar on the street below. The ladies all rushed outside to find the Triangle Shirtwaist Factory, just across the plaza, ablaze. Perkins ran to the factory, in the vain hope of offering some kind of help. Hundreds of workers were trapped inside with no way to escape, and a gruesome scene unfolded, as scores of helpless women and girls jumped to their deaths. Just two years earlier, those same women had engineered a strike to call for more humane working conditions, and a remedy to the very safety concerns that caused the fire. They had been met with violent resistance.

The Triangle Shirtwaist fire was a turning point in Frances Perkins's moral formation, which awakened her to the urgency of fighting for reform. Though her experiences at Hull House had been eye-opening, since moving to New York and circulating once again among the East Coast elite, she had begun to envision her future not as a reformer but as a well-married philanthropist. But the gruesome fire made clear that the factory owners' greed and legislators' indifference had directly resulted in the loss of 146 innocent lives—a fact which could never be remedied with mere charity. She immediately abandoned her vision of a life of gentility and committed herself fully to the "calling" of fighting for workers' rights.

As Perkins plunged into the male-dominated and ethically compromised world of politics, she quickly learned that moral indignation was not enough to win reform. Under the tutelage of progressive Democratic governor Al Smith, she became a shrewd politician, holding several positions in the New York State government, and putting the state in the forefront of legislative reform. She successfully championed more comprehensive factory inspections, safer working conditions for women, reduced working hours, and an end to child labor; and also broke ground on bringing about a minimum wage and unemployment insurance. Perkins became the first woman in American history to hold a cabinet post when she was nominated as secretary of labor by President Roosevelt in 1933, and her expertise and relentless advocacy for labor were instrumental in the design and implementation of the New Deal.[7]

Frances Perkins was one of thousands of middle-class Americans (a great many of them educated women) who, when face-to-face with the deplorable economic and social conditions of the cities, were galvanized—even radicalized—into action. Jane Addams founded the American Settlement House movement and became a vocal advocate for immigrants and the urban poor; Florence Kelley worked tirelessly for labor reform, children's rights, and racial equality; Lillian Wald championed human rights and brought healthcare to tenement-dwellers in New York City; and John Dewey reimagined education as a mode of preparation for engaged democratic citizenship. All exemplified the humane and impassioned spirit of the age. All were private citizens who, heeding both conscience and a growing political consciousness, engaged in countless acts of interclass coalition-building, grassroots organizing, and political advocacy. Together, they formed a groundswell of activism upon which enterprising politicians would draw in marshaling support for the programs and policies that undergirded America's "we" decades.

FROM ISOLATION TO ASSOCIATION

When Paul Harris moved to Chicago in 1896, he was struck by the contrast between the anonymity of life in a busy, congested city and the communal, small-town feel of Wallingford, Vermont, where he grew up. Having recently completed his law degree at the University of Iowa, Harris was one of thousands of enterprising young men just starting out in a new city. "If others were longing for fellowship as I was," he wondered, "why not bring them together?"[8]

Harris soon began talking with friends and business associates about the idea of forming an organization for local professionals. In 1905, he and three other men gathered at an office in downtown Chicago for the first meeting of a new club called Rotary—the name came from the group's early practice of rotating meetings between members' offices. The initial vision for the club was simply to provide "fellowship and friendship" for urban businessmen, and they eventually developed a tradition of noon "luncheon meetings" to accommodate professionals' routines.

When Harris was elected third president of the club in 1907, he expanded the mission of the organization to include service. Their very first project was to construct public toilets in Chicago.

Members were explicitly discouraged from doing business at meetings—the group was meant to provide a cultural counterweight to the relentless press of commerce and competition. Harris instead encouraged a communitarian focus on socializing, service, and mutual aid. In the very first publication of *The National Rotarian*, the club's newsletter, Harris wrote, "If this Rotary of ours is destined to be more than a mere passing thing, it will be because you and I have learned the importance of bearing with each other's infirmities, the value of toleration."[9]

Over the resistance of his fellow founders, who worried about the expense and administrative burden, Harris insisted that the club be expanded to other cities, and by 1910, some fifteen new clubs had been founded across the United States. In August of that year, a national convention was held in Chicago, where the representatives of the various branches voted to create a National Association of Rotary Clubs. In 1911 the organization adopted the motto, "He Profits Most Who Serves Best," and in 1950 added a second, "Service above Self."[10]

Eventually, the organization expanded internationally, and by the time of Harris's death in 1947, his humble effort to bring professionals together in service of the community had grown to include more than 200,000 members in seventy-five countries. Over the past one hundred years, it has acted as clearinghouse for billions of dollars in donated funds, utilized in countless humanitarian projects. In 1987 a decision by the U.S. Supreme Court overturned Rotary's male-only status, and women were finally admitted to full membership. The organization is still active and growing today—now claiming a membership of 1.2 million.

Paul Harris's Rotary Club was one of hundreds of similar organizations and associations started during the Progressive Era, each an outgrowth of a wider cultural turn away from atomization and individualism and toward "association" and communitarianism. From fraternal orders such as the Knights of Columbus, to cultural organizations such as the Sons of Norway; and from trade unions like the United Mine Workers to women's groups such as Hadassah—the range of clubs and societies formed by Progressives and their contemporaries was massive. And, much like Rotary, though these organizations often started as social and leisure groups, a great many eventually oriented their activities toward humanitarian efforts, community issues, and even political activism. These groups and their broad-based memberships proved remarkably enduring, creating a vast store of social capital that fueled the nation's upswing for decades.

FROM DARKNESS INTO LIGHT

Born into slavery in 1862 and freed by the Emancipation Proclamation during the Civil War, Ida B. Wells spent her young life navigating the loss of her parents to disease, and the burden of keeping her siblings from separation by working to support her family. She found a job as an elementary school teacher and in her free time began attending a historically black college in Memphis. In 1884, a train conductor ordered her to give up her seat on a first-class car. Wells refused, citing the 1875 Civil Rights Act, which banned racial discrimination in public accommodations. She was dragged from the train nonetheless. She sued the railroad unsuccessfully, and wrote an impassioned and widely read article about her experience, which launched her career as a journalist relentlessly documenting racial inequality, segregation, and the rise of Jim Crow.

Soon Wells became the editor and co-owner of *The Free Speech and Headlight*, a newspaper based in Memphis. Shortly thereafter, she received word that friends—also business owners in Memphis—were lynched following a dispute over a game of marbles played outside their store. Wells was galvanized to take up the cause of investigating lynching—interviewing people associated with the atrocities and exposing the real reasons behind the brutal acts. She wrote articles, pamphlets, and statistical reports that decried the "Southern Horrors" of lynching. Wells also encouraged blacks to flee the South to seek both safety and a brighter future in the North, which she did herself by moving to Chicago in 1894.

Wells traveled and lectured abroad and gained many international supporters for the antilynching crusade in America. Some of her counterparts in the U.S., including Booker T. Washington and W. E. B. Du Bois, considered her too radical to be effective. Frederick Douglass, however, praised her groundbreaking work in fearlessly shedding light on the true conditions of blacks in the South. Though she never succeeded in convincing whites to criminalize the practice, the number of lynchings began to decline after their peak in 1892, and by the mid-1920s had been reduced by 90 percent—a fact at least partly attributable to Wells's consciousness-raising work.[11]

Wells also fought for civil rights and worked to organize, educate, and build solidarity among African Americans. She helped achieve a successful boycott of the 1893 World's Fair and was instrumental in the founding of the NAACP. She also opened a black settlement house, which offered social services to African American migrants, and cofounded the National Association of Colored Women's Clubs, one of the largest civic organizations of African American women in America—still active today. She was also a suffragist, and even ran for a state Senate seat in Illinois once the state granted limited voting rights to women. However, her vocal position against racism and lynching put her at odds with many white leaders of the women's suffrage movement, including Frances Willard, president of the Women's Christian Temperance Union, with whom she had a public feud. And she directly challenged President Woodrow Wilson's racial resegregation of federal bureaucracies. Wells was indefatigable in speaking and acting out against discrimination.[12]

Ida B. Wells's writing consistently called for honesty and transparency in relation to the realities of life in a segregated America, and she vocally demanded a moral and legal accounting for the injustice and violence done to black Americans under Jim Crow. In so doing, she acted as the conscience of the nation, helped launch the long Civil Rights movement, and laid the groundwork for both black Americans and women to achieve greater equality.

Though her pieces were never published in white-run Progressive magazines of the day, Wells joined the ranks of many Progressive journalists who worked to expose the hypocrisy and brutality of the Gilded Age. Lincoln Steffens uncovered rampant corruption in city politics, Jacob Riis used photojournalism to lay bare the inhumane living conditions in urban tenements, Ida Tarbell exposed the excesses of John D. Rockefeller's monopolistic Standard Oil company, Upton Sinclair took on the abuses of the meatpacking industry, and Ray Stannard Baker covered both brutal crackdowns on striking workers and racism in the South. Known as "muckrakers," these writers produced vivid portraits of the human cost of exploitative and unjust systems, fueling a moral awakening that inspired countless activists and reformers, and stirred the public to take action on the most pressing issues of the day.

FROM TYCOON TO TRANSFORMATIVE LEADER

The son of a Confederate soldier whose fortunes were ruined by the Civil War, Tom Johnson worked to support his family at a very early age by selling newspapers on the railroads in Virginia. Though he completed only one year of formal education, Johnson was eventually hired through a family connection as a clerk in a Louisville streetcar business owned by the DuPont family.

Through hard work and ingenuity, Johnson rose through the ranks of the business quickly. An intuitive understanding of mechanics and a flair for invention won Johnson several patents, the royalties from which gave him the freedom to purchase a business of his own. Johnson soon found himself following in the footsteps of other "rags to riches" robber barons of the day. By the 1890s, he owned a controlling share of the street railway lines in Cleveland, St. Louis, Brooklyn, Detroit, and Indianapolis, and had also invested heavily in the steel business, building mills in Ohio and Pennsylvania, which supplied rails for his multiple streetcar concerns. However, when a train conductor recommended he read Henry George's *Social Problems* (1883), Tom Johnson developed an unexpected sympathy for radical critiques of the capitalist system.

Henry George was a political philosopher who had published his first book, *Progress and Poverty*, in 1879, to enormous commercial success. During the 1890s, its sales exceeded all other books except the Bible, and it had an enormous influence on Progressives—a great many of whom credited an encounter with George's ideas with reorienting their lives toward social and political reform. He argued vehemently for mechanisms to control the astronomical wealth of monopolistic businesses, and their influence on destructive boom-bust cycles in the economy. Tom Johnson was riveted by Henry George's radical rethinking of wealth and poverty, and he spent much of his fortune promoting the spread and implementation of George's ideas.

Johnson's transformation was further spurred by witnessing the Johnstown Flood of 1889, which wiped out an entire community, killing more than 2,200 people. The disaster was caused by a burst dam which had been used to hold a private lake owned by Henry Clay Frick and other business tycoons. The dam had been carelessly constructed and inadequately maintained, and despite several subsequent lawsuits, Frick and his associates were never held accountable. Johnson worked personally to provide relief to the victims but became disillusioned by the inadequacy of charitable responses to problems caused by wider systemic failures. "If we were wise enough to seek and find the causes that call for charity there would be some hope for us," he wrote, reflecting on the devastation at Johnstown.[13]

Acting upon his newfound political consciousness, Johnson ran for office, and served two terms as a U.S. representative, and four terms as mayor of Cleveland. And when fights against monopolistic streetcar barons took center stage in the city, he sold off his own interests in the business and eventually advocated for full public ownership. Johnson relentlessly fought the overreach and undue influence of his former business associates in public life, rooting out corruption with an unremitting zeal. He improved housing conditions, sanitation, and policing. He built public parks, civic centers, and homes for the elderly and indigent. He successfully lowered the cost of utilities by taking them public and established the country's first comprehensive public building code.

Writing in *McClure's Magazine* in 1905, muckraker Lincoln Steffens observed, "Tom Johnson is a reformed business man. . . . He reformed himself first, then he undertook political reform; and his political reform began with the reform of his own class," and pronounced him "the best Mayor of the best-governed city in the United States."[14] Many of Johnson's ideas were truly innovative for the time, establishing new forms of municipal governance, and still others were borrowed from fellow reform-minded mayors across the nation.

Johnson exemplified a generation of charismatic politicians who took the cause of Progressive reform into the halls of power. Including innovative leaders such as Wisconsin's governor and state legislator Robert La Follette, Detroit's mayor Hazen Pingree, and Sam "Golden Rule" Jones, mayor of Toledo, these political entrepreneurs experimented with and proved the efficacy of municipal and state reforms that became models for other cities, states, and even the federal government to follow. To a remarkable degree, the federal policies and programs for which Progressive standard-bearers such as Teddy Roosevelt were famous were the result of local innovations bubbling up from below.

AN AFFAIR OF THE CONSCIENCE

As all of these stories illustrate, the Progressive movement was, first and foremost, a moral awakening. Facilitated by the muckrakers' revelations about a society, economy, and government run amok—and urged on by the Social Gospelers' denunciation of social Darwinism and laissez-faire economics—Americans from all walks of life began to repudiate the self-centered, hyper-individualist creed of the Gilded Age. "It is idle to imagine that changes in our governmental machinery, or in the organization of our industries will bring us peace;" wrote Washington Gladden, an early leader in the Social Gospel movement. "The trouble lies deeper, in our primary conceptions. What we have got to have, if we want the true democracy, is a different kind of men and women—men and women to whom duties are more than rights, and service dearer than privilege."[15]

However, nineteenth-century Progressives understood that true moral and cultural reform would necessarily be a "we" effort. It wasn't enough to point the finger of scorn at the idle rich or the corrupt political machines. Change, they realized, would require more than the identification and expulsion of society's bad apples. As historian Richard Hofstadter has written, "the moral indignation of the age was by no means directed entirely against others; it was in great and critical measure directed inward. Contemporaries who spoke of the movement as an affair of the conscience were not mistaken."[16] A soul-searching effort on the part of these reformers revealed to them their own destructive individualism, and their own complicity in the creation of exploitative systems—and this realization fueled their passionate efforts to right society's wrongs.

This soul-searching was both inspired and fueled by ministers and theologians who not only encouraged individuals to change but called upon religious institutions to more actively critique the "social sins" of the age. Social Gospelers such as Walter Rauschenbusch reframed Christianity itself as a social movement—a blueprint for the building of a more just society.

Today we are seeing a similar drive to uncover corruption, expose exploitation, and lay bare the dark underbelly of the "I" society in which we now live. And we are also hearing calls for reform framed in increasingly urgent and moralistic terms. The 2018 March for Our Lives, in which 1.2 million people gathered at over 880 events in the US and across the globe to protest gun violence and school shootings, is but one example. As is the Families Belong Together initiative, calling for an end to the Trump administration's inhumane treatment of immigrants in border detention facilities. The social media driven #MeToo movement—which is a clarion call for both personal and institutional accountability—is also part of a broader moral awakening in today's America. And the Poor People's Campaign, led by Reverend William Barber, describes its efforts to combat systemic racism and intergenerational poverty as "a national call for moral revival."[17]

The legacy of the Progressives points to the power of moral messaging, but also challenges us to push beyond the idea that silencing or expelling certain elements of our society, punishing offenders, or replacing one faction's dominance with another's, will restore the moral and cultural health of our nation. We must undertake a reevaluation of our shared values— asking ourselves what personal privileges and rights we might be willing to lay aside in service of the common good, and what role we will play in the shared project of shaping our nation's future.

A CIVIC REVIVAL

Another distinct feature of the Progressives' story was the translation of outrage and moral awakening into active citizenship. Throughout the Gilded Age, as the economic, social, and political life of the nation reached a level of complexity barely comprehensible to the average person, many felt an acute loss of control, and a resultant malaise. By the mid-1870s, "Americans had entered a period of radical economic and political instability they were ill-prepared to understand," wrote historian Richard White.[18] To a great degree, Progressive Era innovations were a response to this reality—seeking to reclaim individuals' agency and reinvigorate democratic citizenship as the only reliable antidotes to overwhelming anxiety.

Progressive reformers mustered hope in the face of despair, zeroed in on a vast array of problems, and came up with an astounding number of inventive new solutions which, together, drove our nation's upswing. But to a surprising degree they did not have a national blueprint in mind at the start. In stark contrast to the prescriptive ideology of socialism, which was also gaining adherents at the turn of the last century, Progressive reformers were instead intensely pragmatic, using the new methods of social science to test the merits of different solutions. Such methods, Walter Lippmann had argued, would be the key to mastery. Indeed, true innovation requires openness to experimentation that is not premised upon ideological beliefs. To structure debates within a gridlocked left/right framework precludes the sheer inventiveness that animated our last upswing and generated solutions that appealed to a broad bipartisan swath of Americans.

Perhaps the clearest example of this is the high school movement, which we have pointed to in previous chapters. Universal, free public high schools were an almost entirely local innovation, created in small towns in the early decades of the twentieth century, although academics in places like Harvard had bruited about the idea in the late nineteenth century. At that time, students who wanted to extend their education past "common school" usually had to pay for private instruction, though some cities had selective secondary schools such as Boston Latin, open only to unusually talented youngsters. But recognizing the growing demand for more educated workers in a rapidly changing economy, a handful of communities in the Midwest began rallying citizens to band together and provide free secondary school for all. In towns that successfully raised taxes to pay for them, public high schools were built and, given the growing economic return on education, the idea spread across the country like wildfire—or in a more contemporary metaphor, went viral. Hence, one of the most powerful forces behind America's Great Convergence, as well as our ability to out-compete other nations in a globalizing economy during the upswing, was the vastly expanded education of our workforce—something that, amazingly, came almost entirely from the bottom up.

And another key feature of the Progressives was the wide diversity of issues they took on simultaneously. Because so much of the movement was anchored by citizen activism, Progressivism didn't privilege one type of reform over another, but was instead a holistic reorganizing of society that began at the bottom and was based on a reinvigoration of shared values. As a result, the solutions Progressives championed ranged from free public high schools to women's rights to trustbusting, and everything in between. As we discussed in Chapter 8, our nation's recent downturn has encompassed a stunning variety of economic, social, political, and cultural challenges—none of which can be clearly identified as the "cause" of all the others. Our current problems are mutually reinforcing, and their solutions must be so as well. Thus, today's reformers and policymakers should follow the lead of their Progressive forebearers. Rather than siloed reform efforts competing for resources, the successful engineering of another American upswing will require instead the "immense collaboration" Lippmann and his contemporaries achieved.

"No hard-and-fast rule can be laid down," wrote Theodore Roosevelt in 1901, "as to the way in which such work [reform] must be done; but most certainly every man, whatever his position, should strive to do it in some way and to some degree."[19] The Progressives cannot offer us a blueprint for *what* to do to bring about another upswing. Certainly neither the proliferation of high schools nor the reinvigoration of fraternal organizations is the solution to today's problems. But such successes of the twentieth-century upswing can offer us important lessons in *how* to achieve monumental change: by starting in our own communities and recognizing the latent power of collective action not just to protest, but to build the foundations of a reimagined America.

A GROUNDSWELL OF AGITATION

Though individual and collective action in neighborhoods, cities, and states throughout the country provided the lifeblood of innovation behind the movement, it quickly became clear to Progressives that local solutions were not enough to tackle problems that were systemic in nature, and often extended beyond the bounds of cities and states.

In her book, *Twenty Years at Hull-House* (1910), Jane Addams describes an experience early in her tenure as an advocate for the working poor, in which she tried to negotiate directly with a factory owner whose negligence had caused injury to two young boys, and death to a third. She recounts having naively believed that appealing directly to the owner's conscience would remedy the situation, and was shocked when he refused to do anything. As their experience as changemakers grew, Progressives such as Addams realized that pressure of a different sort would need to be applied, and that government involvement was necessary to ensure fairness, safety, and the common good.

But the idea of large-scale government intervention in society and the economy was still a new and controversial concept at the turn of the twentieth century. Thus, massive grassroots organizing efforts were required to build widespread support for reform legislation. Addams began connecting her efforts on behalf of the poor with those of other settlement workers across the nation, unions began coordinating to bring about larger and more effective strikes, voluntary societies of all stripes utilized their power as federated local chapters to bring about widespread agitation, and suffragists engaged in coalition-building at both the state and national levels. It was when individuals, local groups, and municipal and state actors shared best practices, engaged in complementary bottom-up and top-down strategies, and found common cause with one another that they began to find the full strength of their power.

Today's social entrepreneurs have produced many organizations and initiatives responding to a wide array of problems, but often they are narrowly focused on priorities and proposals benefiting a specific group or cause, which can feel more like a "War of the 'We's'" than a groundswell of citizen activism. We have yet to see a truly nonpartisan movement joining these issue-specific efforts together in a compelling citizen-driven call for large-scale reform. Such a phenomenon would require more than fundraising, nonprofit programming, street protesting, or campaign-based organizing—it would involve the sustained and coordinated efforts of groups spread out across the country. And it would require a new narrative bringing siloed efforts together in a broader vision for the future of America, as well as a retraining and retooling of average Americans for active citizenship.[20]

Another challenge grassroots organizers face today is the critical role of the internet and social media in our modern social and political landscape. The broader effects of these relatively new technologies are still being studied and debated by social scientists, and to a large extent the jury is out on how they affect our communities and our stores of social capital.[21] When it comes to political mobilization, the accepted wisdom is that online organizing is vital to any modern cause, but some research indicates that an overreliance on virtual networks creates fragile movements that rarely achieve their broader aims.[22] Indeed, some of the most encouraging efforts to employ the accelerating power of the internet have been in the creation of new "alloys" of face-to-face and online networks, which rely on social media to spread their message, but use in-person meetings to build the relationships and skills that undergird action.

According to research by sociologist Dana Fisher there are signs that today's "resistance" movements are beginning to take on these characteristics. She has shown that since the Women's March on January 21, 2017, the first mass protest in the Trump era, there has been significant overlap in the various marches, movements, strikes, and coalitions in which protesters are taking part. Participation in demonstrations, which is often prompted by online organizing, also seems to be a catalyst for more localized action when citizens-turned-activists return to their communities. And this movement has so far been led not by far-left political operatives, as many have supposed, but by everyday people working on problems central to their own lives[23] and—in a particularly striking echo of our nation's last upswing—primarily middle-class, middle-aged, college-educated women.[24]

Sociologist Leah Gose, political scientist Theda Skocpol, and historian Lara Putnam have also found that the growing "resistance" movement—encompassing everything from the Women's March, to anti-Trump rallies, to mobilizing turnout in midterm elections—has been sustained to a remarkable extent by thousands of grassroots groups in cities and towns of every size, and has effectively combined traditional forms of organizing with robust online networking.[25] Whether these groups can succeed in formulating, advancing, and sustaining a wider agenda for change remains to be seen.

A POLITICAL RESPONSE

The grassroots organizing of the Progressives was impressive in its scale, in the sheer number of issues it brought to the fore, and in its successful agitation for legislation that genuinely changed the face of America for decades to come. But critical to the Progressive movement was the way political leaders responded to that groundswell of activism. Without astute political entrepreneurs such as Theodore Roosevelt and Woodrow Wilson, who effectively translated the popular uprising into policies and programs that garnered bipartisan support, the movement's legacy would have been much shorter-lived.

But it wasn't only the Progressive presidents who built upon that groundswell. Even Franklin Roosevelt, who came to national power long after the Progressive Era ended, leaned upon seasoned Progressive reformers to staff his administrations, and capitalized on both the communitarian narrative and the grassroots infrastructure they had created to pull America back into an upswing after the backslide of the Roaring Twenties.

Many of the Progressives' campaigns were unsuccessful at first, and much of the legislation passed under the banner of reform proved ineffective. But, as political commentator E. J. Dionne has written, "Democracy is a long game. It involves pressuring those who resist reform . . . and offering proposals future electorates can eventually endorse."[26] Many of the New Deal's signature programs finally realized what a motley coalition of laborers, union leaders, technocratic managers, settlement house workers, middle-class businessmen, activist women, chastened elites, and many others had spent decades organizing to achieve. And one key to understanding their legacy is recognizing that national political leadership came *after* sustained, widespread citizen engagement, not before.

Today's reformers should learn from their forebears, focusing their efforts not only on promoting political candidates, but also on building a grassroots, issues-based movement upon which they and future leaders will be able to draw in order to make lasting change.

A YOUTH-DRIVEN VISION

One final feature of the Progressive movement that is relevant to today's challenges is its youthfulness. All of the reformers and writers whose stories and ideas we have featured in this chapter were in their thirties or younger when they became powerful voices and forces for change. At age forty-two, Teddy Roosevelt was the youngest person ever to assume the office of president.

Then, as now, these young changemakers felt that they had been born into an America completely different from the one in which their parents had been raised. To a great extent, they believed that the logic of a bygone era could never speak to the challenges of a completely altered world. In many ways, they were right, and their reimagining of what America could and should be set our nation on an entirely different course.

Today's challenges will be equally difficult to solve—and will therefore require just as much youthful courage, vigor, and imagination to overcome. And so, to a large extent, America's fate lies in the hands of the post-Boomer generations. Today's young people did not cause today's problems. But like their predecessors 125 years ago they must forgo the cynicism of drift and embrace the hope of mastery.

But unlike the reformers of a bygone era, today we have vastly more tools and resources to help us gain a clearer understanding of where we as a nation have been; what we have succeeded in doing once before; and what problems previous generations have left unsolved. By employing those tools to uncover the I-we-I curve, we hope that this book will be an important contribution to bridging today's generation gap and creating a more fruitful national conversation, which will be a vital component of rebuilding a robust American "we."

Of course, any slate of reforms consequential enough to create a contemporary upswing in America would require a significant change of course that may seem radical to some—just as it did a century ago. As we pointed out in Chapter 3, the issues that rose to the national agenda during the Progressive Era bear a striking resemblance to those being debated today: universal health insurance; safety nets for the elderly, the jobless, and the disabled; progressive income and estate taxation; environmental regulation; labor reform; curtailing the overreach of big business monopolies; gender equality; and campaign finance reform. Progressives were pragmatic but nonetheless uncompromising in pursuit of programs and policies that deeply and fundamentally reshaped America and set the stage for the upswing. Coming together to find common cause, establish common ground, and develop a shared vision of the common good is vitally necessary, but mere "kumbaya we-ness" will not ameliorate vast economic inequalities, curb deaths of despair, or end racism and sexism.

We are beginning to see a synthesis of the strategic lessons of the Progressive Era, most prominently in activism around climate change—the ultimate "we" issue. Activists are pleading for a moral awakening to the costs of inaction. Citizens, municipalities, and states are experimenting with radical innovations, regulations, and laws to curb the effects of environmental degradation at the local level. Organizers are using both internet-based and face-to-face techniques to mobilize mass protests. And youth have taken the lead in creating an urgent, impassioned call for action.

Will we be able to bring this same urgency to all of the challenges now facing our nation? And will these elements ultimately come together successfully to become a catalyst for a new American upswing?

A CAUTIONARY TALE

This book has argued through both historical analysis and statistical evidence that the Progressive Era was a clear turning point in the history of this nation. The Progressives certainly did not solve all the problems of the Gilded Age, but they did manage to engineer an upswing whose effects compounded over time. The changes they set in motion created an America whose prosperity was more equally shared, whose citizens were more engaged and connected, whose politicians were more able to compromise, and whose culture was more oriented toward a common purpose. And yet, the story of these reformers is not all high-minded heroism and altruism—it also contains important cautionary tales of which we cannot fail to make note as we look to generate a similar turning point in our nation today.

First is a caution to avoid the temptation to overcorrect. Progressivism emerged on the heels of populism and in direct competition with socialism, both of which movements advocated many of the same causes, but fell short of their aims because, among other reasons, they failed to appeal to the full range of American values. By contrast, Progressives managed to fashion slow and steady reforms as an alternative to calls for revolution. Progressive reformers quickly learned that in order to succeed they would have to compromise—to find a way to put private property, personal liberty, and economic growth on more equal footing with communitarian ideals and the protection of the weak and vulnerable, and to work within existing systems to bring about change.[27]

However, they were not always so wise. The Eighteenth Amendment, which established the prohibition of alcohol, was a far greater incursion on individual liberty than most Americans expected it to be, and was a far cry from the call for voluntary abstinence promoted for decades by the more moderate advocates of temperance. The law had the unintended effect of encouraging black-market production, emboldening organized crime, and engendering widespread opposition. Finally struck down in 1933, Prohibition was the only constitutional amendment ever to be repealed in its entirety.

Prohibition was an overreach into social control by well-meaning reformers who sought to protect women, children, and the poor. It was aimed at a very real problem, but was ultimately an overcorrection—and one that Americans could and would not bear. This was perhaps a foreshadowing of a similar phenomenon that occurred in the 1950s, when a creeping collectivism and the pressure to conform became a source of resentment and a seedbed of cultural and political backlash. The solution to hyperindividualism is never hyper-communitarianism, nor a repudiation of equally important American values such as liberty and self-determination. For solutions to be long-lasting and to hold widespread appeal, they must respect the full range of American ideals.

Second, and even more significant, is the caution never to compromise on equality and inclusion. To a significant degree, segregationism and white nationalism—undergirded by scientific racism—pervaded the thinking of many Progressives, and limited their understanding of which of the downtrodden deserved to be championed, and just who belonged in a widening circle of "we." The Progressive Era coincided with the rise of Jim Crow; Woodrow Wilson was one of the most openly racist presidents ever to occupy the White House; and much of FDR's New Deal ultimately discriminated against people of color and women—to name just a few examples. On the other hand, the work of Ida B. Wells and W. E. B. Du Bois intertwined with that of white Progressives such as Jane Addams and Florence Kelley, with whom they partnered to found the NAACP, and who were active and articulate models of a more inclusive Progressive agenda.

In assessing such a widely diverse movement, it is nearly impossible to make statements that apply across the board, but most scholars agree

that racism was the norm, not the exception among Progressive reformers. And although it was an incredibly pluralistic movement, Progressivism
was nonetheless largely led and implemented by the white middle class,
who decided not only who would benefit from its reforms, but also what
shape a refashioned America would take. These realities proved problematic because exclusion in any form is antithetical to the founding principles
of this nation. But also because—as the story of America's I-we-I century
has taught us—the failure to take full inclusion seriously compromised the
integrity of America's "we" decades and ultimately sowed the seeds of our
subsequent downturn.

Thus, a critical reading of the moment when we last turned the corner from "I" to "we" offers lessons about how we can put our nation on
an upward course again. But it also cautions us that doing so without fi-
delity to individual liberty, and an unwavering commitment to equality
and inclusion, will ultimately compromise the very best of our efforts. It
is therefore imperative that—alongside the remarkable example of moral
awakening, civic revival, cross-pollination of ideas, grassroots mobilization,
astute political leadership, and youthful mobilization the Progressive Era
provides—we also pay close attention to its failures, and seek to correct
them as we look to turn the corner again.

No one party, no one policy or platform, and no one charismatic leader
was responsible for bringing about America's upswing as we entered the
twentieth century. It was, instead, the result of countless citizens engag-
ing in their own spheres of influence and coming together to create a vast
ferment of criticism and change—a genuine shift from "I" to "we." For
Americans living through the turbulent closing decades of the nineteenth
century, such a turnaround was by no means inevitable or even expected.
And yet it happened, clearly and steadily—a phenomenon that our study
has illustrated in graphic detail. With consciences pricked and patriotism
rallied, an ideologically diverse generation of Progressive reformers arose
who experimented, innovated, organized, and worked for change from the
level of the tenement, neighborhood, ward, and union, all the way up to
the statehouse, the halls of Congress, the Supreme Court, and the White
House. Though historians have debated their motives and their methods,

the Progressives' legacy is nonetheless clear—in hard measures of economic equality, political comity, social cohesion, and cultural altruism they set in motion genuine upward progress that compounded during the first sixty-five years of the twentieth century. "We have felt reality bend to our purposes," Walter Lippmann had concluded hopefully, just fourteen years into that upswing. "We gather assurance from these hints."[28]

The conditions and specific challenges we face today—though often eerily familiar echoes of the past—are of course different in important ways to those faced by Americans in the first Gilded Age. And, accordingly, the paths we follow and the solutions we create will necessarily be different as well. However, looking backward to better understand the mind-set, tools, and tactics employed by early-century reformers may inform and empower us to overcome the drift of our own time, achieve our own form of mastery, and ultimately reverse our course to create a new chapter in the American story. But in engineering a new American upswing, we must set our sights higher than our predecessors did and stay fiercely committed to the difficult but ever-worthy project of fashioning an American "we" that is sustainable because it is inclusive.

A TRADE-OFF BETWEEN INDIVIDUALISM AND COMMUNITY?

What is the proper balance between guarding the interests, rights, and autonomy of the individual on the one hand, and maintaining a strong sense of unity, shared purpose, and common destiny on the other? As the foregoing discussion of the Progressive Era and its modern-day echoes makes clear, this was an urgent question at the beginning of the twentieth century, and it is again today.[29]

Many American political thinkers have argued that these two values are inherently in competition with one another—pitting social solidarity, equality, shared interests, shared destiny, mutual obligations, and shared values *against* individual rights, diversity, freedom, "rugged" individualism, and live-and-let-live tolerance. A simplistic embrace of an I/we dualism implies a zero-sum trade-off between communitarian equality and individualistic freedom. While we acknowledge this timeless tension, we do not believe that we must choose one side or the other, or that all virtue lies at one pole.

Furthermore, it is important to make clear that the I-we continuum is conceptually and empirically distinct from the more familiar left-right spectrum.[30] Both individualists and communitarians can be found on both sides of the political spectrum, because both individualism and community are foundational American ideals.

As political philosopher Danielle Allen has recently observed,

> Political philosophers have generated the view that equality and freedom are necessarily in tension with each other. . . . As a public, we have swallowed this argument whole. We think we are required to choose between freedom and equality. Our choice in recent years has tipped toward freedom. Under the general influence of libertarianism, both parties have abandoned our Declaration; they have scorned our patrimony. Such a choice is dangerous. If we abandon equality, we lose the single bond that makes us a community, that makes us a people with the capacity to be free collectively and individually in the first place.[31]

Like Allen, we reject the view that more freedom necessarily entails less equality and community, believing instead with Alexis de Tocqueville that individualism "rightly understood" is perfectly compatible with community and equality.[32]

As we discussed in Chapters 6–8, from some points of view the post-Sixties trends are welcome—America is now basically a more diverse, tolerant, and open society than it was at mid-century. But from other points of view, the post-Sixties trends have led to a national dead end that few Americans find appealing. And in Chapter 2 we showed that Americans in the first two thirds of the twentieth century enjoyed *both* rapid economic growth *and* greater equality and community—the best of both worlds— and conversely, Americans since the Sixties have had *both* slow growth *and* less equality and community—the worst of both worlds.

Throughout this book we have argued that although America's "we" had gradually become more capacious during the first half of the twentieth century, and as we continued the long historical task of redressing racial and gender inequities, we were in 1960 (and still are) very far from perfection on those dimensions. Americans could have and should have pushed further toward greater equality. Therefore the lessons of history that we glean from the I-we-I century are two-sided: We learn that once before Americans have gotten ourselves out of a mess like the one we're in now, but we also learn that in that first Progressive Era and the decades that followed we didn't set our sights high enough for what the "we" could really be, and we didn't take seriously enough the challenge of full inclusion. Therefore, the question we face today is not whether we can or should turn back the tide of history, but whether we can resurrect the earlier communitarian virtues in a way that does not reverse the progress we've made in terms of individual liberties. Both values are American, and we require a balance and integration of both.

This task will not be an easy one, and nothing less than the success of the American experiment is at stake. But as we look to an uncertain future we must keep in mind what is perhaps the greatest lesson of America's I-we-I century: As Theodore Roosevelt put it, "the fundamental rule of our national life—the rule which underlies all others—is that, on the whole, and in the long run, we shall go up or down together."[33]

ACKNOWLEDGMENTS

This book has a slightly unusual history. While tinkering with several obscure datasets—his favorite pastime—Robert Putnam stumbled over an unexpected confluence of historical patterns, tempting him into reneging on a promise to his long-supportive wife, Rosemary, that *Our Kids* (2015) would be his last book. When framing this quantitative evidence in a broader qualitative narrative threatened to become a Sisyphean task, he turned to Shaylyn Romney Garrett, a former student, collaborator, and friend, and an extraordinary writer who has long been fascinated in her own social activism by Progressive Era reformers.

To our mutual delight the partnership deepened and with it our friendship and mutual respect. While we each took initial responsibility for drafting individual chapters, together we have thoroughly discussed virtually every page, so that it would now be difficult even for us to say who was responsible for which idea in the book. There is no doubt that this is a better book because of the partnership between two people of such different generations and backgrounds.

Pride of place in any account of the background for this book must go to the talented, hardworking team of research associates who toiled collectively on this project for over three years, surveying far-flung previous research on our themes, ranging across more than a century and virtually all of the social sciences, including the indefatigable pursuit of little-known historical archives. This team included Laura Humm Delgado, Meredith Dost, Leah Downey, Ali Hakim, George Kynaston, Alex Mierke-Zatwarnicki, Noah Putnam, Daria Rose, Yael Schacher, Caroline Tervo, and Anna Valuev.

Several members of the team should be singled out for the breadth of their contributions: Aidan Connaughton, Charles (Chaz) Kelsh, Amy Lakeman, Jeff Metzger, and Jonathan Williams. And two team members were crucial as we rushed toward the finish line—Casey Bohlen, whose contributions to our understanding of both the Sixties and the history of racial equality were irreplaceable, and Jonah Hahn, whose role gradually evolved from a research assistant to a full partner on all aspects of the project, as well as becoming our IT consultant. While we appreciated Jonah's running down countless sources and citations, we are most grateful for his critical feedback and astute analysis as we distilled our conclusions.

Harvard University served as the primary host for this research project, as it has for our previous work, and we are especially grateful to the Harvard Kennedy School and its dean, Douglas Elmendorf. Like any large university, Harvard can be terribly fragmented, but it also provides a virtually endless supply of brilliant colleagues, generously willing to offer time and expertise across disciplinary and institutional boundaries. Here we express our profound gratitude to many colleagues who aided our research, though none of them bears any responsibility for our conclusions: Lizabeth Cohen, Matthew Desmond, David Ellwood, Richard Freeman, Jeffry Frieden, Stephen Goldsmith, Peter A. Hall, Jonathan Hansen, Nathaniel Hendren, Gary King, Michèle Lamont, Scott Mainwaring, Robert Manduca, Robert J. Sampson, Mario Small, James H. Stock, Lawrence H. Summers, Moshik Temkin, Mary C. Waters, and Arne Westad.

In addition to our Harvard colleagues, for critical readings of specific chapters and for help with relevant evidence, both quantitative and qualitative, we are deeply indebted to colleagues and friends across many institutions and disciplines, including Joel Aberbach, Dale Bell, Joyce Avrech Berkman, Leo Braudy, Andrew Cherlin, April Clark, Miles Corak, Heidi Hartmann, Daniel J. Hopkins, Paul O. Jenkins, David M. Kennedy, Peter H. Lindert, Anne-Marie Livingstone, Taylor Mann, Robert Mare, Andrew McAfee, Keith Neuman, Paul Pierson, Jonathan F. Putnam, Philip Oreopoulos, Lisa Tetrault, Daniel Wasserman, Harry Wiland, Jeffrey G. Williamson, Scott Winship, and Gavin Wright, though as always we alone are responsible for the remaining errors.

That last caveat also applies to a number of friends who were big-hearted enough to offer advice on the entire manuscript, including Xavier de Souza Briggs, David Brooks, Peter Davis, Angus Deaton, Robert O. Keohane, Michael Meeropol, and Bernard Banet. Bernie, in particular, deserves special mention for sending us, virtually every day over three years, an unending flow of press clippings and academic studies relevant to the full scope of our interests, an extraordinary act of friendship.

We are both grateful, though in different ways, to Professor James T. Kloppenberg, who first introduced each of us to the Progressives and the sweep of twentieth-century American history. Shaylyn took Kloppenberg's intellectual history course as an undergraduate at Harvard and wrote her undergraduate thesis on the social and political legacy of the Settlement House movement and the lives and work of Jane Addams, John Dewey, and their contemporaries. Coincidentally, twenty years later a casual, but enthusiastic lunchtime conversation with Kloppenberg encouraged Bob to move outside his disciplinary comfort zone and undertake the project that has culminated in this book. It is hard to imagine this book being written without Jim's influence on each of us. To Kloppenberg's fellow historians, we plead that you give credit to Jim for whatever of value you see in the book, but absolve him of blame for the errors that remain, which are entirely ours.

Any project of this length and complexity requires staff assistance of the highest caliber. We are delighted to recognize the contribution of Lisa MacPhee, as well as her talented predecessors Kyle Siegel, Louise Kennedy Converse, Tom Sander, and our undergraduate assistant, Cyrus Motanya.

We are also grateful to our skilled editor Bob Bender, his talented collaborator Johanna Li, and their colleagues at Simon & Schuster for guiding this project with their usual acumen, while at the same time adjusting to several unanticipated delays in our writing schedule.

SHAYLYN ROMNEY GARRETT ADDS:

I am grateful first and foremost to Bob Putnam, my longtime mentor, for inviting me to partner with him on this project. I'll always remember the first time he mentioned the idea to me, wide-eyed with wonder at the trends he had discovered. Little did I know I would play a part in bringing this important story to light. The research for this book was nearly complete by the time I joined the team, and I am humbled by the countless hours of investigation and analysis that it represents. It was an exciting challenge to help figure out how to bring coherence to this incredibly broad-based set of stories and to shape the framework for the I-we-I narrative. I learned as much as I contributed along the way. Bob has been tremendously gracious and supportive throughout this writing process. In the now twenty years that we have known one another, through all the various roles I have played in his projects, and through the two books on which we have now collaborated, he has been one of the most important influences in my professional life. And he and his wife Rosemary are shining examples of personal grace, generosity, and kindness.

I am also indebted to David Brooks and his team at the Aspen Institute's Weave: The Social Fabric Project for giving me the opportunity to travel the country during my writing of this book to see firsthand the challenges facing American communities today as well as the myriad grassroots solutions well underway in every corner of our nation. I'd also like to thank David for mentoring me as a writer, helping me rekindle my passion for storytelling, and giving me courage to find my own voice.

To Louise Knight, Ronda Jackson, Ashley Quarcoo, April Lawson, Jake Garrett, Anna Kearl, and many others, thank you for your friendship and support in hashing out how to think about some of the key components of this book.

I'm also sincerely grateful to my family, friends, neighbors, and church congregation—my own little "we"—for supporting (and feeding!) me during some of the more difficult moments of this project. Special thanks go to my parents, Ron and Peggy Romney, and my in-laws, Vern and Nanette Garrett, as well as Maria Vosloo, Gloria Unrein, Jill Phetsomphu, Samira Greenhalgh, Jessica Garrett, and Elizabeth Garrett, all of whom loved and cared for me and my daughter when I needed help the most. And to Holly Wall, thank you for sharing your gifts, and selflessly providing the physical, emotional, and spiritual support I needed to stay well, sane, and centered throughout this project.

To my sweet Sophia Eve, thank you for enduring the endless channeling of mommy's energy into this book, for celebrating every milestone with me, and for offering earnest help and encouragement as only a six-year-old can. May you be blessed to find your passion as your mother has, and pursue your dreams of making the world a better place with wisdom, courage, and conviction!

As I write these words I am awaiting the imminent arrival of my son, whom I thank for allowing me to complete this project without too much discomfort! My sincere hope is that he will be born into an America that is turning the corner toward an upswing, and that my children's generation will be a source of light and hope in a troubled world.

My final and most heartfelt thanks go to my best friend and husband, James Garrett, for encouraging and believing in me throughout this project. Without his love, support, and patience I would not be the woman I am today. To him I direct and dedicate the words with which we closed this book: "the fundamental rule of our . . . life—the rule which underlies all others—is that, on the whole, and in the long run, we shall go up or down together."

ROBERT D. PUTNAM ADDS

Throughout my career I've gotten by with a lot of help from long-time friends, former students, and colleagues. In addition to the colleagues and commentators whom we have jointly acknowledged earlier, I want to single out Larry M. Bartels, David Campbell, Russell J. Dalton, Sergio Fabbrini, Morris P. Fiorina, Carolyn and Norman Fletcher, Kristin A. Goss, David Halpern, Jennifer Hochschild, Ronald Inglehart, Carol Leger, Chaeyoon Lim, Jed Rakoff, Jennifer Rubin, Theda Skocpol, and Paul Solman.

Above all, in this context I want to recognize my lifelong intellectual debt to Robert Axelrod. Bob and I have been best friends since our first day of graduate school at Yale in the fall of 1964. Over the years we developed the habit of spending several days together nearly every summer, exchanging candid, critical thoughts about the evolution of our respective intellectual interests. Having this sort of partnership with someone widely

acknowledged to be among the most creative social scientists of his generation has been of inestimable value and pleasure to me.

Two of America's leading public intellectuals, Michelle Alexander and
Nannerl Keohane, offered incisive critiques of early, private formulations
of my arguments about race and gender. I have no idea what either will
think about our revised formulation, but I want to record publicly my in-
debtedness to each of them. Their forthrightness forced me to think much
more deeply about what racial and gender justice requires.

In addition to Harvard, I'm pleased to recognize several other institutions that provided warm hospitality and generous support for this project.

- Texas A & M University, especially the Hagler Institute for Advanced
  Study; Institute Director John L. Junkins; Dean of Liberal Arts Pamela
  Matthews; two outstanding members of the TAMU Political Science
  Department, Guy Whitten and Paul Kellstedt; two skilled doctoral re-
  search assistants, Janica Magat and Flavio Souza; and the staff of the
  Political Science Department. My "hook 'em horns" stay at TAMU was
  a source of both great pleasure and crucial help with some of the more
  advanced statistical techniques that undergird the curves of this book.
- Oxford University, especially Nuffield College and its exceptional War-
  den Andrew Dilnot and his superb staff, as well as Oxford Professors
  Jonathan Gershuny, Anthony Heath, and Danny Dorling; and Evrim
  Altintas, at the time a British Academy Postdoctoral Fellow of Oxford's
  Centre for Time Use Research. As at several previous moments in my
  career, Nuffield's unique atmosphere—intense and relaxed at the same
  time—provided a wonderful environment for grappling creatively
  with "big" problems.
- For more than twenty years I've enjoyed a most fruitful collaboration with an extraordinary succession of leaders at the New Hampshire
  Charitable Foundation, beginning with its longtime president (and
  dear personal friend) Lew Feldstein. In this book project that partnership continued with its exceptional president and CEO Dick Ober and
  his staff, particularly Katie Merrow, who organized a most constructive
  critical roundtable focused on our treatment of race and gender.

Two long-time professional friends and colleagues deserve special credit for their contributions to this project:

From the mid-1990s, my path began repeatedly to cross that of a precocious deputy mayor of Minneapolis named Rip Rapson. As Rip then rose up first the academic ladder and then the philanthropic ladder, eventually becoming head of the Kresge Foundation, we continued to keep in touch as friends. Over dinner one evening in 2016 Rip asked what I was working on. I replied that I was thinking about retiring, but that I was intrigued by a little puzzle I had stumbled onto. Even before dessert arrived, Rip volunteered that he found the puzzle equally intriguing and that if Kresge could be helpful, I should let him know. On the strength of his trust that I might come up with something worthwhile, the Kresge Foundation provided the sole support for this project for four years, not once questioning me, even about missed deadlines. I am deeply grateful to Rip for his trust and encouragement on *The Upswing*, and my main hope is that this book will not disappoint him.

Rafe Sagalyn has been my good friend and literary agent for a quarter century, and he is always very good at his job. However, in the case of this project his contributions were without parallel—from conception to execution to title. At the very beginning, when I was still unsure whether my statistical curves merited a book, his enthusiasm encouraged me to persevere. When I became unsure whether I was up to finishing a project that was turning out to be much bigger than I had planned, Rafe was the impetus and a continual supporter of my collaboration with Shaylyn. When we found ourselves in a log-jam about the title, Rafe and his colleague Brandon Coward suggested a title that we all now agree is exactly right. For whatever success I've had as a writer over the last quarter century, Rafe Sagalyn is a major part of the explanation.

Of course, my deepest professional obligation for this book is to Shaylyn Romney Garrett. Shaylyn is one of the top students among the thousands whom I've had the pleasure of teaching over the past half century and among the top collaborators with whom I've ever had the good fortune to work. Her very first paper in my class two decades ago considered the Progressive Era and its aftermath, and it is no accident that we return to that topic in this book. Five years after graduating from Harvard she returned as a researcher and writer with me and David Campbell on *American Grace*. Her contribution to *The Upswing* began as a talented writer, but her contributions soon became substantive and intellectual. Because of her prior expertise on the Progressive Era, she was instrumental in the formulation of our narrative, including the sections of the introduction and conclusion that emphasize the parallels between the Gilded Age/Progressive Era and the challenges that face us today. Shaylyn has a great future as a writer and a memoirist, and I'm proud of our friendship.

As in all my previous writings, I continue to be deeply indebted to my wife, Rosemary, to our two children (Jonathan and Lara, both now distinguished authors in their own right), and to our seven grandchildren (Miriam, Gray, Gabriel, Noah, Alonso, Gideon, and Eleanor, some of whom have also begun promising careers as writers). As in the past, my family have made important contributions to this book, especially infusing it with more contemporary sensibilities than I could have mustered on my own.

Rosemary is the only person who has read every word that I have ever published and critiqued every page. Everyone needs a best friend, but I have long had the unusual advantage of being married to mine. Rosemary baked every cookie for every seminar I taught, managed every file for every book I wrote, raised our children and grandchildren, remembered every old friend's name, kept me sane by loving me through every dark moment—all while carrying out a career as a distinguished professional in special education and a real social capitalist—and all this with virtually no public recognition. Hooking up with this remarkable person was the luckiest thing that ever happened to me and the smartest thing I ever did. Everyone who knows us well knows that Rosemary is the senior partner in our relationship, though some of our friends may sometimes have wondered whether I recognized that. I just did.

NOTES

NOTE TO THE READER
The Ngram evidence used in this book is based on the latest data available at the end of 2019. In July 2020 the Ngram website itself cited in Chapter 5 was revised to include data based on a slightly different methodology.

CHAPTER 1: WHAT'S PAST IS PROLOGUE

1   Alexis de Tocqueville, *Democracy in America*, 2nd ed., vol. 2 (Cambridge, MA: Sever & Francis, 1863), chap. 8. Several chapters later he warned of the danger to democracy if the collective interest became overwhelmed by an emphasis on individual rights. See Jonathan M. Hansen, *The Lost Promise of Patriotism: Debating American Identity, 1890–1920* (Chicago: University of Chicago Press, 2003), 189–90.

2   It is of course important to acknowledge that Tocqueville's observations reflect his background as an upper-class white male, and that his descriptions of American society essentially apply only to *white* society. But he did recognize the evils of slavery and the fact that it posed a particular challenge to the new republic and its ideals. (See Alexis de Tocqueville, *Democracy in America*, 2nd ed., vol. 1 [Cambridge, MA: Sever & Francis, 1863], chap. 10.) Scholars have debated exactly how Tocqueville's views on American slavery intersected with his assessment of American democracy. For more on this question, see Sally Gershman, "Alexis de Tocqueville and Slavery," *French Historical Studies* 9, no. 3 (1976): 467–83, doi:10.2307/286232; Richard W. Resh, "Alexis De Tocqueville and the Negro: Democracy in America Reconsidered," *The Journal of Negro History* 48, no. 4 (n.d.): 251–59, doi:10.2307/2716328; and Barbara Allen, "An Undertow of Race Prejudice in the Current of Democratic Transformation: Tocqueville on the 'Three Races' of North America," in *Tocqueville's Voyages: The Evolution of His Ideas and Their Journey Beyond His Time*, ed. Christine Dunn Henderson (Indianapolis: Liberty Fund, 2014), 244–77.

3   Since we speak often in this book about the Gilded Age and the Progressive Era, it may be helpful to note that neither we nor most historians are entirely precise about when the Gilded Age ended and the Progressive Era began. Roughly speaking, "Gilded Age" refers to the period 1870–1900 and

"Progressive Era" to 1900–1915. Like any historical demarcation, this division is not strict, since developments associated with the Progressive movement had clear antecedents during the earlier period, and developments associated with the Gilded Age persisted into the later period.

4   In constructing the composite summary curves in Figure 1.1 and similar summary curves in later chapters, in each case we have used two independent methods of longitudinal factor analysis, the dyad ratio algorithm method of James Stimson and the Expectation-Maximization method of James Stock and M. W. Watson. For the Stock-Watson method, see James H. Stock and Mark W. Watson, "Dynamic Factor Model," in *The Oxford Handbook of Economic Forecasting*, eds. Michael P. Clements and David F. Hendry (New York: Oxford University Press, 2011), and James H. Stock and Mark W. Watson, "Dynamic Factor Models, Factor-Augmented Vector Autoregressions, and Structural Vector Autoregressions in Macroeconomics," in *Handbook of Macroeconomics*, vol. 2 (Amsterdam: Elsevier, 2016), 415–525. For the Stimson approach, see James A. Stimson, "The Dyad Ratios Algorithm for Estimating Latent Public Opinion: Estimation, Testing, and Comparison to Other Approaches," *Bulletin de Méthodologie Sociologique* 137–38, no. 1 (2018): 201–8, doi:10.1177/0759106318761614; unpublished instructional guide available at: http://stimson.web.unc.edu/software/. For an extended example of the use of the Stimson method, see James A. Stimson, *Public Opinion in America: Moods, Cycles, and Swings*, 2nd ed. (London: Routledge, 2019).

The Stock-Watson method is more familiar to econometricians, while the Stimson method is more familiar to political scientists. The Stimson method is better able to deal with missing data (e.g., years for which no measure of split ticket voting is available, because those years had no presidential election), so for calculating the factor scores used throughout the book, we have relied on the Stimson method. However, with our data the two quite different approaches yield essentially the same result in terms of a single dominant factor on which the various measures load very highly.

The curves in Figure 1.1 reflect four separate Stimson-type factor analyses of the key variables used, respectively, in Chapters 2, 3, 4, and 5 on economics, politics, society, and culture. The temporal coverage of each curve varies slightly depending on the timespan of the underlying data; we only included years for which we had nonmissing data for a substantial fraction of the underlying component variables. The summary curve in Figure 1.2 is based on a separate Stimson-type factor analysis that combines all available variables from all four domains. The data points represent standardized factor scores, which can be compared both across the years for a given curve and across the curves for a given year, but do not have a readily interpretable numerical meaning (like percentages or dollars).

We are deeply grateful to Guy D. Whitten, Paul Kellstedt, Janica Magat, and Flavio Souza of Texas A&M University for their invaluable help with this part of the project, though none of them is responsible for the way we have presented and interpreted the results of their work.

5   One exception is Peter Turchin, *Ages of Discord: A Structural-Demographic Analysis of American History* (Chaplin, CT: Beresta Books, 2016).

6   "Bush Hits New Low as 'Wrong Track' Rises," (ABC News, May 12, 2008), http://abcnews.go.com/images/PollingUnit/1064a1Bush-Track.pdf; http://www.pollingreport.com/right.htm.https://www.thedailybeast.com/weve-been-on-the-wrong-track-since-1972.

7   Kim Parker, Rich Morin, and Juliana Menasce Horowitz, "Looking to the Future, Public Sees an America in Decline on Many Fronts," (Pew Research Center, March 21, 2019), https://www.pewsocialtrends.org/2019/03/21/public-sees-an-america-in-decline-on-many-fronts/.

8   "Stress in America: The State of Our Nation" (American Psychological Association, November 1, 2017), https://www.apa.org/news/press/releases/stress/2017/state-nation.pdf.

9   "OK Boomer" is a meme that spread rapidly across the internet in 2019, gaining popularity among younger cohorts as a way to mock attitudes stereotypically attributed to the baby boomer generation. See Karen Heller, "It Was the Year of 'OK Boomer,' and the Generations Were at Each Other's Throats," *The Washington Post*, December 24, 2019, https://www.washingtonpost.com/lifestyle/it-was-the-year-of-ok-boomer-and-the-generations-were-at-each-others-throats/2019/12/24/a2c2b586-1792-11ea-8406-df3c54b3253e_story.html.

10 Rebecca Edwards, *New Spirits: Americans in the Gilded Age, 1865–1905* (New York: Oxford University Press, 2006), 242.

11 Alfred North Whitehead, *The Concept of Nature: Tarner Lectures Delivered in Trinity College, November, 1919,* Tarner Lectures 1919 (Cambridge: University Press, 1920), 143.

12 The scholarly literature on the Progressive Era is broad and deep. For a sampling of the rich accounts of this period in United States history, see Lewis L. Gould, *America in the Progressive Era, 1890–1914*, Seminar Studies in History (Harlow, UK: Longman, 2001); Nell Irvin Painter, *Standing at Armageddon: The United States, 1877–1919* (New York: W. W. Norton, 2008); Richard McCormick, "Public Life in Industrial America," in *The New American History* (Philadelphia: Temple University Press, 1997); John Chambers and Vincent Carosso, *The Tyranny of Change: America in the Progressive Era, 1900–1917* (New York: St. Martin's Press, 1980); Richard Hofstadter, *The Age of Reform: From Bryan to F.D.R*, 1st ed. (New York: Vintage, 1955); Sean Dennis Cashman, *America in the Gilded Age: From the Death of Lincoln to the Rise of Theodore*

Roosevelt, 3rd ed. (New York: New York University Press, 1993); Steven J. Diner, *A Very Different Age: Americans of the Progressive Era* (New York: Hill & Wang, 1998); Samuel P. Hays, *The Response to Industrialism, 1885–1914*, 2nd ed., The Chicago History of American Civilization (Chicago: University of Chicago Press, 1995); Robert H. Wiebe, *The Search for Order, 1877–1920*, 1st ed. (New York: Hill & Wang, 1966); Paul Boyer, *Urban Masses and Moral Order in America, 1820–1920* (Cambridge, MA: Harvard University Press, 1992); Edwards, *New Spirits*; Benjamin Parke De Witt, *The Progressive Movement: A Non-Partisan Comprehensive Discussion of Current Tendencies in American Politics* (New Brunswick, NJ: Transaction Publishers, 2013); Elizabeth Sanders, *Roots of Reform: Farmers, Workers, and the American State, 1877–1917*, American Politics and Political Economy (Chicago: University of Chicago Press, 1999); Allen Freeman Davis, *Spearheads for Reform: The Social Settlements and the Progressive Movement, 1890–1914* (New Brunswick, NJ: Rutgers University Press, 1984); Michael E. McGerr, *A Fierce Discontent: The Rise and Fall of the Progressive Movement in America, 1870–1920* (New York: Free Press, 2003).

CHAPTER 2: ECONOMICS: THE RISE AND FALL OF EQUALITY

1 Steven Pinker, *Enlightenment Now: The Case for Reason, Science, Humanism, and Progress* (New York: Viking, 2018). The standard (and more nuanced) account of American technological change and economic progress is Robert J. Gordon, *The Rise and Fall of American Growth: The U. S. Standard of Living Since the Civil* War (Princeton: Princeton University Press, 2016).

2 Charles I. Jones, "The Facts of Economic Growth," in *Handbook of Macroeconomics*, eds. John B. Taylor and Harald Uhlig, vol. 2A (Amsterdam: Elsevier, 2016), 3–69. Data from 1929 to the present come from NIPA Table 7.1, Line 10. Data from 1870 to 1928 come from Madison project database using the rgdpnapc variable for US per capita GDP. Madison benchmarks with 2011 dollars converted to 2009 values. See also Louis Johnston and Samuel H. Williamson, "What Was the U.S. GDP Then?," accessed November 25, 2019, https://www.measuringworth.com/datasets/usgdp/.

3 Jones, "Facts of Economic Growth."

4 Nicholas Kaldor, "Capital Accumulation and Economic Growth," in *The Theory of Capital*, ed. Douglas Hague (London: Palgrave Macmillan, 1961), 177–222, https://doi.org/10.1007/978-1-349-08452-4_10. Kaldor wrote, "I suggest the following 'stylized facts' as a starting-point for the construction of theoretical models: The continued growth in the aggregate volume of production and in the productivity of labour at a steady trend rate; no recorded tendency for a *falling* rate of growth of productivity."

5 Angus Deaton, *The Great Escape: Health, Wealth, and the Origins of Inequality* (Princeton: Princeton University Press, 2013) and Robert J. Gordon, *The Rise*

and Fall of American Growth have offered abundant evidence for the post-1970 falloff in the long-term annual growth rate.

6   Maria Cecilia P. Moura, Steven J. Smith, and David B. Belzer, "120 Years of U.S. Residential Housing Stock and Floor Space," August 11, 2015, PLOS ONE 10.1371/journal.pone.0134135; Stanley Lebergott, *The American Economy: Income, Wealth and Want* (Princeton: Princeton University Press, 2015); Sue Bowden and Avner Offer, "Household Appliances and the Use of Time: The United States and Britain Since the 1920s," *Economic History Review* 47, no. 4 (1994): 725–48.

7   Transportation Energy Data Book, Edition 36, Office of Energy Efficiency and Renewable Energy, U.S. Department of Energy, Table 3.6, https://cta .ornl.gov/data/chapter3.shtml. Given problems of pollution, global warming, and commuting, not everyone would count the proliferation of automobiles as a plus, but Americans seem to prize them as a symbol of material progress.

8   See Derek Thompson, "The 100-Year March of Technology in 1 Graph," *The Atlantic*, April 7, 2012, https://www.theatlantic.com/technology/archive/2012 /04/the-100-year-march-of-technology-in-1-graph/255573/.

9   The relevant literature on this topic is massive. Three useful overviews are David M. Cutler and Grant Miller, "The Role of Public Health Improvements in Health Advances: The Twentieth-Century United States," *Demography* 42, no. 1 (February 2005): 1–22; "Mortality in the United States: Past, Present, and Future," Penn Wharton Budget Model, June 27, 2016, https://budget model.wharton.upenn.edu/issues/2016/1/25/mortality-in-the-united-states -past-present-and-future; and Maryaline Catillon, David Cutler, and Thomas Getzen, "Two Hundred Years of Health and Medical Care: The Importance of Medical Care for Life Expectancy Gains," Working Paper 25330 (National Bureau of Economic Research, December 2018), https://doi.org/10.3386 /w25330.

10   S. H. Woolf, and H. Schoomaker, "Life Expectancy and Mortality Rates in the United States, 1959–2017," JAMA 322, no. 20 (2019): 1996–2016. Doi:https:// doi.org/10.1001/jama.2019.16932; Gina Kolata and Sabrina Tavernise, "It's Not Just Poor White People Driving a Decline in Life Expectancy," *New York Times*, November 26, 2019, https://www.nytimes.com/2019/11/26/health /life-expectancy-rate-usa.html; Olga Khazan, "Poor Americans Really Are in Despair," *The Atlantic*, June 19, 2018, https://www.theatlantic.com/health/ar chive/2018/06/poor-americans-really-are-in-despair/563105/.

11   For data on suicide increases, see Holly Hedegaard, Sally C. Curtin, and Margaret Warner, "Suicide Mortality in the United States, 1999–2017" (Hyattsville, MD: National Center for Health Statistics, 2018), https://www.cdc.gov /nchs/products/databriefs/db330.htm. On drug overdose deaths, see Holly Hedegaard, Margaret Warner, and Arialdi M. Miniño, "Drug Overdose

Deaths in the United States, 1999–2016" (Hyattsville, MD: National Center for Health Statistics, 2017), https://www.cdc.gov/nchs/products/databriefs/db294.htm. Information on mortality due to cirrhosis comes from Elliot B. Tapper and Neehar D. Parikh, "Mortality Due to Cirrhosis and Liver Cancer in the United States, 1999–2016: Observational Study," *BMJ*, July 18, 2018, k2817, https://doi.org/10.1136/bmj.k2817.

12 Anne Case and Angus Deaton, *Deaths of Despair and the Future of Capitalism* (Princeton: Princeton University Press, 2020).

13 Julia Haskins, "Suicide, Opioids Tied to Ongoing Fall in US Life Expectancy: Third Year of Drop," *The Nation's Health*, vol. 49 (March 2019): 1-10.

14 Noreen Goldman, Dana A. Glei, and Maxine Weinstein, "Declining Mental Health Among Disadvantaged Americans," *Proceedings of the National Academy of Sciences* 115, no. 28 (July 10, 2018): 7290–95, https://doi.org/10.1073/pnas.1722023115. Although the "deaths of despair" narrative largely focuses on poor, middle-aged whites without college degrees, suicide among all racial and ethnic groups and for men and women has gone up since 1999. The CDC report on the rural-urban differences in drug overdose rate demonstrates how opioids such as oxycodone are abused at higher rates in rural counties, although synthetic opioids, such as fentanyl, cause more deaths in urban counties. See Holly Hedegaard, Arialdi M. Miniño, and Margaret Warner, "Urban–Rural Differences in Drug Overdose Death Rates, by Sex, Age, and Type of Drugs Involved, 2017," NCHS Data Brief No. 345, August 2019 (Hyattsville, MD: National Center for Health Statistics, 2019), https://www.cdc.gov/nchs/products/databriefs/db345.htm.

15 Mark Strauss, "Four-in-Ten Americans Credit Technology with Improving Life Most in the Past 50 Years," *Fact Tank—News in the Numbers* (blog), October 12, 2017, https://www.pewresearch.org/fact-tank/2017/10/12/four-in-ten-americans-credit-technology-with-improving-life-most-in-the-past-50-years/.

16 Before Emancipation very few blacks had any formal schooling. Under Reconstruction enrollment rates among black children quickly rose to about one third, but by 1900, two decades after the end of Reconstruction, that figure remained unchanged. Robert A. Margo, *Race and Schooling the South: 1880–1950: An Economic History* (Chicago: University of Chicago Press, 1990).

17 In the short run the rapid expansion of high schools widened the racial gap, since high schools serving blacks, especially in the South, were slower to develop. On the growth of high schools, see Claudia Goldin, "America's Graduation from High School: The Evolution and Spread of Secondary Schooling in the Twentieth Century," *The Journal of Economic History* 58, no. 2 (June 1998): 345–74, https://doi.org/10.1017/S0022050700020544. We discuss the high school movement at greater length in the concluding chapter.

18   The literature on the high school revolution and its effects is vast, but the key work is Claudia Goldin and Lawrence F. Katz, *The Race Between Education and Technology* (Cambridge, MA: The Belknap Press of Harvard University Press, 2008). For a useful overview of statistical evidence of long-term educational change, see also Claudia Goldin, "Education," in chapter Bc, ed. Susan B. Carter et al., *Historical Statistics of the United States, Earliest Times to the Present: Millennial Edition*, ed. Susan B. Carter et al. (New York: Cambridge University Press, 2006), https://doi.org/10.1017/ISBN-9780511132971.Bc.ESS.01.

19   Historical Statistics of the United States, Millennial Edition Bc258-264, http://dx.doi.org/10.1017/ISBN-9780511132971; Trends in High School Dropout and Completion Rates in the United States: 2014 (National Center for Educational Statistics, US Department of Education, 2018), https://nces.ed.gov/pubs2018/2018117.pdf; James J. Heckman and Paul A. LaFontaine, "The American High School Graduation Rate: Trends and Levels," *Review of Economics and Statistics* 92, no. 2 (May 2010): 244–62, https://doi.org/10.1162/rest.2010.12366. Absolute school enrollment peaked in that decade, as the Baby Boomers passed through, but Figure 2.6 shows not absolute numbers but rates, so the halt in the long rise in high school graduation rate cannot be blamed on simple demographics. On the contrary, as the raw numbers of students declined, one might have expected the rate to increase, in order to fill all those newly empty classrooms.

20   The reasons behind this recent uptick are not established. See Richard J Murnane, "U.S. High School Graduation Rates: Patterns and Explanations," *Journal of Economic Literature* 51, no. 2 (June 2013): 370–422, https://doi.org/10.1257/jel.51.2.370, and Mark Dynarski, "What We Don't Know About High Schools Can Hurt Us" (Washington, DC: The Brookings Institution, May 18, 2017), https://www.brookings.edu/research/what-we-dont-know-about-high-schools-can-hurt-us/ and the sources cited there.

21   The "pause" in educational gains in the 1980s and 1990s has also been noted by Peter H. Lindert and Jeffrey G. Williamson, *Unequal Gains: American Growth and Inequality Since 1700* (Princeton: Princeton University Press, 2016), 213; 230–32, and Goldin and Katz, *The Race Between Education and Technology*, though all those authors focus primarily on the "stock" of educated adults, whereas we focus here on the "flow" of graduates among young people, in order to pinpoint more precisely when the slowdown happened.

22   Upon signing the GI Bill in 1944, President Roosevelt summarized the benefits as covering tuition up to $500 per school year and dispensing a monthly stipend. In 1945, tuition at the University of Pennsylvania cost $400 with a $20 "General Fee." See also U.S. Department of Veterans Affairs, "Education and Training," About GI Bill: History and Timeline, November 21, 2013, https://www.benefits.va.gov/gibill/history.asp, and Mark Frazier Lloyd,

"Tuition and Mandated Fees, Room and Board, and Other Educational Costs at Penn, 1940–1949," 2003, https://archives.upenn.edu/exhibits/penn-history /tuition/tuition-1940-1949.

23 We discuss gender and racial differences in educational attainment in Chapters 6 and 7.

24 In drafting this chapter, we have benefited from the important forthcoming work of Charles L. Ballard, "The Fall and Rise of Income Inequality in the United States: Economic Trends and Political-Economy Explanations," in *Inequality and Democracy in America*, ed. Tobin Craig, Steven Kautz, and Arthur Melzer (Philadelphia: University of Pennsylvania Press, forthcoming).

25 Lindert and Williamson, *Unequal Gains*, see chaps. 6 and 7, esp. 173.

26 The narrowing of the income gap between rich and poor during the first half of the twentieth century has been variously termed "Great Convergence," "Great Leveling," and "Great Compression." We generally use the first label, but all three refer to the same phenomenon. This term was popularized by Timothy Noah, *The Great Divergence: America's Growing Inequality Crisis and What We Can Do About It* (New York: Bloomsbury Press, 2017), and Paul R. Krugman, *The Conscience of a Liberal* (New York: W. W. Norton, 2007).

27 Lindert and Williamson, *Unequal Gains*, esp. 194.

28 Ibid., 196. See also Claudia Goldin and Lawrence F. Katz, "Decreasing (and Then Increasing) Inequality in America: A Tale of Two Half Centuries," in *The Causes and Consequences of Increasing Inequality*, ed. Finis Welch (Chicago: University of Chicago Press, 2001), 37–82.

29 Figure 2.8, focused on the share of total income accruing to the top 1 percent of households, is based on the most recent and comprehensive accounting of income distribution (including capital income and nontaxable health and fringe benefits, as well as state and local taxes) over the last ten decades: Thomas Piketty, Emmanuel Saez, and Gabriel Zucman, "Distributional National Accounts: Methods and Estimates for the United States," *The Quarterly Journal of Economics* 133, no. 2 (May 2018): 553–609, https://doi.org/10.1093 /qje/qjx043. See this same source for discussion of the various methodological challenges in compiling these trends. The assumptions underlying this approach remain controversial among economists, but an alternative, more conventional approach yields similar long-term inverted U-curves. See Thomas Piketty and Emmanuel Saez, "Income Inequality in the United States, 1913–1998," *The Quarterly Journal of Economics* 118, no. 1 (February 2003): 1–39, https://doi.org/10.1162/00335530360535135. For a recent independent review of multiple statistical approaches to historical trends in income inequality that confirms the basic inverted-U pattern shown in Figure 2.8, see Chad Stone et al., "A Guide to Statistics on Historical Trends in Income Inequality" (Washington, DC: Center on Budget and Policy

Priorities, August 21, 2019). Generally speaking, conservative analysts argue that mainstream estimates of inequality are too high, but our focus here is not on the absolute level of inequality, but on the long-run trends, up and down, and the basic inverted U curve of income and wealth inequality is essentially accepted by experts of all partisan stripes.

30 Lindert and Williamson, *Unequal Gains*, 194–95.

31 Goldin and Katz, "Decreasing (and then Increasing) Inequality in America," 37–82.

32 For an authoritative account of long-run trends in wealth, see Edward N. Wolff, *A Century of Wealth in America* (Cambridge, MA: Belknap Press of Harvard University Press, 2017).

33 Emmanuel Saez, "Income and Wealth Inequality: Evidence and Policy Implications," *Contemporary Economic Policy* 35, no. 1 (2017), 8.

34 Piketty, Saez, and Zucman, "Distributional National Accounts." See also Emmanuel Saez and Gabriel Zucman, "Wealth Inequality in the United States Since 1913: Evidence from Capitalized Income Tax Data," *The Quarterly Journal of Economics* 131, no. 2 (May 2016): 519–78, https://doi.org/10.1093/qje/qjw004.

35 Using a slightly different time series, Edward N. Wolff shows that the distribution of wealth, as measured, for example, by the share held by the top 1 percent, rose significantly between 2013 and 2016. See Edward N. Wolff, "Household Wealth Trends in the United States, 1962 to 2016: Has Middle Class Wealth Recovered?," Working Paper 24085 (National Bureau of Economic Research, November 2017), https://doi.org/10.3386/w24085.

36 Saez, "Income and Wealth Inequality," 13. Gabriel Zucman, "Global Wealth Inequality," *Annual Review of Economics* 11, no. 1 (August 2, 2019): 109–38, https://doi.org/10.1146/annurev-economics-080218-025852, demonstrates that the top 0.01 percent possess almost 10 percent of total wealth.

37 Saez, "Income and Wealth Inequality," 14–15; Chad Stone et al., "A Guide to Statistics."

38 Saez and Zucman, "Wealth Inequality in the United States Since 1913," 523.

39 Piketty, Saez, and Zucman, "Distributional National Accounts."

40 Saez, "Income and Wealth Inequality," 16.

41 Goldin and Katz, "Decreasing (and then Increasing) Inequality in America." We will discuss the "pause" of progressivism during the Twenties at greater length in Chapters 3 and 5.

42 Émile Durkheim, *Suicide: A Study in Sociology* (New York: Free Press, 1951); Bruce P. Dohrenwend, "Egoism, Altruism, Anomie, and Fatalism: A Conceptual Analysis of Durkheim's Types," *American Sociological Review* 24, no. 4 (August 1959): 466–73, https://doi.org/10.2307/2089533; Walter Scheidel, *The Great Leveler: Violence and the History of Inequality from the Stone Age to*

the Twenty-First Century, Princeton Economic History of the Western World (Princeton: Princeton University Press, 2017).

43   Douglas S. Massey, *Categorically Unequal: The American Stratification System* (New York: Russell Sage Foundation, 2007), 5.

44   Piketty, Saez, and Zucman, "Distributional National Accounts," 577–78.

45   Lindert and Williamson, *Unequal Gains*, 221.

46   Piketty, Saez, and Zucman, "Distributional National Accounts," 577–79.

47   David Leonhardt, "How the Upper Middle Class Is Really Doing," *New York Times*, February 24, 2019, https://www.nytimes.com/2019/02/24/opinion/income-inequality-upper-middle-class.html; Matthew Stewart, "The 9.9 Percent Is the New American Aristocracy," *The Atlantic*, June 2018, https://www.theatlantic.com/magazine/archive/2018/06/the-birth-of-a-new-american-aristocracy/559130/.

48   Jessica L. Semega, Kayla R. Fontenot, and Melissa A. Kollar, "Income and Poverty in the United States: 2016," *Current Population Reports* (Washington, DC: United States Census Bureau, September 2017), Table A-2. Data for top 1 and top 0.1 percent from Piketty, Saez, and Zucman, "Distributional National Accounts," Tables B10 and B11 of Appendix II. These figures are inflation-adjusted, pre-tax, and pre-transfers. The PSZ data for the top 1 and 0.1 percent use a slightly different inflation adjustment and a slightly different estimate of annual income, but the broad comparison in the text is essentially unaffected.

49   Ballard, "The Fall and Rise of Income Inequality in the United States," 4.

50   David Card, Ciprian Domnisoru, and Lowell Taylor, "The Intergenerational Transmission of Human Capital: Evidence from the Golden Age of Upward Mobility," Working Paper 25000 (National Bureau of Economic Research, September 2018), https://doi.org/10.3386/w25000. While they find that high-quality public education improved equality of opportunity over generations during the first half of the twentieth century, the story is not exclusively positive. School quality causally determines upward mobility in education, likely explaining why mobility rates systematically vary by race and location. Racial segregation in education led to a substantial disadvantage for African American children.

51   Raj Chetty et al., "The Fading American Dream: Trends in Absolute Income Mobility Since 1940," *Science* 356, no. 6336 (April 28, 2017): 398–406, https://doi.org/10.1126/science.aal4617. Nathaniel G Hilger, "The Great Escape: Intergenerational Mobility in the United States Since 1940," Working Paper 21217 (National Bureau of Economic Research, May 2015), https://doi.org/10.3386/w21217; and Michael Hout and Alexander Janus, "Educational Mobility in the United States Since the 1930s," in *Whither Opportunity?: Rising Inequality, Schools, and Children's Life Chances*, eds. Greg J. Duncan and

Richard J. Murnane (New York: Russell Sage Foundation, 2011), 165–85 find a similar pattern for absolute educational mobility—rising until roughly 1975 and then falling. Robert M. Hauser et al., "Occupational Status, Education, and Social Mobility in the Meritocracy," in *Meritocracy and Economic Inequality*, eds. Kenneth Arrow, Samuel Bowles, and Steven Durlauf (Princeton: Princeton University Press, 2000), 179–229 find a similar pattern for absolute mobility in occupational status. Research is mixed about whether there was a similar turning point in *relative* intergenerational mobility. Hilger and Hout and Janus find that relative *educational* mobility (which is closely related to income mobility) increased between roughly 1940 and roughly 1970 and then stabilized or even slightly reversed. See also James J. Feigenbaum et al., "The American Dream in the Great Depression: US Absolute Income Mobility, 1915–1940" (unpublished manuscript, 2019), who estimate that absolute mobility rose between roughly 1940 and 1965, thus showing a classic U-curve for this variable, reaching peak mobility in the cohort who reached their adult earning levels in 1965. We follow standard practice among economists by assuming that individuals in a given cohort reach a relatively stable position in the income hierarchy when they reach the age of 30, since income levels before that age are distorted by students and other youth reporting artificially low incomes. By contrast, in later chapters, when discussing intergenerational differences in attitudes, such as trust and racial and gender attitudes, we follow the convention among social psychologists of assuming that attitudes become crystalized on average at roughly 18-21. Both the economists and the social psychologists have good reasons for these contrasting assumptions about stages of the life cycle.

52 See Yonatan Berman, "The Long Run Evolution of Absolute Intergenerational Mobility," (unpublished manuscript, 2018), Table 3, 40-41, https://static.wixstatic.com/ugd/4a2bc3_0d734d65a96b419abacbffe261d85b5d.pdf. The available evidence goes back to the birth cohort of 1917, but until they reached 30, we can't know how they have done compared to their own fathers at the same age. Thus, this measure of mobility can begin only in 1947.

53 Dating of these periods is not precise. See Cutler and Miller, "The Role of Public Health Improvements in Health Advances" and Dora L. Costa, "Health and the Economy in the United States from 1750 to the Present," *Journal of Economic Literature* 53, no. 3 (September 2015): 503–70.

54 Lindert and Williamson, *Unequal Gains*, 7. See also Michael R. Haines, "Inequality and Infant and Childhood Mortality in the United States in the Twentieth Century," *Explorations in Economic History* 48, no. 3 (2011): 418–28, and Aaron Antonovsky, "Social Class, Life Expectancy and Overall Mortality," *The Milbank Memorial Fund Quarterly* 45, no. 2 (April 1967): 31–73, https://doi.org/10.2307/3348839.

55   Jacob Bor, Gregory H Cohen, and Sandro Galea, "Population Health in an Era of Rising Income Inequality: USA, 1980–2015," *The Lancet* 389, no. 10077 (April 8, 2017): 1475–90, https://doi.org/10.1016/S0140-6736(17)30571-8.

56   National Academies of Sciences, Engineering, and Medicine, *The Growing Gap in Life Expectancy by Income: Implications for Federal Programs and Policy Responses* (Washington, DC: The National Academies Press, 2015), 63. In 2019 researchers using a massive CDC annual survey of health among Americans between 1993 and 2017 reported growing divergence by income in health indicators, though *declining* divergence by race. Frederick J. Zimmerman and Nathaniel W. Anderson, "Trends in Health Equity in the United States by Race/Ethnicity, Sex, and Income, 1993–2017," *JAMA Network Open* 2, no. 6 (June 28, 2019): e196386, https://doi.org/10.1001/jamanetworkopen.2019.6386, found that health outcomes for wealthy people remain stable, but the health of the lowest income groups is "declining substantially over time."

57   Case and Deaton, *Deaths of Despair and the Future of Capitalism*.

58   Office of Senator Mike Lee, "Long-Term Trends in Deaths of Despair," SCP Report 4-19, Social Capital Project (Washington, DC: United States Congress Joint Economic Committee, September 5, 2019), https://www.jec.senate.gov/public/index.cfm/republicans/analysis?ID=B29A7E54-0E13-4C4D-83AA-6A49105F0F43.

59   The classic source on the period of regional convergence is Robert J. Barro et al., "Convergence Across States and Regions," *Brookings Papers on Economic Activity* 22, no. 1 (1991): 107–82, https://doi.org/10.2307/2534639. On the impact of federal policies, see Bruce J. Schulman, *From Cotton Belt to Sunbelt: Federal Policy, Economic Development, and the Transformation of the South, 1938–1980* (Durham, NC: Duke University Press, 1994) and Gavin Wright, *Sharing the Prize: The Economics of the Civil Rights Revolution in the American South* (Cambridge, MA: Belknap Press of Harvard University Press, 2013).

60   See C. Cindy Fan and Emilio Casetti, "The Spatial and Temporal Dynamics of US Regional Income Inequality, 1950–1989," *The Annals of Regional Science* 28, no. 2 (June 1994): 177–96, https://doi.org/10.1007/BF01581768; David J. Peters, "American Income Inequality Across Economic and Geographic Space, 1970–2010," *Social Science Research* 42, no. 6 (November 1, 2013): 1490–1504, https://doi.org/10.1016/j.ssresearch.2013.06.009; Orley M. Amos, "Evidence of Increasing Regional Income Variation in the United States: 1969–2006," *Modern Economy* 5 (January 1, 2014): 520–32, https://doi.org/10.4236/me.2014.55049; Peter Ganong and Daniel Shoag, "Why Has Regional Income Convergence in the U.S. Declined?" *Journal of Urban Economics* 102 (November 1, 2017): 76–90; Clara Hendrickson, Mark Muro, and William A. Galston, "Countering the Geography of Discontent: Strategies

for Left-Behind Places" (The Brookings Institution, November 2018), https://www.brookings.edu/research/countering-the-geography-of-dis content-strategies-for-left-behind-places/; and Robert A. Manduca, "The Contribution of National Income Inequality to Regional Economic Diver- gence," *Social Forces* 90 (December 2019): 622–48, https://doi.org/10.1093 /sf/soz013.

61   The causes of the U-curve in economic inequality have been much discussed by economists, though with more attention to the Great Divergence than to the preceding Great Convergence. Here are some of the leading scholars: Lindert and Williamson, *Unequal Gains*, 206–18 and 221–41, emphasize po- litical shocks, including wars, slowdown in labor supply (restricted immigra- tion and smaller families), the rise in mass education coupled with slower technological change, changing times in the financial sector, and perhaps trade. Noah, *The Great Divergence*, emphasizes the education/technology gap, immigration, trade, minimum wage policy, the decline of labor unions, and antipoor attitudes among elites. Anthony B. Atkinson, *Inequality: What Can Be Done?* (Cambridge, MA: Harvard University Press, 2015), and Peter A. Dia- mond, "Addressing the Forces Driving Inequality in the United States," *Con- temporary Economic Policy* 34, no. 3 (July 2016): 403–11, https://doi.org/10.1111 /coep.12184, emphasize globalization, technological change, financialization, unions, changing pay norms, and taxes and transfers by government. Another useful overview is Stone et al., "A Guide to Statistics on Historical Trends in Income Inequality." In addition to other factors, Angus Deaton emphasizes the importance of family formation and collapse—marriage allows couples to pool their *earnings* to form household *income*, which over the last half century has disproportionately benefited upper-income groups, since marriage has declined disproportionately among lower-income groups, as we shall see in Chapter 4. So differences in individual earnings don't capture the difference between two-income power couples and single mothers. In the present chap- ter we set aside those complexities.

62   In Chapter 8 we address the role played by globalization in explaining the broader I-we-I curve, not merely the economic inequality curve.

63   Ronald Findlay and Kevin H. O'Rourke, *Power and Plenty: Trade, War, and the World Economy in the Second Millennium* (Princeton: Princeton Univer- sity Press, 2007), particularly chaps. 7–10; Kevin H. O'Rourke and Jeffrey G. Williamson, *Globalization and History: The Evolution of a Nineteenth-Century Atlantic Economy* (Cambridge, MA: MIT Press, 1999), particularly chapters on the globalization backlash and international capital flows, both of which follow the U-shaped arc; and Jeffrey G. Williamson, *Winners and Losers over Two Centuries of Globalization*, WIDER Annual Lectures 6 (Helsinki: World Institute for Development Economics Research, 2002), which graphically

depicts changes in an index of migration restrictiveness in the decades preceding ~1900. Piketty, Saez, and Gabriel, "Distributional National Accounts," 604, argue that the fact that the collapse of the bottom 50 percent in the US is so much greater than in other advanced, open economies, like France, suggest that domestic factors are very important.

64 For a quick taste of the scholarly debate over the possible impact of immigration on inequality, see Goldin and Katz, "Decreasing (and then Increasing) Inequality in America"; David Card, "Immigration and Inequality," *American Economic Review* 99, no. 2 (May 2009): 1–21, https://doi.org/10.1257/aer.99.2.1; Giovanni Peri, "Immigration, Native Poverty, and the Labor Market," in *Immigration, Poverty, and Socioeconomic Inequality*, eds. David Card and Steven Raphael (New York: Russell Sage Foundation, 2013), 29–59; and George J. Borjas, *Immigration Economics* (Cambridge, MA: Harvard University Press, 2014).

65 For the argument that trade increases inequality at the same time that it increases aggregate welfare, see Hartmut Egger and Udo Kreickemeier, "Fairness, Trade, and Inequality," *Journal of International Economics* 86, no. 2 (March 2012): 184–96, https://doi.org/10.1016/j.jinteco.2011.10.002. For the argument that trade was a source of inequality in the 1970s but not during the 1980s or 1990s, see Bernardo S. Blum, "Trade, Technology, and the Rise of the Service Sector: The Effects on US Wage Inequality," *Journal of International Economics* 74, no. 2 (March 2008): 441–58, https://doi.org/10.1016/j.jinteco.2007.06.003. For the argument that imports from low-wage developing countries have not reduced wages for American workers, see Lawrence Edwards and Robert Lawrence, "US Trade and Wages: The Misleading Implications of Conventional Trade Theory," Working Paper 16106 (Cambridge, MA: National Bureau of Economic Research, June 2010), https://doi.org/10.3386/w16106. For the argument that trade liberalization in itself actually lowers inequality, see Florence Jaumotte, Subir Lall, and Chris Papageorgiou, "Rising Income Inequality: Technology, or Trade and Financial Globalization?," International Monetary Fund Working Paper, 2008. And for the nuanced argument (which we largely share) "that trade played an appreciable role in increasing wage inequality, but that its cumulative effect has been modest, and that globalization does not explain the preponderance of the rise in wage inequality within countries," see Elhanan Helpman, "Globalization and Wage Inequality," Working Paper 22944 (National Bureau of Economic Research, December 2016), https://doi.org/10.3386/w22944.

66 To be sure, many reform efforts of the Progressive Era (like unions or antitrust legislation) had their roots earlier in the Gilded Age, but they gained momentum and power only in the new century.

67 For a very similar argument, see Piketty, Saez, and Zucman, "Distributional National Accounts," 604–5.

68   Goldin and Katz, *The Race Between Education and Technology*.

69   Ibid. They estimate that the supply of high school graduates surpassed the demand by about 1 percent annually during this period.

70   As with all economic theories, the SBTC theory has its critics, and it is not clear that its current dominance in the field will endure. See, for example, Jaison R. Abel, Richard Deitz, and Yaquin Su, "Are Recent College Graduates Finding Good Jobs?," *Current Issues in Economics and Finance* 20, no. 1 (2014): 1–8, and Jonathan Horowitz, "Relative Education and the Advantage of a College Degree," *American Sociological Review* 83, no. 4 (August 2018): 771–801, https://doi.org/10.1177/0003122418785371.

71   Claudia Goldin, "Egalitarianism and the Returns to Education During the Great Transformation of American Education," *Journal of Political Economy* 107, no. S6 (December 1999): S65–S94, https://doi.org/10.1086/250104.

72   In this section we review labor unions primarily as an economic phenomenon, whereas in Chapter 4 we review unions as a social and community phenomenon; clearly, they are both.

73   See Michael E. McGerr, *A Fierce Discontent: The Rise and Fall of the Progressive Movement in America, 1870–1920* (New York: Free Press, 2003), esp. chap. 4.

74   Nell Irvin Painter, *Standing at Armageddon: The United States, 1877–1919* (New York: W. W. Norton, 1987): 44, 95, *et passim*; Lco Troy, *Trade Union Membership, 1897–1962* (New York: National Bureau of Economic Research, 1965): 2. Membership faltered from 1905 to 1909, but then resumed its growth.

75   Philip Taft and Philip Ross, "American Labor Violence: Its Causes, Character, and Outcome," in *The History of Violence in America: A Report to the National Commission on the Causes and Prevention of Violence*, eds. Hugh Davis Graham and Ted Robert Gurr, 1969, http://www.ditext.com/taft/violence.html.

76   Nelson Lichtenstein, *State of the Union: A Century of American Labor*, revised and expanded ed. (Princeton: Princeton University Press, 2013). The related idea of "welfare capitalism" pursued by some industrialists paid homage to the increasingly prominent idea that owners had obligations to their workers, although in practice company-run programs often proved paternalistic and even oppressive of workers' rights. Lizabeth Cohen, *Making a New Deal: Industrial Workers in Chicago, 1919–1939* (Cambridge: Cambridge University Press, 1990).

77   Richard Freeman, "Spurts in Union Growth: Defining Moments and Social Processes," in *The Defining Moment: The Great Depression and the American Economy in the Twentieth Century*, eds. Michael Bordo, Claudia Goldin, and Eugene White (Chicago: University of Chicago Press, 1998), 265–95.

78   August Meier and Elliott Rudwick, *Black Detroit and the Rise of the UAW* (Ann Arbor: University of Michigan Press, 2007), https://doi.org/10.3998/mpub.99863.

79   Gallup Inc., "Labor Unions," Gallup.com, accessed August 26, 2018, http://www.gallup.com/poll/12751/Labor-Unions.aspx.

80   On Figure 2.12 and the growth and decline of unions, see Richard Freeman, "Spurts in Union Growth," esp. 1890–1994; Barry T. Hirsch and David A. Macpherson, "Unionstats.com—Union Membership and Coverage Database from the CPS," Unionstats.com, 2017, http://unionstats.com/, esp. 1995–2015; and Richard Freeman, "Do Workers Still Want Unions? More Than Ever," Briefing Paper 182, Agenda for Shared Prosperity (Washington, DC: Economic Policy Institute, February 22, 2007), http://www.sharedprosperity.org/bp182/bp182.pdf; and Lichtenstein, State of the Union.

81   Gary N. Chaison and Joseph B. Rose, "The Macrodeterminants of Union Growth and Decline," in *The State of the Unions*, Industrial Relations Research Association Series, ed. George Strauss, Daniel G. Gallagher, and Jack Fiorita (Madison, WI: IRRA, 1991), 3–45, esp. 33.

82   G. William Domhoff, "The Rise and Fall of Labor Unions in the U.S.: From the 1830s Until 2012 (but Mostly the 1930s–1980s)," *Who Rules America?*, February 2013, https://whorulesamerica.ucsc.edu/power/history_of_labor_unions.html.

83   Lichtenstein, *State of the Union*.

84   Robert D. Putnam, *Bowling Alone: The Collapse and Revival of American Community* (New York: Simon & Schuster, 2000), 80–82.

85   For comparable evidence linking union membership to the share of income going to the top 10 percent, see Celine McNicholas, Samantha Sanders, and Heidi Shierholz, "First Day Fairness: An Agenda to Build Worker Power and Ensure Job Quality" (Economic Policy Institute, August 22, 2018), FIGURE A: "Union membership and share of income going to the top 10 percent, 1917–2015," https://www.epi.org/publication/first-day-fairness-an-agenda-to-build-worker-power-and-ensure-job-quality/.

86   Lichtenstein, *State of the Union*; Cohen, *Making a New Deal*; Domhoff, "Who Rules America."

87   Henry S. Farber et al., "Unions and Inequality over the Twentieth Century: New Evidence from Survey Data," Working Paper 24587 (National Bureau of Economic Research, May 2018), https://doi.org/10.3386/w24587.

88   Richard B. Freeman and James L. Medoff, *What Do Unions Do?* (New York: Basic Books, 1984). The conclusion of this landmark study has been extended, qualified, and basically confirmed by many recent studies: Unions reduce inequality. See McKinley L. Blackburn, David E. Bloom, and Richard B. Freeman, "The Declining Economic Position of Less Skilled American Men," in *A Future of Lousy Jobs?: The Changing Structure of U.S. Wages*, ed. Gary Burtless (Washington, DC: Brookings Institution, 1990); John DiNardo, Nicole M. Fortin, and Thomas Lemieux, "Labor Market Institutions and the

Distribution of Wages, 1973–1992: A Semiparametric Approach," *Economet-rica* 64, no. 5 (September 1996): 1001–44, https://doi.org/10.2307/2171954; Dierk Herzer, "Unions and Income Inequality: A Panel Cointegration and Causality Analysis for the United States," *Economic Development Quarterly* 30, no. 3 (2016): 267–74, https://doi.org/10.1177/0891242416634852.

89 Jake Rosenfeld, *What Unions No Longer Do* (Cambridge, MA: Harvard University Press, 2014).

90 Jake Rosenfeld, Patrick Denice, and Jennifer Laird, "Union Decline Lowers Wages of Nonunion Workers: The Overlooked Reason Why Wages Are Stuck and Inequality Is Growing" (Washington, DC: Economic Policy Institute, August 30, 2016), https://www.epi.org/publication/union-decline-lowers-wages-of-nonunion-workers-the-overlooked-reason-why-wages-are-stuck-and-inequality-is-growing/.

91 Bruce Western and Jake Rosenfeld, "Unions, Norms, and the Rise in U.S. Wage Inequality," *American Sociological Review* 76, no. 4 (2011): 513–37, https://doi.org/10.1177/0003122411414817; Tom VanHeuvelen, "Moral Economies or Hidden Talents? A Longitudinal Analysis of Union Decline and Wage Inequality, 1973–2015," *Social Forces* 97, no. 2 (2018): 495–529.

92 Carola Frydman and Raven Molloy, "Pay Cuts for the Boss: Executive Compensation in the 1940s," *The Journal of Economic History* 72, no. 1 (March 12, 2012): 225–51, https://doi.org/10.1017/S002205071100249X.

93 DiNardo, Fortin, and Lemieux, "Labor Market Institutions and the Distribution of Wages"; David Card, "The Effect of Unions on Wage Inequality in the U.S. Labor Market," *ILR Review* 54, no. 2 (January 2001): 296–315, https://doi.org/10.1177/001979390105400206; Farber et al., "Unions and Inequality over the Twentieth Century."

94 Obviously education and unionization also were powerfully influenced by public policy.

95 Kenneth F. Scheve and David Stasavage, *Taxing the Rich: A History of Fiscal Fairness in the United States and Europe* (Princeton: Princeton University Press, 2016); Piketty, Saez, and Zucman, "Distributional National Accounts."

96 McGerr, *A Fierce Discontent*, 98.

97 Source for federal income tax rate: Tax Policy Center, http://www.taxpolicy center.org/taxfacts/displayafact.cfm?Docid=543]. Source for total tax rate: Piketty, Saez, and Zucman, "Distributional National Accounts," Appendix Table II-G2: Distributional Series. The correlation between the two smoothed time series is r=.9.

98 Piketty, Saez, and Zucman, "Distributional National Accounts," 599–601.

99 Sources for Figure 2.14: Tax Foundation, "Federal Corporate Income Tax Rates, Income Years 1909–2012," taxfoundation.org; World Tax Database, Office of Tax Policy Research; Internal Revenue Service, Instructions for

Form 1120. An alternative measure of trends in corporate income tax is total corporate tax revenues as a fraction of total national income; that measure, too, shows the same basic U-curve, rising, especially from the mid-1930s to the mid-1950s and then declining. Corporate tax revenue data from U.S. Bureau of Economic Analysis, federal government current tax receipts: Taxes on corporate income [B075RC1Q027SBEA], retrieved from FRED, Federal Reserve Bank of St. Louis, https://fred.stlouisfed.org/series/B075RC1Q027S BEA, November 25, 2019. National income data from U.S. Department of Commerce, Bureau of Economic Analysis, National Data GDP and Personal Income, https://apps.bea.gov/iTable/iTable.cfm?reqid=19&step=2#reqid=19 &step=2&isuri=1&1921=survey.

100 Andrew Carnegie, "Wealth," *North American Review* 148, no. 391 (June 1889): 653–64.

101 Thanks to Eleanor Krause and Isabel Sawhill of the Brookings Institution for making available their unpublished data on this topic, as presented in Figure 2.15. Their sources include Darien B. Jacobson, Brian G. Raub, and Barry W. Johnson, "The Estate Tax: Ninety Years and Counting," Internal Revenue Service (2007), https://www.irs.gov/pub/irs-soi/ninetyestate.pdf; USDA Economic Research Service, "Federal estate taxes," https://www.ers .usda.gov/topics/farm-economy/federal-tax-issues/federal-estate-taxes.aspx. Note: Exemption levels were adjusted for inflation using the CPI for all urban consumers, September–August annual averages. The effective exemption rate has been adjusted for inflation since 2011, when it was $5 million.

102 Kenneth Whyte, *Hoover: An Extraordinary Life in Extraordinary Times* (New York: Alfred A. Knopf, 2017), chap. 15.

103 Piketty and Saez, "Income Inequality in the United States, 1913–1998," quotation at 23.

104 Thomas Piketty, Emmanuel Saez, and Stefanie Stantcheva, "Optimal Taxation of Top Labor Incomes: A Tale of Three Elasticities," Working Paper 17616 (National Bureau of Economic Research, November 2011), https://doi .org/10.3386/w17616.

105 Piketty, Saez, and Zucman, "Distributional National Accounts," 583.

106 Michael Harrington, *The Other America: Poverty in the United States* (New York: Macmillan, 1962), chap. 6.

107 Piketty, Saez, and Zucman, "Distributional National Accounts," 601–3.

108 Robert Sahr, "Using Inflation-Adjusted Dollars in Analyzing Political Developments," *PS: Political Science and Politics* 37, no. 2 (April 2004): 273–84, https://doi.org/10.1017/S1049096504004226. Monthly Benefits for AFDC-TANF Family and Social Security Retired Worker and Wife, Selected Years 1936 to 2001, in Constant (2003) Dollars. Source of current-dollar data: Social Security Bulletin Annual Statistical Supplement, 2002,

Tables 5.H1 and 9.G1, https://www.ssa.gov/policy/docs/statcomps/supple
ment/2002/index.html.

109 AFDC/TANF, commonly called "welfare," is not the only program of government support for poor Americans, but it is a clear indicator of how support
for the elderly poor and support for the non-elderly poor diverged after 1970.

110 Richard White, *Railroaded: The Transcontinentals and the Making of Modern
America* (New York: W. W. Norton, 2011), especially chaps. 5 and 9.

111 Lindert and Williamson, *Unequal Gains*, 217.

112 Thomas Philippon and Ariell Reshef, "Wages and Human Capital in the U.S.
Finance Industry: 1909–2006," *The Quarterly Journal of Economics* 127, no. 4
(2012): 1551–1609, https://doi.org/10.1093/qje/qjs030. See also Lindert and
Williamson, *Unequal Gains*, 201.

113 Jonathan Tepper with Denise Hearn, *The Myth of Capitalism: Monopolies and
the Death of Competition* (Hobokcn, NJ: John Wiley & Sons, 2018).

114 Vivien Hart, *Bound by Our Constitution: Women, Workers, and the Minimum
Wage* (Princeton: Princeton University Press, 1994).

115 Sources for Figure 2.18: 1938–2009: Department of Labor, "History of
Federal Minimum Wage Rates Undcr thc Fair Labor Standards Act, 1938
2009," https://www.dol.gov/whd/minwage/chart.htm; 1968–2020: Federal
Reserve Economic Data (FRED), https://fred.stlouisfed.org/series/STT
MINWGFG; CPI data from FRED https://fred.stlouisfed.org/series/CW
UR0000SA0#0. The fact that many states and localities have recently raised
their minimum wage above the national level means that the nationwide
population-weighted-average minimum wage may have increased somewhat faster over the last decade than Figure 2.18 might suggest.

116 The ups and downs of the federal minimum wage are most tightly correlated
with changes in the 50/20 wage ratio that reflects differences between lower-
and middle-income categories. See also David H. Autor, Alan Manning, and
Christopher L. Smith, "The Contribution of the Minimum Wage to US Wage
Inequality over Three Decades: A Reassessment," *American Economic Journal: Applied Economics* 8, no. 1 (January 2016): 58–99, https://doi.org/10.1257
/app.20140073, as well as "The Effects of a Minimum-Wage Increase on Employment and Family Income" (Washington, DC: Congressional Budget Office, February 18, 2014), https://www.cbo.gov/publication/44995.

117 Piketty, Saez, and Zucman, "Distributional National Accounts," 604–5.

118 One important study that examines the political mobilization of business
in the 1970s as part of the explanation for the Great Divergence is Jacob
S. Hacker and Paul Pierson, *Winner-Take-All Politics: How Washington Made
the Rich Richer—and Turned Its Back on the Middle Class* (New York: Simon &
Schuster, 2010).

119 Piketty and Saez, "Income Inequality in the United States, 1913–1998"; Paul

Krugman, "For Richer," *New York Times Magazine*, October 20, 2002, https://www.nytimes.com/2002/10/20/magazine/for-richer.html; Atkinson, *Inequality: What Can Be Done?*; Diamond, "Addressing the Forces Driving Inequality in the United States."

120 For more on Hoover's outlook and policies during his presidency, see Chapter 3.

121 Sam Pizzigati, *The Rich Don't Always Win: The Forgotten Triumph over Plutocracy That Created the American Middle Class, 1900–1970* (New York: Seven Stories Press, 2012); Krugman, *The Conscience of a Liberal*, 145–47.

122 David Leonhardt, "When the Rich Said No to Getting Richer," *New York Times*, September 5, 2017, https://www.nytimes.com/2017/09/05/opinion/rich-getting-richer-taxes.html; Matt Miller, "What Mitt Romney's Father Could Teach Him About Economic Fairness," *Washington Post*, January 18, 2012, https://www.washingtonpost.com/opinions/what-mitt-romneys-father-could-teach-him-about-economic-fairness/2012/01/18/gIQAB3Wj7P_story.html. See also T. George Harris, *Romney's Way: A Man and an Idea* (Englewood Cliffs, NJ: Prentice-Hall, 1968), where George Romney refers to rugged individualism as "nothing but a political banner to cover up greed."

123 Huma Khan, "Mitt Romney Made $22 Million, Paid Less Than 14 Percent in Taxes," *ABC News*, January 24, 2012, https://abcnews.go.com/Politics/OTUS/mitt-romney-made-42-million-paid-14-percent/story?id=15423615; David Corn, "Secret Video: Romney Tells Millionaire Donors What He Really Thinks of Obama Voters," *Mother Jones*, September 17, 2012, https://www.motherjones.com/politics/2012/09/secret-video-romney-private-fundraiser/; Leonhardt, "When the Rich Said No to Getting Richer." See also Jacob S. Hacker and Paul Pierson, *American Amnesia: How the War on Government Led Us to Forget What Made America Prosper* (New York: Simon & Schuster, 2016), 15–18.

124 See endnote 1.4.

CHAPTER 3: POLITICS: FROM TRIBALISM TO COMITY AND BACK AGAIN

1 For able assistance with exploring and understanding the multiple scholarly literatures used in this chapter, we are grateful to Amy Lakeman. The canonical chart of congressional polarization was initially presented by Nolan McCarty, Keith T. Poole, and Howard Rosenthal, *Polarized America: The Dance of Ideology and Unequal Riches*, 2nd ed. (Cambridge: MIT Press, 2016). We have updated that chart with data from Jeffrey B. Lewis, Keith Poole, Howard Rosenthal, Adam Boche, Aaron Rudkin, and Luke Sonnet, *Voteview: Congressional Roll-Call Votes Database* (2019), https://voteview.com/. The original chart was oriented such that "up" meant more polarized, and we have simply flipped that chart upside down, a transformation that has no effect on the

contours of the trend. Because the separate curves for the House and Senate are so closely aligned, Figure 3.1 shows the basic, smoothed trend for the average of the two curves. Methodologists have debated the details of this chart; for example, roll call votes may overestimate party solidarity, since party leaders seek to prevent issues that divide their party from coming to a vote. We present alternative measures of polarization later in this chapter, which confirm the basic shape of this curve. As Nolan McCarty in his masterful *Polarization* (New York: Oxford University Press, 2019), 30–38, has recently put it, "Ultimately, the use of these different metrics has very little impact on the basic story of legislative polarization in the United States. . . . While any single measure is subject to many caveats and criticisms, the collection of evidence across a wide variety of data tells almost the same story about the increasing polarization of legislators over the past forty years."

2 Dating the beginning of the last half century of increasing polarization is slightly arbitrary, since the curve is smooth, but Nolan McCarty in *Polarization* reflects a general consensus that dates the period from the 1970s. We return to the question of timing later in this chapter.

3 Although McCarty, Poole, and Rosenthal, *Polarized America*, originators of Figure 3.1, view the primary dimension as capturing economic redistribution, others view it simply as a measure of partisan disagreement, whatever the underlying issues on which partisans disagree. See John H. Aldrich, Jacob M. Montgomery, and David B. Sparks, "Polarization and Ideology: Partisan Sources of Low Dimensionality in Scaled Roll Call Analyses," *Political Analysis* 22, no. 4 (Autumn 2014): 435–56, doi:10.1093/pan/mpt048.

4 Helmut Norpoth, "The American Voter in 1932: Evidence from a Confidential Survey," *PS, Political Science & Politics* 52, no. 1 (2019): 14–19, doi:10.1017/S1049096518001014.

5 Sara N. Chatfield, Jeffery A. Jenkins, and Charles Stewart III, "Polarization Lost: Exploring the Decline of Ideological Voting After the Gilded Age," SSRN Scholarly Paper (Rochester, NY: Social Science Research Network, January 12, 2015), https://papers.ssrn.com/abstract=2548551.

6 Michael Kazin, *A Godly Hero: The Life of William Jennings Bryan* (New York: Alfred A. Knopf, 2006), 61.

7 David W. Brady, *Congressional Voting in a Partisan Era: A Study of the McKinley Houses and a Comparison to the Modern House of Representatives* (Lawrence: University Press of Kansas, 1973), chap. 3, as cited in Morris P. Fiorina, *Unstable Majorities: Polarization, Party Sorting, and Political Stalemate* (Chicago: Hoover Institution Press, 2017), 163.

8 B. Dan Wood and Soren Jordan, *Party Polarization in America: The War over Two Social Contracts* (Cambridge: Cambridge University Press, 2017), Fig. 3.3, pp. 84–85 on civil strikes and civil disturbances, especially from 1877 to 1919.

9   Douglas Eckberg, "Crime and Victimization," in *Historical Statistics of the United States: Earliest Times to the Present*, ed. Susan B. Carter, millennial ed. (Cambridge: Cambridge University Press, 2006), Table Ec251-253. On race during this period, see Henry Louis Gates, Jr., *Stony the Road: Reconstruction, White Supremacy, and the Rise of Jim Crow* (New York: Penguin, 2019).

10 On the suppression of racial politics 1910–1960, see Steven Levitsky and Daniel Ziblatt, *How Democracies Die* (New York: Crown, 2018). Edward G. Carmines and James A. Stimson, *Issue Evolution: Race and the Transformation of American Politics* (Princeton: Princeton University Press, 1989), argue that race began to be pushed off the national agenda once Reconstruction ended. After Reconstruction, Congress did not consider any civil rights legislation until 1957, and no president offered a major civil rights program until Truman in 1948. On the other hand, Eric Schickler has argued that as early as the 1930s African Americans and their allies pushed state parties in the North to address racial inequality; see Eric Schickler, *Racial Realignment: The Transformation of American Liberalism, 1932–1965*, Princeton Studies in American Politics (Princeton: Princeton University Press, 2016).

11 Edmund Morris, *Theodore Rex*, 1st ed. (New York: Random House, 2001); Sidney Milkis, *Theodore Roosevelt, the Progressive Party, and the Transformation of American Democracy* (Lawrence: University Press of Kansas, 2009); Lewis L. Gould, *America in the Progressive Era, 1890–1914*, Seminar Studies in History (London: Routledge, 2001); Lewis L. Gould, *The Presidency of Theodore Roosevelt*, 2nd ed., revised and expanded, American Presidency Series (Lawrence: University Press of Kansas, 2011); George E. Mowry, *The Era of Theodore Roosevelt, 1900–1912*, The New American Nation Series (New York: Harper, 1958).

12 Hans Noel, *Political Ideologies and Political Parties in America*, Cambridge Studies in Public Opinion and Political Psychology (New York: Cambridge University Press, 2013), 141.

13 http://teachingamericanhistory.org/library/document/progressive-platform-of-1912/.

14 The White House was controlled by progressive Republicans before 1913 and by a progressive Democrat after 1913. The figures in the text are averaged across both houses and all key votes. Source: https://www.govtrack.us/congress/votes.

15 Erik Olssen, "The Progressive Group in Congress, 1922–1929," *Historian* 42, no. 2 (1980): 244–63, doi:10.1111/j.1540-6563.1980.tb00581.x, as cited in Chatfield, Jenkins, and Stewart III, "Polarization Lost."

16 Jean Edward Smith, *FDR* (New York: Random House, 2007), 177.

17 The only significant exceptions were Alton Parker, the losing Democratic nominee in 1904, Warren Harding, the Republican nominee in 1920, and

John Davis, the losing Democratic nominee in 1924. William McKinley was a nominal exception, elected in 1896 and assassinated just after winning his second term in 1900. Harry Truman and Thomas Dewey, the losing Republican presidential nominee in 1944 and 1948, were too young to have been politically active during the Progressive Era. However, Truman reached national politics as a progressive New Dealer, and Dewey had gotten his start in New York public life under the auspices of the progressive governor Herbert Lehman and Mayor Fiorello La Guardia. All the other Republican nominees of the first half of the twentieth century—TR, William Howard Taft, Charles Evans Hughes, Calvin Coolidge, Herbert Hoover, Alf Landon, and Wendell Willkie—had entered politics as members of the Progressive movement, though Coolidge had become more conservative by the time he was elected president, and Hoover turned sharply more conservative after his defeat in 1932.

18　For biographies of Harding, see Andrew Sinclair, *The Available Man: The Life Behind the Masks of Warren Gamaliel Harding* (New York: Macmillan, 1965); and Robert K. Murray, *The Harding Era: Warren G. Harding and His Administration* (Minneapolis: University of Minnesota Press, 1969). For biographies of Coolidge, see Amity Shlaes, *Coolidge* (New York: Harper, 2013); Donald R. McCoy, *Calvin Coolidge: The Quiet President* (Lawrence: University Press of Kansas, 1988); Claude Moore Fuess, *Calvin Coolidge: the Man from Vermont* (Westport, CT: Greenwood Press, 1976); and Robert Sobel, *Coolidge: An American Enigma* (Washington, DC: Regnery, 1998).

19　Kenneth Whyte, *Hoover: An Extraordinary Life in Extraordinary Times* (New York: Alfred A. Knopf, 2017), quotation at p. 205.

20　David M. Kennedy, *Freedom from Fear: The American People in Depression and War, 1929–1945*, The Oxford History of the United States, vol. 9 (New York: Oxford University Press, 1999), 11–12, 45–48.

21　H. W. Brands, *Traitor to His Class: The Privileged Life and Radical Presidency of Franklin Delano Roosevelt* (New York: Doubleday, 2008).

22　On party politics from the 1920s to the 1940s, see Kennedy, *Freedom from Fear*.

23　Frederick Lewis Allen, *Since Yesterday: The 1930s in America, September 3, 1929–September 3, 1939* (New York: Harper & Brothers, 1940), 189: "If a visitor from Mars had compared the two party platforms of 1936, concentrating his attention not on the denunciations and pointings-with-pride but merely upon the positive recommendations which they contained, he might have wondered why feeling ran so high in this campaign."

24　Hendrik Meijer, *Arthur Vandenberg: The Man in the Middle of the American Century* (Chicago: University of Chicago Press, 2017), 162.

25　On Congressional politics, see Kennedy, *Freedom from Fear*, chap. 11, esp.

341–43; and Eric Schickler, "New Deal Liberalism and Racial Liberalism in the Mass Public, 1937–1968," *Perspectives on Politics* 11, no. 1 (March 2013): 75–98, doi:10.1017/S1537592712003659: "There was a connection between attitudes towards the economic programs of the New Deal and racial liberalism early on, well before national party elites took distinct positions on civil rights. . . . The ideological meaning of New Deal liberalism sharpened in the late 1930s due to changes in the groups identified with Roosevelt's program and due to the controversies embroiling New Dealers in 1937–38."

26 The figures in the text are averaged across all key votes and where available, both houses of Congress. Source: https://www.govtrack.us/congress/votes and https://library.cqpress.com/cqresearcher/.

27 David Levering Lewis, *The Improbable Wendell Willkie: The Businessman Who Saved the Republican Party and His Country, and Conceived a New World Order*, 1st ed. (New York: Liveright, 2018). On the party platforms in 1940, see Gerhard Peters and John T. Woolley, "Republican/Democratic Party Platform of 1940 Online," The American Presidency Project, https://www.presidency.ucsb.edu/node/273387. Democrats did not endorse the ERA until 1944, nor did they refer to lynching and equal voting rights.

28 For data on trends in party identification among blacks, see Philip Bump, "When Did Black Americans Start Voting So Heavily Democratic?," *Washington Post*, July 7, 2015, https://www.washingtonpost.com/news/the-fix/wp/2015/07/07/when-did-black-americans-start-voting-so-heavily-democratic/. Of course, most African Americans were not free to vote until the late 1960s, as we discuss in more detail in Chapter 6.

29 Paul F. Boller, *Presidential Campaigns* (New York: Oxford University Press, 1984), 259–61. "The Republican platform accepted most of Roosevelt's policies, domestic and foreign, but promised to manage them better; and, as usual, denounced excessive governmental interference with business."

30 We are grateful to Daria Rose for her report on inaugural addresses.

31 On the Eisenhower era, see William I. Hitchcock, *The Age of Eisenhower: America and the World in the 1950s* (New York: Simon & Schuster, 2018). Quotation from letter to his brother: https://teachingamericanhistory.org/library/document/letter-to-edgar-newton-eisenhower/.

32 See James T. Patterson, *Grand Expectations: The United States, 1945–1974*, The Oxford History of the United States, vol. 10 (New York: Oxford University Press, 1996), chap. 10.

33 Hitchcock, *The Age of Eisenhower*.

34 See Patterson, *Grand Expectations*, chaps. 8–10.

35 As quoted in Sam Rosenfeld, *The Polarizers: Postwar Architects of Our Partisan Era* (Chicago: University of Chicago Press, 2018), 64.

36   James L. Sundquist, *Politics and Policy: The Eisenhower, Kennedy, and Johnson Years* (Washington, DC: Brookings Institution, 1968), 479.

37   John Morton Blum, *Years of Discord: American Politics and Society, 1961–1974* (New York: W. W. Norton, 1991), 161.

38   This contrast was heightened by the fact that the Civil Rights Act and Voting Rights Act were actually supported by slightly more Republicans than Democrats, because of liberal Northern Republicans and conservative Southern Democrats. However, across all the other topics (War on Poverty, Medicare /Medicaid, immigration, and education), 47 percent of Republicans voted for LBJ's initiatives. The figures in the text are averaged across all key votes and where available, both houses of Congress. Sources: https://www.govtrack.us /congress/votes and https://library.cqpress.com/cqresearcher/.

39   Patterson, *Grand Expectations*, 719.

40   Ibid., 740.

41   John Stoehr, "The Real Romney Legacy," *The American Conservative*, January 28, 2016, https://www.theamericanconservative.com/articles/the-real -romney-legacy/.

42   Patterson, *Grand Expectations*, 762.

43   David S. Broder, "The Party's Over," *The Atlantic*, March 1972, https://www .theatlantic.com/magazine/archive/1972/03/the-partys-over/307016/.

44   Evron Kirkpatrick, "'Toward a More Responsible Two-Party System': Political Science, Policy Science, or Pseudo-Science?," *The American Political Science Review* 65, no. 4 (December 1971): 965–90.

45   After signing the Civil Rights Act of 1964, LBJ reportedly lamented that Democrats "have lost the South for a generation," though no clear source for this oft-repeated assertion has ever been found.

46   Nixon's political strategist Kevin Phillips apparently popularized the term "Southern strategy" in Kevin Phillips, *The Emerging Republican Majority* (New Rochelle, NY: Arlington House, 1969).

47   "Our people look for a cause to believe in. Is it a third party we need, or is it a new and revitalized second party, raising a banner of no pale pastels, but bold colors which make it unmistakably clear where we stand on all of the issues troubling the people?" Ronald Reagan, "Let Them Go Their Way 1975," in *Reagan at CPAC: The Words That Continue to Inspire a Revolution*, ed. Matt Schlapp (Washington, DC: Regnery, 2019), 39–40.

48   For further discussion of the impact of the new articulation of conservative ideology on Republicans' agenda during these years and on partisan polarization, see Chapter 5.

49   Republicans' opposition to "big government" appeared more in their rhetoric than in their actual policies. Reagan did cut regulation and revenues, but increased military spending and failed to cut domestic spending nearly as much

as he had seemed to promise. The GOP spoke of opposing "tax and spend" policies, but they followed through more consistently on revenue than on expenditures.

50 https://www.reaganfoundation.org/ronald-reagan/reagan-quotes-speeches /inaugural-address-2/.

51 Jonathan Freedland, "The Contender Ain't Down Yet; Twice a Presidential Candidate, Twice Defeated, the Rev. Jesse Jackson Is Still Fighting—For Civil Rights and Against the 'Whitelash,' " *The Guardian* (London), June 3, 1995.

52 Throughout this book, for the sake of convenience, we sometimes use the term "church" as a shorthand to cover all religious organizations, not merely Christian ones.

53 Whether party affiliation influences a voter's policy views or the reverse is still somewhat controversial among political scientists. For evidence that individuals shift issue and ideological positions while holding firmly to their partisan affiliation, see Matthew Levendusky, *The Partisan Sort: How Liberals Became Democrats and Conservatives Became Republicans* (Chicago: University of Chicago Press, 2009), chap. 6; Geoffrey C. Layman and Thomas M. Carsey, "Party Polarization and Party Structuring of Policy Attitudes: A Comparison of Three NES Panel Studies," *Political Behavior* 24, no. 3 (2002): 199–236; and Geoffrey Layman and Thomas Carsey, "Party Polarization and 'Conflict Extension' in the American Electorate," *American Journal of Political Science* 46, no. 4 (October 2002): 786–802. Yet abortion seems to make people change parties rather than their stance on the issue: Mitchell Killian and Clyde Wilcox, "Do Abortion Attitudes Lead to Party Switching?," *Political Research Quarterly* 61, no. 4 (2008): 561–73. Recent work indicates that gay rights, along with abortion, tend to produce a greater impact on party identification than the reverse: Paul Goren and Christopher Chapp, "Moral Power: How Public Opinion on Culture War Issues Shapes Partisan Predispositions and Religious Orientations," *American Political Science Review*, 111, no. 1 (2017): 110–28. Most recently, see Michele F. Margolis, *From Politics to the Pews: How Partisanship and the Political Environment Shape Religious Identity* (Chicago: University of Chicago Press, 2018).

54 P. David Pearson, "The Reading Wars," *Educational Policy* 18, no. 1 (2004): 216–52. To be sure, many Democrats favored charter schools as a kind of midway approach between public schools and private schools.

55 For a similar interpretation of the role of racial politics in the origin and timing of polarization, see McCarty, *Polarization*, chap. 5. We return to the issue of race and polarization in Chapter 6.

56 These six key votes were Obama's stimulus package, Dodd-Frank financial regulation, Lily Ledbetter gender pay equity, Obamacare (first creating it and then overturning it), and the 2017 Trump tax cuts.

57 See Jane Mayer, *Dark Money: The Hidden History of the Billionaires Behind the Rise of the Radical Right* (New York: Doubleday, 2016); Theda Skocpol and Alexander Hertel-Fernandez, "The Koch Network and Republican Party Extremism," 14, no. 3 (September 2016): 681–99, doi:10.1017/S1537592716001122; and https://en.wikipedia.org/wiki/Lewis_F._Powell_Jr.#Powell_Memorandum.

58 McCarty, *Polarization*, 3. Thomas E. Mann and Norman J. Ornstein, *It's Even Worse than It Looks: How the American Constitutional System Collided with the New Politics of Extremism*, new and expanded edition (New York: Basic Books, 2016), also have emphasized the asymmetry of the recent polarization. The only exception (minor so far) of the relative stability of the Democrats is a slight shift to the left as a consequence of greater representation of female and minority legislators, but even with this qualification, the overall polarization has been massively asymmetric.

59 Marina Azzimonti, "Partisan Conflict and Private Investment," *Journal of Monetary Economics* 93 (January 2018): 114–31, doi:10.1016/j.jmoneco.2017.10.007. The metric is the fraction of articles in the electronic archives of five major digitized national newspapers that described disagreement among elected officials, standardized at 1990=100.

60 Congressional polarization has been echoed in state politics in recent years. See Boris Shor and Nolan McCarty, "The Ideological Mapping of American Legislatures," *American Political Science Review* 105, no. 3 (August 2011): 530–51, doi:10.1017/S0003055411000153. Polarization has also affected the judiciary and the Supreme Court since 1980, as judicial appointments and confirmation votes have increasingly focused on partisan ideology, and judges have increasingly reflected the party that appointed them. See Richard L. Hasen, "Polarization and the Judiciary," *Annual Review of Political Science* 22, no. 1 (May 11, 2019): 261–76, doi:10.1146/annurev-polisci-051317-125141; Neal Devins and Lawrence Baum, "Split Definitive: How Party Polarization Turned the Supreme Court into a Partisan Court," *Supreme Court Review* (2016): 301–65; Corey Ditslear and Lawrence Baum, "Selection of Law Clerks and Polarization in the U.S. Supreme Court," *The Journal of Politics* 63, no. 3 (August 2001): 869–85, doi:10.1111/0022-3816.00091; and Amanda Frost, "Hasen on Political Polarization and the Supreme Court," SCOTUSblog (Nov. 14, 2018, 10:01 AM), https://www.scotusblog.com/2018/11/academic-highlight-hasen-on-political-polarization-and-the-supreme-court/. However, we lack systematic evidence about polarization in state or judicial politics prior to 1980.

61 Fiorina, *Unstable Majorities*, chap. 7. See also Daniel J. Hopkins, *The Increasingly United States: How and Why American Political Behavior Nationalized*, Chicago Studies in American Politics (Chicago: University of Chicago Press, 2018).

62   For a pioneering use of this measure of polarization covering the period between 1953 and 2001, see Gary C. Jacobson, "Partisan Polarization in Presidential Support: The Electoral Connection," *Congress & the Presidency* 30, no. 1 (2003): 1–36, doi:10.1080/07343460309507855. We've extended this analysis back to the late 1930s by drawing on previously unanalyzed polls from the Gallup archives and forward to 2019 by using the latest data from https://news.gallup.com/poll/203198/presidential-approval-ratings-donald -trump.aspx.

63   The spikes of bipartisan approval of the president in 1989 and 2002 represent the immediate "rally round the flag" effect of the starts of the two Gulf Wars, but those quickly disappeared in intense partisan debates about those wars.

64   Joseph Bafumi and Robert Y. Shapiro, "A New Partisan Voter," *The Journal of Politics* 71, no. 1 (January 2009): 1–24, doi:10.1017/S0022381608090014.

65   Larry Bartels, "Partisanship and Voting Behavior, 1952–1996," *American Journal of Political Science* 44, no. 1 (January 2000): 35–50, doi:10.2307/2669291; Bafumi and Shapiro, "A New Partisan Voter."

66   For a thoughtful analysis of this methodologically complicated issue, see Fiorina, *Unstable Majorities*, chap. 6. See also Jean M. Twenge et al., "More Polarized but More Independent: Political Party Identification and Ideological Self-Categorization Among U.S. Adults, College Students, and Late Adolescents, 1970–2015," *Personality and Social Psychology Bulletin* 42, no. 10 (2016): 1364–1383, doi:10.1177/0146167216660058; and Bartels, "Partisanship and Voting Behavior, 1952–1996."

67   Bafumi and Shapiro, "A New Partisan Voter," 3, 18.

68   Ibid., 8.

69   Some researchers contest this view. See Stephen Ansolabehere, Jonathan Rodden, and James Snyder, "The Strength of Issues: Using Multiple Measures to Gauge Preference Stability, Ideological Constraint, and Issue Voting," *American Political Science Review* 102 (May 1, 2008): 215–32, doi:10.1017 /S0003055408080210.

70   John Zaller, "What Nature and Origins Leaves Out," *Critical Review* 24, no. 4 (December 1, 2012): 569–642, doi:10.1080/08913811.2012.807648.

71   Christopher H. Achen and Larry M. Bartels, *Democracy for Realists: Why Elections Do Not Produce Responsive Government*, Princeton Studies in Political Behavior (Princeton: Princeton University Press, 2016). Morris P. Fiorina, "Identities for Realists," *Critical Review* 30, no. 1–2 (2018): 49–56, doi:10.1080 /08913811.2018.1448513, argues that identities offer a potential heuristic for voters and might not be as baseless as Achen and Bartels suggest.

72   Michael Barber and Jeremy Pope, "Does Party Trump Ideology? Disentangling Party and Ideology in America," *The American Political Science Review* 113, no. 1 (2019): 38–54, doi:10.1017/S0003055418000795. See also Thomas

B. Edsall, "Trump Says Jump. His Supporters Ask, How High?," *New York Times*, September 14, 2017.

73   Marc Hetherington, Meri Long, and Thomas Rudolph, "Revisiting the Myth: New Evidence of a Polarized Electorate," *Public Opinion Quarterly* 80, no. S1 (2016): 321–50, doi:10.1093/poq/nfw003.

74   Bafumi and Shapiro, "A New Partisan Voter," 7–8.

75   Shanto Iyengar, Tobias Konitzer, and Kent Tedin, "The Home as a Political Fortress: Family Agreement in an Era of Polarization," *The Journal of Politics* 80, no. 4 (October 2018): 1326–38, doi:10.1086/698929.

76   On this paragraph, see Robert D. Putnam, *Bowling Alone: The Collapse and Revival of American Community* (New York: Simon & Schuster, 2000), 342. Readers might be surprised that during this period of polarization increasing numbers of Americans are self-described "moderates" ideologically, but that pattern mirrors the growth in the numbers of described "independents" in party identification. In both cases Americans describing themselves as moderate or independent may be seeking to distance themselves psychologically from a politics they find increasingly distasteful. Using other evidence, Alan Abramowitz has also argued that voters who are more engaged in politics tend to choose relatively extreme positions and to identify with the relevant party. See Alan I. Abramowitz, *The Disappearing Center: Engaged Citizens, Polarization, and American Democracy* (New Haven: Yale University Press, 2010).

77   Bartels, "Partisanship and Voting Behavior, 1952–1996"; Bill Bishop, *The Big Sort: Why the Clustering of like-Minded America Is Tearing Us Apart* (Boston: Houghton Mifflin, 2008); Edward L. Glaeser and Bryce A. Ward, "Myths and Realities of American Political Geography," *Journal of Economic Perspectives* 20, no. 2 (Spring 2006): 119–44, doi:10.1257/jep.20.2.119; Bafumi and Shapiro, "A New Partisan Voter"; Samuel J. Abrams and Morris P. Fiorina, "'The Big Sort' That Wasn't: A Skeptical Reexamination," *PS: Political Science & Politics* 45, no. 2 (April 2012): 203–10, doi:10.1017/S1049096512000017; Ron Johnston, Kelvyn Jones, and David Manley, "The Growing Spatial Polarization of Presidential Voting in the United States, 1992–2012: Myth or Reality?" 49, no. 4 (October 2016): 766–70, doi:10.1017/S1049096516001487; and Ryan Enos, "Partisan Segregation," https://scholar.harvard.edu/files/renos/files/brownenos.pdf. The last two studies generally side with Bishop and Cushing and not with Abrams and Fiorina or Glaeser and Ward in finding substantial political segregation and spatial polarization.

78   For recent illustrations, see "The Partisan Divide on Political Values Grows Even Wider," Pew Research Center, October 5, 2017, http://www.people-press.org/2017/10/05/the-partisan-divide-on-political-values-grows-even-wider/#overview; "Extending Political Polarization in the American Public," Pew Research Center, June 12, 2014, http://www.people-press.org/2014/06

/12/political-polarization-in-the-american-public/; and http://www.people -press.org/interactives/political-polarization-1994-2017/, Pew Research Center, October 20, 2017;

79   Lilliana Mason, *Uncivil Agreement: How Politics Became Our Identity* (Chicago: University of Chicago Press, 2018).

80   Ross Butters and Christopher Hare, "Three-fourths of Americans Regularly Talk Politics Only with Members of Their Own Political Tribe," *Washington Post*, May 1, 2017.

81   Yphtach Lelkes, "Mass Polarization: Manifestations and Measurements," *Public Opinion Quarterly* 80, no. S1 (2016): 392–410, doi:10.1093/poq/nfw005; and Marc Hetherington and Jonathan Weiler, *Prius or Pickup?: How the An- swers to Four Simple Questions Explain America's Great Divide* (New York: Houghton Mifflin Harcourt, 2018). Marc Hetherington and his colleagues argue that affective ties is the domain (more than issues or ideology) where we should expect to discover polarization. Marc J. Hetherington and Thomas J. Rudolph, *Why Washington Won't Work: Polarization, Political Trust, and the Governing Crisis*, Chicago Studies in American Politics (Chicago: University of Chicago Press, 2015).

82   Pew Research Center, "Partisanship and Political Animosity in 2016," June 22, 2016, http://www.people-press.org/2016/06/22/partisanship-and -political-animosity-in-2016/.

83   Lelkes, "Mass Polarization"; Gaurav Sood and Shanto Iyengar, "Coming to Dislike Your Opponents: The Polarizing Impact of Political Campaigns," *SSRN Electronic Journal*, 2016, doi:10.2139/ssrn.2840225; Shanto Iyengar, Gaurav Sood, and Yphtac Lelkes, "Affect, Not Ideology: A Social Identity Perspective on Polarization," *Public Opinion Quarterly* 76, no. 3 (Fall 2012): 405–31, doi:10.1093/poq/nfs038. "Political Polarization in the American Public," *Pew Research Center for the People and the Press*, June 12, 2014, https:// www.people-press.org/2014/06/12/political-polarization-in-the-american -public/; Emily Badger and Niraj Chokshi, "How We Became Bitter Political Enemies," *New York Times*, June 15, 2017, The Upshot, https://www.nytimes .com/2017/06/15/upshot/how-we-became-bitter-political-enemies.html.

84   Iyengar, Sood, and Lelkes, "Affect, Not Ideology," 413.

85   Ibid., 416.

86   Shanto Iyengar and Sean J. Westwood, "Fear and Loathing Across Party Lines: New Evidence on Group Polarization," *American Journal of Political Science* 59, no. 3 (2015): 690–707, doi:10.1111/ajps.12152. Iyengar and West- wood tweaked the Implicit Association Test (IAT), which measures the time required to associate ingroups and outgroups with positive or negative quali- ties, to investigate partisan affect. Unlike explicit self-reported survey work, implicit measures are argued to be a more accurate portrayal of subject's

true feelings because they elide cognitive processing. Iyengar and Westwood found a significant racial implicit bias, but despite the substantial gap, "the effect size for race was not nearly as strong as the corresponding effect of party."

87   Iyengar, Konitzer, and Tedin, "The Home as a Political Fortress," quotation at 1326.

88   Iyengar, Sood, and Lelkes, "Affect, Not Ideology," 421–27. This affective polarization does not appear to be driven by ideological divergence, but does appear to be modestly increased by harsh political campaigning.

89   Ibid., 417–18. Using independent evidence, political scientist Lynn Vavreck says in 1958 less than 30 percent of Americans cared about the partisanship of their children's marital choices compared to nearly 60 percent in 2016. Lynn Vavreck, "A Measure of Identity: Are You Wedded to Your Party?," *New York Times*, January 31, 2017.

90   On party polarization of marriage, see Iyengar, Konitzer, and Tedin, "The Home as a Political Fortress," and other work cited there. Note that the Iyengar study compares marriages from mid-1960s (the low tide of polarization) and the mid-2010s. In the earlier period newlyweds agreed politically only about half the time, whereas newlyweds nowadays agree about three quarters of the time. In emphasizing the importance of spousal choice, they discount either gradual convergence after marriage or spurious convergence on the basis of some other trait, like religion or education. On online dating, see Gregory A. Huber and Neil Malhotra, "Political Homophily in Social Relationships: Evidence from Online Dating Behavior," *The Journal of Politics* 79, no. 1 (January 2017): 269–83, doi:10.1086/687533.

91   See Robert D. Putnam and David E. Campbell, *American Grace: How Religion Divides and Unites Us* (New York: Simon & Schuster, 2012), 148–54.

92   Eitan Hersh and Yair Ghitza, "Mixed Partisan Households and Electoral Participation in the United States," *PLOS ONE* 13, no. 10 (October 10, 2018): e0203997, doi:10.1371/journal.pone.0203997, find that married couples over 80 are 66 percent more likely to be in a one-party marriage as compared to married couples age 30. See also https://fivethirtyeight.com/features/how-many-republicans-marry-democrats/.

93   On the increase in religious intermarriage and interfaith good feelings over these very same decades, see Putnam and Campbell, *American Grace*, 148–59, 521–40.

94   For a recent, comprehensive overview of the causes of the post-1970 polarization (though with less attention to the causes of the depolarization in the first two thirds of the twentieth century that we have emphasized), see McCarty, *Polarization*, chaps. 5–6.

95   G. C. Layman, T. M. Carsey, and J. M. Horowitz, "Party Polarization in American Politics: Characteristics, Causes, and Consequences," *Annual*

Review of Political Science 9, no. 1 (2006): 83–110, doi:10.1146/annurev.polisci.9.070204.105138; Marc J. Hetherington, "Review Article: Putting Polarization in Perspective," *British Journal of Political Science* 39, no. 2 (2009): 413–48, doi:10.1017/S0007123408000501; Levendusky, *The Partisan Sort*; James Druckman, Erik Peterson, and Rune Slothuus, "How Elite Partisan Polarization Affects Public Opinion Formation," *The American Political Science Review* 107, no. 1 (2013): 57–79, doi:10.1017/S0003055412000500; Hetherington and Rudolph, *Why Washington Won't Work*; Ryan L. Claassen and Benjamin Highton, "Policy Polarization Among Party Elites and the Significance of Political Awareness in the Mass Public," *Political Research Quarterly* 62, no. 3 (2009): 538–51, doi:10.1177/1065912908322415; and Zaller, "What Nature and Origins Leaves Out."

96 Some scholars, especially Morris Fiorina, are reluctant to consider "sorting" as one form of polarization. On this entire issue of the relationship between elite and mass polarization, see McCarty, *Polarization*, chap. 4.

97 John Zaller, *The Nature and Origins of Mass Opinion* (Cambridge: Cambridge University Press, 1992); Achen and Bartels, *Democracy for Realists*, 258–64.

98 Greg Adams, "Abortion: Evidence of an Issue Evolution," *American Journal of Political Science* 41, no. 3 (1997): 718, doi:10.2307/2111673.

99 Noel, *Political Ideologies and Political Parties in America*, has emphasized, in particular, the role of pundits and public intellectuals in influencing the degree of coincidence of political ideologies and political parties.

100 McCarty, *Polarized America*.

101 Bryan J. Dettrey and James E. Campbell, "Has Growing Income Inequality Polarized the American Electorate? Class, Party, and Ideological Polarization," *Social Science Quarterly* 94, no. 4 (December 2013): 1062–83, doi:10.1111/ssqu.12026; John V. Duca and Jason L. Saving, "Income Inequality and Political Polarization: Time Series Evidence over Nine Decades," *Review of Income and Wealth* 62, no. 3 (September 2016): 445–66, doi:10.1111/roiw.12162. For McCarty's recent recognition that the timing doesn't fit his original hypothesis that inequality caused polarization, see McCarty, *Polarization*, 78–81.

102 McCarty, *Polarization*, chap. 6, reviews in detail the role that gerrymandering, primary elections, and campaign finance rules may have played as causes of polarization and concludes that "the evidence . . . largely rejects the idea that these institutional features are major triggers of increased polarization" (p. 5). He also discounts the idea that party leaders engineered polarization (pp. 81–84).

103 For a useful summary of the mixed evidence on the possible causal role of the media, including social media, see ibid., 88–97.

104 The progenitor of this theory was Joseph A. Schumpeter, *Capitalism, Socialism, and Democracy* (New York: Harper & Brothers, 1942), chaps. 21–22.

105 William H. Haltom Jr., *The Other Fellow May Be Right: The Civility of Howard Baker* (Tennessee Bar Association Press, 2017).

106 Danielle Allen, "An Inspiring Conversation About Democracy," *Ezra Klein Show*, September 30, 2019, https://www.stitcher.com/podcast/the-ezra-klein -show/e/64250447?autoplay=true.

107 McCarty, *Polarization*, chap. 7.

108 Frances E. Lee, *Insecure Majorities: Congress and the Perpetual Campaign* (Chicago: University of Chicago Press, 2016) has made this argument most persuasively. Since polarization and insecure majorities have been closely correlated as an empirical matter, it is not easy to assign the relative blame for gridlock as between those two factors.

109 Six major legislative initiatives of the Reagan administration—three tax and spending bills, savings and loan deregulation, crime legislation, and immigration reform—were supported on the Hill by an average of 74 percent of Republicans and 64 percent of Democrats; as in the case of LBJ, some of Reagan's initiatives had greater support from the opposing party than from his own.

110 Hetherington and Rudolph, Why Washington Won't Work, 4. Figure 3.8 is based on Pew Research Center (April 11, 2019), Public Trust in Government: 1958–2019, https://www.people-press.org/2019/04/11/public-trust -in-government-1958-2019/. The Pew archive compiles results from surveys done over the last sixty years by the National Election Study, CBS/New York Times, Gallup, ABC/Washington Post, and Pew itself.

111 Figure 3.10 draws on two survey archives to construct a composite index of political efficacy. The National Election Study has repeatedly asked respondents to agree or disagree with two survey items: (1) People have a say in government; and (2) Public officials care about what people think. The Harris poll has repeatedly asked respondents to agree or disagree with five comparable survey items: (1) The rich get richer and the poor get poorer; (2) What you think doesn't count very much anymore; (3) Most people with power try to take advantage of people like yourself; (4) The people running the country don't really care what happens to you; and (5) You're left out of things going on around you. In each case to "agree" is to express political cynicism. The items in each index are closely correlated with one another, showing that they are tapping one central dimension. All seven items show the same basic pattern over time. Harris poll: https://theharrispoll.com/wp-content/uploads/2017/12/Harris-Interactive -Poll-Research-ALIENATION-1982-02.pdf and https://theharrispoll.com /in-the-midst-of-the-contentious-presidential-primary-elections-the-har ris-poll-measured-how-alienated-americans-feel-as-part-of-a-long-term -trend-the-last-time-alienation-was-measured-was-in-novemb/.

112 Steven Levitsky and Daniel Ziblatt, "How Wobbly Is Our Democracy?," *New York Times*, January 27, 2018, https://www.nytimes.com/2018/01/27/opinion/sunday/democracy-polarization.html.

113 Ticket-splitting follows the same trend, but with a lag of about ten years, presumably because of the time it takes for party discipline to seep down to congressional nomination contests.

114 See endnote 1.4.

CHAPTER 4: SOCIETY: BETWEEN ISOLATION AND SOLIDARITY

1 Alexis de Tocqueville, *Democracy in America* (Garden City, NY: Doubleday, 1969), 506; Wilson C. McWilliams, *The Idea of Fraternity in America* (Berkeley: University of California Press, 1973); Thomas Bender, *Community and Social Change in America* (New Brunswick, NJ: Rutgers University Press, 1978).

2 For able assistance with exploring and understanding the multiple scholarly literatures used in this chapter, we are grateful to Amy Lakeman. This chapter draws on abridged language and evidence (usually updated) from Robert D. Putnam, *Bowling Alone: The Collapse and Revival of American Community* (New York: Simon & Schuster, 2000), esp. chaps. 3, 7, 8, and 23.

3 Walter Lippmann, *Drift and Mastery* (Englewood Cliffs, NJ: Prentice Hall, 1961 [1914]), 92.

4 William Allen White, *The Old Order Changeth: A View of American Democracy* (New York: Macmillan, 1910), 250–52.

5 John Dewey, "The Democratic State," in *The Political Writings*, eds. Debra Morris and Ian Shapiro (Indianapolis: Hackett Publishing Company, 1993), 180.

6 Jean B. Quandt, *From the Small Town to the Great Community: The Social Thought of Progressive Intellectuals* (New Brunswick, NJ: Rutgers University Press, 1970), 44–45, quoting Mary Parker Follett, *The New State, Group Organization the Solution of Popular Government* (New York: Longmans, Green, 1918), 251.

7 Robert Ezra Park, *Society: Collective Behavior, News and Opinion, Sociology and Modern Society*, Robert Ezra Park, 1864–1944, *Collected Papers*, vol. 3 (Glencoe, IL: Free Press, 1955), 147, as quoted in Quandt, *From the Small Town to the Great Community*, 146.

8 Theda Skocpol et al., "How Americans Became Civic," in *Civic Engagement in American Democracy*, eds. Theda Skocpol and Morris P. Fiorina (Washington, DC: Brookings Institution Press, 1999), 27–80.

9 Theda Skocpol, "United States: From Membership to Advocacy," in *Democracies in Flux: The Evolution of Social Capital in Contemporary Society*, ed. Robert D. Putnam (New York: Oxford University Press, 2002); Mark Wahlgren

Summers, *The Gilded Age, or, The Hazard of New Functions* (Upper Saddle River, NJ: Prentice-Hall, 1997), 49.

10 Gerald Gamm and Robert D. Putnam, "The Growth of Voluntary Associations in America, 1840–1940," *Journal of Interdisciplinary History* 29, no. 4 (Spring 1999): 511–57.

11 Skocpol et al., "How Americans Became Civic." The ratio for those that were *ever* that large is 29 of 58. More than half of all such large membership organizations that are still in existence (however attenuated) were founded in the 1870–1920 period—24 of 43.

12 Theda Skocpol, *Diminished Democracy: From Membership to Management in American Civic Life*, The Julian J. Rothbaum Distinguished Lecture Series, vol. 8 (Norman: University of Oklahoma Press, 2003), 23–24. She goes on to emphasize that these groups "were usually federations that brought together citizens across class lines while linking thousands of local groups to one another and to representatively governed centers of state and national activity."

13 In most of the other measures we deploy in this book, including measures used in this chapter, the nadir in socioeconomic and political solidarity occurs at the turn of the twentieth century, but the upswing in civic organizations we discuss here began in the late nineteenth century.

14 Putnam, *Bowling Alone*, 386–87.

15 See W. S. Harwood, "Secret Societies in America," *The North American Review* 164, no. 486 (1897): 617–20; and David T. Beito, *From Mutual Aid to the Welfare State: Fraternal Societies and Social Services, 1890–1967* (Chapel Hill: University of North Carolina Press, 2000), quotations at 14, 10, 3, 27. Beito makes clear that one central function of fraternal organizations was to provide life, health, and accident insurance, and as those functions were assumed by private enterprise and government, beginning in the 1920s and 1930s, the fraternal orders lost an important part of their rationale.

16 Skocpol, *Diminished Democracy*, esp. 56–59 and 107–9.

17 Richard L. McCormick, "Public Life in Industrial America, 1877–1917," in Eric Foner, ed., *The New American History* (Philadelphia: Temple University Press, 1990): 93–117; Theda Skocpol, *Protecting Soldiers and Mothers: The Political Origins of Social Policy in the United States* (Cambridge, MA: Harvard University Press, 1995), chap. 6; Nell Irvin Painter, *Standing at Armageddon: The United States, 1877–1919* (New York: W. W. Norton, 1989), esp. 105.

18 Theodora Penny Martin, *The Sound of Our Own Voices: Women's Study Clubs, 1860–1910* (Boston: Beacon Press, 1987), quotation at 172.

19 Daniel Okrent, *Last Call: The Rise and Fall of Prohibition* (New York: Scribner, 2010).

20 Howard Husock, "Elks Clubs, Settlement Houses, Labor Unions and the Anti-Saloon League: Nineteenth and Early Twentieth-Century America

Copes with Change" (Harvard University, January 1, 1997), 8, https://case
.hks.harvard.edu/elks-clubs-settlement-houses-labor-unions-and-the-anti
-saloon-league-nineteenth-and-early-twentieth-century-america-copes
-with-change/; Marvin Lazerson, "Urban Reform and the Schools: Kindergartens in Massachusetts, 1870–1915," *History of Education Quarterly* 11,
no. 2 (Summer 1971): 115–42, doi:10.2307/367590; Michael Steven Shapiro,
Child's Garden: The Kindergarten Movement from Froebel to Dewey (University
Park: Penn State University Press, 1983); Skocpol, *Protecting Soldiers and
Mothers*.

21   Elizabeth Anne Payne, *Reform, Labor, and Feminism: Margaret Dreier Robins
and the Women's Trade Union League*, Women in American History (Urbana:
University of Illinois Press, 1988); Annelise Orleck, *Common Sense & a Little
Fire: Women and Working-Class Politics in the United States, 1900–1965* (Chapel
Hill: University of North Carolina Press, 1995); David Von Drehle, *Triangle:
The Fire That Changed America* (New York: Atlantic Monthly Press, 2003),
chap. 3.

22   Rowland Berthoff, *An Unsettled People: Social Order and Disorder in American
History* (New York: Harper & Row, 1971), 273; Steven J. Diner, *A Very Different Age: Americans of the Progressive Era* (New York: Hill & Wang, 1998), 91.

23   Theda Skocpol, Ariane Liazos, and Marshall Ganz, *What a Mighty Power We
Can Be: African American Fraternal Groups and the Struggle for Racial Equality*, Princeton Studies in American Politics (Princeton: Princeton Univer-
sity Press, 2006); W. E. B. Du Bois, *The Philadelphia Negro: A Social Study*
(Philadelphia: University of Pennsylvania Press, 1996), 224–33, as cited in
Loretta J. Williams, *Black Freemasonry and Middle-Class Realities*, University of
Missouri Studies (1926) 69 (Columbia: University of Missouri Press, 1980),
85; Jesse Thomas Moore, Jr., *A Search for Equality: The National Urban League,
1910–1961* (University Park: Penn State University Press, 1981); Ralph
Watkins, "A Reappraisal of the Role of Volunteer Associations in the African
American Community," *Afro-Americans in New York Life and History* 14, no. 2
(July 31, 1990): 51–60; Evelyn Brooks Higginbotham, *Righteous Discontent:
The Women's Movement in the Black Baptist Church, 1880–1920* (Cambridge,
MA: Harvard University Press, 1993); Anne Firor Scott, "Most Invisible of
All: Black Women's Voluntary Associations," *The Journal of Southern History*
56, no. 1 (February 1990): 3–22; Diner, *A Very Different Age*, 141–47; Sum-
mers, *The Gilded Age*, 288.

24   Boyer, *Urban Masses and Moral Order*; LeRoy Ashby, *Saving the Waifs: Reformers and Dependent Children, 1890–1917* (Philadelphia: Temple University
Press, 1984); Dominick Cavallo, *Muscles and Morals: Organized Playgrounds
and Urban Reform, 1880–1920* (Philadelphia: University of Pennsylvania
Press, 1981); Michael B. Katz, "Child-Saving," *History of Education Quarterly*

26, no. 3 (Autumn 1986): 413–24; David I. Macleod, *Building Character in the American Boy: The Boy Scouts, YMCA, and Their Forerunners, 1870–1920* (Madison: University of Wisconsin Press, 1983); Franklin M. Reck, *The 4-H Story: A History of 4-H Club Work* (Ames: Iowa State College Press, 1957); Michael Rosenthal, *The Character Factory: Baden-Powell and the Origins of the Boy Scout Movement* (New York: Pantheon, 1986).

25 Skocpol et al., "How Americans Became Civic," 61. This pattern of growth is substantiated by unpublished evidence from the project described in Gamm and Putnam, "The Growth of Voluntary Associations."

26 Jeffrey A. Charles, *Service Clubs in American Society: Rotary, Kiwanis, and Lions* (Urbana: University of Illinois Press, 1993), esp. 1–33.

27 See many examples, drawn not only from service clubs, ibid., chap. 1.

28 Figure 4.2 is intended only as a rough summary of the experiences of more than thirty separate organizations; interested readers are urged to consult the separate charts for each organization, given in Appendix III of Putnam, *Bowling Alone*. Given the inevitable uncertainty about membership data extending across an entire century and the unavoidable arbitrariness about which groups to include at the margins, the detailed ups and downs of Figure 4.2 should not be overinterpreted. We sought to encompass all large national chapter-based civic organizations from roughly 1910 to 2010 plus a selection of smaller "niche" organizations, like Hadassah, NAACP, Optimists, and the 4-H. (Labor unions and professional associations are excluded from this chart, though they are discussed later in this chapter, as well as in *Bowling Alone*.) Because the broad outlines of Figure 4.2 are echoed in most of this diverse group of organizations, we are fairly confident that it represents broad historical trends in the membership of such organizations. In order to bias Figure 4.2 *against* our hypothesis—declining membership in the last third of the twentieth century—we excluded several large nineteenth-century associations that moved toward extinction in the first half of the twentieth century, such as the Redmen fraternal group, though we included a few that remained strong after World War II, such as the Odd Fellows. These inclusions or exclusions would not, however, significantly alter the broad 120-year profile of Figure 4.2. For each organization listed in Appendix III of *Bowling Alone* we calculated annual national membership as a fraction of the relevant population—PTA membership per 1,000 families with children, American Legion membership per 1,000 veterans, Hadassah membership per 1,000 Jewish women, and so on. For missing years, we interpolated membership from adjacent years. To weight each organization equally, regardless of its size and market share, we computed "standard scores" for each organization, comparing its market share in a given year to its average market share over the century as a whole, and then averaged the standard scores of all

organizations in a given year. Because of this standardization method, the vertical axis measures not absolute membership rates, but trends relative to the century-long average. Taylor Mann (Pine Capital, Brownsboro, Texas 75756, Taylor@Pinecapitalpartners.com), who updated the data in this chart from 1998 to 2016, appears to have followed exactly this same procedure, except that he was unable to find contemporary membership figures for several women's organizations that appear to have lost their original identity, at least in the US, in the less gender-segregated twenty-first century—Business and Professional Women, Women Bowling Congress, and the Girl Scouts. Excluding those groups after 2000 has the net effect of slightly *understating* the decline in the twenty-first century. We are grateful to Mr. Mann for generously sharing his data. We are also grateful to Professor Theda Skocpol for many illuminating discussions about the history of associations in America, as well as for generously sharing data collected in her own research project on this theme. However, we alone are responsible for the evidence and conclusions presented here. See Skocpol et al., "How Americans Became Civic," 27–80; and Skocpol, *Diminished Democracy*.

29   *The Encyclopedia of Associations* (Detroit: Gale Research Company, various years); Kay Lehman Schlozman, John T. Tierney, *Organized Interests and American Democracy* (New York: Harper & Row, 1986); Jack L. Walker, *Mobilizing Interest Groups in America: Patrons, Professions, and Social Movements* (Ann Arbor: University of Michigan Press, 1991); Frank R. Baumgartner and Beth L. Leech, *Basic Interests: The Importance of Groups in Politics and in Political Science* (Princeton: Princeton University Press, 1998), esp. 102–6.

30   David Horton Smith, "National Nonprofit, Voluntary Associations: Some Parameters," *Nonprofit and Voluntary Sector Quarterly* 21, no. 1 (1992): 81–94. We confirmed Smith's findings, comparing random samples of two hundred associations with individual members from various editions of *The Encyclopedia of Associations* (1956, 1968, 1978, 1988, and 1998).

31   Skocpol, *Diminished Democracy*, 13, 138, 219, 159–63, *et passim*.

32   Christopher J. Bosso and Burdett A. Loomis, "The Color of Money: Environmental Groups and Pathologies of Fund Raising," in *Interest Group Politics*, 4th ed., eds. Allan J. Cigler and Burdett A. Loomis (Washington, DC: CQ Press, 1995), 101–30, esp. 117; interviews with Greenpeace staff members.

33   Frank R. Baumgartner and Jack L. Walker, "Survey Research and Membership in Voluntary Associations," *American Journal of Political Science* 32, no. 4 (November 1988): 908–28; Tom W. Smith, "Trends in Voluntary Group Membership: Comments on Baumgartner and Walker," *American Journal of Political Science* 34, no. 3 (August 1990): 646–61; Joseph Veroff, Elizabeth Douvan, and Richard A Kulka, *The Inner American: A Self-Portrait from 1957 to 1976* (New York: Basic Books, 1981).

34   Each of these survey archives is described in detail in Appendix I of *Bowling Alone*, and all are available through the Roper Center for Public Opinion Research.

35   According to the 1987 General Social Survey, in 1987, 61 percent of all organization members had served on a committee at some time or other, and 46 percent had served as an officer. A 1973 Louis Harris survey (study number 2343 at the University of North Carolina Institute for Research in the Social Sciences) found that 48 percent of all organization members had served at one time as a club officer, virtually identical to the 1987 GSS figure.

36   Putnam, *Bowling Alone*, Fig. 10, p. 60

37   The Allen quote is often rendered as "of life," as he himself later acknowledged, though he objected that he recalled having said "of success." (https://en.wikiquote.org/wiki/Woody_Allen).

38   DBB Needham Life Style surveys as cited in Putnam, *Bowling Alone*, Fig. 11, p. 61 and pp. 420–24, updated here for 1999–2005. See Appendix I of *Bowling Alone* for methodological details.

39   We are grateful both to Professor Robinson for sharing the Americans' Use of Time archive and to Dan Devroye for careful analysis of the data. Our results differ slightly from those reported by Robinson and Godbey, because we have weighted the data (1) to correct for sampling anomalies in the 1965 survey and (2) to assure equal weight to diaries from each day of the week. The most important of these adjustments corrects for the fact that the 1965 sample excluded households in communities of less than 35,000 or in which everyone was retired.

40   Putnam, *Bowling Alone*, 61–62. Somewhat surprisingly, the decline in work hours applies to women as well as men. See Robinson and Godbey, *Time for Life*, and Suzanne M. Bianchi, Melissa A. Milkie, Liana C. Sayer, and John P. Robinson, "Is Anyone Doing the Housework? Trends in the Gender Division of Household Labor," *Social Forces* 79 (2000): 191–228.

41   All the trends in time usage reported here are highly significant in statistical terms. Six years after the publication of *Bowling Alone*, this basic pattern of decline was confirmed by Robert Andersen, James Curtis, and Edward Grabb, "Trends in Civic Association Activity in Four Democracies: The Special Case of Women in the United States," *American Sociological Review* 71, no. 3 (June 2006): 376–400.

42   Partial exceptions include self-help support groups and (since 2016) local political reform groups, especially among college-educated women. See Lara Putnam, "Middle America Reboots Democracy: The Emergence and Rapid Electoral Turn of the New Grassroots," in *Upending American Politics: Polarizing Parties, Ideological Elites, and Citizen Activists from the Tea Party to the Anti-Trump Resistance*, eds. Theda Skocpol and Caroline Tervo (New York: Oxford University Press, forthcoming).

43 The following section rests heavily on Putnam, *Bowling Alone*, chap. 4, and Robert D. Putnam and David E. Campbell, *American Grace: How Religion Divides and Unites Us* (New York: Simon & Schuster, 2012), chaps. 3–4.

44 "Church" and "churchgoers" are specifically Christian terms, but for simplicity's sake we use those terms generically to refer to all religious congregations and all religious participants.

45 For evidence in support of the generalizations in the previous two paragraphs, see Putnam and Campbell, *American Grace*, chap. 13.

46 Roger Finke and Rodney Stark, *The Churching of America, 1776–2005: Winners and Losers in Our Religious Economy*, rev. ed. (New Brunswick, NJ: Rutgers University Press, 2005).

47 Ibid., 22–23; Peter Dobkin Hall, *A Historical Overview of Philanthropy, Voluntary Associations, and Nonprofit Organizations in the United States, 1600–2000* (New Haven: Yale University Press, 2006); Walter W. Powell and Richard Steinberg, eds., *The Nonprofit Sector: A Research Handbook* (New Haven: Yale University Press, 2006), 36.

48 Elizabeth Drescher, "Nones by Many Other Names: The Religiously Unaffiliated in the News, 18th to 20th Century," in *Oxford Handbooks Online*, December 5, 2014, https://www.oxfordhandbooks.com/view/10.1093/oxfordhb/9780199935420.001.0001/oxfordhb-9780199935420-e-16.

49 Ray Stannard Baker, *The Spiritual Unrest* (New York: Frederick A. Stokes Company, 1910), 56, as cited in Drescher, "Nones by Many Other Names."

50 Sydney E. Ahlstrom, *A Religious History of the American People*, 2nd ed. (New Haven: Yale University Press, 2004), 952. "Church Members in Population: They Would Fill the White States, and Unchurched Would Fill Dark States," *Washington Post*, September 12, 1909, cited by Drescher, "Nones by Many Other Names." These figures, by including children in the denominator, probably slightly understated church membership as a fraction of the adult population.

51 Ahlstrom, *Religious History of the American People*, 844.

52 A prominent, moderate example of the prosperity gospel is Joel Osteen's mega-best-seller, Joel Osteen, *Your Best Life Now: 7 Steps to Living at Your Full Potential* (New York: Faithwords, 2004).

53 The Social Gospel movement and its links to the Progressive movement were far from simple. For more detail, see Ahlstrom, *A Religious History of the American People*, and Martin E. Marty, *Modern American Religion*, vol. 1: *The Irony of It All, 1893–1919* (Chicago: University of Chicago Press, 1986).

54 Walter Rauschenbusch, *A Theology for the Social Gospel* (New York: Macmillan, 1917).

55 Charles M. Sheldon, *In His Steps: "What Would Jesus Do?,"* author's revised ed. (New York: H. M. Caldwell Company, 1899), 11–12.

56 E. Brooks Holifield, "Toward a History of American Congregations," in *American Congregations*, vol. 2, eds. James P. Wind and James W. Lewis (Chicago: University of Chicago Press, 1994), 23–53, quotation at 39–41.

57 Bruce Duncan, *The Church's Social Teaching: From Rerum Novarum to 1931* (North Blackburn, Australia: Collins Dove, 1991), 48ff.

58 Higginbotham, *Righteous Discontent*, 7.

59 Arthur S. Link and Richard L. McCormick, *Progressivism* (Wheeling, IL: Harlan Davidson, 1983), 23; Cashman, *America in the Gilded Age*, 370; McWilliams, *Idea of Fraternity*, 479–81.

60 In measurement terms, one must distinguish between church attendance and church membership. At both the individual and aggregate level they are broadly correlated, but they are clearly distinct—substantially more Americans claim membership in a congregation than claim regular attendance. Moreover, reliable evidence on church membership covers a much longer period, because it is based to some extent, especially in the early years, on church records, whereas church attendance measures must be based on surveys, and with the exception of a few Gallup polls in the 1940s, surveys using regular, standardized questions begin only around 1960. For both membership and attendance, any given yearly figure is best considered a rough estimate, though broad trends are more reliable. For membership data, we rely in the first place on the *Historical Statistics of the United States* (HSUS). The HSUS series is based on the US Census Bureau's Census of Religions prior to and through the 1930s and data from the *Yearbook of American Churches* after the 1930s. The Yearbook is based in turn on surveys of religious bodies run by nongovernmental organizations after the Census Bureau stopped collecting the information in 1906. What denominator to use is problematic, because some denominations restrict membership to adults, in which case the denominator should be the total adult population of the US, but other denominations allow adolescents to be categorized as members, in which case young people should be included in the denominator, as well. Based on the HSUS's methodological notes, we have settled on population aged 10 and over as the appropriate denominator. The 10+ cutoff represents a good middle ground between these two reporting practices and brings the HSUS membership data closer in line with Gallup polling. Having resolved the denominator issues, we then created a combined curve using the HSUS data prior to the 1990s and the Gallup data afterward. The early Gallup polling numbers relied on a somewhat changing question and were typically based on a single poll in a given year, and early polling practices may have been less reliable, so we relied on the HSUS data where the two diverged; in that early period the Gallup-estimated membership rates were about 10–15 percentage points higher than the HSUS figures during the 1930s and 1940s,

but converged after 1950. Figure 4.4 includes both sets of figures, but uses a LOESS smoothing curve to construct a single continuous, spliced, and plausible time series measure of church membership.

61 On the history of this period, see Ahlstrom, *A Religious History of the American People*, and Robert Wuthnow, *The Restructuring of American Religion: Society and Faith Since World War II* (Princeton: Princeton University Press, 1988), 53.

62 Putnam and Campbell, *American Grace*, 85.

63 This is precisely the same cohort praised as "The Greatest Generation" in Tom Brokaw, *The Greatest Generation* (New York: Random House, 1998), and as "the long civic generation" in Putnam, *Bowling Alone*.

64 Gallup polls provide the longest continuous series of survey data on church attendance, beginning with the first national surveys in the 1940s, and these data are the basis of Figure 4.5. However, there is reason to be cautious about the Gallup data. For decades after 1980 Gallup polls showed remarkably steady or even rising church attendance, whereas other long-term survey series showed slumping church attendance, so that by the 1990s Gallup's figures were substantially and consistently higher than any other regular surveyors. (See Putnam and Campbell, *American Grace*, for much more detail on measuring church attendance and the Gallup anomaly as of 2007.) But just as experts were beginning to voice serious doubts about that discrepancy, the Gallup figures after 2005 began a precipitous decline from 43 percent in 2005 to 37 percent in 2014, bringing their data into much closer alignment with the other houses. No one has a good explanation for that fading "house effect," but it is well known that the church attendance question has a strong "social desirability" bias, and there is reason to believe that that bias was higher in Gallup, but has now declined. For consistency's sake, Figure 4.5 is based entirely on the published Gallup data.

65 Putnam and Campbell, *American Grace*, 374.

66 Ahlstrom, *A Religious History of the American People*, 952.

67 Robert Wuthnow, "Recent Pattern of Secularization: A Problem of Generations?," *American Sociological Review* 41 (October 1976); Wuthnow, *Restructuring of American Religion*, 17.

68 Andrew J. Cherlin, *The Marriage-Go-Round: The State of Marriage and the Family in America Today* (New York: Alfred A. Knopf, 2009), 74.

69 Robert N. Bellah, "Civil Religion in America," *Daedalus* 96, no. 1 (1967): 1–21.

70 Ahlstrom, *A Religious History of the American People*, 954.

71 Will Herberg, *Protestant, Catholic, Jew: An Essay in American Religious Sociology* (Garden City, NY: Doubleday, 1955), 58.

72 As we will show in Chapter 8, the decade of turmoil usually labeled "the Sixties" actually began around 1964 and lasted until about 1974.

73 Ahlstrom, *A Religious History of the American People*, 1080–81.

74 Maurice Isserman and Michael Kazin, *America Divided: The Civil War of the 1960s*, 3rd ed. (New York: Oxford University Press, 2008), 249.

75 For a largely sympathetic account of religious innovations of the 1960s, see Robert S. Ellwood, *The Sixties Spiritual Awakening: American Religion Moving from Modern to Post Modern* (New Brunswick, NJ: Rutgers University Press, 1994). See also Robert Wuthnow, *After Heaven: Spirituality in America Since the 1950s* (Berkeley: University of California Press, 1998).

76 Robert N. Bellah et al., *Habits of the Heart: Individualism and Commitment in American Life* (Berkeley: University of California Press, 1985), 221.

77 Amanda Porterfield, *The Transformation of American Religion: The Story of a Late-Twentieth-Century Awakening* (New York: Oxford University Press, 2001), 18.

78 Wuthnow, *After Heaven*, 2.

79 All data in this paragraph have been compiled from Gallup Poll Reports.

80 Putnam and Campbell, *American Grace*, 92–94, 99, 127–30. The available evidence does not allow us to prove that the shift in sexual norms *caused* the decline in religious affiliation, but the correlation between the two is very close.

81 David Kinnaman and Gabe Lyons, *Unchristian: What a New Generation Really Thinks About Christianity—And Why It Matters* (Grand Rapids, MI: Baker Books, 2007).

82 There was some attention to religious nones as early as 1968: see Glenn M. Vernon, "The Religious 'Nones': A Neglected Category," *Journal for the Scientific Study of Religion* 7 (1968): 219–29. However, they were a very small segment of the population at that time. The first major work on the sharp rise in nones in the 1990s was Michael Hout and Claude S. Fischer, "Why More Americans Have No Religious Preference: Politics and Generations," *American Sociological Review* 67, no. 2 (April 2002): 165–90.

83 The rate of nones depends on how we pose the question, but less than one might think. No matter what wording a survey uses, virtually every long-term survey archive shows a sharp rise in nones beginning in roughly 1990–1992, heavily concentrated among younger people.

84 For a detailed discussion of the varieties of nones and the challenges of identifying them in surveys, see Putnam and Campbell, *American Grace*, 120–27.

85 In general, the level of religious engagement among Latinos is midway between African Americans at the top and whites at the bottom. Ibid., 274–87.

86 Source: General Social Survey. Recent trends among Asian Americans and Latinos are similar to those for blacks and whites, but in the earlier decades their sample sizes are too small for reliable estimation.

87 Michael Hout and Claude S. Fischer, "Explaining Why More Americans Have No Religious Preference: Political Backlash and Generational Succession, 1987–2012," *Sociological Science* 1 (October 2014): 423–47.

88 David Voas and Mark Chaves, "Is the United States a Counterexample to the Secularization Thesis?," *American Journal of Sociology* 121, no. 5 (March 1, 2016): 1517–56.

89 Judged microscopically, it appears that attendance and giving peaked in about 1960 and membership about five years later, but that would probably be to press our microscope beyond its level of precision.

90 John Ronsvalle and Sylvia Ronsvalle, *The State of Church Giving Through 2016: What Do Denominational Leaders Want to Do with $368 Billion More a Year?* (Champaign, IL: Empty Tomb, Inc., 2014), and other annual volumes in this series. We are grateful to the Ronsvalles for their painstaking reconstruction of religious philanthropy over many years and for generously sharing their data.

91 See Patrick M. Rooney, "The Growth in Total Household Giving Is Camouflaging a Decline in Giving by Small and Medium Donors: What Can We Do about It?," *Nonprofit Quarterly*, September 13, 2018; Chuck Collins, Helen Flannery, and Josh Hoxie, "Gilded Giving 2018: Top-Heavy Philanthropy and Its Risks to the Independent Sector," Institute for Policy Studies (November 2018); Nicole Wallace and Ben Myers, "In Search of . . . America's Missing Donors," *Chronicle of Philanthropy* (June 5, 2018); Laurie E. Paarlberg and Hyunseok Hwang, "The Heterogeneity of Competitive Forces: The Impact of Competition for Resources on United Way Fundraising," *Nonprofit and Voluntary Sector Quarterly* 46, no. 5 (October 1, 2017): 897–921.

92 A recent body of literature criticizes the growth in mega-donations. See David Callahan, *The Givers: Wealth, Power, and Philanthropy in a New Gilded Age* (New York: Alfred A. Knopf, 2017); Rob Reich, *Just Giving: Why Philanthropy Is Failing Democracy and How It Can Do Better* (Princeton: Princeton University Press, 2018); Anand Giridharadas, *Winners Take All: The Elite Charade of Changing the World* (New York: Alfred A. Knopf, 2018); Joanne Barkan, "Plutocrats at Work: How Big Philanthropy Undermines Democracy," *Social Research* 80, no. 2 (2013): 635–52; and Nick Tabor, "Why Philanthropy Is Bad for Democracy," *New York* magazine, August 26, 2018.

93 Ralph Chaplin, *Wobbly: The Rough-and-Tumble Story of an American Radical* (Chicago: University of Chicago Press, 1948).

94 James T. Patterson, *Grand Expectations: The United States, 1945–1974*, Oxford History of the United States, vol. 10 (New York: Oxford University Press, 1996), 40.

95 Lizabeth Cohen, *Making a New Deal: Industrial Workers in Chicago, 1919–1939*, 2nd. ed. (Cambridge: Cambridge University Press, 2008).

96 Thomas C. Cochran and William Miller, *The Age of Enterprise: A Social History of Industrial America*, rev. ed. (New York: Harper, 1961), 235.

97   Joshua Benjamin Freeman, *Working-Class New York: Life and Labor Since World War II* (New York: New Press, 2000).

98   General Social Survey, www.norc.org.

99   Nelson Lichtenstein, *State of the Union: A Century of American Labor* (Princeton: Princeton University Press, 2003); Freeman, *Working-Class New York*.

100 Jonah Caleb Saline Hahn, *From Dark to Dawn: How Organizational Social Capital Impacts Manufacturing Workers After Job Loss* (BA Honors thesis, Committee on Degrees in Social Studies, Harvard University, 2017), p. 103. On the collapse of worker solidarity in the eastern Pennsylvania coal fields, see Jennifer M. Silva, *We're Still Here: Pain and Politics in the Heart of America* (New York: Oxford University Press, 2019).

101 On the history of the US family we are indebted to Professor Andrew J. Cherlin, one of America's leading sociologists of the family. See especially Andrew J. Cherlin, *Marriage, Divorce, Remarriage*, rev. and enlarged ed., Social Trends in the United States (Cambridge, MA: Harvard University Press, 1992); Cherlin, *The Marriage-Go-Round*; Andrew J. Cherlin, *Labor's Love Lost: The Rise and Fall of the Working-Class Family in America* (New York: Russell Sage Foundation, 2014); Nancy F. Cott, *Public Vows: A History of Marriage and the Nation* (Cambridge, MA: Harvard University Press, 2002); Arland Thornton and Linda Young-DeMarco, "Four Decades of Trends in Attitudes Toward Family Issues in the United States," *Journal of Marriage and the Family* (November 1, 2001): 1009–37; Shelly Lundberg, Robert A. Pollak, and Jenna Stearns, "Family Inequality: Diverging Patterns in Marriage, Cohabitation, and Childbearing," *The Journal of Economic Perspectives* 30, no. 2 (Spring 2016): 79–102; Stephanie Coontz, *The Way We Really Are: Coming to Terms with America's Changing Families* (New York: Basic Books, 1997); Catherine A. Fitch and Steven Ruggles, "Historical Trends in Marriage Formation: The United States, 1850–1990," in *The Ties That Bind: Perspectives on Marriage and Cohabitation*, ed. Linda J. Waite (New York: Aldine de Gruyter, 2000), 59–88; and Betsey Stevenson and Justin Wolfers, "Marriage and Divorce: Changes and Their Driving Forces," *The Journal of Economic Perspectives* 21, no. 2 (Spring 2007): 27–52.

102 Eric Klinenberg, *Going Solo: The Extraordinary Rise and Surprising Appeal of Living Alone* (New York: Penguin, 2012).

103 The concept of "fragile families" refers to unconventional parent-child groupings with multiple fathers and multiple mothers over time whose pairings are typically non-marital and transitory. See Sara McLanahan, Kate Jaeger, and Kristin Catena, "Children in Fragile Families," in Oxford Handbook of Children and the Law, ed. James G. Dwyer (Oxford Handbooks Online: Oxford University Press, 2019). For more information about the landmark Fragile Families study, see https://fragilefamilies.princeton.edu/.

104 Focusing on the age 30–44 window controls for changes over time at either
     end of the life cycle—delayed marriage and increasing widowhood. There are
     many ways of measuring the incidence of marriage, distinguishing between
     "married now" and "married ever," or focusing separately on men and on
     women or on whites and on nonwhites. But no matter how we measure it, the
     incidence of marriage in America rose and fell over the last 125 years in one
     long pendular swing, exactly as shown in Figure 4.10. See Michael R. Haines,
     "Long-Term Marriage Patterns in the United States from Colonial Times to
     the Present," *The History of the Family* 1, no. 1 (January 1, 1996): 15–39, esp.
     15.

105 Cherlin, *The Marriage-Go-Round*, 68.

106 Ibid., 63–67.

107 Ibid., 71.

108 Ibid., 75.

109 Ibid., 84.

110 Ibid., 85–86.

111 Ibid., 88.

112 Arland Thorton, William G. Axinn, and Yu Xie, "Historical Perspectives on
     Marriage," in *Family, Ties and Care: Family Transformation in a Plural Moder-
     nity*, eds. Hans Bertram and Nancy Ehlert (Leverkusen, Germany: Verlag
     Barbara Budrich, 2011), 57.

113 Cherlin, *Marriage, Divorce, Remarriage*, 7, 20–25.

114 Ibid., 11–12.

115 Catherine Fitch, Ron Goeken, and Steven Ruggles. "The Rise of Cohabita-
     tion in the United States: New Historical Estimates," Minnesota Population
     Center, Working Paper 3 (2005).

116 "Wide Acceptance of Cohabitation, Even as Many Americans See Societal
     Benefits in Marriage," *Fact Tank—News in the Numbers*, November 5, 2019,
     https://www.pewresearch.org/fact-tank/2019/11/06/key-findings-on-mar
     riage-and-cohabitation-in-the-u-s/ft_19-11-05_marriagecohabitation_wide
     -acceptance-cohabitation/.

117 Cherlin, *The Marriage-Go-Round*, 100.

118 "Among Americans with college degrees, we see a much greater centering
     of family life around marriage, whereas for those with less education we see
     a greater reliance on alternatives to marriage, such as cohabiting unions and
     lone parenthood, as well as a higher rate of marital dissolution." Andrew
     Cherlin, "Degrees of Change: An Assessment of the Deinstitutionalization
     of Marriage Thesis," *Journal of Marriage and Family* 82, no. 1 (Feb 2020). See
     also Lundberg, Pollak, and Stearns, "Family inequality"; Sara McLanahan,
     "Diverging Destinies: How Children Fare Under the Second Demographic
     Transition," *Demography* 41, no. 4 (2004): 607–27; and McLanahan, Jaeger,

and Catena, "Children in Fragile Families," 2019. For more information about the landmark Fragile Families study, see https://fragilefamilies.prince ton.edu/.

119 Cherlin, *Marriage, Divorce, Remarriage*, 15–16.

120 Cherlin, *The Marriage-Go-Round*, 102.

121 Lisa Bonos and Emily Guskin, "It's Not Just You: New Data Shows More than Half of Young People in America Don't Have a Romantic Partner," *Washington Post*, March 21, 2019, https://www.washingtonpost.com/lifestyle /2019/03/21/its-not-just-you-new-data-shows-more-than-half-young-peo ple-america-dont-have-romantic-partner/, citing the General Social Survey, https://gssdataexplorer.norc.org/trends/Gender%20&%20Marriage?mea sure=posslq.

122 Cherlin, *Labor's Love Lost*, 17, 18, 21. (This trend is less marked among African Americans.)

123 Robert D. Mare, "Educational Homogamy in Two Gilded Ages: Evidence from Inter-Generational Social Mobility Data," *The ANNALS of the American Academy of Political and Social Science* 663 (January 1, 2016): 117–39, doi:10.1177/0002716215596967.

124 See Donald T Rowland, "Historical Trends in Childlessness" *Journal of Family Issues* 28, no. 10 (2007): 1311–37, doi:10.1177/0192513X07303823.

125 T. J. Matthews and Brady E. Hamilton, "Delayed Childbearing: More Women Are Having Their First Child Later in Life," *NCHS Data Brief*, no. 21 (August 2009): 1–8; S. E. Kirmeyer and B. E. Hamilton, "Transitions Between Childlessness and First Birth: Three Generations of U.S. Women," *Vital and Health Statistics*, Series 2, *Data Evaluation and Methods Research*, no. 153 (August 2011): 1–18.

126 Michael R. Haines, "Demography in American Economic History," *The Oxford Handbook of American Economic History*, eds. Louis P. Cain, Price V. Fishback, and Paul W. Rhode, vol. 1, July 16, 2018.

127 Cherlin, *Marriage, Divorce, Remarriage*, 18–19.

128 Source: B. E. Hamilton and C. M. Cosgrove, "Central Birth Rates, by Live-Birth Order, Current Age, and Race of Women in Each Cohort from 1911 Through 1991: United States, 1960–2005," Table 1 (Hyattsville, MD: National Center for Health Statistics), /nchs/nvss/cohort_fertility_tables.html. The horizontal axis marks the year a cohort of women turned 30 compared to the cohort of women who turned 45 in that year. A mother at 45 in 1960 would have appeared as a mother at 30 in 1945, but some women who were childless at age 30 in 1945 will have had children by age 45 in 1960. For data, see S. E. Kirmeyer and B. E. Hamilton, "Transitions Between Childlessness and First Birth: Three Generations of US Women," Vital and Health Statistics, Series 2, Data Evaluation and Methods Research 153 (August 2011): 1–18;

Rowland, "Historical Trends in Childlessness"; and Tomas Frejka, "Childlessness in the United States," in Childlessness in Europe: Contexts, Causes, and Consequences, eds. Michaela Kreyenfeld, Dirk Konietzka (Cham, CH: Springer Open, 2017), 159–79.

129 Ruth Shonle Cavan and Katherine Howland Ranck, *The Family and the Depression, a Study of One Hundred Chicago Families* (Chicago: University of Chicago Press, 1938). See also Robert D. Putnam, *Our Kids: The American Dream in Crisis* (New York: Simon & Schuster, 2015), 74–75.

130 See endnote 4.101 for full list of sources. Additional texts are S. Philip Morgan, "Late Nineteenth- and early Twentieth-Century Childlessness," *American Journal of Sociology* (1991): 779–807; Jan Van Bavel, "Subreplacement fertility in the West before the baby boom: Past and current perspectives," *Population Studies* 64, no. 1 (2010): 1–18; Cherlin, *Labor's Love Lost*; Kirmeyer and Hamilton, "Transitions Between Childlessness and First Birth"; Daniel T. Lichter et al., "Economic Restructuring and Retreat from Marriage," *Social Science Research* 3, no. 2 (2002); and Michael Greenstone and Adam Looney, "Marriage Gap: Impact of Economic and Technological Change on Marriage Rates" (The Hamilton Project, February 2012), https://www.hamiltonproject .org/assets/legacy/files/downloads_and_links/020312_jobs_greenstone_loo ney.pdf.

131 According to Adam Isen and Betsey Stevenson, "Women's Education and Family Behavior: Trends in Marriage, Divorce and Fertility," Working Paper 15725 (National Bureau of Economic Research, February 2010), doi:10.3386 /w15725, college-educated women in the first Gilded Age were least likely to marry, although now highly educated women are most likely to marry.

132 Sara McLanahan, Kathryn Edin, and their collaborators, https://fragilefami lies.princeton.edu/.

133 Robert D. Putnam, *Our Kids: The American Dream in Crisis* (New York: Simon & Schuster, 2015), 78–79 and sources cited there.

134 Michael Taylor, *Community, Anarchy, and Liberty* (Cambridge: Cambridge University Press, 1982), 28–29. See also Alvin W. Gouldner, "The Norm of Reciprocity: A Preliminary Statement," *American Sociological Review* 25, no. 2 (April 1960): 161–78.

135 Tocqueville, *Democracy in America*, 525–28.

136 Wendy M. Rahn and John E. Transue, "Social Trust and Value Change: The Decline of Social Capital in American Youth, 1976–1995," *Political Psychology* 19, no. 3 (September 1998): 545–65, quotation at 545.

137 Generalized social trust is *not* the same thing as trust in specific people (your neighbor or the president) nor in institutions (unions, police, the federal government, and so on). There is by now an enormous literature on trust in all these senses. For one recent overview, see Kenneth Newton, "Social

and Political Trust," in *The Oxford Handbook of Political Behavior*, eds. Russell Dalton and Hans-Dieter Klingemann (New York: Oxford University Press, 2007), 342–61. For an earlier discussion of generalized social trust and its decline in recent years, see Putnam, *Bowling Alone*, 137–42.

138 For the single-barrel question we have calculated the percentage trusting as a fraction of all valid responses, excluding missing data.

139 Putnam, *Bowling Alone*, 137–41. Most subsequent studies testing Putnam's claim have relied exclusively on the General Social Survey and have not examined a second data archive used by Putnam. An identical decline between 1975 and 2005 appears in the DDB Life Style data archive, using the question "Most people are honest." See Putnam, *Bowling Alone*, Figure 39, p. 141. The DDB Needham Life Style surveys are described in Putnam, *Bowling Alone*, Appendix 2, pp. 429–30, updated subsequently through 2005. For subsequent confirmation of the basic trend and at least a partial generational explanation, see Robert V. Robinson and Elton F. Jackson, "Is Trust in Others Declining in America? An Age–Period–Cohort Analysis," *Social Science Research* 30, no. 1 (March 1, 2001): 117–45, doi:10.1006/ssre.2000.0692; April K. Clark and Marie A. Eisenstein, "Interpersonal Trust: An Age–Period–Cohort Analysis Revisited," *Social Science Research* 42, no. 2 (March 1, 2013): 361–75, doi:10.1016/j.ssresearch.2012.09.006; and April K. Clark, "Rethinking the Decline in Social Capital," *American Politics Research* 43, no. 4 (2015): 569–601, doi:10.1177/1532673X14531071.

140 In virtually all societies "have nots" are less trusting than "haves," probably because haves are treated by others with more honesty and respect. In America, blacks are less trusting than whites, the financially distressed less than the financially comfortable, people in big cities less than small-town dwellers, and people who have been victims of a crime or have been through a divorce less than those who haven't had these experiences. When such people tell pollsters that "most people can't be trusted," they are not simply being paranoid—they are reflecting their personal experience. More sophisticated tests of the argument that trust has fallen since the 1970s generally control for other demographic factors that might affect trust, including race, class, and gender. A good recent overview of the voluminous research on trust and its correlates is Kenneth Newton, "Social and Political Trust."

141 This assumption that generations are formed when their members reach maturity (around 19-21) goes back to the origins of generational analysis: K. Mannheim, "The Problem of Generations," in *Essays on the Sociology of Knowledge: Collected Works*, vol. 5, ed. Paul Kecskemeti (London: Routledge, 1952), 276–322, originally published in German in 1927–28.

142 Stephen W. Raudenbush and Anthony S. Bryk, *Hierarchical Linear Models: Applications and Data Analysis Methods*, 2nd ed., *Advanced Quantitative Techniques in*

the Social Sciences 1 (Thousand Oaks, CA: Sage Publications, 2002); Yang Yang and Kenneth C. Land, "A Mixed Models Approach to the Age-Period-Cohort Analysis of Repeated Cross-Section Surveys, with an Application to Data on Trends in Verbal Test Scores," *Sociological Methodology 2006*, vol. 36 (December 2006): 75–97; Yang Yang and Kenneth C. Land, "Age-Period-Cohort Analysis of Repeated Cross-Section Surveys—Fixed or Random Effects?," *Sociological Methods & Research* 36, no. 3 (2008): 297–326, doi:10.1177/0049124106292360. We here use the CCREM approach, which generates estimates of cohort differences, net of age and period effects and of other demographic factors, such as education. We also explored both CGLIM and Intrinsic Estimator models, which produced cohort curves virtually indistinguishable from the CCREM curve in Figure 4.14. We are grateful to April K. Clark for generous consultation on contemporary APC techniques, though we remain solely responsible for the use to which we put them. For the estimates used in Figure 4.14, we rely on Clark, "Rethinking the Decline in Social Capital."

143 Social isolation and loneliness are related but distinct facets of social solidarity—one sociological and the second psychological. Some evidence suggests that both have been rising in recent decades, though that remains controversial. See Miller McPherson, Lynn Smith-Lovin, and Matthew E. Brashears, "Social Isolation in America: Changes in Core Discussion Networks over Two Decades," *American Sociological Review* 71, no. 3 (2006): 353–75, doi:10.1177/000312240607100301; Miller McPherson, Lynn Smith-Lovin, and Matthew E. Brashears, "Social Isolation in America: Changes in Core Discussion Networks over Two Decades: Correction," *American Sociological Review* 73, no. 6 (December 2008): 1022, doi:10.1177/000312240807300610; Claude S. Fischer, "The 2004 GSS Finding of Shrunken Social Networks: An Artifact?," *American Sociological Review* 74, no. 4 (2009): 657–69, doi:10.1177/000312240907400408; Matthew Brashears, "Small Networks and High Isolation? A Reexamination of American Discussion Networks," *Social Networks* 33, no. 4 (October 2011): 331–41, doi:10.1016/j.socnet.2011.10.003; Keith N. Hampton, Lauren F. Sessions, and Eun Ja Her, "Core Networks, Social Isolation and New Media: How Internet and Mobile Phone Use Is Related to Network Size and Diversity," *Information, Communication & Society* 14, no. 1 (2011): 130–55, doi:10.1080/1369118X.2010.513417; Klinenberg, *Going Solo*; John T. Cacioppo and William Patrick, *Loneliness: Human Nature and the Need for Social Connection* (New York: W. W. Norton, 2009); Jacqueline Olds and Richard S. Schwartz, *The Lonely American: Drifting Apart in the Twenty-first Century* (Boston: Beacon Press, 2009); and *All the Lonely Americans* (Report of the Congressional Joint Economic Committee [August 2018]), https://www.jec.senate.gov/public/index.cfm/republicans/2018/8/all-the-lonely-americans. Since we lack good evidence on either phenomenon

across the full century that is our focus here, we disregard these issues in this book.

144 See endnote 1.4.

CHAPTER 5: CULTURE: INDIVIDUALISM VS. COMMUNITY

1 The original inspiration for this chapter came from a series of conversations with James Kloppenberg, the distinguished Harvard intellectual historian, though he is certainly not responsible for what came from that inspiration. For able assistance with exploring and understanding the multiple scholarly literatures used in this chapter, we are especially grateful to Alex Mierke-Zatwarnicki and Casey Bohlen.

2 John Donne, *Devotions upon Emergent Occasions and Severall Steps in My Sicknes* (London: Printed for Thomas Iones, 1624), Meditation 17. https://www.gutenberg.org/files/23772/23772-h/23772-h.htm.

3 See Dave Nussbaum, "Tight and Loose Cultures: A Conversation with Michele Gelfand," *Behavioral Scientist*, January 17, 2019, https://behavioralscientist.org/tight-and-loose-cultures-a-conversation-with-michele-gelfand/; Michele Gelfand, *Rule Makers, Rule Breakers: How Tight and Loose Cultures Wire Our World* (New York: Simon & Schuster, 2018).

4 Thomas Bender, "Lionel Trilling and American Culture," *American Quarterly* 42, no. 2 (June 1990): 324–47, doi:10.2307/2713020.

5 Jennifer Ratner-Rosenhagen, *The Ideas That Made America: A Brief History* (New York: Oxford University Press, 2019); E. J. Dionne, *Our Divided Political Heart: The Battle for the American Idea in an Age of Discontent* (New York: Bloomsbury, 2012), with whose argument about the back-and-forth between individualism and community over American history this chapter has much in common.

6 Perhaps the single most influential book on individualism and community of the final decades of the twentieth century and one of the first to call attention to the incipient shift toward excessive individualism was Robert N. Bellah, William M. Sullivan, Steven M. Tipton, Richard Madsen, and Ann Swidler, *Habits of the Heart: Individualism and Commitment in American Life* (Berkeley: University of California Press, 1985).

7 "Overton Window," in *Wikipedia*, November 18, 2018, https://en.wikipedia.org/w/index.php?title=Overton_window&oldid=926722212.

8 James T. Kloppenberg, *Toward Democracy: The Struggle for Self-Rule in European and American Thought* (New York: Oxford University Press, 2016), 633–702; Daniel Walker Howe, *What Hath God Wrought: The Transformation of America, 1815–1848*, The Oxford History of the United States (unnumbered) (New York: Oxford University Press, 2009); William Lee Miller, *Lincoln's Virtues: An Ethical Biography* (New York: Alfred A. Knopf, 2002); Richard

Carwardine, *Lincoln: A Life of Purpose and Power* (New York: Alfred A. Knopf, 2006), 11–28.

9 "The Significance of the Frontier in American History" (1893), available at https://www.historians.org/about-aha-and-membership/aha-history-and-ar chives/historical-archives/the-significance-of-the-frontier-in-american-his tory. See also his presidential address to the American Historical Association, 1910, in which he contrasted the individualism of the frontier years with the emerging need for a new democratic sensibility he identified with the progressive reformers: *American Historical Review* 16, no. 2 (1910): 217–33, https://www.historians.org/about-aha-and-membership/aha-history-and-ar chives/presidential-addresses/frederick-jackson-turner.

10 Samuel Bazzi, Martin Fiszbein, and Mesay Gebresilasse, "Frontier Culture: The Roots and Persistence of 'Rugged Individualism' in the United States," Working Paper 23997 (National Bureau of Economic Research), November 2017, 23997, doi:10.3386/w23997.

11 Spencer was allegedly "the single most famous European intellectual in the closing decades of the nineteenth century," according to "Herbert Spencer," in *Wikipedia*, October 26, 2019, https://en.wikipedia.org/w/index.php?title =Herbert_Spencer&oldid=923093648.

12 H. W. Brands, *American Colossus: The Triumph of Capitalism, 1865–1900* (New York: Doubleday, 2010), 558–59.

13 Henry Louis Gates, Jr., *Stony the Road: Reconstruction, White Supremacy, and the Rise of Jim Crow* (New York: Penguin, 2019); Daniel Okrent, *The Guarded Gate: Bigotry, Eugenics, and the Law That Kept Two Generations of Jews, Italians, and Other European Immigrants out of America* (New York: Scribner, 2019).

14 James T. Kloppenberg, *The Virtues of Liberalism* (New York: Oxford University Press, 1998), 126.

15 These lines are paraphrased in part from Ratner-Rosenhagen, *The Ideas That Made America*, chap. 5.

16 For a deeply researched and thoughtful discussion of the history of the term "social capital" during the Progressive Era, see James Farr, "Social Capital: A Conceptual History," Political Theory, 32:1 (February 2004): 6-33. Farr gives some credit to one of us (Putnam) for the reappearance of the term in public discourse at the end of the twentieth century. The N-gram for "social capital" clearly confirms a first blossoming of the term from 1907 to 1910, then a long slump until a massive upsurge after 1993.

17 Marta Cook and John Halpin, "The Role of Faith in the Progressive Movement," https://www.americanprogress.org/issues/democracy/reports/2010 /10/08/8490/the-role-of-faith-in-the-progressive-movement/.

18 In 2000 Google made a technical change in the way books are processed, so there is some concern that the data between 2000 and 2008 may in some way

be incomparable with results from earlier years, but we follow the practice of the majority of researchers in using the full archive up to 2008. To minimize year-to-year fluctuations, we use LOESS-smoothed data, typically with an alpha parameter of .15. We use "case-insensitive" search terms, thus including Social Gospel, social gospel, Social gospel, and even social Gospel.

19 Other key sources for the rapidly expanding field of Ngram-based studies include Patricia M. Greenfield, "The Changing Psychology of Culture from 1800 Through 2000," *Psychological Science* 24, no. 9 (September 2013): 1722–31, doi:10.1177/0956797613479387; Jean-Baptiste Michel et al., "Quantitative Analysis of Culture Using Millions of Digitized Books," *Science* 331, no. 6014 (January 14, 2011): 176–82, doi:10.1126/science.1199644; Jean M. Twenge, W. Keith Campbell, and Brittany Gentile, "Changes in Pronoun Use in American Books and the Rise of Individualism, 1960–2008," *Journal of Cross-Cultural Psychology* 44, no. 3 (2013): 406–15, doi:10.1177/0022022112455100; Rong Zeng and Patricia M. Greenfield, "Cultural Evolution over the Last 40 Years in China: Using the Google Ngram Viewer to Study Implications of Social and Political Change for Cultural Values," *International Journal of Psychology* 50, no. 1 (February 2015): 47–55, doi:10.1002/ijop.12125.

20 Warmest thanks to Andrew McAfee and to Evrim Altintas for independently pointing us to Ngrams.

21 Zeng and Greenfield, "Cultural Evolution over the Last 40 Years in China," 49.

22 An important methodological critique is Eitan Adam Pechenick, Christopher M. Danforth, and Peter Sheridan Dodds, "Characterizing the Google Books Corpus: Strong Limits to Inferences of Socio-Cultural and Linguistic Evolution," *PLOS ONE* 10, no. 10 (October 7, 2015): 1–14. e0137041, doi:10.1371/journal.pone.0137041. Each book appears only once in the Google archive, so more widely read books are not given more weight. There is also some evidence that over the last century or so, scientific and technical books have become relatively more frequent and thus that scientific and technical terminology appears more frequently in the archive. For some purposes those are important constraints, but they are not critical for our purposes of characterizing broad change in American culture along the individual-community axis.

23 "Survival of the fittest" first appeared in American books in any significant way in 1867, seven years after *On the Origin of Species*, and thirty years before the first appearance of "social gospel." The salience of "survival of the fittest" and "social gospel" is measured here on two different vertical axes, since the former almost always appears more frequently than the latter, probably because the former term also appears in scientific publications, not merely books on social philosophy. Measuring both terms on the same axis would obscure the timing of the ups and downs in the salience of each concept.

24 Jane Addams, *Twenty Years at Hull-House*, quoted in Ratner-Rosenhagen, *The Ideas That Made America*, 109.

25 http://www.theodore-roosevelt.com/images/research/speeches/trnation alismspeech.pdf. In December 2011, President Obama, a kind of neo-Progressive, spoke in Osawatomie to echo TR's speech: "And in 1910, Teddy Roosevelt came here to Osawatomie and he laid out his vision for what he called a New Nationalism. 'Our country,' he said, '. . . means nothing unless it means the triumph of a real democracy . . . of an economic system under which each man shall be guaranteed the opportunity to show the best that there is in him.'" https://obamawhitehouse.archives.gov/thepressoffice/2011 /12/06/remarkspresidenteconomyosawatomie-kansas.

26 Michael E. McGerr, *A Fierce Discontent: The Rise and Fall of the Progressive Movement in America, 1870–1920* (New York: Free Press, 2003), 64–67.

27 Ngrams also show a clear rise between 1890 and 1920 in the cultural salience of "neighborliness," "Christian socialism," and "community," though the fate of those terms during the rest of the twentieth century varies.

28 See David M. Kennedy, *Freedom from Fear: The American People in Depression and War, 1929–1945*, *The Oxford History of the United States*, vol. 9 (New York: Oxford University Press, 1999). On the 1930s culturally, see Frederick Lewis Allen, *Since Yesterday: The 1930s in America, September 3, 1929–September 3, 1939* (New York: Harper & Brothers, 1940), 201–24.

29 Herbert Hoover, *American Individualism* (Garden City, NY: Doubleday, 1922). As we noted in Chapter 3, in his later years Hoover became a deeply conservative critic of the New Deal.

30 Kloppenberg, *The Virtues of Liberalism*, 134–38.

31 As quoted in Charles Austin Beard, "The Myth of Rugged American Individualism," *Harper's Monthly* (December 1931). By contrast, for evidence that even in the midst of the Great Depression many Americans were ambivalent about public aid to the jobless, who were thought to be the authors of their own misfortune, see Katherine S. Newman and Elisabeth S. Jacobs, *Who Cares?: Public Ambivalence and Government Activism from the New Deal to the Second Gilded Age* (Princeton: Princeton University Press, 2010), chap. 1.

32 Beard, "The Myth of Rugged American Individualism," 22.

33 *World Film Directors: Volume One 1890–1945*, ed. John Wakeman (New York: H. W. Wilson, 1988), 100.

34 Speech by Franklin D. Roosevelt before the Troy, New York, people's forum, March 3, 1912, https://www.nps.gov/parkhistory/online_books/cany/fdr/part1 .htm.

35 Kennedy, *Freedom from Fear*, 145–46; Ratner-Rosenhagen, *The Ideas That Made America*, chap. 6.

36 See http://library.cqpress.com/cqresearcher/document.php?id=cqresrre193

1120300; Jean Edward Smith, *Eisenhower in War and Peace* (New York: Random House, 2012), chap. 5; and Stuart D. Brandes, *Warhogs: A History of War Profits in America* (Lexington: University Press of Kentucky, 1997), pp. 205–8.

37 Composed initially for the concert hall, "Fanfare for the Common Man" continues to be used frequently for public ceremonial events across the English-speaking world nearly seventy years later. "Fanfare for the Common Man," in *Wikipedia*, November 1, 2019, https://en.wikipedia.org/w/index.php ?title=Fanfare_for_the_Common_Man&oldid=923976555. Of course, in that era no one recognized the male chauvinism implied in the term. Ngram analysis shows no similar pattern for "fanfare" nor for "Common Man," so this chart does not primarily reflect the impact of the musical composition itself.

38 As noted in Chapter 2, from 1945 to 1975 the national distribution of income gradually became somewhat more equal, implying that working-class Americans were getting a slightly larger share of annual growth than upper income Americans, though the actual distribution of income itself remained far from equal. James T. Patterson, *Grand Expectations: The United States, 1945–1974*, *The Oxford History of the United States*, vol. 10 (New York: Oxford University Press, 1996), 321–22.

39 James Truslow Adams, *The Epic of America* (Garden City, NY: Blue Ribbon Books, 1941), 404.

40 See Robert J. Shiller, "The Transformation of the 'American Dream,'" *New York Times*, August 4, 2017.

41 Arthur M. Schlesinger, *The Vital Center: The Politics of Freedom* (Boston: Houghton Mifflin, 1949), 256.

42 Martin Luther King Jr., "Letter from a Birmingham Jail," *African Studies Center—University of Pennsylvania*, accessed November 22, 2019, https://www .africa.upenn.edu/Articles_Gen/Letter_Birmingham.html.

43 John F. Kennedy, "Radio and Television Report to the American People on Civil Rights, June 11, 1963," John F. Kennedy Presidential Library and Museum, accessed November 22, 2019, https://www.jfklibrary.org/archives /other-resources/john-f-kennedy-speeches/civil-rights-radio-and-television -report-19630611.

44 Gary S. Selby, *Martin Luther King and the Rhetoric of Freedom: The Exodus Narrative in America's Struggle for Civil Rights*, Studies in Rhetoric and Religion 5 (Waco, TX: Baylor University Press, 2008).

45 William I. Hitchcock, *The Age of Eisenhower: America and the World in the 1950s* (New York: Simon & Schuster, 2018), chap. 6.

46 Marie Jahoda, "Psychological Issues in Civil Liberties," *American Psychologist* 11, no. 5 (1956): 234–20, quotation at 234.

47   David Riesman, Nathan Glazer, and Reuel Denney, *The Lonely Crowd: A Study of the Changing American Character*, abridged and rev. ed. (New Haven: Yale University Press, 2001).

48   "David Riesman, Sociologist Whose `Lonely Crowd' Became a Best Seller, Dies at 92," *New York Times*, May 11, 2002.

49   William Hollingsworth Whyte, *The Organization Man* (New York: Simon & Schuster, 1956), chaps. 2 4, 5. Another book in this period that emphasized the dangers of blind conformity to rules was Hannah Arendt, *Eichmann in Jerusalem: A Report on the Banality of Evil*, revised and enlarged ed. (New York: Viking, 1964).

50   For example, Dan Reidel, "Oroville Dam: Photos Taken Weeks Before Spillway Broke Show Something Wrong," *Mercury News*, March 11, 2017.

51   For a useful overview of the Asch experiment and its aftermath, see Saul A. McLeod, "Solomon Asch—Conformity Experiment," *Simply Psychology* (Dec. 28, 2018). Retrieved from https://www.simplypsychology.org/asch-conformity.html

52   Quotation from John Greenwood, "How Would People Behave in Milgram's Experiment Today?," *Behavioral Scientist*, July 24, 2018, https://behavioralscientist.org/how-would-people-behave-in-milgrams-experiment-today/.

53   Knud Larsen, "Conformity in the Asch Experiment," *Journal of Social Psychology* 94 (1974): 303–4; Steven Perrin and Christopher Spencer, "The Asch Effect—A Child of Its Time?," *Bulletin of the British Psychological Society* 33 (1980): 405–6; Rod Bond and Peter B. Smith, "Culture and Conformity: A Meta-Analysis of Studies Using Asch's (1952b, 1956) Line Judgment Task," *Psychological Bulletin* 119, no. 1 (January 1996): 111–37, doi:10.1037/0033-2909.119.1.111.

54   Jennifer Burns, *Goddess of the Market: Ayn Rand and the American Right* (Oxford: Oxford University Press, 2009); Daniel Stedman Jones, *Masters of the Universe: Hayek, Friedman, and the Birth of Neoliberal Politics* (Princeton: Princeton University Press, 2013); Angus Burgin, *The Great Persuasion: Reinventing Free Markets Since the Depression* (Cambridge, MA: Harvard University Press, 2015).

55   Rand's quote about "brother's keeper" comes from "The Mike Wallace Interview, Ayn Rand," March 12, 1959, https://www.youtube.com/watch?v=1ooKsv_SX4Y at 18:53. Altruism quotation from Ayn Rand, *The Virtue of Selfishness: A New Concept of Egoism* (New York: Penguin, 1964), 112.

56   David Corn, "Secret Video: Romney Tells Millionaire Donors What He Really Thinks of Obama Voters," *Mother Jones*, September 17, 2012, https://www.motherjones.com/politics/2012/09/secret-video-romney-private-fundraiser/.

57   Alvin Toffler, "Playboy Interview: Ayn Rand," *Playboy*, March 1964, 35–43.

58 James Stewart, "As a Guru, Ayn Rand May Have Limits. Ask Travis Kalanick," *New York Times* (online), July 13, 2017. https://www.nytimes.com/2017/07/13 /business/ayn-rand-business-politics-uber-kalanick.html.

59 Ryan's words come at 2:38 of a 2005 speech to the Atlas Society, "Paul Ryan and Ayn Rand's Ideas: In the Hot Seat Again," *The Atlas Society*, April 30, 2012, https://atlassociety.org/commentary/commentary-blog/4971-paul-ryan -and-ayn-rands-ideas-in-the-hot-seat-again .

60 Francis Fukuyama, *The Great Disruption: Human Nature and the Reconstitution of Social Order* (New York: Free Press, 1999), 13–14.

61 Herbert Marcuse, "Selection from One Dimensional Man," in *The American Intellectual Tradition*, eds. David A. Hollinger and Charles Capper, 6th ed., vol. 2 (New York: Oxford University Press, 2011). On the New Left, see Maurice Isserman, *If I Had a Hammer: The Death of the Old Left and the Birth of the New Left*, rpt. ed. (Urbana: University of Illinois Press, 1993); David Farber, *Chicago '68* (Chicago: University of Chicago Press, 1994); Jim Miller, *Democracy Is in the Streets: From Port Huron to the Siege of Chicago* (Cambridge, MA: Harvard University Press, 1994); Douglas C. Rossinow, *The Politics of Authenticity: Liberalism, Christianity, and the New Left in America*, rev. ed. (New York: Columbia University Press, 1998); and Van Gosse, *Rethinking the New Left: An Interpretative History* (New York: Palgrave Macmillan, 2005).

62 Students for a Democratic Society (U.S.), *The Port Huron Statement: (1962)* (Chicago: C. H. Kerr, 1990).

63 Todd Gitlin, *The Sixties: Years of Hope, Days of Rage*, rev. ed. (New York: Bantam, 1993), 209.

64 Erik H. (Erik Homburger) Erikson, *Young Man Luther: A Study in Psychoanalysis and History*, Austen Riggs Center, Monographs, No. 4 (New York: W. W. Norton, 1958).

65 This paragraph is based on an Ngram analysis (not shown here) of "identity crisis," "racial identity," "gender identity," and "identity politics."

66 "Citizenship Rights and Responsibilities," U.S. Citizenship and Immigration Services, accessed November 22, 2019, https://www.uscis.gov/citizenship /learners/citizenship-rights-and-responsibilities.

67 We use "rights"—the plural—because the singular form is so ambiguous. "Responsibility" is much more common than "responsibilities," though both show the same curve relative to "rights."

68 Mary Ann Glendon, *Rights Talk: The Impoverishment of Political Discourse* (New York: Free Press, 1991).

69 Joseph Bagley, *The Politics of White Rights: Race, Justice, and Integrating Alabama's Schools* (Athens: University of Georgia Press, 2018).

70 Duane F. Alwin, "Cohort Replacement and Changes in Parental Socialization

Values," *Journal of Marriage and the Family* 52, no. 2 (1990): 347–60. See also Michael Hout and Claude S. Fischer, "Explaining Why More Americans Have No Religious Preference: Political Backlash and Generational Succession, 1987–2012," *Sociological Science* 1 (October 2014): 423–47, doi:10.15195 /v1.a24, who emphasize generational differences in "personal autonomy generally and autonomy in the sphere of sex and drugs specifically."

71   Ngram Viewer for "self-help" between 1880 and 2008; and Robert Wuthnow, *After Heaven: Spirituality in America Since the 1950s* (Berkeley: University of California Press, 1998), esp. 153.

72   "Share, v.2," in *Oxford English Dictionary Online* (Oxford: Oxford University Press, 2019), http://www.oed.com/view/Entry/177535.

73   Christopher Lasch, *The Culture of Narcissism: American Life in an Age of Diminishing Expectations* (New York: W. W. Norton, 1979).

74   Jean M. Twenge, *Generation Me: Why Today's Young Americans Are More Confident, Assertive, Entitled—And More Miserable than Ever Before* (New York: Free Press, 2006), 68–69.

75   Jean M. Twenge and W. Keith Campbell, *The Narcissism Epidemic: Living in the Age of Entitlement* (New York: Atria, 2009), 4.

76   Ibid., 67. For a summary of her latest data, see Jean M. Twenge, W. Keith Campbell, and Nathan T. Carter, "Declines in Trust in Others and Confidence in Institutions Among American Adults and Late Adolescents, 1972–2012," *Psychological Science* 25, no. 10 (2014): 1914–23, doi:10.1177 /0956797614545133.

77   See "Graphic detail," The Economist (Feb 16, 2019) https://www.economist .com/graphic-detail/2019/02/16/the-names-of-migrants-to-america-sug gest-they-were-individualists; Geert Hofstede, *Culture's Consequences: Comparing Values, Behaviors, Institutions and Organizations Across Nations.* 2nd ed. (Thousand Oaks CA: Sage Publications, 2001); and https://www.hofstede-in sights.com/models/national-culture/.

78   Jean M. Twenge, Emodish M. Abebe, and W. Keith Campbell, "Fitting In or Standing Out: Trends in American Parents' Choices for Children's Names, 1880–2007," *Social Psychological and Personality Science* 1, no. 1 (2010): 19–25, doi:10.1177/1948550609349515. Knudsen, Anne Sofie Beck, "Those Who Stayed: Individualism, Self-Selection and Cultural Change During the Age of Mass Migration" (January 24, 2019), available at SSRN: https://ssrn.com/ab stract=3321790 or http://dx.doi.org/10.2139/ssrn.3321790; Yuji Ogihara et al., "Are Common Names Becoming Less Common? The Rise in Uniqueness and Individualism in Japan," *Frontiers in Psychology* 6 (2015): 1490, doi:10.3389 /fpsyg.2015.01490; Michael E. W. Varnum and Shinobu Kitayama, "What's in a Name?: Popular Names Are Less Common on Frontiers," *Psychological Science* 22, no. 2 (2011): 176–83, doi:10.1177/0956797610395396. For other

studies in economics and sociology that use birth names for measuring culture, see Samuel Bazzi et al., "Frontier Culture," 2.

79 "Background Information for Popular Names," Social Security Administration, accessed November 22, 2019, https://www.ssa.gov/oact/babynames/background.html.

80 Other studies that use the Gini index in this context include Twenge et al, "Fitting In or Standing Out," Richard Woodward, "Do Americans Desire Homogeneity?;" Twenge et al, "Still standing out: children's names in the United States during the Great Recession and correlations with economic indicators: Names and economic conditions," *Journal of Applied Social Psychology*, 46, no. 11, (2016): 663–670 (2016); Wentian Li, "Analyses of baby name popularity distribution in U.S. for the last 131 years," *Complexity* 18, no.1 (2012): 44-50.

81 Gabriel Rossman, "Now These Are the Names, Pt 2," *Code and Culture*, August 23, 2012, https://codeandculture.wordpress.com/2012/08/23/now-these-are-the-names-pt-2/.

82 Twenge, Abebe, and Campbell, "Fitting In or Standing Out."

83 On pronoun use as associated with relationship strength and stability, see Richard B. Slatcher, Simine Vazire, and James W. Pennebaker, "Am 'I' More Important than 'We'? Couples' Word Use in Instant Messages," *Personal Relationships* 15, no. 4 (2008): 407–24, doi:10.1111/j.1475-6811.2008.00207.x. For language use and depression, see Stephanie Rude, Eva-Maria Gortner, and James Pennebaker, "Language Use of Depressed and Depression-Vulnerable College Students," *Cognition and Emotion* 18, no. 8 (2004): 1121–33, doi:10.1080/02699930441000030. For evidence that pronouns more reliably predict depression than sad words, see Cindy Chung and James Pennebaker, "The Psychological Functions of Function Words," in *Social Communication*, ed. Klaus Fiedler, Frontiers of Social Psychology (New York: Psychology Press, 2007), 343–59. On pronouns and community trauma, see Michael Cohn, Matthias Mehl, and James Pennebaker, "Linguistic Markers of Psychological Change Surrounding September 11, 2001," *Psychological Science* 15, no. 10 (2004): 687–93; and Lori D. Stone and James W. Pennebaker, "Trauma in Real Time: Talking and Avoiding Online Conversations About the Death of Princess Diana," *Basic and Applied Social Psychology* 24, no. 3 (2002): 173–83, doi:10.1207/S15324834BASP2403_1.

84 James W. Pennebaker, *The Secret Life of Pronouns: What Our Words Say About Us* (New York: Bloomsbury, 2011).

85 Greenfield, "The Changing Psychology of Culture from 1800 Through 2000."

86 Twenge, Campbell, and Gentile, "Changes in Pronoun Use in American Books and the Rise of Individualism, 1960–2008."

87   Thomas Wolfe, "The 'Me' Decade and the Third Great Awakening," *New York* magazine, April 8, 2008, http://nymag.com/news/features/45938/.

88   The same basic U-shaped pattern is found for my/our and me/us, but not for he/she/it/they.

89   See endnote 1.4.

90   Technically, we refer here to the loadings of the various measures on the single factor to emerge from the longitudinal factor analysis.

CHAPTER 6: RACE AND THE AMERICAN "WE"

1   Given that our purpose in this chapter is to examine century-long trends in racial equality and compare those trends to the I-we-I curve, our discussion focuses narrowly on African Americans because of a lack of consistent and reliable data on other groups during our period of interest. According to the Pew Research Center, "for most of its history, the United States has had two major races, and until recent decades whites and blacks dominated the census racial categories" (Kim Parker et al., "Race and Multiracial Americans in the U.S. Census," *Pew Research Center's Social & Demographic Trends Project*, June 11, 2015, https://www.pewsocialtrends.org/2015/06/11/chapter-1-race-and-multiracial-americans-in-the-u-s-census/). There are critically important stories to be told about Native Americans, Asians, Latinos, and other peoples of color, who have struggled in unique ways to achieve equality and inclusion. Our purpose is not to diminish or ignore those histories, but rather to base our discussion on the one group for whom we have the most reliable full-century data. We will return briefly to the question of immigration and its relationship to the I-we-I curve in Chapter 8.

2   W. E. B. Du Bois, *The Souls of Black Folk* (Mineola, NY: Dover, 1994).

3   Henry Louis Gates, *Stony the Road: Reconstruction, White Supremacy, and the Rise of Jim Crow* (New York: Penguin, 2019), 8; *The African Americans: Many Rivers to Cross* (PBS Television, 2003).

4   Gates, *Stony the Road*, 26.

5   Georgia's poll tax (1877), South Carolina's eight-box law (1882), and Alabama's Sayre Law (1892) are but three examples.

6   Richard White, *The Republic for Which It Stands: The United States During Reconstruction and the Gilded Age, 1865–1896*, The Oxford History of the United States (unnumbered) (New York: Oxford University Press, 2017), 37–40.

7   Ibid., 101–2; Isabel Wilkerson, *The Warmth of Other Suns: The Epic Story of America's Great Migration* (New York: Vintage, 2011), 41–42.

8   David M. Oshinsky, *Worse than Slavery: Parchman Farm and the Ordeal of Jim Crow Justice* (New York: Free Press, 1996).

9   Wilkerson, *The Warmth of Other Suns*, 53–54.

10 United States Bureau of the Census Administration and Customer Services Division, "Statistical Abstract of the United States, 1999: The National Data Book," Superintendent of Documents, 1999, 847.

11 Thomas D. Snyder, *120 Years of American Education: A Statistical Portrait* (Washington, DC: Department of Education, Office of Educational Research and Improvement, National Center for Education Statistics, 1993), 14.

12 Ibid., 21.

13 William J. Collins and Robert A. Margo, "Race and Home Ownership: A Century-Long View," *Explorations in Economic History* 38, no. 1 (January 2001): 68–92, doi:10.1006/exeh.2000.0748.

14 Peter H. Lindert and Jeffrey G. Williamson, *Unequal Gains: American Growth and Inequality Since 1700*, Princeton Economic History of the Western World (Princeton: Princeton University Press, 2016), 190.

15 It is of course possible to interpret this metaphor as an implicit statement about power dynamics in a multiracial society. (*Who* was in the driver's seat, and *whose foot* was on or off the gas?) Our hope is that we will present enough evidence in this chapter to make clear our belief that both positive and negative change in racial equality and inclusion was driven both from the top down and the bottom up, and was a process that involved the intertwining actions of both white and black leaders and citizens. Certainly power and privilege are important parts of this story. However, "foot off the gas" is intended merely as an objective description of the shape of a statistical trend—a marked slowdown in progress toward racial equality that characterized the latter decades of the century.

16 As we have emphasized throughout this book, because our primary interest is in the rate, timing, and direction of change over the course of approximately 125 years of history, across chapters we have generally focused on *trends* rather than absolute measures. This is especially important to remember when attempting to understand our analysis of racial inequality. When we state that there was improvement or movement toward racial equality, in no way are we arguing that equality was achieved, that the improvement was sufficient, or that the pace of change was rapid enough. Our focus is rather on whether the trends were toward greater or lesser equality between the races, as well as when those trends began, accelerated, decelerated, or reversed—and what that might tell us about the relationship between the I-we-I curve and our nation's ongoing struggle with racial inequality.

17 Data for Figure 6.1 from National Center for Health Statistics, Centers for Disease Control and Prevention, "Death Rates and Life Expectancy at Birth." The spike in the early 1920s is probably attributable to lower than expected black mortality during the influenza pandemic of those years.

See Helene Økland and Svenn-Erik Mamelund, "Race and 1918 Influenza Pandemic in the United States: A Review of the Literature," *International Journal of Environmental Research ond Public Health* 16, no. 14 (2019): 2487. doi:10.3390/ijerph16142487.

18 See Anne Case and Angus Deaton, *Deaths of Despair and the Future of Capitalism* (Princeton NJ: Princeton University Press, 2020), chapter 5.

19 Health data is aggregated from tables in the following sources: W. Michael Byrd and Linda A. Clayton, *An American Health Dilemma: A Medical History of African Americans and the Problem of Race, Beginnings to 1900* (New York: Routledge, 2000); W. Michael Byrd and Linda A. Clayton, *An American Health Dilemma: Race, Medicine, and Health Care in the United States 1900–2000* (New York: Routledge, 2002); Leah Boustan and Robert A Margo, "Racial Differences in Health in Long-Run Perspective: A Brief Introduction," Working Paper 20765 (National Bureau of Economic Research, December 2014), doi:10.3386/w20765; Robert D. Grove and Alice M. Hetzel, *Vital Statistics Rates in the United States, 1940–1960* (Washington, DC: National Center for Health Statistics, 1968), 887, accessed October 22, 2019, https://www.cdc.gov/nchs/data/vsus/vsrates1940_60.pdf; National Center for Health Statistics, "Advance Report of Final Mortality Statistics, 1979," *Monthly Vital Statistics Report* 31, no. 6 (September 30, 1982); Robert N. Anderson and Sherry L. Murphy, "Report of Final Mortality Statistics, 1995," *Monthly Vital Statistics Report* 45, no. 11 (1997): 80; Donna L. Hoyert, Sherry L. Murphy, and Kenneth D. Kochanek, "Deaths: Final Data for 1999," *National Vital Statistics Report* 49, no. 9 (September 21, 2001); Arialdi M. Miniño et al., "Deaths: Final Data for 2000," *National Vital Statistics Report* 50, no. 15 (September 16, 2002).

20 James D. Anderson, *The Education of Blacks in the South, 1860–1935* (Chapel Hill: University of North Carolina Press, 1988), 151, 182.

21 Ibid., 189, 191, 236.

22 M. Richard Cramer, Ernest Q. Campbell, and Charles E. Bowerman, "Social Factors in Educational Achievement and Aspirations Among Negro Adolescents," Cooperative Research Project no. 1168 (U.S. Department of Health, Education, and Welfare, 1966), https://files.eric.ed.gov/fulltext/ED010837.pdf.

23 Robert A. Margo, *Race and Schooling in the South, 1880–1950: An Economic History*, (Chicago: University of Chicago Press, 1990), 10.

24 Anderson, *The Education of Blacks in the South, 1860–1935*, 138–39.

25 James R. Mingle, *Black Enrollment in Higher Education: Trends in the Nation and the South* (Atlanta: Southern Regional Education Board, 1978), 8.

26 Vincent P. Franklin, *The Education of Black Philadelphia: The Social and Educational History of a Minority Community, 1900–1950* (Philadelphia: University of Pennsylvania Press, 1979), 48–50.

27 Southern school quality data come from estimates and calculations in Margo, *Race and Schooling in the South*, 22; Lindert and Williamson, *Unequal Gains*, 188–89; David Card and Alan Krueger, "School Quality and Black-White Relative Earnings—A Direct Assessment," *Quarterly Journal of Economics* 107, no. 1 (1992): 151–200; John J. Donohue, James J. Heckman, and Petra E. Todd, "The Schooling of Southern Blacks: The Roles of Legal Activism and Private Philanthropy, 1910–1960," *The Quarterly Journal of Economics* 117, no. 1 (2002): 230, doi:10.1162/003355302753399490. The most significant and ubiquitous improvements occurred in the fifteen years after 1935, which Donohue, Heckman, and Todd attribute to NAACP litigation and private philanthropy.

28 Lindert and Williamson, *Unequal Gains*, 188–89.

29 Stephen Thernstrom et al., *America in Black and White: One Nation, Indivisible* (New York: Simon & Schuster, 1997), 85. For similar data on selected Southern states between 1940 and 1952, see Charles T. Clotfelter, *After Brown: The Rise and Retreat of School Desegregation* (Princeton: Princeton University Press, 2004), 16.

30 Margo, *Race and Schooling in the South*, 64.

31 Clotfelter, *After Brown*, 16.

32 For a discussion of Northern school segregation, see Gerald N. Rosenberg, *The Hollow Hope: Can Courts Bring About Social Change?*, 2nd ed., American Politics and Political Economy (Chicago: University of Chicago Press, 2008), 98–100; Franklin, *The Education of Black Philadelphia*, 37–47; and Davison M. Douglas, *Jim Crow Moves North: The Battle over Northern School Desegregation, 1865–1954*, Cambridge Historical Studies in American Law and Society (New York: Cambridge University Press, 2005), 139–51.

33 Anderson, *The Education of Blacks in the South*, 1988; Jeannie Oakes, *Keeping Track: How Schools Structure Inequality* (New Haven: Yale University Press, 1985); Jeannie Oakes and Gretchen Guiton, "Matchmaking: The Dynamics of High School Tracking Decisions," *American Educational Research Journal* 32, no. 1 (1995): 3–33, doi:10.3102/00028312032001003; Grace Kao and Jennifer S. Thompson, "Racial and Ethnic Stratification in Educational Achievement and Attainment," *Annual Review of Sociology* 29, no. 1 (2003): 417–42, doi:10.1146/annurev.soc.29.010202.100019.

34 For evidence on this and the subsequent paragraph, see Gavin Wright, *Sharing the Prize: The Economics of the Civil Rights Revolution in the American South* (Cambridge, MA: Belknap Press of Harvard University Press, 2013), esp. 162; Clotfelter, *After Brown*, esp. 56; and Gary Orfield and Chungmei Lee, "Historical Reversals, Accelerating Resegregation, and the Need for New Integration Strategies" (A report of the Civil Rights Project, UCLA: August 2007), 28 and 33. https://civilrightsproject.ucla.edu/research/k-12-education

/integration-and-diversity/historic-reversals-accelerating-resegregation
-and-the-need-for-new-integration-strategies-1/orfield-historic-reversals
-accelerating.pdf.

35   For trends in school integration after 1960, see Clotfelter, *After Brown*: 56;
     Gary Orfield and Chungmei Lee, "Historic Reversals, Accelerating Resegre-
     gation, and the Need for New Integration Strategies" (A report of the Civil
     Rights Project, UCLA, August 2007): 28, 33, https://civilrightsproject.ucla
     .edu/research/k-12-education/integration-and-diversity/historic-reversals
     -accelerating-resegregation-and-the-need-for-new-integration-strategies-1
     /orfield-historic-reversals-accelerating.pdf; and Wright, *Sharing the Prize*,
     161.

36   Longitudinal data is surprisingly scarce on measures of school quality, but
     statistics on modern disparities can be found here: Center for American
     Progress, "Students of Color Still Receiving Unequal Education," August 22,
     2012, https://www.americanprogress.org/issues/education-k-12/news/2012
     /08/22/32862/students-of-color-still-receiving-unequal-education/.

37   James P. Smith, "Race and Human Capital," *The American Economic Review* 74,
     no. 4 (1984): 685–98; Robert A. Margo, "Obama, Katrina, and the Persistence
     of Racial Inequality," *The Journal of Economic History* 76, no. 2 (2016): 301–41.

38   Margo, "Obama, Katrina, and the Persistence of Racial Inequality"; John J.
     Donohue III and James Heckman, "Continuous Versus Episodic Change:
     The Impact of Civil Rights Policy on the Economic Status of Blacks," Work-
     ing Paper 3849 (National Bureau of Economic Research, November 1991);
     Wright, *Sharing the Prize*; James P. Smith and Finis R. Welch, "Black Eco-
     nomic Progress After Myrdal," *Journal of Economic Literature* 27, no. 2 (1989):
     519–64; James P. Smith, "Race and Human Capital," *The American Economic
     Review* 74, no. 4 (1984): 685–98. The studies we cite in this section converge
     on the finding of greatest progress in black-white income equality in the
     1940–1970 period, while using a diverse array of metrics—per capita income,
     male wages, total male earnings including both workers and non-workers,
     and so forth.

39   Thomas N. Maloney, "Wage Compression and Wage Inequality Between
     Black and White Males in the United States, 1940–1960," *The Journal of Eco-
     nomic History* 54, no. 2 (1994): 358–81, doi:10.1017/S0022050700014522.

40   Lindert and Williamson, *Unequal Gains*, 191–92.

41   Robert Manduca, "Income Inequality and the Persistence of Racial Economic
     Disparities," *Sociological Science* 5 (2018): 182–205. See also Patrick J. Bayer
     and Kerwin Kofi Charles, "Divergent Paths: Structural Change, Economic
     Rank, and the Evolution of Black-White Earnings Differences, 1940-2014,"
     Working Paper 22797 (National Bureau of Economic Research, Inc, Septem-
     ber 2017), https://ideas.repec.org/p/nbr/nberwo/22797.html.

42   For a broadly comparable chart, see Margo, "Obama, Katrina, and the Persis-
      tence of Racial Inequality," Figure 1. See also Jennifer L. Hochschild, *Facing
      up to the American Dream: Race, Class, and the Soul of the Nation*, Princeton
      Studies in American Politics (Princeton: Princeton University Press, 1995);
      William A. Darity and Samuel L. Myers, *Persistent Disparity: Race and Eco-
      nomic Inequality in the United States Since 1945* (Northampton, UK: Edward
      Elgar Publishing, 1998); John Bound and Richard Freeman, "What Went
      Wrong? The Erosion of Relative Earnings and Employment Among Young
      Black Men in the 1980s," *Quarterly Journal of Economics* 107, no. 1 (Febru-
      ary 1992): 201–32; Amitabh Chandra, "Is the Convergence of the Racial
      Wage Gap Illusory?," Working Paper 9476 (National Bureau of Economic
      Research, February 2003), doi:10.3386/w9476; Derek Neal and Armin Rick,
      "The Prison Boom and the Lack of Black Progress After Smith and Welch,"
      Working Paper 20283 (National Bureau of Economic Research, July 2014),
      doi:10.3386/w20283; Patrick J. Bayer and Kerwin Kofi Charles, "Divergent
      Paths: A New Perspective on Earnings Differences Between Black and White
      Men Since 1940," SSRN Scholarly Paper (Rochester, NY: Social Science Re-
      search Network, July 5, 2018), https://papers.ssrn.com/abstract=3208755.
43   Margo, "Obama, Katrina, and the Persistence of Racial Inequality," 308.
44   Bayer and Charles, "Divergent Paths," (2018), 1461; Moritz Kuhn, Moritz
      Schularick, and Ulrike Steins, "Income and Wealth Inequality in America,
      1949–2016," IDEAS Working Paper Series from RePEc, 2018, doi:10.21034
      /iwp.9.
45   Bayer and Charles, "Divergent Paths" (2017); Neal and Rick, "The Prison
      Boom and the Lack of Black Progress After Smith and Welch"; Bruce West-
      ern and Becky Pettit, "Black-White Wage Inequality, Employment Rates,
      and Incarceration 1," *American Journal of Sociology* 111, no. 2 (2005): 553–78,
      doi:10.1086/432780; Bruce Western, *Punishment and Inequality in America*
      (New York: Russell Sage Foundation, 2006); Bruce Western, Steve Redburn,
      and Jeremy Travis, "The Growth of Incarceration in the United States: Ex-
      ploring Causes and Consequences," April 30, 2014, doi:10.17226/18613.
46   Hochschild, *Facing up to the American Dream*, 49; William J. Wilson, *The Truly
      Disadvantaged: The Inner City, the Underclass, and Public Policy*, 2nd ed. (Chi-
      cago: University of Chicago Press, 2012).
47   Sources for Figure 6.5: 1900–1970 rates from Steven Ruggles, Sarah Flood,
      Ronald Goeken, Josiah Grover, Erin Meyer, Jose Pacas, and Matthew Sobek,
      IPUMS USA: Version 9.0, 1% Samples, Minneapolis: IPUMS, 2019. 1973–
      2017 rates from US Census Bureau, Housing Survey and US Census Bu-
      reau, Current Population Survey/Housing Vacancy Survey. On black gains
      in homeownership during the Jim Crow era, see William J. Collins and Rob-
      ert A. Margo, "Race and Home Ownership from the End of the Civil War to

the Present," Working Paper 16665 (National Bureau of Economic Research, January 2011), doi:10.3386/w16665.

48 Kuhn, Schularick, and Steins, "Income and Wealth Inequality in America, 1949–2016." Note that Collins and Margo (cited above) argue that this trend takes a slightly different shape because they present the calculation as a gap, not a ratio. However, the underlying figures are the same.

49 Leah Platt Boustan and Robert A. Margo, "White Suburbanization and African-American Home Ownership, 1940–1980," Working Paper 16702 (National Bureau of Economic Research, August 2013), doi:10.3386/w16702.

50 Keeanga-Yamahtta Taylor, *Race for Profit: How Banks and the Real Estate Industry Undermined Black Homeownership, Justice, Power, and Politics* (Chapel Hill: University of North Carolina Press, 2019).

51 Gregory D. Squires, "Predatory Lending: Redlining in Reverse," *Shelterforce*, January 1, 2005, https://shelterforce.org/2005/01/01/predatory-lending-red lining-in-reverse/.

52 Laurie Goodman, Jun Zhu, and Rolf Pendall, "Are Gains in Black Home-ownership History?," *Urban Wire*, February 14, 2017, https://www.urban.org /urban-wire/are-gains-black-homeownership-history.

53 V. O. (Valdimir Orlando) Key, *Southern Politics in State and Nation* (New York: Alfred A. Knopf, 1950); J. Morgan Kousser, *The Shaping of Southern Politics: Suffrage Restriction and the Establishment of the One-Party South, 1880–1910*, Yale Historical Publications, Miscellany 102 (New Haven: Yale University Press, 1974); Laughlin McDonald, *A Voting Rights Odyssey: Black Enfranchisement in Georgia* (Cambridge: Cambridge University Press, 2003), 30–44.

54 Hanes Walton, *The African American Electorate: A Statistical History* (Thousand Oaks, CA: CQ Press, 2012).

55 Milton C. Sernett, *Bound for the Promised Land: African American Religion and the Great Migration*, C. Eric Lincoln Series on the Black Experience (Durham, NC: Duke University Press, 1997), 17.

56 Walton, *The African American Electorate*, 469–79.

57 Dianne M. Pinderhughes, *Race and Ethnicity in Chicago Politics: A Reexamination of Pluralist Theory* (Urbana: University of Illinois Press, 1987), 84, 86. Note that the naturalization process almost certainly had a negative impact on the voter registration rates of Polish and Italian immigrants.

58 Ibid., 77.

59 Ibid., 90–91. For a contemporary analysis that reached much the same conclusions, see Harold F. Gosnell, "The Chicago 'Black Belt' as a Political Battle-ground," *American Journal of Sociology* 39, no. 3 (November 1933): 329–41, doi:10.1086/216435.

60 Wright, *Sharing the Prize*; Figure 6.6 data from 1940 to 1969 are estimates from the Voter Education Project compiled from David J. Garrow, *Protest at*

Selma: Martin Luther King, Jr., and the Voting Rights Act of 1965 (New Haven: Yale University Press, 1978) 7, 11, 19, 189, 200; data from 1970 to 2000 are from the Census Bureau compiled in Stanley, *Voter Mobilization*, pp. 97; 1980–2008 data compiled in Bullock and Gaddie, *Triumph of Voting Right*s, pp. 380–82; 2010–2018 data US Census Bureau, Current Population Survey, P-20 Tables.

61 For another view, see Philip A. Klinkner, *The Unsteady March: The Rise and Decline of Racial Equality in America* (Chicago: University of Chicago Press, 1999), which argues that American racial progress has occurred only in ten- to fifteen-year bursts and then only under specific sets of circumstances: when war required black bodies, when fighting an enemy required egalitarian rhetoric, or when domestic political protest pressured for reforms. Progress, Klinkner notes, has always been followed by years of stagnation and decline, as the white elite reconsolidates its (entrenched) power, blocking reform and embracing inequalities.

62 Data for Figure 6.7 from Ida A. Brudnick and Jennifer E. Manning, *African American Members of the United States Congress: 1870–2018*, RL30378, Congressional Research Service; Jennifer E. Manning, Membership of the 116th Congress: A Profile, RL45583, Congressional Research Service. Evidence indicates that greater black political representation led to strong economic benefits in the South, especially greater provision of local public goods such as education. See Andrea Bernini, Giovanni Facchini, and Cecilia Testa, "Race, Representation and Local Governments in the US South: The Effect of the Voting Rights Act," SSRN Scholarly Paper (Rochester, NY: Social Science Research Network, March 1, 2018), https://papers.ssrn.com/abstract=3138836.

63 Henry Louis Gates, *Stony the Road*.

64 In 1953, under pressure from the NAACP, the racist show *Amos 'n' Andy*, which had been adapted from a radio show with white actors voicing black characters, was canceled. It showed in reruns until 1960, when CBS finally withdrew it altogether. *Sanford and Son* (1972), *Good Times* (1974), and *The Jeffersons* (1975) were the first TV shows featuring all-black casts.

65 Thomas J. Sugrue, *The Origins of the Urban Crisis: Race and Inequality in Postwar Detroit* (Princeton: Princeton University Press, 1996); Herman P. Miller, *Rich Man, Poor Man* (New York: Crowell, 1964), as cited in Charles Willie, "The Inclining Significance of Race," *Society* 15, no. 5 (1978): 14, doi:10.1007/BF02701608.

66 Trevon D. Logan and John M. Parman, "The National Rise in Residential Segregation, *Journal of Economic History* 77, no. 1 (March 2017): 127-170.

67 Richard Rothstein, *The Color of Law: A Forgotten History of How Our Government Segregated America* (New York: Liveright, 2017).

68 See: David M. Cutler, Edward L. Glaeser, and Jacob L. Vigdor, "The Rise and

Decline of the American Ghetto," *Journal of Political Economy* 107, no. 3 (June 1999): 455–506, doi:10.1086/250069. The authors suggest that there are basically three possible ways that segregation can develop: a "port of entry" model, in which black residents prefer to live in majority-black neighborhoods; "collective action racism," in which white residents use formal barriers to restrict black access to certain neighborhoods; and "decentralized racism," in which white residents pay a premium to live in majority-white neighborhoods, generating white flight and pricing black residents out. Using data on average housing costs, they find that the collective action racism model best explains mid-century segregation, on the grounds that black residents paid *more* for equivalent housing than white residents (we would expect them to pay less if they were being priced out of white neighborhoods) and that new black migrants paid no more than longtime residents (we would expect them to pay more in the port of entry model). They find that by 1990 this pattern had reversed, meaning that formal barriers to segregation had given way to the decentralized racism model.

69   Ibid.

70   Key texts on the development of segregated housing in the urban North, particularly in response to the two Great Migrations, include: Arnold R. Hirsch, *Making the Second Ghetto: Race and Housing in Chicago, 1940–1960*, Historical Studies of Urban America (Chicago: University of Chicago Press, 1998); Amanda I. Seligman, *Block by Block: Neighborhoods and Public Policy on Chicago's West Side*, Historical Studies of Urban America (Chicago: University of Chicago Press, 2005); Kenneth T. Jackson, *Crabgrass Frontier: The Suburbanization of the United States* (New York: Oxford University Press, 1985); Sugrue, *The Origins of the Urban Crisis*; Robert O. Self, *American Babylon: Race and the Struggle for Postwar Oakland*, Politics and Society in Twentieth-Century America (Princeton: Princeton University Press, 2003); and Kevin Michael Kruse, *White Flight: Atlanta and the Making of Modern Conservatism*, Politics and Society in Twentieth-Century America (Princeton: Princeton University Press, 2005).

71   Sources for Figure 6.8: Admission rates are from Patrick A. Langan, Race of Prisoners Admitted to State and Federal Institutions, 1926–86, NCJ-125618 (Washington, DC: US Department of Justice, Bureau of Justice Statistics, 1999). Imprisonment rates are from US Department of Justice, Bureau of Justice Statistics, Correctional Populations in the United States Series, 1985–2016 and Prisoners Series, 1980–2017. Population estimates are from national intercensal tables, 1900–2010, US Census Bureau. Figure 6.8 splices the data series for admission rates and imprisonment rates to provide full coverage from 1926 to 2017. Admission rates refer to the number of people admitted to correctional institutions each year and imprisonment rates refer to the total number of people behind bars in each year. Imprisonment rates

are higher than admission rates because prisoners with longer sentences are counted as part of the prison population for multiple consecutive years. Thus, imprisonment rates are a more accurate representation of the full prison population at any given time, but admission rates are more likely to show the effects of prosecutorial reform measures.

72   Henry Louis Gates and Isabel Wilkerson, "A Conversation with Isabel Wilkerson: On America's Great Migration," *Du Bois Review: Social Science Research on Race* 7, no. 2 (Fall 2010): 257–69, doi:10.1017/S1742058X10000433.

73   Zellmer R. Pettet and Charles E. Hall, *Negroes in the United States, 1920–32* (Washington, DC: Bureau of the Census, 1935), http://archive.org/details /negroesinuniteds1920pett.

74   Transcript, *Remembering Jim Crow*, accessed October 23, 2019, http://ameri canradioworks.publicradio.org/features/remembering/transcript.html.

75   Rothstein, *The Color of Law*; Matt Lassiter, "De Jure/De Facto Segregation: The Long Shadow of a National Myth," in *The Myth of Southern Exceptionalism*, ed. Matt Lassiter and Joseph Crestino (New York: Oxford University Press, 2010).

76   Emmett J. Scott, *Negro Migration During the War*, American Negro, His History and Literature (New York: Arno, 1969), 16–18.

77   The Great Migration did, however, introduce economic competition between Northern blacks and new migrants. For the argument that economic gains were not evenly distributed among blacks in the North, see Leah Boustan, *Competition in the Promised Land: Black Migrants in Northern Cities and Labor Markets*, NBER Series on Long-Term Factors in Economic Development (Princeton: Princeton University Press, 2017).

78   Reynolds Farley, *The Color Line and the Quality of Life in America*, Population of the United States in the 1980s (New York: Russell Sage Foundation, 1987), 302.

79   Cheryl Lynn Greenberg, *To Ask for an Equal Chance: African Americans in the Great Depression*, African American History Series (Lanham, MD: Rowman & Littlefield, 2009), 13, 18; James T. Patterson, *Grand Expectations: The United States, 1945–1974, The Oxford History of the United States*, vol. 10 (New York: Oxford University Press, 1996), 387–88.

80   Scott, *Negro Migration during the War*, 79–85.

81   Anderson, *The Education of Blacks in the South*, 202–3.

82   Wilkerson, *The Warmth of Other Suns*, 527.

83   Ibid., 45–46.

84   Ibid., 13.

85   Isabel Wilkerson, "The Long-Lasting Legacy of the Great Migration," *Smithsonian*, accessed October 23, 2019, https://www.smithsonianmag.com /history/long-lasting-legacy-great-migration-180960118/.

86 Most scholars have argued that the benefits of migration for those who left the South were substantial. See Larry H. Long and Lynne R. Heltman, "Migration and Income Differences Between Black and White Men in the North," *American Journal of Sociology* 80, no. 6 (1975): 1391–1409, doi:10.1086/225996; Stanley Lieberson and Christy Wilkinson, "A Comparison Between Northern and Southern Black Residing in the North," *Demography* 13, no. 2 (1976): 199–224, doi:10.2307/2060801; Stanley Lieberson, "A Reconsideration of the Income Differences Found Between Migrants and Northern-Born Blacks," *American Journal of Sociology* 83, no. 4 (1978): 940–66; Stewart E. Tolnay, "The Great Migration Gets Underway: A Comparison of Black Southern Migrants and Nonmigrants in the North, 1920," *Social Science Quarterly* 82, no. 2 (2001): 235–52, doi:10.1111/0038-4941.00020; Christine Leibbrand et al., "Neighborhood Attainment Outcomes for Children of the Great Migration 1," *American Journal of Sociology* 125, no. 1 (2019): 141–83, doi:10.1086/703682. However, others have noted that migrants only reaped relatively modest rewards from relocating: Suzanne C. Eichenlaub, Stewart E. Tolnay, and J. Trent Alexander, "Moving Out but Not Up: Economic Outcomes in the Great Migration," *American Sociological Review* 75, no. 1 (2010): 101–25, doi:10.1177/0003122409357047; Robert Boyd, "Black Women in the 'Black Metropolis' of the Early Twentieth Century: The Case of Professional Occupations," *Journal of Sociology and Social Welfare* 40, no. 2 (2013): 103–17. And when it comes to health specifically, Dan A. Black et al., "The Impact of the Great Migration on Mortality of African Americans: Evidence from the Deep South," *American Economic Review* 105, no. 2 (February 2015): 477–503, doi:10.1257/aer.20120642, have argued that migration to Northern cities was actually detrimental to the longevity of blacks born in the Deep South.

87 Jessica Gordon Nembhard, *Collective Courage: A History of African American Cooperative Economic Thought and Practice* (University Park: Penn State University Press, 2014); Cedric J. Robinson, *Black Movements in America*, Revolutionary Thought/Radical Movements (New York: Routledge, 1997); Gates, *Stony the Road*; Wilkerson, *The Warmth of Other Suns*.

88 Vanessa Northington Gamble, *Making a Place for Ourselves: The Black Hospital Movement, 1920–1945* (New York: Oxford University Press, 1995); Leah Boustan and Robert A. Margo, "Racial Differences in Health in the United States: A Long-Run Perspective," in *The Oxford Handbook of Economics and Human Biology* (Oxford: Oxford University Press, 2016), 742; Edward Beardsley, *A History of Neglect: Health Care for Blacks and Mill Workers in the Twentieth-Century South* (Knoxville: University of Tennessee Press, 1987), 114–16.

89 Anderson, *The Education of Blacks in the South*, 153.

90 Daniel Aaronson and Bhashkar Mazumder, "The Impact of Rosenwald Schools on Black Achievement," *Journal of Political Economy* 119, no. 5 (October 2011): 821–88, doi:10.1086/662962.

91 Anderson, *The Education of Blacks in the South*, 80–83; Robert A. Margo, *Race and Schooling in the South, 1880–1950: An Economic History*. Both Anderson and Margo point out, however, that black communities still retained a significant voice in the school expansion process in this period—in the case of Rosenwald schools because of community participation in both funding and physical construction of the schools, and more generally as a result of the political leverage black communities gained as outmigration from the South produced labor shortages, as well as pressure from the NAACP.

92 Werner Troesken, *Water, Race, and Disease*, NBER Series on Long-Term Factors in Economic Development (Cambridge, MA: MIT Press, 2004); Boustan and Margo, "Racial Differences in Health in the United States"; David M. Cutler and Grant Miller, "The Role of Public Health Improvements in Health Advances: The Twentieth-Century United States," *Demography* 42, no. 1 (February 2005): 1–22; Marcella Alsan and Claudia Goldin, "Watersheds in Child Mortality: The Role of Effective Water and Sewerage Infrastructure, 1880 to 1920," Working Paper 21263 (National Bureau of Economic Research, May 2018), doi:10.3386/w21263.

93 David McBride, *Integrating the City of Medicine: Blacks in Philadelphia Health Care, 1910–1965* (Philadelphia: Temple University Press, 1989), 43–45.

94 Beardsley, *A History of Neglect*, 119–26.

95 Vincent P. Franklin, *The Education of Black Philadelphia: The Social and Educational History of a Minority Community, 1900–1950* (Philadelphia: University of Pennsylvania Press, 1979), 48–50.

96 Beardsley, *A History of Neglect*, 134–37.

97 Byrd and Clayton, *An American Health Dilemma*; Beardsley, *A History of Neglect*, 157–63; McBride, *Integrating the City of Medicine*, 129–30.

98 Beardsley, *A History of Neglect*, 157–63; 177–80; Karen Kruse Thomas, *Deluxe Jim Crow: Civil Rights and American Health Policy, 1935–1954* (Athens: University of Georgia Press, 2011); Byrd and Clayton, *An American Health Dilemma*, 2000, 143, 148–49.

99 Byrd and Clayton, *An American Health Dilemma*, 142.

100 Beardsley, *A History of Neglect*, 169–71.

101 Such accounts include Jennifer A. Delton, *Rethinking the 1950s: How Anticommunism and the Cold War Made America Liberal* (New York: Cambridge University Press, 2013); Mary L. Dudziak, *Cold War Civil Rights: Race and the Image of American Democracy*, Politics and Society in Twentieth-Century America (Princeton: Princeton University Press, 2000).

102 J. D. Hall, "The Long Civil Rights Movement and the Political Uses of the Past," *Journal of American History* 91, no. 4 (2005): 1233–63, doi:10.2307 /3660172.

103 Dorian Lynskey, "How the Fight to Ban *The Birth of a Nation* Shaped American History," *Slate*, March 31, 2015, https://slate.com/culture/2015/03 /the-birth-of-a-nation-how-the-fight-to-censor-d-w-griffiths-film-shaped -american-history.html.

104 National Humanities Center, "NAACP Silent Protest Parade, flyer & memo, July 1917," https://nationalhumanitiescenter.org/pds/maai2/forward/text4 /silentprotest.pdf.

105 Olivia B. Waxman, "The Forgotten March That Started the National Civil Rights Movement Took Place 100 Years Ago," *Time*, accessed October 24, 2019, https://time.com/4828991/east-saint-louis-riots-1917/.

106 Paul Finkelman, *Encyclopedia of African American History, 1896 to the Present: From the Age of Segregation to the Twenty-first Century* (Oxford: Oxford University Press, 2009), 81.

107 For the argument that FDR repeatedly allowed Southern Democrats to write discriminatory clauses into New Deal legislation in exchange for its passage, see Ira Katznelson, *Fear Itself: The New Deal and the Origins of Our Time* (New York: Liveright, 2013). Yet Katznelson also acknowledges that however limited by these clauses, the New Deal nonetheless had the effect of bringing African Americans into the American "we" as never before.

108 David M. Kennedy, *Freedom from Fear: The American People in Depression and War, 1929–1945*, The Oxford History of the United States, vol. 9 (New York: Oxford University Press, 1999), 378.; Christopher Linsin, "Something More than a Creed: Mary Mcleod Bethune's Aim of Integrated Autonomy as Director of Negro Affairs," *Florida Historical Quarterly* 76, no. 1 (1997): 20–41.

109 Eric Schickler, *Racial Realignment: The Transformation of American Liberalism, 1932–1965*, Princeton Studies in American Politics (Princeton: Princeton University Press, 2016).; Eric Schickler, Kathryn Pearson, and Brian D. Feinstein, "Congressional Parties and Civil Rights Politics from 1933 to 1972," *The Journal of Politics* 72, no. 3 (2010): 672–89; Jeffrey A. Jenkins and Justin Peck, "Building Toward Major Policy Change: Congressional Action on Civil Rights, 1941–1950," *Law and History Review* 31, no. 1 (2013): 139–98; Hans Noel, "The Coalition Merchants: The Ideological Roots of the Civil Rights Realignment," *The Journal of Politics* 74, no. 1 (2012): 156–73, doi:10.1017 /S0022381611001186.

110 Patterson, *Grand Expectations*, 20.

111 American Public Media, *Remembering Jim Crow*, Part Two, American RadioWorks, http://americanradioworks.publicradio.org/features/remembering /transcript.html.

112 Patterson, *Grand Expectations*, 25.

113 Kennedy, *Freedom from Fear*, 765–68.

114 In July 1950, UNESCO issued "The Race Question," the first of four statements to clarify what scientists actually knew about race, and to declare a moral condemnation of racism. It was signed by leading researchers at the time in multiple academic disciplines.

115 Delton, *Rethinking the 1950s*, 97.

116 "Executive Order 9981: Establishing the President's Committee on Equality of Treatment and Opportunity In the Armed Forces," *U.S. Equal Employment Opportunity Commission*, accessed November 22, 2019, https://www.eeoc.gov/eeoc/history/35th/thelaw/eo-9981.html.

117 Gunnar Myrdal, *An American Dilemma: The Negro Problem and Modern Democracy*, 20th anniversary ed. (New York: Harper & Row, 1962), Preface, xviiii.

118 Patterson, *Grand Expectations*, 386–87.

119 DC Editorial, "Superman: A Classic Message Restored," *DC*, August 25, 2017, https://www.dccomics.com/blog/2017/08/25/superman-a-classic-message-restored.

120 Patterson, *Grand Expectations*, 386–87.

121 Quoted in ibid., 413.

122 According to Patterson (ibid.), at the end of Eisenhower's administration, only 28 percent of Southern blacks could vote. In Mississippi it was a dismal 5 percent.

123 Ibid., 474–75.

124 LBJ Presidential Library, "President Johnson's Special Message to the Congress: The American Promise," March 15, 1965, http://www.lbjlibrary.org/lyndon-baines-johnson/speeches-films/president-johnsons-special-message-to-the-congress-the-american-promise.

125 The scholarly literature on changes in American racial attitudes is massive. Some key sources include Howard Schuman, Charlotte Steeh, Lawrence Bobo, Maria Krysan, *Racial Attitudes in America: Trends and Interpretations*, rev. ed. (Cambridge: Harvard University Press, 1997); Lawrence D. Bobo, James R. Kluegel, and Ryan A. Smith, "Laissez-faire Racism: The Crystallization of a Kinder, Gentler Anti-Black Ideology," in *Racial Attitudes in the 1990s: Continuity and Change*, eds. Steven A. Tuch and Jack K. Martin (Westport, CT: Praeger, 1997): 15–44; Donald R. Kinder and Howard Schuman, "Racial Attitudes: Developments and Divisions in Survey Research," chap. 13 in *A Telescope on Society: Survey Research and Social Science at the University of Michigan and Beyond*, eds. James House et al. (Ann Arbor: University of Michigan Press, 2004); David O. Sears and P. J. Henry, "Over Thirty Years Later: A Contemporary Look at Symbolic Racism," *Advances in Experimental Social*

Psychology 37 (2005): 95–150; Lawrence D. Bobo, Camille Z. Charles, Maria Krysan, and Alicia D. Simmons, "The Real Record on Racial Attitudes," in *Social Trends in American Life: Finds from the General Social Survey since 1972*, ed. Peter V. Marsden (Princeton: Princeton University Press, 2012), 38–83; Tyrone A. Forman and Amanda E. Lewis, "Beyond Prejudice? Young Whites' Racial Attitudes in Post–Civil Rights America, 1976–2000," *American Behavioral Scientist* 59 (2015): 1394–1428. Though scholars generally agree that "traditional" white racism had mostly faded by the 1970s, they disagree about what replaced it. Some refer to "symbolic" racism and some to "unconscious" or "implicit" racism. When looking at implicit rather than explicit forms of racial prejudice, scholars have found that white respondents exhibited much higher degrees of negative attitudes and a much slower progression toward positive attitudes. Although this data does not stretch back far enough for us to identify a historical trend, it nonetheless indicates higher levels of negative racial attitudes than earlier forms of measurement reveal. See, for example, Lawrence D. Bobo, "Racial Attitudes and Relations at the Close of the Twentieth Century," in *America Becoming: Racial Trends and Their Consequences*, vol. 1 (Washington, DC: National Academies Press, 2001), 276–78, doi:10.17226/9599. Figure 6.9 draws on Schuman et al., *Racial Attitudes in America*, 104–108, and Maria Krysan and Sarah Moberg, *A Portrait of African American and White Racial Attitudes* (University of Illinois Institute of Government and Public Affairs (September 9, 2016): 2, http://igpa.uillinois.edu/files/reports/A-Portrait-of-Racial-Attitudes.pdf.

126 Andrew Kohut, "50 Years Ago: Mixed Views about Civil Rights but Support for Selma Demonstrators," Pew Research Center, accessed October 24, 2019, https://www.pewresearch.org/fact-tank/2015/03/05/50-years-ago-mixed-views-about-civil-rights-but-support-for-selma-demonstrators/.

127 LBJ Presidential Library, "President Johnson's Special Message to the Congress: The American Promise.".March 15, 1965,. http://www.lbjlibrary.org/lyndon-baines-johnson/speeches-films/president-johnsons-special-message-to-the-congress-the-american-promise. "Lyndon Johnson Gave a Speech about Legislation Giving Every American the Right to Vote—LBJ Presidential Library," accessed October 24, 2019, http://www.lbjlibrary.org/lyndon-baines-johnson/speeches-films/president-johnsons-special-message-to-the-congress-the-american-promise.

128 Andrew Kohut, "50 Years Ago: Mixed Views about Civil Rights but Support for Selma Demonstrators."

129 Doug McAdam and Karina Kloos, *Deeply Divided: Racial Politics and Social Movements in Post-War America: Racial Politics and Social Movements in Post-War America* (Oxford University Press, 2014), 104–5.

130 For a list of Civil Rights Martyrs, see Southern Poverty Law Center's Civil

Rights   Memorial: https://www.splcenter.org/what-we-do/civil-rights-me
morial/civil-rights-martyrs.

131 Patterson, *Grand Expectations*, 685–86.

132 McAdam and Kloos, *Deeply Divided*, 109.

133 For a detailed discussion of the Kerner Commission Report, see Fred R. Harris and Lynn A. Curtis, *Healing Our Divided Society: Investing in America Fifty
Years after the Kerner Report* (Philadelphia: Temple University Press, 2018). Evidence for why exactly Johnson rejected the commission's recommendations
is scant, but some discussion of this fact can be found in these two sources:
Lester Graham, "The Kerner Commission and Why Its Recommendations
Were Ignored," July 28, 2017, https://www.michiganradio.org/post/kerner
-commission-and-why-its-recommendations-were-ignored; Alice George,
"The 1968 Kerner Commission Got It Right, But Nobody Listened," *Smithsonian*, March 1, 2018, https://www.smithsonianmag.com/smithsonian-insti
tution/1968-kerner-commission-got-it-right-nobody-listened-180968318/.

134 Patterson, *Grand Expectations*, 704.

135 McAdam and Kloos, *Deeply Divided*, 104–6.

136 Schuman et al., *Racial Attitudes in America*, 123–25. One exception to this opposition is that open housing legislation, by contrast, has seen its levels of
support rise consistently. Schuman et al. ascribe this exception to its being an
extremely close analogue to the abstract principle of equal opportunity and
nondiscrimination, in contrast to a policy like school integration, which may
call to mind "forced" busing programs.

137 Ibid., 172–75. For updated data showing a continuation of this trend, see
M. Krysan and S. Moberg, "Trends in Racial Attitudes," August 25, 2016,
http://igpa.uillinois.edu/programs/racial-attitudes. See also Maria Krysan
and Sarah Moberg, "A Portrait of African American and White Racial Attitudes," University of Illinois Institute of Government and Public Affairs
(September 9, 2016): 2. http://igpa.uillinois.edu/files/reports/A-Portrait-of
-Racial-Attitudes.pdf. This website offers a very useful update of the trends
reported in Howard Schuman et al., *Racial Attitudes in America*.

138 Schuman et al., *Racial Attitudes in America*, 140–43.

139 Ibid., 156–59.

140 National Center for Health Statistics, "Health, United States, 2017—Data
Finder: Table 15" (Hyattsville, MD: U.S. Department of Health and Human
Services,   2018),   https://www.cdc.gov/nchs/hus/contents2017.htm#Table
_015.

141 Corinne A. Riddell, Sam Harper, and Jay S. Kaufman, "Trends in Differences
in US Mortality Rates Between Black and White Infants," *JAMA Pediatrics*
171, no. 9 (2017): 911–913, doi:10.1001/jamapediatrics.2017.1365.

142 Valerie Wilson, "Black Workers' Wages Have Been Harmed by Both Widening

Racial Wage Gaps and the Widening Productivity-Pay Gap," *Economic Policy Institute*, accessed October 24, 2019, https://www.epi.org/publication/black -workers-wages-have-been-harmed-by-both-widening-racial-wage-gaps -and-the-widening-productivity-pay-gap/; Manduca, "Income Inequality and the Persistence of Racial Economic Disparities"; Eileen Patten, "Racial, Gender Wage Gaps Persist in U.S. despite Some Progress," *Pew Research Center*, accessed October 24, 2019, https://www.pewresearch.org/fact-tank/2016/07 /01/racial-gender-wage-gaps-persist-in-u-s-despite-some-progress/; Elise Gould, "The State of American Wages 2017: Wages Have Finally Recovered from the Blow of the Great Recession but Are Still Growing Too Slowly and Unequally," *Economic Policy Institute*, accessed October 24, 2019, https://www .epi.org/publication/the-state-of-american-wages-2017-wages-have-finally -recovered-from-the-blow-of-the-great-recession-but-are-still-growing -too-slowly-and-unequally/; Bayer and Charles, "Divergent Paths," (2018); Rodney E. Hero and Morris E. Levy, "The Racial Structure of Economic Inequality in the United States: Understanding Change and Continuity in an Era of 'Great Divergence,'" *Social Science Quarterly* 97, no. 3 (2016): 491–505, doi:10.1111/ssqu.12327.

143 Alvin Chang, "The Data Proves That School Segregation Is Getting Worse," *Vox*, March 5, 2018, https://www.vox.com/2018/3/5/17080218/school-segre gation-getting-worse-data.

144 Nikole Hannah-Jones, "The Resegregation of Jefferson County," *The New York Times*, September 6, 2017, sec. Magazine, https://www.nytimes.com /2017/09/06/magazine/the-resegregation-of-jefferson-county.html.

145 Robert Reinhold, "Poll Indicates More Tolerance, Less Hope," *New York Times*, February 26, 1978, https://www.nytimes.com/1978/02/26/archives /poll-indicates-more-tolerance-less-hope.html.

146 Bobo et al, "The *Real* Record on Racial Attitudes," 70.

147 Donald Kinder and HowardSchuman, "Racial Attitudes," 379, citing Mary Jackman, *The Velvet Glove: Paternalism and Conflict in Gender, Class, and Race Relations* (Berkeley: University of California Press, 1994).

148 Adam Gopnik, "How the South Won the Civil War," April 1, 2019, https:// www.newyorker.com/magazine/2019/04/08/how-the-south-won-the-civil -war. Gopnik's comment is in direct reference to the difference between the lot of black Americans before and after Reconstruction, but it is a character- ization that proves relevant in later eras as well.

149 Schulman, *The Seventies*, 77.

150 Charles L. Ballard, "The Fall and Rise of Income Inequality in the United States: Economic Trends and Political Economy Explanations," unpublished ms., Michigan State University, October 18, 2017, 59.

151 McAdam and Kloos, *Deeply Divided*.

152   Schulman, *The Seventies*, 76–77. Two additional sources promoting the general view that the rights revolutions of the 1960s effectively caused the shattering of America's "we" include Jefferson Cowie, *The Great Exception: The New Deal and the Limits of American Politics* (Princeton: Princeton University Press, 2017) and Jefferson Cowie, *Stayin' Alive: The 1970s and the Last Days of the Working Class* (New York: New Press, 2010).

153   St. Clair Drake and Horace R. Cayton, *Black Metropolis: A Study of Negro Life in a Northern City*, revised and enlarged ed. (Chicago: University of Chicago Press, 1993), 101.

CHAPTER 7: GENDER AND THE AMERICAN "WE"

1   Intersectionality is the idea that an individual who is a member of multiple historically excluded groups may endure overlapping forms of discrimination that magnify their experience of disadvantage. For more on the concept and consequences of intersectionality, see Angela Y. Davis, *Women, Race, and Class* (New York: Vintage, 1983); Kimberle Crenshaw, "Demarginalizing the Intersection of Race and Sex: A Black Feminist Critique of Antidiscrimination Doctrine, Feminist Theory and Antiracist Politics," *University of Chicago Legal Forum*, vol. 1989, Article 8; *The Combahee River Collective Statement*, https:// americanstudies.yale.edu/sites/default/files/files/Keyword%20Coalition _Readings.pdf.

2   We further acknowledge that gender itself is an increasingly contested form of categorization.

3   Kate Clarke Lemay, ed., *Votes for Women! A Portrait of Persistence* (Princeton: Princeton University Press, 2019), 6–7.

4   Ibid., 5.

5   Among scholars, the idea that feminist activism happened in "waves" is a contested framework (as is exactly when the first wave began). We will address this issue throughout the chapter, ultimately siding with the historians who question the validity and utility of such a narrative.

6   Christine Stansell, *The Feminist Promise: 1792 to the Present* (New York: Modern Library, 2011), 149.

7   Francine D. Blau and Anne E. Winkler, *The Economics of Women, Men, and Work*, 8th ed. (New York: Oxford University Press, 2018), 95.

8   Claudia Goldin, "The Work and Wages of Single Women, 1870–1920," *Journal of Economic History* 40, no. 1 (1980): 81–88; Claudia Goldin, "The Quiet Revolution That Transformed Women's Employment, Education, and Family," *American Economic Review* 96, no. 2 (May 2006): 1–21, doi:10.1257 /000282806777212350.

9   Stansell, *The Feminist Promise*, 150.

10   For more detail on the intersection of race and early-twentieth-century

American feminism, see Estelle B. Freedman, *No Turning Back: The History of Feminism and the Future of Women*, 1st ed. (New York: Ballantine, 2002), 73–81; Martha S. Jones, "The Politics of Black Womanhood, 1848–2008," in *Votes for Women!: A Portrait of Persistence*, ed. Kate Clarke Lemay (Princeton: Princeton University Press, 2019), 6–7.

11   The amendment itself applied to all women but, as we discussed in Chapter 6, ongoing racial discrimination meant that many black women were de facto excluded from the vote.

12   Stansell, *The Feminist Promise*, 154.

13   Claudia Goldin, "A Grand Gender Convergence: Its Last Chapter," *American Economic Review* 104, no. 4 (April 2014): 1091–1119, doi:10.1257/aer .104.4.1091.

14   Historians continue to debate how broadly the second narrative of steady progress applies and whether it adequately acknowledges the slower progress made by women who continue to be marginalized by their race and class.

15   Sources for Figure 7.1: Historical Statistics of the United States, Millennial Edition Bc258-264, http://dx.doi.org/10.1017/ISBN-9780511132971; Trends in High School Dropout and Completion Rates in the United States: 2014 (National Center for Educational Statistics, US Department of Education, 2018), https://nces.ed.gov/pubs2018/2018117.pdf.

16   Nancy Woloch, *Women and the American Experience*, 1st ed. (New York: Alfred A. Knopf, 1984), 543; Susan B. Carter and Mark Prus, "The Labor Market and the American High School Girl, 1890–1928," *The Journal of Economic History* 42, no. 1 (March 1982): 164, doi:10.1017/S0022050700027030.

17   Claudia Goldin, "The Rising (and Then Declining) Significance of Gender," Working Paper 8915 (National Bureau of Economic Research) NBER Working Paper Series, April 2002, 6–9, doi:10.3386/w8915.

18   Figures 7.2 and 7.3 sources: US Department of Commerce, Census Bureau, U.S. Census of Population: 1960, vol. I, part 1; J. K. Folger and C. B. Nam, *Education of the American Population* (1960 Census Monograph); Current Population Reports, Series P-20, various years; Current Population Survey, Annual Social and Economic Supplement, 1970 through 2018; National Center for Education Statistics, Table 104.10. The fraction of all women who became college graduates did not actually fall in the 1950s, but it did not keep up with the rapidly growing share of men who became college graduates. For an interesting overview of women's choices about education, marriage, family, and employment in the postwar era, see Jessica Weiss, *To Have and to Hold: Marriage, the Baby Boom, and Social Change* (Chicago: University of Chicago Press, 2000), which draws on interviews with American couples to create a firsthand account of gender relations in this period.

19 Martha May, *Women's Roles in Twentieth-Century America*, Women's Roles in American History (Westport, CT: Greenwood Press, 2009), 98–99.

20 Blau and Winkler, *The Economics of Women, Men, and Work*, 197.

21 Ibid., 196–99.

22 Goldin, "The Quiet Revolution That Transformed Women's Employment, Education, and Family," 18–19.

23 For more detail on the idea that slow and steady "evolutions" prepared the way for more precipitous "revolutions" later in the century, see Goldin, "The Quiet Revolution That Transformed Women's Employment, Education, and Family."

24 As some scholars have pointed out, there is controversy surrounding how exactly to define and measure women's "work." Many historically female forms of work such as taking in lodgers, farm work, and domestic manufacturing would not be included in typical "labor force" measures. However, this nonwage work is incredibly hard to estimate, which is why, when examining gender inequality, it is largely agreed that using "market work," or work in the wage labor marketplace, is most appropriate. See, for example, Michael B. Katz, Mark J. Stern, and James J. Fader, "Women and the Paradox of Economic Inequality in the Twentieth-Century," *Journal of Social History* 39, no. 1 (2005): 65–88.

25 Claudia Goldin has shown that the one exception to this slow and steady trend is "the labor force participation rate for married women (20 to 44 years old) with a child under the age of one year, which soared from 0.20 in 1973 to 0.62 in 2000." Goldin, "The Quiet Revolution That Transformed Women's Employment, Education, and Family," 8.

26 U.S. Department of Labor, Bureau of Labor Statistics, Table A-1, Employment Status of the Civilian Population by Sex and Age, https://www.bls.gov/news.release/empsit.t01.htm.

27 For example, African American women worked at higher rates early on, which is often attributed to the fact that under Jim Crow African American males were not able to earn enough to support their families, meaning that many wives worked out of necessity. Black women were also hardest hit in terms of unemployment during the Depression, and saw their steepest gains in labor force participation after 1950.

28 Susan B. Carter, "Labor Force," in *Historical Statistics of the United States: Earliest Times to the Present*, ed. Susan B. Carter et al. (New York: Cambridge University Press, 2006), 2–26.

29 Goldin, "The Rising (and Then Declining) Significance of Gender," 36. See also Claudia Goldin, *Understanding the Gender Gap: An Economic History of American Women*, NBER Series on Long-Term Factors in Economic Development (New York: Oxford University Press, 1990), chaps. 3, 4.

30 Freedman, *No Turning Back: The History of Feminism and the Future of Women*, 176–79.

31 Blau and Winkler, *The Economics of Women, Men, and Work*, 173.

32 Elise Gould, "The State of American Wages 2017: Wages Have Finally Recovered from the Blow of the Great Recession but Are Still Growing Too Slowly and Unequally" (Economic Policy Institute, March 1, 2018).

33 "Equal Pay Day: What You Need to Know About the Gender Wage Gap in 2017," *FemChat*, April 4, 2017, https://femchat-iwpr.org/2017/04/04/equal-pay-day-2017/.

34 Ariane Hegewisch and Heidi Hartmann, "The Gender Wage Gap: 2018 Earnings Differences by Race and Ethnicity," March 2019, https://iwpr.org/wp-content/uploads/2019/03/C478_Gender-Wage-Gap-in-2018.pdf.

35 See Figure 2, Ariane Hegewisch et al., "Separate and Not Equal? Gender Segregation in the Labor Market and the Gender Wage Gap," September 2010, https://iwpr.org/wp-content/uploads/wpallimport/files/iwpr-export/publications/C377.pdf.

36 Julie Brines, "Economic Dependency, Gender, and the Division of Labor at Home," *American Journal of Sociology* 100, no. 3 (1994): 652–88, doi:10.1086/230577.

37 Claudia Goldin et al., "The Expanding Gender Earnings Gap: Evidence from the LEHD-2000 Census," *American Economic Review* 107, no. 5 (2017): 110–14, doi:10.1257/aer.p20171065; Erling Barth and Claudia Olivetti, *The Dynamics of Gender Earnings Differentials: Evidence from Establishment Data*, vol. 23381 (Cambridge: National Bureau of Economic Research, 2017).

38 Nikki Graf, Anna Brown, and Eileen Patten, "The Narrowing, but Persistent, Gender Gap in Pay" (Pew Research Center, March 22, 2019), https://www.pewresearch.org/fact-tank/2019/03/22/gender-pay-gap-facts/.

39 Francine D. Blau, Peter Brummund, and Albert Liu, "Trends in Occupational Segregation by Gender 1970–2009: Adjusting for the Impact of Changes in the Occupational Coding System," *Demography* 50, no. 2 (April 2013): 471–92, doi:10.1007/s13524-012-0151-7. Sources for Figure 7.8: Matthew Sobek, *Historical Statistics of the United States, Earliest Times to the Present: Millennial Edition*, Table Ba4207-4213; US Census (1950–2000; Steven Ruggles, Katie Genadek, Ronald Goeken, Josiah Grover, and Matthew Sobek, Integrated Public Use Microdata Series: Version 7.0 [dataset] (Minneapolis: University of Minnesota, 2017); American Community Survey (2001–2016); Ruggles et al. (2017) as calculated by Kim A. Weeden.

40 Research suggests that most of the change in occupational segregation since the 1970s is in fact due to the movement of women into formerly male-dominated jobs. See Blau and Winkler, *The Economics of Women, Men, and Work*, 168.

41 For a more technical explanation of how occupational segregation is calculated, see ibid., 165.

42 Ibid., 159.

43 Woloch, *Women and the American Experience*, 240.

44 Goldin, "The Rising (and Then Declining) Significance of Gender," 10–11.

45 Ibid., 20–22.

46 James T. Patterson, *Grand Expectations: The United States, 1945–1974*, The Oxford History of the United States, vol. 10 (New York: Oxford University Press, 1996), 33.

47 Blau and Winkler, *The Economics of Women, Men, and Work*, 30.

48 Emilie Stoltzfus, *Citizen, Mother, Worker: Debating Public Responsibility for Child Care after the Second World War*, Gender & American Culture (Chapel Hill: University of North Carolina Press, 2003).

49 However, working-class black women were much more supportive of "equal pay for equal work," because they more often found themselves in the "heavier, dirty" jobs that were more "equal" to men's. See Dorothy Sue Cobble, *The Other Women's Movement: Workplace Justice and Social Rights in Modern America*, Politics and Society in Twentieth-Century America (Princeton: Princeton University Press, 2004), 98–101.

50 David M. Kennedy, *Freedom from Fear: The American People in Depression and War, 1929–1945, The Oxford History of the United States*, vol. 9 (New York: Oxford University Press, 2001), 779–81.

51 Goldin, "The Rising (and Then Declining) Significance of Gender," 4.

52 Patterson, *Grand Expectations*, 361–69. This conclusion is also echoed in Kennedy, *Freedom from Fear*, 781–82.

53 Janet E. Halley, Catharine A. MacKinnon, and Reva B. Siegel, *Directions in Sexual Harassment Law* (New Haven: Yale University Press, 2004), 8–11.

54 Ariane Hegewisch and Emma Williams-Baron, "The Gender Wage Gap by Occupation 2016; and by Race and Ethnicity" (Institute for Women's Policy Research, April 4, 2017), https://iwpr.org/publications/gender-wage-gap-occupation-2016-race-ethnicity/.

55 See Ruth Milkman, *On Gender, Labor, and Inequality* (Chicago: University of Illinois Press, 2016).

56 Katz, Stern, and Fader, "Women and the Paradox of Economic Inequality in the Twentieth-Century." For a discussion of the ways in which greater flexibility in work schedules could result in finally closing the gender pay gap, see Goldin, "A Grand Gender Convergence: Its Last Chapter." See also Francine D. Blau and Lawrence M. Kahn, "The Gender Wage Gap: Extent, Trends, and Explanations," Working Paper 21913 (National Bureau of Economic Research, January 2016), doi:10.3386/w21913; and Youngjoo Cha and Kim A. Weeden, "Overwork and the Slow Convergence in the Gender

Gap in Wages," *American Sociological Review* 79, no. 3 (June 2014): 457–84, doi:10.1177/0003122414528936.

57   Sources for Figure 7.9: 1920–1936: J. Kevin Corder and Christina Wolbrecht, *Counting Women's Ballots: Female Voters from Suffrage Through the New Deal* (Cambridge: Cambridge University Press, 2016), 258; 1948–2016: American National Election Study Guide to Public Opinion and Electoral Behavior, "Voter Turnout 1948–2016." See also "Gender Differences in Voter Turnout," Center for American Women and Politics, Eagleton Institute of Politics, Rutgers University (September 16, 1919), https://cawp.rutgers.edu/sites/default/files/resources/genderdiff.pdf.

58   For a representative view of scholarship that promotes the idea of a lull in women's political activity between the two waves of feminism, see Ethel Klein, *Gender Politics: From Consciousness to Mass Politics* (Cambridge, MA: Harvard University Press, 1984), chap. 1. For a revisionist view, see the work of Kristin Goss, cited below. For further documentation of women's ongoing activism, particularly at the local level, see Kathleen A. Laughlin and Jacqueline L. Castledine, *Breaking the Wave: Women, Their Organizations, and Feminism, 1945–1985*, New Directions in American History (New York: Routledge, 2011); and Susan M. Hartmann, *The Other Feminists: Activists in the Liberal Establishment* (New Haven: Yale University Press, 2013). For discussions of working-class and African American activism from the 1930s through the 1960s, see Annelise Orleck, "We Are That Mythical Thing Called the Public: Militant Housewives During the Great Depression," in *Unequal Sisters: An Inclusive Reader in U.S. Women's History*, 4th ed. (New York: Routledge, 2008); Lisa Levenstein, "African American Women and the Politics of Poverty in Postwar Philadelphia," *OAH Magazine of History* 26, no. 1 (January 1, 2012): 31–35, doi:10.1093/oahmag/oar051; Rhonda Y. Williams, *The Politics of Public Housing: Black Women's Struggles Against Urban Inequality* (New York: Oxford University Press, 2004); and Roberta Gold, "'I Had Not Seen Women like That Before': Intergenerational Feminism in New York City's Tenant Movement," in *No Permanent Waves: Recasting Histories of U.S. Feminism* (New Brunswick, NJ: Rutgers University Press, 2010).

59   Scholars vary in their interpretations of women's evolving role in political parties during the first two thirds of the century. Compare, for example, essays in Melanie S. Gustafson, Kristie Miller, and Elisabeth Israels Perry, *We Have Come to Stay: American Women and Political Parties, 1880–1960* (Albuquerque: University of New Mexico Press, 1999).

60   Kristin A. Goss, "The Swells Between the 'Waves': American Women's Activism, 1920–1965," in *The Oxford Handbook of U.S. Women's Social Movement Activism*, Oxford Handbooks Online (New York: Oxford University Press, 2017), 53.

61   For a detailed history of how women's issues interacted with party politics, see Jo Freeman, *A Room at a Time: How Women Entered Party Politics* (Lanham, MD: Rowman & Littlefield, 2000).

62   Kristin A. Goss, *The Paradox of Gender Equality: How American Women's Groups Gained and Lost Their Public Voice*, CAWP Series in Gender and American Politics (Ann Arbor: University of Michigan Press, 2013).

63   Cobble, *The Other Women's Movement*, 145, quoted in Goss, "'The Swells Between the 'Waves': American Women's Activism, 1920–1965," 59–60.

64   Kristi Andersen, *After Suffrage: Women in Partisan and Electoral Politics Before the New Deal*, American Politics and Political Economy (Chicago: University of Chicago Press, 1996), 16, 119.

65   A. W. Geiger, Kristen Bialik, and John Gramlich, "The Changing Face of Congress in 6 Charts," *Fact Tank—News in the Numbers*, February 15, 2019, https://www.pewresearch.org/fact-tank/2019/02/15/the-changing-face-of-congress/.

66   Elaine Martin, "Bias or Counterbalance? Women Judges Making a Difference," in *Women in Politics: Outsiders or Insiders?*, 4th ed. (Upper Saddle River, NJ: Prentice-Hall, 2005), 21.

67   Drew Desilver, "A Record Number of Women Will Be Serving in the New Congress," *Fact Tank—News in the Numbers*, December 18, 2018, https://www.pewresearch.org/fact-tank/2018/12/18/record-number-women-in-congress/.

68   To cite just two examples of such historical interpretations, see William H. Chafe, *The Paradox of Change: American Women in the 20th Century* (Oxford: Oxford University Press, 1992), 157; and Rosalind Rosenberg, *Divided Lives: American Women in the Twentieth Century* (New York: Hill & Wang, 1992), 130–31. Three of the most oft-cited polls used by historians to support the argument that attitudes about women had changed little by mid-century include "The Fortune Survey: Women in America. Part I," *Fortune* 34, no. 2 (August 1946): 5–5; "The Fortune Survey: Women in America. Part 2," *Fortune* 34, no. 3 (September 1946): 5–5; and "The American Woman: Her Attitudes on Family, Sex, Religion and Society," *Saturday Evening Post*, December 22–29, 1962, 15–32.

69   See, for example, Christopher H. Achen, "Mass Political Attitudes and Survey Response," *American Political Science Review* 69, no. 4 (December 1975): 1218–31, doi:10.2307/1955282; Duane F. Alwin and Jon A. Krosnick, "Aging, Cohorts, and the Stability of Sociopolitical Orientations Over the Life Span," *American Journal of Sociology* 97, no. 1 (July 1991): 169–95, doi:10.1086/229744; David O. Sears and Carolyn L. Funk, "Evidence of the Long-Term Persistence of Adults' Political Predispositions," *The Journal of Politics* 61, no. 1 (1999): 1–28, doi:10.2307/2647773; and Gregory Markus, "Stability and

Change in Political Attitudes: Observed, Recalled, and 'Explained,'" *Political Behavior* 8, no. 1 (1986): 21–44, doi:10.1007/BF00987591.

70 There are also differences between female and male respondents within cohorts. In general, women tend to be more feminist in their attitudes than men. However, the same trend is visible when the data is broken down by the respondents' gender: female members of the pre–World War II cohorts are much less egalitarian in their views than female Gen Xers, for example. Interestingly, however, this gendered difference in responses begins to disappear with the Boomers, as men begin to catch up with women in the shift toward a more egalitarian outlook on gender. Male and Female Boomers and Gen Xers tend to hold quite similar views about gender equality. Additionally, there are differences when the respondents are broken down by education level. Those with a high school degree or less are less supportive of gender equality than those with more than a high school degree throughout the 1970s and 1980s. By the 1990s and 2000s, however, these differences tend to disappear. Finally, we note that generational analysis is fraught with methodological complexities. In particular, our analysis here (as in Chapter 6) assumes away any significant life-cycle changes. Most analysts would agree that as a first-order approximation, that assumption is not unreasonable. Relaxing that assumption might somewhat reduce the generational estimates we offer, but is unlikely to cause the differences to vanish.

71 Roberta S. Sigel, *Ambition & Accommodation: How Women View Gender Relations* (Chicago: University of Chicago Press, 1996).

72 Evidence of this leveling off can also be seen in Arland Thornton and Linda Young-Demarco, "Four Decades of Trends in Attitudes Toward Family Issues in the United States: The 1960s Through the 1990s," *Journal of Marriage and the Family* 63, no. 4 (2001): 1009–37; and Kristin Donnelly et al., "Attitudes Toward Women's Work and Family Roles in the United States, 1976–2013," *Psychology of Women Quarterly* 40, no. 1 (2016): 41–54, doi:10.1177/0361684315590774.

73 Figure 7.13 is based on the average cohort score on the index of support for gender equality over the survey years in which that cohort was represented in the GSS. For example, Americans born between 1920 and 1959 appeared in every survey between 1972 and 2014, but Americans born before 1920 disappeared from the surveys after 2002, while Americans born after 1980 appear in the surveys only in 2000. More sophisticated methods of calculating generational differences would yield essentially the same century-long rising curve. In Figure 7.13, cohorts are labeled in terms of not when they were born, but when they "came of age," or turned 20 years old, which is the time most scholars agree that socialization is complete. Attitudes toward abortion show a quite different and independent time trend, as discussed in detail in

Putnam and Campbell, *American Grace*, 406–14, and the sources cited there, which is why they are not included in this index.

74 David Cotter and Joanna Pepin, "Trending Towards Traditionalism? Changes in Youths' Gender Ideology" (Council on Contemporary Families, March 30, 2017), https://contemporaryfamilies.org/2-pepin-cotter-tradi tionalism/.

75 Stephanie Coontz, "Do Millennial Men Want Stay-at-Home Wives?," *New York Times*, March 31, 2017, Opinion, https://www.nytimes.com/2017/03/31 /opinion/sunday/do-millennial-men-want-stay-at-home-wives.html.

76 David Cotter, Joan M. Hermsen, and Reeve Vanneman, "The End of the Gender Revolution? Gender Role Attitudes from 1977 to 2008," *American Journal of Sociology* 117, no. 1 (July 2011): 259–89, doi:10.1086/658853.

77 Virginia Sapiro, "News from the Front: Inter-Sex and Intergenerational Conflict over the Status of Women," *Western Political Quarterly* 33, no. 2 (1980): 260–77, doi:10.2307/447298; Pia Peltola, Melissa A. Milkie, and Stanley Presser, "The 'Feminist' Mystique: Feminist Identity in Three Generations of Women," *Gender and Society* 18, no. 1 (2004): 122–44, doi:10.1177 /0891243203259921.

78 Jennifer Glass, "Parenting and Happiness in 22 Countries" (Council on Contemporary Families, June 15, 2016), https://contemporaryfamilies.org/brief -parenting-happiness/.

79 Keira V. Williams, *Gendered Politics in the Modern South: The Susan Smith Case and the Rise of a New Sexism*, Making the Modern South (Baton Rouge: Louisiana State University Press, 2012). Also interesting to note: in the mid-1990s Republican Party platforms dropped any mention of women's rights, an issue on which they had previously positioned themselves as leaders.

80 For a useful overview of some of the explanations cited here as well as others, see Stephanie Coontz, "Gender and Millennials Online Symposium: Overview" (Council on Contemporary Families, March 30, 2017), https://contem poraryfamilies.org/coontz-overview/.

81 This article surveying the field of political science literature on this topic generally supports these data and our interpretation: "By and large, the trend away from sex-role traditionalism from the early 1960s through the 1990s began before the national rise of the women's movement." N. Burns and K. Gallagher, "Public Opinion on Gender Issues: The Politics of Equity and Roles," *Annual Review Of Political Science* 13, no. 1 (June 15, 2010): 425–43, doi:10.1146/annurev.polisci.12.040507.142213.

82 Sigel, *Ambition & Accommodation*.

83 See, for example, Carol J. Adams, "The Book That Made Us Feminists," *New York Times*, September 7, 2017, Opinion, https://www.nytimes.com/2017/09 /07/opinion/sunday/kate-millet-feminists.html.

84   Goldin, "The Quiet Revolution That Transformed Women's Employment, Education, and Family."

85   See, for example, Kimberle Crenshaw, "Mapping the Margins: Intersectionality, Identity Politics, and Violence Against Women of Color," *Stanford Law Review* 43, no. 6 (1991): 1241–99, doi:10.2307/1229039; and Jocelyn Frye, "Racism and Sexism Combine to Shortchange Working Black Women," *Center for American Progress*, August 22, 2019, https://www.americanprogress.org/issues/women/news/2019/08/22/473775/racism-sexism-combine-short change-working-black-women/.

86   *American Women: The Report of the President's Commission on the Status of Women and Other Publications of the Commission* (New York: Charles Scribner's Sons, 1965) 190, 198.

CHAPTER 8: THE ARC OF THE TWENTIETH CENTURY

1   Thanks to Michael Werner of NASA for this analogy. See Michael Werner and Peter Eisenhardt, *More Things in the Heavens: How Infrared Astronomy Is Expanding Our View of the Universe* (Princeton: Princeton University Press, 2019).

2   Frederick Lewis Allen, *Since Yesterday: The 1930s in America, September 3, 1929–September 3, 1939* (New York: Harper & Brothers, 1940), 241.

3   Because many of the key variables in Chapter 2 on economic equality are missing before 1913, that curve begins only in 1913.

4   Technically, the scores of variables reported in this book are highly multicollinear.

5   Split ticket voting also appears to lag the other variables by about a decade. We have no explanation for that anomaly.

6   Quantitatively inclined readers will recognize that this book focuses on the second derivative of social change.

7   Coincidentally, the US government sponsored just such a study in the early 1930s. In 1930 Herbert Hoover, a firm believer in social science, commissioned a massive interdisciplinary, multivolume study: U.S. President's Research Committee on Social Trends, *Recent Social Trends in the United States; Report of the President's Research Committee on Social Trends* (New York: McGraw-Hill, 1933). Ironically, by the time the volume appeared, Hoover was no longer president. This study was once a familiar source of data for American historians, but in recent decades it has fallen into disuse. Some of the chapters actually provide a prescient analysis of what those then "recent" social trends might mean, but it was far too soon to guess what lay ahead for twentieth-century America. See, for example, Chapter 8, "Changing Social Attitudes and Interests," by Hornell Hart, which explores trends in the then proliferating periodical literature, like *Time* and *Look*.

8   Albert O. Hirschman, *Shifting Involvements: Private Interest and Public Action* (Princeton: Princeton University Press, 1982).

9   Colin Woodard is another scholar who uses the pendular metaphor and offers an account of American history broadly consistent with ours—libertarian dominance in the Gilded Age, communitarian dominance from the New Deal through the Great Society, and renewed libertarian dominance from Nixon to Trump. His interpretation, however, relies on changing dominance among eleven regional cultures or "nations," ranging from communitarian New England to libertarian Appalachia, and offers little help in understanding why the pendulum has swung back and forth. See Colin Woodard, *American Character: A History of the Epic Struggle Between Individual Liberty and the Common Good* (New York: Viking, 2016).

10   Thanks to Jonathan F. Putnam for clarifying this central question for us.

11   This is not a hypothetical example. John V. Duca and Jason L. Saving, using highly sophisticated econometric methods, find evidence for "bi-directional feedbacks between polarization and inequality." See John V. Duca and Jason L. Saving, "Income Inequality and Political Polarization: Time Series Evidence over Nine Decades," *Review of Income and Wealth* 62, no. 3 (September 2016): 445–66, doi:10.1111/roiw.12162.

12   A "narrative" in this sense is not merely an entertaining story, but a series of linked events that helps explain an historical outcome.

13   Robert J. Shiller, *Narrative Economics: How Stories Go Viral and Drive Major Economic Events* (Princeton, NJ: Princeton University Press, 2019), ix. In detail, Shiller's use of narrative in economics is not identical to our use of narrative here, but the parallel is nonetheless instructive.

14   Allen, *Explorations in Classical Sociological Theory: Seeing the Social World*, 3rd ed. (Los Angeles: Sage Publications, 2013), chap. 5; https://uk.sagepub.com /sites/default/files/upm-binaries/6109_Allen__Chapter_5[1]__Authority _and_Rationality___Max_Weber.pdf, 148. Weber quotation is in *From Max Weber: Essays in Sociology*, eds. M. Weber, H. Gerth, and C. W. Mills (New York: Oxford University Press, 1946), 280.

15   Steven Brill, *Tailspin: The People and Forces Behind America's Fifty-Year Fall— And Those Fighting to Reverse It* (New York: Alfred A. Knopf, 2018), blames the Boomers' meritocratic culture; Bruce Gibney, *A Generation of Sociopaths: How the Baby Boomers Betrayed America* (New York: Hachette, 2017), blames the Boomers' sense of entitlement; Francis Fukuyama, *The Great Disruption: Human Nature and the Reconstitution of Social Order* (New York: Free Press, 1999), is more sophisticated, but emphasizes cultural change as the key variable, driven in turn by the pill, the movement of women into the paid labor force, and the consequent collapse of family.

16   This is the thesis of a book that we otherwise greatly admire: Yuval Levin, *The*

Fractured Republic: Renewing America's Social Contract in the Age of Individualism (New York: Basic Books, 2016). We and Levin agree on the basic curvilinear pattern of twentieth-century American history: a pattern of "drawing together and then pulling apart," as he phrases it. However, as discussed in the next chapter, we differ on our interpretation of the Progressive Era. In Levin's view, the Progressives introduced strong, top-down central government into America, which caused the eventual "fracturing" of civil society and of our nation. In our reading, the Progressive movement was much more bottom-up than top-down, and actually brought about an intense flowering of localized solutions and civil society innovations that eventually bubbled up into federal programs. Levin does not discuss the "drawing together" period nearly as much as the "pulling apart" period, so his explanation for the first half of our curve is less clear. Ironically, given these differences between us, we and Levin agree that an important first step toward righting the country is nationwide policy experimentation at the state and local level, what the Progressive jurist Louis Brandeis famously termed "laboratories of democracy."

17 Robert D. Putnam, *Bowling Alone: The Collapse and Revival of American Community* (New York: Simon & Schuster, 2000), 281–82.

18 Federal Reserve Bank of St. Louis and U.S. Office of Management and Budget, Federal Net Outlays as Percent of Gross Domestic Product [FYONGDA188S], retrieved from FRED, Federal Reserve Bank of St. Louis; https://fred.stlouisfed.org/series/FYONGDA188S, December 8, 2019. For total spending by all levels of government as a fraction of GDP, see https://www.usgovernmentspending.com/past_spending. Across the whole period, the two world wars are associated with massive spikes, but our analysis considers those spikes only insofar as they outlast the war.

19 Émile Durkheim, *Suicide: A Study in Sociology* (New York: Free Press, 1951).

20 William Graham Sumner, *Folkways: A Study of the Sociological Importance of Usages, Manners, Customs, Mores, and Morals* (Boston: Ginn & Co, 1911), 12–13.

21 Putnam, *Bowling Alone*, 267–72.

22 See, for example, Richard G. Wilkinson and Kate Pickett, *The Spirit Level: Why More Equal Societies Almost Always Do Better* (New York: Allen Lane, 2009); Eric M. Uslaner and Mitchell Brown, "Inequality, Trust, and Civic Engagement," *American Politics Research* 33, no. 6 (2005): 868–894, doi:10.1177/1532673X04271903; and Keith Payne, *The Broken Ladder: How Inequality Affects the Way We Think, Live, and Die* (New York: Viking, 2017).

23 David Morris Potter, *People of Plenty: Economic Abundance and the American Character* (Chicago: University of Chicago Press, 1954).

24 See Tyler Cowen, *The Great Stagnation: How America Ate All the Low-Hanging Fruit of Modern History, Got Sick, and Will (Eventually) Feel Better* (New York: Dutton, 2011); and John L. Campbell, *American Discontent: The Rise of Donald*

Trump and Decline of the Golden Age (Oxford: Oxford University Press, 2018). For a sophisticated and thoroughly documented argument about the effects of technological innovation and productivity (1920–1970), see Robert J. Gordon, *The Rise and Fall of American Growth: The U.S. Standard of Living Since the Civil War* (Princeton: Princeton University Press, 2016).

25 Sendhil Mullainathan and Eldar Shafir, *Scarcity: Why Having Too Little Means So Much* (New York: Times Books/Henry Holt, 2013). See also Benjamin Friedman, "The Moral Consquences of Economic Growth," *Society* 43 (January/February 2006): 15–22.

26 E. J. Hobsbawm, *The Age of Extremes: A History of the World, 1914–1991*, 1st American ed. (New York: Vintage, 1994), 15–16, 286–87.

27 Interestingly, according to Ngram, the term "self-actualization" exploded into common usage during the 1960s, peaked in 1975, just as Inglehart was formulating his argument, and then virtually disappeared from American culture. Inglehart's initial formulation of his argument was Ronald Inglehart, "The Silent Revolution in Europe: Intergenerational Change in Post-Industrial Societies," *American Political Science Review* 65, no. 4 (1971): 991–1017, doi:10.2307/1953494, and his subsequent book, Ronald Inglehart, *The Silent Revolution: Changing Values and Political Styles Among Western Publics* (Princeton: Princeton University Press, 1977). Like all good empirically rooted theorists, Inglehart has expanded and to some extent modified his theory over the nearly half century since it was first published. For the latest version, see Ronald Inglehart, *Cultural Evolution: People's Motivations Are Changing, and Reshaping the World* (New York: Cambridge University Press, 2018).

28 Jynnah Radford, "Key Findings about U.S. Immigrants" (Pew Research Center, December 6, 2019), https://www.pewresearch.org/fact-tank/2019/06/17/key-findings-about-u-s-immigrants/.

29 Robert D. Putnam, "E Pluribus Unum: Diversity and Community in the Twenty-first Century: The 2006 Johan Skytte Prize Lecture," *Scandinavian Political Studies* 30, no. 2 (2007): 137–74, doi:10.1111/j.1467-9477.2007.00176.x.

30 The best studies of the incorporation of immigrants historically into the United States include *E Pluribus Unum?: Contemporary and Historical Perspectives on Immigrant Political Incorporation*, eds. Gary Gerstle and John H. Mollenkopf (New York: Russell Sage Foundation, 2001); Richard D. Alba and Victor Nee, *Remaking the American Mainstream: Assimilation and Contemporary Immigration* (Cambridge: Harvard University Press, 2003); and Richard D. Alba, *Blurring the Color Line: The New Chance for a More Integrated America*, The Nathan I. Huggins Lectures (Cambridge: Harvard University Press, 2009).

31 Andrew Kohut, "From the archives: In '60s, Americans gave thumbs-up to

immigration law that changed the nation," Pew Research Center Fact Tank (September 20, 2019). https://www.pewresearch.org/fact-tank/2019/09/20 /in-1965-majority-of-americans-favored-immigration-and-nationality-act -2/#more-266999.

32   Anne Case and Angus Deaton, *Deaths of Despair and the Future of Capitalism* (Princeton: Princeton University Press, 2020), 227, 225, citing National Academies of Sciences, Engineering, and Medicine. The Economic and Fiscal Consequences of Immigration (Washington, DC: The National Academies Press, 2017.)

33   Among the debates about the Sixties is exactly what years that label encompasses. For an astute and witty overview of how long or short the "Sixties" were, see M. J. Heale, "The Sixties as History: A Review of the Political Historiography," *Reviews in American History* 33, no. 1 (2005): 133–52, esp. 135. Here we follow the most conventional practice of dating the period from about 1960 to about 1975, a period sometimes called "the long Sixties."

34   Mark Lilla, *The Once and Future Liberal: After Identity Politics* (New York: HarperCollins, 2017), 8.

35   For a range of authoritative perspectives on the Sixties, see James T. Patterson, *Grand Expectations: The United States, 1945–1974,* The Oxford History of the United States, vol. 10 (New York: Oxford University Press, 1996); Arthur Marwick, *The Sixties: Cultural Revolution in Britain, France, Italy, and the United States, c.1958–c.1974* (New York: Oxford University Press, 1998); and Maurice Isserman and Michael Kazin, *America Divided: The Civil War of the 1960s,* 3rd ed. (New York: Oxford University Press, 2008).

36   "Revolution" is from Hobsbawm, *The Age of Extremes,* in the title of chap. 10; "Renaissance" is from 5–18; "Shock wave" and "fracture" are from Daniel T. Rodgers, *Age of Fracture* (Cambridge, MA: Belknap Press of Harvard University Press, 2011), 4; "new America" is from Andrew Hartman, *A War for the Soul of America: A History of the Culture Wars,* 2nd ed. (Chicago: University of Chicago Press, 2019), 2; "everything changed" is from Rob Kirkpatrick, *1969: The Year Everything Changed* (New York: Skyhorse Publishing, 2009).

37   Isserman and Kazin, *America Divided,* 305.

38   Todd Gitlin, *The Sixties: Years of Hope, Days of Rage,* rev. ed. (New York: Bantam, 1993).

39   Not all historians accept the "two Sixties" trope. Van Gosse, *Rethinking the New Left: An Interpretative History* (New York: Palgrave Macmillan, 2005), for example, sees the late Sixties movements as more diversified versions of the early Sixties ethos, still part of a single Movement.

40   Hobsbawm, *The Age of Extremes,* 334.

41   Historians who emphasize the theme of disintegration in the Sixties include William L. O'Neill, *Coming Apart: An Informal History of America in the 1960's*

(Chicago: Quadrangle, 1971); and John Morton Blum, *Years of Discord: American Politics and Society, 1961–1974* (New York: W. W. Norton, 1991); Isserman and Kazin, *America Divided.*

42 Patterson, *Grand Expectations*, 61–73 and 311–23.

43 https://millercenter.org/president/kennedy/campaigns-and-elections.

44 Patterson, *Grand Expectations*, 340–42.

45 It is no accident that Ta-Nehisi Coates's "Letter to My Son" in Coates, *Between the World and Me* (New York: Spiegel & Grau, 2015), echoes Baldwin's "Letter to My Nephew," the first half of James Baldwin, *The Fire Next Time* (New York: Dial Press, 1963), which reflects on the central role of race in American history.

46 This sentence perhaps applies less well to Friedan, who was certainly focused on a widespread issue, but was less focused on collective solutions, though her followers soon moved toward public policy concerns.

47 "Post-Bourgeois Radicalism in France," unpublished manuscript (1969). Later published in French in Ronald Inglehart, "Revolutionnarisme Post-Bourgeois en France, en Allemagne et aux Etats-Unis," *Il Politico: Rivista Italiana di Scienze Politiche* 36, 2 (June, 1971) 209–236. See also Inglehart, "The Silent Revolution in Europe."

48 Charles A. Reich, *The Greening of America* (New York: Random House, 1970), 10, 19.

49 The standard scholarly biography of Dylan is Sean Wilentz, *Bob Dylan in America* (New York: Doubleday, 2010).

50 For extensive conversations about the history of the Beatles, we thank Paul O. Jenkins, librarian of Franklin Pierce University and coeditor of *Teaching the Beatles*, eds. Paul O. Jenkins and Hugh Jenkins (New York: Routledge, 2018).

51 Barry Miles, *The Beatles Diary, Volume 1: The Beatles Years* (London: Omnibus, 2001).

52 Dan Piepenbring, "George Plimpton on Muhammad Ali, the Poet," *The Paris Review*, June 6, 2016, https://www.theparisreview.org/blog/2016/06/06/george-plimpton-on-muhammad-ali-the-poet/. Although many listeners heard "Me? We!" Ali himself recalled it differently. According to a tweet from Muhammad Ali in 2016 (https://twitter.com/MuhammadAli/status/711987024673120256?ref_src=twsrc%5Etfw%7Ctwcamp%5Etweetembed%7Ctwterm%5E711987024673120256&ref_url=https%3A%2F%2Fgenius.com%2FMuhammad-ali-shortest-poem-ever-written-annotated), the poem is "Me? Whee!"

53 At the moment of his death, to be sure, much of the nation, especially in the South, saw him instead as a radical rabble-rouser and possible Soviet dupe. His full resurrection in public opinion didn't come until later.

54 Evan Thomas, *Robert Kennedy: His Life* (New York: Simon & Schuster, 2000);

Larry Tye, *Bobby Kennedy: The Making of a Liberal Icon* (New York: Random House, 2016).

55   *Lord of the Flies* was an iconic 1954 novel by William Golding about a group of young boys who find themselves alone on a deserted island. They develop rules and a system of organization, but without any adults to serve as a "civilizing" impulse, the children eventually become violent and brutal.

56   Robert D. Putnam and David E. Campbell, *American Grace: How Religion Divides and Unites Us* (New York: Simon & Schuster, 2010), 92–93.

57   Todd Gitlin, *The Twilight of Common Dreams: Why America Is Wracked by Culture Wars* (New York: Henry Holt, 1995).

58   Hartman, *A War for the Soul of America*, 2–7.

59   According to monthly Harris poll surveys of political alienation beginning in the early 1960s, much of the total decline in public trust in our political institutions over the last half century was concentrated in (1) the twelve months after Johnson (having promised in the 1964 presidential election not to "send American boys . . . to do what Asian boys ought to be doing") in early 1965 dispatched more than a hundred thousand American troops to Vietnam, and (2) the twelve months immediately after Nixon's 1972 reelection, when the Watergate investigation revealed the depths of the president's involvement in the scandal.

60   U.S. Navy Captain Charlie Plumb, as quoted in *The Seventies: One Nation Under Change*, CNN documentary, 2015, https://www.cnn.com/2015/06/06 /us/seventies-producers-intro/index.html.

61   Compare Peter Turchin, *Ages of Discord: A Structural-Demographic Analysis of American History* (Chaplin, CT: Beresta Books, 2016).

62   Thomas Wolfe, "The 'Me' Decade and the Third Great Awakening," *New York* magazine, (August 23, 1976), http://nymag.com/news/features/45938/.

63   Patterson, *Grand Expectations*, 786–90.

64   Richard Rorty, *Achieving Our Country: Leftist Thought in Twentieth-Century America* (Cambridge, MA: Harvard University Press, 1998), 86.

65   Bruce J. Schulman, *The Seventies: The Great Shift in American Culture, Society, and Politics* (New York: Free Press, 2001), 76–77.

CHAPTER 9: DRIFT AND MASTERY

1   Edward Bellamy, *Looking Backward, 2000–1887* (Boston: Houghton Mifflin, 1898).

2   Walter Lippmann, *Drift and Mastery: An Attempt to Diagnose the Current Unrest* (Madison: University of Wisconsin Press, 1985), 19.

3   Ibid., 99.

4   See, for example, Yuval Levin, *The Fractured Republic: Renewing America's Social Contract in the Age of Individualism* (New York: Basic Books, 2016).

5 Richard Hofstadter, *The Age of Reform: From Bryan to F.D.R.*, 1st ed. (New York: Vintage, 1955), 5. We recognize that Hofstadter represents one school of historical interpretation of the Progressive Era—a school that has many critics. See endnote 1.12 for a brief overview of the massive historiography of the Progressive Era.

6 A full description of how Progressive Era social innovations were accomplished fills many books. We aim here to offer only the briefest overview. For more detailed accounts, consult the sources listed in endnote 1.12.

7 Kirstin Downey, *The Woman Behind the New Deal: The Life of Frances Perkins, FDR's Secretary of Labor and His Moral Conscience* (New York: Doubleday, 2009).

8 "Paul Harris: Rotary's Founder," *Rotary International*, accessed November 25, 2019, https://www.rotary.org/en/history-paul-harris-rotary-founder.

9 Paul P. Harris, "Rational Rotarianism," *The National Rotarian*, January 1911, http://clubrunner.blob.core.windows.net/00000010114/en-us/files/home page/paul-harris-in-the-first-rotarian/pharris_rational_rotarianism_1911 .pdf.

10 After women were admitted to Rotary, the motto "He profits most who serves best" was modified first to "They profit . . ." and then to "One profits . . ." "Rotary's Two Official Mottoes," *Rotary International*, accessed November 25, 2019, https://www.rotary.org/en/rotary-mottoes.

11 Peter H. Lindert and Jeffrey G. Williamson, *Unequal Gains: American Growth and Inequality Since 1700*, Princeton Economic History of the Western World (Princeton: Princeton University Press, 2016), 186; Douglas Eckberg, "Reported Victims of Lynching, by Race: 1882–1964," in *Historical Statistics of the United States, Earliest Times to the Present: Millennial Edition*, eds. Susan B. Carter et al. (New York: Cambridge University Press, 2006): Table Ec251–253.

12 Mia Bay, *To Tell the Truth Freely: The Life of Ida B. Wells*, 1st ed. (New York: Hill & Wang, 2009).

13 Tom L. Johnson, *My Story*, ed. Elizabeth J. Hauser, 1911, 43, http://cleveland memory.org/ebooks/Johnson/index.html.

14 Lincoln Steffens, "Ohio: A Tale of Two Cities," *McClure's Magazine*, July 1905.

15 Washington Gladden, *The New Idolatry: And Other Discussions* (New York: McClure, Phillips & Co., 1905), 210–11.

16 Hofstadter, *The Age of Reform*, 207.

17 www.poorpeoplescampaign.org. Accessed January 9, 2020.

18 Richard White, *The Republic for Which It Stands: The United States During Reconstruction and the Gilded Age, 1865–1896*, The Oxford History of the United States (unnumbered) (New York: Oxford University Press, 2017), 268.

19 Theodore Roosevelt, "Reform Through Social Work," *McClure's Magazine*, March 1901, 576; Quoted in Hofstadter, *The Age of Reform*.

20 Hahrie Han, "When Does Activism Become Powerful?" *New York Times*, December 16, 2019, https://www.nytimes.com/2019/12/16/opinion/activism-power-victories.html.

21 For a fuller overview and analysis of the research addressing this question, see the Afterword in the revised edition of Robert D. Putnam, *Bowling Alone* (Simon & Schuster 2020).

22 See, for example, the work of sociologist Zeynep Tufecki, who has studied the effect of emerging technologies on social movements across the globe.

23 Han, "When Does Activism Become Powerful?"

24 Dana Fisher, *American Resistance: From the Women's March to the Blue Wave* (New York: Columbia University Press, 2019).

25 Lara Putnam and Theda Skocpol, "Middle America Reboots Democracy," *Democracy Journal*, February 20, 2018, https://democracyjournal.org/arguments/middle-america-reboots-democracy/; Leah Gose and Theda Skocpol, "Resist, Persist, and Transform: The Emergence and Impact of Grassroots Resistance Groups Opposing the Trump Presidency," *Mobilization* 24, no. 3 (2019): 293–317, doi:10.17813/1086-671X-24-3-293; Theda Skocpol, "Making Sense of Citizen Mobilizations Against the Trump Presidency," *Perspectives on Politics*, 17, no. 2 (2019): 480–84, doi:10.1017/S153759271900104X.

26 E. J. Dionne, Jr., "This Is What Democracy Looks Like," *Washington Post*, accessed November 24, 2019, https://www.washingtonpost.com/opinions/this-is-what-democracy-looks-like/2019/01/06/489d254a-1087-11e9-84fc-d58c33d6c8c7_story.html.

27 For example, Frances Perkins's victories in securing protective labor laws often meant settling for incremental improvement rather than insisting on revolutionary reforms. See Downey, *The Woman Behind the New Deal*, chap. 5.

28 Lippmann, *Drift and Mastery*, 177.

29 At the turn of the twentieth century, Émile Durkheim—a French intellectual just like Tocqueville—wrote extensively about balancing individual liberty and community cohesion. And, like Tocqueville, he ultimately argued that it was not only possible, but *necessary* to do so in order for modern individuals and societies to flourish. See Galen Watts, "Pioneering Sociologist Foresaw Our Current Chaos 100 Years Ago," *The Conversation*, November 12, 2018, https://theconversation.com/pioneering-sociologist-foresaw-our-current-chaos-100-years-ago-105018.

30 E. J. Dionne, Jr., *Our Divided Political Heart: The Battle for the American Idea in an Age of Discontent* (New York: Bloomsbury, 2012).

31 Danielle S. Allen, *Our Declaration: A Reading of the Declaration of Independence in Defense of Equality* (New York: Liveright, 2014), 23.

32 Alexis de Tocqueville, *Democracy in America*, 2nd ed., vol. 2 (Cambridge, MA: Sever & Francis, 1863), chap. 8.

33 Theodore Roosevelt, "December 3, 1901: First Annual Message," Miller Center, October 20, 2016, https://millercenter.org/the-presidency/presidential-speeches/december-3-1901-first-annual-message.

INDEX

abortion:
  political parties and, 85, 94, 100, 376n53
  Roe v. Wade (1973), 85, 279, 304
Achen, Christopher, 94
Achieving Our Country (Rorty), 312
Adams, James Truslow, 177
Addams, Jane, 171–72, 319, 321, 331–32, 337
advertising, 6–7, 25, 177, 278, 310
Affluent Society, The (Galbraith), 302
African Americans, 200–244
  ban on racial discrimination in federal
    agencies and military, 230
  changing white attitudes and, 233–36,
    423–24n125
  civic associations and, 114, 115–16, 118,
    121, 215, 223, 228–29
  Civil Rights movement, *see* Civil Rights
    movement
  color line and, 200–217, 244
  economic inequality and, 32–33, 202,
    210–14, 229, 240, 429n27, 431n49
  education and, 28–29, 31–32, 202, 205–10,
    223, 225, 226, 240
  federal government programs to support,
    225–27
  in the first Gilded Age (late 1800s), 4, 7,
    73, 201–2
  "foot off the gas" phenomenon and, *see*
    "foot off the gas" phenomenon
  gender equality/inequality and, 247, 259,
    271, 279–80, 281, 429n27, 431n49
  Great Migration and, 207, 213–14, 219–25,
    229, 244
  health disparities and, 27–28, 41–42,
    204–5, 226–27, 240
  "hockey stick" pattern of change, 14–15,
    203–5, 207–9, 211–14, 216–17

  housing and, *see* housing
  incarceration and, 220–21
  I-we-I curves, 242–44, 281
  Jim Crow segregation, *see* Jim Crow
    segregation
  mid-20th century, 11, 14–16, 15–16,
    177–78
  New Deal and, 228–29
  persistence of exclusion, 217–21
  philanthropy to support, 225
  public and private initiatives, 225–27
  public office and, 55, 86, 217–18, 233
  race and political polarization, 73, 78,
    79–80, 82–84, 86–87, 97, 101, 372n10,
    373–74n25
  racial equality rate of change over time, 15
  religion and, 132, 140–41
  slavery/Emancipation of, 2, 4, 33, 167,
    201–3, 224, 247, 318, 323–25
  slowdown in move toward inclusion,
    216–17, 240–42
  social Darwinism/"survival of the fittest,"
    287, 327
  unions and, 53, 143–44, 218–19, 230
  urban riots, 222, 228, 237–38, 308
  voting rights, 201, 214–17, 232, 233,
    247
  white backlash and, 214, 236–40, 243
Agricultural Adjustment Act (AAA, 1933),
  77
Ahlstrom, Sydney, 129–30, 135–36
Ali, Muhammad, 306
Allen, Danielle, 102, 340
Allen, Frederick Lewis, 284, 291
Allen, Woody, 124
"American Century," 18
"American Creed," 231

American democracy:
  cynicism and alienation, 3, 8, 16–17, 103–6
  in the first Gilded Age (late 1800s), 1–9
  Founding Fathers, 69, 81, 102
  political polarization as threat to, 69–71,
    106–8
  Tocqueville on, 1–2, 8, 19, 109, 113, 119,
    158, 340, 351nn1–2
  see also U.S. Constitution
American Dilemma, An (Myrdal), 230–31
American Dream, 3, 5, 177–80, 244
American Federation of Labor (AFL), 49
American Individualism (Hoover), 173
American Liberty League, 76
American Motors Company, 66, 83
American Political Science Association,
    83–84
American Psychological Association, 16–17
American Settlement House movement, 321
Anderson, James D., 206
Anti-Defamation League, 231
anxiety, in the first Gilded Age (late 1800s), 7
Asch, Solomon, 185–86
Asch social pressure effect, 185–86
Asian Americans, 410n1
  educational attainment, 252
  and I-we-I curve, 14
  religious engagement, 393n86
  see also immigrants and immigration; racial
    equality/inequality
associationism, 172–73
Atkinson, Anthony, 65–66
Atlas Shrugged (Rand), 186–87
Audubon Society, 118
automobiles, 24, 25, 80, 355n7
Axinn, William G., 152

Baby Boom/Boomers:
  college education and, 301–2
  gender equality/inequality and, 272–76
  marriage and, 147, 148, 152–53
  1960s as hinge and, 301–2, 308, 312
  "OK Boomer" generation meme, 17, 314,
    353n9
  parenthood and, 154–56
  population shift and, 308
  racial equality/inequality and, 235
  religion/spirituality and, 134, 137, 138
  social trust and, 160–61, 252
  union membership and, 145
baby name trends, 194–96
Baez, Joan, 305
Bafumi, Joseph, 93–94

Baker, Ella, 232
Baker, Howard, 102
Baker, Ray Stannard, 129, 325
Baldwin, James, 303
Ballard, Charles, 243
Barber, Michael, 94
Barber, William, 328
Bartels, Larry, 94
Beard, Charles, 174
Beardsley, Edward, 226–27
Beatles, 151, 189, 305–6
Beecher, Henry Ward, 131
Beito, David, 114
Bellah, Robert, 135, 137
Bellamy, Edward, 315–16, 317
Berthoff, Rowland, 115
Bethune, Mary McLeod, 229
Big Brothers, 116
Big Sisters, 116
Big Sort, The (Bishop and Cushing), 95–96
Bill of Rights, 163, 191–92, 318
birth control, 155, 157, 253, 278, 309
Birth of a Nation (film), 218, 228
Bishop, Bill, 95–96
black Americans, see African Americans
Black Metropolis (Drake and Cayton), 244
Bloody Sunday (1965), 237
B'nai B'rith, 115, 118, 119
Bobo, Lawrence, 241
Boller, Paul, 78
Bowling Alone (Putnam), 283, 293
Boys Clubs, 116
Boy Scouts, 116, 118–19, 121
Broder, David, 83–84
Brooks, Victor, 304
Brotherhood of Sleeping Car Porters, 230
Brown v. Board of Education (1954), 206–7,
    209–10, 227, 231–32
Bryan, William Jennings, 72–73
Buffalo Springfield, 305
Buffett, Warren, 142–43
Bull Moose Party, 73–74, 172–73
Bush, George H. W., 55

Campbell, James E., 100–101
Campbell, W. Keith, 194
Campfire Girls, 116
Capra, Frank, 174
Card, David, 41
Carnegie, Andrew, 57, 142–43
Carnegie Foundation, 230–31
Carson, Rachel, 303, 310
Carter, Jimmy, 84, 269, 311

Carter, Susan B., 249–50
Case, Anne, 28, 43–44, 298
Catcher in the Rye, The (Salinger), 182
Catholicism, 128, 132–34
  Rerum Novarum (1891), 132, 168
  Vatican II (1962-65), 137
Cayton, Horace R., 244
Chaplin, Ralph, 143
Cherlin, Andrew, 135, 150–53, 155, 157
Chetty, Raj, 41
child labor legislation, 74–75, 114, 173, 248, 321
Christianity and the Social Crisis (Rauschenbusch), 130–31
civic associations, 110–21, 123–27
  African Americans and, 114, 115–16, 118, 121, 215, 223, 228–29
  fraternal groups, 112, 114, 116, 117, 323
  I-we-I curves, 112–13, 118–19, 123, 124–26
  membership trends, 118–21, 123–27, 387–88n28
  professional associations, 114, 121–23
  service clubs, 114–20, 321–23
  social class and, 114
  women's groups, 114–15, 116, 121, 267–68, 323, 324
  youth organizations, 116, 118–19, 212, 274
  see also unions
Civilian Conservation Corps (CCC), 228–29
Civil Rights Act (1957), 232
Civil Rights Act (1964), 78, 82, 84, 224, 227, 233, 236–37, 267–68, 300, 375n38, 375n45
  Title VII, 258–59, 264
Civil Rights movement, 14–16, 190, 227–33, 307
  changing white attitudes and, 233–35
  civic associations and, 121
  communitarian values of, 178–79, 180, 189, 244
  integration of U.S. military, 79–80
  Jim Crow and, 178–79, 203, 227–28, 241–42
  "long Civil Rights movement" and, 227–33
  March on Washington (1963), 177, 227, 232
  NAACP and, 116, 121, 215, 228, 229, 324, 337
  white backlash and, 214, 236–40, 243
Civil War:
  political polarization and, 69, 71

Reconstruction, 73, 77, 166, 201–2, 209, 217–18, 356n16
  social solidarity vs. isolation and, 112
Clayton Antitrust Act, 74
Clean Air Act (1970), 82, 85
Clemon, U. W., 241
Cleveland, Grover, 49, 71
Clinton, Bill, 55, 84–85, 103–4
Clinton, Hillary, 89
Cobble, Dorothy Sue, 268
Cochran, Thomas C., 144
cohabitation, 152–53
Cold War, 133–34, 230, 232, 302
Cole, Nat "King," 306
college education:
  gender equality/inequality and, 251–54
  GI Bill (1944), 31–32, 252, 357–58n22
  growth of, 31–32, 47–48, 301–2
  professional degrees and, 226, 252–54, 278
  racial equality/inequality and, 208–9
color line, 200–217, 244
communication, *see* media/communication
communitarianism, 313, 437n9
  of Civil Rights movement, 178–79, 180, 189, 244
  color line vs., 200–217, 244
  dark side of, 178, 180–86
  John Donne on, 163
  New Left, 83, 186, 188–90, 309
  political polarization vs., 70, 75, 79–80
  see also cultural individualism vs. community needs; Great Convergence (1913–70); social solidarity vs. isolation
"companionate" marriage, 150–52, 274
Connor, Bull, 179
contraception, 155, 157, 253, 278, 309
Cook, Marta, 168
Coolidge, Calvin, 76
Copland, Aaron, 175–76, 405n37
corporations:
  executive compensation, 66–67
  federal corporate tax, 56–57, 58–59
  financial regulation and, 61–62
  in the first Gilded Age (late 1800s), 3–5
  franchise-form, 117
  Industrial Revolution, 22, 166
  minimum wage, 54, 62–64, 80, 286, 321, 369nn115–16
  unions and collective bargaining, *see* unions
corruption:
  in the first Gilded Age (late 1800s), 5
  unions and, 52

counterculture, 83, 186, 188–90, 309
Cowen, Tyler, 294
Cox, Harvey, 137
Crash of 1929, 38–39, 76, 173, 174, 228
Cronkite, Walter, 101
Crucible, The (Miller), 184
cultural individualism vs. community needs, 163–99
  baby name trends, 194–96
  balance between, 2, 11–17, 19
  "common man" (1920–50) and, 173–80
  conformity in the 1950s, 178, 180–86, 313
  cultural narcissism and, 5–6, 8, 11, 14–16, 18, 193–94, 304–6
  "culture" as term, 164–65
  dark side of communitarianism, 178, 180–86
  in early American democracy, 1–2, 163
  in the first Gilded Age (late 1800s), 5–8, 166–67, 197, 315–16
  individualism as term, 1–2, 19
  individualism in 1960s and beyond, 186–96, 304–6
  I-we-I curves, 12–14, 169–76, 179–85, 191–99, 284–86
  John Kennedy on, 11–12, 178
  long-term trends (1895–2015), 11–12
  mid-twentieth century, 178, 180–86
  New Right/New Left and, 62, 83, 186–90
  Ngram analysis, 169–70, 172–73, 175–76, 190–95, 197–98, 311, 402–3nn18–23, 439n27
  Overton window and, 165, 173, 175
  in the Progressive Era, 167–73, 176, 197, 325–27
  pronoun usage and, 196–99
  rights and responsibilities, 191–93
  in the second Gilded Age (late 1900s), 16–17, 169
  social Darwinism/"survival of the fittest," 66, 166–70, 187–88, 287, 327
  tradeoff between, 339–41
cultural narcissism, 5–6, 8, 11, 14–16, 18, 193–94, 304–6
  "Me Decade" (Wolfe), 197–98, 301, 311
  see also cultural individualism vs. community needs
culturomics, 169–70
Cushing, Robert, 95–96
cynicism:
  in the first Gilded Age (late 1800s), 3, 8
  in the second Gilded Age (late 1900s), 16–17, 103–6

Darwin, Charles, 166
Davis, Price, 222
Day, Dorothy, 168
DDB Needham Life Style Survey, 124–26, 256–57
Dean, James, 182, 186
"deaths of despair," 28, 43–44, 355–56n11, 356n14
Deaths of Despair and the Future of Capitalism (Case and Deaton), 28
Deaton, Angus, 28, 43–44, 298
Decker, Sarah Platt, 115
democracy, *see* American democracy
Democratic Party:
  Civil Rights movement and, 232–33
  Civil War and, 71
  DINOs ("Democrats in Name Only"), 89
  in Great Convergence, 76–84, 90–91
  in Great Divergence, 6, 16–17, 84–108
  and New Left of the 1960s, 190
  Northern Democrats, 79, 229
  Southern Democrats, 76, 77, 83, 87, 228, 375n38
  see also politics/political polarization *and entries beginning* "election of . . ."
Dettrey, Bryan J., 100–101
Dewey, John, 111, 168, 321
Dewey, Thomas E., 77, 78–79, 81, 90, 372–73n17
Diamond, Peter, 65–66
Diminished Democracy (Skocpol), 122
Dionne, E. J., 334
Dirksen, Everett, 82
divorce, 152, 253, 278, 280
Donne, John, 163
Douglass, Frederick, 324
Drake, St. Clair, 244
Drift and Mastery (Lippmann), 317–18
drug use, 28, 355–56n11, 356n14, *see also* self-destructive behavior
Du Bois, W. E. B., 115–16, 200–201, 228, 244, 324, 337
Duca, John V., 100–101
DuPont, 25, 310, 325
Durkheim, Émile, 39, 293, 444n29
Dyer Anti-Lynching Bill (1919), 228
Dylan, Bob, 305

economic equality/inequality, 21–68
  charitable donations by wealthy, 5, 142–43, 225
  education and, 23, 28–32, 47–48
  financial regulation and, 61–64

in the first Gilded Age (late 1800s), 2–4, 5,
    8, 32–33, 37, 157
GDP growth per capita, 22–23
gender and, 254–65, 429n24, 429n27,
    430–31nn40–42, 431n49, 431–32n56
government transfer payments and, 34, 35,
    59–61
Great Convergence and, 38–39, *see also*
    Great Convergence (1913–70)
Great Divergence and, 40–44, *see also*
    Great Divergence (mid-1970s–)
health and, 25–28, 41–44
history of, 9–10, 11, 21–32
housing and, 23–24
income distribution and, 33–36, 39, 46–47,
    52–53, 59, 63–64, 363n61
I-we-I curve(s), 33–38, 41–44, 47–48, 50,
    51, 55–64, 67–68, 284–87, 294–96
marriage and, 153–54, 156–57
minimum wage and, 59, 62–64, 80, 286,
    321, 369nn115–16
overlap with politics/political parties, 8,
    79–80, 100–101
parenthood and, 156–57
race and, 32–33, 202, 210–14, 229, 240,
    429n27, 431n49
religion and, 131–32
in the second Gilded Age (late 1900s),
    37–38, 313
social norms and, 65–68
taxation and, 54–59
technological change and, 23, 28, 47–48
trade and, 45, 364n65
transportation and, 24–25
unions and, 49–54, 143–45
wealth distribution and, 36–38, 46–47, 53
see also social class
education:
    Brown v. Board of Education (1954), 206–7,
        209–10, 227, 231–32
    college revolution, *see* college education
    economic equality/inequality and, 23,
        28–32, 47–48
    elementary school, 28–29, 206–7, 225,
        330
    in the first Gilded Age (late 1800s), 2–3
    gender equality/inequality and, 31–32, 248,
        249–54, 259, 279, 280, 319–20
    high school revolution, *see* high school
        education
    Jim Crow segregation of schools, 206–7,
        209–10, 227, 231–32
    marriage and, 154

political parties and, 85–86
Progressive Era, 111, 168, 225–26,
    319–21
racial equality/inequality and, 28–29,
    31–32, 202, 205–10, 223, 225, 226,
    240
technological change and, 47–48
Edwards, Rebecca, 17
Eisenhower, Dwight D., 79, 84
    Civil Rights Act (1957), 232
    religion and, 135–36
    taxation and, 80–81
    and War Policies Commission, 175
election of 1896, 72–73, 372–73n17
election of 1904, 372–73n17
election of 1912, 73–74, 132, 172–73, 334
election of 1916, 173
election of 1920, 75, 372–73n17
election of 1924, 372–73n17
election of 1928, 76
election of 1932, 76–77
election of 1936, 76–77, 215, 229
election of 1940, 77–78
election of 1944, 77, 78–79, 372–73n17
election of 1948, 77, 79, 90, 91, 230,
    372–73n17
election of 1952, 80–81
election of 1956, 80
election of 1960, 79, 81, 232–33, 302
election of 1964, 79, 81–82, 83, 91–92,
    442n59
election of 1968, 82–84, 238, 308
election of 1972, 83, 238, 442n59
election of 1980, 46–47, 84, 94
election of 2012, 187
election of 2016, 100
Elementary and Secondary Education Act
    (1965), 85
elementary schools, 28–29, 206–7, 225, 330
Elks Club, 117–20
Encyclopedia of Associations, 121–22
environment:
    civic associations and, 123
    environmental movement, 303, 310
    in the first Gilded Age (late 1800s), 4–5
    political parties and, 82, 85, 94
Environmental Protection Agency (EPA), 82
Equal Credit Opportunity Act (1974), 279
Equal Employment Opportunity Act (1972),
    279
Equal Employment Opportunity
    Commission (EEOC), 259
Equal Pay Act (1963), 268

Equal Rights Amendment (ERA), 78, 267–68, 278, 374n27
Era of Good Feelings (1815–25), 69
Erikson, Erik, 190
eugenics, 167
Evers, Medgar, 237

Facebook, 292
Fair Housing Act (1968), 233, 239
Fair Labor Standards Act (1938), 77
Families Belong Together initiative, 328
family formation, 145–58
  new types of family, 147
  see also marriage; parenthood
"Fanfare for the Common Man" (Copland), 175–76, 405n37
Federal Reserve System, 61, 74
Feminine Mystique, The (Friedan), 254–55, 256, 263, 278–79, 303
feminism/women's movement, 14–16, 152, 246–49, 254–57, 263, 264–65
  abortion, 85, 94, 100, 279, 304, 376n53
  contraception, 155, 157, 253, 278, 309
  Equal Rights Amendment (ERA), 78, 267–68, 278, 374n27
  feminist theory and, 280
  "first wave," 246, 248–49
  "second wave" (1960s and 1970s), 248–49, 258, 260, 265, 268, 274–75, 278–79, 309
  "waves" metaphor and, 267
Finke, Roger, 128
Fire Next Time, The (Baldwin), 303
first Gilded Age (late 1800s):
  American democracy in, 1–9
  cultural individualism vs. community needs and, 5–8, 166–67, 197, 315–16
  cultural narcissism in, 5–6, 8
  as a distant memory, 11
  economic equality/inequality in, 2–4, 5, 8, 32–33, 37, 157
  economics in, 2–4, 5
  family formation, 146–48
  gender equality/inequality and, 2, 4, 7, 246–47
  as hinge point, 17, 285–86, 288
  immigration and, 3–4, 5, 7, 32–33
  lessons of history and, 17–18
  media/communication in, 2–3, 5, 6–7
  parallels with second Gilded Age (late 1900s), 2–9, 17–18
  political polarization in, 70, 71–73, 88, 98, 103, 104

  politics in, 6, 8
  racial inequality and, 4, 7, 73, 201–2
  social solidarity vs. isolation and, 3–4, 5, 7, 110, 112–13, 128–30, 142–43, 147–49, 157
  timing of, 351–52n3
  Tocqueville on, 1–2, 8, 19, 109, 113, 119, 158, 340, 351nn1–2
  transition to Progressive Era, 19–20, 88, 317–19, 336
  unions in, 49–50
Fischer, Claude S., 141
Fisher, Dana, 333
Fitzgerald, Ella, 306
Fitzgerald, F. Scott, 174
Follett, Mary Parker, 111
"foot off the gas" phenomenon:
  in education, 30, 32, 48, 210
  gender and, 275, 281–82, 296
  nature of, 15, 32, 203, 205, 240–42, 243, 281–82, 296, 411n15
  in voting rights, 216–17
Ford, Gerald, 84
Fountainhead, The (Rand), 186–87
4-H, 116, 118, 121
Fox News, 101
franchises:
  civic organizations, 117–19, 322–23
  corporate, 117
Franklin, Vincent P., 207
fraternal groups, 112, 114, 116, 117, 323
Freemasons, 115, 116, 121
Free Speech and Headlight (newspaper), 323–24
Frick, Henry Clay, 326
Friedan, Betty, 254–55, 256–57, 263, 278–79, 303
Friedman, Milton, 84, 186
Fukuyama, Francis, 188

Galbraith, John Kenneth, 302
Gates, Bill, 142–43
Gates, Henry Louis, Jr., 217–18
gay rights/homosexuality, 138, 141, 180, 192, 376n53
Gelfand, Michele, 164–65
gender equality/inequality, 245–82
  abortion rights, 85, 94, 100, 279, 304, 376n53
  changing attitudes toward, 262–63, 270–79, 433–35nn68–73
  civic associations and, 114–15, 116, 121, 267–68, 323, 324

economics of gender equality, 254–65, 429n24, 429n27, 430–31nn40–42, 431n49, 431–32n56
education and, 31–32, 248, 249–54, 259, 279, 280, 319–20
Equal Rights Amendment (ERA), 78, 267–68, 278, 374n27
feminism/women's movement, *see* feminism/women's movement
in the first Gilded Age (late 1800s), 2, 4, 7, 246–47
"foot off the gas" phenomenon and, 275, 281–82, 296
generational differences and, 262–63, 270–77
Great Migration and, 223
homosexuality/gay rights, 138, 141, 180, 192, 376n53
income equality/inequality and, 256–60, 263, 264–65, 431n49, 431–32n56
I-we-I curve, 13–16, 281–82
labor force participation, 246–48, 250–65, 268, 429n24
lesbian rights, 279
long-term trends, 13–16, 247–49, 270–77, 280–81
marriage and, 246, 252, 254–57, 259–60, 262–65
#MeToo movement, 277, 328
mid-20th century, 11, 14–16, 178
motherhood and domesticity, 246, 252, 254–57, 259–60, 262–65, 276–77, 282
occupational segregation, 260–63, 430–31nn40–42
political parties and, 78, 94, 268, 269–70, 278, 320–21
Progressive Era (1900–1915), 247–48, 267–68, 319–21
public office and, 89, 269–70, 278
racial equality/inequality and, 247, 259, 265, 271, 279–80, 281, 429n27, 431n49
sexual harassment, 264, 277, 278, 328
social class and, 246–47, 256–57, 259, 265, 267, 282, 320
Title IX, Education Amendments (1972), 82, 264–65, 279
unions and, 53, 115, 248
voting rights and, 2, 74–75, 114–15, 119, 120, 247–49, 266, 269–70, 324, 428n11
women's groups, 114–15, 116, 121, 267–68, 323, 324
General Federation of Women's Clubs, 115, 121

General Social Survey (GSS), 124
Generation Me (Campbell), 194
Generation X/Gen-Xers, 148, 273–76, 314
George, Henry, 326
Georgetown University, Center on Education and the Workforce, 259
GI Bill (1944), 31–32, 252, 357–58n22
Gilded Age:
first, *see* first Gilded Age (late 1800s)
second, *see* second Gilded Age (late 1900s)
as term, 8, 17–18
Gini index, 195–96
Girls Clubs, 116
Girl Scouts, 116, 118–19, 121, 274
Gitlin, Todd, 189, 300, 309
Gladden, Washington, 327–28
Glendon, Mary Ann, 192
globalization, 296–98
impact of, 45–46
see also immigrants and immigration; international trade
Goldin, Claudia, 38, 47, 48, 248, 252–53, 262, 280–81
Golding, William, 182, 308, 442n55
Goldwater, Barry, 81, 84, 85
Google, Ngram analysis, 169–70, 172–73, 175–76, 190–95, 197–98, 402–3nn18–23, 439n27
Gose, Leah, 333
Goss, Kristin A., 267–68
government regulation:
"big government" as polarizing issue, 84–85
financial regulation, 61–62
in the first Gilded Age (late 1800s), 4–5
New Deal programs, *see* New Deal
Progressive Era, 74–75
unions and, 50, 52
"Grand Expectations" (Patterson), 301
Grange, 116, 118, 120, 121
Grapes of Wrath (Steinbeck), 174
Great Compression, *see* Great Convergence (1913–70)
Great Convergence (1913–70), 38–39, 299
educational innovation and, 47–48
financial regulation and, 61–62
gender equality/inequality and, 247–49, 281–82
Great Migration and, 219–25
income equality/inequality and, 35, 52–53, 211
international factors and, 45–46
minimum wage and, 62–64
New Deal programs and, *see* New Deal

Great Convergence (1913–70) (*cont.*)
origins in the Progressive Era, 38–39,
46–48, 285–86, 288
of politics/political parties, 70–71, 76–84,
88, 90–91, 98, 102–3
public economic policy and, 54
racial equality/inequality and, 227–36
regional equality/inequality and, 44
social innovations and institutional
reforms, 46, 54, 59–61, 65–66, 74–76
taxation and, 54–55, 56–59, 65
technological change and, 48
as term, 33, 358n26
timing of, 33, 281
unions and, 49–51, 53–54
wealth equality/inequality and, 37
Great Depression:
causes of, 291
economic policies in, 173–75
education during, 250–51
financial regulation and, 61–62
GDP growth per capita, 22–23
political parties and, 76–77
social solidarity vs. isolation and, 119–21,
127, 134, 142, 156, 157, 295–96
unions and, 50, 51
see also New Deal
Great Disruption, The (Fukuyama), 188
Great Divergence (mid-1970s–), 40–44
financial deregulation and, 62
"foot off the gas" phenomenon, *see* "foot
off the gas" phenomenon
health measures and, 41–44
income equality/inequality and, 35–36, 53
intergenerational economic mobility, 41, 42
international factors and, 45–46, 296–98
minimum wage and, 63–64
of politics/political parties, 6, 16–17,
84–108
public economic policy and, 54
racial equality/inequality and, 239–42, 243
regional equality/inequality and, 44
reversal of social innovations and
institutional reforms, 46–47, 54, 55–61,
65–68
taxation and, 55–58, 61, 65
technological change and, 48
as term, 35
unions and, 51–54
Greatest, The (film), 306
Greatest (Silent) Generation, 66, 138, 147–
48, 152, 160–61, 234–35, 252, 262–63,
272–73

Great Leveling, 39, *see also* Great
Convergence (1913–70)
Great Migration, 207, 213–14, 219–25, 229,
244, 419n77
Great Recession (2008–2009), 24, 61, 142,
214, 310
Great Society initiatives, 60, 82, 85, 102, 190,
233, 236–39, 300, 375n38
"Greed is Good" ethos, in first Gilded Age
(late 1800s), 5
Greenfield, Patricia, 197
Greening of America, The (Reich), 305
Greenpeace, 123
Greenspan, Alan, 187
gun violence, 328
Guthrie, Woody, 305

Habits of the Heart (Bellah), 137
Hadassah, 118, 119, 121, 323
Halley, Janet, 264
Halpin, James, 168
Hamer, Fannie Lou, 232
Hanifan, L. J., 168
Harding, Warren, 38, 76, 228, 372–73n17
Harrington, Michael, 59–60, 303
Harris, Paul, 117, 321–23
Harrison, George, 305–6
Hayden, Tom, 188–89
Hayek, Friedrich, 186–87
health:
"deaths of despair," 28, 43–44, 355–56n11,
356n14
economic equality/inequality and, 25–28,
41–44
Great Divergence (mid-1970s–) and, 41–44
infant mortality, 25–28, 42, 205, 240
life expectancy, *see* life expectancy
racial equality/inequality and, 27–28,
41–42, 204–5, 226–27, 240
Hearst, Patty, 308–9
Hemingway, Ernest, 174
Herberg, Will, 136, 139
Hetherington, Marc J., 103
Higginbotham, Evelyn, 132
high school education:
"foot off the gas" phenomenon and, 30, 32,
48, 210
gender equality/inequality and, 249–51
high school revolution and, 29–31, 41,
47–48, 329–30, 356–57nn17–21
racial equality/inequality and, 207–9, 223
Hill-Burton program (1946), 226–27
hippie movement, 189, 309

Hirschman, Albert O., 289–90
Historical Statistics of the United States, 133
Hobsbawm, Eric, 295, 300–301
Hofstadter, Richard, 318–19, 328
Hofstede index, 195
Holifield, E. Brooks, 131
Holocaust, 230
homosexuality/gay rights, 138, 141, 180, 192,
    376n53
Hoover, Herbert, 66, 75, 76, 173–75
    Research Committee on Social Trends,
    436n7
    taxation and, 58
    unions and, 50
    War Policies Commission, 175
Hopkins, Harry, 175
housing:
    access to homeownership, 77, 202, 213–14,
        233, 239, 241
    home size trends, 23–24
    residential segregation, 219–20,
        417–18nn68–70
Houston, Whitney, 306
Hout, Michael, 141
How Democracies Die (Levitsky and Ziblatt), 106
How the Other Half Lives (Riis), 167
Hull House, 319, 320, 331–32

identity, 190–91, 243
immigrants and immigration:
    American Dream and, 3
    civic associations and, 110, 115
    in the first Gilded Age (late 1800s), 3–4, 5,
        7, 32–33
    Great Migration and, 419n77
    immigration reform and, 82, 222, 297–98,
        300
    income equality and, 45
    I-we-I curve and, 296–98
    religion and, 128–29, 132–33
    Triangle Shirtwaist Factory fire (1911),
        247, 320
Immigration Act (1924), 222, 297
Immigration and Nationality Act (1965),
    297–98, 300
Implicit Association Test (IAT), 380–81n86
income equality/inequality:
    age distribution of income, 59–61
    executive compensation, 66–67
    gender and, 256–60, 263, 264–65, 431n49,
        431–32n56
    government transfer payments and, 34, 35,
        59–61

Great Migration and, 222–23
immigration and, 45
I-we-I curves, 33–36, 39, 52–53, 59, 63–64,
    358–59n29, 363n61
minimum wage and, 54, 62–64, 80, 286,
    321, 369nn115–16
race and, 202, 211–12, 241, 259
taxation and, 35, 54–59
wealth distribution and, 37–38, 46–47, 53
see also Great Convergence (1913–70);
    Great Divergence (mid-1970s–);
    unions
Independent Order of Odd Fellows, 112,
    116, 117
Index of Dissimilarity, 260–61
individualism, *see* cultural individualism vs.
    community needs
Individualism Reconsidered (Riesman), 182
Industrial Revolution, 22, 166
infant mortality, 25–28, 42, 205, 240
infrastructure, in the first Gilded Age (late
    1800s), 6
Inglehart, Ronald, 295, 304–5, 439n27
Institute for American Democracy, 231
Institute for Women's Policy Research, 259
international trade:
    income equality/inequality and, 45, 364n65
    I-we-I curves and, 296–98
International Women's Strike for Equality
    (1970), 279
internet, 277, 292, 332–33, 336
    Ngram analysis of books, 169–70,
        172–73, 175–76, 190–95, 197–98, 311,
        402–3nn18–23, 439n27
    social media, *see* social media
intersectionality, 245, 427n1, 427–28n10
Interstate Commerce Commission, 74
Interstate Highway system, 80
inverted U-curve, *see* I-we-I curve(s)
isolation, *see* social solidarity vs. isolation
Isserman, Maurice, 136, 300
It's a Wonderful Life (film), 174
I-we-I curve(s), 12–18
    causal analysis and, 286–88, 290–98
    civic associations and, 112–13, 118–19,
        123, 124–26
    cultural individualism vs. community
        needs, 12–14, 169–76, 179–85, 191–99,
        284–86, 339–41
    cultural trends and, 10, 11
    economic equality/inequality and, 33–38,
        41–44, 47–48, 50, 51, 55–64, 67–68,
        284–87, 294–96

I-we-I curve(s) (*cont.*)
  economic trends and, 9–10
  financial regulation and, 62, 63
  gender equality/inequality and, 13–16,
      281–82
  globalization trend and, 296–98
  health trends and, 43–44
  income equality and, 33–36, 39, 52–53, 59,
      63–64, 358–59n29, 363n61
  intergenerational economic mobility and,
      41, 42
  international trade and, 296–98
  marriage and, 147–50
  nature and derivation of, 12–14, 352–53n4
  1960s, as hinge point of twentieth century,
      17, 285–86, 298–314
  parenthood and, 155–56
  pendulum metaphor and, 64, 165, 183–84,
      192, 198, 289–90, 437n9
  politics/political parties and, 10, 11, 69–71,
      86–91, 97, 100–101, 103–8, 284–87
  pronoun usage and, 196–98
  racial equality/inequality and, 242–44, 281
  religion and, 133–35, 139–42
  social spending on elderly and poor, 60–61
  social trends and, 10–11
  social trust and, 159–62
  Stimson composite summary curves, 9–11,
      352–53n4
  Stock-Watson composite summary curves,
      352–53n4
  taxation and, 55–59
  union membership and, 50, 51, 144–45
  wealth distribution and, 36–37, 39, 53
  in wide-angle approach to history, 283–90
Iyengar, Shanto, 97

Jack-and-Jill, 118
Jackman, Mary, 241–42
Jackson, Jesse, 85
Jackson, Jimmie Lee, 237
Jahoda, Marie, 180–81
Jefferson, Thomas, 81
Jews/Judaism, 134
  civic associations, 115, 118, 119, 121, 323
  Nazi Germany/Holocaust, 178, 186, 230
Jim Crow segregation, 323–25
  Brown v. Board of Education (1954), 206–7,
      209–10, 227, 231–32
  Civil Rights movement and, 178–79, 203,
      227–28, 241–42
  economic equality/inequality and, 210–11,
      429n27

Great Migration and, 213–14, 219–25
  housing and, 213–14, 219–20
  lynchings, 73, 201, 218, 228, 323–24
  nature of, 202
  origins in Reconstruction, 201–3, 217–18
  Plessy v. Ferguson (1896), 73, 201
  Progressive Era and, 337–38
  racial polarization and, 73
  of schools, 206–7, 209–10, 227, 231–32
  social Darwinism and, 167
  voting rights, 214–17, 266
Jobs, Steve, 187
Johnson, Andrew, 201
Johnson, Lyndon B.:
  bipartisan approval of social programs,
      91–92, 375n38
  Civil Rights movement and, 233
  election of 1964, 79, 81–82, 91–92, 442n59
  Executive Order 11246 (equal employment
      opportunity), 279
  Great Society initiatives, 60, 82, 85, 102,
      190, 233, 236–39, 300, 375n38
  Kerner Commission (1967), 238, 425n133
  polarization and, 82, 84
  Vietnam War, 310
Johnson, Tom, 325–27
Jones, C. I., 23
Jones, Sam "Golden Rule," 327
journalism, *see* media/communication
Judaism, 118–19, 134

Katz, Lawrence, 38
Kazin, Michael, 136, 300
Kelley, Florence, 321, 337
Kennedy, John F.:
  assassination (1963), 178, 307
  Civil Rights movement and, 232–33, 268
  on cultural individualism vs. community
      needs, 11–12, 178
  election of 1960 and, 79, 81, 232–33,
      302
  New Frontier, 12, 302
  Presidential Commission on the Status of
      Women, 268, 282
  taxation and, 55
Kennedy, Robert F., 307–8
Kerner Commission (1967), 238, 425n133
Kerouac, Jack, 182
Killen, Andreas, 304
Kinder, Donald, 241–42
King, Martin Luther, Jr., 130–31, 232
  assassination (1968), 237, 238, 307, 308
  "beloved community," 180, 244

Birmingham Letter (1963), 178–79
"I Have a Dream" speech (1963), 177, 236
Kirkpatrick, Rob, 304
Kiwanis, 114, 117, 118
Kloos, Karina, 237–38, 243
Kloppenberg, James, 167, 173
Knights of Columbus, 115, 118, 119, 323
Knights of Labor, 49
knowledge economy, 44
Korean War, 81
Kroc, Ray, 117
Krugman, Paul, 65
Ku Klux Klan, 218
Kurlansky, Mark, 304

La Follette, Robert, 327
Lancet, The, 42–43
Landon, Alf, 76–77
La Rochefoucauld, François de, 236
Lasch, Christopher, 194
Latinos, 410n1
  gender pay equity, 259
  and I-we-I curve, 14
  religious engagement, 140, 393nn85–86
  see also immigrants and immigration; racial equality/inequality
Lavender Scare (1950s), 180
League of Women Voters, 119, 120
Lennon, John, 306
Leo XIII, Pope, 132, 168
lesbian rights, 279
Levin, Yuval, 437–38n16
Levitsky, Steven, 106
libertarianism, 437n9
  collective norms vs., 46
  New Right (1960s), 62, 81, 186–91
  see also cultural individualism vs. community needs; first Gilded Age (late 1800s); Great Divergence (mid-1970s–); second Gilded Age (late 1900s); social solidarity vs. isolation
life expectancy, 27–28
  "deaths of despair," 43–44
  in the first Gilded Age (late 1800s), 7
  Great Divergence (mid-1970s–) and, 42–44
  racial equality/inequality and, 202, 204–5, 240
Lilla, Mark, 299
Lincoln, Abraham:
  assassination, 166
  Republican Party and, 78, 201

Whig communitarianism and, 166, 171, 197
  see also Civil War
Lindert, Peter H., 33, 35, 40, 42, 202, 209
Lions Club, 114, 117, 120
Lippmann, Walter, 110, 317–18, 329, 330, 339
literature:
  New Left, 188–89
  New Right, 186–88
  Ngram analysis of books, 169–70, 172–73, 175–76, 190–95, 197–98, 402–3nn18–23, 439n27
  1920s/"Lost Generation," 174
  1950s, 182–84, 186–87, 188, 308, 442n55
  1960s, 188–89, 302–4, 305
Lonely Crowd, The (Riesman), 182
Looking Backward (Bellamy), 315–16, 317
Lord of the Flies (Golding), 182, 308, 442n55

MacKinnon, Catharine, 264
macrohistory, 19, 245–46, 286, see also I-we-I curve(s)
Madison, James, 69, 102
"makers" and "takers" meme, 187
Maloney, Thomas N., 210–11
Manduca, Robert, 211
Man in the Gray Flannel Suit, The (Wilson), 182
Manson, Charles, 308–9
March for Our Lives (2018), 328
March on Washington:
  of 1963, 177, 227, 232
  Women's March (2017), 333
Marcuse, Herbert, 188
Mare, Robert, 154
Margo, Robert A., 207, 211–12
Margolis, John, 304
marriage, 145–54, 157–58
  average age of, 146–51
  cohabitation vs., 152–53
  "companionate," 150–52, 274
  divorce and, 152, 253, 278, 280
  economic equality/inequality and, 153–54, 156–57
  education and, 154
  gender equality/inequality and, 246, 252, 254–57, 259–60, 262–65
  generational differences and, 146–48, 152
  I-we-I curves, 147–50
  politics and, 98, 381n90
  racial intermarriage, 218
  religion and, 134

marriage (*cont.*)
  singletons vs., 146–47, 153, 157
  social class and, 153–54
Marshall, Thurgood, 231–32, 233
Marxism, 172, 287
Masons, 115, 116, 121
Massey, Douglas, 39
McAdam, Doug, 237–38, 243
McCall's magazine, 151
McCarthy, Joseph, 81, 180, 307–8
McCarty, Nolan, 86, 100, 102
McClure's Magazine, 327
McDonald's, 117
McGovern, George, 83
McKinley, William, 72, 74, 372–73n17
Mead, Margaret, 282
"Me Decade" (Wolfe), 197–98, 301, 311
media/communication:
  advertising in, 6–7, 25, 177, 278, 310
  in the first Gilded Age (late 1800s), 2–3,
    5, 6–7
  internet, *see* internet; social media
  political polarization and, 101
  Progressive Era muckrakers, 129, 167,
    325, 327
  racism in, 218, 417n64
  television, 52, 151
  see also literature
Medicare, 59, 82
#MeToo movement, 277, 328
Millennials, 134, 141, 148, 156, 273–77, 314
Miller, Arthur, 184
Miller, William, 144
Mills, C. Wright, 188
minimum wage, 54, 62–64, 80, 286, 321,
  369nn115–16
misery index, 310
Moose, 114, 117, 119
Morgan, Anne, 115
Morgan, J. P., 115
Morgenthau, Henry, Jr., 175
Mr. Smith Goes to Washington (film), 174
Mullainathan, Sendhil, 295
Murray, Pauli, 267
Myrdal, Gunnar, 230–31

NAACP (National Association for the
  Advancement of Colored People), 116,
  121, 215, 228, 229, 324, 337
Narcissism Epidemic, The (Twenge), 194
Narrative Economics (Shiller), 291
narratives, 19, 291
Nast, Thomas, 72

National Academy of Medicine, 43
National Academy of Sciences, 298
National Association of Colored Women's
  Clubs, 116, 324
National Association of Rotary Clubs,
  322–23
National Congress of Mothers, 115
National Congress of Parents and Teachers
  (PTA), 115, 118, 135, 151
National Election Study, "feeling
  thermometer," 96–97
National Endowment for the Arts, 82
National Endowment for the Humanities, 82
National Housing Act (1934), 77
National Industrial Recovery Act (NIRA,
  1933), 77
National Labor Relations Act (NLRA, 1935),
  50, 77
National Organization for Women (NOW),
  279–80
National Urban League, 116, 118, 215
National Youth Association, 229
Native Americans, 410n1
  genocide of, 2
  and I-we-I curve, 14
  natural resources and, 4
  see also racial equality/inequality
natural resources, *see* environment
Nazi Germany, 178, 186
New Age spirituality, 124, 306, 311
New Conservatism, 84–85
New Deal, 226–29, 321, 337
  communitarianism of, 174–75
  Great Convergence and, 38–39, 50–52, 54,
    70–71, 74, 76–79, 102, 289, 373–74n25
  major reforms of, 77–78, 80
  minimum wage and, 62–63
  Progressive Era influence on, 74–75,
    174–75, 334
  taxation and, 57–58
  unions and, 50–51
New Left, 83, 186, 188–90, 309
Newport Folk Festival (1965), 305
New Right (1960s), 62, 81, 186–90
Newton-John, Olivia, 306
"New Women," 246
New York Times, 232, 241
Ngram analysis, 169–70, 172–73, 175–76,
  190–95, 197–98, 311, 402–3nn18–23,
  439n27
1910s, 41, 54, 55, 180
1920s, 37, 39, 48, 50, 54, 55, 66, 73, 75,
  78, 101, 160, 162, 170, 173–74, 175,

176, 179, 196, 198, 173, 288, 291, 324, 385n15, 411n17
1930s, 41, 50, 53, 60, 61, 63, 67, 72, 76, 77, 78, 90, 119, 144, 154, 157, 161, 162, 174, 175, 250, 273, 274, 289, 299, 368n99, 372n10, 374n25, 378n62, 385n15, 391n60, 404n28, 432n58, 436n7
1940s, 41, 55, 119, 120, 134, 144, 147, 159, 160, 210, 215, 229, 263, 267, 269, 274, 289, 312, 391n60, 392n64
1950s:
  conformity and, 178, 180–86, 313
  economic equality and, 16, 313
  as "golden age," 16
  literature and, 182–83, 186–87, 188, 308, 442n55
  Red Scare, 81, 180
  see also Baby Boom/Boomers
1960s:
  causal analysis, 286–88
  crises and, 306–12
  cultural narcissism and, 304–6
  as hinge point of twentieth century, 17, 285–86, 288, 298–314
  historian consensus and, 300–301
  lessons from, 312–14
  literature and, 188–89, 302–4, 305
  pop culture, 151, 189, 304–6, 308, 312
  social solidarity vs. isolation and, 136–39, 149–50
  as "the long Sixties," 310–12, 440n33
  see also Baby Boom/Boomers
1970s:
  Baby Boom/Boomers and, 312
  as "Me Decade," 197–98, 301, 311
  in "the long Sixties," 310–12, 440n33
1980s, 11, 32, 37, 40, 85, 92, 99, 104, 121, 139, 140, 142, 151, 152, 159, 185, 191, 194, 233, 252, 257, 258, 273, 274, 275, 277, 293, 296, 299, 357n21, 364n65, 434n70
1990s, 40, 84, 85, 104, 105, 122, 124, 126, 137, 139, 141, 142, 191, 214, 234, 257, 274, 275, 277, 296, 357n21, 364n65, 392n64, 393n82, 434n70, 435n79, 435n81
Nixon, Richard:
  election of 1960 and, 81
  election of 1968 and, 82–84, 238, 308
  environmental movement and, 82, 85
  polarization and, 84, 238
  Vietnam War, 310
  Watergate, 310

Noel, Hans, 74
Norris-LaGuardia Act (1932), 50

Obama, Barack, 55, 86
Occupational Safety and Health Act (1970), 82
O'Connor, Sandra Day, 269
Odd Fellows, 112, 116, 117
"OK Boomer" generation meme, 17, 314, 353n9
Old Left, 188–90
Old Right, 190
Olney, Richard, 49
One-Dimensional Man (Marcuse), 188
On the Origin of Species (Darwin), 166
On the Road (Kerouac), 182
Organization Man, The (Whyte), 182–83
Other America, The (Harrington), 59–60, 303
Overton, Joseph P., 165
Overton, window (window of discourse), 165, 173, 175

Panic of 1873, 61
Panic of 1893, 61, 72
parenthood, 154–58
  baby name trends, 194–96
  childlessness vs., 155–56
  demographic transition and, 154–55
  generational differences and, 156
  I-we-I curves, 155–56
  single-parent families, 256–57
Park, Robert, 111
Patterson, James, 82, 231, 262, 301, 304, 311
pendulum metaphor, 64, 165, 183–84, 192, 198, 289–90, 437n9
Pennebaker, James, 196–97
People of Plenty (Potter), 294
Perkins, Frances, 175, 319–21
Peter, Paul, and Mary, 305
Pew Research Center, 16, 28, 96
Philadelphia Negro, The (Du Bois), 115–16
philanthropy:
  educational, 225
  in the first Gilded Age (late 1800s), 5, 142–43
  religion-based, 127–28, 142
  in the second Gilded Age (late 1900s), 142–43
Philippon, Thomas, 62
Piketty, Thomas, 39, 58–59, 60, 65–66
Pinderhughes, Dianne, 215
Pingree, Hazen, 327
Pinkert, Otis, 229–30

Playboy, 187
Plessy v. Ferguson (1896), 73, 201
politics/political polarization, 69–108
    affective polarization and, 92–98
    consequences of polarization, 101–8
    cross-party presidential approval, 91–92
    elite polarization, 81–88, 92–93, 99–101
    gender equality/inequality and, 78, 94, 268,
        269–70, 278, 320–21
    generational loyalties, 94–95, 98
    Great Convergence of, 70–71, 76–84, 88,
        90–91, 98, 102–3
    Great Divergence of, 6, 16–17, 84–108
    history of, 71–87
    "independent" voters, 93, 379n76
    I-we-I curves, 10, 11, 69–71, 86–91, 97,
        100–101, 103–8, 284–87
    main polarizing issues, 84–86
    marriage and, 98, 381n90
    mass polarization, 89–98, 99–101
    nature of polarization, 69–71
    New Right/New Left and, 62, 81, 83,
        186–90, 309
    overlap with economic equality/inequality,
        8, 79–80, 100–101
    in the Progressive Era, 73–76, 78, 88, 102,
        372n14
    racial equality/inequality and polarization,
        73, 78, 79–80, 82–84, 86–87, 97, 101,
        372n10, 373–74n25
    religion and, 85, 94, 97
    split ticket voting, 89–91
    third parties, 6, 73–74, 82–83, 104
    trust in government, 101–8
Poole, Keith T., 100
Pope, Jeremy C., 94
populism, 6, 336
Port Huron Statement (1962), 188–89
Potter, David, 294
Pound, Ezra, 174
Powell, Lewis F., Jr., 86
Power Elite, The (Mills), 188
Pregnancy Discrimination Act (1978), 280
Presley, Elvis, 306
Prince Hall Freemasonry, 115
prison reform, 220–21
professional associations, 114, 121–23
Progress and Poverty (George), 326
Progressive Era:
    active citizenship and, 329–34
    cultural individualism vs. community needs
        and, 167–73, 176, 197, 325–27
    education in, 111, 168, 225–26, 319–21

financial regulation in, 61–62
gender equality/inequality and, 247–48,
    267–68, 319–21
influence on New Deal programs, 74–75,
    174–75, 334
Jim Crow segregation and, 337–38
legacy of Progressives, 74–75, 328–29,
    334–39
media/communication in, 129, 167, 325,
    327
nature of, 19–20, 285, 288
origins of Great Convergence in, 38–39,
    46–48, 285–86, 288, *see also* Great
    Convergence (1913–70)
politics/political parties in, 73–76, 78, 88,
    102, 372n14
settlement house movement, 171–72, 175,
    319–21, 324, 331–32
social solidarity vs. isolation and, 110–17,
    120, 130–33, 150–51, 162, 321–23
taxation, 54–58
timing of, 19–20, 351–52n3
transition from first Gilded Age (late
    1800s), 19–20, 88, 317–19, 336
unions and, 49–50
youth-driven vision in, 334–36
Prohibition, 72, 74, 76, 114–15, 132–33, 173,
    336–37
pronoun usage, 196–99
Protestantism, 128–34, 136–37, 168
Prus, Mark, 249–50
PTA, 115, 118, 135, 151
Public Works Administration, 228–29
Pure Food and Drug Act, 74
Putnam, Lara, 333

Race Between Education and Technology, The
    (Goldin), 47
racial equality/inequality:
    ban on racial discrimination in federal
        agencies and military, 230
    gender equality and, 247, 259, 265, 271,
        279–80, 281, 429n27, 431n49
    generational differences and, 234–36,
        271
    Great Divergence (mid-1970s–) and,
        239–42, 243
    income equality and, 202, 211–12, 259
    life expectancy and, 202, 204–5, 240
    media and, 218, 417n64
    scientific racism and, 167, 218, 230, 337
    social Darwinism/"survival of the fittest,"
        66, 166–70, 187–88, 287, 327

see also African Americans; immigrants and
   immigration
Rahn, Wendy M., 158
Rand, Ayn, 186–87
Randolph, A. Philip, 230
Ratner-Rosenhagen, Jennifer, 165
Rauschenbusch, Walter, 130–31, 328
Rayburn, Sam, 81
Reagan, Ronald/Reagan Revolution,46–47,
   52, 65, 84, 85, 92, 102–4, 299, 383n109
Rebel Without a Cause (film), 182
Reconstruction, 73, 77, 166, 201–2, 209,
   217–18, 356n16
Red Cross, 118
Red Scare (1920s), 66
Red Scare (1950s), 81, 180
regional equality/inequality:
   Great Convergence (1913–70) and, 44
   Great Divergence (mid-1970s–) and, 44
   politics and, 71–73, 95–96
Reich, Charles, 305
religion:
   Catholics/Catholicism, 128, 132–34, 137,
      168
   generational differences and, 134, 137–38,
      141
   "Great Awakenings," 128
   I-we-I curves, 133–35, 139–42
   Jews/Judaism, 115, 118, 119, 121, 134, 178,
      186, 230, 323
   "nones" and, 129, 139–41, 146,
      393nn82–84
   philanthropy based in, 127–28, 142
   political parties and, 85, 94, 97
   Protestants/Protestantism, 128–34,
      136–37, 168
   religious institutions and social solidarity
      vs. isolation, 116–17, 120, 127–42
   sexual norms and, 138–39, 141
   Social Gospel movement, 130, 168–70,
      175, 327–28
   World War II and, 133–36
Republican Party:
   Civil War and, 71
   divisions within, 74
   Equal Rights Amendment and, 78,
      268
   in Great Convergence, 76–84, 90–91
   in Great Divergence, 6, 16–17, 84–108
   and New Right of the 1950s, 190
   Northern Republicans, 79, 201, 375n38
   Reagan Revolution, 46–47, 52, 65, 84, 85,
      92, 102–4, 299, 383n109

RINOs ("Republicans in Name Only"),
   89, 188
"Southern strategy," 84, 238
see also politics/political polarization *and*
   entries beginning "election of . . ."
Rerum Novarum (1891), 132, 168
Reshef, Ariell, 62
Riesman, David, 182, 185, 186
Riis, Jacob, 167
Road to Serfdom (Hayek), 186–87
Roaring Twenties, 37–39, 46, 67, 70, 173–74,
   288, 334
Robenalt, Jim, 304
Robert, Henry Martyn, 112
Robert's Rules of Order, 112
Rockefeller, John D., 57, 142–43, 325
Rockwell, Norman, 177
Roe v. Wade (1973), 85, 279, 304
Romney, George, 66, 83
Romney, Mitt, 66–67, 83, 187
Roosevelt, Eleanor, 175, 268
Roosevelt, Franklin D., 75, 299
   Executive Order 8802 (banning racial
      discrimination), 230
   GI Bill (1944), 31–32, 252, 357–58n22
   New Deal, *see* New Deal
Roosevelt, Theodore:
   Anthracite Coal Commission, 49–50
   Bull Moose Party, 73–74, 172–73
   election of 1912 and, 132, 334
   Progressivism, 73–75, 132, 171–73, 318,
      327, 331, 333, 334–35, 341
   Square Deal, 318
Roper Social and Political Trends archive,
   124, 125–26
Rorty, Richard, 312
Rosenthal, Howard, 100
Rosenwald Foundation, 225
Rosenwald schools, 225
Rosie the Riveter, 262
Rossman, Gabriel, 195
Rotary, 114, 117, 118, 321–23
Rudolph, Thomas J., 103
Ryan, Paul, 187, 188

Saez, Emmanuel, 37–38, 39, 58–59, 60,
   65–66
Salinger, J. D., 182, 186
Saturday Evening Post, The, 177
Savage, Jon, 304
Saving, Jason L., 100–101
SBTC (skill-based technological change)
   theory, 48, 365n70

scandals, in the first Gilded Age (late 1800s), 5

Schlesinger, Arthur, Jr., 178

Schulman, Bruce, 242–43, 312

Schuman, Howard, 241–42

scientific racism, 167, 218, 230, 337

second Gilded Age (late 1900s):
cultural individualism vs. community needs and, 16–17, 169
cynicism in, 16–17, 103–6
economic equality/inequality in, 37–38, 313
parallels with first Gilded Age (late 1800s), 2–9, 17–18
social solidarity vs. isolation in, 110, 142–43

Secret Life of Pronouns, The (Pennebaker), 196–97

Secular City, The (Cox), 137

Seeger, Pete, 305

self-destructive behavior:
data sources, 355–56nn11–14
"deaths of despair," 28, 43–44, 355–56n11, 356n14
in the first Gilded Age (late 1800s), 8

self-interest, 156, 294–95
in early American democracy, 1–2
in the first Gilded Age (late 1800s), 5
in the second Gilded Age (late 1900s), 16–17
as Tocqueville term, 2, 109, 157, 340

Seneca Falls convention (1848), 246

service clubs, 114–20, 321–23

settlement house movement, 171–72, 175, 319–21, 324, 331–32

sexual harassment, 264, 277, 278, 328

sexual norms, 138–39, 141, 152–53, 309

Shafir, Eldar, 295

Shakespeare, William, 1, 18, 19

Shapiro, Robert Y., 93–94

Sheldon, Charles, 131

Shifting Involvements (Hirschman), 289–90

Shiller, Robert, 177–78, 291

Shore, Dinah, 151

Siegel, Reva, 264

Sigel, Roberta, 274

Silent (Greatest) Generation, 66, 138, 147–48, 152, 160–61, 234–35, 252, 262–63, 272–73

Silent Spring (Carson), 303, 310

Sinatra, Frank, 151

Sinclair, Upton, 325

Singer Sewing Machines, 117

Skocpol, Theda, 112, 114, 117, 122, 333

slavery, 2, 4, 33, 167, 201–3, 224, 247, 318, 323–25

Smith, Al, 76, 320–21

Smith, David Horton, 121–22

Smith v. Allwright (1944), 215

social capital, 12–13, 293, 323
civic organizations and, 114–16
religion and, 116–17
social media and, 332–33
as term, 168, 402n16

social class:
civic associations and, 114
in the first Gilded Age (late 1800s), 3, 4
gender equality/inequality and, 246–47, 256–57, 259, 265, 267, 282, 320
health disparities and, 27–28, 41–44
income disparities, see Great Divergence (mid-1970s–)
intra-racial divides in, 212–13
marriage and, 153–54
worker solidarity and, 143–45
working women and, 246–47, 265, 282, 320

social Darwinism/"survival of the fittest," 66, 166–70, 187–88, 287, 327

Social Gospel movement, 130, 168–70, 175, 327–28

socialism, 6, 131, 172–73, 328, 336

social media, 332–33
Facebook, 292
#MeToo Movement, 277, 328
"resistance" movements and, 333
Twitter, 101, 292

Social Problems (George), 326

Social Security Act (1935), 55, 59–61, 77, 78, 80, 176, 226

social solidarity vs. isolation, 109–62
civic associations and, see civic associations
family formation and, 145–58
in the first Gilded Age (late 1800s), 3–4, 5, 7, 110, 112–13, 128–30, 142–43, 147–49, 157
Great Depression and, 119–21, 127, 134, 142, 156, 157, 295–96
I-we-I curves, 10–11, 284–86
philanthropy and, 127–28, 142–43
Progressive Era, 110–17, 120, 130–33, 150–51, 162, 321–23
religious institutions and, 116, 120, 127–42
in the second Gilded Age (late 1900s), 110, 142–43
social trust and, 158–62, 398–99n137

unions and worker solidarity, 49–54,
143–45
World War II and, 119–20, 133–36, 147,
159
social trust, 158–62, 398–99n137
generational differences in, 160–62, 252
I-we-I curves and, 159–62
Southern Christian Leadership Conference
(SCLC), 232
Spencer, Herbert, 166–67
split ticket voting, 89–91
stagflation, 310
Stansell, Christine, 246, 248
Stark, Rodney, 128
Steffens, Lincoln, 325, 327
Stein, Gertrude, 174
Steinbeck, John, 174
Stevenson, Adlai, 80
Stimson, James, 352–53n4
Stimson composite summary curves, 9–11,
352–53n4
Stock, James, 352–53n4
Stock-Watson composite summary curves,
352–53n4
Stony the Road (Gates), 217–18
stress:
in the first Gilded Age (late 1800s), 7
in the second Gilded Age (late 1900s),
16–17
Student Nonviolent Coordinating
Committee (SNCC), 232
Students for a Democratic Society (SDS),
188–89
Sugrue, Thomas J., 218–19
suicide, 28, 355–56n11, 356n14
Summer of Love (1967), 309
Sumner, William Graham, 166–67, 293–94
Sun Belt, unions and, 52
Symbionese Liberation Army (1974-75),
308–9

Taft, William Howard, 55, 74
Taft-Hartley Act (1947), 52
Tarbell, Ida, 325
taxation, 54–59, 74
Eisenhower administration, 80–81
estate/inheritance tax, 54–55, 57–59, 173
federal corporate tax, 56–57, 58–59
federal income tax progressivity, 54–56,
173
Great Divergence and, 55–58, 61, 65
I-we-I curves, 55–59
Taylor, Michael, 158

Teamsters Union, 52
technology:
automobiles, 24, 25, 355n7
economic equality/inequality and, 23, 28,
47–48
education and, 47–48
in the first Gilded Age (late 1800s), 6
internet and social media, *see* internet;
social media
New Right and, 187
skill-based technological change (SBTC)
theory, 48, 365n70
utopian vision of advances, 111
television, 52, 151
Tempest, The (Shakespeare), 1, 18, 19
Tennessee Valley Authority (TVA), 77, 78
terrorism:
in the first Gilded Age (late 1800s), 7, 73
9/11 terrorist attacks, 105, 196
white, 221
Thatcher, Margaret, 187
Thornton, Arland, 152
time diaries, 125–26
Title IX, Education Amendments (1972), 82,
264–65, 279
Title VII, Civil Rights Act (1964), 258–59,
264
Tocqueville, Alexis de, 1–2, 8, 19, 109, 113,
119, 158, 340, 351nn1–2, 444n29
trade, *see* international trade
trade unions, *see* unions
transportation:
automobile, 24, 25, 80, 355n7
in the first Gilded Age (late 1800s), 2–3, 6
Transue, John E., 158
Triangle Shirtwaist Factory fire (1911), 247,
320
Trilling, Lionel, 165
Truman, Harry, 52
election of 1948 and, 79, 91, 230,
372–73n17
Republican approval of, 91–92
Trump, Donald J.:
conservatism and, 188
Families Belong Together initiative and,
328
"Make America Great Again," 296
polarization and, 44, 86, 89, 100
regional disparities, 44
taxation and, 55, 57, 58
Women's March on Washington (2017),
333
Turner, Frederick Jackson, 166

turning point (esp. 1960s–1970s), 46, 53, 55,
    60, 67, 70, 90, 92, 140, 141, 142, 198,
    216, 226, 230, 238, 288, 290, 299, 300,
    301, 306, 312, 316, 319, 320, 336, 361
Twain, Mark, 8
Twenge, Jean, 194, 195, 197
Twenty Years at Hull-House (Addams), 331–32
Twilight of Common Dreams, The (Gitlin),
    309
Twitter, 101, 292
2000s, 125, 434n70
2010s, 51, 89, 154, 159, 296, 381n90

U-curve, see I-we-I curve(s)
unions, 49–54, 143–45, 323
    gender equality/inequality and, 53, 115,
        248
    I-we-I curve(s), 50, 51, 144–45
    membership trends, 50–52, 144–45
    racial equality/inequality and, 53, 143–44,
        218–19, 230
    strikes and collective bargaining, 49–50,
        52, 53, 143, 144
    worker solidarity and, 49–54, 143–45
United States Commission on Civil Rights,
    232
U.S. Congress:
    cross-party collaboration, 70–71
    Joint Economic Committee, 43–44
    polarization by political party, 86–87, 99,
        377n60
    women in, 269
U.S. Constitution:
    Fifteenth Amendment (black male
        suffrage), 247
    Sixteenth Amendment (income tax), 55
    Eighteenth Amendment (Prohibition),
        114–15, 132–33, 336–37
    Nineteenth Amendment (female suffrage),
        114–15, 247–48, 266, 279, 428n11
    Bill of Rights, 163, 191–92, 318
    Equal Rights Amendment (ERA,
        proposed), 78, 267–68, 278, 374n27
U.S. Department of Health, Education, and
    Welfare, 80
U.S. Department of Labor, Women's Bureau,
    267
U.S. Securities and Exchange Commission
    (SEC), 61–62
U.S. Social Security Administration:
    baby name trends, 195–96
    Social Security Act (1935), 55, 59–61, 77,
        78, 80, 176, 226

U.S. Supreme Court:
    African American justices, 233
    birth control and, 309
    Brown v. Board of Education (1954), 206–7,
        209–10, 227, 231–32
    female justices, 269
    Plessy v. Ferguson (1896), 73, 201
    political polarization, 377n60
    racial intermarriage and, 218
    Roe v. Wade (1973), 85, 279, 304
    Smith v. Allwright (1944), 215
    taxes as unconstitutional, 55
United Way, 142
Urban League, 116, 118, 215

Vandenberg, Arthur, 77
Vanity Fair, 187
Vatican II (1962–65), 137
Vietnam War, 84, 103, 189, 300, 307–10
Vital Center, The (Schlesinger), 178
voting rights:
    female suffrage, 2, 74–75, 114–15, 119,
        120, 247–49, 266, 269–70, 324, 428n11
    racial equality/inequality and, 201, 214–17,
        229, 232, 233, 247
    Voting Rights Act (1965), 82, 215–17, 227,
        233, 236, 237, 300, 375n38

Wald, Lillian, 321
Wallace, George, 83–84, 238
Wallace, Henry A., 175–76
Wall Street (film), 187
War on Drugs, 220–21
War on Poverty, 62, 82, 85
Washington, Booker T., 324
Washington Post, 129
Watergate scandal, 310
Watson, M. W., 352–53n4
wealth distribution:
    first Gilded Age (late 1800s), 37
    income equality/inequality and, 37–38,
        46–47, 53
    I-we-I curves and, 36–37, 39, 53
    wealth, defined, 36
Weathermen bombings (1969–74), 308–9
Weber, Max, 292
welfare capitalism, 365n76
welfare spending, 59–61
Wells, Ida B., 323–25, 337
Whig Party, 166, 171, 197
White, Richard, 329
White, William Allen, 111
Whitehead, Alfred North, 19

Whyte, Kenneth, 76
Whyte, William H., 182–83, 186
Wilkerson, Isabel, 223, 224
Willard, Frances, 115, 324
Williamson, Jeffrey G., 33, 35, 40, 42, 202, 209
Willkie, Wendell, 77–78, 90
Wilson, Sloan, 182
Wilson, Woodrow, 38, 74, 172–73, 324, 333, 337
Wolfe, Tom, 198, 311
Woman's Christian Temperance Union (WCTU), 115
women, *see* gender equality/inequality
Women's Christian Temperance Union, 324
Women's Educational Equity Act (1974), 279
Women's March on Washington (2017), 333
Women's Strike for Equality (1970), 279
Women's Trade Union League, 115
Works Progress Administration (WPA), 77, 226, 228
World's Fair (1893), 166, 324
World War I:
  economic equality and, 39
  Great Migration and, 221

Progressive movement following, 75–76, 173–76
  unions and, 50
World War II, 175–77, 294
  economic equality and, 39, 66
  educational attainment and, 29, 31–32, 250–51, 252
  gender equality/inequality and, 262–63
  GI Bill (1944), 31–32, 252, 357–58n22
  as the "good war," 301, 302
  Greatest (Silent) Generation and, 66, 138, 147–48, 152, 160–61, 234–35, 252, 262–63, 272–73
  political parties and, 79, 88, 90
  racial equality/inequality and, 229–30
  religion and, 133–36
  social solidarity vs. isolation and, 119–20, 133–36, 147, 159
  unions and, 50–51

Xie, Yu, 152

youth organizations, 116, 118–19, 121, 274

Ziblatt, Daniel, 106
Zuckerberg, Mark, 142–43
Zucman, Gabriel, 37–38, 39, 60, 65